A to Z

OF AFRICAN AMERICANS

African-American Business Leaders and Entrepreneurs

Rachel Kranz

Facts On File, Inc.

≈

This book is dedicated to the women and men of the Civil Rights movement,
who made a new world for us all to live in.

≈

Note on Photos
Many of the illustrations and photographs used in this book are old, historical images. The quality of the prints is not always up to current standards, as in some cases the originals are from old
or poor-quality negatives or are damaged. The content of the illustrations, however, made their
inclusion important despite problems in reproduction.

African-American Business Leaders and Entrepreneurs

Copyright © 2004 by Rachel Kranz

Facts On File, Inc.
132 West 31st Street
New York NY 10001

Library of Congress Cataloging-in-Publication Data

Kranz, Rachel.
African-American business leaders and entrepreneurs/Rachel Kranz.
    p. cm.—(A to Z of African Americans)
Includes bibliographical references and index.
ISBN 0-8160-5101-1
1. African American businesspeople—Biography—Dictionaries. 2. African American execu-
tives—Biography—Dictionaries. I. Title. II. Series.
HC102.5.A2K73 2004
338.092—dc21   2003008700

Facts On File books are available at special discounts when purchased in bulk quantities for businesses, associations, institutions, or sales promotions. Please call our Special Sales Department in
New York at (212) 967-8800 or (800) 322-8755.

You can find Facts On File on the World Wide Web at http://www.factsonfile.com

Text design by Joan M. Toro
Cover design by Nora Wertz

Printed in the United States of America

VB Hermitage 10 9 8 7 6 5 4 3 2 1

This book is printed on acid-free paper.

CONTENTS

LIST OF ENTRIES

ACKNOWLEDGMENTS

This book would not have been possible without the extraordinary assistance of Amy Goldberger. Thanks also to Nicole Bowen for the usual staunch editorial guidance and support and to Laura Shauger for her unfailingly cheerful and helpful editorial assistance. Thanks to all the women and men who generously assisted in the preparation of this book by contributing photographs and information. And finally, a profound thanks to all the African-American business leaders without whose extraordinary lives this book would not have been possible in the first place.

A very warm and heartfelt thank-you to my parents, Bea and Murray Kranz, who first started me thinking about race, politics, and history, and particularly to my father, who in the 1960s and 1970s helped pioneer the new move to study and teach African-American history.

Author's Note

The figures in this book represent a largely neglected portion of U.S. history and contemporary life: African-American business leaders, from colonial times to the present. People were chosen for this book according to a number of criteria. First, of course, I wanted to include the most significant figures from every era—the ones who have had an unmistakable influence on American and African-American life. Then, I wanted a broad balance across time periods, geographical areas, types of industry, and size of enterprise. It seemed important to include the owners of small businesses as well as large; independent entrepreneurs as well as corporate executives; pioneers in new fields as well as more traditional businesspeople. I also wanted to include as many women as possible, as women have always been a bulwark of the African-American community.

Every effort has been made to find complete, up-to-date, and accurate information on the figures listed in this book, along with substantial and accessible suggestions for further reading. Whenever possible, contemporary figures have been approached with requests for information, and an extensive search has been made for biographical source material. Generally, I have not included obscure or purely scholarly material in these bibliographies but have rather chosen sources more easily available to the general reader.

However, because of the general neglect of this aspect of U.S. history and culture, many of the figures in this book—including some who are still living—remain somewhat obscure. Whenever possible, obscurities or uncertainties in the historical record have been noted, and every effort has been made to convey a lively and useful account of each person's life, even if certain historical details are occasionally missing.

Working on this book was a profound experience for me personally. Although I have been writing and thinking about African-American history for more than three decades, I had never really considered the role of African Americans in the business world. I was struck by how crucial African-American entrepreneurs often were to their community, as well as moved by the enormous obstacles that they invariably had to overcome. I was also intrigued by the often contradictory nature of their efforts—on the one hand, they frequently strove to "uplift the race"; on the other hand, they were sometimes accused of profiting unduly from their own people, particularly when they themselves owned slaves, as occasionally happened in the 19th century, or rented out substandard, segregated housing, as sometimes occurred in the 20th. In many cases, these contradictions seemed to embody the American love of upward mobility and personal achievement, even as they pointed out the shortcomings of an individual approach to social and community problems.

In the end, I came away with a new appreciation for the strength, diversity, and resourcefulness of the African-American community and with profound gratitude for the men and women who over the centuries have found such creative and meaningful ways of serving their people. In this book you will find a rich array of business leaders who made a wide variety of choices. Over the centuries, African-American business leaders have included slaves and slaveholders, conservatives and civil rights leaders, small proprietors and corporate giants. It is impossible to understand the richness of African-American life without them.

INTRODUCTION

Since there have been Africans in the Americas, there have been African-American entrepreneurs—men and women of business. Before the Civil War, free people of color worked as dressmakers and tailors, carpenters and masons, barbers and hairdressers, tavernkeepers and restaurateurs, caterers and cooks. Enslaved African Americans might be found managing plantations, trading goods on behalf of their owners, conducting their own trade among other slaves, and setting up their own small businesses in various communities. A small but significant number of African Americans even owned slaves of their own—inherited from white planter fathers or purchased with their own accumulated earnings as planters, land speculators, barbers, and craft workers. After the Civil War, African Americans founded enterprises to serve their own community—funeral parlors, insurance agencies, newspapers, companies that manufactured beauty products. Later in the 20th century, African Americans founded new types of businesses—advertising agencies, electronics firms, asset-management companies, ventures involving music, television, film, and the Internet. They also rose to the top of the corporate hierarchies in a number of industries, heading such internationally famous companies as American Express and AOL Time Warner. Faced with daunting obstacles and armed with enormous determination, African-American men and women of business have always managed to carve out a place for themselves in all sorts of industries and enterprises.

Although African Americans have achieved a remarkable amount of success as entrepreneurs, they have always occupied a contradictory position. The difficulties they have faced, as well as the accomplishments they have achieved, point up some contradictions in the very nature of U.S. society.

From the founding of the first colonies, America was perceived as a land of economic opportunity, a place where an enterprising man—or, occasionally, an ambitious woman—could make a fortune and rise to the highest level of society. An important aspect of U.S. political and social life was the notion of this land as a place where "all men were created equal," endowed with the inalienable rights of life, liberty, and property—rights that were later extended, at least partially, to women.

Yet many people did not consider that African Americans—male and female—had been created equal, nor that they shared the same inalienable rights as other ethnic groups. The question of slavery was hotly debated when the U.S. Constitution was being written and during the early days of the new Republic: politicians from New England and Pennsylvania argued that liberty was the right of all humans, while many political leaders from both South and North were well aware that their states' economies depended upon slave labor. Africans who had been forcibly brought to the United States were crucial to the enormous plantations of rice and tobacco that helped to fund the development of the new nation, and to the crops of sugar and cotton that would later prove even more important to the national economy. New England traders had long relied upon business from the British West Indies, societies in which slave-grown sugar was such a profitable crop that all other commodities—including food, furniture, housewares, and clothing—were imported whenever possible from Europe and North America. In the late 18th and early 19th centuries, New York and other northern states relied upon enslaved Africans to develop their own budding economies, while in the first half of the 19th century, slave-grown cotton provided New England mills and New York traders with one of their most valuable commodities.

Clearly, enslaved labor of all types was vital to the U.S. economy—yet the principles of political equality and economic opportunity were also crucial to the new nation. As a result, politicians, revolutionaries, and ordinary citizens of all races and colors engaged in passionate debate about the role of Africans in America. Were the Africans who were forcibly brought to these shores human beings, endowed with the inalienable rights described in the Declaration of Independence and protected by the Constitution? Or were they themselves the property whose ownership was also protected in the Constitution?

Given this contradiction, how could an African American become an entrepreneur, a property owner and citizen entitled to freely operate his or her business? Did the African-American entrepreneur look to the promise of American economic opportunity for all or to the reality of racial discrimination in law and custom? And what about the fact that most enterprises required some form of additional labor? What did it mean when African Americans also owned slaves, profiting from their free labor just as white people did?

When African Americans became employers, were they providing a service by creating jobs, or were they taking advantage of their fellow African Americans, who often worked for low wages while their employers got rich? Likewise, did African-American landlords benefit their communities by providing housing to black people who were often not allowed to live anywhere else—or were they simply profiting from their own people, who sometimes had to pay black landlords higher rents to live in substandard housing?

These questions, too, were hotly argued within the black community, and they continue to be debated today. Whether rich and powerful African Americans benefit their community or simply take advantage of it—or both—has been a controversial topic for at least two centuries.

Consider the case of black slaveowner Andrew Durnford, the owner of a Louisiana sugar plantation who, like his white neighbors, beat the enslaved people who worked for him and routinely sold parents away from children, husbands away from wives. Or look at William Johnson, "the barber of Natchez," who owned a few enslaved African Americans and hired several free people of color to work in his prestigious barbershop—where only white people were accepted as customers.

In the 20th century, landlords like Oscar DePriest, Philip A. Payton, and Dempsey Travis were greatly admired for providing needed housing to the thousands of African Americans coming up from the South to live in New York and Chicago—even as these entrepreneurs were criticized for presenting needy people with high rents and substandard housing. Music entrepreneurs like Berry Gordy were admired for making black music available to a mainstream audience—and criticized for steering such music away from its rough urban roots into a more soft and acceptable sound. Fight promoter Don King remains the only African American to have reached the highest level of the fight game—which relies upon the work of black and Latino fighters—and many of

King's fighters signed with him precisely because they wanted to be represented by someone who was black like them. Yet many of King's fighters have also accused him of taking advantage of them, of being more concerned with his money than with their careers. The debate within the black community over the role of the entrepreneur and business leader has historically been part of a larger argument about how African Americans should advance within U.S. society. As the Civil War was ending, two major figures offered two alternative viewpoints.

Frederick Douglass, the abolitionist leader, proclaimed that African Americans should press for full legal, social, and political equality in society. Douglass was inspired by the fight to end slavery and to win full rights for African Americans. As the Civil War ended and slavery was abolished, Douglass and his allies pressed for America's first civil rights legislation, establishing political and civil rights for African Americans in the southern states where they had formerly been slaves. The old southern leadership that had supported the Confederacy was temporarily removed from power, while new state constitutional conventions began the process known as Reconstruction—literally, reconstructing and rewriting the political basis for southern life, in which black men now had the right to vote, run for office, sit on juries, testify in court, and participate in political life. (At the time, women of all races were unable to engage in those activities—though Douglass fully supported their right to do so as well.) Douglass and his followers were inspired by the possibility that, at long last, African Americans could take their place as full citizens in U.S. society—no matter how much struggle it took to fulfill that promise. Douglass and his allies believed that black people had created much of the wealth that had made America great. Now African Americans should finally be entitled to their full share of the country they had helped to build.

Douglass's major opponent was Booker T. Washington, founder of the Tuskegee Institute in Alabama. Tuskegee was a school where the focus was not on reading, writing, and academic subjects, but rather on useful trades, such as carpentry and farming. Washington and his followers considered Douglass's militant approach not only wrong but dangerous. Such radical demands, Washington warned, would only alienate white people, leading to greater repression of the black community. Instead, Washington put forth a policy that he called "accommodationism," arguing that black people should accommodate to, or accept, the political and social limits that white-dominated society set forth. Within those limits, Washington suggested, black people could learn useful trades—such as were taught at Tuskegee. They might also found their own enterprises, businesses that could serve the black community while being supported by it. This would free black people from dependence on white people, Washington argued, without angering white people or directly confronting them.

Both views ran into severe difficulties in the years after Reconstruction. Although black political rights were guaranteed for a time, the 1876 Tilden-Hayes compromise settled a very close presidential election by throwing the presidency of the United States to Rutherford B. Hayes in exchange for Hayes's agreement to withdraw federal troops from the South. When the federal troops left the southern states, the old white leadership of the society took it as a signal that they could restore white political dominance. Legislatures began passing laws restricting the voting rights of black people. They also began to institute segregation—racial separation—also known as "Jim Crow." Black people were gradually prevented from sharing public space with white people in much of the South, forbidden from riding on the same streetcars, shopping at the same stores, or eating at the same restaurants. In this political climate, Douglass's vision of full civil rights seemed unrealistic to many people.

But Washington's vision of black self-help was also problematic. Washington had to call upon white philanthropists (wealthy people who donate money) to support his activities at Tuskegee, and indeed, all of the black colleges and universities set up during the post–Civil War period relied upon the generosity of wealthy white people. There simply was not enough money in the black community to fund all the activities needed to educate and support the newly freed African Americans. How could there be? Most African Americans had been slaves until 1865, denied the right to keep any share of the wealth they had created during long hours of backbreaking labor in the fields and workshops of the South and in many northern states as well. Likewise, black enterprises such as banks and insurance companies, while sometimes successful, often failed. They had the noble aim of providing loans to black homeowners and start-up money for black businesses, and these black financial institutions did indeed manage to help many in the African-American community achieve their goals. But for a bank to be successful, it must avoid loaning money to people who cannot pay it back—so black banks often either withheld money from poor African Americans, or went bankrupt, or both.

After Douglass died, his side of the debate was taken up by the writer, scholar, and agitator W. E. B. DuBois. DuBois argued that the black community would be best served by a "talented tenth" becoming successful in all areas of social life—as professors, scientists, writers, artists, lawyers, doctors, and political leaders. Such outstanding African Americans, DuBois believed, would demonstrate to both white and black Americans that there was nothing African Americans might not achieve, if given a fair chance. Black intellectuals and artists would also help lead and inspire their own people to fight for their rights in the political and social world, opposing Jim Crow and restricted voting rights, struggling for full social and political equality.

Washington considered DuBois to be even more unrealistic than Douglass had been. He argued that black intellectuals of the kind DuBois supported would only enrage white people, who thought African Americans should stay in their place. What kind of work could these intellectuals get, Washington argued, when white society was so closed to them? Better for black people to be educated in useful trades, where they could clearly function as productive members of society—skilled workers and farmers improving their own condition and that of their people little by little. Through the virtues of thrift, modesty, and hard work, black people could begin to care for themselves and their families in ways that would not alienate white society but would improve the black community. Meanwhile, black businesses could serve African-American customers. So what if white restaurants and banks and insurance companies failed to allow African Americans to use their services? Black entrepreneurs would simply start their own businesses.

To promote black enterprise and self-help, Washington founded the National Negro Business League (NNBL) in 1900, to promote the "commercial, agricultural, educational, and industrial advancement" of African Americans. Its main purpose was to encourage more black people to go into business, steering black people away from political issues and toward the economic issues that Washington thought were so important. The NNBL exists today in the form of the National Business League, but it lost most of its influence during the 1950s, when the Civil Rights movement called for black people to demand their full rights throughout society, rather than to start their own separate institutions that left white dominance unchallenged.

Many of the entrepreneurs in this volume were members of the NNBL. Many more were influenced by Washington. Yet even those who followed Washington could also admire Douglass and DuBois. In reality, the world of the black entrepreneur was far more complicated than a simple choice between two different philosophies. Many black entrepreneurs were leaders in the fight for civil rights, both in the early 20th century and during the Civil Rights movement. In Nashville, in 1905, for example, such business leaders as James Napier and Richard Boyd helped to found a streetcar company of their own so that black citizens did not have to ride the segregated white streetcar. Napier and Boyd put their wealth and prominence to the service of organizing a streetcar boycott much like the one that would be so successful in Montgomery, Alabama, a half-century later, under the leadership of Martin Luther King, Jr., and Rosa Parks. Napier and Boyd's action was ultimately unsuccessful, while King and Parks succeeded. Yet without the resources that Napier and Boyd had accumulated, it is unlikely that the first boycott would ever have taken place. And even though it was ultimately unsuccessful, the very effort made a difference to the residents of Nashville's African-American community, setting the stage for future struggles that would have better outcomes.

Likewise, during the 1960s, business leaders like motel owner Arthur Gaston in Birmingham, Alabama, and contractor Herman J. Russell in Atlanta, Georgia, helped bankroll the Civil Rights movement with the resources they had amassed in their enterprises. Gaston offered meeting facilities to King and his colleagues, while Russell was called on to bail out numerous Civil Rights workers and leaders who were repeatedly sentenced to jail as they fought for African-American rights. This tradition of social activism and political engagement continues today as black entrepreneurs support the campaigns of black politicians, donate money to activist groups, and work with such political leaders as civil rights activist Reverend Jesse Jackson.

Another function of the black entrepreneur has been to help make visible the African-American experience, both within the black community and to the society at large. In the 1920s and 1930s, filmmaker Oscar Micheaux operated his own production company because his type of film would not have been acceptable to the Hol-

lywood studios: They restricted black actors to the most stereotyped and limited roles, while Micheaux expanded the options for black film. In the 1950s and 1960s, black music entrepreneurs such as Berry Gordy, Dick Griffey, and Suzanne De Passe promoted the new urban sounds of African Americans, while in the 1970s, 1980s, and 1990s, De Passe, Yvette Lee Bowser, and Oprah Winfrey were among those who created new African-American images for television.

The end of the 20th and the beginning of the 21st centuries saw a dramatic rise in the number of black business leaders who headed major corporations, as well as those who have high places within the corporate hierarchy. American Express's Kenneth Chenault, AOL Time Warner's Richard Parsons, and MSNBC's Pamela Thomas-Graham are all African-American chief executive officers of previously white-dominated companies. Their rise has been made possible by the Civil Rights movement of the 1950s and 1960s and by the affirmative action policies that followed from it—a type of integration and access to power that opened the doors of the corporate world to at least some African Americans.

Yet even as the larger U.S. society becomes more available to black business leaders, the world of black business is becoming ever more white-dominated. As part of a larger trend for big businesses to acquire smaller ones, formerly black-owned companies, such as Berry Gordy's Motown Records or Wally Amos's Famous Amos Cookies, become the property of white owners as soon as they are profitable enough. Even *Essence* magazine, founded in 1975 by Edward T. Lewis and Clarence O. Smith, has been bought up by AOL Time Warner, though the magazine is still technically 51 percent black-owned. Likewise, hip-hop magnate Russell Simmons's DefJam records is now owned by Polygram.

In the same way, integration has ironically weakened the foundation on which many black-owned businesses rest. As white-owned insurance companies accept black policyholders, black-owned insurance companies suffer; as white-owned inns and restaurants accept black customers, black-owned establishments like Odetta and Albert Murray's Hillside Inn run into trouble. When the Murrays founded Hillside in the highly segregated Poconos region of Pennsylvania, in the late 1940s, black people were not allowed to stay at local inns and hotels. Today, those barriers have come down, creating unprecedented new opportunities for African Americans, in the business world and elsewhere. At the same time, the Murrays' business has declined.

The contradictions remain for African-American entrepreneurs—and so do the opportunities. Meanwhile, the stories in this volume remain inspiring. These tales of men and women who triumphed against almost unimaginable odds to create new businesses and new opportunities for African Americans are a dramatic example of the enormous determination, creativity, strength, and spirit that have always characterized the U.S. black community.

Abbott, Robert Sengstacke
(Robert Sengstacke, Robert S. Abbott)
(ca. 1870–1940) *publisher*

Robert Sengstacke Abbott was one of the most important publishers in the United States during the early 20th century. The newspaper he founded, the *Chicago Defender,* was one of the leading voices in the African-American press for many years, and Abbott's editorials in that publication have been credited with playing an influential role in the Great Migration of African Americans from the U.S. South to northern industrial cities, including Chicago.

Abbott was born on Saint Simons Island, Georgia. Many reputable sources list his birthdate as November 28, 1870, though some sources put the date at 1868. His parents were both former slaves. His father, Thomas Abbott, enjoyed the relatively privileged status of house servant to Captain Charles Stevens, while his mother, Flora (Butler), had a far harder life as a field slave. The two were married in 1867, though the Abbott family disapproved, considering that their son was marrying beneath him.

As the Civil War ended, the newlywed couple began a life of freedom. Thomas Abbott worked as a surveyor for a streetcar line in Savannah, Georgia, then began a grocery business on Saint Simons Island serving recently freed slaves.

In 1869, Thomas Abbott died, and Flora married John H. H. Sengstacke, with whom she had seven children. Abbott used his stepfather's surname for many years but later took his father's name again and built a monument to him on Saint Simons Island. Sengstacke was a minister and missionary of German and African descent. Because of his light skin, he was more easily accepted into the African-American elite, who tended to have fairer complexions and connections with white families. Yet Flora—and Robert—were dark-skinned and therefore rejected by the elite. Robert Abbott later spoke angrily of the poor treatment he received at Beach Institute, the Savannah private school for upper-class black students. (In those days, education in the South was strictly segregated, or separated by race.)

Before he had finished his studies at Beach, he went on to Claflin University in Orangeburg, South Carolina, where he worked on the school's farm and received some basic education. He then apprenticed at the Savannah *Echo,* the more militant of Savannah's two black-owned papers.

In November 1889, John Sengstacke began to publish the *Times* in Woodville, Georgia, and the man who was still calling himself Robert Sengstacke worked there for a while, studying at Hampton Institute in Virginia, where he heard a number of militant African-American leaders speak about black politics and economics. As a member of the Hampton Quartet, he was able to travel throughout the United States, and at the World's Columbian Exposition in Chicago in 1893, he heard the speeches of crusaders Frederick Douglass and Ida B. Wells.

Eventually, he, too, settled in Chicago, where he was rejected for a series of jobs in the printing trades—even as non-English-speaking white immigrants were hired in his place. In 1897, he began to study at Kent College of Law under the name Robert Sengstacke Abbott, the first time he used that last name. When he graduated, he was told by an older, light-skinned lawyer that his skin was too dark for him to be successful practicing in Chicago, so Abbott tried working first in Gary, Indiana, then in Topeka, Kansas, both times without success. In Topeka, however, Abbott arranged to distribute the Topeka newspaper, the *Plaindealer,* in Chicago, where he took a number of small print jobs.

Abbott tried to publish a daily newspaper in Chicago, but went out of business after only a few issues. Then, in 1905, Abbott founded the Chicago *Defender.* Perhaps ironically, the militant tone that would characterize the later *Defender* was not in evidence at first; instead, the newspaper focused on black achievement. The paper certainly represented Abbott's own achievement, as he scraped together investors and small lines of credit and somehow managed to put out the entire paper himself, even selling it personally at places where African-American customers might want to buy it—churches, bars, pool rooms, and nightclubs.

Still, the paper was foundering when Abbott's landlady, Henrietta Lee, offered to open her home to the newspaper as well. With Lee's help, the *Defender* began to do better, as Abbott began to bring in volunteers to write about sports, health, and social events. He also improved the paper's layout and design, imitating the *Evening American,* a tabloid newspaper owned by white newspaper magnate William Randolph Hearst. Hearst

sued Abbott for copyright infringement, and Abbott changed his own masthead. (The masthead is the newspaper's title, including both words and design.)

In 1910, Abbott hired J. Hockley Smiley, who made a huge difference in the paper's style and content. Smiley changed the look of the paper once again, making it appear more as a standard weekly newspaper. The words "The World's Greatest Weekly" were added to the masthead, and the *Defender* began to take more militant stands on racial issues. Abbott and Smiley even decided that their paper would no longer use terms they found offensive, including *Negro, colored,* and *Afro-American.* Only the word *race* would be used.

Smiley realized that Chicago was a major railroad terminal and also a major destination for theatrical performers. He began promoting the *Defender* to railway workers and theater people, and their interest in the paper quickly made it a national venture. On this national stage, Abbott promoted his own principles: the ending of all race prejudice and segregation, equal opportunity in employment and education, extension of the vote to all African Americans, and an end to lynching—a form of terror that kept black people from enjoying the few political and economic rights they did have.

By 1916, the *Defender* was sold in 71 different locations throughout the United States, making it the first black newspaper with a mass circulation. It was particularly well read in Kentucky, Tennessee, and the Gulf states, giving Abbott a platform for the crusade he began in 1917: encouraging southern black people to move North. Over the next few years, a million black people left the South, with several hundred thousand settling in Chicago. For many years, black southern schools actually held their reunions in Chicago, while southern authorities condemned the *Defender.* Many cities actually passed laws making it a criminal offense to "entice" African Americans to leave town. Sometimes officials in the South actually attempted to confiscate the *Defender* or punish those who had it in their possession.

A major turning point in the *Defender*'s history took place in 1919, when the Chicago riots resulted from rising racial tensions that were partly a result of the vast, sudden increase in the city's black population. Racial hostility escalated, and when some white people drowned an African-American youth, black people began to riot. The *Defender* covered the riots, and eventually, Abbott spoke out, counseling African Americans to exercise restraint. The military eventually had to restore order, and a Commission on Race Relations was formed to explore the problem, including three white members and three black members, one of whom was Abbott. During the commission's meetings, Abbott was criticized for excessive militance, and as a result, he began to modify the newspaper's approach. Rather than insisting that black people's demands be met immediately, he called for a more gradual approach and also began publishing articles about black achievement.

Meanwhile, Marcus Garvey was gaining enormous popularity among African Americans. The West Indian Garvey preached African pride and urged black people in the United States and the Caribbean to return to their African homeland. His United Negro Improvement Association (UNIA) had hundreds of thousands of members, while his newspaper, *Negro World,* reached many readers. Abbott strongly opposed Garvey and criticized him frequently.

When rioters had gathered in front of the plant where the *Defender* was printed, production stopped, and Abbott had to publish his paper at a plant in nearby Gary, Indiana. In response, Abbott bought his own printing presses and established the Robert S. Abbott Publishing Company in 1918. Because so few black people had been trained in the printing trades, Abbott hired a white foreman who helped unionize the shop. The *Defender* signed a contract with Chicago Typographical Union No. 16—the same all-white

Robert S. Abbott edited the *Chicago Defender,* a newspaper for African Americans that soon achieved distribution nationwide. *(Chicago Defender)*

union that had once refused to allow Abbott to join. The *Defender* became the first black-owned union shop, and Abbott hired an integrated staff of skilled workers—another first.

By 1920, the *Defender* was being read by 230,000 African Americans. Two-thirds of those issues were sold outside Chicago, with 23,000 per week being sold in New York City. Abbott's biographer, Roi Ottley, wrote in 1955 that "until recently, with the exception of the Bible, no publication was more influential among the Negro masses." The *Defender* gave birth to *Abbott's Monthly,* an arts magazine that was soon reaching 100,000 readers. Until JOHN H. JOHNSON's *Ebony* appeared in 1945, no publication equaled the national success of the *Defender.*

During the 1930s, the *Defender* was hurt by the Great Depression, which damaged many black-owned businesses. The aging Abbott was also losing touch with the times, as well as suffering from tuberculosis and Bright's disease. When he died on February 29, 1940, the paper passed into the ownership of John Sengstacke, the son of Abbott's stepbrother. Sengstacke built an even larger empire than Abbott had created, and the *Defender* remains in print. Likewise, the Robert S. Abbott Publishing Company continues to operate as a holding company for several firms, including Sengstacke Enterprises and Amalgamated Publishers. Abbott continues to be honored as a pioneer in black publishing and an integral part of the Great Migration.

Further Reading

The Black Press: Soldiers without Swords. "Newspapers: The Chicago *Defender:* Founder Editor—Robert S. Abbott." PBS Online. Available online. URL: http://www.pbs.org/blackpress/news_bios/defender.html. Downloaded on February 6, 2003.

Drake, St. Clair, and Horace Cayton. *Black Metropolis: A Study of Negro Life in a Northern City.* New York: Harcourt Brace and World, 1970.

Fitzgerald, Mark. "Robert Sengstacke Abbott." *Editor & Publisher* 132, no. 44 (October 30, 1999): 18.

Ottley, Roi. *The Lonely Warrior: The Life and Times of Robert Abbott.* Chicago, Ill.: Regnery, 1955.

Alexander, Archie Alphonso

(1888–1958) *contracting engineer, governor*

Archie Alexander was a highly successful contracting engineer who pioneered the entry of African Americans into that field. The founder and operator of several engineering enterprises, he also had an unsuccessful term as governor of the U.S. Virgin Islands.

Alexander was born on May 14, 1888, in Ottumwa, Iowa, to Price and Mary Alexander. He grew up in the overwhelmingly white communities of Ottumwa and Des Moines, where his father worked as a janitor and where Alexander graduated in 1905 from Oak Park High School. He attended Highland Park College and Cummins

Art School before becoming the first African-American student at the State University of Iowa in Iowa City, from which he graduated in 1912 with a B.S. in civil engineering.

At first, Alexander worked at odd jobs and as a laborer, but by 1914, he had formed his own general contracting firm, A. A. Alexander, Inc., where he was joined by George F. Higbee, a white colleague. As Alexander and Higbee, the new firm built bridges, viaducts, and sewage systems in Iowa until Higbee died in an accident in 1925. Alexander continued to operate the company by himself, building a $1 million heating plant for Iowa State University in 1926 and a new power plant and tunnel system in 1928.

In 1929 he was joined by another white colleague, Maurice A. Repass, and the firm was renamed Alexander & Repass. The company's work force was integrated, though most of the skilled workers were white. When Alexander worked in the highly segregated city of Washington, D.C., whose union rules required separate restrooms and drinking fountains for white and black workers, Alexander provided paper drinking cups for his employees and offered two restrooms: "skilled" and "unskilled."

Alexander & Repass undertook projects in virtually every state in the nation and maintained offices in Des Moines and Washington, D.C., where their most renowned projects were located: a $1.5 million Tidal Basin bridge and seawall; the K Street elevated highway and underpass from Key Bridge to 27th Street, N.W.; and the $3.35 million Whitehurst Freeway along the Potomac River. The firm was also responsible for building railroad bridges throughout Iowa and Missouri; a $1 million apartment building for the National Association for Colored Women, located in Anacostia, Maryland; and the Moton Airfield in Tuskegee, Alabama.

Despite the move of many African Americans into the Democratic Party in the 1930s, Alexander remained a staunch Republican, supporting Dwight D. Eisenhower's 1952 presidential campaign. In response, Eisenhower appointed him to be the second black governor of the U.S. Virgin Islands, a former Danish colonial outpost populated largely by the descendants of former African slaves. (The Virgin Islands was a U.S. possession but not a state, so its governor was appointed by the president.) Alexander took office on April 9, 1954, but his administration was generally viewed as a failure. In his biographical article, Charles E. Wynes wrote that Alexander's relationship to the islanders was "dogmatic, paternalistic, undemocratic, and [marked by] . . . an openly stated contempt." The legislature accused him of illegal expenditures of public funds and asked him to resign in 1955.

Alexander was involved in a number of other businesses, and he was active with the National Association for the Advancement of Colored People (NAACP) and with other racial causes. He died of a heart attack at his home in Des Moines on January 4, 1958.

Further Reading

"Archie Alphonso Alexander." *American National Biography 1.* Oxford, England: Oxford University Press, 1999, pp. 262–263.

Boyer, William W. *America's Virgin Islands: A History of Human Rights and Wrongs.* Durham, N.C.: Carolina Academic Press, 1983.

Wynes, Charles E. "'Alexander the Great,' Bridge Builder." *The Palimpsest* 46 (May–June 1985): 78–86.

Allensworth, Allen
(1842–1914) *developer of an all-black town*

Allen Allensworth was the founder of Allensworth, California, an all-black town where African Americans were supposed to be able to live in freedom and equality. Although the town was not ultimately successful, it stands as the powerful symbol of a dream of black independence, in an era when the rest of U.S. society was highly segregated (separated by race) and offered only limited opportunities to people of color.

Allensworth was born into slavery in Louisville, Kentucky, in April 1842. Little is known about his early life, though scholars believe he was sold downriver to Mississippi at the age of 12 for trying to learn to read and write. He made two unsuccessful attempts to escape from slavery, finally succeeding during the early years of the Civil War, when he ran away to join the Union army. During 1862, he worked as a civilian aide to the 44th Illinois volunteer infantry (foot soldiers). On April 3, 1863, he became a first-class seaman in the Union navy, serving on various gunboats, including the *Queen City* and the *Pittsburg* (sic). By the time he left the navy in April 1865, at the end of the Civil War, Allensworth had achieved the rank of first-class petty officer.

After the Civil War, Allensworth decided to become a minister. He studied theology at Roger Williams University in Nashville, Tennessee, where he met and later married Josephine Leavell. After he graduated, Allensworth preached from several pulpits in and around Louisville. He was also active in politics, serving as a Kentucky delegate to the Republican National Conventions in 1880 and 1884. (In those days, the Republican Party was the party of Abraham Lincoln and civil rights, and thus the party of choice for most African Americans.)

In 1882, an African-American soldier approached Allensworth to complain about the lack of chaplains for black soldiers. The armed forces of the time were segregated, and the all-black units were left without religious leadership. After a long campaign, in which he solicited letters of support from a variety of southern politicians of both parties, wrote to President Grover Cleveland, and approached the Office of the Adjutant General (a high army post), Allensworth managed to become the army's first black chaplain in April 1886, when he was assigned to the 24th Infantry with the rank of captain.

Allensworth's 20-year army career had him serving in various posts throughout the West, including Fort Apache in the Arizona Territory, Camp Reynolds in California, and Fort Missoula in Montana. When he retired in 1906, he had attained the rank of colonel and was the army's highest-ranking black officer.

Allensworth and his family initially settled in Los Angeles, California. But Allensworth had been inspired by the teachings of Booker T. Washington, the African-American leader who preached self-reliance, self-help, and thrift to the black community and encouraged black people to form their own institutions and take care of themselves. Allensworth began a speaking tour preaching thrift, education, and racial uplift, offering such lectures as "The Five Manly Virtues Exemplified," "The Battle of Life and How to Fight It," and "Character and How to Read It."

Then Allensworth met teacher and scholar William Payne, who was living in Pasadena, California. Together the two men conceived the idea of an all-black community where African Americans could enjoy the opportunities denied them by the larger white society. At the time, many scientists argued that black people were inherently inferior as a result of their genetic inheritance, a movement known as "eugenics." Allensworth and Payne though that an all-black community would give black people a chance to prove what they were capable of. Allensworth also thought that such a community could be a haven for the soldiers in the United States's four all-black regiments. There, every person might afford a home, and soldiers' families might live in peace while their military men were off fighting.

On June 30, 1908, Payne and Allensworth created the California Colony and Home Promoting Association with the goal of buying land and establishing their dream community. The association was unable to obtain land, however, until the white-owned Pacific Farming Company offered 800 acres of land in Solito, a rural area in Tulare County 30 miles north of Bakersfield. The community was renamed Allensworth in honor of its founder. The land was fertile and seemed to be well supplied with water—a key consideration in the arid California climate—and it included a depot station on the Santa Fe Railroad that ran between Los Angeles and San Francisco.

Black families moved into the new community with enthusiasm. Within a year, some 35 families lived there, and by 1912 the town's official population had reached 100, including Alwortha Hall, the first baby born there. In 1910, Allensworth and his wife built their own home in the community, which had grown to include two general stores, a post office, a school, and even a library, reflecting the town's preoccupation with education and self-improvement. Social clubs and organizations abounded, including such groups as Campfire Girls, Girls' Glee Club, and Children's Saving Association for children, with a Sewing Circle, Whist Club, Debating Society, and Theater Club for adults. The First Baptist Church had its own building in Allensworth, while the First AME (African Methodist Episcopal) Zion Church held services in the local school.

From 1912 through 1915, the community flourished, populated by some 300 settlers and winning national attention from black newspapers during an era that saw many other setbacks for black Americans. This was a time of increasing segregation and discrimination, so the image of a town run by black people for black people was enormously attractive to many. In keeping with Booker T. Washington's belief that black people should focus on learning useful trades rather than on becoming scholars or professionals, Colonel Allensworth tried to form an educational institute modeled after Washington's own Alabama-based Tuskegee: a school offering courses in agriculture, carpentry, and masonry. When a bill to establish such a school was introduced in the California state legislature in 1914, the town's success seemed assured.

Then the community encountered a number of difficulties. In 1914, the Santa Fe Railroad built a line to a neighboring town, allowing rail traffic to bypass Allensworth. The railroad had always shown prejudice against the town, refusing to use the name Allensworth on their schedules or to hire African Americans as managers or ticket agents in the community depot. In 1915, the legislature voted down plans for the school, partly because African Americans in San Francisco and Los Angeles opposed the project,

Allen Allensworth achieved the rank of lieutenant colonel in the U.S. Army before he founded the all-black town of Allensworth, California. *(California Historical Society; FN-32157)*

which they saw as a way to segregate black people into separate and lesser institutions rather than allowing them into the state university system. And the Pacific Farming Company failed to honor its commitment to supply water to the town, leading to legal battles and environmental problems that ultimately caused water shortages and other insurmountable problems for the young town.

The most serious blow to the town was the death of Colonel Allensworth himself, who was hit by a speeding motorcycle driven by two white youths on September 13, 1914. Allensworth died the following day. He was later given a military service at the Second Baptist Church of Los Angeles, with an honor guard that included both black and white soldiers. Gradually, the town of Allensworth declined, and by World War II, it had become a ghost town. In 1976, the state of California designated the 800-acre community as Colonel Allensworth State Historic Park. Although the town of Allensworth is long gone, its memory lives on.

Further Reading

"California's Black Utopia." *Sunset* 180, no. 3 (March 1988), p. 78.

"Colonel Allensworth's Black Colony in the San Joaquin Valley." *Sunset* 171, no. 9 (September 1983), p. 48.

Fisher, Edith Maureen. "Pioneer in Black Librarianship: Ethel Hall Norton and the Allensworth Colony." *American Libraries*, February 1987, p. 140.

Hamilton, Kenneth. *Black Towns and Profits*. Champaign: University of Illinois Press, 1991.

Radcliffe, Evelyn. *Out of Darkness: An African-American Man's Success, the Story of Colonel Allen Allensworth.* Menlo Park, Calif.: Inkling Press, 2002.

Wheeler, B. Gordon. "Allensworth: California's All Black Community." *Wild West*, February 2000. Available online on African-American History, About.com. URL: http://afroamhistory.about.com/library/prm/blallensworth1.htm. Downloaded on December 28, 2002.

Amos, Wally
(Famous Amos, Wallace Amos, Wallace Amos, Jr.)
(1936–) *cookie company founder*

Better known as "Famous Amos," Wally Amos is the creator of the first "celebrity cookie"—a food product that achieved success because of its association with such celebrities as Carol Burnett, Marvin Gaye, and Elton John. Although Amos has had his financial ups and downs, his marketing concept has been widely imitated, and he remains famous enough to publish a series of top-selling books.

Wallace Amos, Jr., was born on July 1, 1936, in a poor, black neighborhood in Tallahassee, Florida, the son of Wallace Amos, a local employee of the gas company, and Ruby Amos. Neither of his parents could read, and they reportedly raised Amos with little affection as they struggled to make it through the hard economic times of the Great Depression and the severe racial discrimination of the South.

When Amos was 12, his parents divorced, and his mother moved in with her own mother in Orlando, Florida, sending her son to live with his Aunt Della in New York City. Amos's aunt was the first person to give him chocolate-chip cookies. While living in New York, he attended Edwin W. Stitt Junior High School—the first integrated school he had ever attended. It was difficult for him to cope with the adjustment and with the street gangs that demanded money from him regularly. Amos worked part-time while attending school, delivering newspapers, groceries, and ice.

Amos attended Food Trades Vocational High School with the goal of becoming a chef. He was particularly excited about the second year of school, when he would alternate a week of classes with a week of on-the-job training at the first-class Essex Hotel—but racism, he felt, kept him away from cooking main courses and restricted him to other kinds of food preparation. Amos dropped out of school, gambled away the money his aunt needed to pay her bills, and ran off to live

on the streets. He eventually reconciled with his aunt and, at 17, went to join the air force in 1953.

In 1957, Amos left the air force and began studying at the Collegiate Secretarial Institute while working part-time at Saks Fifth Avenue department store. He did well at Saks, which put him on an executive-training track and sent him to New York University's retail and merchandising course. Amos had trouble with math, however, so he left Saks in 1961 to work at William Morris Talent Agency. He began in the mailroom, studying and practicing his typing during his lunch hour, and soon became a substitute secretary, then one of two secretaries to Howard Hausman, a top executive in the music department. Amos wanted to become an agent, and he invited Hausman to a local club to hear an act that turned out to be the hit musical duo Simon and Garfunkel. Hausman signed the singers and promoted Amos to assistant agent, making him the first black agent at William Morris.

Amos did well at William Morris, booking the Supremes, the Temptations, and Marvin Gaye. But by 1967, he felt the music scene was changing from the rhythm and blues sound he enjoyed so much to hard rock and acid rock, which he did not understand as well. He also felt that he had gone as far as an African American would be allowed to go at William Morris. So he moved to Hollywood and began working independently, managing singers Abbey Lincoln and Oscar Brown, Jr., actress Pat Finley, and comedian Franklin Ajaye. For a while, he was concentrating on only one client, trumpeter Hugh Masakela, but then the relationship dissolved and Amos bounced around from one job to the next. He was also involved in two failed marriages, which produced three sons.

To cheer himself up, Amos began baking his Aunt Della's cookies. Believing that these cookies could lead him into a new career, he started bringing bags of the cookies to parties, complete with his card, hoping that the gimmick would jump-start his fledgling business. Although it did not, the cookies did lead to a chance remark from

QUINCY JONES's secretary, who suggested that they go into business together selling the cookies.

Amos approached his friend, singer Helen Reddy, who urged him to find other investors. She and her husband put up $10,000; recording executive Artie Mogull put up $5,000; and Marvin Gaye put up the final $10,000. Under the name "Famous Amos," which Jones's secretary also suggested, he rented a storefront and started marketing "the superstar of cookies," giving a huge, celebrity-studded party on March 10, 1975, to launch the new product.

Amos's cookies were an instant hit, both because the homemade-style cookies were a more luxurious type of food than was commercially available at the time and because he succeeded in making the cookies themselves a status symbol through their association with celebrities. In 1976, a designer friend took the cookies to Bloomingdale's in New York, where they soon became a hit, starting a whole new trend—gourmet foods at non-food stores. Amos set up a factory in Nutley, New Jersey, to support the Bloomingdale's operation while opening new shops in Southern California. Soon, Neiman Marcus and Macy's department stores were selling his cookies. When Amos was part of the famous Macy's Thanksgiving Day parade, his cookies really took off.

In 1979, Amos married Christine Harris, a flight attendant who would later design Famous Amos key rings, T-shirts, and posters. Eventually the couple had a daughter, Sarah Kapiolani. By 1979, Amos was also doing extremely well financially, with his company netting $4 million in annual revenue. His cookies also became available in supermarkets. But in a few years, Amos ran into difficulties. Other upscale companies, such as Mrs. Fields and David's, cut into his business. He also failed to franchise his operation—to sell small operators licenses to market the cookies—focusing entirely on wholesale (large-scale) business. The newer companies were making money by selling their cookies in small booths,

Wally Amos became known as "Famous Amos," after the brand of cookies he founded and promoted. (AP/Wide World Photos)

rather than in department stores or supermarkets, and Amos was losing out.

Eventually, too, the enormous amount of positive publicity began to turn sour. People complained that the picture on the bag did not match the cookies inside. Moreover, Amos was a great promoter but a poor businessman. In 1985, although Amos's company was selling more than $10 million worth of cookies a year, he was facing bankruptcy. New management bought out the company, with Amos keeping just 8 percent of the stock. Amos continued to promote the cookies, but he was no longer in control of their production—or their quality. Eventually, he lost all equity in (ownership of) the firm.

In 1989, Amos left the company he had founded, having signed a two-year agreement not to compete with the Famous Amos brand. He gave motivational speeches and lived on fees and his retirement fund. In 1992, he went back into business with Wally Amos Presents Chip & Cookie, using his original recipe, even as the owners of the original company had cheapened his product considerably. Amos employed his skillful promotional methods, selling dolls, books, cookie jars, and T-shirts associated with his new brand.

The Famous Amos company sued Amos for using his own name and picture to promote his new cookie. Amos countersued. In the final settlement, Amos was not allowed to use his name or image on any packaging, only in promotions. Amos capitalized on the controversy by starting the Uncle Noname (pronounced "no-NAHM-ay") Cookie Company. He included a story about making lemons into lemonade with each cookie package, turning the difficulties he had encountered into an opportunity for success.

Amos continued to give generously to charities, promising 1 percent of all Uncle Noname sales to Cities in Schools, a program to keep students from dropping out. He also published several books about his experiences. When the large-size packages of his cookies did not sell well, he switched in 1995 to making only two-ounce packages of Uncle Noname cookies, to be distributed by 7-Eleven convenience stores. In 1996, he started selling fat-free and sugar-free muffins. He filed for bankruptcy once again in 1997. Then the Keebler company acquired Famous Amos, and in 1999, they asked him to accept a salary to promote his own brand—complete with his name and likeness on the package. On condition that they improve the quality of the recipe, he agreed, and he has gone on to promote the new cookie, although he has no ownership in that company. Amos continues to promote his muffins, to work for charities, and to be a spokesperson for the Literacy Volunteers of America.

Further Reading

Amos, Wally, and Camilla Denton. *The Power in You: Ten Secret Ingredients for Inner Strength.* Laredo, Tex.: Nightingale-Conant, 1988.

———. *Man with No Name: Turn Lemons into Lemonade.* Fairfield, Conn.: Aslan, 1994.
Amos, Wally, and Stu Glauberman. *Watermelon Magic: Seeds of Wisdom, Slices of Life.* Hillsboro, Ore.: Beyond Words, 1996.
Amos, Wally, and Eden Lee-Murray. *The Cookie Never Crumbles: Inspirational Recipes for Everyday Living.* New York: St. Martin's Press, 2001.
Amos, Wally, and Leroy Robinson. *The Famous Amos Story: The Face That Launched a Thousand Chips.* New York: Doubleday, 1983.
Applegate, Jane. "How Cookie Crumbles—Famous Amos Misfortune." *San Diego Business Journal,* December 9, 1997, p. 12.
Candy, Dana. "A Famous Cookie and a Face to Match." *New York Times,* July 3, 1999, p. C1.
Gale Group. "Wallace Amos, Jr." *Contemporary Authors Online,* The Gale Group, 2002. Reproduced in *Biography Resource Center.* Farmington Hills, Mich.: The Gale Group, 2002. Available online. URL: http://www.galenet.com/ servlet/BioRC. Downloaded on December 4, 2002.
———. "Wally Amos." *Business Leader Profiles for Students,* vol. 1, Gale Research, 1999. Reproduced in *Biography Resource Center.* Farmington Hills, Mich.: The Gale Group, 2002. Available online. URL: http://www.galenet.com/servlet/BioRC. Downloaded on December 4, 2002.
———. "Wally Amos." *Newsmakers 2000,* Issue 1, Gale Group, 2000. Reproduced in *Biography Resource Center.* Farmington Hills, Mich.: The Gale Group, 2002. Available online. URL: http://www.galenet.com/servlet/BioRC. Downloaded on December 4, 2002.
Heuslein, William. "Famous, Shmaymous." *Forbes,* December 20, 1993, p. 146.

Antoine, Cesar Carpentier
(1836–1921) *publisher, life insurance executive, politician*

Like THOMY LAFON, Antoine was a relative newcomer to the prestigious Creole community of

New Orleans, Louisiana, one of the transitional generation that helped preside over the many changes that took place during and after the Civil War. Antoine acquired his money and status through his political activities, most notably a term as state lieutenant governor during the Reconstruction era, when black politicians were being elected for the first time.

For Antoine's life to make sense, it is crucial to understand the class and color lines in Louisiana. Most African Americans in that state were dark-skinned and enslaved. There were also thousands of free people of color, however, many of whom were light-skinned. These light-skinned free black people were known as Creoles, which originally meant only "the children of foreigners." The word has come to mean many things in Louisiana, but in this context, it means "light-skinned African-American elite." However, Antoine, who was free and who seems to have been dark-skinned, was also considered a Creole because he had French ancestry. Much of Antoine's life can be seen as a conflict between his involvement with the Creole elite and his efforts to represent the interests of all black people.

A lot of what is known about Antoine comes from his own account, which historians do not consider to be entirely reliable. He claimed that his mother was descended from an African chief and that his grandmother had been brought to New Orleans as a slave. His father, a free man of color, served as a soldier in the battles around New Orleans during the War of 1812.

Born in New Orleans, Antoine was also educated in private schools there, suggesting that his parents had a certain degree of wealth. As a Creole, he learned both French and English. He became a barber—one of the few professions open to free black people in New Orleans at the time, but one of the least prestigious. In 1860, Antoine was a successful small businessman but yet was not wealthy enough to be mentioned in the census. Perhaps significantly, the census listed him as "black" (dark-skinned) rather than "mulatto" (the

term used for lighter-skinned people of mixed African and European backgrounds).

When Union troops occupied New Orleans during the Civil War, Antoine saw a political opportunity that he quickly seized. He allied himself not with the Creole elite but with a group of free black people, whom he began recruiting into the "Native Guards," later Company I, Seventh Louisiana Colored Regiment, of which he was captain. (Even though the Union troops were from free states, they were racially segregated.)

In 1864, before the Civil War had ended, the light-skinned Creole aristocracy, including Thomy Lafon, had formed the *Tribune,* a newspaper supposedly dedicated to fight for the rights of all black people. But many dark-skinned blacks and recent slaves, including Antoine, suspected that the Creoles were more interested in proving their superiority to darker-skinned African Americans than in winning equal rights. Antoine worked with others, including businessman P. B. S. PINCHBACK, to organize the *Black Republican,* a newspaper that would represent the poorer and darker-skinned African Americans who felt left out by the Creole elite.

Antoine lived for a time in Shreveport, Louisiana, where he owned a small grocery store. He was a delegate to the Louisiana Constitutional Convention in 1867–68, helping to draft the new state constitution, which was supposed to reflect the new world after slavery and to include African Americans in political representation. When the constitution was completed, Antoine was elected state senator from Caddo Parish (in the Shreveport area), a post he held until 1872.

Meanwhile, he engaged in several partnerships with Pinchback, including a New Orleans cotton-selling business in 1869 and a semiweekly newspaper, the *New Orleans Louisianian,* in the same year (Antoine left the paper in 1872, when Pinchback became sole owner). Antoine was involved with a number of other New Orleans ventures, including a questionable scheme with Pinchback to sell some land to the city as parkland. Pinchback, a city parks commissioner in 1871, joined with other commissioners to buy the land at a low price and then sell it to the city at a much higher price. Reportedly, Antoine complained that Pinchback owed him money as a result of the deal.

In 1872, Antoine was nominated for lieutenant governor on the Republican ticket. (Before and for many years after the Civil War, the Democrats were considered the party of slavery and the old South, while the Republicans were the party of Abraham Lincoln, Reconstruction, and "the Negro.") The Republican nominee for governor was a northern white man, and when the Republicans won, elite white politicians and newspapers objected that the city government was "to be delivered over to the rule of the recently emancipated Africans," in the words of a June 25, 1872, editorial in the New Orleans *Times.*

After the election, Antoine joined a group called the Unification Movement that attempted to unite black and white citizens in support of equal opportunity for both races, in the workplace and in political office. The Creole elite favored this plan, but it never received widespread support. Meanwhile, Antoine, a Creole, was viciously attacked by the Creole elite, which claimed that he did not have the education or breeding to be a leader.

In 1876, Antoine was nominated for lieutenant governor again, but the election was disputed. Federal troops, which had been stationed throughout the South to prevent the old slaveholding planter aristocracy from resuming control after the Civil War, were withdrawn that year, leading to the expulsion of Republicans—and people of color—from politics.

For a while, Antoine was on the school board in Caddo Parish, and during the 1870s, he was involved in various businesses, including investing in railroads and lotteries, raising racehorses, and assuming the presidency of the Cosmopolitan Life Insurance Company in 1880. He also purchased a Caddo Parish plantation and several lots in New Orleans, as well as an expensive city home. In 1891, he joined the Comité des Citoyens (Citizens Committee), a group formed by the Creole elite to protest their poor treatment. Some have viewed this committee as fighting for black-white equality; others have accused it of being more concerned with reestablishing Creole privilege at the expense of other black people. This is the committee that brought the suit *Plessy v. Ferguson* to the Supreme Court, objecting to the segregation of black people in New Orleans railway cars. The Supreme Court eventually ruled that "separate but equal" accommodations for black people were acceptable, and this remained the law of the land until the 1954 decision *Brown v. Board of Education.* The committee also fought against the segregation of Catholic churches, which was established in New Orleans in 1895 (previously pews had been segregated, but not whole buildings). The committee was generally unsuccessful: By the 20th century, strict segregation was the rule, and the Creole elite had lost much of its separate status. Antoine died in obscurity in September 1921. The new black leadership that came after him focused more on building independent black communities than on engaging in the kind of political activism that he had led.

Further Reading

Blassingame, John. *Black New Orleans 1860–1880.* Chicago: University of Chicago Press, 1973.

McCants, Dorothea Olga, Sr. *Our People and Our History.* Baton Rouge: Louisiana State University Press, 1973.

Simmons, William J. *Men of Mark, Eminent, Progressive, and Rising.* Reprint, New York: Arno Press, 1968.

B

Banks, Charles
(1873–1923) *banker, town developer, entrepreneur*

Charles Banks was an integral part of the development of Mound Bayou, Mississippi, an idealistic black community founded in the late 19th century. Although Mound Bayou flourished for a while, it eventually fell on hard times, evidence that all-black communities—like most small communities—could not ultimately marshal enough resources to live separately from the larger society for long periods of time.

Banks was born on March 25, 1873, the son of Daniel and Sallie Ann Banks. Little information is available on his early years, though it is known that he was born in a log cabin in Clarksdale, Mississippi; that he grew up in extreme poverty; and that he attended public schools and Rust University in Holly Springs, Mississippi. After college, he returned to Clarksdale, where he became a speculator in real estate and cotton, buying land and cotton at low prices and reselling them at a profit. He formed Banks & Co. to continue his activities.

In 1893, Banks married Trenma O. Booze of Natchez, Mississippi, and began a business association with her brother, Eugene Parker Booze, starting with Banks taking young Eugene as an apprentice in his enterprises. (An apprentice works for no or low wages in exchange for learning a trade or business.)

In 1903, Banks visited the community of Mound Bayou, which had been founded by ISAIAH T. MONTGOMERY. In 1904, he moved to the new community with the intention of opening the Bank of Mound Bayou. Booze came with him and eventually married Montgomery's daughter.

Although Banks made Mound Bayou resident John W. Francis bank president, he owned some two-thirds of the bank's stock and served as cashier, and it was under his leadership that the bank proceeded. By 1910, the bank had moved into a two-story building with plate-glass windows and more than $100,000 in assets. The Mound Bayou community benefited enormously from having its own bank, as it meant that the community kept control of its own resources and had a source of money that local businesspeople could borrow to create new enterprises. In 1909, Banks and Booze began another business, the Farmer's Cooperative Mercantile Company, intended to sell farmers the basic things they needed at affordable prices.

The Mound Bayou bank faced a number of financial difficulties, however, in part due to Banks's weaknesses as a manager. In 1914, the country faced a recession that resulted in the bank's failure, even though it had received a loan from Julius Rosenwald, the white president of

Sears, Roebuck and a supporter of black civil rights. Banks and Montgomery set up a new bank in 1916, the Mound Bayou State Bank, which survived only until 1926.

Banks worked with Montgomery's brother, William Thornton Montgomery, to found and operate the Mound Bayou Loan and Investment Company. As with the bank, it was intended to keep the community's money within the community and to help local farmers hold onto their farms. He also worked with Isaiah Montgomery to found the Mound Bayou Oil and Manufacturing Company, a cottonseed oil company, but the company had difficulties from the start and finally stopped operating in 1915.

Banks's and Montgomery's partnership fell apart over political differences in 1917, a split that basically lasted until Banks's death. By 1922, the Mercantile company had failed, and Banks died in poverty presumably a year later in 1923, though records are uncertain about the exact date. The Mound Bayou community that he had helped found, however, stands as a testimony to the power of a dream of black freedom and autonomy—even if that dream could not be achieved by means of black withdrawal from the larger society.

Further Reading

Chambers, Caneidra. "Mound Bayou: Jewel of the Delta." Department of Anthropology and Sociology, University of Southern Mississippi website. Available online. URL: http://ocean.otr.usm.edu/~aloung/mbayou.html. Downloaded on January 16, 2003.

Hamilton, Kenneth. *Black Towns and Profits.* Urbana, Ill.: University of Illinois Press, 1991.

Jackson, David H., Jr. *A Chief Lieutenant of the Tuskegee Machine: Charles Banks of Mississippi.* Gainesville: University of Florida Press, 2002.

Young, Amy L., and Milburn J. Crowe. "Descendant Community Involvement in African-American Archaeology in Mississippi: Digging for the Dream in Mound Bayou." Arkansas Archaeological Survey, University of Arkansas Web Site. Available online. URL: http://www.uark.edu/campusresources/archinfo/SHACyoung.pdf. Downloaded on January 16, 2003.

Barden, Don
(Don H. Barden)
(1943–) *real estate speculator, automotive dealer, cable executive, casino owner*

Over the course of his entrepreneurial career, Don Barden has moved from one business to another, with a seemingly unerring instinct about when to enter an industry and when to leave it. He has also proven skilled at developing political connections that enhance his business dealings. He rose to fame with a cable television empire when the cable industry was still in its infancy. His latest venture is in the world of casino gambling, in Las Vegas, Nevada, and elsewhere.

Don Barden was born on December 20, 1943, in Detroit, Michigan, the son of Milton Barden, a laborer, and Hortense (Hamilton) Barden, a homemaker who raised 13 children. As a child growing up in the then rural suburb of Inkster, Michigan, Barden saw his father working as a farmer, mechanic, auto-plant laborer, and in a variety of other jobs. Barden attended public school in Detroit, where at one point he was captain of both the football and the basketball teams. In 1963 he enrolled in the predominantly black Central State University in Wilberforce, Ohio, working part-time as a barber to pay his tuition. Even so, he had to drop out after one year due to lack of finances. He moved to Lorain, Ohio, where one of his brothers lived, working as a shipyard laborer, plumber, and restaurant worker.

Barden managed to save $500, with which he opened a record store. Soon he was booking bands and promoting shows, leading to the creation of his own record label. Barden discovered that he was good at promotion, and so he started his own public relations firm in Lorain. Although the firm was ultimately not successful, it provided a valuable foundation for Barden's entrepreneurial career.

When Barden learned that the U.S. government was looking for a new building to house its military recruiting station in Lorain, he offered to find the property—and then used the promise of a big tenant to secure financing to buy a suitable building. Barden invested $25,000 of his own savings in the deal—and then sold the building two years later for $50,000.

For a time, Barden and a colleague tried to start a newspaper, an enterprise that failed in 1967 but that led to his more successful founding of the *Lorain County Times,* which he ran for five years, writing the stories, selling the ads, and delivering the paper to subscribers. He also became the first black person to be elected to the Lorain City Council, where he served two terms, from 1972 to 1975. In 1977, he began hosting a talk show at Cleveland's WKYC-TV, a National Broadcasting Company (NBC) affiliate, a position he held for three years.

After Barden failed at an effort to run for Ohio state senate, he moved into a new industry: cable. He helped arrange a deal in which 4 percent of the cable franchises of Lorain and nearby Elyria, Ohio, would be set aside for African Americans. Then he bought 2 percent of each franchise for $2,000 apiece—and sold them two years later for $200,000.

Barden went on to seek communities in the Midwest where he could run cable franchises for black viewers. At the time, other cable operators focused on more upscale customers who were largely white and suburban. Barden saw an untapped market among African Americans. His first contract was for wiring his old hometown of Inkster, Michigan, in suburban Detroit. He engaged in other cable business ventures throughout 1981 and 1982, acquiring his biggest prize in 1982: the city of Detroit.

The Detroit deal was large enough that Barden needed a partner to help finance the huge costs involved, so in 1984 he went into business with the Canadian communications company Maclean Hunter, Ltd., of Toronto. Barden began

wiring Detroit in 1986, and by 1994, Barden Cablevision—a division of Barden Communications, Inc.—had won some 120,000 subscribers out of Detroit's 375,000 households. But Barden had discovered that less affluent customers were problematic, since they frequently had trouble paying their monthly bills and often cancelled their service. Still, Barden continued to operate profitably, and in 1991, Barden Communications Inc. had even expanded into the field of personal communications services—wireless devices that could transmit phone signals for phone, fax, and computer communication. As few black firms got into the personal-communications field so early, this was a tribute to Barden's farsightedness.

In 1994, however, Barden decided to leave the cable business. Maclean Hunter had already sold its share to Comcast Corp., a Philadelphia company, and Barden sold his own share to the same company for a $100 million profit. Meanwhile, he had already moved on to a new field: casino gambling. He won a contract to build the Majestic Star Casino, a riverboat gambling facility in Gary, Indiana. In 1998, when the possibility of casino gambling opened up in Detroit, entrepreneur Donald Trump solicited Barden's partnership. Although the two men were unable to win the gambling contract from the city, Barden continued to seek other casino ventures. He tried again to win a Detroit contract in partnership with entertainer Michael Jackson, but once again his bid was rejected.

In 1996, Barden had entered the automotive field with a deal to supply the southern African nation of Namibia with 824 Chevrolet pickup trucks to be delivered in 1998. Some scandal attached to the arrangement, however, when it was discovered that Barden had sold cars designed to drive on the right side of the road, while Namibians drive on the left. Namibia had to pay an additional $15 million to convert the cars, and Barden won that contract as well. Barden countered his critics by saying that some people had difficulty accepting a black man's success.

In 2001, Barden expanded his casino activities by purchasing Fitzgeralds' chain of hotels and casinos, including properties in downtown Las Vegas and in the regions of Memphis, Tennessee, and Denver, Colorado. This purchase made Barden the only African-American owner of a casino chain and put him into three of the top five gaming markets in the United States.

Barden continues to operate in a number of arenas, including real estate. He seems poised to expand further in the casino field—and perhaps to enter new industries as he identifies future prospects for success.

Further Reading

Dietderich, Andrew. "Barden Buys 3 Casinos." *Crain's Detroit Business,* February 25, 2002, p. 18.

Dingle, Derek T. *Black Enterprise, Titans of the B.E. 100s.* New York: John Wiley & Sons, Inc., 1999, pp. 213–230.

"Don H. Barden." Barden International. Available online. URL: http://www.barden.com.na/Players/DonBarden.html. Downloaded on January 13, 2003.

Gale Group. "Don Barden." *Contemporary Black Biography.* Vol. 20. Farmington Hills, Mich.: The Gale Group, 1998.

Neusom, James I., II. "Don Barden, The New Black Face of Vegas." The City Lights Reporter, 5, Issue 1. Available online. URL: http://www.citylightssoftware.com/reporter0102.html. Posted January 2002.

Slavin, Al. "Barden, Trump, Team Up on $38M Parking Garage." *Crain's Detroit Business,* August 14, 2000, p. 2.

Bartholomew, Joseph Manuel

(1890–1971) *contractor, real estate developer, golf course designer, insurance company executive*

Joseph M. Bartholomew was one of the major designers and builders of golf courses in New Orleans, Louisiana, but because of segregation, he was never allowed to play on most of the courses he created. A fearless and determined entrepreneur, Bartholomew created several successful companies. Throughout his life, however, golf remained his first love.

Bartholomew was born on August 1, 1890, in New Orleans, to Manuel and Alice Bartholomew. His parents' professions are unknown, but the Bartholomews were not members of the city's predominantly Creole black elite, and Joseph Bartholomew had only an elementary education at one of New Orleans's public schools. At age seven he began working after school as a caddie at Audubon Golf Course, where he fell in love with the game. He taught himself to play golf and went on to manage the club's greens and to become its assistant pro, giving lessons to white men who would eventually become the premier golfers of the city.

When the new Metairie golf course was being planned in 1922, a club member named H. T. Cottam convinced the club to send Bartholomew to New York, where he attended Golf Architectural School and visited various golf courses. Bartholomew returned to New Orleans to build the Metairie Country Club course. He then rented his construction equipment to white contractors, giving him a chance to observe construction firsthand. Meanwhile, he used a wagon and two mules to run a cartage business.

Bartholomew went on to expand his construction business, while also building a number of Louisiana golf courses, including City Park No. 1, City Park No. 2, and the New Orleans Country Club. Because city facilities were segregated, he was not allowed to play on the courses he had built. Eventually, he built Crescent City Golf Club, a private "black golf course" on his own property in the New Orleans suburb of Harahan.

Bartholomew's construction activity included work for the historically black universities Dillard and Xavier, Charity Hospital, and all the New Orleans public housing projects of the 1930s and 1940s. During World War II, he was a subcontractor on the largest shipyard building program in Louisiana history, working at Higgins Industries. He also laid the foundations for the Johns-Manville plant in New Orleans, as well as several other factories and office buildings. After the war, he built the New Orleans County Club and Pontchartrain Park, a black housing project. His crews included both black and white workers, highly unusual for the time.

Working with a white partner to make savvy real estate investments, Bartholomew expanded his fortune, which he used in 1940 to purchase the financially troubled black-owned Douglas Life Insurance Company. This enterprise, too, he made successful, along with an ice-cream plant that he built with his partner, John Creech.

The dark-skinned, rags-to-riches Bartholomew was something of an anomaly in New Orleans, whose historically light-skinned Creole elite is known for being one of the nation's most influential black bourgeoisies. Despite his alienation from the city's upper class, Bartholomew was a leader in race matters, participating in the National Association for the Advancement of Colored People (NAACP) and the Urban League. He was married to Ruth Segue, with whom he had two daughters and one son. He died of a stroke on October 12, 1971. In 1972, he became the first black man to be named to the Greater New Orleans Sports Hall of Fame, and in 1979, the Joseph M. Bartholomew Golf Course in New Orleans was named in his honor.

Further Reading

"History: Joseph M. Bartholomew." ourGOLF.: Minority Golf Online. Available online. URL: http://www.ourgolf.com/history/bartholomew.html. Downloaded on September 14, 2002.

Ingham, John N., and Lynne B. Feldman. *African-American Business Leaders: A Biographical Dictionary.* Westport, Conn.: Greenwood Press, 1994, pp. 54–58.

McDaniel, Pete, Geoff Russell, and Martin Davis. *Uneven Lies: The Heroic Story of African-Americans in Golf.* Chicago, Ill.: The American Golfer, Inc., 2000.

Beavers, George Allen, Jr.
(1891–1989) *insurance company founder, executive*

George Allen Beavers, Jr., helped found and operate Golden State Insurance (now Golden State Mutual), the major African-American-owned insurance company in California and one of the major such companies in the nation. Beavers helped build the company into a multimillion-dollar business that survived the Great Depression and continues to flourish today.

Beavers was born in Atlanta, Georgia, on October 30 or 31, 1891, the son of George Allen Beavers, Sr., a laborer in a wholesale grocery; his mother was a laundress. The family moved to Los Angeles when George was 12, hoping to escape the increasingly violent and discriminatory atmosphere of the U.S. South. George, Sr., got work as a laborer at Pacific Electric Railway while George worked as a water boy for the same company on summer vacations from Los Angeles High School.

Beavers graduated from high school, got married in 1911, and went to work as an elevator operator at the German-American Bank, later Security Pacific National Bank. Beavers went on to become stock clerk, then messenger at the bank. In World War I, he was unable to serve in the army because he had lost an eye as a teenager, so he worked as a molder's helper in the Los Angeles Foundry. Formerly active in the African Methodist Church, he went on to help establish the People's Independent Church of Christ. He also began selling real estate at G. W. Wheatley Real Estate.

In spring 1922, Beavers met the men who had founded an insurance company known as American Mutual—Norman Oliver Houston and William Nickerson, Jr. Beavers was initially approached to buy a policy; he soon became a part-time agent for the company, started studying the business under Houston and Nickerson, and took classes at the extension division of the University of California, Los Angeles. In 1923,

Houston left American Mutual, and Beavers took over Houston's job as superintendent of agents.

In 1924, Nickerson, Beavers, and Houston decided to form their own company, with Nickerson as president. They named their venture the Golden State Guarantee Fund Insurance Company, in honor of California's nickname, the Golden State. Beavers took the post of vice president and director of agencies in 1925, a position he held until Nickerson's death in 1945.

The new company expanded rapidly from its Los Angeles office, adding divisions based in Oakland, Pasadena, Bakersfield, San Diego, and Fresno. In 1928, the company moved to a new building that was designed and built entirely by African Americans, from the architect to the contractor to the construction firm. The insurance company shared space there with several other black merchants.

From 1931 to 1932, Beavers served as vice president of the National Negro Insurance Association, a group founded to promote black insurance companies. During the same year, the company changed its name to Golden State Mutual Life Insurance Company to reflect some adjustments in the type of insurance business it conducted. Despite the Great Depression of the 1930s, Golden State continued to do well, expanding into Chicago in 1938 and into Texas in 1944. By the end of World War II, the company possessed more than $2 million in assets, $1 million in policy reserves, and nearly $24 million of insurance.

In 1945, William Nickerson died, and Norman Houston became the company's second president, with Beavers moving up to serve as chairman of the board. Although Houston became president, it was generally recognized that Beavers and Houston were equals in running the company.

In 1949, Golden State moved from its old headquarters to a new six-story building, which was visited by more than 10,000 people from all over the nation during its grand opening week—a major event in Los Angeles's African-American community. The company continued to expand throughout the 1950s, opening offices in Oregon, Washington, and Arizona. By 1960, the company had more than $16 million in assets and $133 million of insurance in force.

From 1962 to 1963, Beavers served as president of the National Negro Insurance Association. During the same year, he retired from active management, though he continued as chairman of the board until 1965 and then served on the board of directors until 1980. Between 1980 and his death on October 13, 1989, he acted as chairman emeritus and director emeritus ("emeritus" means "retired," and a person with that title has honorary involvement in an institution).

Throughout his life, Beavers was active in Los Angeles community affairs, including a time as president of the Los Angeles Urban League. He received honors from presidents Franklin D. Roosevelt and Harry S. Truman, and was a close friend of Los Angeles Mayor (later governor) Tom Bradley. He also worked with the National Association for the Advancement of Colored People (NAACP), the Los Angeles County Conference on Community Relations, and the National Conference of Christians and Jews. Golden State continues to operate as a major insurance company in the western United States, a monument to Beavers and his colleagues.

Further Reading

Golden State Minority Foundation website. Available online. URL: http://www.gsmf.org. Downloaded on January 14, 2003.

Golden State Mutual Web Site. Available online. URL: http://www.gsmlife.com. Downloaded on January 14, 2003.

Ingham, John N., and Lynne B. Feldman. *African-American Business Leaders: A Biographical Dictionary*. Westport, Conn.: Greenwood Press, 1994, pp. 58–75.

Big Red   See GREENLEE, GUS.

Binga, Jesse
(1856–1950) *banker, realtor*

Jesse Binga was Chicago's leading African-American businessperson in the early part of the 20th century and the owner of the first privately owned African-American bank in the North. Although he finished life penniless and disgraced, for several decades he was at the center of Chicago's black business development, and his reputation as realtor, banker, and entrepreneur survives.

Binga was born on April 10, 1865, the youngest in a family of eight girls and two boys. His parents were free people of color who had moved to Detroit, Michigan, in the 1840s. Robert Binga, Sr., a barbershop owner, had come to Detroit from Ontario, Canada. Adelphia Powers Binga had grown up in Rochester, New York. The tenement houses she built in Detroit were known as "Binga rows." She also worked as an entrepreneur, shipping whitefish and sweet potatoes across state lines.

As a young man, Binga learned barbering from his father while helping his mother collect rents and repair rental properties. When he was in his third year of high school, he dropped out to work for African-American attorney Thomas Crispus, who also taught him law. In 1885, despite the beginnings of a business career in Detroit, Binga headed west, visiting cities in Missouri, Minnesota, Montana, Washington, California, Utah, and Idaho, working variously as a barber and a Pullman porter. In Pocatello, Idaho, he profited from buying land on a former Indian reservation. In the mid-1890s, he settled in Chicago, where he was to make his mark as one of the city's leading entrepreneurs.

Despite his good fortune in Pocatello, Binga arrived in Chicago with very little money, suggesting that he might have been heavily in debt before the Idaho deal. Sources differ on his early days in Chicago: Some believe that he ran a fruit stand, others that he sold coal oil and gasoline from a wagon that he drove, and still others that he shined shoes. Historians do agree, however, that in 1898 he opened a real estate business that soon prospered, despite its humble beginnings: With five dollars (half the money he possessed), Binga paid the rent on his office, and with the other five dollars, he bought a desk, three old chairs, and a used stove.

Binga's experience working for his mother in Detroit along with his hard work, soon paid off. He often stayed up all night repairing boilers and plumbing, hanging wallpaper, and doing other jobs to renovate the buildings he owned and rented. Having renovated his own shabby office building, he rented it out and moved to a more prestigious location, in a building that he first rented and then owned. He began buying up other properties, finding ways to buy properties on formerly all-white streets and then renting or selling them to black people. Because white people often feared black neighbors, this practice was known as "blockbusting," since once a single black family had moved into the neighborhood, white people often moved out, leaving their properties at lower rents or sale prices for black families to acquire. According to a 1912 article in the *Chicago Defender*, Chicago's premier black newspaper, Binga might lease a home to a white person for $20 or $25 per month in order to fool the owner into allowing the transaction. Then he would proceed to re-rent the property to a black tenant for up to $40. Other real estate dealers soon followed suit in this profitable practice, which had the mixed effect of opening up new areas of the city to black tenants and owners, while associating black residents with falling property values.

Meanwhile, in 1908, Binga opened the Binga Bank, which quickly became famous as the first black-owned bank in the North. Then, in 1912, Binga further increased his wealth and prominence by marrying Eudora Johnson, sister of the late gambling kingpin John "Mushmouth" Johnson. Because of her wealth and age, contemporaries speculated that Binga had married Johnson for her money, and indeed, their wedding was a huge extravagant affair that led to increased wealth and an improved social position for Binga. The couple's Christmas parties became famous, and Binga's wealth continued to grow. He prospered as the African-American population of Chicago grew—the result of the black migration northward after World War I, with African Americans seeking better jobs and freedom from the harsh racial laws of the South. At the height of his prosperity, Binga owned 1,200 residential leases in Chicago, and by 1926, he was the largest owner of frontage on State Street, at the center of Chicago's black business district. He also owned a group of storefront apartments known as "the Binga Block."

Many white people did not take kindly to Binga's wealth and power. Between 1917 and 1921, his properties were vandalized, especially during the 1919 race riots, known as "Red Summer," when many white people took to the streets to express their frustration with the increasing influx of black people into Chicago. Binga's own home was bombed five times, partly because it was located in an otherwise all-white area. Binga refused to back down, however, and continued to lead a public and prominent life, despite hiring armed guards and arming himself.

As the so-called Great Migration of blacks continued northward, Binga Bank attracted many new customers, and its business increased dramatically between 1917 and 1921. Binga Bank had originally operated as a private bank—a bank that operated without any state charter (contract with the state). In 1919, Binga was finally able to obtain a charter, however, and he renamed his enterprise Binga State Bank.

As with many black enterprises, Binga's bank offered many opportunities for young African Americans to find jobs in a sector that had previously been closed to them. The bank also served as a financial center for Chicago's African-American community. Although Binga was the bank's largest shareholder, *Chicago Defender* publisher ROBERT SENGSTACKE ABBOTT was also a shareholder and a member of the board of directors.

Binga's bank was also a haven for many black customers who had been discriminated against or treated discourteously at white-owned banks. Loan sharks, private individuals who offered loans at huge interest rates, were less able to prey on Chicago's African Americans, because Binga's bank—unlike many white banks—would lend them money. Binga went on to form the Binga Safe Deposit Company, where black customers could store their valuables, as well as an insurance company.

Binga had a mixed reputation during the years of his success. He was known for his generous donations to charity, including the Young Women's Christian Association (YWCA), an Old Folks Home, and various local charities for children and the elderly. He also gave to Fisk, Howard, and Atlanta Universities, historically black institutions. And he was prominent in the Associated Business Club, an affiliate of Booker T. Washington's National Negro Business League, a group set up to promote black self-help and focus on black enterprise. On the other hand, Binga was also known as mean and arrogant, someone who charged his low-income tenants the highest rents he possibly could, taking advantage of the fact that they had nowhere else to go. He obviously enjoyed his wealth and his ability to display it, and he was accused of taking advantage of his wife and her fortune.

Yet, when hard times came, Binga was able to rely on the support of the black community. In 1929, the U.S. stock market collapsed and the Great Depression began. Black people in Chicago felt the hard times keenly, but for a while Binga was able to expand, constructing a five-story office building, complete with a rooftop ballroom, known as the Binga Arcade. However, in 1930, Binga's bank collapsed. Not only did Binga lose his personal fortune of $400,000—an enormous sum at the time—but the savings of thousands of Chicago's African Americans were lost.

On March 5, 1931, Binga was arrested for banking irregularities but was acquitted at trial. In 1933 he was tried again and this time he was convicted of embezzlement (stealing money for personal use from his company). He was sentenced to ten years in prison, but the black community rallied behind him—despite their own losses from his dealings—and he was freed in 1938.

Binga's wife had died in 1933, and by the time of his release from jail, Binga had become a Catholic. He went to work as a handyman at St. Anselm's Catholic Church, a position he held the rest of his life. He died in Chicago on June 13, 1950, from a stroke that caused him to fall down the stairs of his nephew's house, where he had gone to live. Although most of his properties are no longer standing, his memory endures as one of the leaders of Chicago's early black business community.

Further Reading

American Council of Learned Societies. "Jesse Binga." *Dictionary of American Biography, Supplement 4: 1946–1950.* New York: Scribner's, 1974.

Chicago Tribute Markers. "Jesse Binga." Chicago Tribute Markers of Distinction. Available online. URL: http://www.chicagotribute.org/Markers/Binga.htm. Downloaded on December 4, 2002.

Logan, Rayford, W., and Michael R. Winston, eds. *Dictionary of American Negro Biography.* New York: Norton, 1982.

Osthaus, Carl R. "The Rise and Fall of Jesse Binga, Black Financier." *Journal of Negro History* 58 (January 1973): 39–60.

Spear, Allan H. *Black Chicago: The Making of a Negro Ghetto, 1890–1920.* Chicago: University of Chicago Press, 1969.

Blayton, Jesse

(1897–1977) *banker, bottling company executive, radio station executive, CPA*

Jesse Blayton is known for founding financial institutions that serve Atlanta's black community, for becoming the first African-American owner of a U.S. radio station, and for his place in the Radio Hall of Fame. As Georgia's first black certified public accountant (CPA), he also served as mentor to a new generation of black professionals.

Blayton was born on December 6, 1897, in Fallis, Oklahoma, to Lester B. Blayton and Mattie E. Carter. He graduated from Langston University in Oklahoma in 1918, and served in the 92nd Division of the U.S. Army during World War I. From 1922 to 1929, he worked as an auditor. In 1925 he joined with 14 other black investors, each of whom put in $100 to form the Mutual Federal Savings and Loan Association. Also in 1925 he began teaching at Atlanta's historically black Atlanta University (which later combined with Clark University under its current name of Clark Atlanta University). He became Carnegie Professor of business administration at Atlanta University in 1930.

Meanwhile, in 1928, Blayton became Georgia's first African-American CPA and in the same year formed his own accounting firm, J.B. Blayton and Company. According to *A White-Collar Profession: African American Certified Public Accountants Since 1921,* by Theresa A. Hammond, "Interviews with dozens of African American CPAs from all regions of the country revealed that many of them received early encouragement from one influential man, Jesse B. Blayton, Sr., an accounting professor. . . ."

In 1928 Blayton also joined fellow black businessmen Lorimer D. Milton and Clayton R. Yates to reorganize Citizens Trust Bank, which in 1936 became the first black bank to join the Federal Reserve. Mutual Federal and Citizens Trust became two of the three largest black financial institutions in Atlanta by the mid-1950s, and the companies played a key role in financing homes for African Americans. In 1940, Citizens Trust worked with the Federal Housing Administration to develop the area around Hunter Road—now known as Martin Luther King, Jr., Drive—creating an extremely prestigious neighborhood where Blayton himself had a home. Ku Klux Klan crosses burned on residents' lawns indicated some white resistance to the development.

Citizens Trust also helped finance many black-owned businesses, including the newspaper, the *Atlanta Daily World,* and the city's first black night club, the Top Hat Club, which Blayton, Milton, and Yates bought through their BLMIYA (BLayton, MIlton, YAtes) corporation. The club, modeled on New York City's Cotton Club, generally attracted a black audience, though Saturday evenings were reserved for whites only. It was later sold and renamed the Royal Peacock.

Citizens Trust provided key financial support to Robert and James Paschal, brothers whose La Carousel Lounge (1960) and Paschal's Motor Hotel (1967) served as the unofficial headquarters of the Southern Christian Leadership Conference (SCLC) and the Freedom Riders during the Civil Rights movement and for the city's black politicians in the 1980s and 1990s.

In 1949, Blayton obtained a Federal Communications Commission (FCC) license to operate WERD in Atlanta, the first black-owned long-wave radio station in the United States. He founded Midway Television Institute, which trained radio and television mechanics, and the Blayton Business School. He was also the first president of the Atlanta Negro Chamber of Commerce. Blayton was a major financial supporter of the Civil Rights movement and was active in the National Association for the Advancement of Colored People (NAACP) and the Urban League, while remaining a lifelong conservative Republican. At the same time, during the 1960s, he allowed his radio station to share building space with the SCLC, offering a platform for civil rights leaders to reach radio listeners in the South. Blayton sold WERD in 1968 while remaining active in community affairs until his death on September 7, 1977. He was inducted into the Radio Hall of Fame in 1995.

Further Reading

Alexander, Robert J. "Negro Business in Atlanta." *Southern Economic Journal* 17 no. 4 (April 1951): 456–458.

Hammond, Theresa A. *A White Collar Profession: African American Certified Public Accountants since 1921.* Chapel Hill: University of North Carolina Press, 2002.

Opdyke, Tom. "Life As It Used to Be: Werd Is a Word in Black History." *Atlanta Journal-Constitution,* October 31, 1994, Section C, p. 2.

Boutte, Alvin Joseph
(1929–) *banker*

Alvin Boutte is the founder and CEO of Indecorp, which in its time was the largest black-owned financial institution in the United States.

Boutte was born on October 10, 1929, in Lake Charles, Louisiana, to parents about whom little is known. He graduated from historically black Xavier University in 1951 with a bachelor's degree in pharmacology. He then competed for the first time in his life against a racially mixed group when he took the tests for the U.S. Army Officer's Candidate School. After finishing second in a pool of 220, Boutte remained in the army until 1954 and then settled in Chicago. He worked as a pharmacist at Lakeside Drugstore, whose owner planned to sell him the business after one year. Boutte prepared by observing other drugstores and taking business courses at the University of Chicago. He financed his purchase with a loan from Sealtest Dairy, since banks at the time were unwilling to make small business loans to African Americans, whereas the ice cream company was always seeking drugstores and other new outlets for its products.

By the mid-1960s, Boutte had created Independent Drug Store, a four-store chain. In 1964, he joined with George Johnson, head of a major black cosmetics firm, to organize Independence Bank. Initially, the black bank owners hired a white president, but the bank foundered under his leadership. In 1967, Boutte took over as president, selling his drugstore chain, investing $400,000 in the bank, and increasing his holdings to 25 percent of what many financial experts saw as an extremely risky investment. Nevertheless, the bank prospered as Boutte developed a new management team, sought white corporate mainstream accounts, and expanded the bank's retail consumer base.

By the 1970s, Boutte had acquired corporate accounts from CBS, Chrysler, and General Motors; an operating account for Delta Airlines and for a CBS-owned radio station; and the payroll account for a division of Johnson & Johnson baby products. He also held accounts for several black businesses. By 1973, Independence was the largest black bank in the United States.

In 1977, Boutte became the first nonemployee to join the board of directors of Chicago Metropolitan Mutual Assurance Company, a major black insurance company. Chicago Metropolitan and Independence Bank played major roles in financing black business activity in Chicago through the 1970s and 1980s.

In 1979 Boutte acquired the failing black banks, Gateway National Bank and the Nation of Islam's Guaranty Bank & Trust, which each served many of Chicago's black working families. In 1980, he formed Indecorp, the bank holding company that holds Independence Bank. He acquired Drexel National Bank in 1988, the first time a black bank had acquired a healthy white-owned bank. In 1993, he acquired black-owned Highland Community Bank, though the bank was sold to the white Shorebank holding company in 1995.

Boutte saw the development of black business as a way of supporting the progress of the black community, and to that end, he served on the board of the Small Business Administration and as president of the Freedom Development Corporation, which Dr. Martin Luther King, Jr., had founded to help black people acquire property. From 1969 to 1974, he served on the Chicago School Board. A married man, he and his wife have four children.

Further Reading

Brimmer, Andrew, "The Black Banks: An Assessment of Performance and Prospects." *Journal of Finance* 26 (May 1971): 379–405.

Grzywinski, Ronald. "The New Old-Fashioned Banking." *Harvard Business Review* 60, no. 3 (May–June 1991): 87–98.

Ingham, John N., and Lynne B. Feldman. *African-American Business Leaders: A Biographical Dictionary.* Westport, Conn.: Greenwood Press, 1994, pp. 91–97.

Lash, Nicholas A. "Banking, Chicago Community Development Banks and Community Reinvestment Act (CRA)," in Walker, Juliet E. K., editor, *Encyclopedia of African American Business History.* Westport, Conn.: Greenwood Press, 1999, pp. 55–59.

Taub, Richard. *Community Capitalism.* Cambridge, Mass.: Harvard Business School Press, 1994.

Bowser, Yvette Lee

(ca. 1965–   ) *television producer, production company head*

Yvette Lee Bowser is the first African-American woman to have created her own successful television situation comedy, not to mention the only black woman to have two shows on the air at the same time. Her achievement is all the more notable for having taken place before she reached the age of 31. Bowser is the head of her own production company, SisterLee Productions, with which she continues to create and produce shows.

Born Yvette Lee sometime around 1965 to parents of mixed heritage, the young woman grew up around Philadelphia and studied political science and psychology at Stanford University, thinking she would become a lawyer. There, she had the chance to meet Bill Cosby, who was in nearby Oakland, California, filming the movie *Leonard Part VI.* She showed Cosby her writing samples and asked for a job. Cosby refused, but Lee was persistent, and in 1987 Cosby hired her as an apprentice writer on his television show, *A Different World,* which related the stories of a group of African-American college students at a traditionally black college.

Lee gradually worked her way up from fetching sandwiches and coffee to pitching her own ideas. Eventually she became a writer, then a producer. She went on to work briefly as a producer for the TV show *Hangin' with Mr. Cooper,* the story of an African-American high school teacher. Lee was frustrated by that experience, feeling that women's views were not welcome and that her own sense of the show's black characters was not respected, even though she was for a short time the only black person on staff.

When Lee left *Mr. Cooper,* she was committed to creating her own show, hoping to portray African-American women in their twenties, women who resembled her and her friends. In 1992, the film *Waiting to Exhale* seemed to establish that stories about black women could be commercially successful. So when Bowser was offered a development deal at Warner Brothers, she developed *Living Single,* the story of four black professional women living in Brooklyn.

Because Lee had not yet created her own show, she was partnered with Tom Anderson, who had worked on the hit sitcom *Cheers.* Lee was initially concerned that the pairing would mean her loss of control of the show, but she found Anderson respectful of her leadership and she appreciated his support.

Living Single debuted on the Fox network in August 1993 and quickly became a hit. Although it garnered critical praise as well as popular support, it was still the victim of stereotyping to some extent; for example, *Newsweek* dubbed it the "Booty-Shakin' Sugar Momma" show. Nevertheless, nearly 10 million viewers watched every week during the show's five years on the air. Now in syndication, *Living Single* was the top-rated show in black and Latino households for all five years that it was on the air, and Bowser's efforts to portray positive but diverse images of African-American women was widely praised for its success at overcoming stereotypes and opening the door to more accurate and interesting portrayals of young black professionals. Warner Brothers was so

pleased it offered Lee a production deal to form her own company, SisterLee Productions.

Meanwhile, in 1994, Lee married Kyle Bowser, a television executive. Through SisterLee, she developed *Lush Life,* a 1996 Fox show starring the white actress Lori Petty and the black actress Karyn Parsons as lifelong friends and roommates. The show did not survive the season, but Lee went on to work as a creative consultant to *The Wayans Brothers,* a comedy show featuring several of the Wayans, and continued to develop her own sitcoms.

In 1997, Bowser gave birth to Evan Justice Bowser, her first son. In 1998 her comedy *For Your Love* aired as a mid-season replacement (a show brought in during the year rather than in the fall) on NBC. Although the show had a short life on its first network, airing only eight times, it was picked up by the new WB network, which had a reputation of being more friendly to black-themed shows than the "big three" networks: CBS, NBC, and ABC. *For Your Love* features three couples at different stages of their relationship, with a mixed black and white cast. The WB put the show in its 1998 fall lineup, and as of this writing, it is still on the air.

In 2002, Bowser debuted a show on UPN, the smallest of the six non-cable networks and the one that seemed to have taken over the WB's role as home to black-themed shows. The program *Half and Half* tells the story of two half sisters who share the same father but grew up very differently, one with a bohemian single mom, the other with a social-climbing second wife.

Bowser feels a sense of mission about her work, which she sees as providing a much needed vision of the lives of black professionals, and of black women in particular. She is frustrated that more black women have not been brought into the industry, which heightens her own sense of needing to get her message on the air and of wanting to mentor other black writers. She also works with a number of community groups, including the National Association for the Advancement of

Colored People (NAACP), the African-American sorority Alpha Kappa Alpha, and the Los Angeles Mission, as well as sponsoring four children in an inner-city arts program, All God's Children Performing Arts Conservatory.

Further Reading

Gale Group. "Yvette Lee Bowser." African American Publications, Biography Resource Collections, Gale Group. Available online. URL: http://www.africanpubs.com/Apps/bios/0600BowserYvette.asp?pic=none. Downloaded on November 12, 2002.

"Living Single." Written By, January 1997. Available online on Writers Guild of America, West website. URL: http://www.wga.org/WrittenBy/1997/0197/livingsingle.html. Downloaded on November 12, 2002.

Sanko, Alana Burgi. "Witty Women." Written By, August 1998. Available online on Writers Guild of America, West website. URL: http://www.wga.org/WrittenBy/1998/0898/WittyWomen.html. Downloaded on November 12, 2002.

Boyd, Richard Henry

(1843–1922) *publisher, banker, manufacturer*

Although Richard Henry Boyd was unable to read or write while he lived as a slave, he went on to own the largest black publishing house in America, own and edit a black newspaper, write several books and articles, and become president of the first black-owned bank of the 20th century. Boyd's achievements were indicative of the extraordinary strides made against tremendous odds by the first generation of freed African Americans.

Boyd was born into slavery on March 15, 1843, in Noxubee County, Mississippi, and given the name Dick, after his mother's father. His last name, Gray, was that of his owner Martha Gray, according to the custom for slaves. His mother went by the name Indiana; little is known about his father except that he was a slave in Mississippi.

In 1849, the Grays moved to Washington County, Texas, taking Dick and Indiana with them. When Martha Gray died in 1858, Indiana and Indiana's daughter ended up in Grimes County, Texas, while Dick remained in Washington County as the property of Benonia W. Gray, where he became an efficient manager in the production and sale of the plantation's cotton, selling the cotton to Mexico.

After the Civil War broke out, Benonia's husband and three sons signed up with a Confederate regiment, taking Dick with them as their personal servant. All of the men were killed except for one son, whom Dick nursed back to health and then accompanied back to Texas in 1864, where he continued to work for the Gray family even after slavery.

In 1866, however, the Grays decided not to reestablish their farm, and Dick went on to take several other jobs, including cowboy, cotton trader, and sawmill laborer. He married Laura Thomas in 1868, but she died less than a year later. In 1867, he left behind his slave name of Dick Gray to become Richard Henry Boyd, and in 1869, he was baptized in a Baptist church. He then decided to become a minister and enrolled in Bishop College in Marshall, Texas, although he never graduated. In 1871, he married Hattie Albertine Moore, with whom he had nine children.

Boyd soon revealed the entrepreneurial and organizational talents that would characterize the rest of his career. In 1870 he organized the first Negro Baptist Association in Texas. He also took a number of positions in various Baptist groups, organized several churches, and developed enormous influence among Texas Baptists. He began to resent the lack of literature published by black Baptists, however, frustrated with the fact that all available materials came from the white northern group, the American Baptist Home Mission Society, which funded schools and missionary activities in the South. Like many other black Baptists,

Boyd viewed this group as paternalistic (patronizing, treating black people as children), and he participated in a number of battles over this issue at various Baptist conventions and meetings.

Finally, in 1894 and 1895, he published his own pamphlets for use in black Sunday schools, and in 1895, he argued at the National Baptist Convention—the convention of black Baptist churches—that black Baptists needed their own religious materials. Although the group was reluctant to offend northern white Baptists, Boyd would not give up, and in 1896 he established the National Baptist Publishing Board in Nashville.

Boyd faced several difficulties as an African-American businessman in the South, which at that time set up many barriers for black people. For example, Boyd could not buy his own printing equipment but had to find a white man to front for him. Nevertheless, that purchase helped to make his company the most successful black publishing firm in the United States, and the only sector of the Baptist Church to make money.

In 1898, Boyd incorporated the board as a separate body with an independent charter, making it both a private company and a wing of the church group—an ambiguous status that would eventually cause trouble for Boyd, leading to criticisms that he was operating the enterprise for personal gain and efforts to bring the group under the control of the larger church body. Boyd had put his own money into the enterprise, however, and he fought for financial and editorial control.

A legal battle resulted from the bitter debates of the 1915 convention, resulting in a new split-off group associated with Boyd. This group allowed Boyd to retain control of the National Baptist Publication Board, which flourished.

Boyd also started a number of other enterprises, including the National Baptist Church Supply Company, founded in 1902, and the National Negro Doll Company, founded in 1908. Although these companies were technically separate entities, they were all housed at the National Publishing Board's headquarters. The doll company, while not financially successful, operated for two decades as a groundbreaking company that sold dolls resembling African Americans, a highly unusual product for the time.

In 1903, JAMES CARROLL NAPIER, the Nashville politician and entrepreneur, arranged with Booker T. Washington to hold the annual convention of the National Negro Business League (NNBL) in Nashville. The NNBL was a group that Washington and others had founded to promote black enterprise, and at its Nashville meeting, Boyd was elected vice president. The 1903 convention helped create closer ties among Boyd, Napier, and other black Memphis leaders, who went on to found the One Cent Savings Bank and Trust Company.

As soon as it opened in 1904, the new bank found itself torn between the wish to invest in the black community by making loans for homes and small businesses—its original purpose—and the need to maintain a conservative financial policy to protect its funds. Under the leadership of Boyd, its first president, the bank came down on the conservative side, protecting its stability but enjoying a very slow rate of growth. Many scholars believe that Boyd was more of a figurehead, with Napier bearing the true responsibility for the policy; indeed, Napier had pledged his own fortune as security for the bank.

Boyd, meanwhile, continued to fight for black civil rights. White Nashville residents were beginning to press for segregation—the separation of black and white citizens in public accommodations, such as restaurants, stores, and streetcars. In 1903, when the local streetcar company added a car reserved for black workers at the local fertilizer plant, white residents used that as an opportunity to push for further segregation. In 1905, the state legislature instituted complete racial segregation of the trolley lines, to go into effect on July 5 of that year. Boyd, Napier, and others fought back by forming their own firm, the Union Transportation Company. They called for a boycott of the white-owned company, offering their own streetcars as an alternative. Although Union Transportation was ultimately unable to stay in business and the boycott did not succeed, the efforts of Boyd and his colleagues were a precursor of the militant civil rights activities in the 1950s.

In response to the boycott, Boyd began publishing the *Nashville Globe* in 1906, to give the black community a stronger voice. Boyd's son Henry ran the paper, as he had run many of Boyd's other enterprises. When another group of Memphis community leaders founded the People's Savings Bank and Trust Company in 1909, hoping to create a financial institution with a less conservative policy than the One Cent Bank, the *Nashville Globe* said that the rival bank would ultimately be good for the black community. In 1920, meanwhile, the One Cent Bank reorganized itself as the Citizens Savings Bank and Trust, though its policies did not change. After Boyd died, his son, Henry A. Boyd, took over as president, a post he held until his own death in 1959.

Boyd had been a strong supporter of Booker T. Washington and the NNBL. Eventually, though, the *Globe* began to criticize Washington's policy of "accommodationism"—avoiding political confrontation with white people to focus on black self-help. Instead, the *Globe* began to praise Washington's rival, W. E. B. DuBois, who supported a militant political approach and full social equality for black people. DuBois also suggested that local organizations would be more effective than national groups, such as those Washington advocated.

In this spirit, both Richard and Henry Boyd supported better public schools for black children. In those days, all schools in the South were strictly segregated (separated by race), but the Boyds were less concerned with segregation than with quality. They also fought for improved colleges and universities for black students.

When Richard Boyd died on August 23, 1922, some 6,000 people turned out to mourn for him. Twenty-five years after that the National

Baptist Publishing Board dedicated a life-sized bronze statue to their founder. Boyd continues to be remembered as a pioneer in black publishing and in African-American civil rights.

Further Reading

Gale Group. "Richard Henry Boyd." *Notable Black American Men.* Farmington Hills, Mich.: Gale Research, 1998.

Haskins, Jim. *Black Stars: African American Entrepreneurs.* New York: John Wiley & Sons, 1998, pp. 52–56.

Lovett, Bobby L. *A Black Man's Dream: The First 100 Years; Richard Henry Boyd and the National Baptist Publishing Board.* Nashville, Tenn.: R. H. Boyd Publishers, 1993.

McDougald, Lois C. "Richard Henry Boyd" (1815–1912). *Profiles of African Americans in Tennessee,* edited by Bobby L. Lovett and Linda T. Wynn. Nashville, Tenn.: Annual Local Conference on Afro-American Culture and History, 1996. Available online on University of Tennessee Web Site. URL: http://www.tnstate.edu/library/digital/RHBoyd.htm. Downloaded on January 23, 2003.

Thompson, Nolan. "Boyd, Richard Henry." The Handbook of Texas Online, TSHA Online. Available online. URL: http://www.tsha.utexas.edu/handbook/online/articles/view/BB/fbo60.html. Downloaded on January 23, 2003.

Bragg, Janet Harmon (Janet Waterford)
(1907–1993) *pilot, nursing home owner*

Janet Harmon Bragg is an example of an African American becoming an entrepreneur in response to racial segregation. Although Bragg was the first African-American woman to own an airplane and obtain a commercial pilot's license, she could not earn a living in aviation. Eventually, she became a successful owner of a health-care facility, but the vocation was far from her first choice.

Janet Harmon was born on March 24, 1907, in Griffin, Georgia, the daughter of brick con-

Janet Bragg was the first African-American woman to obtain a commercial pilot's license—but because of racial discrimination, she could not earn a living in aviation. *(National Air and Space Museum, Smithsonian Institution [SI Neg. No. 91-15485])*

tractor Samuel Harmon and his wife, Cordia Batts. She graduated with a nursing degree from Spelman Seminary (now Spelman College) in 1929. During her first month as a nurse in a segregated Griffin hospital, she witnessed two incidents in which black patients died from inadequate treatment, leading her to leave the South and go to live with relatives in Chicago.

After racial discrimination forced her into a series of menial jobs, she became night supervisor at Wilson Hospital's emergency room while studying laboratory procedures and radiology at Chicago Medical School. Sometime around 1931, she married Evans Waterford.

In 1933, her marriage ended, her father died, and her mother and two nieces moved in with her. Her new financial responsibilities led her to take a better-paying job in a medical office and to complete her graduate work in pediatric nursing at Cook County School of Nursing. After obtaining a graduate certificate in public health administration from Loyola University, she became a health inspector for the black-owned Metropolitan Burial Insurance Company. With her new financial security, Waterford turned to her true interest—learning to fly.

At the time, black pilots were not allowed to fly out of airports used by whites, so a group of black would-be flight students formed the Challenger Aero Club, bought their own land, and made an airfield with their own hands in the all-black town of Robbins, Illinois. Waterford obtained her private pilot's license and wrote a column, "Negro Aviation," in the black newspaper the *Chicago Defender.*

In 1943, Waterford applied for the Women's Auxiliary Service Pilots (WASPS) but was rejected on racial grounds. She sought to join the military nurses corps but was told that the quota for black nurses had been filled. Waterford then enrolled in the Civilian Pilot Training Program (CPTP) at Tuskegee, Alabama, a division of a federal program that had been specially set aside for black pilots. She recounts in her autobiography, *Soaring Over Setbacks,* that she passed the test, but that the federal flight examiner refused the license, saying, "I've never given a colored girl a commercial license, and I don't intend to now." Waterford later obtained the license in Chicago.

Meanwhile, Waterford continued to work as a health inspector at Metropolitan Burial. She and her brother planned to buy a two-apartment house in Chicago, but when her brother withdrew from the arrangement, Waterford took a friend's suggestion to turn the building into a convalescent home for patients on welfare.

For a time, Waterford continued as a health inspector, with cousins from Georgia helping her run the nursing home. Then, in 1951, she married Sumner Bragg, a supervisor at Metropolitan, and resigned from her job to devote herself full-time to the nursing-home business. In 1953 she bought a 22-room mansion that she converted into a health-care facility. With her husband, she bought the adjacent mansion, and together they expanded their business to serve 60 patients. Bragg's nursing home also housed students from Ethiopia. As a result, she was invited to spend three months in Ethiopia in 1955 as the guest of Emperor Haile Selassie.

Bragg retired from commercial flying in 1965 because of her husband's health problems but continued to fly for pleasure into the 1970s. Also for her husband's health, Bragg retired from nursing in 1972 and moved with her husband to Tucson, where she became involved with such community groups as the Urban League and Habitat for Humanity. She also lectured widely on aviation, and on women in science and aerospace. In 1982 she was deemed "Outstanding Citizen of Tucson" by Mayor Lewis Murphy, and in 1985, she received the Bishop Wright Air Industry award. She died on April 11, 1993.

Further Reading

Bragg, Janet Harmon, as told to Marjorie M. Kriz. *Soaring Above Setbacks: The Autobiography of Janet Harmon Bragg, African American Aviator.* Washington, D.C.: Smithsonian Institution Press, 1996.

Cochrane, D., and P. Ramirez. "Janet Bragg." National Air and Space Museum, Smithsonian Institution website. Available online. URL: http://www.nasm.si.edu/nasm/aero/women_aviators/janet_bragg.htm. Posted on December 15, 1999.

Haskins, Jim. *Black Stars: African American Entrepreneurs.* New York: John Wiley & Sons, 1998, pp. 101–105.

Bricktop
(Ada Smith, Ada Beatrice Queen Victoria Louise Virginia Smith)
(1894–1984) *nightclub owner, entertainer*

Bricktop is best known for her Paris club, Bricktop's, where she performed as a jazz singer; taught people the latest New York City dances; and hosted the royalty, writers, and artists of Europe and the Americas. Although Bricktop's performances were legendary, her entrepreneurial spirit found its expression in her clubs, which she opened successfully in Paris, Mexico City, and Rome.

Originally named Ada Beatrice Queen Victoria Louise Virginia Smith, Bricktop was born in Alderson, West Virginia, on August 14, 1894, the youngest of four children raised by Thomas Smith, a barber, and Hattie E. Smith, a woman of African and Irish heritage who had been born in slavery. When Thomas died, Hattie moved the family to Chicago, where Ada attended an integrated public school on the city's South Side. The young woman quit school at 16 to join the chorus of dancers that was touring with Miller and Lyles, a black comedy and musical team.

Bricktop herself began singing at Chicago clubs, including one owned by black heavyweight boxer Jack Johnson. In 1922, she moved to New York to sing and dance at Baron Wilkins Club and Connie's Inn in Harlem. In 1924, she went on to Paris, where she sang at Le Grand Duc, "a room so tiny that it felt crowded with six pairs of elbows leaning on the bar," according to *Bricktop,* her autobiography. Before she found success, she bused tables with the then unknown writer Langston Hughes. Famed composer Cole Porter once wandered into Le Grand Duc and asked Bricktop to teach him the Charleston, the latest New York dance craze. When Bricktop gave him a lesson, he exclaimed, "What legs! What legs!" and began bringing his glittering circle of friends to the club, including millionaires, royalty, and international artists. Writer F. Scott Fitzgerald once said his main claim to fame was discovering Bricktop before Cole Porter.

Bricktop soon took over the club's management, renamed the place "Chez Bricktop" ("At the Home of Bricktop"), and created a truly homelike atmosphere for the famous and infamous guests whom she attracted. Despite the economic chaos

Bricktop was world-famous for her club, Bricktop's, where she hosted royalty, writers, and artists. *(Library of Congress)*

of the depression, Chez Bricktop flourished until the eve of World War II, when Bricktop left Paris at the last possible moment before the German invasion, assisted by the duchess of Windsor. Although her attempts to start a club in New York were unsuccessful, she had better luck in Mexico City, where heiress Doris Duke helped her open a café in 1944. She returned to Paris in 1949, but the new Bricktop's was unsuccessful there, and in the early 1950s, Bricktop moved her club to Rome, where her establishment was frequented by such movie stars as Frank Sinatra, Ava Gardner, Elizabeth Taylor, and Richard Burton.

Bricktop's was closed for good in 1961, and although Bricktop occasionally sang after that, she herself pointed out, "I'm not a singer. I'm not a dancer. I'm a performer and a saloon-keeper." In the last few years of her life, Bricktop was in semiretirement, working on her autobiography, which appeared in 1984. She died soon after on February 1.

Further Reading

Bricktop (Ada Smith), with James Haskins. *Bricktop.* New York: Atheneum, 1983. "Bricktop." West Virginia Archives and History, West Virginia Division of Culture and History. Available online. URL: http://www.wvculture.org/history/notewv/bricktop.html. Downloaded on September 15, 2002.
Shack, William A. *Harlem in Montmartre: A Paris Jazz Story Between the Great Wars.* Berkeley: University of California Press, 2001.

Brimmer, Andrew F.
(Andrew Brimmer, Andrew Felton Brimmer, Andrew Brimmer, Jr.)
(1926–) *first African American on the Federal Reserve Board, economic consultant, economist, educator*

Andrew Brimmer was the first African American to serve on the Federal Reserve Board, a post he held from 1966 through 1974, from an appointment by President Lyndon B. Johnson. Brimmer is a noted economist who specializes in monetary policy (policies regarding money and currency), banking, and economic issues affecting the black community. He currently heads Brimmer and Co., Inc., a consulting firm on economic issues.

Brimmer was born on September 13, 1926, in Newellton, Louisiana, the son of Andrew Brimmer, a sharecropper and warehouse worker, and Vella Davis Brimmer, a homemaker. In 1944, at age 17, he graduated from the all-black Tensas Parish Training School in St. Joseph, Louisiana, then moved to Bremerton, Washington, to live with one of his sisters. In 1945, he enrolled in the U.S. Army, serving as a staff sergeant until November 1946, which entitled him to a federal education grant for former servicemen. In January 1947, he used that grant and his own savings to enroll in the University of Washington, where he initially majored in journalism. His faculty adviser steered him away from that field, however, claiming that the opportunities for African Americans would be severely limited, so Brimmer switched his major to economics, which he thought would help him answer questions about U.S. society. He graduated in 1950 with a bachelor's degree, going on to pursue his master's with a John Hay Whitney Foundation fellowship.

Initially, Brimmer was interested in foreign economies, going in 1951 to study at the Delhi School of Economics and the University of Bombay in India, funded by a Fulbright fellowship. He went on to publish a number of articles about the Indian economy and started work on his doctoral degree in economics at Harvard University. At the same time, he worked as a research assistant at the Massachusetts Institute of Technology's Center for International Studies.

In 1953, Brimmer married Doris Millicent Scott, with whom he eventually had one child, Esther Diane. From 1955 through 1958, Brimmer worked as an economist for the Federal Reserve Bank of New York, while in 1956 he was appointed to a fact-finding mission to Sudan, a developing country in Africa.

Brimmer received his Ph.D. in 1957, and went on to work as assistant professor of economics at Michigan State University. In 1963, he took a job with the U.S. Commerce Department in Washington, D.C., where he was eventually promoted to assistant secretary for economic affairs. One of his key responsibilities at the Commerce Department was to promote overseas investment by U.S. companies as a way of reducing the international deficit.

In 1966, Brimmer received what was probably the key appointment of his life, to the Federal Reserve System Board of Governors. The Federal Reserve sets monetary and banking policy for the United States and has a huge influence on the U.S. economy. Brimmer was the first African American to serve on that body, and his appointment was considered another milestone in the process of establishing equality for African Americans in all sectors of the economy. Brimmer advocated fighting inflation by implementing a tax increase, a policy implemented by President Johnson in 1968.

Although Brimmer's term on the Fed was not due to expire until 1980, he left his post in 1974

to become the Thomas Henry Carroll Ford Foundation professor at Harvard University's School of Business Administration, a post he held until 1976, when he went on to found his own economic consulting firm. He continued to teach at various institutions, later becoming the Wilmer D. Barrett Professor of Economics at the University of Massachusetts at Amherst.

Brimmer has gradually gained a reputation as an expert on the black business community and black economic affairs, writing regular articles for the magazine *Black Enterprise* and coming out against discrimination against black-owned busi-

Andrew Brimmer was the first African American to serve on the Federal Reserve, the institution that sets U.S. monetary policy. (*Library of Congress*)

nesses. He has also criticized the black community for failing to take responsibility for its own development, arguing that black workers will need more skills and education as the economy becomes more competitive.

In 1995, Brimmer was appointed by President Bill Clinton to head a five-member board intended to help the District of Columbia resolve its increasingly severe financial problems. As chair of the Columbia Financial Responsibility and Management Assistance Authority, Brimmer attempted to balance the district's budget and put its finances on a stronger footing. He received severe criticism for his role on the authority, however, which may have led to his resignation in 1998.

Brimmer has served as director of a number of corporations, including United Airlines, Equitable Life Assurance, Maryland National Bank, Mercedes Benz Corporation of North America, Bell-South Corporation, E.I. du Pont de Nemours, Navistar International Corporation, Airborne Express, and Gannett Company. He has published numerous books, articles, and studies, and continues to receive awards, honors, and honorary degrees.

Further Reading

"Brimmer to Quit as Head of Washington, D.C. Panel." *Wall Street Journal*, March 23, 1998, p. B9B.

"Brimmer Will Head District of Columbia's New Financial Board." *Wall Street Journal*, June 1, 1995, p. A4.

"Congress Gives Noted Economist Andrew Brimmer Authority to Oversee D.C. Financial Recovery." *Jet*, August 18, 1997, p. 39.

Edwards, Tamala M. "Disaster on the Potomac: How Not to Run a City." *Time*, August 18, 1997, p. 22. Available online. URL: http://www.cnn.com/ALLPOLITICS/1997/08/11/time/marion.barry.html. Downloaded on January 16, 2003.

Gale Group. "Andrew F. Brimmer." *Notable Black American Men*. Farmington Hills, Mich.: Gale Research, 1998.

Norton, Eleanor Holmes. "Notes from Congress." *Straight From the Streets*, Summer 1998. Available online. URL: http://www.crosstownarts.com/sfts/norton.htm. Downloaded on January 16, 2003.

Vise, David A. "Brimmer's Term Extended 90 Days." *Washington Post*, May 30, 1998, p. A1.

Brown, Willa Beatrice
(Willa Brown Chappell)
(1906–1992) *flight school founder, operator*

Willa Brown is an example of an African American becoming an entrepreneur so as to have scope for another type of activity. A trained pilot and airplane mechanic, she cofounded and helped to run the Coffey School of Aeronautics at Harlem Airport in Oak Lawn, Illinois, an institution that was central in enabling African-American pilots and mechanics to enter civil aviation in the years before World War II. She was also the first black female officer in the Civil Air Patrol and the first African-American woman to hold a commercial pilot's license.

Willa Beatrice Brown was born on January 22, 1906, in Glasgow, Kentucky, to Reverend Eric and Mrs. Hallie Mae (Carpenter) Brown. She grew up in Indiana, where she received a B.A. from Indiana State Teacher's College in 1927. In 1935, she earned a master mechanic's certificate from Chicago's Aeronautical University. In 1937 she received an M.A. in business administration from Northwestern University. The following year, she got her commercial pilot's license after studying with Cornelius R. Coffey, a certified flight instructor and expert aviation mechanic working at Harlem Airport outside of Chicago.

At the time, airports in Chicago were segregated by race; indeed, the entire field of civil aviation was highly segregated. As an African-American woman, Brown knew that she would have few opportunities to work in aviation, so she went into business instead, founding the Coffey School of Aeronautics with Coffey in 1937 and marrying her business partner in 1939.

In 1939, Congress authorized the Civilian Pilot Training Program (CPTP), a system established by the Civil Aeronautics Authority to ensure that there would be a pool of civilian pilots available to fly during national emergencies. As the bill was being considered, Brown, Coffey, and Enoch P. Walters formed the National Negro Airmen's Association, with the goal of integrating civil and military aviation. The group lobbied Congress to include black pilots in the CPTP and won an amendment banning racial discrimination in the bill that authorized funding; however, the training of pilots continued on a "separate but equal" basis. (After the 1896 Supreme Court case *Plessy v. Ferguson*, U.S. law allowed separate public accommodations for African Americans so long as these accommodations were equal to those of whites.)

Yet in January 1940, the Coffey School won a contract from the Civil Aeronautics Authority to teach a racially mixed group of 30 students. Coffey was one of two flight instructors, while Brown served as ground instructor. Many of their students became U.S. Air Force pilots, while Brown became the CPTP coordinator for Chicago.

Brown continued her efforts to end discrimination in aviation. As national secretary and president of the Chicago branch of the National Airmen's Association, she lobbied for the integration of black pilots into the segregated Army Air Corps. During World War II, Brown served as a second lieutenant in the Illinois Civil Air Patrol. She and Coffey continued their efforts to oppose segregation, taking part in the controversy over the creation of the segregated 99th Pursuit Squadron at Tuskegee Institute, the famous "Tuskegee Airmen." When the War Department refused to create an integrated air force, the Coffey school was selected to provide black trainees for the segregated unit. However, Brown and Coffey's efforts were part of the campaign that eventually brought about the integration of the U.S. military in 1947.

The Coffey school continued to operate throughout the war, winning both government

Second Lieutenant Willa Beatrice Brown of the Illinois Civil Air Patrol enjoys a soft drink during a break. (*National Archives*)

and private contracts until most of its assets were destroyed by fire in 1945. Brown went on to win election in 1948 as Republican committeewoman for Chicago's Second Ward. She became the coordinator of war-training service for the Civil Aeronautics Authority and served on the Federal Aviation Administration's Women's Advisory Committee from 1971 to 1974. She later divorced Coffey to marry Reverend J. H. Chappell, and has sometimes been referred to as Willa Brown Chappell. She died on July 18, 1992.

Further Reading

Jakeman, Robert J. *The Divided Skies: Establishing Segregated Flight Training at Tuskegee, Alabama,*

1934–1942. Tuscaloosa: University of Alabama Press, 1992.

Octave Chanute Aerospace Museum. "Willa Beatrice Brown (1906–1992)." Octave Chanute Aerospace Museum website. Available online. URL: http://www.aeromuseum.org/willa.html. Downloaded on February 11, 2002.

Strickland, Catherine Patricia. *The Putt-Putt Air Force: The Story of the Civilian Pilot Training Program and the War Training Service (1939–1944).* Washington, D.C.: U.S. Federal Aviation Administration, 1970.

Writer's Program of the Work Projects Administration. *Who's Who in Aviation: A Directory of Living Men and Women Who Have Contributed to the Growth of Aviation in the United States, 1942–1943.* Chicago: Ziff-Davis Publishing Company, 1942.

Browne, William Washington
(Ben Browne)
(1849–1897) *founder of fraternal organization, banker*

William Washington Browne helped found one of the major African-American organizations of the 19th century, the United Order of True Reformers. In the harsh climate of the late 1800s, in which African Americans faced increasingly violent and discriminatory treatment by white people, particularly in the U.S. South, many African Americans believed that the black community had to pull together and form its own institutions. Browne helped launch one of the most powerful black self-help groups, as well as starting the nation's first black-owned bank.

Much of the information available on Browne's early years is unreliable and uncertain. He is believed to have been born on October 20, 1849, a slave on the Habershaw County, Georgia, plantation owned by Benjamin Pryor. The son of Virginia natives Joseph and Maria Browne, he was originally named Ben. As a child, he worked as a servant in the Pryor household. Pryor died soon

afterwards, and his widow sold the plantation and Ben's parents, married A. G. Pitman, and moved with her new husband—and Ben—to her husband's home in Rome, Georgia.

In Georgia, Ben was hired out to work for a local storekeeper and then to a lawyer. He requested that his name be changed to Washington, and then added William to it. As William Washington Browne, he was sold to a horse trader who trained him as a jockey. After being beaten for having insulted his owner, Browne was sent to a Mississippi plantation. The Civil War had begun, and Browne managed to escape north in search of the Union army. Eventually, he worked as a servant in a saloon in Cairo, Illinois—where he developed a lifelong distaste for liquor—and then joined the navy as a bootblack, serving aboard the gunboat *National.* Browne participated in several battles, then went to Wisconsin and joined the 18th U.S. Infantry, becoming a sergeant major by the war's end. He attended school in Prairie du Chien, Wisconsin, for a time and then returned to Georgia.

Browne soon became a community leader in Georgia, where he began teaching in the so-called freedmen's schools that had been set up to educate newly freed slaves. When the Ku Klux Klan arose as a terrorist organization designed to frighten black people out of participating in the community's political and economic life, Browne spoke out against it and urged black people to arm themselves in self-defense. He also became a leader in the temperance movement—the movement to outlaw liquor and stop people from drinking. In Browne's view, African Americans were undermining their new freedom by wasting their money on liquor, particularly since public drunkenness—which was illegal—often led to black citizens being imprisoned on chain gangs.

Browne approached the Grand Lodge of Good Templars, a white self-help organization based in Alabama, with the idea of starting a black chapter of the group. The leaders suggested that he organize a group under a separate name, so Browne founded the United Order of True Reformers. He also married Mary A. (Molly) Graham, with whom he adopted two children.

Browne had been working as a teacher in Georgia, but in 1874 he left that job to work full-time for the True Reformers in Alabama. In 1876 he also became a minister of the A.M.E. (African Methodist Episcopal) Church, which enhanced his status in the black community.

Although Browne was relatively successful in organizing the True Reformers in Selma and Montgomery, Alabama, he was frustrated by the white leaders' ultimate control over his work. In 1875 he had organized a branch of the group in Richmond, Virginia, and in 1880 he decided to relocate there. He became a minister at Leigh Street A.M.E. Church until church leaders felt that his work with the True Reformers interfered with his ministerial duties; then he left the church to work for the True Reformers full-time.

Although the group's roots were initially in the city's black elite and middle class, Browne gradually built a mass organization that was attractive to the city's ordinary black citizens. Known as "True Reformer Browne," he helped the group expand rapidly throughout the state and to incorporate formally in 1883. He also set up a system of levying fees on members based on how old they were, with the understanding that when a member died, he would receive $100 toward burial costs. Thus the True Reformers became a kind of insurance company, guaranteeing that its members could at least afford the cost of a funeral and a grave.

As the group accumulated more money, Browne devised the idea of establishing a bank. On March 2, 1888, he obtained a charter for the True Reformers Bank from the Virginia legislature, making his the first black-owned bank in the nation, although by the time the institution actually began to operate, on April 3, 1889, the Capitol Savings Bank had been running for several months in Washington, D.C.

Browne put many key Richmond leaders on the bank's board of directors, including JOHN MITCHELL, JR., editor of the *Richmond Planet*. The bank became the foundation of a number of businesses, including Browne's real estate agency, founded in 1892, and his newspaper, *The Reformer*, established in 1895.

Browne's politics became a source of controversy as he continued to prosper. In 1895 he actually criticized Mitchell and a black Massachusetts legislator for visiting the governor's mansion along with some white Massachusetts legislators: In Browne's view, by "going too far," the black men were provoking white racism. When criticized for his views, Browne countered that the black men in question were light-skinned men of mixed race who were eager to gain white approval, while he himself, dark-skinned and of purely African heritage, was more proud and independent.

Browne died of cancer on December 21, 1897, so he did not live to see some of his organization's most successful ventures. In the late 1890s, the Reformer's Mercantile and Industrial Association was founded to operate a chain of stores and to build a 150-room hotel for black people, who were not allowed to stay in white-owned hotels. The association took over the real estate agency and newspaper, and formally incorporated in 1900. The group also founded an Old Folks Home in 1898, as well as the Westham Farm, a 634-acre property established for agricultural production and to be broken up into lots for black people's homes, an all-black town known as Browneville.

Nor did Browne live to see the 1910 financial scandal that brought about the downfall of the bank he had founded, resulting from the bank's cashier embezzling (stealing) $50,000. Despite the ultimate failure of Browne's enterprises, his work served as a model for other entrepreneurs, including JOHN MERRICK, founder of the North Carolina Mutual Insurance Company, and fellow Richmond resident MAGGIE LENA WALKER.

Further Reading

Ingham, John N., and Lynne B. Feldman. *African-American Business Leaders: A Biographical Dictionary*. Westport, Conn.: Greenwood Press, 1994, pp. 112–120.

Williams, Michael Paul. "William Washington Browne." Richmond Times-Dispatch website. Available online. URL: http://www.timesdispatch.com/blackhistory/MGBK577B61C.html. Posted February 1, 2002.

Willis, Anita. "The Founder of the Order of True Reformers: The Story of William Washington Browne." African American Genealogical Society of Northern California. Available online. URL: http://www.aagsnc.org/columns/feb99col.htm. Posted February 1999.

Brunson, Dorothy
(Dorothy Edwards Brunson)

(1938–   ) *radio station owner, television station owner*

Dorothy Brunson was the first African-American woman to own a radio station, and for many years, she was the only black woman to have achieved that stature. After acquiring a total of three radio stations, she eventually sold them to focus on WGTW-TV, a Philadelphia-based television station that she built up from a broken-down operation into a successful—though relatively small—competitor in the local market, which reaches into New Jersey and Delaware as well as Pennsylvania. Brunson's ownership of WBTW makes her the first and so far the only African-American woman to own a full-power television station.

Born Dorothy Edwards on May 13, 1938, in Glensville, a small town in Georgia, the future executive was the daughter of Wadis and Naomi (Ross) Edwards. Her father was a laborer who worked in painting and construction. Her mother was employed by United Airlines for more than 30 years as a matron (attendant), and was one of the first African Americans to fly out of John F. Kennedy Airport in New York. The family moved to Harlem in 1940, where Dorothy was raised. She went on to graduate from Empire State College, in New York City, with a B.S. in business and finance. In 1964, she married James Brunson, an electrician with whom she had two children, Edward and Daniel.

Initially, Brunson worked in advertising, placing ads in newspapers for the curtain division of a discount department store known as W.T. Grant. But she was always interested in radio and television, and she moved on to work at Sonderling Broadcast Group when the company began programming some of its stations for black listeners in 1962. She became assistant controller of WWRL-Radio on Long Island, New York, obtaining her position both for her skill and for her ability to reach out to the black community that suddenly interested the company's owners.

Brunson rose rapidly through the ranks, becoming controller in only three months and later becoming assistant general manager and corporate liaison to the company's board of directors. In 1969, she cofounded Howard Sanders Advertising, one of the first black-owned ad agencies in the United States. In 1969, the business world was highly segregated (separated by race), as was the world of media, and for African Americans to develop black-oriented ad campaigns was virtually unheard of. High-level black executives were also rare, and Brunson faced an uphill battle in the business world as both an African American and a woman.

Nevertheless, she left the ad agency in 1970 with $115,000 in buyout money (money given to buy part of a business from one of its owners), which she used to purchase a dress shop. When that enterprise failed, Brunson helped cofound Inner City Broadcasting, a new communications company that owned the black-oriented radio station WLIB-AM. The call letters "LIB" were short for "liberation," reflecting the station's commitment to black empowerment. Brunson was brought into the group in order to seek investors.

After four months in operation, Inner City Broadcasting hired Brunson as general manager. The job was not an easy one—the fledgling company was already more than one million dollars in debt—but Brunson had several ideas for how to improve the operation's finances. She cut the staff from 35 to eight and restructured the station's debt (made new arrangements with lenders for how interest would be charged and payments would be made). Despite these cost-cutting measures, Brunson also made a bold move: She obtained a loan to buy WLIB-FM, a black-oriented music station that she renamed WBLS. Her plan was to operate both stations with a single staff, increasing the potential for ad revenues while keeping costs low. She also had WBLS expand their playlist past rhythm and blues—known as exclusively "black" music—to include some white artists that black audiences liked. This mix became known as "urban contemporary," and it made the station very popular with both listeners and advertisers.

Inner City Broadcasting profited accordingly. By 1978, their annual sales had skyrocketed from $500,000 to $23 million, and they had gone from owning a single radio station to having seven. Meanwhile, sometime around 1976, Brunson was divorced.

Brunson wanted her own chance to build a radio corporation, so in 1979 she bought WEBB-Radio in Baltimore when singing star James Brown was forced to sell it in a bankruptcy proceeding, making her the first—and for a while, the only—African-American woman to own a radio station. She soon discovered, however, that her station owed a huge sum in back taxes and had several Federal Communications Commission (FCC) violations to its name. (The FCC is responsible for supervising U.S. radio and television stations.) Local stations with minority programming resented Brunson adding another black-oriented station to their city, while neighborhood organizations protested her construction of radio towers in an area where they feared

the towers would interfere with existing radio and TV reception. For the first four years of operation, WEBB ran a deficit—and for the first year, Brunson refused to take a salary.

Nevertheless, somehow Brunson managed to raise the capital that she needed, and within seven years she had lifted her station's ratings from the bottom of her 35-station market all the way up to 10th place, while she raised advertising sales from $100,000 to more than $800,000. Meanwhile, in 1981, she bought WIGO-AM in Atlanta, Georgia; within a few years, the station's revenues had more than doubled. In 1984 she acquired WBMS-AM in Wilmington, North Carolina, under the umbrella of her media company, Brunson Communications.

Brunson saw her work in radio as giving the black community a voice as well as reaching black people with educational, enlightening messages. In Baltimore, she engaged in such community activities as sponsoring a basketball team and offering Father's Day awards for black fathers.

In 1984, Brunson began negotiations for WGTW-TV, a Philadelphia television station. It took her two years to obtain the station's license. To build the station, she sold all her radio proper-

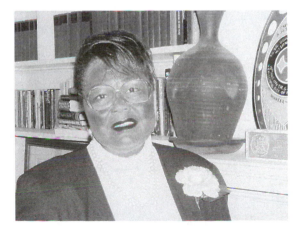

Dorothy Brunson was the first African-American woman to own a radio station—and for years she was the only black woman to do so. *(With permission of Dorothy Brunson)*

ties for about $3 million. It was difficult to get the station on the air, as it had been out of operation for ten years. The building had been vandalized, and the equipment had broken down. Yet in August 1992, after two and a half years of work, the station began to broadcast again.

WGTW-TV competes with much larger and better-funded corporations, but it has managed to hold its own. The station features mainstream programming with some minority focus, and is committed to having a racially mixed staff.

Brunson was always aware that her position as an African-American female executive was a precarious one. In a 1996 *Black Enterprise* article, she spoke of needing to find additional financing, which she said was difficult despite her company's solid rate of profit and its annual growth rate of 30 percent. "Most people would look at these barometers and say that the company is doing well," she said. "But because I am a woman, my company is seen as a fluke."

Brunson is currently working with her sons on their ventures. Daniel started one of the first black Internet Service Providers (ISP), Nuroots.com, in Baltimore, Maryland, while Edward founded a Philadelphia-based production company, Amina, to produce documentaries and record black historical events for syndication. Brunson is also currently working on an autobiography.

Further Reading

Gale Group. "Dorothy Brunson." *Contemporary Black Biography,* Vol. 1. Farmington Hills, Mich.: Gale Research, 1992.

Hayes, Cassandra, and Carolyn M. Brown. "Sister CEOs Speak Out." *Black Enterprise,* August 1996, p. 68.

Lafayette, Jon. "WGTW Offers Another View in Philadelphia." *Electronic Media* 18, no. 5 (February 1, 1999): 12.

Burrell, Thomas J.

(1939–   ) *advertising agency founder*

Thomas J. Burrell is one of the pioneers in African-American advertising. Not only was he one of the few African Americans working in advertising in the 1960s and 1970s, he also founded his own agency; captured the African-American-related accounts of major corporations at a time when such companies barely acknowledged that a black market existed; and helped to develop the concept of niche marketing, which has become a standard approach in the advertising industry. (Niche marketing is the idea that some products should be marketed to a targeted audience, such as young people, or snowboarders, or fans of rock music, rather than to a more general audience.)

Thomas Burrell was born on March 18, 1939, in Chicago, the son of a tavern owner and a beautician. Little is known about Burrell's parents, except that, according to Burrell, his father tended to discourage him while his mother gave him love and support. Burrell grew up in Chicago's Englewood neighborhood, a community within the South Side black ghetto that underwent a stormy transition from all white to largely black during the years of Burrell's childhood. In November 1949, when Burrell was only 10, the Englewood Riot shook the neighborhood, sealing its future as a poor area marked by gangs and violence.

Burrell was an undistinguished student who was something of an outsider during his years in public elementary schools and at Englewood High School. When he transferred to Parker, another public high school, he was given an aptitude test that revealed high scores in the areas of artistic and persuasive abilities. Burrell was puzzled by the results and asked a teacher what they meant. When the teacher suggested that they indicated success in advertising, Burrell seized upon this image of his future. He enrolled in Chicago's Roosevelt University on probation but failing grades sent him to a job on the assembly line of a local paint factory. Burrell so disliked factory work that he managed to return to Roosevelt, where he majored in English and advertising, graduating in 1962.

The previous year, Burrell had found a job as a mailroom clerk in the now defunct Wade Advertising Agency in Chicago. After six months in the mailroom, he marched into the creative director's office and told the man that he could solve some of his problems. In two weeks, he had a job as a copywriter trainee, a job that Burrell believes made him the only black person working on the creative side of advertising in Chicago.

After Burrell got his college degree, he was promoted to copywriter, where he worked on the television and print ads for such clients as Alka-Seltzer, One-a-Day vitamins, and Falstaff beer. In those days, all of the nation's large ad agencies were white-owned, and all of them essentially ignored African Americans. While some black-owned agencies existed, they focused largely on black-made products and black consumers. The white agencies behaved as though the United States were one large melting pot with a homogeneous and unified audience. Thus it was an unusual triumph for Burrell when he landed the account for Toni home permanents, which was trying to market one particular product to black women.

In 1964, Burrell took a job as a copywriter at the huge Leo Burnett Company in Chicago, moving on in 1967 to write copy for the London office of Foote, Cone, & Belding. Frustrated by the low salary he was making, Burrell returned to Chicago in 1968 as a copy supervisor for Needham, Harper & Steers. Despite his apparent progress, Burrell was frustrated by the world of advertising, which tended to either ignore African Americans altogether or to portray them in stereotypical roles—the smiling cook Aunt Jemima or the happy chef Uncle Ben—rather than as complex, interesting, and diverse people. Black people in the media were rarely portrayed as educated, professional, or family-oriented; rather, they were almost always portrayed in relation to white people, in positions of service.

The Civil Rights and Black Nationalist movements led many civil rights groups to press major ad agencies to develop new images of black people, even as African Americans began to start their own ad agencies. In 1971, Burrell went into partnership with Emmitt McBain and Frank Mingo, two advertising colleagues with whom he hoped to start his own agency. Mingo left before the business got started, going on to form his own company. The two remaining partners started the Burrell McBain Advertising Agency in a tiny one-room office with no secretary, one telephone, and three old desks, which they painted red, green, and orange—the colors of the African continent, and a symbol of black pride. Another dozen or so black-owned agencies were started during the 1970s. Many failed, some succeeded—but for most of the next three decades, Burrell's company would be the largest.

It took Burrell six months to land his first account, which paid only $3,000 per month. Eventually, though, Burrell moved on to the large white-owned clients he had always sought. In 1972, he landed the Coca-Cola soft drink account for the black market, convincing the giant cola company that it needed a special campaign to reach black consumers. While the 1974 Coke slogan was "Look up, America, and see what you've got," Burrell felt that black people were not yet ready to focus on being part of a country that until recently had denied them their civil rights. He convinced Coke to target black consumers with a different slogan: "For the real times, it's the real thing." Likewise, when Burrell landed the McDonald's black advertising account, he counseled the company not to use "You deserve a break today" for black consumers, who, unlike white customers, tended to patronize McDonald's not just "for a break" but several times a day. "McDonald's is good to have around" is the slogan Burrell suggested instead.

In 1974, McBain left the company to pursue a career in art, and the company became known as Burrell Communications, Inc., an umbrella group that later housed public relations firms as well as advertising enterprises. Burrell continued to garner white-owned accounts, though he also handled two black-owned businesses: Johnson Publishing, the Chicago company owned by JOHN H. JOHNSON, who published *Ebony* and *Jet;* and Johnson Products, George Johnson's Chicago-based hair products company.

Burrell carved out a niche by offering special expertise in reaching African-American consumers. But he also argued that he and his black colleagues were particularly skilled at reaching white customers. He believed that the very sensitivity to racial differences that black people needed to survive in a white world also enabled black people to read white consumers' needs and

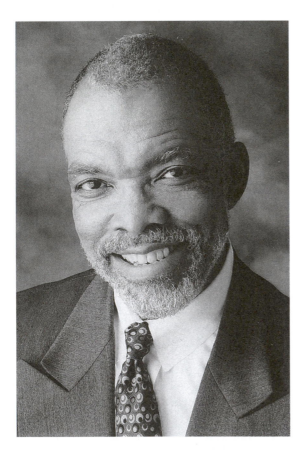

Thomas Burrell was a pioneer in advertising, founding his own agency and developing new concepts in marketing. *(Victor Powell Photography)*

desires, designing ad campaigns that would reach whites as well as blacks.

In 1983, Burrell landed the Crest toothpaste account for the black market. Doing business with Crest's parent company, Procter & Gamble, was a breakthrough for Burrell since P&G and its household products represented a departure from the traditional "black" categories of fast food restaurants, soft drinks, and liquor. Still, Burrell continued to work in those categories, landing the Martell Cognac account from the Jos. Garneau Company, the first time he had been asked to develop ads for both black and white consumers. His success led to a new account in 1984, for Garneau's Jack Daniel's whiskey, a white-oriented product that Burrell managed to sell successfully.

Another breakthrough came in 1983, when Burrell regained the Coca-Cola account (which he had temporarily lost to another agency). Commissioned to reach consumers on the continent of Africa, Burrell's became the first black-owned ad agency to receive an international contract.

Burrell's company has continued to grow, maintaining its status as the largest U.S. black-owned ad agency throughout most of the 1980s and 1990s. The company's latest target is what it calls the "Yurban Market," the young people known as "Generation Y" who live in urban areas and relate to a hip, contemporary approach. Burrell continues to stress niche marketing, as well as to argue that the general-interest mainstream market is now far more diverse than ever before, offering new kinds of opportunities for black-owned agencies who are sensitive to national trends.

Burrell's clients include such corporate giants as Coca-Cola Co.; Procter & Gamble Co.; McDonald's Corp.; Sears, Roebuck & Co.; Toyota; and Verizon. For much of its corporate life, Burrell Communications Inc. was the largest black-owned ad agency in the United States. In 2001 and 2002 it was the third-ranking black ad agency, with some 150 employees and close to $200 million in billings.

Further Reading

Moses, Kimberly. "Thomas Burrell and Yurban Marketing." The Center for Interactive Advertising, University of Texas at Austin. Available online. URL: http://www.ciadvertising.org/student_account/fall_01/adv382j/kimcutie/practitioner/page1.htm. Last updated November 1, 2001.

Fudge, Ann. "Shop Has the Answer in Researching Stove Top." *Advertising Age*, June 3, 1996, p. C12.

Kern-Foxworth, Marilyn. *Aunt Jemima, Uncle Ben, and Rastus: Blacks in Advertising, Yesterday, Today, and Tomorrow.* Westport, Conn.: Greenwood Press, 1994.

"Toyota Announces Partnership with African American Advertising Agency." Automotive Intelligence. Available online. URL: http://www.autointell.com/News-2001/November-2001/November-2001-2/November-14-01-p10.htm. Posted on November 14, 2001.

Bush, John Edward

(1856–1916) *real estate speculator, self-help group founder, federal officeholder, civil rights activist*

John Edward Bush was a supporter of black self-help in the mold of Booker T. Washington, the African-American leader who advocated that black people form their own institutions so that they would not have to rely on resources from white society. Bush is best known for founding the Mosaic Templars, a black-owned and -operated group that founded several businesses of its own under his leadership.

Bush was born in Moscow, Tennessee, on November 15, 1856, the son of a white planter and an enslaved African-American woman. Like many other slave children, he knew little of his father, and few records survive about his mother. In 1862, as the Civil War was getting underway, Bush and his mother were brought north to Little Rock, Arkansas, by their owner, who was seeking to escape Union troops. Bush's mother died soon

thereafter, and, when young Bush gained his freedom during the war, he became a drifter. In 1869, he entered the newly opened Capitol Hill public school in Little Rock, the region's first public school for black people. (In those years, public education was strictly segregated [divided by race] in the South.) Although Bush was initially forced to enter the school, he became a bright and ambitious student. Because he had to work his way through high school, it took him seven years before he finally graduated in 1876, when he became one of the school's teachers.

Meanwhile, in 1875, at the age of 19, Bush had begun to speculate in real estate, buying a city lot for $150. He later sold the lot at a profit and bought three more properties. Also in 1875, Bush had received a government appointment: night postal clerk in the Arkansas Railway Service, a job he kept even while teaching. Bush may have gotten the job because of his participation in the Republican Party, which in those days was considered the party of Abraham Lincoln, civil rights, and support for African Americans. Starting in 1883 he was elected delegate to various Republican state conventions and in 1884 served as the state convention's secretary. In 1892 he was chosen a delegate to the national Republican convention. In 1898, Bush received his highest federal appointment yet, an appointment by President William McKinley to the post of Receiver of United States Lands (Monies) at Little Rock, making him the highest-ranking federal officer in the state until 1913, when Democrat Woodrow Wilson became president and Republican appointees, including Bush, had to leave their posts.

Bush's role as a federal officeholder gave him a platform from which to lobby the Republican Party to appoint still more African Americans to government posts and to solicit help in combating the increasingly discriminatory laws—known as "Jim Crow" laws—being passed in Arkansas and elsewhere in the South. In 1891, he opposed the "Separate Coach Law," which required black people to ride in separate cars in public transportation. Although the law passed, Bush was undaunted, going on in 1905 to lobby successfully against a statute that would have funded black public schools entirely out of taxes paid by African Americans, reserving white people's taxes for white-only schools.

Meanwhile, Bush had founded the Mosaic Templars in 1882, helping the group obtain a state charter in 1883. Bush led the group to greater financial strength, helping the Templars to found their own savings and loan association and insurance company. By 1918, the Templars had expanded to found international chapters in Central America, Panama, and the West Indies. They boasted more than 80,000 members and assets of more than $300,000.

Bush's involvement in the Templars grew out of his support of Washington's philosophy of accommodationism, which held that black people should accommodate themselves to racial discrimination rather than organizing political activity against it. When Washington founded the National Negro Business League in 1900 to support black business, Bush became a charter mem-

ber. Meanwhile, Bush continued to remain active in the real estate market, and by 1907, he had acquired $30,000 worth of property in the Little Rock area. Three years later, he had built himself a Victorian home worth $10,000, having acquired a personal fortune worth $100,000. When Bush died on December 11, 1916, he was remembered as a "race man"—someone who had dedicated himself to both personal achievement and the betterment of his people.

Further Reading

Bush, A. E., and P. L. Dorman. *History of the Mosaic Templars of America. Its Founders and Officials.* Little Rock, Ark.: Central Printing Company, 1924.
Gatewood, Willard. *Aristocrats of Color: The Black Elite, 1880–1920.* Bloomington, Ind.: Indiana University Press, 1990, pp. 92–93.
Smith, C. Calvin. "John E. Bush: The Politician and the Man, 1880–1916." *Arkansas Historical Quarterly* 52, no. 2 (summer 1995): 115–133.
———. "John Edward Bush." *Encyclopedia of African American Business History,* ed. Juliet E. K. Walker. Westport, Conn.: Greenwood Press, 1999, pp. 99–101.

Chappell, Emma

(1941–) *banker, executive director of RAINBOW/PUSH's Wall Street Project*

Emma Chappell is the first African-American woman to found a full-service commercial bank, and the second to ever found a bank in the United States. She has won numerous awards for her work as the founder and CEO of United Bank of Philadelphia, which was the first black bank in Philadelphia in 35 years.

Emma Carolyn Bayton was born in the black working-class neighborhood of West Philadelphia on February 18, 1941, the daughter of George and Emma Bayton. Her mother died when Emma was only 14, and her father, a chef at Horn & Hardart Restaurant, raised her. An important influence on the young Emma was the Reverend Leon Sullivan, the pastor at her Zion Baptist Church (and later, the anti-apartheid leader who gave his name to the "Sullivan Principles," rules for helping companies and local governments boycott South Africa). Although Emma wanted to be a nurse, Sullivan gave her an aptitude test, discovered her talent for math, and encouraged her to go into banking. Emma graduated from public school in 1959 and went to work as a clerk-photographer at Continental Bank. (Today, a clerk or secretary would make photocopies on a machine, but in the late 1950s, a clerk-photog-

rapher used a camera to make copies of documents known as photostats.)

Emma married Verne Chappell and began working her way up in the bank hierarchy while attending evening classes at Temple University. She obtained her degree in 1967, having been promoted to teller and loan review specialist; the bank went on to put her in an executive training program, which she completed in 1971. By 1977, she had become the bank's first black vice president as well as its first woman in that position.

Chappell's devotion to her community was always a large part of her personal and professional life. She worked with the National Association for the Advancement of Colored People (NAACP) and the Southern Christian Leadership Conference (SCLC), two major civil rights groups, although she backed off from her involvement as her conservative employer objected. Then, in response to the civil rights movement, the federal government began to engage in efforts to help poor and minority communities, and Chappell was able to integrate her social ideals with her work at the bank. In 1971, she established a program at Continental designed to offer loans to minority businesses and low-income customers. In 1974, she took a leave to help Philadelphia city officials organize the Model Cities Business and Commercial Project (later renamed the Philadelphia Commercial Development Project), which brought together a consortium of lenders dedicated to revitalizing business activity in the inner city. She went on to found the Delaware Valley Mortgage Plan, an effort to help low- and moderate-income people become home-owners.

Despite her commitment to her community, Chappell was able to exercise stringent judgment in the awarding of loans. According to *U.S. Banker*, during her 20 years at Continental, her loan-loss ratio was less than 1 percent (that means that very few people to whom she lent money defaulted on, or refused to pay back, their loans).

By now Chappell had divorced her husband and was raising her daughters, Tracey and Ver-daynea, as a single mother. In 1984, she took another leave to serve as treasurer of Jesse Jackson's campaign for president, and she later helped Jackson found the Rainbow Coalition, a group dedicated to racial equality. She was also working toward her master's degree at Rutgers's Stonier School of Banking.

Inspired by Jackson's focus on self-determination for the black community, Chappell was receptive to the group of black Philadelphia financiers and commercial leaders who approached her in 1987 and asked her to found a black bank in Philadelphia, on the theory that a minority-owned bank would be more likely to fund community development in low-income and inner-city neighborhoods. The stock market crash of October 1987 threatened to scuttle the plan, but Chappell was committed to founding the new black bank, and in addition to seeking large investors, she also developed an innovative plan of soliciting funds from moderate-income members of the black community. She went to church after church, explaining why such a bank would help black people in Philadelphia and selling blocks of stock in the bank in units of $500. In an epic five-year fundraising process, she eventually managed to raise an impressive $3.3 million from 3,000 small investors. This enabled her to exceed

the $5 million minimum required by federal law as she was able to bring $6 million to the founding of the bank.

The United Bank of Philadelphia opened on March 23, 1992, and although the institution had its ups and downs, it eventually achieved financial stability while winning widespread recognition. In 1995, it was named Financial Company of the Year by *Black Enterprise*. In 1997, the bank had amassed $106 million in assets and began issuing its own credit cards. It had also developed a partnership with American Express to offer investment advice and financial services to bank customers, a continuation of the kinds of educational services that United had always sought to offer.

In June 1999 Chappell received the Blue Chip Enterprise Initiative Award of the U.S. Chamber of Commerce, which honors small-business owners who have overcome obstacles to create opportunities for themselves and their communities. President William Clinton also made her a presidential appointee to the Board of Trustees of the Malcolm Baldridge Quality Service Award, the highest award given to Fortune 500 companies for exceptional customer service.

Chappell remained head of United until 2000, when she stepped down in what at first looked like a voluntary decision. When the bank sued her a few months later, in 2001, it emerged that she had been asked to leave and was accused of engaging in fraudulent real estate dealings, charging bank employees inflated parking fees, and requiring the bank to pay thousands of dollars for her own limousine service and parking spaces. Chappell agreed to a settlement that required her to remain silent about what had happened at the bank. She has gone on to become executive director of Jesse Jackson's Wall Street Project, an effort to make Wall Street firms more responsive to African Americans. She also lectures nationwide and continues to remain active in Philadelphia community affairs.

Further Reading

"Dr. Emma Chappell." Harry Walker Agency. Available online. URL: http://www.harrywalker.com/speakers_template.cfm?Spea_ID=73&SubcatID=176. Downloaded on November 11, 2002.

Fairley, Juliette. "Emma Chappell: From Presidential Campaign Treasurer to Founder of United Bank: Excerpts from *Money Talks*. BusinessWeek, December 31, 1998. Available online at BusinessWeek online. URL: http://www.businessweek.com/smallbiz/news/coladvice/book/bk981231.htm.

———. *Money Talks: Black Finance Experts Talk to You About Money*. New York: John Wiley & Sons, 1998.

Gale Group. "Emma C. Chappell." African American Publications, Biography Resource Center. Available online. URL: http://www.africanpubs.com/Apps/bios/0185ChappellEmma.asp?pic=none. Downloaded: November 11, 2002.

Harris, Hamill R. "Emma Chappell Drops CEO Status." *Black Enterprise,* August 2000.

Jones, Joyce. "Chappell and United Bank Settle." *Black Enterprise,* January 2001.

Quittner, Jeremy. "A Community Bank Founder's Secret: Never Take No for an Answer." *BusinessWeek,* July 6, 1999. Available online at BusinessWeek online. URL: http://www.businessweek.com/smallbiz/news/coladvice/reallife/rl990706.htm. Downloaded on November 11, 2002.

Chappell, Willa Brown   See BROWN, WILLA BEATRICE.

Chase, Calvin
(William Calvin Chase, Sr., W. Calvin Chase, Sr.)
(1854–1921) *publisher, editor*

Calvin Chase was the editor and publisher of the *Washington Bee,* the African-American newspaper serving the Washington, D.C., area in the late 19th and early 20th centuries. During an era when black-owned newspapers flourished across the United States, Chase was known as one of the country's most outspoken editors.

Chase was born into a prosperous middle-class Washington family on February 2, 1854, the son of William H. Chase, a blacksmith, wheelwright, and mechanic, and Lucinda Seaton Chase, a dressmaker whose wealthy father had owned a large grocery store and served in the Virginia legislature. Unusual for black people at the time, these free people of color knew how to read and owned their own home. When Calvin was nine, however, his father was killed in an accident, and the family fell on hard times. Calvin's mother struggled to raise him and her five daughters, for a time operating an ice cream and candy store out of her home. Calvin sold newspapers while attending a private school for black children. (Washington, D.C., schools were at that time strictly segregated [separated by race].)

Calvin so impressed one of his white customers that she arranged for him to work for a Massachusetts hat manufacturer, but he did not like the business and soon returned home to attend public school and work in the printing trade. Although he never attended college, he enrolled in Howard University's preparatory department—a course intended to help students prepare for college. Several years later, in 1883 or 1884, he took courses at Howard Law School, and was admitted to the Virginia and the District of Columbia bars in 1889. By this point, Chase was running the *Bee,* but needed another source of income, so he practiced law for the rest of his life.

Meanwhile, in 1875, Chase had begun working as a temporary clerk in the tax collector's office run by John F. Cook, Jr., who had administered the private school Chase once attended. He also became the Washington correspondent for the *Boston Observer,* a black-owned paper. Chase hoped at this point to gain a political position, and he turned to African-American leader Frederick Douglass for help. When Douglass refused to support him, he published a blistering attack on Douglass.

The *Observer* went out of business, and Chase went on to work for the Washington office of the *Boston Co-operator* in 1879, moving on that year to a post at the *Washington Plain Dealer,* and then to an editorial position at the *Argus,* whose name Chase changed to the *Free Lance.* Through each of these positions, Chase's quick temper and strong opinions got him into trouble. Finally, in 1880, Chase settled in at the *Washington Bee,* of which he soon became editor and publisher. Chase continued to run that paper for the rest of his life, making it a well-known Washington institution.

Chase took firm stands on many key civil rights issues of the day, particularly lynching, a growing problem for African Americans after the end of Reconstruction in 1877. Lynching was a form of terror that kept African Americans from full political and economic participation in the society, a response to the increased political power that black people had gained after the Civil War. Chase wrote editorials and published cartoons critical of lynching and other violence against African Americans, calling for black self-defense and arguing that any means of resistance, including "devastation, destruction, blood, tears, misery and starvation," would be justified.

Chase was also critical of anti-black discrimination in the federal civil service, and he attacked local courts, which he claimed scapegoated black criminals and sought to blame them for the rising crime rate. In one article, Chase cited a report by the city's mayor and police department, which found that the number of crimes committed by white people was far higher than those committed by black people.

A number of racial incidents drew Chase's attention as well. In 1906, when the U.S. Army was still strictly segregated, black troops stationed in Brownsville, Texas, were accused of rioting. As a punishment, President Theodore Roosevelt dismissed three black companies allegedly involved

in the incident. Many black people felt that the whole issue had been distorted, and Chase criticized the president for more than a year over the way he handled the situation. Chase had also been critical of discrimination against black troops during the Spanish-American War of 1898, and he refused to support U.S. entry into World War I until black people were better treated.

On the other hand, Chase tended to keep quiet about private instances of discrimination. He felt that social clubs, universities, and churches had the right to bar black people, and he strongly opposed integrated schools, which he considered a betrayal of those black people who had founded their own educational institutions.

A major issue of the time was the conflict between W. E. B. DuBois, an advocate of militant political action for black equality, and Booker T. Washington, who believed that black people should accommodate themselves to existing political realities and focus on black self-help and entrepreneurship. Chase sometimes attacked and sometimes supported each of these leaders. He also turned to each of them for financial support of the *Bee.* Some scholars believe that Chase's editorials about the two men had more to do with their support—or lack of support—for his paper than with their actual ideas.

One leader whom Chase ignored was Marcus Garvey, whose efforts to get black people to return to Africa were a subject of controversy in the early 20th century. Although Chase had vigorously criticized other back-to-Africa movements, he was silent where Garvey was concerned.

In 1886, Chase married Arabella Virginia McCabe, a fellow graduate of Howard's preparatory department, a writer, and a musician. The couple had a son, William Calvin, Jr., and a daughter, Beatriz, both of whom eventually went to work for the *Bee.* Chase's editorial slogan for the *Bee* was "Honey for Friends, Stings for Enemies," an approach that won him respect from both black and white citizens in the Washington, D.C., community. Both black and white mourners were among the 3,000 people who attended his funeral, after Chase died of a heart attack on January 3, 1921.

Further Reading

Howard-Pitney, David. "Calvin Chase's Washington *Bee* and Black Middle-Class Ideology, 1882–1900." *Journalism Quarterly* (spring 1986): 86–97.

Ingham, John, and Lynne B. Feldman. *African American Business Leaders: A Biographical Dictionary.* Westport, Conn.: Greenwood Press, 1994, pp. 130–134.

Logan, Rayford W., and Michael R. Winston. *Dictionary of Negro Biography.* New York: W. W. Norton & Co., Inc., 1982, pp. 99–101.

Chenault, Kenneth Irvine
(1951–   ) *corporate executive*

As chair and chief executive officer (CEO) of American Express Company, Kenneth I. Chenault is one of a handful of African-American CEOs of Fortune 500 companies (the top 500 companies in the nation according to *Fortune* magazine) and one of the most powerful people on Wall Street.

Chenault was born on June 2, 1951, on Long Island, New York. He is the son of Hortenius Chenault, a dentist, and Anne N. (Quick) Chenault, who sent him to the prestigious Garden City, New York, private high school, the Waldorf School, from which he graduated in 1969. He went on to get a B.A. in history from Bowdoin College in 1973 and a J.D. from Harvard Law School in 1976.

Chenault began his working life as a management consultant for Bain & Co. in Boston, moving on to become an associate at the New York City law firm of Rogers and Wells. In 1981, he began a long and productive career with American Express when he was made the company's director of strategic planning. In 1989, he became president of American Express's Consumer Card Group, charged with reviving the sagging fortunes of the elite charge card. When Chenault took over the consumer-card division, American Express was known as the card that served high-end, well-off consumers. The American Express card had to be paid off in full each month, and it tended to be accepted only at elite, upscale businesses, a market position that was causing the company to lose business to competitors like MasterCard and Visa. Although these other companies charged high interest rates, they allowed customers to pay only a portion of their bills each month, making them more appealing to low- and middle-income spenders.

Moreover, American Express charged merchants 4 percent of each purchase price for the use of the card, whereas competitors charged far less—in Visa's case, less than half. This meant that many companies did not want to accept the American Express card, particularly companies that sold low-cost products—American Express's fees were simply too high.

Chenault moved aggressively to solve the company's problems. He improved relationships with merchants, cutting fees and signing up more low-end businesses, such as gas stations, discount stores, and supermarkets, vastly expanding the kinds of places where customers could use their American Express cards. He started Membership Rewards, a program that rewarded customers with points each time they used their cards—points that could be exchanged for prizes and bonuses. As a result, customers used their American Express cards more often and to charge higher amounts. In addition, Chenault began offering cards that customers could pay off over longer periods, such as the Optima card. He also offered cards in partnership with such companies as Delta Air Lines and Costco Wholesale Corp.

Chenault's activities vastly increased business for American Express, and his management moves looked like financial genius. The U.S. economy was taking off in the 1990s, and American Express profited with it, positioning Chenault as an

Chairman and chief executive officer Kenneth I. Chenault of American Express is one of the top black corporate leaders in the United States. *(Courtesy of American Express Company)*

up-and-coming manager. In 1993, he was named president of American Express Travel Related Services (TRS). He was promoted to vice chair of the entire company in 1995 and was made responsible for TRS International. In 1997, he became the company's president and chief operating officer, second-in-command to Chair and CEO Harvey Golub, who in 1999 announced his upcoming retirement and designated Chenault as his successor. When Golub retired, he handed the company over to Chenault, who assumed responsibilities as CEO and chair in 2001.

Initially, Chenault seemed poised to inherit a company in excellent financial shape. For eight years in a row, charge-card volume had increased, and since 1995 the company's earnings had risen as well, hitting a record $2.8 billion in 2000. More than $1.9 billion of this amount came from Travel Related Services, the division that Chenault had headed for so many years. Chenault's reputation on Wall Street was solid, and he was considered one of the most widely respected executives in the business world.

Then came the recession of 2001 followed by the disastrous events of September 11. Consumer spending—and credit-card use—dropped precipitously, as did travel, a business on which American Express depended. Chenault was held responsible for difficulties that the company had with various investments, and he found himself leading a company whose stock prices were falling, whose market value had dropped, and whose earnings were down.

Chenault's personal response to the September 11 attack, however, won him increased respect from his employees and his colleagues. When the first plane crashed into the tower, Chenault was on a business trip, speaking on the phone with a New York colleague from his hotel room in Salt Lake City, Utah. As soon as Chenault heard the news, he asked to be transferred to security for the company's building in lower Manhattan, the American Express Tower. Responding far more effectively than many others to the disaster, he told security to evacuate all employees immediately. Unable to travel back to New York, Chenault continued to keep a firm hand on the reins long-distance. An October 29, 2001, cover story in *BusinessWeek* reported that American Express's head of Global Corporate Services, Edward P. Gilligan, got a call from Chenault on the afternoon of September 11, as soon as Gilligan had reached his home in New Jersey. First, Chenault wanted to make sure Gilligan was safe. Next, he wanted to call a meeting of the company's top executives. Though Chenault could not return home for two days, his company knew that he was in charge, a leadership role that

Chenault continued to play through subsequent weeks, as he called a town meeting of 5,000 company employees to process the emotions relating to the event. In the weeks following the attacks, he joined New York City Mayor Rudolph Giuliani and New York Governor George Pataki in requesting federal funds for New York City and steered American Express through the troubled financial waters that followed.

Chenault has continued to cope with both the recession and the aftermath of September 11. He has increased the company's use of technology in an effort to cut costs. He has moved some clerical operations overseas to places like India, where lower rent and lower wages will further cut costs even as the company has access to many English-speaking employees. He is aggressively moving to expand the company's corporate travel and charge card accounts with a wide variety of corporations. And, he is working to improve the company's performance in the stock and bond markets, bringing in new personnel to review the investments that American Express has made. He has also had to lay off thousands of employees in New York City as a result of these changes. Nevertheless, he continues to win acclaim: In 2001, *BusinessWeek* called him one of the top 25 managers of the year, while *Worth* magazine listed him among the top 50 CEOs in the United States.

Chenault is married to Kathryn Cassell Chenault, a non-practicing attorney with whom he has two sons, Kenneth, Jr., and Kevin. He serves on a number of corporate and community boards and is a member of the prestigious Council on Foreign Relations, a group that studies U.S. foreign policy and publishes the influential journal *Foreign Affairs*.

Further Reading

Ashby, Meredith, ed. *Leaders Talk Leadership: Top Executives Speak Their Minds*. New York: Oxford University Press, 2002.

Byrne, John A., and Heather Timmons. "Tough Times for a New CEO." *BusinessWeek*. October 29, 2001. Available online at BusinessWeek online. URL: http://yahoo.businessweek.com/magazine/content/01_44/b3755001.htm. Downloaded on November 23, 2002.

Cable News Network. "Kenneth Chenault: Corporate CEO." CNN.com. Available online. URL: http://www.cnn.com/SPECIALS/2002/black.history/stories/08.chenault. Posted in February 2002.

Clarke, Marilyn. *Take a Lesson: Today's Top Black Achievers Talk About How They Made It and What They Learned Along the Way*. New York: John Wiley & Sons, 2001.

Cose, Ellis. "Rethinking Black Leadership." *Newsweek*, February 18, 2002, p. 40.

Gale Group. "Kenneth Irvine Chenault." African American Publications, Biography Resource Center. Available online. URL: http://www.africanpubs.com/Apps/bios/2005ChenaultKenneth.asp?pic=none. Downloaded on November 23, 2002.

"Harvey Golub and Kenneth I. Chenault, American Express." *BusinessWeek*, January 8, 2001. Available online at BusinessWeek Online. URL: http://www.businessweek.com/2001/01_02/b3714003.htm. Downloaded on November 22, 2002.

Norment, Lynn. "3 at the Top." *Ebony*, February 2002, p. 133.

TopBlacks. "Kenneth Chenault—President and Chief Operating Officer of American Express." TopBlacks: Positive Profiles of People of Color. Available online. URL: http://www.topblacks.com/business/kenneth-chenault.asp. Downloaded on November 23, 2002.

Church, Robert Reed, Sr.

(1839–1912) *real estate developer, banker, businessman*

Robert Church founded what was virtually a Memphis dynasty, a family that in its day was considered one of the most prestigious African-American families in the United States. According to Stephen Birmingham, author of a study of upper-class African Americans, "The Churches *are* Memphis."

Church was born in Holly Springs, Mississippi, on June 18, 1839, the son of Charles B. Church, a wealthy white owner of two luxury steamboats, and Emmaline, one of the man's slaves who worked as a seamstress on the Church plantation. Robert Reed Church always maintained that neither he nor his mother had ever been treated as a slave, even though that was their legal status. He insisted that his fair-skinned mother had been the daughter of a Malaysian princess and once testified before a congressional committee that he himself had little African blood, saying, "My father is a white man; my mother is as white as I am."

Captain Church apparently treated his son with affection but never legally or formally recognized the kinship. Although he did not educate his son, he did train him in the steamboat business, having him work as dishwasher, cook, and finally steward, the highest position on a steamboat that an African American could then achieve. The young Church was known as a ready fighter with a quick temper, always ready to use his fists or a pistol to settle a dispute. In 1857, he married Margaret Pico, another slave, who gave birth to one daughter, Laura Napier.

In 1862, Church was working as a steward on the steamer *Victoria* when it was captured by Union troops during the Civil War. The Union left the 23-year-old Church in Memphis, and the young man decided to make his fortune there, becoming involved in the saloon business.

Church was personally threatened during the Memphis riots of 1866—a time when white Irish police brutally attacked a group of recently discharged black soldiers and eventually rampaged through the entire black community, leaving 46 black people and two white people dead. The largely Irish white police force took the side of the rioters, and Church learned that a group of police wanted to put him out of business. He insisted on opening his saloon nevertheless and was shot in the back of the head while defending his business from the police, who were stealing his liquor and

his cash. Church later testified against police when federal officials came to investigate the riot.

For the rest of his life, Church faced trouble with the police, as well as with the many underworld elements who frequented his establishments, and with white hoodlums. Church's businesses—including saloons and billiard rooms—promoted drink, gambling, and probably prostitution, and they were often a center for violence and crime. In 1878, Church was shot by a local sheriff, supposedly in a fight over a black woman. In 1903, when Church was 64, he got into a brawl with two white brothers, who ended up in jail.

Meanwhile, Church had married Louise Ayers, a maid in Bluff City, Tennessee, with whom he had Thomas Ayers Church and Mary Church Terrell, a major leader of African-American women. Church divorced Ayers in 1870. He was by this time a wealthy man, having bought up huge amounts of real estate in black neighborhoods, and he continued to purchase property throughout all of the city's ups and downs. During the late 1870s, Memphis was struck by several yellow fever epidemics, and white people were often willing to sell their homes at bargain prices as they fled the cities. Church moved his own family out of town but he himself continued to buy for hundreds of dollars properties that had once been worth thousands. He became a wealthy landlord by the time of his death in 1912.

Despite the seamy side of Church's business dealings, he was known as a benefactor of the black community. In 1899, he gave his own land to create Church Park, which included a playground and concert hall that hosted such prestigious guests as Booker T. Washington, President Theodore Roosevelt, and black entertainer W. C. Handy. Church's contribution was particularly important at a time when black people were not allowed in Memphis's city parks or public auditoriums.

In 1885, Church married the fair-skinned African American Anna Wright, who became an unquestioned social leader in Memphis black society. The couple produced Robert Church, Jr., and Annette Church.

In 1906, Church helped to found the Solvent Savings Bank and Trust Company, with HARRY H. PACE serving as cashier and sitting on the board of directors along with the rest of Memphis's black business leaders. When the Panic of 1907 (an economic depression) hit the financial community, a number of banks faced ruin as their depositors asked for all their money back. (Most banks loan out the majority of their funds, so if every depositor wants his or her money back, the bank will be unable to pay.) Church had a creative way to calm depositors' fears: He put sacks of money in the bank's windows with a sign reading, "This Bank Is Paying off All Depositors." The bank survived and flourished well past Church's death, although bad financial investments in the 1920s led to its ultimate downfall.

Church insisted on always riding on the white section of streetcars, at a time when few black people could get away with such defiance. He supported black voting rights at a time when it could be physically dangerous to do so. He ran for city government positions in 1882 and 1886, but more popular black candidates defeated him. However, in 1900, he was chosen to be a delegate to the Republican national convention. (In those days, Republicans were considered the party of Abraham Lincoln and black civil rights.) In 1906, he offered Church Park for a rally to oppose a proposed Jim Crow law. (Jim Crow was the system of separating and discriminating against black people throughout the South.) He also played a political role behind the scenes, helping two black Memphis citizens to get appointments to the State Department's foreign service.

In 1909, Church stepped down as bank president, and his son Robert took over until his father's death on August 2, 1912. Unusual for the time, Memphis's white newspapers printed long obituaries, indicating Church's importance to the community. His life is a central part of the history of his adopted city.

Further Reading

Birmingham, Stephen. *Certain People: America's Black Elite.* Boston, Mass.: Little, Brown & Co., 1977.

Coppock, Paul R. *Memphis Memoirs.* Memphis, Tenn.: Memphis State University Press, 1980.

Gale Group. "Robert Reed Church, Sr." *Notable Black American Men.* Farmington Hills, Mich.: Gale Research, 1998.

Gatewood, Willard B. *Aristocrats of Color: The Black Elite, 1880–1920.* Bloomington, Ind.: Indiana University Press, 1990.

Lee, George W. *Beale Street: Where the Blues Began.* College Park, Md.: McGrath Publishing, 1934.

Miller, M. Sammye. "Portrait of a Black Urban Family." *Negro History Bulletin* 42 (April/May/June 1979): 50–51.

Mitchell, Reavis L. "Robert Reed Church, Sr. (1839–1912)." *Profiles of African Americans in Tennessee,* edited by Bobby L. Lovett and Linda T. Wynn. Nashville, Tenn.: Annual Local Conference on Afro-American Culture and History, 1996. Available online at Tennessee State University website. URL: http://www.tnstate.edu/library/digital/churchrs.htm. Downloaded on January 15, 2003.

Cohen, Walter I.

(1860–1930) *insurance executive, drugstore owner, government official*

Walter I. Cohen rose to prominence in Louisiana politics, getting his start during the Reconstruction era, when African Americans were allowed for the first time to take an active role in southern political life. Although he managed to hang on for a time after Reconstruction ended, southern opposition to black politicians eventually interfered with his political career and deprived him of his government job. Cohen responded by founding two successful businesses, People's Industrial Life Insurance and People's Drug Stores, which flourished in New Orleans for many years after his death.

Cohen was born on January 22, 1860, in New Orleans, Louisiana, the son of Amelia Bingaman, an African-American woman who had received her freedom in 1857, and Bernard Cohen, a Jewish man. Walter, however, was raised Catholic, and attended St. Louis Catholic School until he was in fourth grade, when both of his parents died. Very little information is available on Cohen's early life, but he seems to have worked for a while as a cigar maker—a skilled trade in those days— and also spent four years working in a saloon. He managed to attend Straight University for several years as well.

During the 1870s, Reconstruction was in force, and federal troops were stationed throughout the South to protect African-American political rights. During this era, many African-American politicians came to prominence, particularly in New Orleans, where even before the war the city had included a large population of free people of color, wealthy and powerful people who were poised to enter politics as soon as the law allowed it. While working as a page for the legislature, Cohen met politicians CESAR CARPENTIER ANTOINE and P. B. S. PINCHBACK, both of whom helped Cohen make his own entry into politics.

These men, however, were forced to retreat from politics as Reconstruction ended and federal troops were withdrawn as part of the 1876 compromise that put President Rutherford B. Hayes in power. As soon as federal support ended, black voting rights were swiftly curtailed and black politicians generally lost power. Cohen, however, managed to keep various government posts even as the men who had mentored him were withdrawing from the political arena. Cohen became secretary of the Republican State Central Committee—in those days, the Republican Party was seen as the party of Abraham Lincoln and black political rights—and was able to remain in that influential (though unpaid) position until President Herbert Hoover ended the appointment when he took office in 1929.

Despite the opposition from white politicians who hated the thought of black political power,

Cohen also held various paying government appointments until 1910, when President William Taft abolished the position that Cohen held. Taft offered Cohen a similar job that would have required leaving New Orleans, but Cohen was unwilling to leave his hometown. He decided instead to found the People's Benevolent Life Insurance Company, becoming its president. Black politician Booker T. Washington had supported Cohen in his efforts to remain in politics, and he now sent a letter of support for Cohen's new enterprise. When Cohen founded People's Drug Store, Washington sent a similar letter and even backed Cohen for a loan.

In the highly segregated (divided by race) city of New Orleans, Cohen's drugstore was designed to appeal to African-American customers, who patronized the store and its soda fountain and ice cream parlor. Eventually, Cohen was able to open a second store. He dabbled for a time in the roof garden business—a kind of restaurant and drinking establishment popular at the time—but withdrew from that enterprise in 1912, focusing on his drugstore and insurance ventures. He was also active in the National Negro Business League, an organization founded by Washington to promote black enterprise.

In 1882 Cohen had married Wilhelmina Selden. When she died in 1920, Cohen soon remarried, to Antonia Manade. In 1924, he was appointed to another federal post, controller of the Port of New Orleans. President Warren Harding had tried to secure this position for Cohen some years earlier, but white opponents of black civil rights had opposed the move, and the U.S. Senate rejected Cohen's appointment three times. Finally, President Calvin Coolidge was able to give Cohen the position. While Cohen held that job, his daughter from his first marriage, Camille, ran the insurance company while he focused on the drugstores.

The controller's job was abolished by President Herbert Hoover in 1929, when Hoover offered Cohen the ambassadorship to Liberia, a West African nation originally founded by freed slaves. Cohen again asserted his wish to remain in New Orleans, where he was active in a number of civic and civil rights groups, including the National Association for the Advancement of Colored People (NAACP), the Knights of Pythias, the Odd Fellows, and the Elks, as well as several exclusive organizations patronized by New Orleans's black elite, the Iroquois Literary and Social Club and the Société d'Economique. He continued to operate his drugstores and insurance business for the rest of his life.

Like many prominent African Americans of the era, Cohen also faced legal attacks. In 1908, his son was sentenced to two years in prison for a crime involving his work as a postal carrier. In 1925, Cohen himself was accused of accepting bribes in a liquor-smuggling scandal, along with 52 white officials, but he was fully exonerated at trial. He died, a respected and prominent figure, on December 29, 1930, in New Orleans.

Further Reading

Ingham, John, and Lynne B. Feldman. *African American Business Leaders: A Biographical Dictionary.* Westport, Conn.: Greenwood Press, 1994, pp. 145–151.

Roussève, Charles B. *The Negro in Louisiana: Aspects of His History and His Literature.* New York: Johnson Reprint Corp., 1937, pp. 130–131.

Coincoin   See METOYER, MARIE-THÉRÈSE.

Coleman, Warren Clay
(1849–1904) *textile manufacturer, banker, merchant, insurance company owner*

Warren Coleman dreamt of founding a black-owned textile mill in North Carolina. Although he was a successful entrepreneur in other fields, he was not able to make the mill succeed—in part because of the discrimination that black people faced in the South at that time. Nevertheless, his efforts stand as a story of great ambition and energy in the service of a difficult goal.

Coleman was born on March 28, 1849, as a slave on the Cabarrus County, North Carolina, plantation belonging to William M. Coleman. His mother was a slave named Roxanna Coleman, and his father is believed to have been Rufus Clay Barringer, a white man who later became a Confederate army general, lawyer, and farmer. Barringer certainly helped Coleman as a young man and invested in many of his ventures. Roxanna Coleman, meanwhile, went on to marry John F. Young, another slave who was also a skilled blacksmith.

Plantation owner William Coleman allowed Warren to learn the shoemaking trade on his plantation through the end of the Civil War in 1865, with Warren making shoes and boots for the Confederate army. Later, the owner took Warren as his own apprentice (someone who works for a person for little or no wages while learning a trade). When Warren Coleman later recalled this time, he felt that he had not in fact been trained but only required to perform menial tasks. When he was 18, in 1867, his apprenticeship ended and he was free to engage in trading and peddling. He established his own barbershop and a cake and candy store. Two years later, he bought his first piece of property for $600, a substantial achievement for a 20-year-old ex-slave.

Coleman went to Alabama for a year, seeking new opportunity, but returned to the town of Concord, North Carolina, near the Coleman plantation, in 1871. He peddled groceries, started some other small enterprises, and began farming. In 1873, he sold his business and enrolled at Howard University, an all-black school in Washington, D.C., but he was uninterested in formal education and by 1874 had returned to Concord permanently, having bought up more property and married Jane E. Jones, a woman eight years older than he whom he had met in Alabama. That year, he began to work as a moneylender, and by 1876, he was selling land as a real estate agent and brokering (arranging trades of) various goods. He continued his real estate activities throughout the 1870s, when he also became active in the AME (African Methodist Episcopal) Zion Church in Concord.

In 1881 he bought from William Coleman a half-interest in a lot on Main Street, fulfilling his dream of buying property in downtown Concord. He built a wooden building on the lot and began lending money there to local farmers, until it burned to the ground in 1885, costing him $7,000—a huge amount for the time. In 1887, he bought more land on the plantation where he had once been a slave, and he eventually expanded his real estate holdings within and even beyond Concord. Besides buying up the land, he had houses built on them, especially in nearby Coleberg, where he rented cabins to black tenants, creating what today is Concord's major African-American community. By 1895, Coleman had become one of the wealthiest African Americans in the South, and one of the largest merchants and landowners in Concord.

Coleman was also interested in promoting black enterprise and black education, as well as supporting the AME Zion Church. He was also active as a Republican (in those days considered the party of Abraham Lincoln, civil rights advocates, and African Americans), becoming a justice of the peace in 1895—a controversial position for a black man. In 1896 he got the Republican nomination to run for county commissioner, but he was pressed to withdraw because of his race.

Sometime in 1895 or 1896, meanwhile, Coleman began to consider the possibility of building a cotton mill. At that time in the South, most cotton was grown by African-American sharecroppers, poor farm laborers who were allowed by large landowners to farm small plots of land in exchange for a percentage of their crop. Although they grew the cotton, black people were not allowed to take the better-paying jobs of turning it into cloth. Cotton mills at the time were primarily located in New England, but an increasing number were being built in the South, including

Concord. Black people were considered incapable of working the machinery; many people in the political power structure also wanted to segregate southern society (to keep it divided by race) and to preserve the mill jobs for white workers.

Coleman decided to build a cotton mill of his own, both as a source of profit for himself and to demonstrate the capabilities of black workers. He founded Coleman Manufacturing in Concord, and set about seeking financing. In 1897, Coleman finally obtained financing from two wealthy black men from Durham, North Carolina: Richard B. Fitzgerald, a brickworks owner who would soon serve as company president, and Dr. James E. Shepherd. Funds were not sufficient, however, and Coleman had enormous trouble raising money, partly because the textile business was in trouble in the late 1890s and partly because white people feared supporting a black enterprise in a climate of increasing violence against black people and their white supporters. Eventually, after making an appeal to the black people of North Carolina, Coleman was able to raise the needed funds from black ministers; the presidents of black colleges; a black doctor; Fitzgerald; and Edward A. Johnson, an attorney from Raleigh, North Carolina, who was also an ex-slave. He also relied upon the financial help of the Duke family, wealthy white tobacco planters.

Financing continued to be a problem even after the mill building was completed. Yet Coleman decided that he needed to build a larger operation than the one he had originally planned, and he returned to the Dukes to borrow funds. By February 1900, the machinery was in place but the mill was not operating because the company could not afford to buy cotton. The Dukes were approached for another loan, but they did not respond until March 1901, when they made additional funds available—but also deducted interest from the first loan.

The mill was finally able to begin operations in June 1901, but unfortunately, the cotton market was at its lowest point since the Civil War. Many mills had to close, and Coleman's mill faced obvious difficulties. In December 1903, Coleman was asked to resign from his post as secretary treasurer, and he was replaced by a white merchant and cotton buyer. Finally, in June 1904, Benjamin M. Duke foreclosed on the property to get back the funds that he and his family had loaned. In 1906, the mill became the property of J. W. Cannon, the white textile entrepreneur whose Cannon Mills still operates the property today as Fieldcrest Cannon Plant #9. Coleman did not live to see the loss of his mill: He died on March 31, 1904.

Years later, however, Coleman was honored by his community. In February 2000, the Concord City Council voted to rename in his honor the section of Highway 601 that runs by his old plant. The newly named road, Warren C. Coleman Boulevard, was unveiled in March 2001.

Further Reading

Clark University. "Discover! Promise and Disappointment: Black and White Americans after Emancipation." Clark University website. Available online. URL: http://www.clarku.edu/research/access/history/greenwoodD.shtml. Downloaded on December 18, 2002.

Greenwood, Janette. *Bittersweet Legacy: The Black and White "Better Classes" in Charlotte, 1850–1910.* Chapel Hill: University of North Carolina Press, 1994.

North Carolina Department of Transportation (NCDOT). "Approval—Resolution for Warren C. Coleman." NCDOT website. Available online. URL: http://www.ncdot.org/board/minutes/years/01/january/Add9_ResoluColeman_0101.html. Posted in January 2001.

Cuffe, Paul
(Paul Cuffee)

(1759–1817) *shipbuilder, shipping company owner, trader, merchant, philanthropist*

By the time of his death in 1817, Paul Cuffe was probably the richest black man in America, as well as being the wealthiest man in his hometown of Westport, Massachusetts. He had amassed a fortune of $20,000 (a huge sum for the time), a fleet of ships, and several profitable businesses. He used his position as an African-American entrepreneur to fight for black equality and civil rights. He was also a strong supporter of colonization, a policy that sought to return free black people to Africa.

Cuffe was born on the island of Cuttyhunk, off the coast of New Bedford, Massachusetts, in 1759. He was the seventh of 10 children born to Cuffe Slocum and Ruth Moses. Slocum was an African-born Ashanti and former slave who had purchased his freedom from his master, Captain John Slocum in Dartmouth, Massachusetts. Moses was a Wampanoag Indian. As a young man, Cuffe had the family name changed, so that the family would no longer bear the name of his father's owner. Cuffe is an English version of *Kofi,* a West African name that means "born on Friday."

Slocum died when Cuffe was 13 years old, and Cuffe went on to fulfill several ambitious plans for himself. He learned to read and write and mastered the art of navigation. When he was 16 years old, he found a place on a whaling ship. In 1776, he was on his third voyage when the Revolutionary War broke out. Cuffe's ship was captured by the British, who put him in a New York prison for three months. When he was released, he settled in Westport, a Massachusetts town that was home to many Friends (also known as Quakers). The Friends were generally supportive of abolition (ending slavery) and often worked for black equality.

During the Revolutionary War, the British established a blockade (an effort to prevent all goods from entering or leaving U.S. ports). Cuffe made a living smuggling goods in and out of American harbors, but this dangerous occupation put him at risk from pro-British pirates as well as the British themselves, so Cuffe also worked as a hired hand on a farm and continued his studies of navigation. From his trading by boat along the Connecticut shore, sometimes in partnership with his brother, John, he made a handsome profit that enabled him to buy an 18-ton ship and hire other sailors.

In 1780, Paul and John refused to pay their taxes in protest of the Massachusetts laws that forbade black men from voting or owning a business, referring to the central principle of the American Revolution, "No taxation without representation." The Cuffes were thrown into the Taunton town jail in December. When they were released the following spring, they brought the issue to a Taunton town meeting, along with five other black people. Their taxes were lowered, and in 1783, free black people won the right to vote in Massachusetts.

Shipbuilder and trader Paul Cuffe is portrayed here with one of his ships crossing the ocean between Africa and North America. *(Courtesy of The New Bedford Whaling Museum. © The New Bedford Whaling Museum)*

Also in 1783, Cuffe married Alice Pequit, a Wampanoag Indian, with whom he eventually had seven children. The couple rented a house in Westport as Cuffe sailed to Ontario, Canada, to purchase dried codfish. Dried cod was a staple food in the early days of the United States, because it would keep for a long time without being refrigerated. The profits from this journey helped Cuffe establish a shipping business, trading with Europe and the Caribbean. He often worked in partnership with his brother-in-law, Michael Wainer, and he gave employment to many black sailors, with whom he sailed to Sweden, Russia, and France. In 1793, he became a whaler, sailing with his 42-ton schooner *Mary* and personally harpooning two whales. With the profits from that voyage, he went to Philadelphia, where he outfitted the *Ranger,* a 69-ton schooner in which he sailed south to Norfolk, Virginia. He bought corn in Virginia, which he sold back in Westport.

Cuffe continued to trade in various commodities (products offered for sale), including corn, gypsum (a mineral used to make plaster), and fish. His longest voyage was on the 268-ton ship known as the *Alpha.* With a seven-member black crew, he sailed south to Wilmington, Delaware, and Savannah, Georgia, then crossed the ocean to Helsingor, Denmark, and Göteborg, Sweden, before returning to Philadelphia carrying passengers and freight. Cuffe used only black crews on his ships, hoping to prove that black people were as capable as whites.

Over the course of his lifetime, Cuffe owned part or all of 10 ships, building or supervising the construction of seven of them at his own shipyard. He operated businesses in whaling, trading, farming, and fishing and often engaged in partnerships with prominent white Quakers, including William Rotch, Jr. By 1806, his holdings were worth approximately $10,000, a huge sum for the time. In 1808, he was made a member of the Society of Friends, which his parents had not been allowed to do because of their race.

Cuffe donated large amounts to build a Quaker meeting house in Westport and an interracial Quaker schoolhouse in the Cuttyhunk area, where he had also bought a farm. He worked with abolitionists in the United States and England, and England's Royal African Institution invited him to visit Sierra Leone, a nation that England had established on the coast of West Africa to serve as a new home for enslaved Africans captured during the now illegal slave trade.

On January 1, 1811, Cuffe sailed for Sierra Leone on his own ship, the *Traveller,* a journey that inspired him with hopes for trade among black people in the United States, England, and Sierra Leone. He also wanted to bring skilled free black Americans to Sierra Leone, as he was beginning to believe that black people had better prospects for true equality in Africa than in America. The War of 1812 made Atlantic travel impossible, but after the war, on December 15, 1815, Cuffe and nine families—a total of 38 people—sailed for Sierra Leone, where the families resettled.

Cuffe returned to the United States determined to work for colonization. He began an alliance with the American Colonization Society, a group of white southerners who supported the idea of sending free black people back to Africa. Though most black Americans opposed this plan, believing that colonization would divide free black people from their brothers and sisters in slavery, many black leaders agreed with Cuffe's ideas. Historians believe that his commitment to Africa inspired generations of black nationalists, including the 1930s leader Marcus Garvey.

Cuffe died in Westport on September 9, 1817, and his position as wealthy businessman was recognized in the large funeral he was given by the Society of Friends. However, he was buried in a far corner of the Quaker cemetery, separate from the white people buried there. Today Cuffe Farm in Westport, Massachusetts, is a National Historic Landmark, and Mystic Seaport, Connecticut, offers the Paul Cuffe Memorial Fellowship for the study of minorities in U.S. maritime (sea-related) history.

Further Reading

Africans in America. "Forten Letter to Cuffe." PBS.org. Available online. http://www.pbs.org/wgbh/aia/part3/3h484.html. Downloaded on November 10, 2002.

———. "Historical Documents: Memoir of Captain Paul Cuffee [sic], Liverpool *Mercury.*" PBS.org. Available online. URL: http://www.pbs.org/wgbh/aia/part3/3h485.html. Downloaded on November 10, 2002.

Harris, Sheldon. *Paul Cuffe: Black America and the African Return.* New York: Simon & Schuster, 1972.

Mystic Seaport. "Paul Cuffe Memorial Fellowship." Mystic Seaport website. Available online. URL: http://www.mysticseaport.org/learn/lo-Cuff.htm. Downloaded on November 10, 2002.

Salvador, George. *Paul Cuffe, the Black Yankee, 1759–1817.* New Bedford, Mass.: Reynolds-DeWalt, 1969.

Wiggins, Rosalind Dobb, ed. *Captain Paul Cuffe's Logs and Letters, 1808–1817: A Black Quaker's "Voice from Within the Veil."* Washington, D.C: Howard University Press, 1996.

D

Davis, Willie D.

(1934–) *entrepreneur, professional football player, beverage distributor, radio station owner*

Willie Davis was a football star who typified a certain type of black entrepreneur: After achieving success and fame in sports, he moved into business when his athletic career was over. Many other African-American sports figures have followed this model, including MEL FARR, Dave Bing, Julius Erving, Oscar Robertson, and Gale Sayers, while such superstars as "Magic" Johnson and Michael Jordan have built successful business careers for themselves while still playing. Unlike the others, however, Davis never made a huge salary while he was playing, and his success in business depended less on his athletic fame and fortune than on his entrepreneurial skills.

Davis was born on July 24, 1934, in Lisbon, Louisiana, His family had very little money as Davis was growing up, especially since his mother was raising her three children as a single parent. Out of fear for his safety, she forbade Davis to play football—but he insisted on joining the team, playing at the segregated (separated by race) public schools of the time. When he graduated from Booker T. Washington High School in 1952, his classmates voted him "Least Likely to Succeed," but as a star in three different sports, he was able

to win an athletic scholarship to Grambling College in Louisiana, where he became the football team's captain and star player as well as making the Dean's List (a list of students with top grades) several times. He graduated in 1956 with a B.S. in industrial arts, going on to spend two years in the U.S. Army, winning further honors as a football player.

When Davis entered professional football in 1958, he seemed headed for obscurity. He was drafted in the 17th round by the Cleveland Browns, and then, two years later, was sent to the Green Bay Packers. In those days, the standard threat of National Football League (NFL) coaches was, "If you don't like it here, we'll send you to Green Bay." But Vince Lombardi had just come on the team as its coach, and his legendary leadership turned the team into one of the greatest football clubs of all time. While Davis was on the team, they won six division championships and five world championships, and Davis himself became defensive team captain and was selected to the All-Pro team for six years. Later, in 1981, he was chosen for the NFL Hall of Fame.

Despite his success, Davis was well aware that a football career was short, and during his last five years on the team, he studied for an M.B.A. (master's in business administration) at the University of Chicago. Davis found it difficult to attend school and play professional football at the same time, not least because when the team was playing a world championship, he had to start the semester two or three weeks late. In 1968, Davis was flunking a course, and he went to Lombardi for advice. "You've never been a quitter, have you?" Lombardi asked him, inspiring Davis to return to his coursework. He was able to bring his grades up so far that he eventually made the Dean's List.

During his football career, David had invested in real estate, purchasing an apartment building in Green Bay with former teammate Herb Adderley and buying a portion of Valley School and Office Supplies in Appleton, Wisconsin, with former teammates Bob Skronski and Rob Kostelnick. Davis had also sought employment in business before he actually retired, applying in 1964 to the Joseph Schlitz Brewing Company in Milwaukee—where he was turned down. Schlitz was more receptive to Davis in 1969, however, when Davis retired from football. At that time, Davis received more than 50 job offers, but he chose to take an executive training position with Schlitz while continuing to pursue the M.B.A. that he finally received in 1970.

Also in 1970, Schlitz offered Davis the chance to buy a distributorship in Los Angeles. The business cost $500,000, and Davis had only $150,000 in savings, but he managed to get a loan against the value of his home and other businesses. He chose not to apply for government programs that supported minority-owned businesses, feeling that too much paperwork would be involved.

Willie Davis Distributing, located in the African-American neighborhood known as Watts, was phenomenally successful, doubling its business in the first three years, achieving sales of $4.5 million by 1973, and expanding to $17.5 million in sales by 1982. Also in that year, the National Black MBA Association named Davis MBA of the Year for his contributions to the black business community. In addition, Stroh's Brewing took over the Schlitz company—but Davis's business

Football star Willie Davis went on to become an entrepreneur in real estate, radio, and the beverage business. *(AP/Wide World Photos)*

continued to prosper, remaining the largest beer distributorship on the West Coast. Davis added wines to his inventory, and in 1986 moved into a Coors distributorship, West Coast Beverage, in partnership with actors Tom Selleck and Larry Manetti. This company was also hugely successful. But Davis saw that sales of beer were declining generally, and the largest companies were fighting bitterly for market share. He decided to leave the beer business and sold his interests in that industry in 1988.

Meanwhile, he had begun working in radio, a field he preferred. In 1976, he had bought L.A. station KAGB-FM, whose call letters later changed to KACE. Davis had bought the station in a run-down state for the relatively low price of $225,000—by 1983, it was worth $4 million. The station was oriented to middle-class black professionals, playing a variety of music that it called "Soulful Bouillabaisse" (bouillabaisse is a kind of fish stew with many ingredients), including rhythm and blues, jazz, and pop. The success of KACE led Davis to acquire several other radio stations. With Northwestern Mutual in Milwaukee, he bought Milwaukee stations WLUM-FM and WAWA in 1979. In 1981, he bought KQIN-AM in Seattle and he added KYOK-AM in Houston to his holdings in 1982. Later he bought KDHT-FM in Denver. The stations are held through a company called "All-Pro Broadcasting."

Davis also serves on the boards of directors of many corporations, including Dow Chemical; Sara Lee Corporation; Kmart Corporation; MGM, Inc.; and Alliance Bank. He is a trustee of the University of Chicago, Marquette University, and Occidental College and is a member of the Grambling College Foundation. In the 1960s, he was active with former NFL star Jim Brown in the Negro Industrial Economic Union, which helped small black businesses get loans. Davis's approach to race issues has generally been low-key, conservative, and nonconfrontational, though his friends and colleagues say that he has never forgotten his responsibilities to the black community.

Further Reading

Gale Group. "Willie D. Davis, Mr." *Who's Who Among African Americans*, 14th ed. Farmington Hills, Mich.: Gale Research, 1992.

Ingham, John, and Lynne B. Feldman. *African American Business Leaders: A Biographical Dictionary.* Westport, Conn.: Greenwood Press, 1994, pp. 168–174.

Day, Thomas

(1801–1861) *furniture manufacturer, master carpenter, woodworker, artist*

Thomas Day has won acclaim in recent years for his extraordinary furniture and cabinetry, which

has led the Craftique company to its creation of its Thomas Day collection. Though Craftique had previously specialized in reproductions of 18th-century U.S. furniture, Day's work inspired them to create a special a special line of 19th-century reproductions devoted to his work. Day's work has also been the subject of shows at the DuSable Museum in Chicago and the North Carolina Museum of History in Raleigh.

During his own lifetime, Day's clients included the governor of North Carolina as well as many wealthy residents of the state. Scholars have speculated that some of his works resemble art made in West Africa, particularly the image of the sankofa, a mythic Ghanaian bird that looks backward while flying forward, symbolizing the need to move forward on the basis of a strong connection with the past.

Day was born near Petersburg, Virginia, in 1801 to a free black woman and a cabinetmaker father, who moved the family to North Carolina in 1817. Because early records on African Americans tend to be sparse, little is known about his early life, though he seems to have been taught reading and writing (he was known to write eloquently, with elegant handwriting), and to have been apprenticed to a local carpenter. (An apprentice works for a skilled craftsperson for free or at very low wages in order to learn the skill.) His brother, John, went to Milton, North Carolina, in 1821 to study theology. (John would later lead the Southern Baptist mission in Liberia, a country founded in west Africa to be a home for freed U.S. and British slaves.)

A year or two later, Day followed his brother to Milton, a prosperous town in the heart of a wealthy tobacco-growing region. Many cabinetmakers were located in Milton, and Day might have found work with any of them. By 1827, he had bought his own shop on the town's Main Street for the substantial sum of $550. His business grew as he made cabinets, interior trim, and furniture for the area's wealthy tobacco growers. In 1830, the local census records that Day was a black artisan who owned two slaves. Records also indicate that Day employed white apprentices.

In 1830, Day married Acquilla Wilson, a free black woman from Virginia, and for a time, he thought he might have to join her there. An 1826 law had made it difficult for free black people like Wilson to enter North Carolina, a sign of how anxious white people of the time were about both the possibility of slave revolts, which they felt free black people encouraged, and about the presence of free blacks generally, who upset the notion that black people were somehow naturally intended for slavery and incapable of surviving outside it. Day was so popular in Milton, however, that when he threatened to leave on account of this law, 60 white citizens of the tiny town petitioned the General Assembly (part of the state legislature) for a waiver of the law, and a letter in support of the petition was sent by state attorney general Romulus Saunders. Day was able to bring his wife to Milton, where the couple had three children. As an 1844 North Carolina law prohibited the education of free black people, all three children were educated in Wilbraham, Massachusetts, at the school now known as Wilbraham & Monson Academy. Similar laws forbade free black people from serving in the military except as musicians, bearing witness against white people in court, or collecting money owed to them by whites unless they themselves were property owners.

In 1848, Day bought the Yellow Tavern, a prestigious residence on the town's Main Street, to which he added a two-story wing. He established his home and business in the same building, which became the most expensive on that street. Day's prominence in Milton is also indicated by the fact that he was an elder in the local Presbyterian Church. At one time he owned a 270-acre tobacco farm and three town properties, and the 1850 census records him as employing more people (12) and producing more goods than any of the 51 cabinetmakers listed in the census, with an estate valued at $8,000. However, the Panic of 1857 (an economic crisis) hurt his business, and

in 1858 he was about to close his doors. His son, Thomas Day, Jr., bought the shop instead, operating the business until 1871. Thomas Day, Sr., died sometime in 1861.

Today Day is honored by Milton's inclusion of his home among valued local landmarks, and by a fellowship that bears his name, in which North Carolina teachers of art, social studies, and language arts participate in an intensive study of African-American history and culture.

Further Reading
Day, Tom, and Mary E. Lyons. *Master of Mahogany: Tom Day, Free Black Cabinetmaker.* Glenview, Ill.: Scott, Foresman, 1995.
Lyons, Mary E. *Master of Mahogany: Tom Day, Free Black Cabinetmaker.* The Lyons Den: Books for Young Readers. Available online. URL: http://www.lyonsdenbooks.com/html/mahogany.htm. Downloaded on November 14, 2002.
Rogers, Patricia Dane. "Carved in History. Thomas Day: A Success in an Unlikely Time and Place." *Washington Post,* February 13, 1997, p. T10.
Tamulevich, Susan. "A Carolina Legacy Carved in Wood." *Washington Post,* March 10, 1991, p. W22.

DeBaptiste, George
(ca. 1815–1875) *abolitionist, entrepreneur, restaurateur, steamboat owner*

George DeBaptiste is an example of an African-American entrepreneur who used his position as business owner to aid other members of the black community, particularly through his work on the Underground Railroad (a nationwide network that helped runaway slaves escape to freedom). Although DeBaptiste was active in antislavery and civil rights work for many years before and after the Civil War, he was most known for owning a steamship that enabled him to ferry former slaves across Lake Erie into Canada, where they could be free.

Little is known about DeBaptiste's early life, partly because records kept on black people in the 19th century were often scanty. It is known that he was born free in either 1814 or 1815 in Fredericksburg, Virginia, and that his father, John DeBaptiste, was a successful man of business who seems to have apprenticed his son to a barber in Richmond, Virginia. From his early adult years, DeBaptiste began helping enslaved African Americans escape to the North, moving to Madison, Indiana, in 1837 or 1838, where he worked as a barber—and as a conductor on the Underground Railroad. Since under the law, slaves were viewed as human property, helping them to escape was legally considered analogous to stealing and/or disposing of stolen goods, and DeBaptiste was forced to leave Indiana due to his growing reputation as an abolitionist (an opponent of slavery).

DeBaptiste moved on to Ohio, where he met the politician William Henry Harrison. He worked as Harrison's servant during his campaign for the U.S. presidency, then as his White House steward (the person responsible for running the household) until Harrison died in 1841. DeBaptiste probably returned to Ohio, where he continued to work as a barber and an abolitionist.

DeBaptiste went farther north to settle in Detroit in 1846, where he worked with a wholesale clothing business, ran a bakery, operated a catering service, ran an ice cream parlor, and owned two restaurants. He seemed to have belonged to a secret abolitionist group that had several different names over its lifetime, including Order of the Men of Oppression, African-American Mysteries, and the Order of Emancipation (freeing slaves). He was also a delegate to the Cleveland National Convention of Colored Citizens, a national effort to oppose slavery and improve conditions for all African Americans, and he served as president of the Black Union League, another African-American community group. As before, he continued to work with the Underground Railroad.

In 1847, an incident occurred that illustrates how important community support was to the abolitionist effort. An escaped slave, Robert Cromwell, was captured in Detroit by his former owner David Dunn and an agent whom Dunn had hired to help him catch Cromwell. Although slaves were considered the property of their owners no matter what state they were in, some communities opposed slavery and sought to bend the law. In this case, Cromwell was rescued through the intervention of a judge, his clerk, and a high-spirited crowd, including Underground Railroad conductors William Lambert and George DeBaptiste. Dunn and his helper, fearing the crowd, gave up Cromwell, who was taken safely to Canada, while Dunn was arrested on kidnaping charges.

In 1859, DeBaptiste is known to have met with a group of abolitionists that included African-American leader Frederick Douglass and white activist John Brown, who had come to Detroit to rally support for an armed insurrection (uprising) Brown planned to lead at Harpers Ferry, West Virginia. Brown hoped that this uprising would inspire a nationwide rebellion of slaves and force an end to slavery. It is not clear whether or not DeBaptiste supported Brown, but his presence at the meeting suggests his prominence in the abolitionist community.

In 1860, DeBaptiste bought the steamboat *T. Whitney,* hired white pilots, and ran a service connecting various Canadian ports. Later, his boat sailed across Lake Erie between Sandusky, Ohio, and Detroit, stopping on each trip to pick up wood in Amherstburg, Ontario, in Canada. This route gave him occasion to pick up runaways in Ohio and Michigan, taking them to freedom and safety in Canada. He apparently listed the black people in his cargo as "black wool," his way of concealing their presence on board while making a private joke.

When the Civil War ended in 1865, DeBaptiste's property holdings in Detroit were valued at $10,000, a huge sum at the time. He went on to work for the Freedmen's Association, a group dedicated to helping the newly freed slaves find work and other resources in the new society. On April 7, 1870, during a Detroit celebration of the Fifteenth Amendment (which had given black people the right to vote), DeBaptiste put up a sign saying, "Notice to Stockholders—Office of the Underground Railway: This office is permanently closed." The sign was another of DeBaptiste's jokes, echoing the language of a typical going-out-of-business sign, as though the Underground Railroad had been a business instead of a political organization. The fact that the organization was no longer necessary held deep meaning to DeBaptiste, who later attached the sign to his office building in downtown Detroit. DeBaptiste died in Detroit in 1875.

Further Reading

African-American Registry. "George DeBaptiste, a Michigan Abolitionist." Media Business Solutions Presents the African American Registry. Available online. URL: http://www.aaregistry.com/detail. php3?id=1245. Downloaded on November 14, 2002.

Brennon, James. "George DeBaptiste Homesite." Mich Markers.com: The Michigan Historical Markers website. Available online. URL: http://www.mich markers.com/Pages/S0452.htm. Downloaded on November 14, 2002.

Detroit Historical Museums and Society. "The Doorway to Freedom." Detroit Historical Museums website. Available online. URL: http://www. detroithistorical.org/exhibits/index.asp?MID= 1&EID=161. Downloaded on November 14, 2002.

————. "New Exhibit Opening at the Dossin Great Lakes Museum Tells the Story of African American Sailors." Detroit Historical Museums website. Available online. URL: http://www.detroithistori cal.org/news/pressreleases.asp?ID=18. Posted January 25, 2002.

New Detroit, Inc. "Underground Railroad Monument." New Detroit: The Coalition. Available online. URL: http://www.newdetroit.org/under ground_railroad.asp. Downloaded on November 14, 2002.

De Passe, Suzanne Celeste

(1947–   ) *Motown executive, music producer, television producer, entertainment company founder*

Next to OPRAH WINFREY, Suzanne de Passe may well be the most powerful African-American woman in television. She is the founder of de Passe Entertainment, where she produces television series and specials. She also had a long history with BERRY GORDY, JR.'s Motown record label and with the many companies he founded to produce music, television, theater, and film. With her own company, she has produced documentaries, miniseries, situation comedies, and awards shows.

De Passe is private about her past; only limited information is available on her early years. Records indicate that she may have been born in New York City in 1947, a member of the city's African-American elite. Her father worked for Seagrams, a liquor company, while her mother taught school. The young de Passe grew up in a middle-class Harlem neighborhood and attended the Jack and Jill School, a prestigious integrated facility. Summers were spent on the luxurious Martha's Vineyard resort in Massachusetts. De Passe's parents divorced when she was three, and as a consolation gift, her grandfather sent Suzanne and her mother on a trip to Europe. Her father remarried when she was nine, and de Passe has said that she felt well supported by all three parental figures.

De Passe attended New Lincoln, a progressive, integrated school where fellow students recall de Passe as extremely popular, self-assured, talented, and independent. She graduated in 1964 and went on to Syracuse University, where she found herself lonely and isolated as one of only 80 African Americans among 20,000 students. She transferred to Manhattan Community College the following year but found college dull. Against the strenuous objections of her parents, she dropped out to work at Cheetah, a New York disco where she had been spending most of her time. She began telling the manager and the owner what she thought of the various acts they booked, and they were so impressed with her judgment that they invited her to attend their weekly auditions for new acts. Eventually, they fired their booking agent and hired her as talent coordinator.

Artists from Berry Gordy's Motown often appeared at Cheetah, which was also a popular party spot for the label's biggest stars. She met Gordy briefly, then spoke with him a year later when she had gone on to work for a booking agent. Reportedly, in 1968, de Passe told Gordy that she had tried to book his acts but that no one would return her phone calls; Gordy, amused, invited her to work for Motown to come "straighten it out." Three weeks later, de Passe had moved to Detroit and become Gordy's assistant. She later helped him set up offices in Hollywood, having been named vice president in charge of creative operations.

As part of the Motown story, de Passe is known for guiding Lionel Richie's solo musical career, launching Rick James and the funk era, and discovering Michael Jackson and the Jackson 5. As Motown expanded into numerous fields, de Passe was there, co-writing the 1972 Oscar-nominated screenplay for the company's *Lady Sings the Blues* and taking over in 1981 as president of Motown Productions to supervise television production, charged with developing the company's movie, theater, and television products on a $10 million budget. She went on to produce some very successful television specials that drew on Motown's musical history, including the Emmy-winning "Motown 25: Yesterday, Today, Forever" (NBC, 1983), a salute to the company's 25-year anniversary that brought the Supremes back together and featured Michael Jackson's ability to moonwalk. In 1985, she produced a summer variety show, *Motown Revue* (NBC), the Emmy-winning special "Motown Returns to the Apollo" (NBC, 1985), and the Showtime series *Motown on Showtime* (1986–90). In 1987, she produced "Motown Merri X-mas"

for ABC; in 1990, she produced the company's 30th anniversary special, "Motown 30: What's Goin' On" (CBS); and in 1998, she produced a four-hour documentary commemorating the company's 40th anniversary, "Motown 40: The Music Is Forever" (ABC).

De Passe and Motown's forays beyond African-American culture were not successful at first. She produced some relatively unsuccessful television movies in the 1980s and in 1985 backed an unprofitable feature film called *The Last Dragon*. Meanwhile, Gordy sold Motown Records in 1988, though de Passe continued to work with him at the Gordy Company, the umbrella group overseeing Gordy's other record labels as well as Motown Productions, his media company.

De Passe and Berry scored their big television breakthrough in February 1989, when de Passe produced the highest-rated miniseries in five years, a western called *Lonesome Dove*, based on the novel of the same name by Larry McMurtry. Besides being a huge success, winning Emmys, Golden Globes, and Peabody Awards, *Lonesome Dove* demonstrated that neither de Passe nor Motown was limited to African-American themes. The series brought $10 million in profits to Motown Productions at a time when the company was floundering. De Passe went on to produce several sequels, including *Return to Lonesome Dove* (CBS, 1993), *Larry McMurtry's Streets of Laredo* (CBS, 1995), and a syndicated series, *Lonesome Dove: The Outlaw Years* (1994–1996).

De Passe continued to work with Gordy as she oversaw a wide variety of television shows. Her credits include *Night Life* (1986–87), a syndicated comedy series starring David Brenner; *Rollergames,* a syndicated update of *Roller Derby* (1989); and the Emmy-nominated miniseries *Small Sacrifices* (ABC, 1989), starring Farrah Fawcett as a woman who tries to kill her own children. That program also won two Golden Globe Awards and the prestigious Peabody Award for best miniseries.

In 1991, Gordy withdrew from an active role in producing, letting de Passe take a majority control of the properties in their joint company over to her own de Passe Entertainment. There, in 1992, she produced "Liberators," a PBS special about African-American troops who liberated concentration camps in World War II. She also produced the Emmy-nominated miniseries about the Jackson 5, *The Jacksons: An American Dream* (ABC, 1992). In 1995, she executive-produced the Emmy-nominated miniseries *Buffalo Girls* for CBS, followed by *Larry McMurty's Dead Man's Walk,* a miniseries for ABC in 1996, both from Larry McMurtry novels. In 1998, she produced *The Temptations*, an NBC miniseries that won the NAACP (National Association for the Advancement of Colored People) Image Award, as well as an Emmy and numerous other awards.

During the 1990s, de Passe began producing situation comedies, including *Sister, Sister* (ABC, 1994–95, The WB, 1995–99), about two young African-American twins who were reunited after being separated at birth and adopted by different families; *On Our Own* (ABC, 1994–95), about a family of six performing siblings that resemble the Jacksons; and *Smart Guy* (The WB, 1997–99), about an African-American boy genius.

De Passe has produced a number of other television movies, including *Zenon, Girl of the 21st Century* (1999) and *Zenon: The Zequel* (2001), both for The Disney Channel; *The Loretta Claiborne Story* (2000) for ABC; and *Cheaters* (2000) for HBO. In 2001, she produced the 32nd NAACP Image Awards for Fox. She continues to develop television productions, drawing both on her Motown history and on her wide variety of other interests. In addition to her numerous Emmy Awards, de Passe has received the AWRT (American Women in Radio and Television) Silver Satellite Award (1999), Women in Film Crystal Award (1988), Revlon Business Woman of the Year Award (1994), and Essence Business Award (1989), as well as being inducted into the Black Filmmakers Hall of Fame in 1990.

Further Reading

Duffy, Mike. "How Suzanne de Passe Made It Happen." *Detroit Free Press*, July 19, 1992. Available online. URL: http://www.freep.com/motownat40/archives/920719.htm.

Gordon, Tim. "Now Playing: Conversation with . . . Suzanne de Passe." reel images Magazine.com. Available online. URL: http://www.reelimagesmagazine.com/txt_features/conversations/reel_conversation_suzanne_depasse.htm. Downloaded on November 12, 2002.

Hollywood.com, Inc. "Suzanne de Passe." Hollywood.com. Available online. URL: http://www.hollywood.com/celebs/detail/celeb/188861. Downloaded on November 12, 2002.

De Priest, Oscar Stanton

(1871–1951) *congressman, entrepreneur, realtor*

Oscar Stanton De Priest was the first African-American congressman to be elected from a northern state. He rose to political prominence in part because of his striking success in real estate, using his entrepreneurial abilities to support both his political and his business career.

De Priest was born on March 9, 1871, in a cabin in Florence, Alabama, the fifth child of the ex-slaves Neander R. and Martha Karsner De Priest. His father had a hauling business and farmed part-time while his mother worked as a laundress. Neander De Priest was a friend of Republican congressman James T. Rapier, and once sheltered the black politician from an angry mob that resented his efforts to win black civil rights. In the years after the Civil War, the Republican Party was considered the party of Abraham Lincoln and black political activism, while the Democratic Party was seen as the party of the Old Confederacy. Neander De Priest insisted on his right to vote Republican even in the face of threats to his business.

When Oscar was a child, he discovered a neighbor who had been lynched outside his door and shot several times. Although the De Priests left the South in 1878 when Oscar was only seven, Oscar never forgot the racial violence within which he had grown up.

In Florence, Oscar studied in a Congregational church school for freedmen (newly freed slaves). When his father moved the family to Salina, Kansas, Oscar studied in the public elementary school there, going on to a two-year business and bookkeeping course at Salina Normal School. He also learned the painting and decorating trade from his uncles and from a painter to whom he was apprenticed. (To apprentice means to work for no or low wages in order to learn a trade.)

When De Priest was 17, he and two white companions ran away to Dayton, Ohio. The next year, he went on to Chicago, alone. De Priest had fair skin and light-brown hair, and he occasionally passed for white in Chicago in order to get better jobs. He started out working as a house painter. In 1897 he married Jessie L. Williams of Rockford, Illinois, with whom he had two sons. By 1905, De Priest owned a successful painting and decorating firm, which specialized in renovating run-down buildings.

De Priest became active in Republican Party politics and was skilled at manipulating events to enhance his own success. He became a county commissioner at age 33, and while he held office, his decorating business won $25,000 worth of contracts from the Chicago Board of Education. He served two terms as commissioner but was unable to win a third term—so he returned his focus to expanding his decorating business. By the 1920s, he had amassed a fortune from managing real estate on Chicago's South Side, a black neighborhood that was expanding rapidly with emigrants from the South, who, like De Priest's father, were seeking both economic opportunity and freedom from the violence of the South.

Meanwhile, in 1915, De Priest became the city's first black alderman. Two years later, he was indicted for bribery, but he was eventually acquitted, with famed lawyer Clarence Darrow defending him. Temporarily at odds with the local Republicans, he ran as an independent in 1918 and 1919, but was defeated by black Republicans. De Priest patched up his difficulties with the party and became a delegate to the 1920 Republican convention.

De Priest continued to prosper in real estate as he tried various strategies to gain political success, playing off different factions within the Republican Party and occasionally even supporting Democratic candidates. In 1927, he threw both his financial support and his political influence behind Republican William Hale Thompson, who became Chicago's mayor—and rewarded De Priest by helping him get appointed assistant Illinois commerce commissioner.

In 1928, De Priest supported a white congressional candidate over a black opponent. The white candidate won the primary—and then died. The mayor once again helped De Priest, supporting him for the nomination. Even though De Priest faced new criminal charges—he was accused of helping racketeers operate gambling houses on the South Side with police protection—he went on to defeat a white Democrat and a black independent, becoming the first black African-American congressman to be elected from the North. As there had been no black people in Congress for 28 years, De Priest was a pioneer of sorts.

De Priest did well as long as the Republican Party remained the party of civil rights and black advancement. He was a follower of Booker T. Washington, a believer in entrepreneurship and self-help, and he bitterly opposed any kind of government aid to the poor. In 1929, however, the Great Depression hit Chicago hard, with particular difficulties for black voters. When Democrat Franklin D. Roosevelt was elected president in 1932, he stood for government assistance in creating jobs, offering training, and providing relief until the economy improved. Black voters flocked to support him—and De Priest became politically isolated. In 1934, he was defeated by a black Democrat and lost his congressional seat.

De Priest remained an active Republican, serving as vice chair of the Cook County Republican Central Committee from 1932 to 1934, as delegate to the 1936 Republican convention, and as alderman from the Third Ward from 1943 to 1947. He also remained active in the real estate business, which made him an enemy of the Communist Party. Communists in those days were extremely active with tenants' rights and civil rights. They accused De Priest of "blockbusting"—buying apartment buildings in white neighborhoods and then moving in black tenants. When white people left these buildings in a panic, De Priest moved in more black tenants—and then raised their rents. Some people defended De Priest as a man providing needed housing for black citizens who were flocking to the city. But the Communists and others saw him as a greedy landlord who took advantage of his own people.

De Priest died on May 12, 1951, several months after having been hit by a bus. He is remembered as a contradictory figure whose historic achievements are complicated by the criticism he received.

Further Reading

American Council of Learned Societies. "Oscar Stanton De Priest." *Dictionary of American Biography, Supplement 5, 1951–1955.* New York: Scribner's, 1977.

Branham, Charles. "Oscar Stanton De Priest." *Encyclopedia of African American Business History,* ed. by Juliet E. K. Walker. Westport, Conn.: Greenwood Press, 1999, pp. 182–184.

Christopher, Maurine. *America's Black Congressmen.* New York: Thomas Y. Crowell, 1971.

Day, David S. "Herbert Hoover and Racial Politics: The De Priest Incident." *Journal of Negro History* 65 (winter 1980): 6–17.

Gale Research Group. "Oscar Stanton De Priest." *Notable Black American Men.* Farmington Hills, Mich.: Gale Research, 1998.

Mann, Kenneth Eugene. "Oscar Stanton De Priest: Persuasive Agent for the Black Masses." *Negro History Bulletin* 35 (October 1972): 134–137.

Dickerson, Earl Burrus
(1891–1986) *insurance executive*

Earl Burrus Dickerson helped to operate Supreme Liberty Life Insurance, the oldest black-owned insurance company in Chicago and at one time the largest African-American owned business in the North. By the 1990s, it was a relatively insignificant part of JOHN H. JOHNSON's empire, but for much of its history, the company had been a central part of Chicago's black business history.

Dickerson was born in Canton, Mississippi, on June 23, 1891, the son of Edward and Emma (Garrett) Dickerson. (Some sources give his birthdate as June 22.) Dickerson's mother worked as a laundress, and as a child, Dickerson used to pick up and deliver clothes to his mother's customers in the white section of town, using his little wagon. On one of these trips, at the age of five or so, he was knocked unconscious by a rock thrown by one of a group of white boys who was harassing him.

Dickerson went to school in Canton, but in 1907, at the age of 16, he went north to Chicago for more education. He was part of the wave of immigrants moving to Chicago in search of a better life and more opportunity at a time when the laws and customs restricting the lives of black people in the South were growing ever more severe. In 1909, he graduated from Evanston Academy, the school set up to prepare students for Northwestern University, from which he graduated in 1914. He then taught for two years at Booker T. Washington's Tuskegee Institute in Alabama and at a high school in Vincennes, Indiana, before enrolling at the University of Chicago for further studies.

Then the United States entered World War I and Dickerson became a first lieutenant, serving in France. He returned to Chicago in 1919 and completed his law degree in 1920. Also in 1919, he helped found the American Legion, a group whose conservative politics he later had cause to criticize.

In 1921, he passed the bar exam and was asked to draw up the articles of incorporation for Liberty Life Insurance, becoming general counsel for the firm. Dickerson had always been interested in politics, and in 1923, he became head of the Negro Division of William Dever's campaign for mayor. Dever, a Democrat, won the election and made Dickerson assistant corporation counsel for the city. In those years, most black people were affiliated with the Republican Party, which was still seen as the party of Abraham Lincoln and civil rights. Dickerson was a staunch Democrat, however, continuing to work for his party's candidates throughout the 1920s. In 1929, he ran as an independent for the position of alderman, but he lost the election badly, and in 1931 he was once again a Democrat.

Meanwhile, he had become a civil rights leader, going on to be active with the National Association for the Advancement of Colored People (NAACP) and the Urban League, as well as an activist for public housing. In 1931, he protested police brutality in Chicago, and in 1939, he took on the case of Carl Hansberry, the father of playwright Lorraine Hansberry, as Carl tried to win the right to buy a house in an area where property owners had agreed not to sell to black people. (Lorraine Hansberry was then a child; she later used this incident as the basis of her famous play, *Raisin in the Sun.*)

When Franklin D. Roosevelt was elected president in 1932, promising increased social services and government assistance, he helped convince many black people to switch from Republican to Democrat. As a longtime Democrat, Dickerson was in a good position, and he was made assistant attorney general of the state of Illinois in 1933. When he ran for alderman in 1939, he won easily. Meanwhile, he made a deal with the longtime

incumbent, William Dawson, to join forces after the election, when the African-American Dawson crossed over to the Democrats as well.

Despite his support of Roosevelt's New Deal, Dickerson took positions that annoyed many of Chicago's more conservative Democratic leaders. He joined such left-wing groups as the Midwest Committee for Protection of the Foreign Born, National Lawyers Guild, Free Earl Browder Conference, Abraham Lincoln School, International Labor Organization, and the Progressive Party— forerunners of the Civil Rights movement of the 1950s in calling for full freedom and equality for black people. Dawson was more conservative and frequently opposed Dickerson's actions.

Meanwhile, in 1940, the Supreme Court found for Hansberry, who along with HARRY H. PACE had bought property in a "restricted" (white-only) area in 1937. The victory meant that at least one Chicago neighborhood became open to black people. Although Dickerson was proud of helping black homeowners expand the areas where they could buy property, he was equally concerned with low-income apartment residents, pushing the Chicago Housing Authority to build more public housing and rehabilitate more old buildings.

In 1941, Dickerson was appointed by President Roosevelt to serve on the Committee of Fair Employment Practices, charged with investigating complaints of discrimination and recommending government employment policy. Dickerson focused on an aircraft plant in Melrose Park, Illinois, which he claimed discriminated against black people. He also pushed for African Americans to be included in craft unions, which had historically been all white.

In 1942, Dickerson ran for U.S. Congress as an independent, with Dawson running against him as a Democrat. Although he was endorsed by the city's major black newspaper, the *Chicago Defender*, as well as by the Chicago American Federation of Labor (AFL) and the Congress of Industrial Organizations (CIO) (the two groups had not yet united), he had made enemies in the

Democratic Party and he finished third in the race. In 1943, he ran for reelection as alderman, and he was defeated by a Dawson supporter.

Although Dickerson got out of electoral politics as a result, he continued to be a civil rights leader throughout the next three decades, serving as president of the Chicago Urban League for a time and as a director of the National Urban League and the NAACP. In 1954, he also became executive vice president at Liberty Life, and one of the major figures calling for sweeping changes in the company's practices. In 1955, he was made general manager, and in 1956 he went on to become the company's president and chief executive officer.

When Dickerson took over the company, his main goal was to increase its rate of growth. His policies were successful, for in 1961, the company was the largest black-owned business in the North and the third in the nation. This had happened partly as a result of absorbing several other firms: Friendship Mutual Life Insurance Company; the Beneficial Life Insurance Company of Detroit, Michigan; the Dunbar Life Insurance Company of Cleveland, Ohio; the Federal Life Insurance Company of Washington, D.C.; and the Domestic Life Insurance Company of Louisville, Kentucky. By 1962, the company was making record profits of half a million dollars, and it was newly positioned to compete in the modern market.

Dickerson ran the company until he was 80 years old, in 1971, when John Johnson, the company's majority stockholder, took over its management, with Dickerson continuing as chairman of the board until 1973. After that, he was honorary chairman emeritus ("emeritus" means "retired") until his death. In the 1970s, the company was not doing as well, partly because the Civil Rights movement had meant that white-owned companies were now willing to accept black customers and to treat them more fairly.

Perhaps in response, Dickerson became disillusioned later in life with the goals he had fought for. In 1973, when he was 82, he said that he had

begun to question whether integration into mainstream white-dominated society was a useful goal for black people. He died on September 1, 1986. Despite his later discouragement, he continues to be honored by both black and white members of society, with his company's building designated an historical landmark in 1998, and with the Chicago Bar Association's establishment of the Earl Burrus Dickerson award, given to minority lawyers and judges who have worked to give minorities fair representation in the courts.

Further Reading

Gale Group. "Earl Burrus Dickerson." *The Complete Marquis Who's Who.* New Providence, N.J.: Marquis Who's Who, 2001.

Ingham, John, and Lynne B. Feldman. *African American Business Leaders: A Biographical Dictionary.* Westport, Conn: Greenwood Press, 1994, pp. 198, 207–209, 216–219.

Puth, Robert C. "Supreme Life: The History of a Negro Life Insurance Company." *Business History Review* 43, no. 1 (spring 1969): 1–21.

Travis, Demsey J. *An Autobiography of Black Chicago.* Chicago, Ill.: Urban Research Press, 1981.

———. *An Autobiography of Black Politics.* Chicago, Ill.: Urban Research Press, 1987.

Downing, George Thomas

(1819–1903) *restaurant owner, caterer, hotel owner, civic leader*

Before the Civil War, George T. Downing was one of the most successful of the northern African-American entrepreneurs. He ran a catering business that served the elite families of New York City, and of Providence and Newport, Rhode Island. He owned the Sea-Girt House, a luxury hotel in the elite resort of Newport. And he ran the restaurant of the U.S. House of Representatives from 1865 through 1877. Through it all, he agitated against slavery, for equal opportunity, and for equal education.

George Downing was born in New York on December 30, 1819, the son of Thomas Downing, who owned New York City's famous Oyster House Restaurant. No information is available on Downing's mother.

Downing was educated at Hamilton College. By the time he reached his mid-twenties, he had founded his own catering business on New York City's fashionable avenue, Broadway. Catering was a popular business for many African-American entrepreneurs of the 18th and 19th centuries, as it was considered a "servile" occupation suited to people of color, although many entrepreneurs grew rich in the process of running their businesses. In those days, wealthy families hired caterers to provide them with all or most of their meals, so the field was a rapidly growing one before it became fashionable instead to hire a household staff to prepare gourmet meals at home. Downing took full advantage of the trend to establish his business in New York, using the profits to lease property in Newport, Rhode Island, which was just then becoming an extremely fashionable resort where elite families from New York City and Boston spent their summers.

Downing's involvement with civil rights had a long history: At age 14 he had organized a literary society whose members boycotted the Fourth of July, on the grounds that African Americans were not allowed to participate in the promise of American liberty. Before the Civil War, he took part in antislavery societies and various conventions held by African Americans to press both for the end of slavery and for the expansion of African-American rights.

On November 24, 1841, he married Serena Leanora de Grasse, whose father, George de Grasse, was considered a protégé of famed U.S. politician Aaron Burr. He went on to open a catering business in Providence by the end of the 1840s and to expand his activities in Newport. In 1854, he built a fancy hotel in Newport, the Sea-Girt House ("Sea-Girt" means "surrounded by the sea), though on December 15, 1860, the hotel was

attacked by an arsonist who caused $40,000 worth of damage. Downing responded by building Downing Block in the same location—a huge building whose upper floors he leased to the U.S. Naval Academy during the Civil War, when hostilities forced Union naval education to be moved out of the southern city of Annapolis, Maryland.

During the Civil War, Downing fought to include black men in the Union army, and then helped recruit and organize African Americans when they were finally allowed to serve in the military. He was clearly doing well financially, for in 1865, he was one of 26 Newport residents to donate money for what became Touro Park, where a stone marker still bears his name. He also participated in a committee that made various town improvements, such as the extension of Newport's main street, Bellevue Avenue, all the way down to Bailey's Beach. During that year, he also pressed for integrating the Newport public schools (allowing black and white students to attend the same schools).

In 1865, Downing went to Washington, D.C., to run the House of Representatives' restaurant, a post he held until 1877. The appointment was an indication of how widespread his reputation was and in what high esteem he was held. He was a strong supporter of Massachusetts senator Charles Sumner, one of the leading Radical Republicans (a group of congresspeople who fought for African-American equality after the Civil War), and pressed for the passage of Sumner's civil rights bill. He also fought against discrimination that black people suffered on the Baltimore and Ohio Railroad, which ran between the District of Columbia and the city of Baltimore. In 1869, he served as vice president of the National Negro Labor Union, which fought for the rights of black workers. He died in Newport on July 21, 1903.

Further Reading

Davis, Kay. Class and Leisure at America's First Resort: Newport, Rhode Island, 1890–1914. University of Virginia website. Available online. URL: http://

xroads.virginia.edu/~MA01/Davis/newport/home/
home.html. Downloaded on November 15, 2002.

Medford, Edna Greene. "Downing, George Thomas."
Encyclopedia of African American Business History,
ed. by Juliet E. K. Walker. Westport, Conn.:
Greenwood Press, 1999, pp. 188–189.

Newport Notables. "George T. Downing." Redwood
Library and Athenaeum website. Available online.
URL: http://www.redwoodlibrary.org/notables/
downing.htm. Downloaded on November 15, 2002.

Stokes, Theresa Guzman. "Black History." Eyes of
Glory. Available online. URL: http://www.
eyesofglory.com/blkhist.htm. Downloaded on
November 15, 2002.

Dudley, Joe L., Sr.

(1937–   ) *hair-care products executive*

Joe L. Dudley grew up in a three-room farmhouse in North Carolina and was mistakenly labeled "mentally retarded" by his teachers. But he managed to work his way up to founding a company that now generates an annual revenue of more than $30 million. Mentored by S. B. FULLER, who founded the Fuller Products Company, Dudley is a good example of an African-American entrepreneur who worked within the African-American business community to achieve success of his own through the help of other successful black entrepreneurs.

Some 80 percent of the ethnic hair-care and cosmetic market operates on the retail level—that is, selling directly to consumers or through stores. Dudley products are unusual in that they are sold only to beauty salons. Since Dudley also owns several beauty schools, he has a natural outlet for promoting his products, which include more than 200 professional hair-care and personal-care items.

Dudley was born in Aurora, North Carolina, on May 9, 1937, the fifth of 11 children born to the farmers Gilmer L. and Clara Yeates Dudley. In the first grade, due to a speech impediment, teachers perceived him as developmentally chal-

lenged and he was held back. He credits much of his ability to persevere throughout difficulties to his mother, who he says always believed in him.

In 1957, Dudley was studying business administration at A & T State University in Greensboro, North Carolina, when he invested 10 dollars in a sales kit so that he could sell Fuller Products door to door. The Fuller company was set up so that people around the country could sell products with very little investment, keeping a percentage of the profits. Dudley graduated with a B.S. in 1962 and moved to Brooklyn, New York, where he sold Fuller products full time.

In 1960, Dudley had married Eunice Moseley, who had come with him to Brooklyn. In 1967, the couple returned to Greensboro, North Carolina, where they opened a Fuller Products distributorship. Soon they were outselling all other branches, even those in larger communities such as New York. Thanks to his success, Dudley developed a close relationship with Fuller, who frequently visited him in North Carolina and became his mentor.

In 1969, the Fuller company ran into financial problems and had trouble providing its sales force with enough products. The Dudleys responded by starting their own company: At night, Eunice and their children—Joe, Jr., Ursula, and Genea—made beauty products on their kitchen stove and poured them into mayonnaise jars and the washed-out jars of other cosmetics; during the day, Joe and his sales force sold them. By 1975, Dudley had launched the Dudley Products Company, with a sales force of more than 400. He had also founded a beauty school and a chain of beauty supply stores that operated throughout the South.

In 1976, Fuller asked Dudley to come to Chicago to take over as president of Fuller Products. Dudley ran both companies until 1985, purchasing the rights to Fuller in 1984 and returning to North Carolina so that he could open a new headquarters and manufacturing plant in Kernersville.

The company continued to grow and flourish, making Dudley a millionaire by the time he turned

40. The enterprise has been listed in *Black Enterprise*'s "Top 100 List of Black Businesses," and Dudley has won numerous other awards, including the Maya Angelou Tribute to Achievement Award (1992) and induction into the National Black College Alumni Hall of Fame (1995), the Horatio Alger Association of Distinguished Americans (1995), and the Direct Selling Hall of Fame (2001). His company operates in Canada, Brazil, Zimbabwe, South Africa, Bahama, and throughout the Caribbean. Dudley Cosmetology University in Kernersville, founded in 1989, along with a chain of eight beauty schools throughout the South, help promote Dudley products. Dudley also sponsors a number of mentoring, training, and scholarship programs, hoping to help other young people as Fuller helped him.

Further Reading

Dudley, Joe L., Sr. *Walking by Faith: I Am, I Can, and I Will*. Greensboro, N.C.: Executive Press, 1997.

Dudley Products, Inc. "Joe L. Dudley, Sr.: Entrepreneur and Humanitarian." Welcome to the World of Dudley. Available online. URL: http://www.dudleyq.com/Corporate/joedudley.html. Downloaded on November 14, 2002.

Horatio Alger Asosciation of Distinguished Americans. "Joe L. Dudley, Sr., 1995." Horatio Alger Association of Distinguished Americans website. Available online. URL: http://www.horatioalger.com/member/dud95.htm. Downloaded on November 14, 2002.

Durnford, Andrew

(1800–1859) *sugar planter, land speculator*

Andrew Durnford is an example of how African Americans became slave owners during the period when slavery was legal. Durnford was known as a stern master who worked his slaves hard and punished them often in his efforts to make his Louisiana sugar plantation a success. Although he lived comfortably, he never made the kinds of profits from his sugar enterprises that the wealthiest planters accrued and was able to cover the costs of running his plantation for only two out of the 26 years that he owned it.

Durnford was born in 1800 in New Orleans, Louisiana, the son of Thomas Durnford, a wealthy English merchant, moneylender, and slave owner, and Rosaline Mercier, a free woman of color. In New Orleans, there were many such liaisons, in which free women of color—usually but not always light-skinned—established long-lasting legal relationships with white men, whom they were legally unable to marry but who might support them and their children financially. The system was known as *plaçage* ("placement") and Mercier was referred to as the *placée* ("the woman who has been placed"). She seems to have lived with Thomas Durnford, and when he died in 1826, his will guaranteed $1,716 to Mercier for services rendered.

Thomas had previously had a relationship with a free woman of color in Pensacola, Florida, where the *plaçage* system did not exist. Their son, Joseph Durnford, was a free black man who visited his half-brother Andrew frequently in New Orleans. Like most New Orleans free people of color, Andrew seems to have identified himself as quite separate from other African Americans, identifying more with the white elite that ruled Louisiana than with the black slaves who worked there.

When Thomas Durnford died, he designated his friend, white planter and slave owner John McDonough, as the curator of his estate, and McDonough acted as Andrew's guardian, friend, and protector, enabling his later prosperity. Some scholars believe that McDonough had a homoerotic (romantic same-sex) attachment to Durnford, though their exact relationship is impossible to determine. A wealthy man who never married, McDonough was known for his affectionate relationships with a number of men. He was also known for allowing his slaves to work off their purchase price through years of labor, after which McDonough would help them immigrate to the newly forming nation of Liberia in Africa. McDonough was a prominent supporter of the American Colonization Society, which sought to resettle free black people in Africa, an idea embraced by some black leaders but strongly opposed by many others, including JAMES FORTEN, SR.

Little is known about Andrew Durnford's life before 1828, though scholars know that he was well educated in both French and English, as was customary for much of the Louisiana elite. He also knew enough mathematics to practice medicine, and had probably received business training from his father and McDonough, who may also have taught him about cultivating sugar. In 1828, Durnford bought 14 slaves and 10 arpents (about $8^1/_2$ acres) of land to establish a plantation in Louisiana's Plaquemines Parish on the Mississippi. He had already married Charlotte Remy, a free woman of color, whose dowry may have formed part of his fortune, along with cash left to him by his mother and tracts of land left to him by his father, which he sold. The land he bought for his plantation, which he named St. Rosalie, was sold to him by McDonough at a 6 percent mortgage, considerably less than the 10 percent interest rate that McDonough had charged Andrew's father.

Durnford continued to acquire adjacent plots of land from McDonough, with whom he also formed a partnership to cultivate and produce sugar and molasses. He also continued to acquire slaves—according to historian David O. Whitten, too many slaves for the size of his plantation and the degree of his profit. By the time of his death he owned some 75 slaves. He seems to have kept them on a tight rein, so that when the African-American engineer Norbert Rillieux offered Durnford $50,000 for the use of his plantation to test the sugar-refining process Rillieux was developing, Dunford refused, saying that he could not "give up control of his people."

In 1835, Durnford traveled to Virginia to buy additional slaves for himself and McDonough, a trip on which he realized that southerners looked down on those who traded slaves for a living while admiring the planters who bought and worked the slaves. He took advantage of his own position as a planter to get cheaper prices for his slaves, which included several children who, he wrote in a letter to McDonough, had trouble walking with the rest of the group. Durnford frequently spoke or wrote contemptuously about his human property, saying that it was impractical to free slaves because they could not take care of themselves and that it was unlikely that slaves could save up to buy their own freedom because, like their owners, they did not "have the moral courage to deprive themselves of luxuries."

Durnford had his oldest son, Thomas McDonough Durnford, educated privately in New Orleans and then at Lafayette College in Easton, Pennsylvania. The young Thomas went on to become a New Orleans physician who lived part-time in Paris. He too seems to have identified with white owners, saying that African slaves should be freed and then sent to Africa, the land of "their" fathers.

Andrew Durnford died on July 12, 1859, in Louisiana, still owing $13,000 to the estate of John McDonough. After his death, another son, Andrew, Jr., tried to run the family plantation, along with his sister, Rosema, but, like most planters, they foundered after the Civil War, unable to make farming pay without the free labor of slaves. In 1874, overwhelmed by debt, they sold St. Rosalie for an extremely low price. Andrew, Jr.'s daughter, Sarah Mary Durnford, taught in New Orleans public schools—most of which had been endowed by and named for John McDonough—until she retired in 1952.

Further Reading

Rankin, David. "Black Slaveholders: The Case of Andrew Durnford." *Southern Studies* 21, no. 3 (1982): 343–348.
Whitten, David O. *Andrew Durnford—A Black Sugar Planter in the Antebellum South.* Berkeley, Calif.: Transactions Publishers, 1995.

Wilson, W. Scott. "One Black Master." *American Renaissance* 7, no. 5 (May 1996). Available online at the Common Sense Club. URL: http://www.common senseclub.com/Slavery.html. Downloaded on November 12, 2002.

Du Sable, Jean-Baptiste Pointe
(Jean-Baptiste DuSable)
(1745–1818) *explorer, trader, founder and developer of Chicago*

Jean-Baptiste Pointe Du Sable helped develop the region that later became the city of Chicago from a relatively uninhabited marshy area into a thriving settlement of Europeans and other non-Native Americans. Indians in the Chicago region still comment that "the first white man in Chicago was a black man." Du Sable established other trading posts throughout the region as well, helping to develop that part of the Northwest Territory for non-Native Americans.

Much confusion and many legends have sprung up around Du Sable's early life, and little is known for certain. He seems to have been born sometime in 1745 in the community of St-Marc, on the western part Hispaniola, which later became known as Haiti. In 1745, the island was still a French colony inhabited by a few French planters and a large number of African slaves, including Suzanne, a Congolese woman who was Du Sable's mother. His father, also called Du Sable, has been reported as a French mariner, but some accounts have him as a French coffee and hardwood planter who bought and later freed Suzanne, going on to live with her although laws against interracial mixing prevented him from marrying her.

According to one account, while the planter Du Sable was away from the island on business in 1755, the Spanish burnt his home to the ground and killed Suzanne. In response, the planter took his son to school in France, enrolling him at the St-Thomas school in St-Cloud, near Paris, along with Jacques Clemorgan, the white son of a planter from Martinique. Clemorgan and the young Jean-Baptiste Du Sable went on to become lifelong friends and business allies.

Still according to these accounts, the two men returned to Haiti for a time, where Jean-Baptiste worked as a seaman on his father's ships and learned the business of his father's trading post at Cap Français. In 1764, the young Du Sable and Clemorgan set sail for the French colony in North America, then called New France, later known as Louisiana. Du Sable lost his papers of French citizenship on the voyage and feared that he might be treated as a slave in the North American colony, so he sought protection from Father Pierre Gilbault, a priest who hired him to work as groundskeeper in the Catholic mission. Clemorgan went to work as a clerk at a merchandising house. The two young men kept in touch occasionally despite the laws in the area that discouraged friendship across racial lines.

Another account has Du Sable working in New Orleans on behalf of his father, to develop new business for his father's enterprises. In any case, Du Sable was frustrated with the racial restrictions of the North American colony, and when the Spanish took over the colony under the Treaty of Paris, he had even more reason to leave. In 1765, he, Clemorgan, and Choctaw, a Native American friend, set sail up the Mississippi in a boat they had built themselves from cottonwood trees.

In those years, the Mississippi had barely been explored by people who were not Native Americans, and indeed, the native peoples in the region were largely hostile toward the outsiders who tried to penetrate their lands. According to some accounts, however, Choctaw spoke many of the region's languages and made it possible for Du Sable to become relatively well accepted. Some accounts also have it that in or around 1766, Du Sable met the great leader Pontiac, who became his friend and tried to use Du Sable as part of his plan to unite the warring native nations in the region against the British, who had claimed all land east of the Mississippi after the French and Indian Wars ended in 1763. In 1769, Pontiac was assassinated by a member of another tribe. Nevertheless, Du Sable tried to fulfill Pontiac's mission and was able to bring his message of unity to the Native American nations.

Then, according to some historians, Du Sable and Choctaw moved farther north on the Mississippi, to St. Louis, now in Missouri, then another French-controlled city, where Du Sable traded with the Indians. Du Sable went on to establish a store in St. Louis until the British wrested that city from the French in 1767. Du Sable moved yet again, to Peoria, Illinois, then a frontier outpost, sending furs down to Clemorgan for the two men's joint fur-trading business in New Orleans.

In Peoria, Du Sable lived among the Peoria and Potawatomi Indians, and he eventually married a Potawatomi woman named Chikiwata, who sometimes went by the European name of Catherine. Some accounts have him trapping and trading in Canada in 1769, along the Illinois River and Lake Michigan.

Historians agree, however, that in 1772, Du Sable decided to live in Eschikagou, "the place of bad smells," a marshy area between Canada and the southern ports where he had previously been trading. In 1773, he and his wife had their first child, Jean-Baptiste Pointe Du Sable, Jr. In 1774, Du Sable brought his family to live with him in Eschikagou and encouraged other Native Americans to join them. This was the beginning of what would later become the city of Chicago. When Du Sable's child, Suzanne, was born in 1775, she became the first person to be born in the new settlement.

Du Sable started a trading post in the new settlement and sold his own milk, cheese, beef, and corn throughout the region, eventually reaching markets as far away as Louisiana and Quebec. Sometime around 1777, a French Canadian group asked Du Sable for permission to build on his land, seeking safety from the British. Since the British had been at odds with the French for a

long time, and since the Revolutionary War had begun the year before, the British were highly suspicious of all French in the region, and the settlers sought safety with Du Sable. He and the Potawatomi elders agreed to give land to the French Canadians, who became dairy farmers, trappers, and lumbermen in the region. One of these men, Jean LeLime of Quebec, later became a full-time employee at Du Sable's trading post, where his partner, Choctaw, continued to work. Later, Du Sable brought Gibault to Chicago to help educate the local children.

Some accounts say that Du Sable spied for the British during the Revolutionary War. Others say that Du Sable refused to let the British build a fort at Chicago in 1779. All sources agree that he was arrested by the British, who seem to have feared his power with the French and Indians in the area, and his potential support for the Americans. He was released from jail within a few months, and made liaison officer between Indians and Europeans. Some accounts say this was at the request of the Native Americans in the region. Others say it was because British territorial governor Patrick Sinclair had been impressed with his prisoner, who had convinced him that his loyalty was to the British.

In any case, by 1782, Du Sable had returned to Chicago, where he continued to trap furs, run his trading post, and expand his property, including his livestock holdings. His home was known for its beauty and elegance, and for the 23 works of European art that decorated its walls. His estate was an enterprise in itself, including a mill, a bakehouse, two barns, a dairy, and a poultry house.

In 1796, Du Sable tried and failed to become chief of the local tribes. In 1800, he was approached by U.S. government agents who wanted to buy his land for a fort. Unhappy with the U.S. plans for disposing of land in the Northwest Territory, Du Sable sold his Chicago holdings to Jean LeLime for the then enormous sum of $1,200. In 1804, LeLime sold the estate to John

Kinzie, who for many years was mistakenly considered to be the founder of Chicago, based partly on false claims by his daughter-in-law.

Du Sable, meanwhile, went back to Peoria, where he had extensive land holdings and a trading post. When his wife died in 1809, he gave the Peoria property to his son and daughter-in-law and went on to St. Charles, Missouri, with his daughter and her family. There he bought a house from another black man, Pierre Rodin—a house that would eventually become the home of Missouri's first governor, Alexander McNair.

In 1813, his granddaughter, Eulalie, married, and Du Sable was wealthy enough to transfer a house, a lot, and half his stock of animals to the new couple. Yet in 1814, he filed for bankruptcy, and he died, penniless, on August 29, 1818. Chicago's Du Sable Museum of African-American History, founded in 1961, helped to keep his memory alive, as did his inclusion as one of eight historical figures shown in the Illinois Centennial Building in Springfield, erected in 1965. Not until 1968, though, was he officially recognized as Chicago's founder, when a memorial marker was put on his formerly obscure grave. The site of his cabin—now in Chicago's business district—was designated a National Historic Site in 1986. In 1987 he became the first Haitian-born person to be honored on a U.S. postage stamp. Chicago's Du Sable High School has also been named in his honor.

Further Reading

Chicago: City of the Century. "People & Events: Jean-Baptiste du Sable (1745?–1818)." American Experience, PBS.org. Available online. URL: http://www.pbs.org/wgbh/amex/chicago/peopleevents/p_dusable.html. Downloaded on January 23, 2003.

Cortesi, Lawrence. *Jean Du Sable: Father of Chicago*. Philadelphia: Chilton Book Co., 1972.

Franklin, John Hope, and Albert Moss. *From Slavery to Freedom, A History of African Americans*, 8th ed. New York: Knopf, 2000.

Gates, Henry Louis. *African-American Voices of Triumph: Perseverance*. Alexandria, Va.: Time-Life Books, 1993.

Green, Richard L., ed. *A Gift of Heritage: Historic Black Pioneers*, vol. 3. Chicago: Empak Enterprises, 1990.

Katz, William Loren. *Black People Who Made the Old West*. Trenton, N.J.: Africa World Press, 1992.

Lowe, David. *Lost Chicago*. Boston, Mass.: Houghton Mifflin, 1975.

Robinson, Susan. "Jean-Baptiste Point Du Sable: Early American Trader, Pioneer, and Founder of Chicago." Gibbs Magazine. Available online. URL: http://www.gibbsmagazine.com/dusable.htm. Posted March 19, 2001.

Zellner, Dan. "Jean-Baptiste Pointe DuSable (1745?–1818)." Studio Z. Available online. URL: http://www.studioz.org/dusable/index.html. Downloaded on January 23, 2003.

Dutrieuille, Albert E. (1877–1944) and Peter Albert Dutrieuille (1838–1916)
caterers

Peter Albert Dutrieuille and his son, Albert E. Dutrieuille, were among the last of the great black caterers of Philadelphia. Because meal preparation was considered a "servile" profession, African Americans were allowed to enter it, and in both New York and Philadelphia this business provided the foundation for an African-American elite.

The first Dutrieuille to come to America was Pierre Albert, who came from Bordeaux, France, after spending some time in the French West Indies. He and his wife, Mary Lambert, had two sons, one of whom was Peter Albert Dutrieuille, born in 1838, educated in Philadelphia's public schools, and put to work as a shoemaker for seven years.

In November 1864, Peter Dutrieuille married Amelia Baptiste, a child of the local elite, and decided to enter the catering business. From colonial times through the 1870s, catering was a major business in the United States, as wealthy families typically hired catering firms to provide all or some of their daily meals. Dutrieuille worked as an apprentice (trainee) at the prestigious firm of Augustine and Baptiste, and set up his own business in 1873. His home-based operation soon attracted a prestigious clientele, including the wealthy businessman T. DeWitt Cuyler, who tried to interest Dutrieuille in opening a branch in New York. Dutrieuille's wife supposedly opposed the idea, and Dutrieuille remained in Philadelphia, where he helped to organize the Caterer's Manufacturing and Supply Company, which furnished caterers with tables, chairs, linens, china, silver, and glassware. Dutrieuille served as president of the company for several terms and was also active with the Philadelphia Caterers Association, a kind of trade union for the city's black caterers.

In addition, Dutrieuille engaged in a number of civic activities, serving as treasurer of the Pioneer Building and Loan Association, a group set up to help finance local home ownership; the Negro Historical Society; St. Mary's Catholic Beneficial Society; Quaker City Beneficial Association; and several literary clubs. He was also a devout Roman Catholic who belonged to St. Joseph's Catholic Church.

In the 1870s, catering became less popular with the rich as they turned to upscale restaurants and hotels. Middle-class families supported catering firms to handle special events, but the growing racism of the period made such business more difficult for black-owned companies to acquire. At the same time, the wave of immigration made various types of European cooking popular, putting the old-line caterers at a disadvantage. All of these factors contributed to the decline of Philadelphia's black catering elite, but the Dutrieuille family managed to remain successful long after other firms had closed their doors.

Dutrieuille's son, Albert E. Dutrieuille, was born in Philadelphia on July 26, 1877, and was educated in city schools. As a young man, he helped his father in the family business and went on to marry Florence May Waters in 1900. Although Peter Dutrieuille retained control of his own business throughout his life, Albert gained more authority as he got older. Independently, he obtained and fulfilled contracts for supplying several area army camps during World War I.

In 1916, Peter Dutrieuille died. Albert changed the company's name to Albert E. Dutrieuille in 1917 and continued to run the company successfully. In 1937, Dutrieuille prepared a typical meal for the Mutual Assurance (Insurance) Company, whose menu survives: various hors d'oeuvres (appetizers), caviar on toast, a horseradish chili sauce, bisque of mushroom soup, currant jelly, spinach and eggplant, Virginia ham, celery salad, ice cream cakes, and coffee. He was known for his fashionable clientele—many of whom had been his father's customers—and for his popularity among Roman Catholic clergy, who often chose his firm to cater church-related events.

Dutrieuille took great pride in his family's role in the city's black elite and helped cofound the Olde Philadelphia Club, an organization of wealthy African Americans. He continued to operate his business successfully until 1967, when he retired at the age of 89. He died in Philadelphia on April 25, 1974, at the age of 97.

Further Reading

Fleming, G. James, and Bernice D. Shelton. "Fine Food for Philadelphia." *The Crisis*, April 1938, pp. 107, 114.

Gatewood, Willard B., Jr. *Aristocrats of Color: The Black Elite 1880–1920.* Fayetteville: University of Arkansas Press, 2000.

Willson, Joseph. *The Elite of Our People: Joseph Willson's Sketches of Black Upper-Class Life in Antebellum Philadelphia.* University Park: Pennsylvania State University Press, 2000.

Eldridge, Elleanor

(ca. 1784–ca. 1845) *entrepreneur,
laundress, home improvement worker*

Elleanor Eldridge was a free black woman living in
New England during a time when slavery was
legal throughout the United States. Although she
had no formal education, she was able to found
and operate a number of successful businesses,
amass an estate worth $4,800 at the time of her
death (a substantial sum for the time), and defend
herself in court at a time when the word of
African Americans carried far less weight than
the word of white people. Her autobiography,
Memoirs of Elleanor Eldridge, written with Frances
H. Green, was published in 1838 and provided
one of the few accounts of a free black woman's
life in early America.

Eldridge was born free in Warwick, Rhode
Island, in 1785, though slavery was legal in that
state. Indeed, her father, Robin Eldridge, had been
brought with two brothers to Rhode Island on a
slave ship but had earned their freedom by fighting in the American Revolution. They had been
promised 200 acres of land in New York for their
service to the new country but were given only a
small amount of money. Elleanor's mother, Hannah Prophet, who was part Narragansett Indian,
was a laundress who worked for local families
until she died, when Elleanor was only 10.

Robin Eldridge had managed to save enough
money to buy a small piece of land and build his
own home. He was frustrated and angry when his
10-year-old daughter went to work as a live-in
servant in the home of a local family, the Bakers,
for whom her mother had worked. Indeed, her
mother had named her for Elleanor Baker, who
took special notice of the child. At the Bakers,
Eldridge learned how to spin, weave, and do arith-
metic, becoming a skilled weaver by age 14.

When Eldridge was 17, she started working as
a dairy woman in the family of Captain Benjamin
Greene at Warwick Neck, winning acclaim for her
excellent cheese. Two years later, her father died,
and Eldridge occupied herself with his estate
while continuing to work five more years for
Greene, until his death.

The 26- or 27-year-old Eldridge then went to
the home of her sister, Lettise, in Adams, Massachusetts, where she and her siblings started a
business of weaving, washing, and soap boiling.
The business was so successful that Eldridge was
able to buy land and build a house, which she
rented out for $40 a year.

Three years later, she moved again, to Providence, Rhode Island, where she hired herself out to
do whitewashing (washing walls with lime, a disin-
fectant), wallpapering, and painting when it was
warm; and laundry and housework for families,
hotels, and boarding houses when the weather was

cold. By 1822, she had saved enough to buy another lot and build a $1,700 house in Providence, where she was able to both live and take in a renter. She continued to work and save, putting her money into additional lots, as well as a house in Warwick, winning a certain amount of prestige among both white and black people for her success as an entrepreneur.

In 1831, the middle-aged Eldridge contracted typhus (a potentially fatal disease) for the second time. She went to recuperate with relatives in Massachusetts, and rumors began to circulate that she had died. When Eldridge returned to Providence in 1832, she discovered that the rumor had enabled a local resident to petition for the sale of her property, so that he could recover a $420 loan. She quickly made a deal with her creditor to stop the sale.

Then, that summer, a cholera epidemic hit Providence. Eldridge took a job nursing a sick child and went with the family to Pomfret, Connecticut. She fell behind on her loan payments, and when she returned to town, her property had all been sold and her tenants evicted. But the sale had never been advertised, which was a legal requirement. The state attorney general advised her to sue the person who had bought her property, but the local sheriff maintained that he had advertised the sale, so she lost her suit, despite the support of several white people in the community. Then she hired two detectives to find someone who had actually seen the alleged advertisements. When no one was found, she sued the sheriff for perjury. Finally, the buyer agreed to sell the property back to Eldridge for several hundred dollars more than Eldridge had originally paid for it—and she dropped the suit. Her white supporters believed that race was definitely a factor in Eldridge's legal troubles, since even free black people simply did not receive the same respect or legal treatment as white people in that era.

Despite her difficulties, Eldridge continued her business activities as well as writing her memoir. The exact date of her death is uncertain. Some scholars have placed it at 1845, while others cite 1862 or 1865.

Colonial entrepreneur Elleanor Eldridge, a free black woman, built up a number of businesses at a time when many African Americans were enslaved. *(Portrait of Elleanor Eldridge in Frances H. Green,* Memoirs of Elleanor Eldridge *[1838], Duke University Rare Book, Manuscript, and Special Collections Library)*

Further Reading

Cottrol, Robert J., ed. *Memoirs of Elleanor Eldridge*, in *From African to Yankee: Narratives of Slavery and Freedom in Antebellum New England*. Armonk, N.Y.: M.E. Sharpe, Inc., 1998.

Davis, Karen. "Black Women: Then and Now. Elleanor Eldridge: Entrepreneurial Pioneer." Providence Journal Digital Extra. February 20, 1997.

Eldridge, Elleanor, with Frances H. Green. *Memoirs of Elleanor Eldridge*. Providence, R.I.: B.T. Albro, 1838. Available online. URL: http://docsouth.unc.

edu/neh/eldridge/menu.html. Downloaded on November 14, 2002.

Ziner, Karen Lee. "Making a Difference. Elleanor Eldridge (1785–1862). Businesswoman Stood Up to Injustice." *Providence Journal* Digital Extra.

Ellison, William
(April Ellison)

(1790–1861) *planter, slaveholder, cotton gin maker, repairer*

William Ellison began his life as a slave and ended it as one of the largest slaveholders in South Carolina. Ironically, Ellison's rise was enabled by the fact that his father was almost certainly a wealthy white planter and slave owner who had had a relationship with a female slave; although no information is available about his mother, his father was probably his owner, William Ellison, or his owner's father, Robert. Ellison became one of the richest African Americans in the pre–Civil War South— a prosperity that was enabled by slavery itself.

At birth, Ellison was given the first name "April," perhaps from the African custom of naming children after the month they were born. His tombstone, however, records only that he was born in 1790 in Fairfield District, South Carolina. In 1802, instead of being sent to the fields as was customary for enslaved children, April was apprenticed to William McCreight, a maker of cotton gins. (An apprentice works for little or no money in order to learn a skill; the cotton gin was a machine that took seeds out of cotton bolls, enabling the cotton to be spun into thread.) Historians consider that April's unusually good treatment is further evidence that his father was one of the white Ellisons.

April worked for McCreight until 1806, learning how to read, write, keep books, deal with customers, and run a business, as well as mastering all the mechanical skills involved in making and repairing gins. April's owner apparently intended the young man to have his freedom,

since these skills would be of little use to a field-worker. In January 1811, April, then 20 years old, had a daughter named Eliza Ann with a slave woman named Matilda. In 1815, he had another daughter, Maria.

On June 8, 1816, William Ellison, the white owner, undertook the elaborate legal steps necessary to give April his freedom, appearing with his slave to ask a magistrate and five free white property holders to let him set April free. Apparently, April had also paid his father/owner for his own freedom.

The newly freed 26-year-old April moved to Stateburg, in the Sumter District of South Carolina. The following year, he bought the freedom of Matilda, who became his wife, as well as buying his daughter, Eliza Ann. On June 20, 1820, April appeared before a magistrate asking to change his name to William, pointing out that "April" was recognizable as a slave name and so might hurt his business.

The newly named William Ellison had three sons between 1816 and 1821, Henry, William, Jr., and Reuben, all of whom grew up to help their father in his gin business. When his sons were still young, however, Ellison bought two male slaves in 1820, using the labor of these skilled workers to expand his business. In 1822, he bought an acre of land on which he founded a factory, and his reputation grew. He helped develop the design of an improved cotton gin, and he was known throughout the region for his high-quality products. Planters from as far away as Mississippi bought his gins, enabling Ellison to become a cotton planter himself in the 1830s.

Ellison got his start as a planter by using his slaves as collateral for an 1837 loan of about five thousand dollars. Ellison used the loan to buy field workers, and their labor in turn enabled him to expand his plantation. By 1840, he owned 30 slaves, including women and children, 11 field workers, and 12 artisans. By 1860, he owned 44 field hands who worked 800 acres of land and produced 80 bales of cotton, in addition to peas and corn. He had also founded a profitable black-smithing and carpentry business.

Historians have found no evidence in any of Ellison's letters that he felt any guilt or regret over his ownership of slaves. In part, this is because owning slaves was the key to prosperity, and Ellison wanted to become rich. Also, owning slaves made it less likely that proslavery white people would accuse Ellison and his family of being anti-slavery. Finally, as a light-skinned "mulatto" (someone of mixed race), Ellison considered himself to be racially distinct from his slaves who, whatever their actual heritage or color, were all counted in the federal census as "black."

Ellison seems to have been an unusually harsh owner who had no reservations about selling female children born on his plantation, as they could not do the field work he required. Indeed, he used the profits from their sale to buy more adult men to work in his fields. He was also quick to hire slave catchers—people who made a profession of finding and returning runaway slaves.

Meanwhile, in 1830, Ellison had purchased his daughter, Maria, but did not free her. South Carolina law made it very difficult to give slaves their freedom—special permission from the state assembly was required—and once free, a slave had to leave the state—again, unless the legislature gave special permission. Maria seems to have lived as though she were free, but legally, Ellison owned his daughter just as his father had once owned him.

Socially, Ellison and his family took their place among the mulatto elite of Charleston, while Ellison sought acceptance among local whites as well. His was one of the few African-American families allowed to worship at the Holy Cross Episcopal Church in Stateburg, and in 1844, after 20 years of sitting upstairs with the other black families, his was the first African-American family to be allowed to buy a pew at the back of the "white" section downstairs.

When the federal census was taken in 1860, William Ellison was 70 years old, the owner of 63 slaves and nearly 900 acres of land. Historians esti-mate that his slaves were probably worth between $100,000 and $150,000, and that his land was worth more than $16,000. Soon after the Civil War broke out in 1861, Ellison fell into a coma and died at his house in Stateburg. Both black and white people served as his pallbearers. Although his sons tried to keep up the family business, much of their wealth was tied up in Confederate notes. Eventually, the Ellisons lost their plantation and most of their fortune. In 1920, the last family member still in residence died, alone and forgotten, in the hall that William Ellison had built.

Ellison's story reveals the extent to which, as long as slavery was in force, it was virtually impossible to either gain or maintain wealth in the South without making use of slave labor. His life also shows how the slave system led to an irrational preoccupation with race. In a world where white people had rights and privileges that African Americans were denied, free people of mixed race often sought to distance themselves from "black" slaves even as the law refused to allow them the rights and privileges given to whites. Ellison seemed to identify more closely with white slaveholders than with black slaves—yet despite his wealth and his ownership of slaves, he never attained the legal status or social freedom of a white person.

Further Reading

Grooms, Robert M. "Dixie's Censored Subject: Black Slaveholders." AmericanCivilWar.com. Available online. URL: http://americancivilwar.com/authors/black_slaveowners.htm. Downloaded on November 16, 2002.

Johnson, Michael P., and James L. Roark. *Black Masters: A Free Family of Color in the Old South.* New York: W. W. Norton & Co., 1986.

Koger, Larry. *Black Slaveowners: Free Black Masters in South Carolina 1790–1860.* Columbia: University of South Carolina Press, 1995.

Schweninger, Loren. *Black Property Owners in the South, 1790–1915.* Urbana: University of Illinois Press, 1990.

F

Famous Amos   See AMOS, WALLY.

Farr, Mel
(Melvin Farr, Sr.)
(1944–   ) professional football player, automotive entrepreneur

In 1998, Mel Farr's chain of auto dealerships and related industries was ranked by *Black Enterprise* magazine as the nation's largest African-American-owned business. By 2000, the company's fortunes had fallen, and as of 2003, Mel Farr's holdings were relatively small though still prosperous. Despite his recent decline, Farr had spent two decades as a pioneer in the automotive industry, opening the ranks of what had been a predominantly white sector of the economy to African-American entrepreneurs.

Mel Farr was born on November 2, 1944, in Beaumont, Texas, the son of Miller Farr, a truck driver who also owned his own used-car lot, and Doretha Farr, a domestic worker. Farr grew up washing cars at his father's lot and later spent his weekends scouting junkyards for good deals. He won a football scholarship to the University of California, Los Angeles, in 1963, but left UCLA before he graduated to play professional football, becoming the Detroit Lions' number-seven draft pick in 1967. In 1968, he was named Rookie of the Year—an honor that netted him only an additional $500.

Farr had already married Mae and had two sons, Mel, Jr., and Michael. (Later the couple had a daughter, Monet.) He was concerned about supporting his family—yet was unable to renegotiate his contract or to win commercial endorsements. When he became injured, Farr realized that an athlete's career is often limited. At the time, there were no black coaches with the National Football League, so Farr resolved to build up his entrepreneurial skills to guarantee himself a future after his football career was over. He enrolled in the University of Detroit, where he earned his B.S. in 1970. He also sought employment with Ford Motor Company, whose owners also owned Farr's football team.

Ford offered Farr a choice: a job in public relations helping to promote the company's racing division, or a lower-paying position in dealer development. Farr chose the latter and spent seven years learning the car dealership business. In the late 1960s, companies in predominantly black cities, like Detroit, were under a great deal of pressure to expand their minority representation, so Farr was asked to find suitable black candidates to become auto dealers. He found only five, none of whom had sufficient funds to meet Ford's requirements. Farr went on to help design a black dealer training program, in which he also enrolled.

Farr retired from professional football in 1974, intending to open his own dealership. Ford insisted that he find an experienced partner, however, so he went into business with John Cook, a former dealer he had met while working in the dealer development program. Each man put up $40,000 to buy a Detroit-area franchise in the suburb of Oak Park, which opened in 1975. Farr later discovered that the dealership had been on the verge of bankruptcy. Nevertheless, by 1977, the enterprise was grossing $9.8 million in revenue. Farr was one of only about two dozen African-American new-car dealers at the time.

Farr bought out his partner in 1978 and continued to prosper. Then the 1979 oil crisis and recession brought new challenges to the U.S. automotive industry, whose low-mileage cars fell out of favor with consumers. Though Farr's revenue had reached $14.6 million in 1978, by 1980, they had dropped to $8.6 million, and Farr had to cut his staff from 90 to 38, bringing in his teenage sons to help him do janitorial work on nights and weekends.

Farr's business was saved by two factors: First, with the help of civil rights activist Jesse Jackson, Farr mobilized other black auto dealers to lobby Ford for help. He was able to borrow money from the Small Business Administration and from Ford to help him stay afloat.

Second, Farr began an innovative advertising campaign that capitalized on his fame as a former football player. Dressed in business suit and red cape, he portrayed himself as flying over Detroit over theme music and lyrics that proclaimed, "Mel Farr to the rescue." Farr wrote, shot, directed, and produced the ads himself. They were a huge success, as were ads starring Detroit Lions star Billy Sims.

In 1986, Farr was able to buy his second dealership in another Detroit suburb, managed by his brother Miller. He went on to acquire or launch dealerships in several other states, including New Jersey, Ohio, Maryland, and

In the late 1990s, Mel Farr's chain of auto dealerships and related industries were among the nation's largest black-owned businesses. *(Mel Farr Automotive Group)*

Texas, financing his purchases through loans from banks and from Ford, and hiring his sons in various positions.

In the early 1980s, Farr tried to expand into a Toyota dealership but ran into trouble: Only four black dealers had been able to purchase outlets from that company. Farr lobbied with civil rights groups, other black dealers, and the National Association of Minority Auto Dealers, calling once more on Jesse Jackson and taking several trade missions to Japan to lobby government and industry there. In 1989, he finally opened his first Toyota franchise in Bloomfield Hills, Michigan—becoming only the fifth African

American to run a Toyota dealership. In 1992, he went on to buy Mazda and Volkswagen franchises as well.

Farr attempted several other ventures: in 1985, he and two colleagues bought a 7 UP bottling franchise, which they sold in 1987. In 1995, he bought 22 percent of Bing Manufacturing, an auto parts supplier owned by former Detroit Pistons basketball player Dave Bing. And in 1997, he attempted an abortive casino venture with magnate Donald Trump.

Most noteworthy, however, was his 1990 establishing of Triple M Financing, a finance company geared to car customers whom other sources considered bad credit risks. In 1998, he attempted to get Wall Street's backing for these loans, seeking high-yield bonds that would use the auto debt as collateral. Farr also opened a used-car lot that likewise targeted poor, inner-city residents as potential customers, offering them credit through his finance company.

This was the beginning of his downfall. Farr's used-car enterprise engaged in practices that drew negative publicity, including the controversial "On-Time device," an electronic instrument that prevented a car from starting if the weekly payment was not made. Farr maintained that only such devices enabled him to extend credit to customers that others had shunned—but he later settled two class-action suits from people who alleged that his device had stopped their cars while in motion, even though they had made their payments.

Farr ran into further financial problems from his efforts to back auto debt with Wall Street bonds, and in 2000, he was forced to sell a number of his dealerships. As of 2003, he retained only his Hyundai and Kia Franchises, used-car superstore, finance company, and service and repair shop. He plans to continue expanding his used-car enterprises, a reflection of the economic difficulties faced by Detroit in general and black consumers in particular.

Further Reading

Dingle, Derek T. *Black Enterprise, Titans of the B.E. 100s.* New York: John Wiley & Sons, Inc., 1999, pp. 115–136.

Gale Group. "Mel Farr." *Contemporary Black Biography,* Vol. 24, ed. by Shirelle Phelps. Famington Hills, Mich.: Gale Group, 2000.

Gite, Lloyd and Alan Hughes. "Driving in a New Direction?" *Black Enterprise,* April 2002, p. 25.

Sawyers, Arlena. "Farr: Critics Won't Disable Plans for Growth." Payment Protection Systems. Reprinted from *Automotive News.* Available online. URL: http://www.ppsontime.com/news/news5.html. Downloaded on December 28, 2002.

Snavely, Brent. "Mel Farr Empire Falls to Earth." *Crain's Detroit Business,* April 1, 2002, p. 3.

Suhr, Jim. "Farr Can Use Shutoff Switch on Leased Cars." Payment Protection Systems. Reprinted from *Detroit News.* Available online. URL: http://www.ppsontime.com/news/news8.html. Posted December 21, 1999.

Faustina, Gilbert

(ca. 1878–1941) *cigar maker, real estate developer, recreational property developer, civil rights activist, religious leader*

Gilbert Faustina achieved remarkable success in a number of enterprises at a time when African Americans faced enormous discrimination in virtually all political, economic, and social spheres, particularly in the Deep South, where Faustina lived. Faustina founded a successful factory, opened a prosperous beach resort, and became one of the first African-American bail bondspeople in Mobile, Alabama (a bail bondsperson puts up money for the bail of those who have been arrested).

Faustina was born sometime around 1878 in New Orleans, Louisiana, the second son of a Cuban father, a sea trader, and a French mother, Angela, who died soon after his birth. Faustina's father left Gilbert and his brother Manuel to be raised by two unmarried aunts. Later, the young men moved to Mobile, Alabama, where Manuel sought work as a musician and music teacher before eventually moving to Los Angeles. Gilbert, meanwhile, apprenticed himself to a cigar maker (an apprentice takes a job at no or low wages in order to learn a skill). In those days, cigars were rolled by hand, a highly skilled profession that generally paid well. According to the racially coded legal system of the time, both young men were considered "colored."

When the factory where Faustina worked closed in the early 1900s, the owner paid off the wages he owed by giving each worker a packet of tobacco leaf. Faustina used the tobacco to make his own cigars, an enterprise that by 1918 had grown into a fully incorporated company located in a two-story factory. Both local custom and racially biased laws restricted black people to certain locations in Mobile, so Faustina, living in one of the town's poorest black neighborhoods, built his factory there, too.

Based on its name, the business—High Grade Union Made Cigars—seems to have employed unionized workers (a union is an organization of workers who have banded together to demand higher wages and better working conditions). Popularly known as Faustina's Best, the company produced several different brands, including G. F. Tampa Smokers, Little Orco, Porto Rico Specials, and Excelsior, which was the name of Manuel's jazz band. Faustina employed nine full-time workers and was known for the high quality of his product and the outstanding creativity of his marketing techniques. He gave out business cards and calendars with the company's name on them, and he had special wrappers and cigar boxes made that were noted for their beautiful and original designs. Predominantly white wealthy customers in Mobile and New Orleans supported the brand until the early 1920s, when cheaper machine-made cigars came into vogue and Faustina went out of business.

With the money he had made in the cigar business, Faustina went on to buy several old and run-down houses, which he then repaired, turning them into decent, low-cost rental units. His status as property owner enabled him to start a bail bond business as well. Usually, someone seeking bail puts up 10 percent of the amount that the judge sets, while a bail bondsperson guarantees the other 90 percent in exchange for a fee. If the arrested person leaves before his or her trial, all the bail is forfeited—and the bail bondsperson takes a loss. Legend has it that none of Faustina's clients ever ran out on him: They all knew and respected him too much for that.

Faustina sometimes had to post bail for himself, as he frequently got into trouble with the law for refusing to pay the poll tax when he voted. The poll tax was one of the many ways in which southern and other states tried to keep African Americans and other poor people from voting—by literally charging a tax to vote. Later, this practice was ruled unconstitutional, but meanwhile, Faustina protested it in his own way.

Although the racially biased laws of the time restricted the most desirable land to whites only, Faustina found ways around these laws. When he wanted to buy seven acres of prime beachfront on Mon Luis Island, 20 miles south of Mobile on Mobile Bay, he found a way to make the purchase, perhaps through using a white lawyer who had always enjoyed his cigars. In 1922, he opened Faustina Beach, a five-acre picnic ground and bathing area open to African Americans—the only place anywhere in the entire Gulf of Mexico where black people could go swimming. Whites in the region who wanted to keep the area segregated (whites only) were enraged, even though Faustina promoted his beach as a place for families, churches, and community groups.

Because Faustina Beach was the only recreational site of its kind available, people came from as far away as Birmingham, Alabama; Pascagoula, Mississippi; and Pensacola, Florida. Faustina never charged more than 10 cents per adult, while always allowing children to swim free. He was continually harassed on account of the beach, but he managed to keep it open and even to make a profit from it until the late 1950s, when the Civil Rights movement opened other beachfront areas to people of color, and Faustina Beach closed. Ironically, as black professionals began to purchase their own land on Mon Luis Island, they, too, objected to the "riffraff" that Faustina had allowed onto his public beach.

Meanwhile, Faustina had expressed his devotion to Catholicism by founding the Knights of Peter Claver in 1909. This group for Catholic men of color was the result of the many refusals Faustina received when he tried to found his own chapter of the Knights of Columbus, a Catholic group that at the time did not allow black people. Frustrated at being shut out of a religious group, Faustina started his own all-black group with the help of two other black laymen (people who are not religious leaders) and four white priests. The Knights of Peter Claver helped needy members financially while providing a social group. Faustina led the group for 17 years, and chapters formed throughout Alabama, Louisiana, Mississippi, Texas, Oklahoma, and Missouri, even as the Catholic hierarchy continued to oppose the group's existence. Today, the Knights of Peter Claver has 25,000 members in 23 states and the District of Columbia.

Faustina died in 1941 of a heart attack, leaving behind six sons and three daughters. His message to them was one of his favorite sayings: "Lost time is never found again."

Further Reading

Chachere, Bernadette P. "Gilbert Faustina." *Encyclopedia of African American Business history,* ed. by Juliet E. K. Walker. Westport, Conn.: Greenwood Press, 1999, pp. 299–331.

Foley, Albert S. *Gold's Men of Color: The Colored Catholic Priests of the United States, 1854–1954.* New York: Farrar, Straus & Co., 1955.

O'Neal, Michael J. *Some Outstanding Colored People: Interesting Facts in the Lives of Representative Negroes.* Baltimore, Md.: Franciscan Sisters, 1943, pp. 148–149.

Felton, William McDonald ("Hack" Felton)
(ca. 1876–1930) *owner of flying school, automotive entrepreneur, theater and club owner*

In his time, William McDonald Felton was the owner of the largest black-owned automobile business in New York when he owned the Auto Transportation and Sales Company, a combined auto dealership and repair shop that he opened in 1902 and expanded in 1910. At its peak, the business took up four floors of a seven-story building, giving employment to 15 people. Felton also owned clubs and theaters, as well as becoming the owner of the first black-owned school to teach airplane mechanics when he founded the Auto and Aeroplane Mechanical School in 1919.

Felton, the son of Sonnay Felton, was born in Marshallville, Georgia, sometime around 1876. Because poor records were kept about African Americans in those days, his exact birth date and year are unknown, and little is known about his early life. Sometime during the 1890s, he became a watch repairer, working first in Marshallville, then migrating to New York City in 1898.

When Felton arrived in New York, he opened a store to repair clocks, bicycles, and guns. He was perceptive enough to see that automobiles were the wave of the future, so even though very few people owned cars in 1901, Felton became a partner in a school that taught chauffeurs (drivers). (Because cars were so new, the rich people who could afford them did not necessarily learn how to drive but rather hired chauffeurs to drive for them.) In 1902, Felton opened a garage, which became a profitable enterprise. With the money he made, Felton opened the Fifty-ninth Street Theater in New York City, in what was then a black neighborhood.

In 1914 Felton relocated to Steelton, Pennsylvania, where he opened a school to teach auto and airplane mechanics. Both automobiles and airplanes were relatively new inventions just coming into widespread use, and by learning and then teaching about these new machines, Felton was getting in on the ground floor of two growing industries. Indeed, schools that taught either of these subjects were rare—and thousands of young men were just then returning from World War I, which had ended in 1919. Both black and white men came to Felton's school. Felton also welcomed women into this school, an unusual move for the time. He even advertised that he would offer separate classes for men and women, on alternate days of the week. In 1921, he expanded and relocated his school, moving it to nearby Harrisburg, Pennsylvania.

After the move, Felton hired Walter Diehl, a World War I pilot, to offer flying lessons. By this time, Felton had bought his own airstrip, becoming the first African American to own a flying school. He was able to advertise nationally in African-American publications such as the *Chicago Defender* and the *Crisis* that students could learn piloting, chauffeuring, automobile repair, and airplane mechanics.

In 1923, Felton had constructed a new two-story building, worth $100,000, for his Auto and Aero Mechanical School. In the same year, he announced his intentions for the further expansion of his airfield, though objections from local white people interrupted those plans. In 1924, however, he did manage to expand his school, offering a home study program whereby students could take correspondence courses (lessons received and sent by mail) in the repair of automobile and aircraft engines. Meanwhile, Felton had taken some of his profits from his enterprises to open a small dance club in Harrisburg.

Felton married Josephine Souza, of St. Kitts, British West Indies. The couple had one surviving son, William McDonald Felton, Jr., and a daughter, Evelyn, who died while still a child. In May 1927, a fire destroyed Felton's school. He died three years later, in Harrisburg, in November 1930.

Further Reading

"Automobile Instructions Now Given in Your Own Home." *Chicago Defender*, December 13, 1924.

"Conduct Automobile Schools in New York." *New York Age*, February 13, 1913.

"New $100,000 Auto and Aero Mechanics' School in Harrisburg to be Dedicated." *Pittsburgh Courier*, October 27, 1923.

"Scenes Typical of the Automobile and Aeroplane Mechanical School." *Harrisburg Telegraph*, March 15, 1919.

Snider, Jill D. "William McDonald Felton." *Encyclopedia of African American Business History*, ed. by Juliet E. K. Walker. Westport, Conn.: Greenwood Press, 1999, pp. 251–252.

Fletcher, Alphonse, Jr.
("Buddy" Fletcher)
(1966–) *founder of asset management company*

Alphonse "Buddy" Fletcher is the founder of Fletcher Asset Management, Inc., a Wall Street firm with a strong reputation as a consistently good adviser in money matters. According to its own website, "Fletcher-related entities have assets under management totaling roughly $500 million." The Fletcher funds include Fletcher International, Ltd., a pioneer in direct-investment approaches—investments that are large enough to affect companies' subsequent decisions—and the Fletcher Foundation, which is active in a number of charitable endeavors.

Fletcher was born on December 19, 1965, in New London, Connecticut. His father, Alphonse

Fletcher, Sr., was a technician at General Dynamics who continually attempted to operate various small businesses, including a chicken restaurant, a moving company, and some apartment buildings. Fletcher's mother, Dr. Bettye Fletcher, was an elementary school principal who worked part-time as a licensed real estate broker. Fletcher, the oldest of three sons, attended public schools in Waterford, Connecticut, where the family lived. When he was 11, he created a computer program that could predict the outcome of dog races with 80 percent accuracy, early evidence of a fascination with being able to make profitable financial predictions.

Fletcher went on to Harvard University, where he majored in applied mathematics and started a small T-shirt company with his roommate. He soon sold out to his partner, however, since sales were lower than he had expected. He enrolled in the Air Force R.O.T.C. (Reserve Officers Training Corps, a college program that allows students to train for officer-level positions in the military while continuing to attend school), intending to serve in the military for four years, but that plan was frustrated by air force budget cuts. So when Fletcher graduated in 1987, he went to work as a trading associate with the Wall Street brokerage firm Bear, Stearns. His prowess with mathematics and computers led to a job offer at another broker, Kidder, Peabody.

Fletcher claimed that Kidder, Peabody had offered him a large salary plus a percentage of the profits he earned for the company. At the end of his first year, he received only 10 percent of the profits he had earned, which he considered smaller than what the company had promised. He resigned and sued the company, winning $1.26 million in back pay in 1992.

Fletcher was concerned that he now had a reputation as a troublemaker, so he decided to start his own company, renting temporary space at Bear, Stearns. A successful $100 million deal enabled him to found Fletcher Asset Management, which continues to be a major Wall Street firm. His personal wealth has been estimated at around $50 million, and he is known for his extensive philanthropic activities, donating large sums to the National Association for the Advancement of Colored People (NAACP) and to Harvard University, where his gift of $4 million established the Alphonse Fletcher, Jr., University Professorship, a permanent chair that was initially held by Cornel West. Fletcher's gift was in response to the efforts of Henry Louis Gates, Jr., to establish a preeminent African-American studies department, following Fletcher's philosophy of giving to places where he believes he can make a difference.

Further Reading

"Answering the Question, Who Am I?" *The American Benefactor* (winter 1998). Available online through Fletcher Asset Management website. URL: http://www.fam-inc.com/profiles.jsp. Downloaded on November 4, 2002.

Birger, Jon. "Forty and Under: Alphonse Fletcher, Jr." *Crains New York Business*, January 26, 1998. Available online through Fletcher Asset Management website. URL: http://www.fam-inc.com/profiles.jsp. Downloaded on November 4, 2002.

"The Buddy System." *The New Yorker*, April 29/May 6, 1996, pp. 82–86.

Fletcher Asset Management website. Available online. URL: http://www.fam-inc.com. Downloaded on November 4, 2002.

Haskins, James. *African American Entrepreneurs (Black Stars Series)*. New York: John Wiley & Sons, 1998, pp. 156–159.

"Spotlight." *Crains New York Business*, January 11, 1999. Available online through Fletcher Asset Management website. URL: http://www.fam-inc.com/profiles.jsp.

"University Professorship Named for Fletcher." *Harvard University Gazette*, April 25, 1996. Available online. URL: http://www.news.harvard.edu/gazette/1996/04.25/UniversityProfe.html.

Flora, William

(unknown–ca. 1818) *Revolutionary War soldier, businessperson, trader*

William Flora fought in the American Revolution's Battle of the Great Bridge during the winter of 1775–76. After the Revolution, he become a major black property owner in Portsmouth, Virginia, where he maintained a wagon and freight business.

Virtually nothing is known about Flora's early life, except that he was born free, probably in Portsmouth, Virginia. In 1775, the Revolutionary War was threatening the stability of the British-ruled colonies, and many British leaders sought to obtain the support of free and enslaved Africans for their cause, recognizing that since black people made up one-fifth of the people in the colonies their support would be worth having. As part of this trend, Virginia governor Lord Dunmore proclaimed that any black slaves who were willing to fight for the British would be set free. Hundreds of former slaves flocked to his banner and were organized into a company known as the Ethiopian Regiment. In those days, Ethiopia, the name of an African country, was often used by white people as an umbrella term for all of Africa. Sadly, many of these soldiers died of smallpox contracted on the overcrowded ships that the British used to transport them.

Flora was a free black man, and an American patriot, so he was not interested in Dunmore's offer, nor in joining the Ethiopian Regiment. Instead, he fought with the Americans, serving with Colonel William Woodford's Second Virginia Regiment. In fact, Flora fought against the Ethiopian Regiment when they successfully engaged in combat with Woodford's men. In this way, Flora was like many other African-American patriots, such as Crispus Attucks, who was killed in the Boston Massacre of 1770; Prince Estabrook, who fought in the Battle of Lexington; and Peter Salem, who killed Major John Pitcairn at Lexington and later fought at the Battle of Bunker Hill.

The battle in which Flora won fame is less well known than these Massachusetts encounters, but Flora's heroism is noteworthy nonetheless. In the winter of 1775 and 1776, he joined in the Battle of the Great Bridge, in which a small Patriot force attempted to hold Great Bridge, near the town of Norfolk, Virginia. Flora gained renown for standing his ground and firing eight times as British forces overwhelmed the American position. Even as the other American soldiers ran away, Flora remained, winning the admiration of his fellow soldiers.

After the Revolution, Flora bought property in Portsmouth, building up a wagon and freight business. He did so well that he was able to buy the freedom of his wife and children, who were enslaved. He was also able to buy horses, wagons, and carriages and to set up a business of hauling freight and hiring out horses and carriages.

Shortly before his death, Flora applied for one of the land grants that the state of Virginia was offering to Revolutionary War heroes. Although there were many areas in which black people were not recognized as equal to whites or as having the same rights, the government of Virginia did recognize Flora as a veteran and awarded him the land. He died in Virginia sometime around 1818.

Further Reading

"Blacks in the Revolution." New York Freedom Trail. Available online. URL: http://www.nyfreedom.com/blacks.htm. Downloaded on November 14, 2002.

Kaplan, Sidney. *The Black Presence in the Era of the American Revolution.* Reprint, 1973. Amherst, Mass.: University of Massachusetts Press, 1989.

Kranz, Rachel, and Philip, J. Koslow. *Biographical Dictionary of African Americans,* Revised Edition. New York: Facts On File, 1999.

Forten, James, Sr.
(1766–1842) *sailmaker, abolitionist*

By 1832, James Forten had amassed a fortune of $100,000 from his sailmaking business. He was responsible for inventing and perfecting a new kind of sail design, which greatly contributed to his prosperity. He also became one of America's most prominent black abolitionists (opponents of slavery) and used a great deal of his wealth to buy freedom for slaves and support abolitionist political activity.

Forten was born free in Philadelphia in 1766, the child of Thomas and Sarah Forten. Although they were born free, their parents had been

Sailmaker James Forten used the fortune he made in business to buy slaves' freedom and work for the abolition of slavery. *(The Historical Society of Pennsylvania, James Forten)*

brought to America as enslaved Africans. As a child, Forten attended a colored children's free school in Philadelphia run by Anthony Benezet, an abolitionist who belonged to the Society of Friends (Quakers), a religious group that opposed slavery and often worked for black equality.

James's father, Thomas, worked in a sail loft (sailmaking business) owned by Robert Bridges, and at the age of eight, James went to work there, too. When Thomas died in a boating accident in 1775, James had to leave school and go to work in a grocery store to help support his mother. At the age of 14, he signed on as a powder boy (someone who loaded the guns with gunpowder) on the *Royal Lewis*, a privateer (a ship that seized goods from enemy ships). On his second voyage, he was captured by the British, who normally sold captive black people into slavery. The British captain noticed, however, that Forten had proven a good companion to the captain's son. He offered Forten the chance to be educated in England, but Forten refused on the grounds that he was an American patriot who would never betray his country. He was sent to a prison ship called the *Jersey*, from which he barely escaped with his life.

After the war, in 1785, Forten returned to Bridges's loft as an apprentice (a person who learns a skill by working for someone more skilled). Within a year, he had been promoted to foreman. In 1798, Bridges retired. Hoping that his own sons would becomes merchants, Bridges lent Forten the money to buy his loft, and by the time Forten was 32, he was employing a workforce of 38 men, half of whom were white.

Sometime after 1800, Forten invented a device that helped control sails, which is now credited with beginning the era of modern sailing. Forten never patented (recorded and licensed) his invention, so its exact date is not known. However, this innovation helped to make his fortune, and he went on to obtain many contracts from the U.S. Navy. A staunch patriot, he later recruited black soldiers to serve in the War of 1812. He might have made an even greater fortune had he worked with slave traders, but he always refused to do business for such vessels. His aunt, however, owned slaves and may have been involved in slave trading.

Forten himself was a devoted abolitionist. In 1800, he helped lead a petition drive calling on Congress to emancipate (free) all slaves. In 1813, he wrote a pamphlet protesting a move by the Pennsylvania senate to prevent the migration of free black people from other states. On January 15, 1817, he and other black leaders called a meeting known as the Convention of Color, a black abolitionist gathering of nearly 3,000 black men convened to consider the idea of colonization (a policy to relocate free black people in Africa). Many black leaders supported this idea, believing that free black people would never achieve equality in the United States. But most black people of the time were highly suspicious of this idea, which was supported by white southern slaveholders and the American Colonization Society (ACS). Many black people felt that the ACS supported colonization so that free black people would leave America, abandoning those black people who were still in slavery.

Three prominent black ministers—Richard Allen, Absalom Jones, and John Gloucester—spoke in favor of colonization at this meeting, and then Forten called for a vote. As he later recounted in a letter to black abolitionist and shipping merchant PAUL CUFFE, "there was not one single sole [sic; soul] that was in favor of going to Africa." Forten still privately supported the notion of colonization, but publicly he aligned himself with the men at the meeting he had called, who voted unanimously to remain in America and fight for freedom and equality there. Forten became chair of a committee formed at that meeting to oppose the ACS, joined by committee members Allen, Jones, and Gloucester.

In 1833, Forten helped to form the American Anti-Slavery Society and to rally black support for the group's newspaper, *The Liberator*. He obtained many of the first 1,700 black subscrip-tions to this paper, and bought the first 27 sub-scriptions himself. His wealthy home on Lombard Street, in Philadelphia, served as a stop on the Underground Railroad, where he helped many runaway slaves to escape to freedom. He died on March 4, 1842, in Philadelphia, having created two generations of black sailmakers who went on to start businesses in California, Haiti, and Liberia. He expanded his fortune by investing his profits in real estate and stock.

Further Reading

Africans in America. "Forten Letter to Cuffe." PBS.org online. Available online. URL: http://www.pbs.org/ wgbh/aia/part3/3h484.html. Downloaded on November 10, 2002.

———. "The Forten Women, 1805–1883." PBS.org online. Available online. URL: http://www.pbs.org/wgbh/aia/part3/3p477.html. Downloaded on November 10, 2002.

Gale Group. James Forten." Biography Resource Center, African American Publications. Available online. URL: http://www.galegroup.com/free_resources/bhm/bio/forten_j.htm. Downloaded on November 10, 2002.

"James Forten." Black Inventor Online Museum. Available online. URL: http://www.blackinventor.com/pages/jamesforten.html. Downloaded on November 10, 2002.

"James Forten." Spartacus Educational. Available online. URL: http://www.spartacus.schoolnet.co.uk/USASforten.htm. Downloaded on November 10, 2002.

Krebs, Laurie. *A Day in the Life of a Colonial Sailmaker.* New York: Powerkids Press, 2003.

Taylor, L. Allison. "James Forten: A Port Personality." L. Allison Taylor Personal website. Available online. URL: http://www.columbia.edu/~lt165/forten.html. Downloaded on November 10, 2002.

White, Monica. "James Forten, Sr. (1766–1842)." Monica A. White Personal website. Available online. URL: http://www.geocities.com/Heartland/Prairie/7824/forten.html. Downloaded on November 10, 2002.

Winch, Julie. *A Gentleman of Color: The Life of James Forten.* New York: Oxford University Press, 2002.

Fortune, Amos
(ca. 1710–1801) *tanner, carpenter*

Amos Fortune's resilience and determination led him to create a remarkable life for himself beginning at the age of 60, when after some 45 years as a slave he bought his own freedom, built up a prosperous business as a tanner, bought the freedom of several other enslaved Africans, and became one of the most respected men in the predominantly white town of Jaffrey, New Hampshire, where he finally settled.

Because good records were not kept on the Africans who were kidnaped from their native land, Amos Fortune's African name is not known, nor are any of the details of his early life. Scholars believe that he was born around 1710 in western Africa, either on the Gold Coast (which today includes regions in Nigeria, Sierra Leone, Liberia, and Ghana), or in the West African country that is today known as Guinea. The earliest records on Fortune date from 1752, when he was owned by Ichabod Richardson, a tanner in Woburn, Massachusetts. Although Richardson had promised Fortune his freedom several times, when he died unexpectedly in 1768, his new will made no mention of Amos Fortune. In theory, Fortune was still a slave, but since he was 58, it was unlikely that anyone would want to buy him. In November 1769, papers were finally drawn up giving Fortune his freedom.

There is no information about Fortune's life between the years 1770 and 1774, but he must have found ways to earn and even to save money, for on July 20, 1774, he bought a half-acre of land in Woburn, Massachusetts, where he built a small house.

Unusually for most people of the time, Fortune knew how to read and write, and enjoyed a high level of trust among his fellow African Americans. In 1777, for example, an enslaved man in

Lexington, Massachusetts, Pompey Blackman, authorized Fortune to act as his business representative. On June 23, 1778, Fortune bought the freedom of the African American Lydia Somerset from her owner in Billerica, Massachusetts. He married her on July 8, 1778, in Lexington; sadly, she died three months later, on October 3, 1778. On November 9, 1779, Fortune went on to buy the freedom of Violate Baldwin from her owner James Baldwin of North Woburn. He married her the following day. At the time, Violate was 50, while Amos was 69. Violate remained his wife for the rest of his life. Fortune later bought the freedom of other enslaved Africans, including four-year-old Celyndia, whom he and Violate adopted.

In the summer of 1781, the couple moved to Jaffrey, New Hampshire. When the Fortunes arrived in Jaffrey, they were "warned out" by town constable Joseph Thorndike. Although some historians have interpreted the incident as racially based, all new arrivals were given a similar warning, so that if they were unable to support themselves, the town would not be required to take care of them. The Fortunes ignored the warning, stayed in Jaffrey, and built up a prosperous business.

For eight years, Fortune lived on land owned by the town, but in 1789, he bought his own 25 acres on a road that is now known as Amos Fortune Road. It was here that he dug tanning pits, built a house, and erected a barn. The house and barn are still standing today. Fortune's tannery quickly prospered, and Fortune became known as one of the best tanners in the area, drawing business from eastern Massachusetts as well as New Hampshire. He was a full member of the local church (as he had been in Woburn), and an active supporter of its activities. He is listed as the town's first benefactor (meaning that he made the first donation to support the town). He helped to found the local library and reportedly bound several of the library's books (books were then bound in leather, to which, as a tanner, Fortune would have had easy access).

On November 17, 1801, Fortune died at the age of 91. He was buried in the Old Burying

Ground behind the Meetinghouse, where one year later Violate was interred beside him. His inscription reads, "Sacred to the memory of Amos Fortune who was born free in Africa, a slave in America, he purchased liberty, professed Christianity, lived reputably [with a good reputation] and died hopefully Nov. 17, 1801 . . ."

Fortune left a $100 legacy to the church and $243 to the local school. When the school closed, the money was unused for many years. Eventually the funds, which with interest have grown to about $10,000, were put into trust for the Jaffrey Public Library children's department. The library helped publish a biography of Fortune and is exploring other ways to honor his memory.

Further Reading

Hendryx, Nancy. "Kindred Spirits." *Concord Monitor,* October 20, 1999. Available online. URL: http://www.concordmonitor.com/stories/top100/fxb_yates.shtml.

Lambert, Peter. *Amos Fortune, The Man and His Legacy.* Jaffrey, N.H.: The Amos Fortune Forum, 2000.

———. "Amos Fortune." Peter Lambert's homepage. Available online. URL: http://www.geocities.com/prlambert76/afortune/fortune1.html. Last updated August 29, 2002.

New Hampshire Division of Historical Resources. "Hannah Davis-Amos Fortune." New Hampshire Historical Markers. Available online. URL: http://www.state.nh.us/markers/mo13.html. Downloaded on November 14, 2002.

Yates, Elizabeth. *Amos Fortune, Free Man.* New York: Penguin, 1989.

Fraunces, Samuel
(ca. 1722–1795) *tavern keeper*

Samuel Fraunces owned and ran a tavern in 18th-century New York that George Washington liked to frequent. The Sons of Liberty—a group of men dedicated to freeing America from British colonial rule—used to meet there, as did British officers committed to suppressing the American Revolution. Fraunces reportedly eavesdropped on the British conversations and reported them to American revolutionaries. He is noteworthy both for his services to the American Revolution and for being an entrepreneur at a time when most African Americans in New York were slaves.

Little is known about Fraunces's early life, though scholars believe that his name may at some point have been spelled "Frances." Scholars also believe that he was born and raised in the West Indies, one of seven children, though a 1790 census lists him as a native of New York. Since the same census lists him and his wife as "free whites," however, this appears to be an unreliable source.

Fraunces seems to have arrived in New York in 1755, when he was about 33 years old. He was apparently an accomplished cook who had accumulated a fair amount of capital, since he was able to start a catering business almost as soon as he entered the city. Some scholars believe that he had been an officer's cook on an English ship, which was how he obtained passage to New York.

When Fraunces first arrived, the city's population included about 2,500 enslaved African Americans and a far smaller number of free black people. Catering was one of the few enterprises open to African Americans, who could take advantage of the custom of rich families to engage caterers that would regularly provide them with some or all of their meals. When Fraunces entered the city, some black men and even a few black women were working as caterers, and Fraunces went into partnership with one man for about five years. During this time, he married Elizabeth Dalles. In 1759, the couple established their own business, a tavern called Mason's Arms that served regular meals and the colonial version of "bar food": soup, ketchup, bottled gooseberries, pickled walnuts, pickled and fried oysters, and pickled mushrooms.

In 1762, the couple moved to a new building near the wharves so that they could both serve people and supply ships. They converted this building into the Queen's Head Tavern, which offered complete meals at a fixed price and soon became popular all over town. In 1767, Fraunces opened Vauxhall, a garden—an early version of an amusement park—in upstate New York, where customers could visit a wax museum, but in 1770 he sold this unsuccessful venture to focus on his tavern.

As tensions rose between Britain and America in the early 1770s, many prominent people from both sides of the conflict met at Fraunces's tavern. The Sons of Liberty met there in 1774 before throwing imported tea into the river, a New York version of the more famous Boston Tea Party protest against import taxes on tea. Although Fraunces was a loyal American and seemed to have spied for the revolutionary side, he may also have wished to avoid trouble, for he tried to sell his inn in 1775 but was unable to find a buyer. When revolution broke out in 1776, Fraunces changed the name from "Queen's Head Tavern," which sounded like British royalty, to "Fraunces Tavern" (later, City Tavern).

George Washington gradually became a close associate of Fraunces's, both through Washington's own visits to the tavern and through Fraunces's daughter Phoebe, who seemed to have worked as Washington's housekeeper at his Mortimer House residence on Richmond Hill. Phoebe supposedly discovered and reported a plot to assassinate Washington. When Washington was ready to draw up peace terms with the British, the men met at Fraunces Tavern. Washington also made an emotional farewell speech to his officers there.

In 1785, Fraunces sold his inn and retired to country life in the neighboring state of New Jersey. In 1788, though, he returned to open a new tavern in downtown New York. When Washington set up the new U.S. capital in Philadelphia, Fraunces went with him as his personal steward (an employee who runs a household on behalf of the owner), remaining at the executive mansion for several years. In 1794, he left Washington's household to establish two taverns in Philadelphia, where he also owned two houses, one of which he gave to his son, Andrew Gautier Fraunces. Both men were called "gentlemen" in the city directory.

Samuel Fraunces died in Philadelphia on October 10, 1795. His Philadelphia properties were eventually destroyed, but his New York tavern has been preserved, partly through the early efforts of the Sons of the Revolution, a group of descendants of those who participated in the Revolutionary War dedicated to keeping that history alive. In 1965, the building was the oldest in New York and was made a historical landmark by the New York City Landmarks Preservation Committee. However, despite efforts to preserve the building, Fraunces's African-American identity has rarely been acknowledged in information about the site.

Further Reading

DeWan, George. "Washington Says Thanks." Long Island Our Story/LIHistory.com, Newsday.com. Available online. URL: http://www.newsday.com/extras/lihistory.com/4/hs430a.htm. Downloaded on November 12, 2002.

Fraunces Tavern Restaurant. "The Birth of a Landmark." Fraunces Tavern website. Available online. URL: http://www.frauncestavern.com/fraunces_history.htm. Downloaded on November 12, 2002.

Ingham, John, and Lynne B. Feldman. *African American Business Leaders: A Biographical Dictionary.* Westport, Conn.: Greenwood Press, 1994, pp. 240–244.

Fudge, Ann
(Ann Marie Fudge)
(1951–) *business executive*

Ann Fudge has been one of the most powerful corporate executives in North America in her role as executive vice president of Kraft Foods, Inc., North America's largest food company. In 2001,

Fudge was the top African-American woman in a U.S. corporation, famous for her career-long success at marketing old brands in new ways. Yet in that year, she left the corporate world, hoping to rediscover a more personal side of life. She returned in 2003 to head Young & Rubicam, a major advertising agency.

Fudge was born Ann Marie Brown on April 23, 1951, in Washington, D.C., the daughter of Malcolm R. and Bettye (Lewis) Brown. Her father was an administrator at the U.S. Post Office and her mother was a manager at the National Security Agency. She attended Catholic schools through high school. Also in high school, she became a member of a local department store's Teen Board, advising buyers what teenagers might like to purchase.

In 1968, when Martin Luther King, Jr., was assassinated, the young high school student was deeply moved. African Americans across the country were rioting in anger and frustration over the murder, and Brown herself felt a strong sense of determination that she later credited with helping her to advance in her corporate career.

Brown went on to Simmons College, in Boston, where she became the advisee of Margaret Henning, author of *The Managerial Woman* and later the founder of Simmons's business school. In the late 1960s and early 1970s, very few women of any color had been hired at top corporate positions or even as lower-level managers, but Henning encouraged Brown to pursue corporate life. Meanwhile, Brown married Richard E. Fudge during her sophomore year and gave birth to Richard, Jr., before she graduated. She graduated with honors in 1973. Soon after, her son Kevin was born.

Fudge, meanwhile, began to work as a personnel executive at General Electric in Bridgeport, Connecticut. In 1975, she started studying at Harvard Business School, receiving her M.B.A. in 1977. From there, she went to General Mills in Minneapolis, Minnesota, to work as a marketing assistant.

Fudge set for herself the personal goal of becoming a general manager of a brand division by the time she was 40; indeed, she rose rapidly through the ranks. In 1978, she became an assistant product manager; in 1980, she was made product manager; and from 1983 to 1986, she was marketing director, the first woman and the first African American to hold such a post at General Mills. As marketing director, she was responsible for four brands. She also helped to develop Honey Nut Cheerios, one of the best-selling brands in the United States.

In 1986, Fudge had a chance to move up to general manager at General Mills. Instead, she moved east to be closer to her sick mother, taking the post of strategic planning director at General Foods in White Plains, New York. General Foods is the nation's largest food company, and, as a division of tobacco company Philip Morris, part of a major U.S. corporation. She rose rapidly there, too, becoming vice president for marketing and development in the "Dinners and Enhancers" division in 1989. In 1991, she became general manager of the whole brand division, which gave her responsibility for $600 million worth of company business—and enabled her to beat her personal goal by one year. Brands that Fudge supervised included Stove Top Stuffing Mix, Minute Rice, Log Cabin Syrup, and Good Seasons salad dressing. Fudge was responsible for helping these labels meet the competition from cheaper store brands. Although most of General Foods saw a 1 percent revenue increase in 1991, Fudge's division attained double-digit sales and earnings, primarily through her talent for ad campaigns, her inventive promotional ideas, and her ability to repackage familiar products in new and exciting ways.

In the 1990s, a trend toward healthier eating was sweeping the nation, and Fudge found ways to capitalize on this development when she became head of the marketing team that developed the "Why Fry?" campaign for Shake 'n' Bake. The product was a breaded coating for chicken that enabled customers to imitate the taste of fried chicken while baking their food—a healthier alternative. Fudge's ad campaign capitalized on the national health-consciousness, as well as focusing on the product's new flavors and offering such enticements as discount coupons.

Fudge was doing well in the corporate world, but the interviews she gave sometimes revealed the strains of combining corporate life with her role as mother. She spoke of needing to plan the family's meals for several days in advance, and once she turned down a choice promotion that would have involved moving to another city, explaining that it would have entailed having one of her sons switch schools in his senior year.

In 1994, General Foods merged with Kraft Foods, and Fudge moved up to the presidency of Maxwell House Coffee while becoming an executive vice president of the whole corporation. When Fudge took over, Maxwell House Coffee was second in sales revenues in the coffee market, with 24.6 percent of the market share; Folger's, with 27.6 percent, was first. Fudge focused on beating Folger's so that her own brand could take first place, but also she faced stiff competition from the new trend of coffeehouses such as Starbucks and the rise of gourmet coffees sold by other specialty companies.

Accordingly Fudge began her presidency by going to Seattle, where Starbucks had first begun to operate and where many gourmet coffee blends were routinely served in coffeehouses. As a result of her research, Fudge opened up a line of flavored Maxwell House coffees, seeking to create a coffeehouse image at a lower price and a convenient supermarket location. Capitalizing on the popularity of "retro" ads—ads that evoked the past— Fudge also revived Maxwell House's famous "Good to the last drop" slogan—and doubled her division's earnings.

In 1997, she was rewarded with a promotion, taking over as president of Kraft's new "Coffee and Cereals" division, a move that put her in charge of $2.7 billion worth of the company's

$16.8 billion in sales. It was this promotion that led *Fortune* to dub her one of the nation's 50 most powerful women in business in 1998 and 1999.

Like most corporate leaders, Fudge acquired responsibilities in other corporations as well, serving on various boards of directors throughout her career, including stints with the Federal Reserve Bank of New York, General Electric, Liz Claiborne, Inc., and other companies. She has also served as an officer of the Executive Leadership Council, a nonprofit group of African Americans working in corporate leadership positions as managers and directors.

In 2001, many were predicting that Fudge might become the first African-American woman to run a major U.S. company. Her story seemed to prove that an African-American woman could succeed in a top executive position. Already dubbed one of the 50 most powerful businesswomen, Fudge was also called one of the 12 most powerful black people in corporate America by *Ebony* magazine.

Observers were surprised, therefore, when she abruptly left her post at Kraft. Although Fudge had originally planned to take another top-level job, instead she took some time off and went on a biking trip through Corsica and Sardinia with her husband and sons. She intended to reenter corporate life—but in a different spirit from the first time, allowing more time for personal growth and family connections. In 2003 she took over as chair and chief executive officer of Young & Rubicam Inc., one of the largest U.S. advertising agencies.

Further Reading

"Ann Fudge Gets Top Y&R Post As Dolan Quits." *Wall Street Journal,* May 13, 2003, p. B1.

Baskerville, Dawn M., Sheryl Hilliard Tucker, Donna Whittingham-Barnes. "21 Women of Power and Influence in Corporate America." *Black Enterprise,* August 1991, p. 39.

Fudge, Ann. "Shop Has the Answer in Researching Stove Top." *Advertising Age,* June 3, 1996, p. C12.

Hodges, Jane. "Top Corporate Women are Quitting to 'Have It All.'" *Career Journal Asia,* from *The Asian Wall Street Journal* and *Far Eastern Economic Review.* Available online. URL: http://www.career journal.com/myc/workfamily/20020716-hodges. html. Downloaded on December 4, 2002.

McCauley, Lucy. "Next Stop—The 21st Century." *Fast Company* 27 (September 1999): 108. Available online. URL: http://www.fastcompany.com/online/ 27/one.html.

McDonald, Marci. "They Love Me—Not: Once Hailed as Heroes, Female CEOs Now Face Harsh Critiques." *U.S. News & World Report,* June 24, 2002. Available online at Kellogg School of Management, Northwestern University. URL: http://www.kellogg.northwestern.edu/news/hits/ 020624usn.htm.

O'Connell, Vanessa. "Starbucks, Kraft, Align for Pact to Sell Coffee." *Wall Street Journal,* September 28, 1998, p. B4.

Pollack, Judann. "Team-builder Fudge Likes the Problem-Solving Aspect." *Advertising Age,* February 3, 1997, p. S2.

"Working Moms Who Broke Through." *Working Mother,* May 1995, p. 37.

Fuller, S. B.
(Samuel B. Fuller)
(1905–1988) *beauty supply firm founder, publisher, department store owner*

S. B. Fuller founded one of the first modern multimillion-dollar businesses owned and operated by an African American, a large and diversified hair-care and cosmetics company that eventually included a line of 300 products and employed 5,000 people. Yet his business was brought low by boycotts from white organizations who convinced southern white people not to buy products made by an African American—and by boycotts inspired by civil rights leaders who felt that Fuller's own statements were anti-black.

Fuller was born on June 4, 1905, in Monroe, Louisiana, the son of sharecroppers whose poverty forced him to drop out of school after the sixth grade. As early as age nine, however, Fuller was selling products door to door, an experience that became the foundation for his later success as an entrepreneur who relied upon such salespeople. When Fuller was 15, his family moved to Memphis. No further information is available about his father, but his mother died two years later, leaving behind seven children who somehow managed to support themselves, being too ashamed to accept government assistance.

In 1928, Fuller hitchhiked to Chicago with no money but lots of ambition. He worked for a while in a coal yard, then as an insurance representative for Commonwealth Burial Association, an African-American firm. Meanwhile, he dreamt of owning his own business, and with his friend Lestine Thornton—the woman he later married—he invested $25 in soap, which he sold himself, door to door. The profits he made convinced him to invest another $1,000, and soon he had founded Fuller Products Company, which he incorporated in 1929 while continuing to work for Commonwealth.

Four years later, he was promoted to a manager's job even as he built his own business, establishing a line of 30 products and hiring more door-to-door salespeople. Chicago's South Side included a substantial number of black families who became Fuller's target customers, and their business enabled him to start a small factory in 1939. Fuller was now one of the major black business owners in Chicago.

In 1947, Fuller bought the white cosmetics company Boyer International Laboratories, which made Jean Nadal Cosmetics and HA Hair Arranger, sold primarily in the U.S. South. In those days, white people, especially in the South, were often reluctant to accept African Americans in positions of power, so Fuller kept his purchase secret, allowing customers to believe that his products were made by a white-owned company.

S. B. Fuller, an entrepreneur who made and distributed beauty products, gave many inspirational speeches to community and business groups. *(Library of Congress)*

Fuller's success continued through the 1950s, as his Chicago plant made creams, lotions, perfumes, and household goods for black people, while Boyer made similar products marketed to whites. Fuller was known for motivating his salespeople to ever greater efforts and to instilling a sense of pride and "family" in his people, who called themselves "Fullerites." Many African-American entrepreneurs got their start selling for Fuller, including George Johnson and JOE L. DUDLEY, SR. Fuller was able to build himself and his wife a quarter-million-dollar home in suburban Illinois, a luxurious showplace that revealed the wealth and success he had achieved.

In the early 1960s, Fuller could boast of $10 million worth of sales and a customer base that was 60 percent white. He established 85 branches of his business in 38 states, in addition to buying an interest in other cosmetics companies—J. C. McBrady and Co. and Patricia Stevens Cosmetics—and becoming a major shareholder in the Pittsburgh Courier Publishing Company, which owned the country's oldest black newspaper, *New York Age*, as well as its largest black newspaper, the *Pittsburgh Courier*. He invested in real estate, farming, cattle, and the Regal Theater, Chicago's premier center of black entertainment. He also founded the Fuller Guaranty Company, which made loans, and the Fuller-Philco Home Appliance Center.

Then a series of financial disasters struck. In 1964, Fuller was accused of improprieties and was placed on probation for five years and ordered to repay $1.6 million to people who had lent him money. More seriously, the White Citizens Council—an anti-black group—discovered Fuller's ownership of "white" companies. They urged white southerners to boycott Fuller's products and destroyed his business in the South: Jean Nadal sales actually fell to zero. Fuller tried to sell Jean Nadal to a New York liquor company, using the company's promise to pay as the basis for a $500,000 loan to open Fuller Department Store (formerly the South Center Department Store) on Chicago's South Side. When the liquor company reneged on its promise, Fuller was in serious financial trouble, which deepened when a Chicago social worker accused him of extending credit to welfare clients, which was against welfare regulations. The social worker urged his customers on welfare not to honor their debts to his department store, which cost him more than $1 million and eventually led to him losing the store. His publishing interests were costing him money, as well, so Fuller sold them in 1968 to Sengstacke Enterprises (founded by ROBERT SENGSTACKE ABBOTT). The combination of difficulties proved too much for Fuller, who declared bankruptcy in 1969.

Fuller faced further troubles from the black community, resulting from a speech he had made in 1963 to the National Association of Manufacturers (NAM), of which he was the first African-American member. Fuller had told the NAM that black people's problems stemmed from "lack of understanding of the capitalist system" and from the fact that "they have nothing to sell." Later, he accused the National Association for the Advancement of Colored People (NAACP) of trying to change white people's attitudes rather than focusing on the more pressing problem of black people's lack of motivation and entrepreneurship. Although Fuller was the former president of the NAACP's South Side chapter, many civil rights leaders saw him as blaming black people for the results of racism, and they urged the black community to boycott his products.

Fuller went on to reorganize his bankrupt business with the help of Dudley, and by 1972, he was reporting profits of $300,000. Although this was far less than the $10 million figure he had once enjoyed, it testified to his ability to withstand even the harshest setbacks. On June 4, 1975, the day of his 70th birthday, he was honored by Illinois governor Daniel Walker, who declared it "S. B. Fuller Day," as well as by black entrepreneurs George Johnson and JOHN H. JOHNSON, who cosponsored a testimonial dinner. The June 16, 1975, issue of *Jet* reported that at the dinner,

George Johnson acknowledged Fuller's pioneering role as a black entrepreneur, saying, "If there had been no you, there would have been no us."

Fuller died of kidney failure on October 24, 1998, survived by his wife, five daughters, 13 grandchildren, and 18 great-grandchildren, his memory honored by several succeeding generations of black entrepreneurs. His company continues to distribute products in Atlanta; Los Angeles; New York City; Richmond, Virginia; Washington, D.C.; Greensboro, North Carolina; Cleveland, Ohio; and Newark, New Jersey.

Further Reading

Gale Group. "S. B. Fuller." Notable Black American Men. Farmington Hills, Mich.: Gale Research, 1998.

Ingham, John N., and Lynne B. Feldman. *African-American Business Leaders*. Westport, Conn.: Greenwood Press, 1994, pp. 244–249.

Walton, Charles. "Bronzeville Conversation—47th Street and South Park Boulevard—Bronzeville's Downtown." Jazz Institute of Chicago website. Available online. URL: http://jazzinstituteofchicago.org/index.asp?target=/jazzgram/bronzeville/fortyseventhstreet.asp. Downloaded on November 18, 2002.

Wright, Elizabeth. "S. B. Fuller: Master of Enterprise." Issues & Views. Available online. URL: http://www.issues-views.com/index.php/sect/1000/article/1003. Downloaded on November 18, 2002.

G

Gardner, Barbara See PROCTOR, BARBARA GARDNER.

Gardner, Edward G.
(Edward George Gardner)
(1925–) *hair-care products company founder*

Edward G. Gardner is the founder of the company Soft Sheen Products, Incorporated, a company that Gardner started in his own basement that grew to become one of the largest black-owned businesses in the United States. His products—Soft Sheen Hair and Scalp Conditioner, and Care Free Curl—were used by millions of people in the United States and internationally, and his community effort, Black on Black Love, an attempt to stop black-on-black violence, reached African Americans throughout his hometown of Chicago.

Gardner was born in Chicago on February 15, 1925. Little is known of his early life, but he graduated from Fenger High School, a public school, in 1943. He himself said that his business training came "from the streets."

World War II was raging when Gardner graduated, and he was drafted into the U.S. Army. There he faced the kinds of prejudice that were common against African Americans in those days. During his basic training in Pennsylvania, a military police officer hauled him out of a movie the-ater for daring to sit in the middle rather than in the balcony. He served in the Pacific and was discharged as a staff sergeant, becoming eligible for the G.I. Bill, a program designed to help pay the tuition of returning soldiers.

Using that federal subsidy, Gardner obtained his B.A. from Chicago Teachers College and became an elementary teacher in Chicago's public schools. He earned his master's degree at the University of Chicago and became an assistant principal, eventually working at the school that served one of the city's roughest housing projects. In 1957, he also began working part-time as a salesman for a friend who sold hair-care products. In those days, most beauty salons were strictly segregated (separated) on the basis of race, partly because African Americans had different hair needs and partly because society was segregated in so many ways. Gardner started as a businessman by visiting black-owned beauty salons with a cardboard box full of his friend's products.

In 1962, he began making his own products, setting up the E. G. Gardner Beauty Products Company—later Soft Sheen—in his basement with his wife Bettiann. He left his job in the schools, a move that he later said reflected his own ignorance of the business world. Nevertheless, because in those days white-owned hair products companies tended to ignore black hair needs completely, many black-owned businesses made hair products in a basement or back room and distributed them from the trunk of somebody's car. The market at the time was dominated by George Johnson's Johnson Products, which marketed Afro Sheen, a product that supported the tightly curled Afro hairstyle and won Johnson 80 percent of the market in the 1960s. JOHN H. JOHNSON and, earlier, S. B. FULLER had also been major players in the industry. Gardner and many other small entrepreneurs divided up the rest of the market.

Initially Gardner's products smelled so unpleasant and worked so poorly that stylists threw him out of their salons. Eventually, he developed Soft Sheen Hair and Scalp Conditioner, which he sold directly, with Bettiann keeping the books and their four children filling the bottles and packing the boxes.

Soon Gardner was able to set up a plant outside of his apartment, but his family continued to work there, making four or five dozen bottles a week. Then, in the 1970s, the Afro went out of style and Soft Sheen began to capture a greater share of the market. By 1979, the company was employing some 100 people and selling $500,000 worth of products a year.

In 1978, Michael Jackson and other celebrities had popularized the Jheri curl, a loosely curled look that required most black people to first straighten their hair and then recurl it, using huge amounts of hair-care product to preserve the loose, curly look. In 1979, Soft Sheen introduced Care Free Curl, which greatly added to the company's profits. Although white-owned Revlon had a Jheri curl product on the market, it was a liquid, while black stylists tended to prefer creams. Revlon's product was also time-consuming and expensive. By 1983, Gardner's company had outstripped Johnson's, controlling 55 percent of the new hair-curl market. By 1987, Soft Sheen's total sales had risen to more than $81 million, as compared to $38 million for Johnson Products.

Meanwhile, the white-owned companies were fighting to expand their 50 percent share of the so-called ethnic hair-care products market, which by 1988 was worth some $1 billion. Gardner said at the time that he would not mind competition from the white companies, with their huge capital resources, if only he were able to sell to white customers.

Then Revlon executive Irving Bottner made the mistake of saying that black-owned firms produced poor-quality products. Reverend Jesse Jackson's People United to Save Humanity (PUSH)—a civil rights group that sometimes focuses on expanding black business opportunities—started a boycott of Revlon products. Gardner led the American Health and Beauty Aids Institute (AHBAI), a minority trade association, in a $3 million campaign to promote black-owned companies among black consumers. Edward T. Lewis (see EDWARD I. LEWIS AND CLARENCE O. SMITH) refused to accept Revlon ads in *Essence,* the major magazine for black women, and John H. Johnson did the same at *Jet* and *Ebony.*

Although black-owned cosmetic companies were treated by some activists as a basis for black pride, other African Americans have criticized them. Some in the black community view it as demeaning for black people to straighten their hair, which they see as imitating a white standard of beauty. Moreover, black people spend far more per capita than white people on hair-care products and cosmetics, which many feel drains money from the black community that could better be used for other things.

Meanwhile, Gardner made some changes at Soft Sheen between 1986 and 1988. He sold off Perfect Pinch, a condiments company, and founded Brainstorm Communication, an ad agency; Bottlewerks, a bottler; and *Shoptalk,* a black beauticians' trade magazine. He enlisted Anita Baker as celebrity spokeswoman for Soft Sheen to counter the celebrities used by white-owned companies, such as Billy Dee Williams and Jayne Kennedy. And he bought Dyke and Dryden, the largest black-owned importer, manufacturer, and distributor of black cosmetic products in

Great Britain. He went on to establish Soft Sheen West Indies, Ltd., to reach the Jamaican market, and he bought Alaion Products, a men's hair-care company based in Newark, New Jersey.

Much of this reorganization was the work of Gardner's son Gary. In the late 1980s and 1990s, Gardner left much of the business to his children: Gary; Guy, who managed the bottling operation; and Terri, who headed the advertising agency. He and his wife focused instead on civic products, helping to renovate S. B. Fuller's old Regal Theater—Chicago's equivalent of Harlem's famed Apollo Theater, a black entertainment center—and founding Black on Black Love, a response to the attack of a black female employee by a black male. In the early 1980s, Gardner also donated $200,000 to a black voter registration drive that helped elect Chicago's first black mayor, Harold Washington.

Gardner has expressed his distress that the new generation of black M.B.A.s is not founding black-owned companies to employ black employees, but rather going to work for white-owned corporations that take money out of the African-American community. Nevertheless, in 1998, he sold Soft Sheen to the French company L'Oréal, although his daughter Terri stayed on as head of the company. The business Gardner built continues to enjoy massive sales in the United States, Canada, Africa, and the Caribbean.

Further Reading

HistoryMakers, The. "Bettiann Gardner: Biography." BusinessMakers, on The HistoryMakers. Available online. URL: http://www.thehistorymakers.com/biography/biography.asp?bioindex=233&category=businessMakers. Downloaded on January 24, 2003.

———— "Ed Gardner: Biography." BusinessMakers, on the HistoryMakers. Available online. URL: http://www.thehistorymakers.com/biography/biography.asp?bioindex=44&category=businessMakers. Downloaded on January 27, 2003.

Ingham, John, and Lynne B. Feldman. *African American Business Leaders: A Biographical Dictionary.* Westport, Conn.: Greenwood Press, 1994, pp. 250–258.

L'Oréal. "L'Oréal Acquires Soft Sheen in the United States." L'Oréal website. Available online. URL: http://www.loreal.com/us/press-room/full_article.asp?id_Art=1423&id_sousrubrique=1. Posted July 1, 1998.

Gaston, Arthur G.
(Arthur George Gaston)

(1892–1996) *banker, insurance executive, real estate developer, motel owner*

As Arthur Gaston approached his 100th birthday, *Black Enterprise* magazine dubbed him "Entrepreneur of the Century." As the owner of multiple enterprises, he was known for providing jobs and resources to the African-American community at a time when the Alabama region in which he lived was dominated by white-owned businesses that practiced segregation (racial separation) with both workers and customers. He was also known for being a key figure in the Civil Rights movement, providing resources and meeting spaces for Martin Luther King, Jr., and the Southern Christian Leadership Conference (SCLC) at a crucial stage in its history.

Gaston was born on July 4, 1892, in Demopolis, Alabama, in a log cabin constructed by Joe and Idella Gaston, the former slaves who were his grandparents. His father, a railroad worker, died when Arthur was a baby, and he was raised by his mother, Rosie, a cook and domestic worker. Arthur was raised in the South at a time when black people had very few political or civil rights, and as a child, Arthur believed deeply that white people were honest and just. Thus, when he witnessed a lynching, he thought that justice had prevailed.

Gaston lived with his grandparents as a child and—a budding entrepreneur—charged the neighborhood children a button or a pin to use the swing in their yard. He then sold the buttons and pins to local women for their sewing.

Rosie Gaston and her son moved to Birmingham in 1900 to work as a cook for department store owners A. B. and Minnie Loveman. She and Arthur lived in servant's quarters over the stables. Later, she opened a catering business, with the Lovemans among her main customers.

Gaston attended the Carrie Tuggle Institute, a boarding school run by a former slave. He went as far as the 10th grade—all the education that the school offered. Although he wished for more schooling, he was unable to afford it and began instead to sell subscriptions to the *Birmingham Reporter,* a local black newspaper. He moved to Mobile, Alabama, where he worked for the Battle House Hotel and began to operate a number of small businesses as well.

In 1910, Gaston joined the U.S. Army, later serving as a sergeant in France in an all-black unit (the army was segregated in those days). In 1918, he left the army and became a laborer at the Tennessee Coal and Iron Company of Westfield, Alabama. He began selling his fellow workers the box lunches that his mother prepared, as well as lending them money when they ran short—charging 25 cents on the dollar for the privilege. He also operated a popcorn and peanut stand.

Gaston then came up with the idea for his first major enterprise: a burial society. At the time, most black people in the South were not served by white funeral homes, and they were used to taking up collections in church to pay for their burial costs. In 1923, Gaston began Brother Gaston's Burial Society, later the Booker T. Washington Burial Society, with customers paying a regular fee in exchange for the security of knowing that when they died, their expenses would be covered. Around this time, Gaston married his childhood sweetheart, Creola Smith, who became the company's secretary. Her father, A. L. "Dad" Smith, served as vice president of the company and pro-

vided financial support. In 1932, the business was incorporated as the Booker T. Washington Insurance Company, which became the foundation for all of Gaston's later businesses, the source of financial support that enabled him to branch out in the business world while supporting the black community in various ways.

After Creola died, Arthur went on in 1939 to marry Minnie Gardner, with whom he had one son, Arthur George Gaston, Jr. In the same year, he founded the Booker T. Washington Business College to train clerks for his other businesses. Gaston's school was one of the only places that African-American women could receive business training, and eventually he expanded the college, which was headed by his wife. Also in 1939, he founded the Brown Belle Bottling Company, one of his only unsuccessful businesses. Gaston attributed the lack of success to the fact that the bottling company was founded purely to make money; he saw his other enterprises as motivated by the wish to provide services to the black community.

Many of the services that Gaston provided were a result of the segregated society in which he lived. For example, white motels at the time did not accept black guests, so Gaston founded the A. G. Gaston Motel to serve black travelers. This motel became a historic site for the Civil Rights movement, headquarters for the SCLC, and a resting place for leaders and activists. As a result, the motel was frequently bombed by white opponents of civil rights.

Gaston was often at odds with Martin Luther King, Jr., whom he nonetheless admired and supported in various ways. In 1957, he helped black people in Tuskegee, Alabama, who were agitating for voting rights by means of an economic boycott. Gaston made available mortgage and business loans to people who were in danger of losing their homes and businesses in the face of economic pressure from white people who objected to the boycott and to black civil rights. He also offered the Gaston Motel to civil rights activists for lodging and meetings, and when King was arrested for marching without a permit, Gaston put up his $5,000 bail.

Some people considered Gaston an "Uncle Tom" for his willingness to accommodate white southern politicians, but Gaston saw himself as someone who could facilitate negotiations and peaceful settlements after "agitators" like King and the other demonstrators had stirred things up. He admired Booker T. Washington, who had preached the gospel of accommodation—getting along with the white power structure—in addition to black self-help and private enterprise. Yet in his support of King and the SCLC, Gaston took

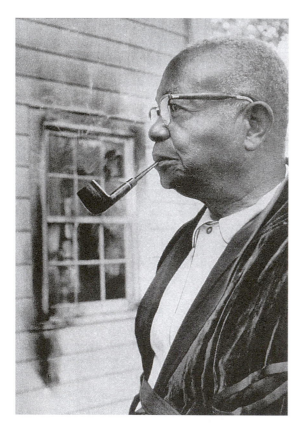

The burn marks are still visible from where Arthur G. Gaston's home was firebombed during the entrepreneur's involvement in the Civil Rights movement. *(Library of Congress)*

political action of a kind that Washington would never have approved.

Meanwhile, Gaston continued to expand his operations. In 1955, he opened the Vulcan Realty and Investment Corporation to manage the real estate being purchased by his insurance company. In 1957, he founded the Citizens Federal Savings and Loan Association, which made mortgage money available to black people who wanted to buy homes through his realty company. In 1963, he started the A. G. Gaston Home for senior citizens, so that his friends and former employees would have a place to spend their old age.

Gaston was an active supporter of the black community, in part by forming the A. G. Gaston Boys and Girls Club in 1966, so that young people could engage in sports while receiving adult supervision and guidance. Meanwhile, in 1975, Gaston entered the radio business by acquiring WENN-FM, now a rhythm and blues station, and WAGG-AM, now a gospel station. He saw the stations as another way to give black people a voice in their community. In 1986, he went on to found the A. G. Gaston Construction Company. His holdings also included Citizens Drugstore and Zion Memorial Gardens and Mausoleum.

Ironically, Gaston's role in the black community began to change as the Civil Rights movement became victorious, for once the South was no longer segregated, black people no longer depended upon African-American entrepreneurs to get decent treatment as either workers or customers. While Gaston himself continued to be successful, the type of enterprise he founded no longer served as the same kind of model for other black entrepreneurs.

In 1978, Gaston was ready to reduce his involvement in the business world, and he came up with an innovative approach that once again was intended to benefit the black community: He devised an employee stock option plan and sold his Booker T. Washington Insurance Company to its workers for a small percentage of its market value. In Gaston's view, this way of ending his career was consistent with the way he had lived his whole life. He told *Black Enterprise* in 1992 that becoming rich had been accidental—his main goal was playing a helpful role in the African-American community.

Even after he sold his insurance company, Gaston remained active in the business world. Although he lost a leg to diabetes in the mid-1980s and was confined to a wheelchair, and though he suffered a mild stroke in 1992, he continued to return to work nearly every day, serving as chairman of the board of Citizens Federal and Booker T. Washington Insurance Company until virtually the end of his life. After he suffered his second stroke, Gaston died on January 19, 1996, leaving behind grandchildren and great-grandchildren to carry on his legacy. His motel has become a civil rights museum, and his memory lives on among both entrepreneurs and activists.

Further Reading

Gaston, A. G. *Green Power: The Successful Way of A. G. Gaston.* Birmingham, Ala.: Southern University Press at Birmingham Publishing Co., 1968. Reprint, Troy, Ala.: Troy State University Press, 1977.

———. "How to Make a Million." *Ebony,* January 1963, pp. 110–116.

Haskins, Jim. *African American Entrepreneurs.* Black Stars Series. New York: John Wiley & Sons, 1998, pp. 88–92.

Jackson, Harold. "True Grit." *Black Enterprise,* June 1992, pp. 230–234.

Lloyd, Foda Marie. "Footprints in Time." *Black Enterprise,* August 1995, pp. 109–120.

Marshall, David. "A. G. Gaston." *Black Enterprise,* July 1976, pp. 31–33.

Nelson, Stanley. "The Chicago Defender." The New West Indian. Available online. URL: http://www.awigp.com/default.asp?numcat=Chicago. Posted January 2003.

Smith, Eric L. "Blazing a Path for 100 Years." *Black Enterprise,* March 26, 1996, pp. 15–16.

Gates, Clifton W.
(1923–   ) *banker, realtor, mortgage broker*

Clifton Gates helped bring black enterprise in St. Louis, Missouri, out of the ranks of the small businesses and onto a citywide and statewide scale. The cofounder of Gateway Bank, one of the publishers of the *St. Louis Sentinel,* and a major presence in the city's real estate market, Gates rose to prominence in the wake of the Civil Rights movement though he faced scandal later in his career.

Gates was born on August 13, 1923, in Moscow, Arkansas, the son of Mattie and Lance Gates. His mother had died by the time his family moved to St. Louis in 1926, when Gates was 3, and his father died when Gates was 12. Gates and his brother were raised by an uncle during the depression, yet he managed to graduate from Sumner High School and attend two years at St. Louis's Stowe College before joining the U.S. Army and being sent to Europe.

Upon his return to St. Louis, Gates worked for 12 years at the U.S. Post Office, selling real estate after hours. He drove himself quite hard, surviving on four hours of sleep a night during his last years with the Post Office. In 1958, he finally left the security of that job to form C. W. Gates Realty, which prospered—in part because black-owned real estate firms were able to focus on the black portions of the city's segregated housing market. Gates also became vice president of Mid-Central Mortgage and Investment Company, a business he helped found. Since most white-owned companies refused to give mortgages to black people, Mid-Central was another example of how black-owned businesses were needed to serve black customers in the discriminatory environment before the Civil Rights movement.

By 1964, Gates was a prominent African-American businessman, and as such, was part of a group of local black leaders—including JAMES HURT, JR.—who applied for a national bank charter. Gateway National Bank was to be the first all-black-owned bank in Missouri, and the first bank of any kind chartered in St. Louis since the depression. He became president and chief executive officer of Gateway, which had a slow start but picked up after Gates was made the first black member of the St. Louis Board of Police Commissioners in 1966. Also in 1966, Gates and his colleagues brought in I. Owen Funderburg, a dynamic young man who became executive vice president at Gateway.

In 1968, Gates and some other black entrepreneurs were licensed to operate a local radio station, which he was ultimately unable to keep on the air. In that year, too, Gateway was showing a profit. Although the bank had been founded with the idea of helping black individuals get loans for housing and small businesses, Funderburg suggested seeking commercial accounts from white businesses as well. They also lengthened their hours, expanded their operations, and began training bank workers.

In 1970, Gateway's officers could claim a long list of black businesses that they had helped fund, including an excavating company, several service stations, a McDonald's franchise, a moving company, and two trash-hauling companies. Many of these companies had had trouble getting funding from white-owned banks, although Gateway also came in for criticism from some black businesses whom it did not fund. The bank was also hurt by the involvement of its employees in several robberies.

In 1972, Funderburg went on to Atlanta's Citizen's Trust Bank, a serious blow to Gateway but one that did not prevent the bank from growing. In 1980, however, Gateway was found to be holding more than $173,000 in bad checks—a crisis it had weathered by 1981, when Gates became chairman of the board.

By this point, Gates was a prominent political and civic leader in St. Louis, though one who had come in for his share of criticism. In 1968, his home was firebombed by a militant black group that felt he was hurting the African-American community, while in 1974 he failed to win the Democratic congressional nomination. However,

Gates also served as president of the Urban League and worked with the National Association for the Advancement of Colored People (NAACP).

In the 1980s, Gates set up Lismark Distributing Company to market products made by the Miller Brewing Company, the third black-owned firm to distribute Miller's products. In 1987, Lismark began distributing 7-Up as well, and by 1990 the firm had made the *Black Enterprise* list of the top 100 black-owned firms. In 1984, Gates was also put on the St. Louis Housing Authority.

At Gateway, however, a power struggle began in which Gates was ousted from the board in 1987, in the wake of several scandals. In 1989 he was back in power, and he remains the bank's largest shareholder. Gateway has had its ups and downs, but it continues to operate in St. Louis, while Gates remains head of Lismark and a prominent civic leader. In 1997, Gates became one of the major investors on a renovation of the Gateway Hotel, then an 80-year-old hotel in downtown St. Louis. The $172 million project was slated to include a renovation of the nearby historic Lennox Hotel, several restaurants, and other amenities, as well as a convention center. The hotel was expected not only to bring construction jobs and, eventually, convention and tourist business into St. Louis, but also to inspire other development projects in the city's downtown. Gates was clearly continuing his tradition of combining the entrepreneurial search for profit with an effort to improve conditions in urban St. Louis.

Further Reading

Gateway National Bank. "About Us." Gateway Bank website. Available online. URL: http://www.gatewaybank.com/about_us.cfm. Downloaded on January 27, 2003.

———. Gateway Bank & Trust Co. Online. Available online. URL: http://www.trustgateway.com. Downloaded on January 27, 2003.

Ingham, John, and Lynne B. Feldman. *African American Business Leaders: A Biographical Dictionary.*

Westport, Conn.: Greenwood Press, 1994, pp. 271, 274–276, 280.

Magrath, Betty. "Marriott Renaissance/HRI Selected to Build New St. Louis Convention Hotel." *Saint Louis Front Page* 2, no. 51 (December 22–28, 1997). Available online. URL: http://www.slfp.com/1222BIZp.htm.

Nicklaus, David. "St. Louis's Banks New Owners Have a Plan to Turn Things Around." *St. Louis Post-Dispatch,* January 22, 2001, Business Section Plus, p. 8.

Geddes-Willis, Gertrude Pocte   See WILLIS, GERTRUDE.

Gibson, Vivian
(1949–   ) *food products company founder*

Vivian Gibson is the founder and sole owner of the Mill Creek Company, which produces Vib's hot sauces and seasonings. Gibson's products are sold in more than 100 food stores throughout Missouri and Illinois, in Paradies shops at the Lambert–St. Louis International Airport, and online.

Vivian Ross was born in St. Louis, Missouri, the child of Randle H. Ross and Frances Elizabeth Hamilton Ross. Her father was a truck driver and a janitor at the family church. Her mother raised nine children and worked at home making objects for sale: hats, purses, crocheted doilies, and other handmade crafts.

Ross initially wanted to be a fashion designer, choosing industrial sewing as her focus at Vashon High School in St. Louis. After graduating in 1968, she spent two years at Tarkio College in Tarkio, Missouri, then went to Fashion Institute of Technology (FIT) in New York, where she worked as a receptionist while going to school at night.

Ross graduated from FIT in 1976 and started a millinery business, designing and selling women's hats to congregations at black churches. Although the venture was lucrative, Gibson grew discouraged about the prospects for a black woman designer in the fashion business. She gave

Vivian Gibson's hot sauces and seasonings are sold in more than 100 stores and other venues. *(Andrea Randolph)*

up her enterprise and focused on work at the consulting firm where she had been promoted from receptionist to head of personnel.

In 1977, Gibson married Walter Mayo, an executive at Chemical Bank, and the following year, the couple had a child, Elizabeth. In 1979, the family moved to Liberia, where Walter helped set up the Bank of Liberia. Vivian bought U.S. clothing and jewelry on her frequent trips to the United States and sold them to Liberians; however, her second enterprise was interrupted by Liberia's revolution.

Eventually, she divorced her husband and returned to St. Louis, where she began working full-time for the St. Louis public school system. She took various culinary courses and in 1990, she formed a partnership with a classmate to start a catering business, Moveable Feast. The two were unable to sustain the growth of the business, however, and sold it to a larger catering company in 1993.

By now Gibson had remarried and had two children, Elizabeth Mayo and Ross Gibson. She enrolled in St. Louis's Fontbonne College to take business courses, with the goal of figuring out why her earlier ventures had failed. When she graduated from Fontbonne in 1994 with a B.S. in business administration, she was planning to launch Vib's Caribbean Heat, a hot sauce. Then a cerebral aneurysm left her partially paralyzed and unable to speak for several weeks.

When Gibson recovered, she realized that she needed more support for her business than she could afford to pay for. She went to a marketing professor at Washington University School of Business and offered her business, the Millcreek Company, as a class project for his marketing students. The students prepared an elaborate marketing campaign, and Gibson began her operation as a one-woman project, working out of the bowling alley that she had used for her catering business. When she realized that the facility had no loading dock or elevator for transporting 55-gallon drums of vinegar to her second-floor kitchen, she purchased the vinegar in one-gallon containers and lugged them up the stairs herself, one by one.

In 1995, Gibson made an arrangement to sell her sauce through Paradies airport souvenir shops. She then got an account with Shnucks, an 85-store supermarket chain based in the Midwest. To fulfill her first order, she enlisted the help of family members to hand-pour sauce into five-ounce bottles.

Business was slow for Gibson initially, but a 1995 article in the *St. Louis Post-Dispatch* brought her needed publicity and enabled her to make a deal with Dierbergs, an upscale 22-store chain. She managed to find a food broker (an agent that places products in grocery stores); started writing a cooking column for the *St. Louis American*, a black weekly newspaper; and began teaching cooking classes. Her promotional efforts paid off, and in 1998, she debuted Vib's Southern Heat, a red hot sauce. Later she added other hot sauces to her product line, bought a bottling machine, and began contracting out some of the manufacturing work. She plans to add other products and to bring investors into her business. She also continues to recruit volunteers for the St. Louis public schools.

Further Reading

Beech, Wendy. "Recipe for Success." *Black Enterprise* August 1997. Available online. URL: http://www.blackenterprise.com/ArchiveOpen.asp?Source=ArchiveTab/1997/08/0897-24.htm.

Fiery Food Connection. "Vib's Sauces & Seasonings." Fiery Food Connection.com. Available online. URL: http://www.fieryfoodconnection.com/mfg-Vibs.asp. Downloaded on November 5, 2002.

Harris, Wendy. *Against All Odds, Ten Entrepreneurs Who Followed Their Hearts and Found Success.* New York: John Wiley & Sons, 2001, pp. 47–69.

Gidron, Dick
(Richard D. Gidron)
(1938–   ) *car dealer*

Dick Gidron rose to success in the automotive industry, owning top-performing car dealerships in the New York City area. As of this writing, he is the owner of Dick Gidron Ford and Dick Gidron Fleet and Leasing in the Bronx, a New York City borough, and of Dick Gidron Oldsmobile/Cadillac in Yonkers, a New York City suburb.

Gidron was born on October 10, 1938, in Chicago's South Side, a black neighborhood, the son of a railroad chef and a schoolteacher. When Gidron turned 14, his father died in a railway accident and his mother was left to raise three children on her own with the help of Gidron's grandmother, a strict disciplinarian.

Gidron attended Bryant Stratton College as a business major while receiving financial help from General Motors (GM) and working for GM part-time. He graduated in 1959 to become the first black person to sell Cadillacs in the history of the company. At the time, Cadillacs were considered a major luxury car, and Gidron's ability to sell them represented a pioneering step for African Americans. By 1967, he was earning $100,000 per year as the top Cadillac salesman in the country, a position he kept for four years running.

Gidron's success enabled him to become assistant branch manager of the Chicago dealership where he was working, despite the fact that some three-fourths of the outlet's customers were white. He went on to become general manager of the dealership, and then, in 1972, to take over a GM dealership that opened up in the Bronx, working closely with two African-American executives at the car company. Gidron was only the second black person to own a GM dealership—the first was ALBERT W. JOHNSON—and he made the New York franchise a success with the help of such highly placed connections as media executive and politician PERCY E. SUTTON and entrepreneur J. BRUCE LLEWELLYN.

Gidron was able to succeed despite the recessions and oil crises of the 1970s, which caused many other black-owned—and white-owned—dealerships to founder. Moreover, within two weeks of his taking over the company, he faced a labor dispute involving the sales force that eventually resulted in a citywide strike. Somehow, Gidron managed to make money even during the strike.

Gidron's dealership is located in an ethnically diverse part of New York City, but a sizable portion of his clientele is white. Yet Gidron has been able to increase his black customer base through persistent efforts at customer service and outreach. When he took control of the company in 1972, the white/black customer ratio was 75:25; by 1975 the ratio had shifted to 62:38.

Although Gidron felt a strong loyalty to GM, he wanted to branch out to Ford, which in 1983 had the nation's top-selling car, the Escort. Despite the ongoing difficulties facing black car dealers, Gidron managed to buy a Ford dealership in the Bronx, where he did very well. In 1982, the year before Gidron bought the outlet, it sold 395 cars and 166 trucks; by 1988, it sold 1,120 cars and 52 trucks.

In 1989, Gidron's chain of stores seemed to be flourishing, and he owned a total of four franchises: the Cadillac dealership where he got his start, two Ford stores in the Bronx, and a third in Mount Kisco, a New York City suburb. In that year, *Black Enterprise* dubbed him "Auto Dealer of the Year." Gidron had also branched out into insurance and real estate ventures in the Bronx and in Scarsdale, and bought a stake in NYT Cable TV.

In 1996, GM cancelled Gidron's Bronx franchise. Gidron responded by bringing suit against General Motors, which he claimed failed to support his business. Gidron argued that the dispute began when GM wanted to relocate his dealership, a move Gidron initially opposed but to which he eventually agreed. Negotiations ceased, however, when the dealership was closed for several months due to a tax dispute with the Internal Revenue Service. By the time the IRS claim was settled, GM had told Gidron that they were giving his franchise to another dealer. Gidron responded by suing GM, charging that GM was "redlining" the Bronx—refusing to offer services to this racially diverse community—a charge that GM has denied. However, at the time, only 1.2 percent of GM's dealers were black, a figure that Gidron cited to substantiate his claim of racial bias.

Over the years, Gidron has become involved in Bronx and New York City politics, although he turned down an offer to run for Bronx borough president when he decided that the position did not carry enough clout. His political connections have helped him with his business but have also caused him some trouble. Gidron had been a strong supporter of state senator Guy Villela, and when Manhattan district attorney Robert Morgenthau began investigating Villela on various charges, his suspicions fell on Gidron as well. In 2002, Morgenthau indicted Gidron for failure to pay income taxes and sales taxes. In June 2003, Gidron pled guilty to evading state and city sales taxes in exchange for five years probation and $1.6 million in restitution. He was sentenced for three years to restrict himself to only four locations—home, work, doctor, and church—and his car dealership was overseen by a court-appointed monitor.

Further Reading

"Black Dealer Alleges 'Redlining' by GM in Loss of Franchise." *Wall Street Journal,* July 16, 1996, p. B10.

Connors, Cathy. "Dick Gidron Sues GM in $257 Mil. Bias Suit." *New York Amsterdam News,* July 20, 1996, p. 5.

Gidron.com. Available online. URL: http://www.gidron.com/. Downloaded on January 15, 2003.

Hocker, Cliff. "Gidron's Ride with GM Comes to an End." *Black Enterprise,* February 1997, p. 30.

Hughes, Bill. "Manhattan D.A. Indicts Gidron in Fraud." The Journal News, November 27, 2002. Available online URL: http://www.thejournalnews.com/newsroom/112702/A327gidron.html.

Mangan, Dan. "Tax-Rap Car Dealer Looks for a Bargain." *New York Post,* November 26, 2002, p. 6.

Martin, D. "Luck and Pluck: From Poverty to Mega-Dealing." *New York Times,* May 19, 1990, p. 1.

Maull, Samuel. "Car Dealer Gidron Pleads Guilty in Tax Dodge." *Newsday,* June 23, 2003.

Thompson, Barbara. "District Attorney—New York County." New York County District Attorney's Office website. Available online. URL: http://www.manhattanda.org/whatsnew/press/2002-11-25.htm. Posted on November 25, 2002.

Swarms, Rachel L. "From Showroom to Courtroom." *New York Times,* November 16, 1996, p. 25.

Thompson, K. D. "Driven by Excellence." *Black Enterprise,* June 1989, p. 236.

Gordy, Berry, Jr.

(1929–   ) *record company founder, songwriter, media producer*

Berry Gordy founded what is arguably the most successful African-American enterprise of all time, Motown, the record company that grew to define the sound of an era and expanded to include enterprises in music publishing, artist management, film and television production, and other related businesses. The city of Detroit is now nicknamed Motown, after the company that Gordy founded there, while numerous artists— Gladys Knight, Diana Ross, Michael Jackson, Stevie Wonder, and many others—owe their beginnings to Gordy's company.

Gordy was born on November 26, 1929, in Detroit, the son of Berry "Pops" Gordy, Sr., and Bertha Gordy. Berry, Sr., was the son of a successful Georgia landowner and businessman; he himself was forced to leave Georgia because local white people were jealous of his success. He worked first as a plasterer, then as the owner of a print shop, where he eventually employed all eight of his children; he also owned a grocery store named for the African-American pioneer of self-help, Booker T. Washington. Bertha Gordy worked as an insurance agent.

Although Berry Gordy, Jr.'s family was relatively prosperous, segregation (the separation of people by race) forced Gordy, Jr., to grow up in the Detroit ghetto of the 1930s, where he attended public schools and dreamed of becoming a professional boxer like his hero, Joe Louis. He dropped out of Northeastern High School in his junior year to pursue that career and managed to win 12 of his 15 fights. Then he realized that, as a welterweight, he would never have the commercial success of a heavyweight boxer.

In 1951, still trying to settle on a career, Gordy was drafted into the army. In 1953, he was released, having received his high school equivalency diploma. He borrowed $700 from his father to open the Three-D Record mart, where he could sell the jazz he loved. The store soon went bankrupt, though, and Gordy worked for his father as a plasterer, wrote songs, and hung around Detroit's R&B (rhythm and blues) clubs.

Later that year, he married Thelma Coleman, with whom he eventually had three children. To support his family, he got a job at the Ford Motor Company's Wayne Assembly plant, but the monotony of the work drove Gordy to compose songs in his head, which he then tried to get performed at the R&B clubs.

Eventually, Gordy achieved some success writing songs for Jackie Wilson, who recorded "Reet Peteet" (written with Gordy's sister Gwen), "Lonely Teardrops," "To Be Loved," and "That's Why I Love You So," all for Decca Records. Gordy realized, though, that Decca made huge profits while paying small royalties, and he decided to found his own company.

Then, in 1958, he met Raynoma Liles, a musician whom he would marry in 1959. With Liles's advice and with another $700 borrowed from his family, he founded Motown Records (short for "Motor Town," a reference to Detroit's automotive industry). He ran the company on the first floor of a modest house while living on the second floor. In 1959, he released "Bad Girl," recorded by William "Smokey" Robinson and the Miracles—the beginning of a historic partnership.

Robinson convinced Gordy to market his records nationally, advice that paid off in 1960, when Gordy and Robinson wrote and recorded "Shop Around," whose 1 million sales made it Motown's first gold record. Gordy had grand ambitions for Motown, and when his single-home business blossomed to include several other buildings on the same street, he called his recording studio Hitsville, U.S.A.

In the early 1960s, white audiences were still somewhat threatened by black music, but Gordy reasoned that black women might frighten white people less than black men. At that time, R&B music was considered "black," while pop music was largely reserved for white people. Gordy determined to break down those categories. He discovered African-American teenager Mary Wells and began preparing her to become a star. She and Robinson sang a number of hits together, and Wells topped the charts in 1964 with "My Guy." Motown, meanwhile, was producing hits from a girl group called the Marvellettes, including "Please Mr. Postman" in 1961—Motown's first act to head the pop charts. In 1963, he had another hit with Martha and the Vandellas' "Heat Wave," and he also enjoyed success with the songs recorded by Marvin Gaye.

In October 1962, Gordy sent out the first Motown Revue, a 10-week tour featuring the Marvellettes, Marvin Gaye, the Supremes, and many other groups. During the same period, the Freedom Riders were touring the South, registering black people to vote and promoting the Civil Rights movement. The Motown Revue seemed to some white southerners the musical equivalent of this political activity, and the group's bus was shot at, while the artists were denied access in white-only hotels and restaurants. The group tried to perform for integrated audiences, but racial segregation was still in force.

Gordy had discovered the Supremes in the early 1960s, with Flo Ballard as the lead singer. Initially, the group was a black-identified R&B act. But Diana Ross rose from backup to lead singer as Gordy discovered that her voice was more suited for the more commercial sound that could make the group a pop success. Indeed, during the 1960s, the Supremes sold more records than any other group except the Beatles, with more than 12 million records to their credit. When Diana Ross left the group (by then called Diana Ross and the Supremes) in 1969, the Supremes continued to turn out hits with Cindy Birdsong as the lead singer.

Gordy struggled with Motown in the early years. The small size of his company meant that he had little financial margin for error. He had to depend on smaller and less reliable distributors to get his records into stores and he lacked the clout with radio stations that a larger company might have. Yet Gordy was able to create a sense of family among Motown artists, and a sense of excitement about the company's ambitions. Some artists found Gordy's supervision frustrating and overly paternalistic (too much like a father's). Others complained that Motown artists were encouraged to compete against one another to an almost unendurable extent. But many raw, young artists blossomed under Gordy's care, even if later, older and wiser, they sought to strike out on their own.

Gordy's next big success was the Jackson 5, headed by preteen Michael Jackson. Gladys Knight and the Pips were another Motown success, winning a number of Grammy Awards for the company. Gaye, Robinson, and later, Stevie Wonder also added to the company's roster of hits.

Capitalizing on his enormous success, Gordy went on to establish eight record labels, a management service, and a publishing company called Jobete. From 1964 to 1967, he had 114 top pop singles, 20 top R&B singles, 46 top-20 pop singles, and 75 top-15 R&B singles. Then, in 1967, the Detroit riots exploded, even as black and white audiences alike turned to a less pop and more inner-city sound, exemplified by such urban artists as James Brown, Aretha Franklin, and Otis Redding. White audiences were also turning to the psychedelic music of the Grateful Dead and similar groups. Motown responded by adding more African rhythms to its sound, and creating a more complex musical style. But Gordy recognized that an era had ended, and in 1970, he began to establish operations in Los Angeles, moving the company there officially in 1972.

Part of Gordy's interest in Hollywood was to make Diana Ross a movie star, an effort he began by producing the Oscar-nominated film *Lady Sings the Blues,* which starred Ross and which was co-written by his associate SUZANNE CELESTE DE PASSE. He went on to produce *The Bingo Long Traveling All Stars and Motor Kings,* about the Negro Baseball Leagues, starring Billy Dee

Williams and the young Richard Pryor; *Mahogany,* directed by Gordy and starring Ross as a supermodel; and *The Wiz,* starring Ross and Michael Jackson in an African-American version of *The Wizard of Oz.* Critics were not kind to most of these films, though some of them made money.

In 1983, Motown's 25th anniversary, the company was celebrated as the largest black-owned business in the United States—though it would soon be overtaken by JOHN H. JOHNSON's Johnson Publications and then by REGINALD FRANCIS LEWIS's TLC Beatrice International. But as early as the 1970s, Gordy had begun delegating Motown's leadership to others, and by this time, De Passe was clearly his second in command. She managed to win success for Motown in the television field, producing several successful specials and TV movies, but Motown was no longer defining the era's musical styles, despite the addition of such artists as Lionel Richie.

In 1986, rumors began to circulate that Gordy was going to sell his company, and in 1988, MCA and Boston Ventures bought the company for $61 million. Although DICK GRIFFEY had tried to buy Motown and to keep it a black-owned business, the company passed to white ownership, though Gordy held onto the publishing company (and the library of Motown's hits) and Hitsville, the Detroit recording studio. Gordy also controlled Motown Production, the media arm of the company. He went on to form the Gordy Company to contain these businesses, and in 1990, the firm boasted $100 million in revenue. By 1992, however, the Gordy Company was no longer considered to be 51 percent black-owned, and Berry Gordy was no longer considered an important force on the music scene.

Although many record companies before Gordy's had marketed black music and developed African-American performers of all types, Motown was the first record company to successfully market black music to a mainstream white audience. Gordy's success helped change the nature of popular music in America, establishing black artists on a hitherto unknown scale. His legacy continues to be honored as both a cultural and a political achievement for African Americans.

Further Reading

"Berry Gordy Resigns Post as Motown Records Chief." *Detroit Free Press.* Available online. URL: http://www.freep.com/motownat40/archives/0112 73mo.htm. Downloaded on November 12, 2002.

Gordy, Berry. *To Be Loved: The Music, the Magic, The Memories of Motown: An Autobiography.* New York: Warner Books, 1994.

Posner, Gerald. *Motown: Money, Power, Sex, and Music.* New York: Random House, 2002.

Singleton, Raynoma Gordy. *Berry, Me and Motown* (audio book). Los Angeles, Calif.: Publishing Mills, 1991.

Graves, Earl G.
(Earl Gilbert Graves, Earl Gilbert Graves, Jr.)
(1935–   ) *publisher, entrepreneur*

By founding the magazine *Black Enterprise,* Earl Graves has been one of the nation's major promoters of African-American entrepreneurship at all levels. Graves's magazine has both spread the word about successful black entrepreneurs and provided information and resources for running a business. In 2002, *Fortune* magazine called him one of the 50 most influential African Americans in corporate America.

Graves was born on January 9, 1935, in the Bedford-Stuyvesant neighborhood of Brooklyn, New York, a poor black community in New York City. His father was Earl Godwin Graves, a shipping clerk, and his mother was Winifred Sealy Graves. Graves's father always urged him to own something, since he saw self-employment and ownership as the key to success.

Graves graduated from Erasmus Hall High School, a well-known public school—the second-oldest high school in America—with few black students. He won a scholarship to Morgan State University in Baltimore, Maryland, where he made the dean's list (an honor given to those with high grades) and participated in a number of campus groups. When Graves was 19, his 47-year-old father died, so Graves had to work summers as a New York City lifeguard, as well as operating several campus enterprises during the year, among them a food and snack service, and a landscaping and gardening service. (Years later, Graves endowed Morgan with a $1 million gift to advance business education, and the university renamed its business school, in his honor, the Earl G. Graves School of Business and Management.)

While in school, Graves was also a member of the Reserve Officer Training Corps (R.O.T.C.), a program whereby college students could also qualify to be officers in the armed forces. When he graduated in 1958 with a B.A. in economics and joined the U.S. Army, his time in R.O.T.C. meant that he entered the service with the rank of second lieutenant. He served in the 19th Special Forces Group—the famous Green Berets—and was promoted to captain. When he left the service, he worked for a time as a narcotics agent with the U.S. Treasury Department but soon returned to New York, working at a real estate firm in Bedford-Stuyvesant.

In 1965, Graves volunteered to help out in Senator Robert Kennedy's office. Kennedy was widely viewed as a dynamic and exciting politician who stood for the rights of the oppressed. Graves was given a full-time position on Kennedy's staff within a year, and he worked for Kennedy until the senator's assassination in 1968. Graves then went on to form Earl G. Graves Associates, a consulting company to advise corporations on urban issues. Although he numbered many large, multinational firms among his clients, Graves wanted to have a broader impact on black economic development.

In 1969, Graves had gone on to work in Fayette, Mississippi, supporting Charles Evers's campaign to become the city's first black

Earl Graves's *Black Enterprise* magazine has promoted African-American entrepreneurs for more than 30 years. *(Courtesy of Earl G. Graves Publishing)*

The time seemed right for a magazine focusing on black entrepreneurs, but with a focus on how black-owned businesses would help the community as a whole. In August 1970, the first issue of *Black Enterprise* appeared, with the goal of showing that black people could aspire to wider career choices than working in civil service or teaching jobs.

From the first, Graves had a base of support that went far beyond the entrepreneurial world to include many of the key political leaders and organizations from the Civil Rights movement. He was endorsed by Whitney Young, Jr., head of the National Urban League, as well as by such groups as the National Association for the Advancement of Colored People (NAACP) and the Congress of Racial Equality (CORE). He also received support from business groups, including the National Business League, the Interracial Council for Business Opportunity, the National Association of Marketing Developers, the Office of Minority Business Enterprise, and the Black Advisory Council of the Small Business Administration. Eventually, Graves had amassed a list of 100,000 "present and future leaders of the black community" who had endorsed his magazine—and who would receive a free subscription in exchange. Graves then approached Chase Manhattan Bank's Capital Corporation president Lewis Allen for financing, and chose Pat Patterson of *Newsday* as his editor. Their first cover featured Charles Evers.

By 1973, readership had reached 125,000, but Graves still had trouble convincing large companies to advertise. Pulling advertisers is difficult for any new magazine, but a magazine with primarily black readers had an especially difficult time in the early 1970s, when most companies had not yet begun to target African-American consumers as an important segment of the market. Indeed, stereotypes prevailed at the time of "lazy" African Americans "who were all on welfare." By the 1990s, however, the magazine was selling ads to large corporations as well as to small businesses.

mayor. When Evers won, Graves began to think in new ways about the connection between entrepreneurial success—which Evers had achieved—and making a contribution to the black community. President Richard M. Nixon had won the 1968 presidential election, and it was clear that, unlike previous presidents, he had little sympathy for civil rights or black political struggle. Black enterprise, on the other hand, seemed popular with the new administration as a way of turning African Americans' attention away from politics and toward an allegiance to U.S. capitalism.

Meanwhile, Graves set up other enterprises of his own. Earl G. Graves Marketing and Research led to the formation of a related company, Minority Business Information Institute, a library with census tract data and two full-time professional researchers. EGG Dallas Broadcasting operated AM and FM radio stations in Dallas. In the mid-1980s, Graves also started a series of "networking seminars" to help black entrepreneurs meet one another and share information.

In 1990, Graves joined with L.A. Lakers starter Earvin "Magic" Johnson to obtain the Pepsi-Cola franchise in the Washington, D.C., area—the largest minority-owned Pepsi franchise in the United States, which handles accounts for the White House, the Capitol, Air Force One, and the vice president's residence. Graves sold his stake in the franchise back to the company in 1998, though he remains with the franchise as chair of the company's Customer Advisory and Ethnic Marketing Committee, and his youngest son, Michael, got an executive position with the company after the sale.

Also in 1998, Graves found a place for his son, Earl "Butch" Graves, who became president and chief executive officer (CEO) of Earl G. Graves Publishing, which includes *Black Enterprise*. Graves's middle son, John, was made head of Black Enterprise Unlimited, a company that markets products and services to the magazine's readers.

In 2000, *Black Enterprise* celebrated its 30th anniversary. At the time, the magazine had a circulation of 375,000, reached 3.1 million readers, and earned $47.9 million in annual revenue. By 2003, the magazine's circulation was more than 450,000, with a readership of at least 4.1 million. In a letter to his grandchildren that he published in the anniversary issue, Graves celebrated the gains of the Civil Rights movement but warned that African Americans continue to be impoverished by racism and discrimination. Ironically, Graves has been criticized for being harmful to the affirmative action programs that he himself supports: In 2000, president of the National Black Chamber of Commerce Harry Alford accused Graves of presenting an overly optimistic view of black enterprise, leading opponents of affirmative action to conclude that no such programs are necessary. Likewise, such critics as Manning Marable, author of *How Capitalism Underdeveloped Black America*, believe that Graves's faith in black entrepreneurship is misguided, as ultimately the business world will be harmful to African Americans as a group (as well as to white people), even if certain successful individuals benefit.

Graves, meanwhile, continues to speak out on the political issues that concern him, even as he publishes his magazine and pursues his other enterprises. In 1997, for example, Graves told then-president Bill Clinton that he was wrong to expect the private sector to train and hire the large number of people that were being thrown off welfare. People on welfare needed enormous support to enter the workplace, Graves pointed out, and it was unreasonable to expect business to shoulder those costs—particularly black-owned businesses, whose profit margins were low enough as it was. Graves's remarks made it clear that, in his own mind at least, a commitment to black entrepreneurship and a dedication to social justice can go hand in hand.

Further Reading

Browne, J. Zamgba "'We Won't Do Your Work for You,' Graves to Prez." *New York Amsterdam News*, March 1, 1997, p. 10.

Gale Group. "Earl B. Graves." *Business Leader Profiles for Students*. Vol. 1. Farmington Hills, Mich.: Gale Research, 1999. Reproduced in *Biography Resource Center*. Farmington Hills, Mich.: The Gale Group, 2003. Available online. URL: http://www.galenet.com/servlet/BioRC. Downloaded on January 12, 2003.

Gite, Lloyd. "Marathon Men Revisited." *Black Enterprise*, June 2002, p. 92.

Graves, Earl G. *How to Success in Business Without Being White: Straight Talk on Making It in America*. New York: Harper Business, 1998.

Haskins, Jim. *Black Stars: African American Entrepreneurs*. New York: John Wiley & Sons, 1998, pp. 135–140.

Smith, Ethan. "Eyes on the Enterprise." *New York*, April 10, 2000, p. 13.

Yazigi, Monique P. "Bringing a Son Up Right (Right Up to the Top)." *New York Times*, June 21, 1968, Section 9, p. 1.

Gray, Simon

(ca. 1800–unknown) *enslaved flatboat captain, enslaved lumber entrepreneur*

Simon Gray achieved remarkable success as an entrepreneur—while always remaining legally enslaved. Although he seems to have operated as a free man in practice, the slave system maintained him as the property of another man until the Civil War ended U.S. slavery.

Historians know little of Gray's early life, but he seems to have been born sometime around 1800, to enslaved parents. In the 1840s, Andrew Donnan, a blacksmith and merchant, hired Gray out to Andrew Brown to work in Brown's lumber company, which operated along the Mississippi. Gray quickly rose through the ranks. Within three years after he first appeared in the company records, he was directing a crew of rafters as they brought logs to a lumber mill in Natchez, Mississippi. In 1856, Brown promoted Gray to captain of a flatboat—a flat-bottomed boat used to transport merchandise up and down the Mississippi—and assigned Gray to make trips between Natchez and the company's operations in New Orleans, Louisiana. Gray worked as chief boatman until 1863. His duties included delivering lumber to New Orleans, selling lumber along the river, taking new orders, discussing prices with customers, and sometimes even deciding which customers might buy on credit.

Although he was legally a slave, Gray commanded free white employees of the company as well as other slaves, and his role as occasional paymaster for the white workers must have made his managerial position seem even more firmly established. His story illustrates some of the more surprising contradictions of slavery, a system in which African Americans were enslaved and yet could also work for wages, a system in which they were considered inferior and yet were often given managerial and entrepreneurial responsibilities, a system in which they were theoretically supposed to be closely supervised and yet were often allowed an astonishing degree of apparent freedom and mobility while still remaining legally enslaved.

Thus Gray was allowed to travel and to handle his employer's money, apparently trusted neither to escape nor to run off with company funds. He seemed to serve more as a manager and supervisor than as the lowest-ranked worker that his legal status would suggest.

In 1850, Brown purchased some members of Gray's family for $500, and in 1856, he purchased Gray's son, Washington, also for $500. Gray himself seems to have earned the money for these purchases (though as a slave he would have had no legal title to it), through his own ventures in carrying sand to New Orleans.

Although most slaves were forbidden to learn to read and write, Gray often wrote detailed reports of his activities for Brown, keeping records of his business transactions. After 1853, according to historian David F. Herr, he "lived as a free black in all but name." During the 1850s, Brown's business was doing well. He made Gray responsible for buying and transporting lumber in the Yazoo River area. Eventually Gray was in charge of all the company's logging business in the Mississippi River Delta.

Even after the Civil War broke out, Gray continued to work for Brown. Not until July 1863, when the Union army took Vicksburg, Mississippi, did Gray leave Brown's service—six months after the Emancipation Proclamation that had theoretically freed all the slaves in the Confederacy. There is no further record of Gray's life after that time.

Further Reading

Herr, David F. "Simon Gray." *Encyclopedia of African American Business History,* ed. Juliet E. K. Walker. Westport, Conn.: Greenwood Press, 1999, pp. 278–279.

Moore, John Hebron. "Simon Gray, Riverman: A Slave Who Was Almost Free." *Mississippi Valley Historical Review* 49 (December 1962): 472–484.

Greenlee, Gus
(William Augustus Greenlee, Big Red)

(1897–1952) *baseball team owner, ballpark owner, boxing promoter, saloon and nightclub owner, numbers operator, politician*

Gus Greenlee owned what is arguably one of the greatest baseball teams of all time: the Pittsburgh Crawfords, which included five future Hall of Famers: Leroy "Satchel" Paige, "Cool Papa" Bell, Josh Gibson, Judy Johnson, and Oscar Charleston. Greenlee helped to revive the Negro National League, built the first black-owned ballpark in America, and then worked with Branch Rickey to integrate professional baseball. He is a legendary figure in black baseball history who was active in a number of other enterprises as well.

Greenlee was born on December 26, 1897, in Marion, North Carolina, the son of a masonry contractor who built the town courthouse, hotel, and other important buildings. Although Greenlee's mother stressed education and racial pride—her sons became doctors and lawyers; her daughters teachers and businesswomen—Greenlee himself dropped out of his second year of college and migrated north to Pittsburgh in 1916 at age 19.

Greenlee's arrival in Pittsburgh later became legendary, as he described riding in on a freight train and shining shoes for a living. He went on to work at the Jones and Laughlin steel mill and drove a cab for a local undertaker. Eventually he acquired his own taxi. He was shipped overseas during World War I and wounded in battle, then returned to Pittsburgh. Soon, Prohibition—the federal law against buying or selling liquor—was in force, and Greenlee became known for selling bootleg (illegal) liquor out of his taxi. This made him a prominent figure in "the Hill," a black neighborhood that was home to many African Americans migrating north to escape the restrictive racial laws and lack of economic opportunity in the South.

Greenlee's fame led him to open the Paramount Club, a speakeasy (illegal nightclub) where bootleg liquor was served and jazz artists were booked. Although the police closed his club in 1922, Greenlee and a partner reopened in 1924. A local newspaper alleged that young white girls were "running wild" in Greenlee's club, and he lost his dance license—but soon he was able to open again.

Because of his experience booking acts into his club, Greenlee went on to found the Musical Booking Agency, with offices upstairs from the Paramount. His agency booked acts for many local clubs as well as his own. Greenlee also owned the Sunset Café, the Workingmen's Pool Hall, and the Crawford Grill, a major jazz club where such stars as Count Basie, Duke Ellington, Cab Calloway, Louis Armstrong, and the Mills Brothers performed regularly, and where singer Lena Horne got her start. Both black and white customers frequented the grill, which was the hub for all of Greenlee's activities, including the illegal ones.

Greenlee by this time had moved into the numbers racket, a lotterylike system that enabled poor people to bet regularly on three-digit numbers that came up every day. This kind of illegal gambling flourished in poor neighborhoods, enabling Greenlee to make as much as $20,000 to $25,000 per day when his business was at its height. His wealth and style earned him the nickname of "Caliph [Emperor] of 'Little Harlem,'" referring to his power in Pittsburgh's black neighborhoods.

Organized crime tried to enter the numbers game and cut into Greenlee's take, but he was able to pay off the police and politicians so as to retain his position. He was known for using his gains to help others in the black community, paying the college tuition of many young people, helping homeowners with their mortgages, providing poor people with food, handing out turkeys on holidays, and running a soup kitchen across from the Crawford Grill throughout the Great Depression.

Then Greenlee became known as the "Jesus of Negro Sport" for his support of black baseball.

Gus Greenlee owned one of the greatest baseball teams of all time—the Pittsburgh Crawfords, which included such superstars as Satchel Paige, Josh Gibson, and "Cool Papa" Bell. *(Carnegie Library of Pittsburgh)*

Until 1947, U.S. baseball was strictly segregated, with professional teams remaining all-white as black teams scraped along as best they could. In 1930, Greenlee bought the Crawford Colored Giants and took the unprecedented step of putting them on salary. He built an extraordinary team, throwing local players off the Giants as he replaced them with stars he had raided from other teams.

In 1933, Greenlee also built Greenlee Field, which cost the then enormous sum of $100,000 and was the first black-owned ballpark in the United States. Until that time, black baseball teams had "barnstormed"—traveling around from town to town, playing wherever they could. Occasionally they were able to use a professional team's park, as with the Pittsburgh Pirates' Forbes Field, but even then they were rarely allowed to use the locker room or other facilities and had to suit up and shower in a local YMCA. Greenlee's construction of a ballpark made a significant statement about the right of black ballplayers to be treated as equals and taken seriously.

A number of efforts had been made to organize black teams into a league, as far back as 1889. The most successful had been Rube Foster's effort in the 1920s to form the Negro National League (NNL), but this effort had failed by 1930. In 1933, Greenlee resurrected the NNL so that his team would have a league to play in—the most successful effort of them all. Like Greenlee, many team owners in the NNL were in black organized crime, since these were the African Americans of the time who could afford to own a team.

For a time, Greenlee had an astonishingly good team—but by 1937, he was facing difficulties. Though he had never expected his team to turn a profit, he was losing money in the numbers racket as the police stepped up their raids. He lost some of his players to the Pittsburgh Grays, a rival team run by CUM POSEY, and even more players to the Dominican Republic, when dictator Rafael Trujillo offered star pitcher Satchel Paige the staggering sum of $10,000 to play in his country's Dominican League. Paige left the Crawfords, taking nine other players with him. Greenlee disbanded the Crawfords in 1938, and his ballpark was demolished the same year to make room for a public housing project.

Greenlee had been promoting boxers since the 1930s. His greatest champion was John Henry Lewis, the 1935 world light-heavyweight champion. Lewis found few men to fight in his own weight class, so he began fighting heavyweights. He was successful until 1939, when he lost in 149 seconds to "Brown Bomber" Joe Louis. Lewis retired, and Greenlee got out of the fight game.

Greenlee continued to try to reenter baseball, eventually forming a semipro Crawfords team and raiding the NNL for players. In 1945 and 1946 he worked with the Brooklyn Dodgers' Branch Rickey to form the United States League, headquartered upstairs from the Crawford Grill. At that point, Rickey wanted to integrate professional baseball, and many people believed that the new league was primarily intended to provide him with a source of players. Indeed, six months after the league was formed, Rickey announced that he had signed Jackie Robinson to a contract, and in 1947, Robinson became the first African-American player in professional baseball.

Greenlee's involvement with the United States League enraged many in black baseball. When he raided teams for their best players, the Negro League teams suffered—and, eventually, both the white teams and Greenlee profited, along with the individual black players. Greenlee was helping to destroy black baseball, even as he was opening up new opportunities for black athletes.

Greenlee was eventually forced out of the numbers racket and faced even greater financial difficulties after the Crawford Grill burned down in 1951. He died on July 7, 1952, and his memory was honored with an enormous funeral. In 1988, the Pittsburgh Pirates and the Pittsburgh city government honored Greenlee further with a plaque commemorating his team and that of Cum Posey, who had "made Pittsburgh the center for Black Baseball in America during the years when the color line barred blacks from the major leagues."

Further Reading

Bankes, James. *The Pittsburgh Crawfords: The Lives and Times of Black Baseball's Most Exciting Team.* Dubuque, Iowa: William C. Brown Publishers, 1991.

Gardner, Robert. *Forgotten Players: The Story of Black Baseball in America.* New York: Walker & Co., 1993.

Holway, John B. "Cum Posey and Gus Greenlee: The Long Gray Line." *Blackball Stars.* Westport, Conn.: Meckler Books, 1991, pp. 299–328.

———. *Josh and Satch: The Life and Times of Josh Gibson and Satchel Paige.* Westport, Conn.: Meckler Books, 1991.

Mullen, Phil, and Mark Clark. *Blacks in Baseball: An Historical Perspective, 1867–1988.* Westport, Conn.: Meckler Books, 1991, pp. 123–138.

Ribowsky, Mark. *Don't Look Back: Satchel Paige in the Shadows of Baseball.* New York: Simon & Schuster, 1994.

Leonard, Buck, with James A. Riley. *Buck Leonard: The Black Lou Gehrig, the Hall of Famer's Story in His Own Words.* New York: Carroll & Graf Publishers, 1995.

Paige, Leroy "Satchel," as told to Hal Lebovitz. *Pitchin' Man: Satchel Paige's Own Story.* Westport, Conn.: Meckler Publishing, 1992.

Paige, "Leroy Satchel," as told to David Lipman. *Maybe I'll Pitch Forever: A Great Baseball Player Tells the Hilarious Story Behind the Legend.* Lincoln: University of Nebraska Press, 1993 (reissue of 1962 original).

Peterson, Robert. *Only the Ball Was White.* Englewood Cliffs, N.J.: Prentice-Hall, Inc., 1970.

Ribowsky, Mark. *The Power and the Darkness: The Life of Josh Gibson in the Shadows of the Game.* New York: Simon & Schuster, 1996.

Santa Maria, Michael. "King of the Hill." *American Visions* 6, no. 3 (June 1991): 20.

Griffey, Dick

(1932–   ) *concert promoter, record company founder*

Dick Griffey followed in the footsteps of such recording industry pioneers as BERRY GORDY, JR., to bring black music to white audiences. During the 1980s, his SOLAR (Sounds of Los Angeles Records) was one of the major black entertainment companies in the United States. By the end of that decade, it was the nation's 11th largest black-owned firm.

Dick Griffey was born on November 6, 1943, in Nashville, Tennessee. No information is available on his father, but his mother was Juanita Hines, an enormously popular gospel singer and later one of Griffey's own recording artists. Griffey went to public schools in Nashville and went on to Tennessee State University. From an early age, Griffey dreamed of owning a business—although he played football and was a musician, he dreamt not of a career as an athlete or artist, but rather as the man who owned the team or the record company. His mother once said in an interview that, even as a small boy, Griffey never wanted to work for white people.

After graduating from college, Griffey joined the air force, where he remained until 1966. He and former classmate Dick Barnett, who had become a player-coach for the New York Knicks basketball team, became co-owners of Guys and Dolls, an L.A. nightclub. Griffey did the bookings, which put him in touch with such popular groups as the Temptations, the Impressions, and the Four Tops.

Eventually, Griffey decided there was more money in filling a concert hall periodically than in trying to pack a club every night. He became a concert promoter at a time when there were relatively few black people in that field. His first concert—Count Basie and the Four Tops at an auditorium in San Bernardino, California—sold only 85 tickets to a hall of 10,000 seats, and the concert had to be cancelled. Griffey lost his back-

ers' money, but he continued to find support and to book concerts. Indeed, by the early 1970s, he was a major L.A. concert promoter who was beginning to develop a national reputation. As a cofounder of the Black Concert Promoters Association, he was also playing a national role in supporting African-American music as well as meeting such superstars as Stevie Wonder, whose 1974 tour Griffey organized.

In 1973, Griffey had been approached by producer and television personality Don Cornelius, who was then hosting the popular black music show *Soul Train*. Cornelius asked Griffey to book acts onto the show. In 1975, they cofounded Soul Train Records, getting a limited deal with RCA Records to distribute their albums. Although it took the company a while to get started, Griffey bought the recording rights for the Whispers, a group he managed, and RCA went on to distribute the groups' records.

Then the disco craze hit, and Griffey capitalized on it to establish his company. He helped form the group Shalamar, whose "Uptown Festival" became a huge success, and he discovered Carrie Lucas, whose "I Gotta Keep Dancin'" single likewise took off. Griffey later married Lucas as he went on to build his reputation in the music world.

In 1978, Griffey and Cornelius dissolved their partnership, and Griffey changed the company's name to SOLAR, signing another distribution contract with RCA. Griffey knew that to be successful, he had to find the right formula: black music that retained some of its gritty urban roots while softening the edges enough to appeal to a mainstream white audience. He created a blend of pop, soul, funk, and disco—somewhat similar to the sound developed by producer QUINCY DELIGHT JONES, JR., during the same era—and he continued to work with the highly successful Shalamar as well as with the funk band known as Lakeside. SOLAR was so successful in the early 1980s that the pop music magazine *Rolling Stone* compared the company to Motown as a veritable factory of hits.

Meanwhile, Griffey expanded into gospel, signing his mother and several other gospel artists. In 1981, he dropped his distribution deal with RCA to switch to Elektra-Asylum. His reputation as the producer of solid, middle-of-the-road hits was secure, supported by his insistence that all of his artists keep up a "squeaky-clean" image and avoid what he called the self-destructive behavior of drugs and other "negative" activities.

Griffey has continued to work as a concert promoter, as well as serving as president of United Black Concert Promoters. He has worked in a number of related areas, as well, founding Griff-co Management to manage his artists; Spectrum Seven and Hip Trip publishing companies, to handle the rights to SOLAR's songs; and Dick Griffey Productions, a video production company whose series *Sultans of Soul* was sold to cable. Running Solar Stables, where Griffey houses and trains his thoroughbred horses, is a beloved hobby of Griffey's.

Griffey's entrepreneurship has made him a major community leader in Los Angeles as well as nationwide. He has worked with youth gangs in Los Angeles, supported the Boys Clubs, and given money to the Sugar Ray Youth Foundation. When Jesse Jackson ran for president in 1984 and 1988, Griffey was a key adviser.

One of Griffey's ongoing frustrations is the tendency of black artists to prefer size and prestige over a loyalty to the black community, starting their careers with black managers, promoters, and record labels and then passing over to larger and more prestigious white companies as they become successful. He was also upset that when Berry Gordy sold Motown, the company went not to him, another black owner, but to MCA and Boston Ventures.

Despite his frustrations, Griffey's business ventures continue to find success. His African Development Public Investment Corporation, which trades African commodities (items for sale) and runs an air travel service, was a growing business in the early 1990s, even as Griffey's other businesses continued to do well. Griffey stands firm in his belief that black music is at once a spiritual, political, and financial base for the African-American community, and that it must be treated as a valuable resource by black Americans.

Further Reading

Graff, B. "Carrie Lucas." All Things Deep.com. Available online. URL: http://www.allthingsdeep.com/dge/carrie_lucas.htm. Downloaded on November 18, 2002.

Ingham, John, and Lynne B. Feldman. *African American Business Leaders: A Biographical Dictionary.* Westport, Conn.: Greenwood Press, 1994, pp. 307–312.

Lamb, Bill. "And We Danced. Solar Records." Dance Music of the 80s website. Available online. URL: http://www.andwedanced.com/1980/so1980.htm. Last updated on September 22, 1998.

H

Henderson, Henry F., Jr.
(Hank Henderson)
(1928–) *manufacturer*

Henry F. Henderson, Jr., is one of the few African-American entrepreneurs who founded his own manufacturing company, as well as one of the few to have entered the world of high-tech electronics. His H. F. Henderson Industries has been a major supplier of electronic products to such major corporations as Dow Chemical, Hershey Chocolate, Union Carbide, Goodyear, and General Electric and works extensively with the U.S. government.

Henderson was born on March 10, 1928, in Paterson, New Jersey, the son of Henry F. Henderson, Sr., the only black general contractor in northern New Jersey at that time. His mother was Elizabeth (Hamond) Henderson. Young "Hank" Henderson, Jr., was likewise the only black male at Passaic Valley Regional High School in Little Falls, New Jersey, while his cousin was the only black female. He was an outstanding athlete in baseball, basketball, and track, and he also managed the football team.

Henderson went on to the pre-law program at New York University but transferred to the State University of New York (SUNY) in Alfred after a year and a half when he realized that he was less interested in law than in engineering. In

1950, he graduated with an associate degree in electrical machinery and power distribution. Later he did graduate work at William Paterson College, Seton Hall University, and New York University.

A budding entrepreneur, Henderson hired other SUNY–Alfred students to work for him in a painting business for which his father supplied the equipment. After he graduated, he went to work for aircraft manufacturer Curtiss-Wright in Caldwell, New Jersey, grinding the insides of propeller blades. The work did not require the skill level that Henderson had acquired, and he wanted to transfer to the electronics department but eventually realized that such a position would not be open to an African American. In the early 1950s, color barriers were very strong, and Henderson was one of the few black people with his skills. He faced discrimination a second time when he applied for a job at Richardson Scale Company in Clifton, New Jersey, but by chance, as he was leaving the building after his interview, he met a high school colleague who introduced him to chief electrical engineer Enrico Klein. A second interview with Klein led to Henderson being hired, and he worked for the firm until 1967.

Meanwhile, in 1952, Henderson had built his own home in an all-white neighborhood, and in 1954 he used that home to found a part-time business. He and retired postal worker John Dotson began an electrical contracting company, with Dotson obtaining the contracts and Henderson doing the work at nights and on weekends—primarily in commercial and industrial buildings that preferred such after-hours work. When Richardson developed a backlog of work orders, Henderson offered to subcontract the work, a substantial boost to his company, which he then named H. F. Henderson Industries.

Like most new businesses, Henderson Industries (HI) had to take some initially low-paying jobs where the profit was minimal. Because of his dual role—as both employee and subcontractor to Richardson—Henderson also had to be careful not to compete with his employer. Still, HI prospered. On one occasion, Henderson built a console that was so large he had to take three beams out of his garage to get it out—but the business eventually expanded beyond Henderson's home into ever larger quarters, eventually locating in a 5,000-square-foot building in Paterson, New Jersey.

In 1967, Dotson sold his interest in the company, making Henderson a 99 percent shareholder, with his wife owning the other 1 percent. That was the year in which Henderson left his full-time job to focus on his own company. His business grew rapidly from that point on, with Henderson moving onto three acres of land in West Caldwell Industrial Park in 1971. He mortgaged his own house to finance the move, but he had to turn to his father to co-sign the other loan he needed. Eventually, Henderson was able to convince the bank to give him a loan on his own recognizance.

HI grew into a high-tech electronics company that specializes in various types of weighing systems and control panels. The company has relied heavily upon the 8(a) program of the Small Business Administration (SBA), a set-aside program that guarantees a certain number of contracts to minority-owned businesses.

Henderson has many firsts to his credit, including becoming proprietor of the first black-owned company to engage in a venture with a Chinese business—the Ta Chung Hua Rubber Tire Plant, with whom Henderson signed a contract in 1983. Although the contract was small, it opened the door to further international activity.

Also in 1983, Henderson became the first black person to serve as a commissioner on the Port Authority of New York and New Jersey, a post he held for 14 years. He chaired a number of committees during his tenure, including the prestigious Audit Committee, which had both financial and operational responsibilities. He was also chosen to head the Essex County Economic Development Commission.

Henderson has had a certain amount of criticism over the way he has handled racial issues. Very few of his employees are African American, and in the early days of his business, he often had a white employee stand in for him so that clients would not realize the company was black-owned. Henderson defends his hiring policies on the grounds that there are few black people with the skills he needs, and he felt that his other practices were necessary in a time when African Americans faced enormous discrimination.

Meanwhile, Henderson has been honored for his achievements. In 1985 he was named Small Business Person of the Year by the SBA and in 1986, he received an award from the National Black MBA Association for his contributions to the business community. He has received numerous other awards, including the James Cogswell Award from the Department of Defense in 1995.

Further Reading

Dingle, Derek. "The Next Generation of CEOs." *Black Enterprise,* February 1997, pp. 159–168.

Ingham, John, and Lynne B. Feldman. *African American Business Leaders: A Biographical Dictionary.* Westport, Conn.: Greenwood Press, 1994, pp. 313–322.

Henson, Josiah

(1789–1883) *enslaved plantation manager, free entrepreneur in Canada*

Josiah Henson was a slave of extraordinary entrepreneurial skill who managed his owner's plantations for many years while he himself was still enslaved. When he finally sought freedom in Canada, he put his skills to work in founding a number of enterprises within a free black community. The model for Harriet Beecher Stowe's famous character, Uncle Tom, who figured in *Uncle Tom's Cabin,* the real-life Henson showed extraordinary patience with and charity toward the people who enslaved him, but unlike Stowe's character, he eventually rebelled.

Henson was born on June 15, 1789, in Charles County, Maryland, the son of a man he called "Dr. Josiah McP." in the narrative he later published about his life. Henson remembered his first owner as unusually kind, but when he died, Henson was sold to a crueler man. The white overseer on the new plantation turned out to be a thief whom Henson exposed. He was rewarded with the position of superintendent while he was still only a teenager. According to his own account, Henson raised double the crops that had previously been grown on the estate, with fewer problems among his fellow slaves.

Sometime around his 18th year, Henson heard his first preacher, a powerful experience that eventually led to his own conversion. Later he, too, became a preacher, an influential position in slave society. At age 22, Henson married a woman with whom he eventually had 12 children, eight of whom survived.

When Henson was in his mid-30s, his owner married a much younger woman, whose spending habits Henson saw as bringing ruin to the plantation. At one point, Henson's owner believed that all his possessions, including the humans he owned, might be seized by the people to whom he owed money. He made Henson promise to take a group of 18 slaves to a new plantation in Kentucky. The trip involved pass-

Plantation manager and entrepreneur Josiah Henson was the real-life model for "Uncle Tom" in Harriet Beecher Stowe's famous novel, *Uncle Tom's Cabin.* (*From* Father Josiah Henson's Story of His Own Life, *in the Albert and Shirley Small Special Collections Library, The University of Virginia Library, Charlottesville, Virginia*)

ing through the free state of Ohio, where abolitionists approached the group and suggested that they escape to freedom. Henson, however, had always intended to buy himself rather than run away, and he also believed he was bound by his promise to his owner. He convinced the rest of the group to remain enslaved and continued on with them to Kentucky. For a while, Henson was happy on the new plantation. Then, a few years later, word arrived that all the slaves except Henson's family had to be sold, and Henson was racked with regret over his part in convincing the slaves to forgo their chance to be free.

Henson tried to raise money to buy his freedom, but his owners cheated him in various ways. Then he was ordered to accompany Amos, the 21-year-old son of the man who ran the Kentucky plantation, on a trip to New Orleans. Henson knew that he would be sold into the harsh slavery of the Deep South, where he would almost certainly die. He decided to kill the other men on the boat and make a break for freedom—but on the night of the murder, he realized that, as a Christian, he could not commit such an act, no matter what the consequences to himself.

Henson was saved at the last moment from being sold when Amos came down with a severe case of river fever and Henson was needed to care for him. Even after this act of devotion, however, his owners did not offer him freedom, and in 1830, Henson finally resolved to escape with his wife and all his children. Both Indians and sympathetic white people helped the Hensons reach Canada, where Henson found employment among a colony of escaped slaves.

In Canada, Henson's son Tom discovered that his father could not read, and offered to teach him. Although Henson felt shame at his illiteracy, he realized that it was more important to learn how to read than to preserve his pride.

In 1841, Henson engineered a scheme where he and a group of abolitionists could purchase 400 acres near Dresden, Ontario, to found the Dawn Settlement, a community where free black people could begin a new life. In 1842, Henson and his colleagues founded the first black vocational school in North America, the British American Institute for fugitive slaves. Students spent their mornings working in local industries, gristmills, sawmills, and farms, while spending their afternoons learning basic skills.

Henson also worked with the Underground Railroad to help others escape U.S. slavery. He is credited with helping 118 people find freedom in Canada. His descendants later founded the Uncle Tom's Cabin Museum in Dresden so people could learn the truth of Henson's legacy.

Further Reading

Brown, Cheryl. "'Uncle Tom's Cabin'—The Josiah Henson Historical Centre." Footsteps to Freedom 2001. Available online. URL: http://rims.k12.ca. us/ugr/urg_2001/day5_01/htm1/henson.html. Downloaded on January 11, 2003.

Henson, Josiah. *The Life of Josiah Henson.* Boston, Mass.: A. D. Phelps, 1849. Available online. URL: http://docsouth.unc.edu/neh/henson49/menu.html.

Railton, Stephen. "The Original 'Uncle Tom'?" Uncle Tom's Cabin & American Culture, The Institute for Advanced Technology in the Humanities. Available online. URL: http://www.iath.virginia. edu/utc/africam/henson5881.html. Downloaded on January 11, 2003.

Uncle Tom's Cabin Historic Site. Available online. URL: http://www.uncletomscabin.org. Downloaded on January 11, 2003.

Hobbs, Elizabeth   See KECKLEY, ELIZABETH.

Holland, Jerome Heartwell
("Brud" Jerome H. Holland)
(1914–1985) *educator, diplomat, New York Stock Exchange director, member of many boards of directors*

Jerome "Brud" Holland had a number of "firsts" to his credit: He was the first African American to play football for Cornell University, the first to chair National Planned Parenthood and World Population (1970) and the U.S. Red Cross (1979–1985), and, most significantly, he was the first to serve as a director of the New York Stock Exchange (NYSE), a position he held from 1972 through 1980. Although Holland's main interests were in scholarship and education, throughout his life he found himself active in a wide range of activities.

Holland was born on January 9, 1916, in Auburn, New York, the son of Robert Howard Holland, a gardener and handyman, and Viola

(Bagby) Holland, a homemaker who sometimes worked in a local factory. The Hollands had 13 children and not much money, so Jerome began working for his father at age eight, even as he attended Auburn Public Schools.

In the 1920s, African Americans were steered onto what was known as the "commercial" or "business" track in high schools, which led to work immediately after high school, as opposed to the "academic" track, which led to college. At first Holland accepted this discriminatory pressure and completed the commercial track, but he spent an additional year after graduating high school taking academic subjects so that he would be eligible for college.

Jerome "Brud" Holland was the first African American to serve as a director on the New York Stock Exchange. *(AP/Wide World Photos)*

Holland entered Cornell University in Ithaca, New York, in the fall of 1935—a time when it was unusual for anyone to attend college, much less an African American from a poor family. Because the tuition was lower, he studied in the agricultural college, though his interest was in sociology. To make ends meet, he worked at various jobs, including cleaning a fraternity house. In those days, dormitories and on-campus housing at Cornell was restricted to white students, so Holland was forced to live off campus. Despite financial and social pressures, he made the honor society in his junior and senior years.

At the time, discrimination against African Americans extended to the sports world, yet Holland became the school's first black football player, making the varsity (top-level) team and becoming an All-American left end in 1937 and 1938, a prestigious achievement that ought to have improved his chances at finding a job. However, unlike his fellow white students, Holland was ignored by the job recruiters who came to campus seeking new employees. (His achievements were recognized years later in 1965, when he was elected to the National Football Hall of Fame.) After he graduated in 1939, he found a job at Lincoln University in Oxford, Pennsylvania, where he taught sociology and coached football, studying during the summers for his M.S. degree in sociology, which he received from Cornell in 1941. He married Madeline Smalls, with whom he had two children before divorcing her in 1944.

In 1941, the United States entered World War II, and Holland went to work in 1942 as director of personnel for the Sun Shipbuilding and Drydock Company of Pennsylvania. Like so much else in U.S. society, war production work was segregated, so Holland worked at the construction yard set aside for black workers. He remained there until 1946, a year after the war ended, when he took a job as chair of the Department of Political and Social Sciences and football coach at Tennessee State College in

Nashville (later Tennessee Agricultural and Industrial State University). On August 22, 1948, he married Laura Mitchell, with whom he had two children.

Holland had been studying for his Ph.D. in sociology, which he obtained in 1950 from the University of Pennsylvania. He went on to work as a social research consultant for the Pew Charitable Trust in 1951. The trust, located in Philadelphia, was known for its support of black higher education, which may have explained its interest in Holland. In 1953, he became president of a black college, Delaware State College in Dover. Enrollment at the school was so small that the school was on the verge of closing, but Holland built new buildings, increased enrollment, gained accreditation (validation of the school's academic credentials), and turned the all-black college into an integrated institution.

In 1960, Holland moved on again, to take the presidency of a private Virginia college known as the Hampton Institute. He showed the same business flair at Hampton that he had displayed at the shipyard and at Delaware State: He increased the school's endowments (money invested so that the school can receive the income) and again expanded the school's physical plant.

In 1970, Holland received his greatest honor so far: appointment to the ambassadorship to Sweden by President Richard M. Nixon. At that time, Sweden had been greatly critical of the U.S. role in pursuing the Vietnam War. U.S. citizens who wished to escape the draft—including numerous African Americans—were offered asylum (safety) in Sweden, which strained relations between the two countries. Holland was expected to restore goodwill between the two nations, which he managed to do, although at great personal cost. He reported that his visibility as a black man in the largely white nation led to him being publicly insulted and that he had heard racial slurs in Sweden that were rare in the United States.

In 1972, Holland resigned the ambassadorship and moved to Yonkers, a suburban community outside of New York City. This is when he began his long term of community service, his tenure on the Stock Exchange, and his service on a number of corporate boards, including AT&T, Chrysler, Federated Department Stores, General Foods, Union Carbide, and Manufacturers Hanover. He was a trustee and officer of many nonprofit and service organizations, including the Institute of International Education, the United Negro College Fund, the northeast region of the National Council of Christians and Jews, the Salvation Army, Cornell University, Massachusetts Institute of Technology, and the American Academy of Arts and Sciences.

Holland exemplifies the kind of groundbreaking African American who opened doors for himself and others in the wake of the Civil Rights movement, approaching the issue of racial discrimination with strength, determination, humor, and a profound commitment to education. In his book, *Black Opportunity*, which he published in 1969, he argued for education as the route to black self-empowerment, commenting that through education "we acquire and believe in our own dignity, self-respect, and assurance. . . . [We] accept equality as a natural right." It makes sense, then, that most of Holland's life was spent as an educator—yet his role on the New York Stock Exchange was a significant one for black entrepreneurs and business leaders, as his presence was a silent assertion of the rights of African Americans to participate in U.S. business life.

Holland was known as a charming, attractive, and friendly man whose warm manner and powerful speaking ability made him particularly effective in community service. He became fatally ill with lung cancer in the 1980s and died of that disease in New York City on January 13, 1985. That year, his contributions were recognized by President Ronald Reagan, who posthumously (after his death) awarded him the Presidential Medal of Freedom.

Further Reading

Hill, Marilyn Wood. "Jerome Heartwell Holland." *The Scribner Encyclopedia of American Lives, Volume 1: 1981–1985.* New York: Charles Scribner's Sons, 1998.

Holland, Jerome. *Black Opportunity.* New York: Weybright and Talley, 1969.

Netter, Richard. "Commemorating 40 Years." Workplace Diversity Network, School of Industrial and Labor Relations, Cornell University. Available online. URL: http://www.ilr.cornell.edu/extension/wdn/pdf/n etter_remarks.pdf. Posted on May 5, 1998.

Thomas, Sasha. "Jerome Heartwell Holland." *Encyclopedia of African-American Culture and History.* 5 vols. New York: Macmillan, 1996.

Hughes, Cathy
(Catherine Elizabeth Hughes)
(ca. 1947–   ) *owner and chief executive of radio network*

Cathy Hughes runs the largest African-American-owned radio broadcasting company in the United States, Radio One, Inc., a 29-station radio network that makes her the most powerful woman in radio and the first African-American woman to head a publicly traded company. In an economic climate that has seen a steady decline in the number of black-owned stations, Hughes's empire has grown, making hers a highly unusual type of success story.

Hughes was born Catherine Elizabeth Woods sometime around 1947 in Omaha, Nebraska, where she grew up with three younger siblings in a public housing project, the children of accountant William Alfred Woods and musician Helen Jones Woods. She was the first African-American student at a local Catholic girls' school, where she did well until she became pregnant at age 16. She married Alfred Liggins, the baby's father, before their son, Alfred Liggins, Jr., was born, but although her son continued to be "my motivation

and my inspiration," in her oft-quoted words, her marriage lasted only two years.

Nevertheless, she finished high school and began taking courses in business administration. In 1971, she began working as the administrative assistant of noted broadcaster Tony Brown, founder of the communications department at the historically black Howard University in Washington, D.C. In 1973, Brown gave her a job at WHUR-FM, the school's radio station, and in 1975, he promoted her to vice president and general manager—the first female general manager in that media market. She claims to have increased the station's billing from $250,000 per year to $3 million in 18 months, and to have invented the radio format that she called "The Quiet Storm," the now ubiquitous format in which a sexy-voiced announcer plays love songs with sexual overtones. She tried without success to get the university to license the format, leading her to dream of owning her own station where she might profit from her own ideas.

Later, she married Dewey Hughes, a television producer. She had moved to the D.C. gospel station WYCB-AM in the late 1970s, where she spent six months as president and general manager before joining with her husband in an effort to purchase their own station. In 1980, the couple bought the D.C. station WOL-AM, which they purchased with $100,000 from their own savings, $150,000 from investors, and $300,000 from an African-American-owned venture capital firm. They had to approach 32 banks before obtaining the loan that enabled them to raise the additional $400,000.

Hughes's plan was to have an all-talk radio station that focused on African-American issues, and hers was the first such station in the Washington, D.C., area. When her second marriage ended, she was in a tough financial position, particularly in early 1982, when the bank threatened to cut her funding unless she switched from talk to music. Hughes negotiated a compromise: music during all but the morning hours, when she herself became the talk-show host for lack of funds to hire a professional. Her show became vastly influential, offering her a power base within the black community. In 1987, she led a 13-week protest among the black community against alleged racial insensitivity at the *Washington Post* magazine—an action that ultimately led to an on-air apology from the newspaper's publisher and editor. She continued to host the show until 1995.

Hughes had managed to make her station profitable by 1986, and in 1987, she went on to buy another local station, WMMU-FM, for $7.5 million. When federal regulations against multiple ownership within a single market were relaxed in the mid-1990s, Hughes further expanded her network, at a time when the number of African-American stations was dropping rapidly. In 1999, Radio One went public, raising $172 million in an initial public offering.

Hughes's son went on to get his M.B.A. at Wharton University in Pennsylvania, even as he took an active part in Hughes's radio network and eventually went on to purchase his own separate station. Hughes claimed to have been harder on her son than on any other employee, paying him on commission rather than on salary. Meanwhile, she continued to maintain her own interest in creating jobs for black broadcasters and particularly for women.

Hughes has been a controversial figure throughout her career. While some have applauded her evident devotion to the black community, others have accused her of putting herself and her drive for profits first. She has also been charged with a pro-black attitude that some people consider prejudicial to other races. Meanwhile, her radio empire continues to grow, and she continues to win a number of awards for her contributions to African Americans, including the first annual Black History Hall of Fame Award (2000) and the National Action Network's "Keepers of the Dream" Award (2000), given to those who carry on Martin Luther King, Jr.'s legacy.

Further Reading

Anthony, Florence. "Life Beat Goes On." *New York Amsterdam News*, October 21, 2000, p. 32.

Brown, Jeremy. "Cathy Hughes." *Current Biography* 61, no. 2 (February 2000), p. 33.

Gale Group. "Cathy Hughes." *Newsmakers* 1999, no. 1, Farmington Hills, Mich.: Gale Research, 1999.

———. "Cathy Hughes." *Contemporary Black Biography*. Vol. 27, ed. Ashyla Henderson. Farmington Hills, Mich.: Gale Research, 2001.

Jones, Charisse. "Owning the Airwaves." *Essence*, October 1998, p. 112.

Jones, Joyce. "Keeping It in the Black." *Black Enterprise*, May 1995, p. 22.

Norment, Lynn. "Cathy Hughes: Ms. Radio." *Ebony*, May 2000, p. 100.

Stark, Phyllis. "Radio One Owner/CEO Building an Empire." *Billboard*, January 14, 1995, p. 61.

Hurt, James, Jr.

(1923–unknown) *banker, newspaper publisher, grocery store owner, developer*

James Hurt helped to raise a St. Louis, Missouri, business from the mom-and-pop level to a grander scale. For a while, he was a director and cofounder of Gateway Bank, owner of a major grocery store, and a primary developer in black neighborhoods in the city. Yet ultimately, his empire dissolved in a scandal that caused him to leave the city and mysteriously disappear, having lost the fortune he had once enjoyed.

Hurt was born sometime in 1923, the son of James Hurt, Jr., a respected physician and entrepreneur, who founded the Employees Loan and Investment Company in 1938 with the goal of helping black people obtain loans after white institutions had refused them. The young James grew up and attended public schools in St. Louis, working as a janitor at his father's company from the age of 12. He wanted to attend college in St. Louis but both Washington University and St. Louis University refused to accept African-American students, so Hurt enrolled for a while in Ohio State University in nearby Athens, Ohio.

Then World War II caused Hurt to interrupt his studies with military service in Asia, where he served three years. After the war, he was finally able to enter St. Louis University, graduating with a B.A. in commerce and finance in 1948. He then went to work for seven years with his father's company.

Eventually, Hurt moved on to the St. Louis Housing Authority, where he managed a troubled housing project for two years. In 1956, Hurt's father gave up active management of his company to take the less-active role of chairman of the board, and in 1957, Hurt, Jr., took over as president and chief executive officer, with an aggressive asset-management plan of selling stock and investment certificates.

In 1960, Hurt was asked by the Citizen's Association for the Public Schools to run for a seat on the School Board, a post he held for many years, going on to become president in 1967. He had become a prominent and well-respected black businessman—but his very reputation for compromise and accommodation earned him the distrust of some segments of the black community, who viewed him as an "Uncle Tom" who was too closely linked to white power structures.

Meanwhile, in 1964, Hurt joined with CLIFTON W. GATES and some other black businessmen to found Gateway National Bank, where he served on the board of directors. The bank had its ups and downs, but it continues to operate to this day. Hurt served as a director of the bank but took a more active role in other enterprises.

Throughout the 1960s and into the 1970s, Hurt ran the finance company his father had founded, which eventually became the foundation for a mini-empire of related enterprises. For example, he discovered that his company was financing furniture that other companies were selling. So he moved into the furniture business, setting up Vanguard, Inc., as a company that would eventually include many subdivisions. He also formed Vanguard Bond and Mortgage Company to run a public housing project, supervise the construction of two others, and sell subsidized one-family homes to low-income families. That company also won a government contract to provide training and orientation to low-income homeowners.

In 1968, Hurt cofounded the *St. Louis Sentinel.* The following year he opened Central City Foods, a supermarket in a black neighborhood, built, run, and primarily staffed by African Americans. The store represented a dream of black entrepreneurship and self-sufficiency, a way of keeping black people's money within the community. Hurt's Vanguard Redevelopment Corporation helped finance the construction of the store, with Vanguard owning the land, constructing the facility, and renting it to Central City. The U.S. Small Business Administration subsidized the project by guaranteeing that the rent would be paid. Hurt also leased some of the land to Ralston Purina, which built a Jack-in-the-Box fast-food restaurant there.

Black Power activists saw entrepreneurs like Hurt as too closely allied with the white power structure, and in 1969, his company was fire-bombed. But Hurt continued to prosper. In 1970, he set up Vanguard Volkswagen, the first black-owned Volkswagen dealership in the United States. He later announced his plan to expand his grocery store into a national chain, and he started working with black architects and subcontractors to develop more black construction projects. Hurt's Vanguard Bond went on to work on the redevelopment of a troubled black neighborhood in St. Louis, an ambitious project that would have involved many of Hurt's businesses.

Then he began to face an increasing number of difficulties. After his father died, Hurt fell behind with tax payments on his father's estate. He was hit with a number of court decisions that challenged his operation of various companies and ordered him to repay funds that had been spent improperly. A group of stockholders sued for the dissolution of his father's company and for Hurt's removal from his post there. His Vanguard Construction and Development company defaulted twice on low-income apartments that it was supposed to build for the St. Louis Housing Authority. Hurt was accused of passing bad checks and was arrested twice for brief periods in 1975 and 1976. After being released from his second arrest, he disappeared from St. Louis, and no further information is available on him.

Further Reading

Gateway National Bank. "About Us." Gateway Bank website. Available online. URL: http://www.gatewaybank.com/about_us.cfm. Downloaded on January 27, 2003.

———. Gateway Bank and Trust website. Gateway Bank & Trust Co. Online. Available online. URL: http://www.trustgateway.com. Downloaded on January 27, 2003.

Ingham, John, and Lynne B. Feldman. *African American Business Leaders: A Biographical Dictionary.* Westport, Conn.: Greenwood Press, 1994, pp. 271–280.

J

James, Charles Howell (1862–1929) and
Charles H. James III (Chuck James) (1959–)
food processing company executives, whole-sale/retail distributors

C. H. James & Co. is one of America's oldest continuously existing black businesses, despite the fact that it is located in West Virginia, a state with a small black population and little tradition of hospitality to African Americans. Nevertheless, this venerable food-processing company has survived for over a century, through four generations of African-American ownership, changing to fit the times but always supporting the James family.

Charles Howell James was the founder of the enterprise. He was born sometime in 1862 in Gallia County, Ohio, the son of Francis and Elizabeth Courtney James. Little is known about Charles's mother, but his father was fighting for the Union when Charles was born. After the war, Francis James moved his family to West Virginia, where he became a Baptist minister and taught for a time in the new public schools set up for black people. As a child, Charles was sent to live with his grandfather in Ohio, returning in 1880 to rejoin his father in West Virginia.

Charles James became a teacher for a time, but he soon decided that he preferred the world of business. Perhaps as early as 1881 and certainly by 1883, he and his three brothers had become peddlers, pooling their little bit of money to buy merchandise to sell, including ginseng, medicinal herbs and bark, and novelty items, such as pictures of recently assassinated president James A. Garfield. The James brothers were trading among extremely poor farmers, so they began bartering their items for local produce instead of cash—produce that they then sold at a profit in Charleston, West Virginia. Soon they had bought a mule and wagon to transport their goods, establishing a profitable trade: They bought their goods on credit from wholesale houses in Charleston; traded them to poor farmers; sold the farmers' produce to Charleston hotels, restaurants, and grocers; and then paid their bills at the wholesale houses.

In 1885, James married Roxy Ann Clark, with whom he had six children. Meanwhile, the family business continued to prosper. Although this was a period when anti-black legislation was increasing throughout the South, along with severe violence against African Americans, the James family's customers were almost entirely white. In 1894, Charles's brother Garland was shot while on one of his trading trips, but the other family members simply avoided that area and continued doing business as before.

Around this time, another brother died, and a third brother decided to immigrate to New

Zealand and later to São Paulo, Brazil. Meanwhile, Charles's only son to reach adulthood, Edward Lawrence James, was growing up. In 1916, Charles asked his son to leave school and help with the business, which was being transformed from a retail business to a wholesale food distributor. With Edward as his partner, Charles went on to build a three-story warehouse in Charleston for the business now called "C. H. James & Son, Wholesale Produce."

The James family imported fresh fruit and vegetables from as far away as Cincinnati, Ohio, and Richmond, Virginia, distributing their produce with a fleet of 10 trucks and operating with a staff of 30 employees. All of the company's sales agents were black, and each had a company car. James was active in a number of enterprises, including serving as director of the Mutual Savings and Loan and the Mountain State Building and Loan Association in Charleston. A follower of Booker T. Washington, who preached black self-help and black business ownership, James was a longtime supporter of Washington's National Negro Business League, helping the group to set up local chapters across the United States. He also served as an elder in the local black Baptist church, and helped to found a local chapter of the civil rights group, the National Association for the Advancement of Colored People (NAACP), leading a protest against the film *Birth of a Nation*, which portrayed black people as dangerous rapists and the Ku Klux Klan as heroic guardians of the white race.

Charles James retired from his prosperous company in 1926, leaving it in the care of his son. He died on February 2, 1929, and soon after, his son petitioned for bankruptcy, for the company his father left him was owed money by many customers and was then unable to weather the stock market crash. Although Edward James lost everything he had and was forced to take a job on a federal assistance project, he found a way to reestablish the family business, selling eggs and, later, fresh-killed poultry. By 1940, the company

was showing a profit, but hard times were still ahead. In 1952, their poultry-processing plant was destroyed by two suspicious fires, so Edward James left the processing side of the business and began simply distributing fresh-dressed poultry (chickens that had already been plucked) and brokering sales of frozen food. Eventually, he bought the warehouse and freezer facilities that enabled him to sell frozen food full-time, as well as selling canned goods to hotels, restaurants, and other large customers.

In 1961, James Produce was incorporated, and Edward retired, handing the business to his son, Charles Howell James II. Under the third generation's leadership, the business prospered in the 1960s but its growth slowed or stopped in the 1970s and 1980s. In 1989, the fourth generation, Charles H. James III, joined the company.

Charles James III was an ambitious young man, the son of Charles James II and Lucia Jeannette Bacote James. Born in 1959 and educated at Morehouse College, he had worked for two years as a banking associate at Continental Illinois Bank, a Chicago company. Then he attended Wharton School of Business, where he got an M.B.A. and wrote a thesis analyzing his family's business. In 1985, he returned to Charleston, running the company unofficially until 1988, when a series of heart attacks led his father to liquidate the business and sell it to his son. In 1989, Charles James III founded the James Corporation as a holding company, with the business operating through a wholly owned subsidiary known as C. H. James & Co. These legal and financial maneuvers were designed to separate the family's personal assets from the business, in case there should ever be another bankruptcy.

Charles James III renovated the company's employment practices so that its 25 employees were encouraged to participate more actively in the life of the firm. He sought national contracts, feeling that unless the company became a national and international presence, it would fail. Although in 1987 the company had no national contracts, by 1991, half the firm's business came from such arrangements. The younger James also pursued minority set-aside contracts—business that the federal government reserved for minority-owned companies through the 8(a) program of the Small Business Administration. For example, the James company was able to supply Veterans Administration hospitals with canned goods and juices.

James is active in local civic affairs, serving on the board of trustees of Charleston University and the board of directors of the Charleston Area Medical Center. He has been the treasurer of the West Virginia Economic Development Authority, and has received a number of awards and honors from various levels of the Small Business Administration. He has said that when he walks into his office every day, he is well aware of his responsibility as the fourth-generation leader of a family business. His goal, he says, is not simply to make money but to preserve the business for the generations to come.

Further Reading

Dingle, Derek T. *Black Enterprise, Titans of the B.E. 100s.* New York: John Wiley & Sons, Inc., 1999, pp. 173–192.

Gale Group. "Charles Howell James II." *Who's Who Among African Americans.* 15th ed. Farmington Hills, Mich.: Gale Group, 2002.

Ingham, John, and Lynne B. Feldman. *African American Business Leaders: A Biographical Dictionary.* Westport, Conn.: Greenwood Press, 1994, pp. 339–351.

Jefferson, Lucy C.
(Lucy Crump Jefferson)

(1866–1953) *funeral home owner, civic leader, philanthropist, educator*

Lucy Crump Jefferson was the first African American to own and operate a business in the state of Mississippi when she and her husband opened their funeral home in 1894, pioneering a new type of black business and changing the way African Americans handled their funeral arrangements. Jefferson used the profits from her extremely successful business to support a number of charities in the African-American community and was a major supporter of African-American education in her home of Vicksburg, Mississippi.

Lucy Crump was born on November 3, 1866, in Jackson, Mississippi. Because there were so few records kept about African Americans during this era, there is no information about her father, but she is known to have been one of two children of Alice (Reynolds) Crump. Likewise, little is known about her education, although she apparently attended Vicksburg public schools.

On June 20, 1889, she married William Henry Jefferson, whose father had been a free and relatively well-off man of color in Virginia. Lucy Jefferson and her husband founded the W. H. Jefferson Funeral Home on December 1, 1894, which was reported to be the first black business in Mississippi and was certainly the first black funeral home in the state. Lucy Jefferson continued her involvement with the company until her death in 1953, and as of 2003, the business she founded has been in continuous operation for more than one hundred years, managed by three generations of the Jefferson family.

In the late 19th century, segregation (separation by race) was in full force in the southern United States, and white-owned businesses often refused to serve African Americans or to treat them on an equal footing with white people. The notion that a black-owned funeral home might treat African Americans better than a white-owned business, and that they and their families might be more comfortable there, seemed clear to those who founded such businesses—but, according to Jefferson, the concept took a while to catch on. In an interview published some time after death in the Vicksburg *Evening Post* on April 16, 1965, Jefferson was quoted as saying that "Negroes had to be taught to use Negro funeral directors. . . . We were an oddity and doomed to early failure—so thought many of our friends." As a result, her husband kept his job as a railroad worker while the business was getting started.

Within five years, though, the business was a success—in Jefferson's view, because of the support of loyal friends in the community. In 1914, Jefferson and her husband founded the Jefferson Burial Association. This was another common type of black-owned business in the early 20th century, in which membership in an association guaranteed an individual or family coverage for the costs of a funeral, embalming, and burial. For poor families who had difficulty raising ready cash, paying membership dues in an association insured that they would be able to bury their dead with dignity whenever the time came.

In addition to her association with the funeral home, Lucy Jefferson was an active philanthropist, supporting the Margaret Murray Washington Home for delinquents and funding the Lucy C. Jefferson scholarship for a local graduating high school student. From 1928 to 1934, she was president of the Mississippi Federation of Colored Women's Clubs, part of a national black women's club movement that offered a way for African-American women to become active in civic affairs and to support the black community. For a time, Jefferson was also vice president of the National Association of Colored Women's Clubs. Locally, Jefferson was active with the Camille Art and Literary Club, the first Interracial Council of Vicksburg, and a trustee of Campbell College in Jackson, Mississippi, as well as a number of other civic groups.

Jefferson also worked as a teacher for a time, and was a strong supporter of black education in her community. She circulated a petition to establish a junior high school for Vicksburg's black community so that students would not have to travel to schools in nearby towns. Her efforts were not successful until after her death—the school was built in 1966 and was then named in her honor.

Jefferson died of cancer on April 24, 1953, at Mercy Hospital in Vicksburg, Mississippi. Her name and memory live on in the business and the tradition that she and her family helped to build.

Further Reading

Gale Group. "Lucy C. Jefferson." *Notable Black American Women*, Book 1. Farmington Hills, Mich.: Gale Research, 1992.

Mosley, Mrs. Charles C., Sr. *The Negro in Mississippi History*. Jackson, Miss.: Hederman Brothers, 1969.

Sewell, George Alexander, and Margaret L. Dwight. *Mississippi Black History Makers*. Jackson: University Press of Mississippi, 1984.

Jennings, Thomas L.
(1791–1859) *tailor, dry cleaner, inventor*

Thomas L. Jennings was the first African American to receive a patent for an invention. (A patent is a legal document indicating who is responsible for the invention; a patented invention cannot be used without the permission of the patent owner, who must usually be paid for that use.) On March 3, 1821, Jennings patented a method of dry cleaning known as dry scouring. He used the money he earned from his patent to buy and free enslaved family members and to support abolitionism (the movement against slavery). Jennings developed his invention through the operation of his successful tailoring and dry cleaning business in New York City. He also ran a boardinghouse.

Little is known of Jennings's early life. As an adult, he is known to have been a leading member of the National Colored Convention Movement, an African-American organization designed to improve conditions for black people. He was also a founder of an organization that aided widows and orphans, the New York African Society for Mutual Relief, which was chartered (given legal recognition) on March 23, 1810. In 1831, he became assistant secretary for the First Annual Convention of the People of Color in Philadelphia.

In the early 19th century, Americans were engaged in a national debate about how black people should be treated. Some people supported slavery, while others opposed it. People also debated whether African Americans should remain in the United States or be returned to Africa. Jennings believed strongly that African Americans had helped to build America and ought to remain there. In 1828, speaking at the New York African Society for Mutual Relief, he said:

> Our claims are on America; it is the land that gave us birth. We know no other country. It is a land in which our fathers have suffered and toiled. They have watered it with their tears and fanned it with their sighs. Our relation with Africa is the same as the white man's is with Europe. We have passed through several generations in this country and consequently have become naturalized. Our habits, our manners, our passions, our dispositions have become the same. The same mother's milk has nourished us both in infancy; the white child and the colored have both hung on the same breast. I might as well tell the white man about England, France or Spain, the country from whence his forefathers emigrated, and call him a European, as for him to call us Africans. Africa is as foreign to us as Europe is to them.

Jennings's son, Thomas L. Jennings, Jr., studied dentistry in Boston and went on to practice in New Orleans, Louisiana. His daughter, Matilda Jennings, became a dressmaker who went to live in San Francisco.

In 1854, Jennings helped finance a suit brought by his sister, Elizabeth, against the Third Avenue Railway Company, the New York City horsecar company that required black people to ride in separate cars marked "Colored." Her lawyer was Chester A. Arthur, who would later become president of the United States. Jennings wrote many appeals in support of his sister's suit, including one in which he pointed out that there was no law segregating the cars; rather, the separation of black and white people was merely a matter of custom and of transit company rules. Elizabeth won her suit, ending segregation on New York City's public transportation. Jennings died in New York in 1859.

Further Reading

Bellis, Mary. "Thomas Jennings." Inventors, About.com. Available online. URL: http://inventors.about.com/library/inventors/bljennings.htm. Downloaded on November 4, 2002.

Hewitt, John H. "The Search for Elizabeth Jennings, Heroine of a Sunday Afternoon in New York City." *New York History.* Cooperstown, N.Y.: New York State Historical Association, October 1990, pp. 387–415.

McManus, Edgar J. *A History of Negro Slavery in New York.* Syracuse, N.Y.: Syracuse University Press, 1966.

Ottley, Roi, and William J. Weatherby, eds. *The Negro in New York.* New York: New York Public Library, 1967.

Sterling, Dorothy, ed. *Speak Out in Thunder Tones: Letters and Other Writings by Black Northerners, 1787–1865.* New York: Doubleday, 1973.

Johnson, Albert W.
(Al Johnson)
(ca. 1923–) *car dealership owner, cable systems owner*

Albert W. Johnson is the first African American to own a General Motors franchise. For a time, he was one of the most successful black car dealers in the country, though DICK GIDRON later outstripped him with a larger chain of dealerships. Still, Johnson was a pioneer who helped African Americans enter a field of business that had previously been whites-only.

Johnson was born on February 23, 1920, in East St. Louis, Illinois, the son of a physician. He graduated with a B.S. in business administration from the University of Illinois in 1943, moving on to a graduate degree in hospital administration from Northwestern University. His first job was with the United Public Workers union, whom he served as regional director. He went on to take an administrative job at Homer Phillips Hospital in St. Louis, Missouri, which his father had helped to found.

Johnson spent 20 years at the hospital, always under the shadow of his father's expectation that he should have become a doctor. But in 1953, Johnson had started selling cars on commission and realized how much he loved the automobile business. He worked after hours for a dealer in Kirkwood, Illinois, taking advantage of the fact that many in the all-white world of auto dealers did not particularly want black customers. Johnson did, and as a result he was selling twice as many cars in his 18-hour week as some of the white dealers who worked full-time.

Although Johnson was doing well, he was not allowed to sell on a showroom floor because of the color of his skin. Indeed, he became known as "the man who sold cars from a briefcase." The Civil Rights movement, however, was bringing pressure on General Motors and the other big auto manufacturers to include black people in their dealership ranks. In 1967, Johnson was allowed to buy an Oldsmobile franchise in Chicago, and he left the hospital and his home to take advantage of the opportunity.

For a while, he faced hard times, as the dealership he had been offered was a failing business. He also had to realize that while he was a superb salesman, he knew nothing about the other parts of his business. In a dramatic story of generosity, Johnson's white competitor, John Watson, gathered four white dealers who gave Johnson a series of informal lessons in how to run his business. This shared expertise enabled Johnson to make a success of his enterprise, and he was turning a profit in his third month. Within three years, Johnson had raised his net yearly profits from $20,550 to $142,405.

In 1971, he sold his franchise to another black businessman and purchased a Cadillac dealership. Johnson did so well selling the luxury cars that he was able to pay back the loans he had needed to obtain the business, so that he became

the first black man to fully own a General Motors (GM) dealership. By 1974, he was worth almost $3 million and was named one of the top 10 dealers in the country by *Time* magazine. In 1972, meanwhile, he helped GM start a training program for new dealers, and a number of other black entrepreneurs were able to enter the field, including Dick Gidron, who opened the first black-owned Cadillac dealership in the Bronx.

In 1981 Johnson branched out into foreign-made automobiles, becoming the first black person to receive a Saab dealership. In 1986 he was racking up some $21.4 million in sales from his Cadillac and Saab dealerships, ranking 71st in *Black Enterprise*'s list of 100 black businesses. (Gidron's chain ranked 14th, with gross sales of $57.5 million.) Johnson became known for his luxurious lifestyle, featuring such extravagant gestures as chartering a jet to see a boxing match. He also became a partner in a cable television group; served as adviser and supporter to Chicago's first black mayor, Harold Washington; and donated generously to a number of civic and church groups.

Johnson is a treasurer of Jesse Jackson's Operation PUSH, which he helped to found, and a member of the National Association for the Advancement of Colored People (NAACP). In 1994, he sold his companies to focus on civic and political activism. He has received a number of honors, including induction to the Entrepreneurship Hall of Fame and being named Man of the Millennium by the University of Illinois School of Business.

Further Reading

The HistoryMakers. "Albert W. Johnson: Biography." BusinessMakers, The HistoryMakers. Available online. URL: http://www.thehistorymakers.com/biography.asp?bioindex=241&category=businessMakers. Downloaded on January 25, 2003.

Ingham, John, and Lynne B. Feldman. *African American Business Leaders: A Biographical Dictionary.* Westport, Conn.: Greenwood Press, 1994, pp. 351–356.

Johnson, John H.
(John Harold Johnson)
(1918–   ) *publisher, beauty products manufacturer, insurance company executive*

John H. Johnson has built one of the most significant black publishing companies in the United States, reaching millions of readers with such publications as *Ebony, Jet,* and *Negro Digest.* He has also achieved success running a major black-owned insurance company, an upscale cosmetics company, and a number of other enterprises. For many years, his was the only name that came to mind when most white Americans thought of black-owned businesses or black millionaires, and as a result, he was the first African American to sit on many corporate boards in the 1970s, when corporate leaderships tried to diversify and become more representative of the U.S. population.

Johnson was born on January 19, 1918, in the rural mill town of Arkansas City, Arkansas. He was the son of mill worker Leroy Johnson and Gertrude (Jenkins) Johnson, a field worker and domestic. Gertrude was the daughter of two former slaves who managed to achieve barely a third-grade education before she was forced to go to work. When John Johnson was six years old, his father was killed in a mill accident and his mother married James Williams, another mill worker, whose drinking and gambling led the family to live in extreme poverty. Gertrude ran field kitchens for work crews, and did washing and ironing for laborers, with John's help.

Johnson attended segregated (separated by race) schools in Arkansas City, but there was no public high school for African Americans. Both Johnson and his mother were determined that he should go to school, so she had him repeat eighth grade while trying to save money to send him to private school. Then she decided to move to Chicago with her son, leaving her husband behind. They arrived in Chicago in 1933, when the Great Depression was at its most severe. Gertrude found work as a domestic, and John

attended first Wendell Phillips High School, then, when the building burned down, Du Sable High School. This became the premiere black high school in the city, and Johnson's classmates included future mayor Harold Washington, jazz musician Nat "King" Cole, the comedian who would one day be known as Redd Foxx, and entrepreneur DEMPSEY J. TRAVIS.

At first the other students made fun of Johnson's homemade clothes, but when Johnson complained to his mother, she made sure he was well dressed. His stepfather joined the family a year after their arrival in Chicago, but he was unable to find a job for a few years, so from 1934 to 1936, the family was on relief, a kind of welfare program founded by President Franklin D. Roosevelt as part of his New Deal array of social-service programs to pull the country out of the depression. Meanwhile, John Johnson was an honor student, president of the student council and the senior class, and a member of the debating team. In 1936, he spoke at his school's commencement and received a $200 scholarship to the University of Chicago.

Johnson's stepfather had managed to get a Works Progress Administration (WPA) job—another Roosevelt innovation—and Johnson himself was working with the National Youth Administration (NYA), yet another program that Roosevelt had founded. Still, Johnson was unsure of how he would pay for his college education—until he met HARRY H. PACE at an Urban League dinner. Pace was then president of Supreme Liberty Life Insurance, the largest black business in Chicago, and he offered Johnson a part-time job to help finance his studies.

Johnson became more interested in the world of business than in his studies, and he dropped out of college after two years to work full-time. Pace had started a monthly company newspaper, *The Guardian,* and in 1939, Johnson became assistant editor. Because Supreme Liberty Life was at the center of Chicago's black social life, the magazine was of broader interest than most company magazines, and it proved to be good training for Johnson.

Supreme Life executive EARL BURRUS DICKERSON became Johnson's mentor, and working on Dickerson's unsuccessful 1939 campaign for alderman gave Johnson a useful introduction to Chicago city politics. In 1941, Johnson took another step up by marrying Eunice Walker, a member of the Chicago black elite with whom he later adopted two children, John Harold, Jr., and Linda.

The last year Pace was alive, he asked Johnson to create a digest of events in the African-American world. Johnson was so intrigued with the project he decided to create a black version of *Reader's Digest,* a popular monthly magazine that presented excerpts from various magazines. Johnson sought investors, but everyone he approached discouraged him from what seemed like a foolhardy effort. Johnson got permission from Pace to use Supreme Liberty Life's mailing list, and mortgaged his mother's furniture to acquire $500 worth of postage. He wrote to all of Supreme Liberty Life's customers, offering subscriptions for $2 each. The 3,000 answers he received netted him the $6,000 he used to put out the first issue of *Negro Digest* in November 1942, with a press run of 5,000.

It took the new magazine a while to get off the ground, and Johnson faced periodic financial crises. Then he instituted a feature called "If I Were a Negro," written by prominent white people, including department store magnate Marshall Field and Nobel Prize–winning author Pearl Buck. When he convinced First Lady Eleanor Roosevelt to write a column, his circulation jumped almost immediately to 150,000—and the magazine's success was assured. Johnson later added other features, including "My Most Humiliating Jim Crow Experience," written by prominent African Americans. ("Jim Crow" was the name for the set of discriminatory laws and customs that barred black people from mainstream white society.)

Johnson left his job at Supreme Liberty Life and soon became interested in a new project,

John H. Johnson founded *Ebony,* the first black mass-market publication in the United States. *(Property, Johnson Publishing Co., Inc.)*

Ebony, a glossy magazine that ran features and photographs showing black people doing "normal" things—a magazine with an upbeat focus rather than one that stressed discrimination and racism. He sold out his first press run of 25,000 almost immediately and disposed of his second run soon afterwards, quickly reaching a readership of more than 400,000 per issue. However, for the first several months of the magazine's life, Johnson had no advertisers, and he was losing money with every issue, subsidizing *Ebony* with the profits from *Negro Digest.* He wanted to keep the price of each issue low, to encourage readers, but it was difficult to convince white-owned businesses to advertise in a black-owned magazine, even one with a large readership.

In May 1946, Johnson got his first big ads, for Chesterfield cigarettes and Kotex menstrual pads, as well as selling ads to Murray's Hair Pomade—

a black-owned hair products company—and Supreme Liberty Life. He went on to sell ads to Zenith by pointing out that almost all black people owned radios, most of which seemed to be made by Zenith. The head of Zenith helped him reach a number of other mainstream corporations, and *Ebony* was off and running.

At first, *Ebony* portrayed black life in a glamorous and somewhat sexualized way, but soon the magazine became more sedate. It included articles on civil rights and other social issues, but many people criticized it for being too moderate. Sociologist Kenneth B. Clark, however, thought it was important for African Americans to have access to positive images of themselves and their community, particularly since the white-owned media virtually ignored African Americans, or else presented almost uniformly negative images.

In 1950, Johnson brought out *Tan*, a true-confessions magazine that later became a general women's magazine. In 1951, he published another journal called *Hue*, which was dropped soon after it started publication. Also in 1951, Johnson added *Jet* to his portfolio, a pocket-sized newsweekly that was flashier and more colorful than *Negro Digest*. *Jet* still appears today; *Negro Digest* stopped publication in 1951 but was brought back 10 years later. In the 1950s, Johnson also started a book-publishing division.

As a result, by 1972, Johnson's company was worth between $50 million and $60 million, owned completely by Johnson, his wife, and his mother. Johnson could afford to build an $8 million office building in Chicago's downtown Loop area—the first black-owned property in that part of town.

Johnson was diversifying into other areas as well. He started Beauty Star Cosmetics and Linda Fashions, and sold a number of other products, such as vitamins, wigs, and books. These companies evolved into Supreme Beauty products, which sold Duke and Raveen hair-care products; Ebony Fashion Fair; and Fashion Fair Cosmetics,

which Johnson managed to get into Marshall Field & Co. department stores, and from there into Bloomingdale's, Neiman-Marcus, Dillards, and a number of other major outlets.

In 1972, Johnson bought radio station WGRT and renamed it WJPC. The AM station was not very profitable, but owning it did make Johnson the first African-American station owner in Chicago. He also bought AM station WLOU in Louisville, Kentucky, and finally, WLNR, an FM station in a suburb from which the broadcast signal could reach Chicago.

In television, Johnson sponsored the Ebony Music Awards and the American Black Achievement Awards. He also invested in Lawson Gardens, a middle-income subsidized complex in Chicago. He made several other real estate investments as well.

Johnson became the largest stockholder in Supreme Liberty Life, and when the company seemed to be making less money than it could, he took over as chief executive officer. Meanwhile, he was grooming his daughter, Linda Johnson Rice, to take over as president and chief operating officer of Johnson Publishing, a job she assumed in 1987 at a relatively young age. Nevertheless, as of early 2003, Johnson remains chief executive officer (CEO) and chairman of the board and shows no signs of retiring or even slowing down.

Meanwhile, Johnson has won numerous honors and awards. In 1996, President Bill Clinton awarded him the Medal of Freedom Award. In 1997, he was welcomed into the Junior Achievement National Business Hall of Fame. Also in 1997, he was named a "captain of industry" by *Black Industry*, indicating that his company has been a top black-owned company for more than 25 years.

Further Reading

Birmingham, Stephen. *Certain People: American's Black Elite*. Boston: Little, Brown & Co., 1977, pp. 19–35.

Dingle, Derek T. *Black Enterprise, Titans of the B.E. 100s.* New York, John Wiley & Sons, Inc., 1999, pp. 1–26.

Gite, Lloyd. "Marathon Men Revisited." *Black Enterprise,* June 2002, p. 92.

Haskins, Jim. *Black Stars: African American Entrepreneurs.* New York: John Wiley & Sons, 1998, pp. 114–119.

Johnson, John H., with Lerone Bennett, Jr. "'Are You Trying Real Hard?'" *Ebony,* May 1994, p. 145.

———. "The Best Christmas I Ever Had." *Ebony,* December 1993, p. 17.

———. *Succeeding Against the Odds.* New York: Amistad Press, 1993.

Johnson, Robert L.
(Robert Louis Johnson)
(1946–) *media executive*

Robert L. Johnson is one of the richest men in the United States and the first African-American billionaire to make his fortune in business rather than as an athlete or entertainer, a position he achieved by founding Black Entertainment Television (BET), a 24-hour cable station featuring black-oriented entertainment. In 1991, Johnson became the first black head of a company to be traded on the New York Stock Exchange (NYSE). Johnson also runs a number of other media enterprises and commercial ventures. In 2002, he became the first African American to hold a principal interest in a professional major sports team.

Johnson was born on April 8, 1946, in Hickory, Mississippi, a rural town near Meridian, Mississippi, the son of Archie and Edna Johnson, who were both factory workers. When Johnson was a child, the family moved to Freeport, Illinois, where, as the ninth of 10 children, Johnson learned how to work hard but also how to rely on his older brothers and sisters for support.

Johnson wanted to become a U.S. Air Force fighter pilot, but he did not meet the physical requirements. He went on to graduate high school with honors in history, winning an academic scholarship to the University of Illinois. He graduated in 1968 with a B.A. in history and was accepted into Princeton University's Woodrow Wilson School of Public and International Affairs, despite his lack of the usual entrance credentials. In 1972 he graduated sixth in his class with an M.P.A. (master's in public administration).

The Vietnam War was in its final stages, so Johnson joined the U.S. Army Reserve, while drawing on his Princeton connections to become public affairs officer at the Corporation for Public Broadcasting. He went on to become director of communications for the Washington Urban League, press aide for the District of Columbia (D.C.) city councillor Sterling Tucker, and press secretary for the D.C. nonvoting member of Congress, Walter Fauntroy. Then, in 1976, Johnson got into the world of cable, which was to make his fortune, serving until 1979 as vice president of government relations for the National Cable and Television Association (NCTA).

In 1979, black faces on television were still few and far between, even though A. C. Nielsen ratings had discovered that black viewers watched television for an average of 70 hours per week, as opposed to 48 hours for white people. Programming on network television was overwhelmingly directed to white viewers, and the roles that did exist for black people tended to be secondary characters in white comedies or dramas. Cable, however, allowed for more targeted marketing than was possible at the networks, and Johnson came up with the idea of creating a cable network company specifically directed to African Americans.

Johnson got a $15,000 consulting contract from his NCTA supervisor, which gave him leverage to obtain a matching loan from the National Bank of Washington. With that seed money, he was able to borrow $320,000 from John C. Malone, head of Tele-Communications Inc. (TCI), a major builder of cable systems. Johnson also received $180,000 from TCI in exchange for a 20 percent share in the new network.

Black Entertainment Television (BET) started broadcasting on January 25, 1980, with *A Visit to the Chief's Son*, a low-budget two-hour movie with an all-black cast. BET found ways of keeping costs low by playing free promotional music videos; films with black themes, such as *Lady Sings the Blues;* and talk shows with black hosts and guests. Later, BET began broadcasting black college sports.

It took Johnson several years to get the new venture off the ground. In 1982, he went into

BET executive Robert L. Johnson is the first African-American billionaire to make his fortune as a businessman, rather than as an athlete or entertainer. *(BET)*

partnership with Taft Broadcasting Company. In 1984, he got a break when Home Box Office (HBO), a subsidiary of Time Inc. (now AOL Time Warner), invested in BET, which by then was on the air 24 hours a day, with 7.6 million subscribers. In 1984, meanwhile, Johnson started District Cablevision Incorporated, which was 75 percent owned by TCI. The new venture was supposed to wire homes in the District of Columbia, but competitors filed suit against the company, claiming that TCI might obtain a monopoly in the D.C. area.

By 1989, BET was finally beginning to pay back its investors, although it was still the smallest cable network and the one least available through the major cable carriers. Nevertheless, Johnson went on to form BET Holdings II Incorporated as a parent company for BET, and in 1991, the firm became the first black-owned corporation to be traded on the NYSE and only the fourth black-owned firm to become a public company (a company whose stock is traded on the open market rather than held privately). Investors bid their stock prices up rapidly when the new company went on the market, and at the end of the first trading day, the company—which had reported $9 million in earnings—was worth $475 million. Johnson sold several thousand of his own shares at this new high price and earned $6.4 million in that one day. His controlling interest in the company was now worth $104 million. (A controlling interest is the ownership of enough stock to control the company's decisions.)

BET went on to acquire controlling interest in *Emerge: Black America's News Magazine,* a young-adult publication, and began to publish *YSB (Young Sisters and Brothers)*, a teen publication. In 1994, BET set up a radio network that provides news and music to black-oriented radio stations across the country.

The cable system, meanwhile, continued to grow, adding a children's literature hour, a weekly show for teenagers, town hall meetings, and a public affairs show. BET also owned the Cable Jazz Channel, and in 1996, it launched BET Movies/STARZ!3, the first black-controlled cable movie premium channel, featuring movies of interest to African Americans. In 1998, Johnson started BET Gospel, a gospel-oriented cable station; and BET Pictures II and BET Arabesque Films, to make films, documentaries, and television movies that would appeal to African Americans. BET Arabesque books became the only publisher of black-oriented romance novels. The company brought out *BET Weekend,* the third-largest black publication in the nation, and *Heart & Soul,* a beauty, health, and fitness magazine.

BET also reached out to the Internet in a joint venture with a number of other companies, including Liberty Digital; LLC News Corporation, Inc; USA Networks, Inc; and Microscoft Corp., and BET.com became a website for African Americans. Under the auspices of BET Interactive LLC, Johnson expanded his holdings to include 360hiphop.com, a hip-hop music and culture website. Johnson also created a number of other restaurants and clubs in Orlando, Florida; Las Vegas, Nevada; and elsewhere, including one restaurant in partnership with Walt Disney World Resort.

In 1998, Johnson took his company off the stock exchange and went private again (meaning that anyone wishing to buy stock in the company would have to approach a stock owner directly, rather than being able to trade on the open market). At that point, the company was valued at $1.3 billion. In 2001, the company was acquired by Viacom for $3 billion, with Johnson receiving $1.5 billion for his 63 percent share and staying on as chairman of the board and chief executive officer (CEO). This arrangement made Johnson the first African-American billionaire, and as of 2003, he ranked among the top 200 wealthiest Americans, according to the ratings done by *Forbes* magazine.

However, the Viacom deal also provoked angry charges within the African-American community that Johnson had "sold out"—that once again, an African-American company was being controlled by white people. BET was also accused of lacking a social consciousness and promoting outdated images of African Americans. Johnson has responded by saying that no one network can appeal to everyone, and that the criticisms are the result of BET being "the only black network in town."

BET has come in for other criticisms as well. Lesbian/gay and feminist groups have occasionally found fault with its portrayal of women and with comments made by some on-air personalities that were considered to be homophobic.

Johnson, meanwhile, has gone on to invest in other ventures beyond BET. Through RLJ Development LLC, he bought seven hotels from Hilton for $95 million, as well as buying and then selling several of the restaurants that had been created under the auspices of BET. In 2000, Johnson tried to create a new airline, DC Air, from a merger of United Airlines and US Airways but the federal government would not accept the merger. In 2002, he became the first African American to be the principal owner of a major professional sports team when the National Basketball Association (NBA) awarded him an expansion franchise in Charlotte, North Carolina. Although professional basketball depends on African-American players—as do many other sports—African Americans had not yet been able to rise into the highest ranks of the game.

Johnson remains a powerful and somewhat controversial figure in black enterprise, admired for his power and success, while questioned occasionally about the content of his media ventures. It is clear, however, that BET and its various holdings have made new images and artists available to the American public, as well as to African-American viewers and readers.

Further Reading

Black Entertainment Network (BET). "Robert L. Johnson, Founder." BET.com. Available online. URL:

http://www.bet.com/articles/0,1048,c15-225,00.html. Downloaded on January 31, 2003.

Dingle, Derek T. *Black Enterprise, Titans of the B.E. 100s.* New York: John Wiley & Sons, Inc., 1999, pp. 27–50.

Hocker, Cliff. "Suite Success." *Black Enterprise,* April 2001, p. 20.

Miller, Robert G. "Robert L. Johnson: A Business Titan Redefining Entrepreneurial Success." The Black Collegian Online. Available online. URL: http://www.black-collegian.com/issues/1stsem00/titan2000-1st.shtml. Downloaded on January 31, 2003.

Pulley, Brett. "Oprah Who?" *Forbes,* November 27, 2000, p. 56.

Rhoden, William C. "Finally, a Member of the Club." *New York Times,* December 19, 2002, p. D1.

Sandomir, Richard. "Founder of TV Network Becomes First Black Owner in Major Sports." *New York Times,* December 19, 2002, p. A1.

"10 Most Powerful Blacks in TV." *Ebony,* October 2002 p. 86.

Johnson, William Tiler

(1809–1851) *barber, landowner, slave owner, land speculator, stock investor, moneylender*

William Johnson was a remarkably successful businessman and barber in Natchez, Mississippi, before the Civil War, an era when there were very few free black people in Mississippi, and when free black people labored under an enormous set of legal and social restrictions. Johnson, however, was highly respected and successful, serving white clients in his prestigious barbershop and engaging in a number of other business activities.

William Johnson was born a slave in 1809, in Natchez, the son of Amy, an enslaved African-American woman; his father was almost certainly the white man William Johnson, who was also Amy's owner. Antebellum (pre–Civil War) Mis-

sissippi had a number of laws on the books that made it difficult to emancipate (free) enslaved people, but Johnson went through the legal processes to free Amy on March 20, 1814. Her children, however, remained slaves until they became older: Johnson freed Delia (also called Adelia) in 1818, when she was 13, and William on February 20, 1820, when he was 11.

Also in 1820, Delia married a 20-year-old free black man named James Miller, a Philadelphia-born barber who had a shop in Natchez. Young William went to apprentice (learn the trade) with him, and by 1827, at the age of 18, he had achieved such stature in the Natchez community that 44 white men petitioned the state legislature for William to be given the same legal rights as a white man except the right to vote and serve on juries. Free black people were very threatening to a white-dominated slave society, because they reminded people that African Americans were not necessarily limited to the role of slaves and also because they seemed to provide a base of support for slave revolts and antislavery activity. William, however, found a way to make himself acceptable to white people of the era.

When Johnson turned 19, in 1828, he went on to run his own barbershop in nearby Port Gibson, Mississippi. In 1830, when James Miller moved to New Orleans, he sold his Natchez shop to Johnson, who quickly prospered. By 1833, he moved from a rented store to a fancy brick building on Main Street, and two years later, he owned four slaves, had other property worth at least $2,700 (a considerable sum for the time), and had married Ann Battles, a young free black woman. Eventually, he and Ann had 10 children.

Johnson's ownership of slaves was key to his expanding prosperity. Skilled white people would not work for him, and illiterate white people were not good employees. Free black people did apprentice with Johnson to become full-fledged barbers, but they often left to start their own shops and they would do only barbering, not the many other kinds of work he required. Like white slaveholders of the time, Johnson took advantage of the financial opportunities that slaveholding offered. In addition, his status as slaveholder must have reassured local whites that he was no threat, that he would support the institution of slavery on which their own livelihood and/or status depended.

In this era, most slaves were counted in the federal census as "black," while many free African Americans were recorded as "mulatto," of mixed black and white parentage, as Johnson was. Probably Johnson did not consider himself racially similar to the slaves whose labor he used, and, based on the diary he kept, he seems to have had no compunction about whipping them or selling them.

By the mid-1830s, Johnson usually owned four or five slaves, a number that rose to eight or nine by the mid-1840s and to 15 at the time of his death in 1851. His barbering business catered exclusively to white customers, with all of his barbers either free men of color or skilled slaves whom he had trained. He was able to make several improvements in his barbershop as his prestige and prosperity grew, as well as expanding his business: Eventually, he owned a bathhouse (since most homes had no running water in those days), some smaller barber shops, various other real estate, farmland, and timberland. He also hired out his slaves at a profit. By the time of his death, his estate was worth at least $25,000, enough to make him a rich man.

Johnson was fatally shot on June 16, 1851, in an ambush on a rural road, and he died the next day. He named the culprit before his death—Baylor Winn, who had been engaged in a land dispute with Johnson for some time. Though Winn was a free black man, he was able to claim in court that he was really white. Since all of the witnesses to the shooting were black, and since Mississippi law prohibited black people from testifying against whites, Winn was eventually acquitted—even though Johnson was highly beloved in the town and Winn had been tried three times. Ironically, despite Johnson's many successes, racial prejudice played a role in the aftermath of his death.

Further Reading

Davis, Edwin Adams, and William R. Hogan, eds. *The Barber of Natchez.* Baton Rouge: Louisiana State University Press, 1973.

Johnson, William. *William Johnson's Natchez: The Antebellum Diary of a Free Negro.* Edited by Edwin Adams Davis and William R. Hogan. Baton Rouge: Louisiana State University Press, 1993.

McCallum, Gloria, Georgia Wise, and Bill Mudd. "William Johnson House." An Adams County Mississippi Slave Record Book. Available online. URL: http://pages.prodigy.net/gmccallum/_import/pages.prodigy.net/gmccallum/index10.html. Downloaded on November 22, 2002.

Jones, John
(ca. 1816–1879) *tailor, clothier, abolitionist*

John Jones was one of Chicago's wealthiest and most important 19th-century entrepreneurs. He was also a major community leader who fought for the abolition of slavery and African-American civil rights.

Jones was born sometime around 1816 on a plantation in Greene County, North Carolina, the son of a German man named Bromfield and a free woman of color. Although little information is available on Jones's early years, his mother seemed to fear that his father's relatives would try to treat her son as a slave, so she apprenticed him to a Mr. Sheppard, who took him to Tennessee. Apprenticeship is the practice of hiring someone out for little or no wages so he or she can learn a trade. Apparently Mr. Sheppard "bound over" Jones to Richard Clere—that is, he transferred Jones's apprenticeship to Clere, a tailor. When Jones's term was up he worked for himself as a tailor in Memphis, Tennessee, until he met Mary Richardson, a blacksmith's daughter. When she moved to Illinois, he followed her, and the couple was married, living first in Alton, Illinois, and then going on to Chicago in 1845.

Chicago was a new city in those days, having been founded just 12 years previously. The Jones family rented a one-room cottage and opened up a tailoring shop, where Jones slowly but surely won the business of several wealthy white families, including many abolitionists.

Jones also became an abolitionist. He taught himself to read and write and became politically active, hosting such civil rights leaders as Frederick Douglass and John Brown in his home. He helped organize a meeting of 300 black people at an African Methodist Church (later known as Quinn Chapel) to protest the 1850 passage of the Fugitive Slave Law, which required Northerners to help return escaped slaves to their Southern owners. He was also a leader of a local Vigilance Committee, set up to help slaves escape, as well as offering his home as a station on the Underground Railroad, a network of people assisting runaway slaves.

In 1853, the Colored National Convention was held in Rochester, New York, to advance civil rights and oppose slavery. Jones was elected vice president of that convention. In 1856 he went on to organize a state convention in Illinois to petition for black legal rights. Jones also agitated against the so-called Black Laws, a body of laws that sought to keep black people from voting and testifying in court. Toward that end, Jones published a 16-page pamphlet, "The Black Laws of Illinois and a Few Reasons They Should Be Repealed." His campaign was successful and the discriminatory laws were indeed repealed. After the Civil War, he helped lobby for the passage of the Thirteenth Amendment, abolishing slavery, and he was a major reason that Illinois became the first state to ratify that amendment.

Meanwhile, Jones's entrepreneurial activities continued to prosper. Although he had come to Chicago with only $3.50, he had amassed a fortune of between $85,000 and $100,000 by the time of the Chicago Fire of 1871. Although he lost a great deal of money and property in the fire, he was still one of the wealthiest black men in the United States.

Jones was active with the Republican Party, which in those days was considered the party of Abraham Lincoln and civil rights. In 1871, he ran for county board on a bipartisan (two-party) ticket known as the Fire Proof Ticket. He won a year-long term, then a three-year term that kept him in office until 1875, when he and other Republicans were defeated. During his tenure, he helped pass the law that abolished local segregated schools.

Jones died in 1879. His obituaries describe him as an important city leader and a key force in the campaign to repeal the Black Laws, as well as a prosperous entrepreneur.

Further Reading

Bontemps, Arna, and Jack Conroy. *Anyplace But Here.* New York: Hill and Wang, 1966.

Butler, Dominique. "John Jones." Illinois History, February 1996, p. 27. Available online. Illinois Periodicals Online (IPO). URL: http://www.lib.niu.edu/ipo/ihy960227.html.

Gosnell, Harold F. *Negro Politicians: The Rise of Negro Politics in Chicago.* Chicago: University of Chicago Press, 1935.

Sawyers, June Skinner. *Chicago Portraits.* Chicago: Loyola University Press, 1991.

Travis, Dempsey J. *An Autobiography of Black Chicago.* Chicago: Urban Research Press, 1981.

Jones, Quincy Delight, Jr.

(1933–) *owner of a multimedia production company, television producer, composer, music arranger*

Quincy Jones is a good example of how African Americans have often become entrepreneurs while working in the arts in order to have control of their artistic work as well as to promote their vision of African-American culture. Jones has won a number of awards for his work as a composer and music producer, including 26 Grammy Awards (second on the all-time list) and 77 Grammy nominations (the most anyone has ever received). He produced and conducted the "We Are the World" recording, the best-selling single in history, as well as Michael Jackson's multiplatinum solo albums, *Off the Wall, Bad, and Thriller,* which became the best-selling album in history.

Jones was born on March 14, 1933, in Chicago, Illinois, the child of Quincy Jones, Sr., a carpenter, and Sarah, who worked at home. When Jones was three, his mother was taken to a mental institution. Later, Jones's father remarried, and when Quincy was 10, the family moved to the Seattle suburb of Bremerton, Washington.

Jones loved music from an early age and was composing by age 15. He made friends with a local singer-pianist three years older than he was, named Ray Charles, and the two young men played together at clubs and weddings, establishing a lifelong friendship that led to many subsequent artistic partnerships.

When jazz bandleader and trumpeter Lionel Hampton played an engagement in Seattle, Jones went backstage to show the jazz great his own composition, *The Four Winds.* Hampton hired the teenager to play third trumpet while the band stayed in Seattle.

At age 18, Jones won a scholarship to study with trumpeter Clark Terry at the Boston school that later became known as Berklee School of Music. Despite his scholarship, he had to keep playing professionally to support himself and dropped out of school to go on the road with Lionel Hampton, which led to work as a freelance arranger. Throughout the 1950s, Jones worked in New York writing charts for a number of world-class jazz musicians.

In 1956, Jones went on a State Department–sponsored tour of the Middle East and South America with the Dizzy Gillespie Band, which had hired him as a trumpeter and music director. When he returned, he recorded the first album of his own band for ABC Paramount.

Quincy Jones has achieved fame in a number of arenas, including as a musician, composer, producer, and entrepreneur. *(AP/Wide World Photos)*

In 1957, Jones studied in Paris with the famous musicologist Nadia Boulanger and the composer Olivier Messiaen while working as a music director for Mercury Records's French distributor, Barclay Disques. He went on tour as musical director for Harold Arlen's jazz musical, *Free and Easy,* and when the tour closed in Paris in February 1960, he attempted to form his own 18-person band with musicians from the show. Touring with his musicians and their families, he garnered good reviews but low cash flow, and the experience left Jones in serious debt.

Jones managed to get a loan from Mercury Records head Irving Green and went to work in

New York as Mercury's music director. When he became vice president in 1964, he also became the first African-American executive with a white-owned label.

In 1964, Jones also began working as a composer of film scores, writing music for *The Pawnbroker* at the request of director Sidney Lumet. Jones was the first black composer for major Hollywood movies and went on to write a total of 33 major motion picture scores. He also wrote a number of theme songs for television shows, including *Ironsides* (the first synthesizer-based television theme song), *Sanford and Son,* and *The Bill Cosby Show.* Meanwhile, he supported Dr. Martin Luther King, Jr.'s Operation Breadbasket, which promoted economic development in inner cities, and became a board member of Rev. Jesse Jackson's People United to Save Humanity (PUSH), an organization that works to make the corporate world more responsive to African Americans.

From 1969 to 1981, Jones was known for the many Grammy-winning albums he produced. During that time, however, in 1974, he was laid low by a near-fatal cerebral aneurysm (the bursting of blood vessels that lead to the brain). In the 1980s he gained more fame as producer of Michael Jackson's best-selling songs and albums. In 1985, he became a filmmaker, coproducing Steven Spielberg's adaptation of Alice Walker's novel *The Color Purple,* which introduced Whoopi Goldberg and OPRAH WINFREY to a mass audience.

Jones and his company, Quincy Jones Enterprises, have continued to produce numerous media projects. His Qwest Records has earned gold records and continues to support a number of artists. In 1993, he and David Salzman formed a partnership known as Quincy Jones/Salzman Entertainment (QDE), a co-venture with Time-Warner, Inc., in which Jones serves as co-CEO and chair. QDE publishes *Vibe* magazine and produced the long-running television show *Fresh Prince of Bel Air,* now in syndication. In 1994 Jones

formed Qwest Broadcasting in partnership with a group of businessmen, including football Hall of Famer Willie Davis, television producer Don Cornelius, journalist Geraldo Rivera, and entrepreneur Sonia Salzman. Qwest, the owner of TV stations WATL in Atlanta and WNOL in New Orleans, Louisiana, is one of the largest U.S. minority-owned broadcasting companies, and Jones serves as its chairman and CEO. In October 1998, he formed Quincy Jones Media Group, Inc., to produce film and television projects.

Jones's philanthropic projects, designed to further black culture, include helping to form IBAM (the Institute for Black American Music), which helps to fund a national library of African-American art and music, and the annual Black Arts Festival in Chicago. He continues to expand his activities in music, publishing, philanthropy, and support of the black community.

Further Reading

American Masters. "Quincy Jones." PBS Online. URL: http://www.pbs.org/wnet/americanmasters/database/jones_q_homepage.html. Downloaded on November 10, 2002.

Bayer, Linda N. *Quincy Jones: Overcoming Adversity.* New York: Chelsea House Publishers, 2003.

Jones, Quincy. *Q: The Autobiography of Quincy Jones.* New York: Doubleday, 2001.

Quincy Jones Music Publishing. Available online. URL: http://www.quincyjonesmusic.com/. Downloaded on November 10, 2002.

Ross, Courtney, and Nelson George. *Listen Up: The Lives of Quincy Jones.* New York: Warner Books, 1990.

Jones, Wiley
(1848–1904) *entrepreneur in real estate, public transportation, and entertainment; and racetrack owner*

By the turn of the 20th century, Wiley Jones had become the richest African-American man in

Arkansas and one of the richest in the South. He amassed his fortune through a variety of shrewd investments in his community, ironically profiting from the fact that life in the South was strictly segregated (separated) by race. Thus, among other properties, he owned the "black" streetcar company and organized a profitable Colored State Fair, as well as engaging in joint ventures with local white entrepreneurs.

Jones was born on July 14, 1848, in Madison County, Georgia, one of six children born to white planter George Jones and his African-American slave "wife," Anna. Before George Jones died in 1858, he had promised to free his wife and children, but since no freedom papers were ever found, the family remained enslaved until the Civil War ended in 1865. During the war, Jones was owned by Confederate general James Yell, for whom he worked as camp servant until Yell's death, after which he lived with the Yell family in Waco, Texas, where he worked as a wagon driver.

In 1868, Jones went to Pine Bluff, Arkansas, where he worked as a farm laborer, mule skinner, and finally, a night porter in a hotel. During the day he worked as a barber, a common occupation for African Americans at the time. Between saving his earnings and investing his extra money, Jones was able to buy a saloon, whose profits he reinvested in the real estate market, making him a prosperous local property owner by 1880.

Jones went on to build the Wiley Jones Race Track, at which he raced his own 24 stallions. He organized the Colored State Fair at the Colored State Fair Grounds, which he owned. The event attracted 20,000 visitors to Pine Bluff each year, a boost to local business generally. Then, in August 1886, Jones began his biggest venture yet: He received a franchise from the Pine Bluff City Council to build and operate a mule-drawn streetcar system that would serve black people in the region. The Jones Street Railway and Equipment Company was intended to serve a dual purpose: It allowed Jones to profit from the local population

explosion (Pine Bluff grew from 3,000 to 9,000 between 1880 and 1890), and it enabled him to transport residents out to his racetrack.

Jones's company ran side by side with the Citizens Street Railway Company, which had received its franchise in 1885. The white-owned Citizens company served the white community, while Jones's operation served black people; in downtown Pine Bluff, the two companies literally ran on parallel tracks. Although Jones's company was profitable only when the Colored State Fair was in operation, he was able to operate it every day throughout the year. Citizens, on the other hand, could not maintain continuous operation, and the company was sold in 1890 to Jones, Thomas S. James, and Arthur Murray, the owner-publisher of the local black weekly newspaper, the *Pine Bluff Press Eagle*. Jones and his associates went on to operate the consolidated (combined) Citizens Railway Company and Jones Street Railway Company for three years, but the company was never particularly profitable and they sold it back to the original owners for $90,000 in 1894.

Meanwhile, in 1885, Jones had established a venture with local white developer Edward Houston to create White Sulphur Springs, Pine Bluff's first modern suburb. In 1892, the partners incorporated the White Sulphur Springs Land and Improvement Company, a fashionable summer resort for many years. In 1888, Jones also founded a wholesale supply house known as the Southern Mercantile Company, yet another profitable business. When Jones died in 1904, he failed to leave a will, so his properties were managed by his brother, James Jones. Eventually, James had to sell most of Wiley's holdings to settle the estate, but Wiley Jones's memory lived on as one of the state's most successful entrepreneurs.

Further Reading

Gatewood, Willard B. "Arkansas Negroes in the 1890s: Documents." *Arkansas Historical Quarterly* 33 (1974): 305–306.

Gordon, F. L. *Caste & Class: The Black Experience in Arkansas, 1880–1920.* Athens: University of Georgia Press, 1995, pp. 78–79.

Smith, C. Calvin. "Wiley Jones." *Encyclopedia of African American Business History,* ed. Juliet E. K. Walker, Westport, Conn.: Greenwood Press, 1999, pp. 345–346.

Joshua, Ernest P.

(1928–   ) *founder of hair-care products company*

Ernest P. Joshua is the founder of J. M. Products, Inc., the largest minority-owned aerosol manufacturing company in the United States, and a multimillion-dollar manufacturer of ethnic hair-care products. His company is one of the largest U.S. makers of ethnic hair-care products and the largest black-owned company in Arkansas, a corporation employing some 100 people that began life in the mid-1970s as a one-person operation.

Ernest P. Joshua, Sr., was born in 1928. Little is known of his childhood. In 1969, he started Ravel Products, a small hair-care company based in Chicago, but he soon sold his share in the company to his partner. In 1970, he and his family moved to Los Angeles, where he started "M. N. and Company by Ernest P. Joshua, Jr.," selling products door to door at barbershops and beauty salons, as was then common in the ethnic hair-care business. His major product was called ISODINE (now ISOPLUS), a lotion designed to eliminate the thinning of hair commonly resulting from chemical treatments such as perms and straightening.

In 1977, Joshua was diagnosed with lymphatic cancer, leading him to return with his family to Little Rock, Arkansas. There he opened a small, $28,000-a-year storefront operation. In 1982, he named this company J. M. Products, Inc. As Joshua fought cancer—with eventual success—his company grew into an operation that currently operates two manufacturing facilities in Little Rock and North Little Rock, comprising more than 252,000 square feet of production space, in addition to the affiliates abroad. As Joshua's four children grew up, they, too, became involved in J. M. Products, Inc. His son, Michael W. Joshua, currently acts as president and general manager of the company.

Joshua's line of hair-care products includes four nationally recognized brands that he developed himself—ISOPLUS, ISOPLUS for Kids, UpTURN, and Oil of K—as well as Black Magic, which he purchased in 1994 from American Beauty Products of Tulsa, Oklahoma. His products include aerosol hair sprays, shampoos, conditioners, hair relaxers, styling aids, and scalp oils. His other enterprises include a construction company and an entertainment and supper club.

Joshua's products are sold in South Africa, Jamaica, the United Kingdom, and various West African countries, as well as throughout the United States via such major chains as Walgreen's, Rite Aid, CVS, Kroger, Food Lion, A&P, Winn-Dixie, Wal-Mart, Kmart, Target, Family Dollar, and Dollar General. His products are also sold through beauty and barber-supply schools, at armed forces outlets, and at beauty schools and salons throughout the world.

Joshua has been named Arkansas Small Business Person of the Year (1986), an award given by the U.S. Small Business Administration; Six-State Regional Small Businessman of the Year (1987); and runner-up for National Small Businessman of the Year (1987). His company is active in civic affairs and contributes to many scholarship funds and community projects. In 1987, Joshua was the first Arkansas businessperson to be honored at the White House for his achievements in business (by President Ronald Reagan), and in 1994 he was selected by President Bill Clinton to take part in the first U.S. trade mission to South Africa.

Further Reading

Dawson, Nancy J. "Ernest P. Joshua." *Encyclopedia of African American Business History,* edited by E. K.

Walker. Westport, Conn.: Greenwood Press, 1999, pp. 330–331.

J. M. Products, Inc. "About J. M. Products Inc." ISO-PLUS by J. M. Available online. URL: http://www.isoplus.com/aboutjm.htm. Downloaded on November 14, 2002.

——. *Company History.* Little Rock, Ark.: J.M. Products, 1994.

——. *Ernest P. Joshua, Sr., Biography.* Little Rock, Ark.: J. M. Products, 1994.

Joyner, Marjorie Stewart

(1896–1994) *hair-care business executive, inventor, educator, community leader*

Marjorie Stewart Joyner was the first African-American woman to hold a patent (a license certifying that she had invented a particular device or process), which she received for her innovative method of giving "permanent waves," hairstyles for women that would last for several days or even weeks. She was a prominent executive in the beauty company founded by MADAME C. J. WALKER and helped found several organizations and institutions to advance black beauty culture.

Joyner was born on October 24, 1896, in Monterey, Virginia, in the Blue Ridge Mountains. She moved to Chicago as a child, and as a teenager, began studying cosmetology (beauty and hair care). In 1916, she went to work as an agent (saleswoman and teacher) for the Madame C. J. Walker Manufacturing Company, and quickly rose in Walker's enterprise to become Walker's confidante (the person in whom she confided, a close personal friend), chief spokesperson, and organizer for the city of Chicago.

In 1919, Joyner became vice president and national supervisor for the beauty schools run by the Walker company. Since the Walker company sold beauty and hair-care products, the next natural step was to establish its own beauty schools, where black beauticians were taught how to use the products in their work. Joyner's job was to recruit and train the teachers and saleswomen, known as agents, including some 15,000 women.

In 1921, Joyner helped found the National Beauty Culturalist League, a professional organization for black women working in the beauty field. Because of the intense discrimination against black women in all walks of life, it was extremely important to establish these women as professionals—trained people with credentials that ought to be taken seriously. Indeed, for a time, Joyner traveled in a large van, which she used to demonstrate products and give classes to black beauticians, since racial discrimination often made it impossible for her to rent other venues to work with these professionals.

In 1924, Joyner worked with two other women to write the nation's first state law regulating the beauty business. In 1928, she received a patent for her permanent wave machine, a device that fit over a woman's head like a metal hood and zapped her hair with electricity in one-inch sections. Joyner's invention meant that a woman could go to the beauty parlor and then keep the same well-groomed look for several days

Hair-care products executive Marjorie Stewart Joyner *(in front, with cane)* attends the funeral of her friend, Mary McLeod Bethune, a pioneer in African-American women's education. *(Bethune-Cookman College Photo)*

or even weeks, rather than losing the benefits of the visit as soon as she washed her hair.

Joyner saw organizations as an important route for the advancement of black women. In 1935, she became a founding member of the National Council of Negro Women, a civil rights group organized by Mary McLeod Bethune. In 1938, she became president of the National Beauty Culturalist League that she had cofounded. She was a leader in the Democratic Party during the 1940s, and in 1945, she worked with Bethune and Chicago congressman William L. Dawson to organize the sorority and fraternity Alpha Chi Pi Omega, a group dedicated to raising the educational standards for black beauticians and to promoting black-owned businesses. In the same year, she also helped found the United Beauty School Owners and Teachers Association.

Besides her work with professional organizations, Joyner worked with Bethune to raise money for Bethune-Cookman College, a school for black women. And for more than 50 years she chaired the charities program of the *Chicago Defender,* a black newspaper. She was particularly active with the Bud Billiken parade, which the *Defender* had originally started to reward its paperboys and which has gone on to become the largest annual parade in the United States, attracting more than a million viewers. In the political arena, Joyner chaired the Women's Division of the Democratic National Campaign Committee in 1944, at a time when it was highly unusual for a black woman to head a multiracial nationwide group. She took the post at the request of First Lady Eleanor Roosevelt and went on to raise funds and support for President Franklin D. Roosevelt and Congressman Dawson.

Joyner remained active until the end of her life, which lasted almost 100 years. In 1987, her achievements were recognized at an exhibit at the Smithsonian Museum of American History in Washington, D.C. Joyner is a good example of the kind of African-American entrepreneur who works to better the lives of black people in many areas—business, education, politics, and community affairs—using the resources and achievements gained in one domain to make progress in another. She died in Chicago on December 27, 1994, at the age of 98.

Further Reading
Amram, Fred M. B., and Jerry Kahn. *African-American Inventors: Lonnie Johnson, Frederick McKinley Jones, Marjorie Stewart Joyner, Elijah McCoy, Garrett Augustus Morgan.* Minneapolis, Minn.: Capstone Press, 1996.

Arnold, Latasha. "Marjorie Stewart Joyner." Troy State University Student WWW Server. Available online. URL: http://prism.troyst.edu/~arnold/final%20%20mojo_files/frame.htm. Posted August 25, 2001.

Inventors Museum. "Marjorie Stewart Joyner: First African American Female Patent Holder." Inventors Online Museum. Available online. URL: http://www.inventorsmuseum.com/MarjorieJoyner.htm. Downloaded on November 15, 2002.

Lemelson Center for the Study of Invention and Innovation. "Marjorie Stewart Joyner." Smithsonian Institution website. Available online. URL: http://www.si.edu/lemelson/centerpieces/iap/inventors_joy.html. Downloaded on November 15, 2002.

Julian, Percy Lavon
(1899–1975) *scientist, inventor, executive, owner of laboratory and research institute*

Percy Lavon Julian overcame enormous obstacles to become a scientist at a time when African Americans faced severe restrictions in most forms of employment and particularly in the sciences. Yet he went on to make numerous significant discoveries and to found his own laboratory and research institute. He is a good example of the African-American entrepreneur whose main interests lie outside of business, but who becomes an entrepreneur so that he can work for himself.

Percy Lavon Julian was born on April 11, 1899, in Montgomery, Alabama, the grandson of a slave. He was the son of James Sumner Julian, a railroad mail clerk, and Margaret Julian, a schoolteacher. Since there was no public high school open to African Americans in Montgomery, he went to a private school instead, graduating in 1916 at the head of his class. Then he was accepted into DePauw University in Greencastle, Indiana, as a "subfreshman," and was required to attend the local Ashbury Academy during his first two years in school to catch up with the school's academic requirements, even as he also worked to support himself.

Julian graduated in 1920 with a major in chemistry, was invited to join Phi Beta Kappa (an honors fraternity and sorority), and was class valedictorian (head of his class). He wanted to go on to graduate school but universities refused to accept him on the grounds that a black scientist would never find work and so should not be given advanced training. Reluctantly, he went to teach chemistry at Fisk University, an all-black school in Nashville, Tennessee.

In 1922, Julian won an Austin Fellowship and enrolled at Harvard University, where he studied with the well-known chemist E. P. Kohler, earned straight A's, and was awarded a master's degree in organic chemistry in 1923. He went back to teaching, first at West Virginia State College, then as the head of the chemistry department at Howard University, another all-black school.

In 1929, Julian was honored with the General Education Fellowship from the Rockefeller Foundation, which he used to attend the University of Vienna in Austria. He learned German so that he could study there with famed chemist Ernst Spath, and earned a Ph.D. in organic chemistry in 1931.

In 1932, Julian had an appointment at DePauw that allowed him to conduct research with two German assistants from the University of Vienna. In 1935, he made his first great discovery when he and his assistant Josef Pikl synthesized a drug that could treat the eye disease glaucoma—a task that other chemists had said could never be done.

Julian was at DePauw only because his old teacher and friend, Dean William Blanchard, had managed to get him a temporary position there. Despite Julian's achievement, he was rejected for a permanent appointment to the faculty. He had an offer to work for a Wisconsin firm, but the offer was withdrawn when the company discovered that a local town law forbade black people from staying overnight within city limits. In 1936, therefore, Julian went to work for Glidden Paint Company in Chicago as director of research in its Soya Products division, concerning products made from soybeans.

Meanwhile, in 1935, Julian had married Anna Johnson, also a member of Phi Beta Kappa and the first African American to get a Ph.D. in sociology from the University of Pennsylvania. They had two children.

Julian's position at Glidden was highly unusual for an African American, but the company's courage was rewarded when Julian turned the previously failing soybean division into a profitable wing of the company. One of Julian's discoveries enabled the mass production of cortisone, a drug used to treat arthritis and many other ailments. He and his team also produced a number of hormones, including progesterone and testosterone; a fire-resistant foam used for fires at sea; the food supplement lecithin, recommended for people with high cholesterol; and ingredients used in poultry and animal feed. Besides working in applied science, Julian also engaged in basic research and published numerous articles on organic chemistry and biochemistry.

Julian continued to encounter racism throughout his life. In 1950, when he and his family bought a house in the all-white suburb of Oak Park, Illinois, he received threatening phone calls and had difficulties getting the water commissioner to turn on the water; the house was once bombed, although no one was inside. In 1951, he was one of several scientists invited by the Research Corporation of New York City to hear a

Inventor and scientist Percy Lavon Julian went on to own his own laboratory, where he developed many new products. *(Library of Congress)*

Chicago headquarters he opened in 1954, followed by a subsidiary in Mexico in 1955, where his associates studied the benefits of the Mexican yam. In 1961, he sold his businesses to the Philadelphia company Smith, Kline, and French for nearly $2.4 million but continued to work as president of Julian Laboratories until 1964. That year, in semiretirement, he founded two more companies, the Julian Research Institute and Julian Associates.

In 1974, Julian was diagnosed with cancer of the liver, but he continued to work at his companies and as a consultant for Smith, Kline, and French. He died on April 19, 1975. In 1993, the U.S. Postal Service memorialized him with a stamp in its Black Heritage series, while the city of Oak Park, Illinois, named a middle school in his honor.

Further Reading

Aaseng, Nathan. "Julian, Percy L." *Black Inventors.* New York: Facts On File, 1997.

Chemical Heritage Foundation. "Percy Lavon Julian and Carl Djerassi." Chemical Heritage Foundation website. Available online. URL: http://www. chemheritage.org/EducationalServices/chemach/ ppb/ld.html. Downloaded on November 15, 2002.

———. "Percy L. Julian." *Notable Black American Men.* Farmington Hills, Mich.: Gale Research, 1998.

National Academy of Sciences. "Percy Lavon Julian." The National Academies website. Available online. URL: http://www.nas.edu/history/members/ julian.html. Downloaded on November 15, 2002.

National Inventors Hall of Fame. "Inventor Profile: Percy Lavon Julian." National Inventors Hall of Fame website. Available online. URL: http://www. invent.org/hall_of_fame/84.html. Downloaded on November 15, 2002.

Yount, Lisa. "Julian, Percy L." *Black Scientists.* New York: Facts On File, 1991.

talk at Chicago's Union League, but the club's manager told the corporation that no black people were allowed in the building. Julian became more involved in the Civil Rights movement later in the 1950s, helping to organize a group to raise money for the National Association for the Advancement of Colored People (NAACP).

In 1953, Julian left Glidden to form his own company, Julian Laboratories, whose suburban

K

Keckley, Elizabeth
(Elizabeth Hobbs)
(1818–1907) *seamstress, dressmaker to Mary Todd Lincoln*

Elizabeth Keckley, born a slave, earned enough money from her haute couture (high fashion) dressmaking business in St. Louis to purchase her freedom and that of her son. She employed some 20 people in a similar business in Washington, D.C., where she went on to become the private dressmaker to First Lady Mary Todd Lincoln, as well as the author of a memoir about her life as a slave and as a free employee of the Lincolns.

Elizabeth Hobbs was born in 1818 to George and Agnes Hobbs, enslaved parents in Dinwiddie Courthouse, Virginia. As she wrote in her autobiography, "I came upon the earth free in God-like thought, but fettered in action." She and her mother were owned by Colonel A. Burwell, who put the four-year-old Elizabeth in charge of minding his infant daughter. Burwell's financial circumstances caused him to move several times, leading to the separation of Elizabeth's parents, who had different owners. George Hobbs was allowed to visit his wife and daughter only at Christmas and Easter, and after Elizabeth was about seven or eight (because slave records were poorly kept, the time is uncertain), her father's

owner moved away, taking George with him. Elizabeth never saw her father again.

Elizabeth's mother was charged with a number of household duties, and Elizabeth learned to become a seamstress in order to help her mother. At age 14, she was given to the colonel's son and his bride as a wedding gift. When Elizabeth was nearly 18, the family moved to Hillsborough, North Carolina, taking Elizabeth with them. There she was raped by a white man who forced a four-year relationship with her, resulting in the birth of Elizabeth's only child, George, named for her father.

Hobbs and her son were purchased in 1845 by the daughter of her original owner, who took them to her home in St. Louis. She had probably been sought out because of her exceptional dressmaking skills, which enabled her to start a business so prosperous that it supported her owners, their five children, herself, and her son.

In 1852, Elizabeth married James Keckley, through whom she hoped to obtain her freedom. She later discovered that he was a slave and an alcoholic, and the couple separated, though Elizabeth kept his surname.

At the age of 37, in 1855 Keckley managed to obtain $1,200 worth of loans from her customers, enabling her to buy her freedom. She continued to run her business for another five years, until she had paid back the loans, and then moved first to Baltimore, then to Washington, D.C., in 1860. There she became the dressmaker to many of the leaders of capital society, including the wife of Jefferson Davis, future president of the Confederacy, who was then a senator from Mississippi. Keckley met Mary Todd Lincoln the day after Abraham Lincoln was inaugurated president and soon became Mary Todd's dressmaker. Eventually she moved into the White House, where she worked as Mary Todd's dressmaker and personal maid. Mrs. Lincoln was known to be unstable and possibly mentally disturbed, and Keckley was apparently the only person in whom the first lady could confide.

During the Civil War, Keckley's son passed for white and enlisted in a white regiment in the Union army, where he was killed in action. After President Lincoln was assassinated in 1865, both Mary Todd and Keckley left the White House, but Keckley remained a close friend of the former first lady until 1868, when she published her memoir, *Behind the Scenes; Thirty Years a Slave, and Four Years in the White House,* in collaboration with James Redpath. The book gave intimate details of the Lincolns' lives in the White House, and Mary Todd considered it a personal betrayal, refusing to see Keckley again after it was published.

Keckley showed a remarkable amount of political principle. When President Andrew Johnson vetoed the Civil Rights Act of 1866, she refused to do business with his daughters—a courageous stand both because it cost her some business and because she risked losing other white customers. With both Mary Todd Lincoln and the Johnsons withdrawing their support, Keckley fell on extremely hard times and lived in poverty.

In 1892, Keckley went to Wilberforce University in Xenia, Ohio, where she taught domestic science. In 1898, she returned to Washington, where she spent the rest of her life, ultimately supported by her son's army pension. She died of a paralytic stroke on May 26, 1907, in the boardinghouse for destitute (poor) women and children that she had helped found many years before.

Further Reading

Keckley, Elizabeth. *Behind the Scenes: Thirty Years a Slave and Four Years in the White House.* New York: Oxford University Press, 1997. Available online at Digital Schomburg African American Women Writers of the 19th Century. URL: http://149.123.1.7/dynaweb/digs/wwm9713. Downloaded on November 10, 2002. Also available online at the University of North Carolina at Chapel Hill Libraries: Documenting the American South. URL: http://docsouth.dsi.internet2.edu/keckley/menu.html. Downloaded on November 10, 2002.

Rutberg, Becky. *Mary Lincoln's Dressmaker: Elizabeth Keckley's Remarkable Rise from Slave to White House Confidante.* New York: Walker & Co. Library, 1995.

Smithsonian Institution Press. "Gown Made by Elizabeth Keckley for Mary Todd Lincoln, about 1864." Legacies: Collecting America's History at the Smithsonian. Available online. URL: http://www.smithsonianlegacies.si.edu/objectdescription.cfm?ID=258. Downloaded on November 10, 2002.

Women in History. "Elizabeth Keckley." Lakewood Public Library. Available online. URL: http://www.lkwdpl.org/wihohio/keck-eli.htm. Downloaded on November 10, 2002.

Kennedy, William Jesse, Jr. (1889–1985) and William J. Kennedy, III (1922–   )
insurance company executives

The Kennedys were part of a network of family and associates who founded and operated North Carolina Mutual Insurance, which was for a time the largest black-owned business in the United States. Their civic and corporate activities in Durham, North Carolina, have been an important element of the African-American community there.

William Jesse Kennedy, Jr., was born on June 15, 1889, in Andersonville, Georgia, the grandson of a slave who was a skilled carpenter and bridge-builder and who became the owner of a successful farm after emancipation. His parents were William Jesse Kennedy, Sr., the owner of a meat market, and Katie C. Kennedy, who worked at home.

Young William learned carpentry from his grandfather and also worked in his father's market in Andersonville. In 1912 he graduated from the Americus Institute, a Baptist school in Americus, Georgia. He went on to work—as a carpenter, then as a sales agent for a custom-tailoring shop—while taking correspondence courses from LaSalle University, studying the law, and taking courses in business administration through Columbia University's extension division.

Kennedy got into the insurance field by selling policies for the Guaranty Mutual Health and Life Insurance Company in Athens, Georgia, where he became district manager within a year. He was soon promoted to traveling inspector, then to district manager of the office in Augusta, Georgia, the company's largest district. JOHN MERRICK, CHARLES CLINTON SPAULDING, and Aaron Moore were touring the South, promoting their life-insurance company, and they inspired Kennedy to get into that field. He began reading every textbook in the field and seeking to educate himself about the profession, and in September 1916 he became manager of North Carolina Mutual's Savannah office. He was a remarkable sales agent and manager: When he came on board, there was only $7,500 worth of insurance in force in that office, while two years later there was more than $100,000.

In 1917, Kennedy married Margaret Lillian Spaulding, Charles Spaulding's sister, extending the complex web of family relationships that ran the company. When company president Merrick died in 1919, Kennedy became manager of the Ordinary Department, and in 1920 he was given a seat on the board of directors. In 1923 the next president died, leading to another shakeup, in which Kennedy was made assistant secretary. In 1924, he also became office manager for the home office, and in 1931, he went on to be the company's vice president and secretary.

Kennedy was known as a "detail man" who solved problems and made things work, a useful second in command for the company's president, the energetic, dynamic, and visionary Charles Spaulding. When Spaulding died in 1952, Kennedy became North Carolina Mutual's fourth president, a position he held for seven years. Kennedy presided over a period of growth for the insurance company, with a quiet, steady management style. In 1959, at the age of 70, Kennedy went on to become chairman of the board for two years, then went on to become honorary chair. He was also chairman of the board of Mechanics and Farmers Bank and of the Mutual Savings and Loan Association.

Kennedy was active in Durham political and civic affairs, though typically, he took a backstage

William Jesse Kennedy, Jr., was the grandson of a slave—and the founder of one of the largest black insurance companies in the nation. *(Courtesy of North Carolina Mutual Life Insurance Company)*

William J. Kennedy III helped modernize and diversify North Carolina Mutual Life Insurance Company, the firm his family helped to found. *(Courtesy of North Carolina Mutual Life Insurance Company)*

sylvania, where he got his M.B.A. in 1946, followed by a second M.B.A. from New York University in 1948. He held various positions at North Carolina Mutual, including controller in 1959, vice president in 1970, and president and chief executive officer in 1972, a position that he held until 1990.

Kennedy III presided over North Carolina Mutual during a difficult phase of the company's history. Although the black-owned insurance company was founded at a time when African Americans were rarely served by white-owned companies—due partly to the racial segregation of the early 20th century and partly to the widespread poverty among African Americans—the situation had changed in the 1960s and 1970s. The Civil Rights movement helped to break down racial barriers and to create a black middle class that was more attractive to white-owned companies. Moreover, by 1972 many white people bought their insurance from North Carolina Mutual. In response, Kennedy hired more white salespeople—for which he was criticized by many African-American community groups. Kennedy also had to find a way to make the company profitable during a period when its traditionally black customer base was now free to buy insurance from white-owned companies.

Kennedy's answer was to diversify and to focus on investment opportunities. In 1986 he set up NCM Capital, an investment advisory company geared to attract such large-scale investors as pension funds and corporate funds. By 1990, this company was managing $500 million worth of assets for a number of high-profile clients, including Chrysler, IBM, and the Chicago Transit Authority.

Some of Kennedy's ventures have been similarly profitable, while others have floundered or failed. In 1988, the company lost a $3 million investment in a Durham residential housing subdivision, though it did well with a $500,000 apartment building in Winston-Salem, North Carolina. Kennedy continued to be committed to helping

role. He was a member of the North Carolina State Board of Higher Education and a local founder of the National Association for the Advancement of Colored People (NAACP). He died on July 8, 1985.

After Kennedy stepped down in 1959, the company presidency passed into the hands of Asa T. Spaulding, Charles Spaulding's second cousin. Then, in 1972, another Kennedy took over the company—William J. Kennedy III, son of William Jesse Kennedy, Jr., and Margaret Lillian (Spaulding) Kennedy. Born in Durham on October 24, 1922, Kennedy III attended local schools and graduated in 1942 from Virginia State College. He saw some action in World War II, then went on to the Wharton School of Business in Penn-

North Carolina Mutual regain its former prominence and size. Ironically, even as the company has become integrated into white society, it has seen the increasing impoverishment of large sectors of the black community—a very different outcome from the dream of its first founders.

Further Reading

Alston, R. "North Carolina Mutual's Policy for Growth." *Black Enterprise,* June 1990, p. 214.

Carstensen, Fred. "William Jesse Kennedy, Jr." *The Scribner Encyclopedia of American Lives, Volume 1: 1981–1985.* New York: Charles Scribner's Sons, 1998.

Gale Group. "William J. Kennedy, III." *Who's Who Among African Americans,* 15th ed. Farmington Hills, Mich.: Gale Research, 2002. Reproduced in *Biography Resource Center.* Farmington Hills, Mich.: The Gale Group, 2003. Available online. URL: http://www.galenet.com/servlet/BioRC. Downloaded on January 28, 2003.

North Carolina Center for the Study of Black History. "William Jesse Kennedy, Jr. Exhibit." The University of North Carolina at Chapel Hill School of Information and Library Science. Available online. URL: http://www.ils.unc.edu/~rothj/exhibit/kennedy.htm. Downloaded on January 28, 2003.

Ingham, John N., and Lynne B. Feldman. *African-American Business Leaders: A Biographical Dictionary.* Westport, Conn.: Greenwood Press, 1994, pp. 387–402.

King, Don
(Donald King)
(1931–   ) *boxing promoter, music promoter*

One of the most recognizable and colorful figures in the boxing world is Don King, the only top-level African-American promoter in an industry that relies upon African-American fighters. Although King has sustained his share of criticism from sportswriters, government officials, and many of the boxers he has represented, he has also won admiration as a successful African-American businessman who has prospered in a field whose most profitable sectors are otherwise dominated by white people.

King was born on August 20, 1931, in Cleveland, Ohio, the son of Clarence King, a steelworker, and Hattie King, a home-based entrepreneur who baked pies and sold peanuts to raise money. When King was 10 years old, his father was killed in an explosion at the steel mill, and his mother had seven children to raise. She used the insurance money from Clarence's death to move out of their low-income neighborhood into a middle-class area, enlisting her sons in selling her pies and peanuts to the neighbors for extra cash. The King boys would put a paper with a lucky number in each bag of peanuts, making the product popular with local gamblers and bringing Don into contact with some of the city's numbers racketeers. ("Numbers" is a kind of lottery, in which people bet on a three- or four-digit number each day, popular in poor neighborhoods but illegal.)

When King was in high school, he became interested in boxing, initially as a fighter. However, he seemed to have little talent as an athlete and was knocked out cold in one of his first fights. King was then working as a numbers runner (someone who collected bets and paid out winnings) for one of Cleveland's top racketeers. He planned to attend Kent State University, but he misplaced a winning betting slip, which he had to repay from his own funds, leaving him without enough money to attend college. Instead, he began his own numbers business while taking classes for a year at Case Western Reserve University in Cleveland. By age 20 he had become a successful racketeer and was married to Luvenia Mitchell.

By age 30, he was one of the city's top racketeers who was well known for his extravagant style of dress and behavior. He also began getting into various kinds of trouble. In 1954, he had killed a man named Hillary Brown who was allegedly trying to rob one of his numbers stations. King was able to get off by claiming self-defense. Later, the front of his house was blown up by a gangster who wanted protection money that King refused to pay. King was planning to testify against the man on extortion charges when he was shot in the head—but emerged without serious injury.

In 1960, King went on to make the acquaintance of a brilliant young fighter, an Olympic champion then called Cassius Clay. King followed Clay across the country to attend his fights, and a friendship grew between the two men. Meanwhile, King's marriage had fallen apart and he married Henrietta King.

In 1966, King got into an argument with an employee, Sam Garrett, who owed him money. By the time the argument was over, Garrett was dead

Fight promoter and manager Don King is the only top-level African American in a field that relies upon black athletes. *(AP/Wide World Photos)*

from head injuries that resulted when his head hit the pavement. By some accounts, King brutally beat the smaller, weaker man; by his own account, King was once again acting in self-defense. This time, King was convicted of manslaughter and sent to prison, where he began studying the classics of literature and philosophy. He was released on parole in 1971 and granted a full pardon in 1983.

Prison had a transformative effect on King, though at least one of his biographers claims that he has remained a charlatan and a hustler throughout his career. King himself said that God gave him a sign by making his hair stand up in its trademark style, and he continues to maintain that he has never cut or styled his hair since he first received that heavenly message. In any case, King left the numbers game and sought a legitimate business career. In 1972, he organized a benefit to keep open Cleveland's only black hospital, inviting Muhammad Ali—the former Cassius Clay—to fight 10 rounds against four different opponents. The event was so successful that King became a fight promoter.

In 1974, King became nationally and internationally known for promoting the "Rumble in the Jungle," a fight that he organized with the closed-circuit TV company Video Techniques, between Ali and champion George Foreman in Kinshasa, Zaire. King convinced the Zaire government to back the event at a cost of more than $10 million. The event was hugely successful and it made King's reputation.

In 1975, King went on to promote the "Thrilla in Manila," a fight in the Philippines between Ali and Joe Frazier. He continued to promote Ali, though his friend later went to Bob Arum for representation, along with Arum's closed-circuit company, Top Rank. Many other fighters wanted to work with King, however, including Larry Holmes, Michael Dokes, Mike Weaver, Tim Witherspoon, Bonecrusher Smith, Trevor Berbick, and, most famously, Mike Tyson. Many of these top fighters wanted to work with a black promoter, and King was the only African-American high-level promoter in the fight industry. Some observers have charged that King exploited his fighters, while others applaud him for opening the top ranks of the industry to people of color, especially since so many fighters are African-American or Latino.

In 1977, King set up a series of fights with ABC-TV, but the fights were cancelled when the Federal Bureau of Investigation (FBI) found evidence that King had altered some of the boxers' records. In the early 1980s, the FBI investigated King again, as part of a large-scale look into the boxing industry. In neither case did charges result, but in 1984, King and his secretary Constance Harper were indicted on tax evasion—although the jury acquitted King and convicted Harper. King responded in a typically extravagant manner, buying the jury members first-class plane tickets and ringside seats for heavyweight bouts.

King expanded his promotional activities into the music business in 1984, when he promoted the Victory Tour of singer Michael Jackson and his brothers. The tour was enormously profitable.

King's public statements have been as contradictory as his reputation. Sometimes he expresses his deep patriotism and repeats his famous catchphrase, "Only in America." At other times, he speaks of the racism that he believes is an integral part of American life, and points to his role in such civil rights groups as the National Association for the Advancement of Colored People (NAACP), the United Negro College Fund, and Jesse Jackson's Operation PUSH. He has been accused of using his blackness to exploit other black people, even as he has been praised for using his position to further the position of African Americans in society.

The early 1990s were difficult years for King, as many of his fighters claimed that he had cheated them. Witherspoon sued King, Tyson lost the championship and was then jailed for rape, and King lost the close relationship he had developed with HBO. In 1992, a former accountant revealed

evidence of insurance fraud, leading to an indictment of King. Yet eventually, Tyson was released and began earning money again, King developed a partnership known as King Vision with cable network Showtime, and King was vindicated of the insurance-related charges in 1995. King continues as one of the major players in the boxing industry and in African-American enterprise.

Further Reading

Carey, Charles W., Jr. "King, Don." *American Inventors, Entrepreneurs, and Business Visionaries.* New York: Facts On File, 2002.

Gale Group. "Don King." *Contemporary Black Biography,* Vol. 14. Farmington Hills, Mich.: Gale, 1997.

Newfield, Jack. *Only in America: The Life and Crimes of Don King.* New York: William Morrow, 1995.

Don King Productions, Inc. Available online. URL: http://www.donking.com/popup.htm. Downloaded on January 28, 2003.

King, Horace
(1807–1885) *covered-bridge builder, contractor*

Although he was a slave for half his life, Horace King left a legacy in the form of more than 100 covered bridges that he built throughout Georgia, Alabama, and Mississippi. He created a prosperous construction company, based on the skills, reputation, and connections that he developed while still a slave, winning the respect of both black and white residents of the southern towns in which he lived.

King was born a slave in South Carolina's Chesterfield District on September 8, 1807, the son of a mixed-race slave named Edmund King and a woman named Susan or "Lucky," of Catawba Indian and African-American heritage. King and the rest of the family's slaves were sold in 1829 when his owner died, and King was eventually sold to John Godwin, a house builder and bridge contractor who may have worked with

Horace King became famous for the covered bridges he built throughout the South. *(Alabama Department of Archives and History, Montgomery, Alabama)*

King in building a bridge over the Pee Dee River in 1822 under the supervision of famed Connecticut architect Ithiel Town. Town had developed an innovative new technique for building bridges, and it was this technique that King would employ for the rest of his life.

Godwin was the son of a South Carolina businessman who wanted to make a life for himself on the frontier and decided that the new, raw country of the West would need bridges. In 1832, when the state of Alabama acquired territory from the Creek Indians, Godwin bid for the contract. Reportedly, his bid was the highest but had the earliest completion date, and he was awarded the job of building a bridge across the Chattahoochee River, connecting the older portions of Alabama with the part that had once been Indian territory.

The Chattahoochee was a difficult river to span, but Godwin and King managed to build what was first called the City Bridge, later the Dillingham Street Bridge. From the first, Godwin treated King more as a junior partner than as a slave, respecting his technical skills and engineering ability. Godwin's role in the business was to develop proposals and enter bids, while King supervised the actual construction. After their success with the Chattahoochee, the two men went on to build bridges at Irwinton, Alabama (now Eufala); West Point, Georgia; Tallassee, Alabama; and Florence, Alabama. King's workmanship was renowned throughout the region, and his ingenious ability to overcome technical problems won him the admiration of many. King also built many houses in Girard (now Phenix City), Alabama, and Columbus, Georgia.

In 1839, King married Frances Thomas, a free-born woman of mixed race: African American, Creek, and white. Their four sons and one daughter later joined King in his bridge-building business.

In the 1840s, King began to work with Robert Jemison, Jr., a wealthy lawyer, planter, and Alabama state senator who owned a number of other businesses, including a stagecoach company, a sawmill, and a turnpike and bridge company. In their three-way partnership, Jemison supplied the lumber, Godwin organized the work crews, and King supervised the building of the bridges. Godwin began to suffer financial reverses during this period, but although he received many offers to purchase King, one as high as $6,000, he always refused to sell King and indeed, went to a great deal of trouble to see that he could not be sold. Godwin feared that if his creditors seized his property in payment of his debts, King might be taken. However, a number of states had made it extremely difficult to set slaves free in the 1840s, including Alabama, where a ruling of the state legislature was required to set even a single black person free. Godwin asked Jemison to petition the legislature on King's behalf, and in 1846, King received his freedom. Godwin also arranged for a petition to the Georgia state legislature, so that King's freedom would be recognized in both states.

As a free man, King continued to engage in the bridge-building business, working both on his own and with Jemison, who, as a member of the state Ways and Means Committee, was in line for many government contracts. The two built the Alabama Insane Hospital in 1860, as well as several bridges and other buildings. There was clearly respect on both sides of the relationship; however, Jemison wrote to King as "Dear Horace" and signed his letters "your friend," while King wrote to Jemison as "Mr. Jemison, Dear Sir" and signed his letters "Your humble servant," even in the 1870s, when slavery had ended.

Godwin's finances continued to decline and he died in 1859, penniless. His children were still concerned with King's freedom, however, and they recorded his emancipation (freedom) in the Russell County courthouse. King missed his friend so much he spent $600—a huge sum at the time—to put up a marker on his grave, "in lasting remembrance of the love and gratitude he felt for his lost friend and former master." Ironically, this marker became known as a sign of the love that slaves felt for their owners, and became quite famous when a picture of the stone was put in Robert Ripley's *Believe It or Not,* a newspaper column of unusual occurrences.

During the Civil War, King worked a number of construction jobs, but as he was paid in Confederate currency, he did not prosper much from that period in his life. He was also occupied with managing the Godwin Sawmill and contracting business, even as he kept his own businesses going. King's wife died in 1864, adding to his troubles.

In 1869, King married Sarah Jane McManus and became somewhat involved in politics, serving in the Alabama House of Representatives from 1868 to 1872, and becoming a magistrate for Russell County and a registrar for the town of Girard. He seems to have run for office at the urging of white friends, who feared the more radical African Americans seeking political office in the years after the Civil War.

In the mid-1870s, King and his family moved to LaGrange, Georgia, where King worked with the Freedman's Bureau, an organization set up to help newly freed African Americans. King was especially interested in education and at one point thought of establishing a trade school. His company, now called King Brothers, built a chapel for Southern Female College and the LaGrange Academy, the city's first black school.

King retired in the early 1880s, and his sons and daughter continued to run the family business. He died on May 28, 1885, honored by a funeral procession that marched through the town's center. All business stopped, and people of all races came out to pay their respect. The local newspaper said that King had "risen to prominence by force of genius and power."

Further Reading

French, Thomas L., Jr., and Edward L. French. "Covered Bridge Builders of Georgia." Georgia Department of Transportation website. Available online. URL: http://www.dot.state.ga.us/specialsubjects/specialinterest/covered/builders.shtml. Downloaded on December 27, 2002.

Gibbons, Faye. *Horace King: Bridges to Freedom.* Birmingham, Ala.: Crane Hill Publishers 2002.

Osinski, Bill. "Former Slave Turned Bridge Builder." *Atlanta Journal-Constitution.* December 7, 1997, p. F3. Available online at Fort Tyler: Battle of West Point, Georgia. URL: http://www.forttyler.com/king.htm. Downloaded on December 27, 2002.

L

Lafon, Thomy
(1810–1893) *businessman, philanthropist, real estate broker, store owner*

Thomy Lafon was one of the most prominent black philanthropists of the 19th century. Part of the group of free black people in New Orleans, Louisiana, he left a huge estate of more than $600,000 when he died in 1893, which, without wife or children, he left to a number of charitable institutions. He also gave enormous sums to charity during his lifetime, from the money he made as a merchant and speculator in real estate.

Lafon was born on December 28, 1810, into a poor family in New Orleans. His mother was a woman named Modeste Foucher, probably of Haitian background, while his father was probably Pierre Laralde, who may have been either a white man from France or a black man with some French heritage. Because records kept about black people in the 19th century tend to be incomplete, little is known about Lafon's early life, though historians believe that his father may have deserted the family during Lafon's childhood. Nevertheless, Lafon received a good education, and he himself later claimed that he was partly educated in Europe, citing his fluency in languages as evidence. Indeed, in 1935, his lawyer, René Metoyer, claimed that Lafon had attended the School of Louis XIV in Paris.

Myths and popular stories abound concerning Lafon's life before the Civil War. He may have sold cakes to the workers on the wharves, or perhaps he taught school. In 1842, when he was 32, he was listed as a merchant in the New Orleans city directory; the next time he appears in the directory is 1861, associated with a different New Orleans business. Some historians claim that he ran a small store and then, just before the Civil War, began lending money at extremely high interest rates while investing in real estate. In the 1867 directory, he is listed at a new business address, and for the first time, he has a separate residence, suggesting that he has prospered. His business was then listed as "broker," suggesting that he was buying and selling various commodities (items for sale) and/or real estate.

In any case, by 1870, Lafon was a rich man with thousands of dollars in real estate. Yet he lived very simply, with his sister, in a shabby house. He never married, and he dressed in clean but very simple and unfashionable clothes. He was on the boards of several banks, was generally respected by people of all races, and was known to be very cultured, with an interest in music and art.

Before and after the Civil War, Lafon was part of the move to fight for equality and the social position of free black people. He formed the Radical Club in New Orleans, a group that supported the Union occupation troops, demanded the vote, and sought to integrate white public schools. They formed a newspaper called the *Tribune*—the first black-owned newspaper in the South after the Civil War—but were unable to prevent the trends after the war of increasing segregation (separation of black and white) and the erosion of black civil rights.

Depressed by their political failures and loss of status, many of New Orleans's black elite committed suicide. Lafon seems to have chosen more private ways of doing good, giving to established charities, helping individuals, and founding the Lafon Orphan Boys' Asylum and the Home for Aged Colored Men and Women. After his death in New Orleans on December 22, 1893, he left money for a hospital, for Straight (later Dillard) University, and for New Orleans University, as well as to rest homes, religious orders, and other Catholic institutions—constituting the largest philanthropic gift ever given by a New Orleans black person. The Thomy Lafon Public School was named for him in 1898.

Further Reading

Ingham, John N., and Lynne B. Feldman. *African-American Business Leaders*. Westport, Conn.: Greenwood Press, 1992, pp. 410–414.

Kranz, Rachel, and Philip J. Koslow. *The Biographical Dictionary of African Americans*. New York: Facts On File, 1999, p. 145.

Wynes, Charles E. "Thomy Lafon: Black Philanthropist," *The Midwest Quarterly* 22, no. 2 (winter 1981): 105–112.

Lee, George Washington
(1894–1976) *insurance executive, community leader, author*

George Washington Lee is best remembered for the book he wrote about Beale Street in the heart of the African-American community in Memphis, Tennessee: *Beale Street: Where the Blues Began,* which he published in 1934. He was also a key figure in the African-American insurance industry.

Lee was born on January 4, 1894, in the tiny village of Heathman, Mississippi, four miles west of Indianola, in the same state. His father, Reverend George Lee, preached on Sundays and worked during the week on his small farm, supporting himself with the nickels and dimes he collected in church. His mother, Hattie Stringfellow Lee, left her husband soon after George was born. When the Reverend died after that, his brother took the family farm and Hattie became a sharecropper, working a piece of someone else's land in exchange for the right to live in a small cabin and to collect a small allowance of cornmeal at the plantation store.

When the owner of the land forced Hattie Lee to leave, she and her family went to join her oldest son, Abner, who was working at a cotton-seed mill in Indianola. The town of 2,000 people was strictly segregated (separated by race), and white residents periodically resorted to violence rather than see black people rise economically. As a youth, George Washington Lee got a job running errands for a local white-owned grocery store, because the white youth who had previously had that job had been caught stealing. Community pressure forced the owner to fire Lee, however, who said he had hired Lee only because he thought he would not have the nerve to steal as much as a white person.

Lee went on to work as houseboy for cotton planter and merchant Charles Klingman, who later got him a position as a driver making deliveries for a local store. Then Hattie Lee insisted that her son quit his job to study at Alcorn Agricultural and Mechanical College, which provided him with the equivalent of a high school education.

In 1912, Lee went on to Memphis, where his brother had moved earlier. Although Tennessee was segregated, as Mississippi had been, there was a huge black business community in Memphis, and the city of 100,000 offered many more opportunities for a budding entrepreneur. Lee began by working as a bellhop at the Gayoso Hotel.

When the United States entered World War I, the National Association for the Advancement of Colored People (NAACP) protested the racial segregation of the U.S. armed forces; in response, the army set up a black officer training camp in Des Moines, Iowa. Lee managed to be accepted there in 1917, even though he was only 23, younger than the minimum age. He was sent to France and eventually achieved the rank of first lieutenant. He liked to be known thereafter as "Lieutenant Lee of Beale Street." At a time when white people referred to black people by their first names only, Lee managed to get white people to call him "Lieutenant," though they would never have called him "Mister."

In 1919, Lee returned to Memphis and began selling policies for Mississippi Life Insurance. He was soon promoted to district manager of the Memphis office, where he recruited and trained new agents. Although the company had begun in Mississippi, its president moved the home office to Memphis, feeling that race relations were better there. The company specialized in so-called industrial insurance, in which poor people could pay a nickel or a dime each week in order to guarantee that their families could collect burial expenses when they died. This was a common form of insurance for black-owned companies to sell: It meant that they dealt with customers whom white companies ignored, and it allowed them to serve the large segment of the black community that was then very poor.

Lee and his sales agents were very successful, and in 1920, he was promoted to vice president of the company. The same year, he attended a meeting of the National Negro Business League (NNBL), an organization founded by Booker T. Washington to promote self-help and black enterprise. The largest black enterprises at the time were indeed insurance companies—but Lee found that the NNBL was dominated by companies associated with so-called fraternal orders, volunteer self-help organizations that also offered burial insurance for small weekly fees. Larger companies,

like his own, had less power in the NNBL, so Lee, CHARLES CLINTON SPAULDING, and others organized the National Negro Insurance Association (NNIA), based in Durham, North Carolina.

In 1923, Mississippi Life was sold to Heman Perry, an Atlanta entrepreneur. Perry owed a lot of money to the white-owned Southeastern Trust company. To pay back this debt, he began stealing money from Mississippi Life, which he then sold to a white firm, Southern Life. Lee organized a revolt to keep the black-owned company under African-American control. He and his agents refused to work for the new company, and he organized sales managers from three states to resign their positions and picket the new company. In the racially divided climate of the South at this time, only African-American agents could collect the weekly premiums from the company's black customers—white agents would probably have refused such "demeaning" work, and black customers would in any case have mistrusted white agents—so Lee and those who stood with him had made the company worthless to its new owners.

Lee refused a $7,000 salary—a huge amount in those days—to call off the strike, and continued to fight for black control of the company. Because he found it so difficult to accept that an African American had sold the company to white people in the first place, he claimed that Perry had been tricked by the Ku Klux Klan, a belief that seems to have no basis in fact. Indeed, when Perry came to Memphis, the former employees of Mississippi Life spit on him and threw bottles at him, driving him out of town with threats of greater harm.

Lee might then have organized his own company, but he preferred to approach Atlanta Life Insurance Company executive Alonzo Herndon, who made Lee the manager of a new Memphis branch of his company. Lee and his agents continued to serve his old customers, and Lee remained with Atlanta Life for the rest of his life, becoming senior vice president and a member of the board of directors. He also helped found the company magazine, *The Vision*.

In 1927, Lee also became a member of the board of directors of Universal Life Insurance, the black-owned company organized from the remains of Mississippi Life. Throughout the 1920s, Lee supported black capitalism and stressed that black people had to create their own financial institutions in order to succeed in America. He also advocated black pride, arguing in favor of civil rights. In those years, a group of African-American ministers in Memphis argued that black people should accommodate themselves to white people's restrictions, with some even agreeing that black people were biologically inferior to whites. Lee wrote articles and gave speeches arguing strongly against that view and also joined the NAACP, the major civil rights group of the time.

Meanwhile, Lee got involved in politics as an associate of Robert Church, Jr., a key figure in state Republican politics. In those days, the Republican Party was seen as the party of Abraham Lincoln and civil rights, and church enjoyed a certain amount of power behind the scenes. Lee became a leading orator under Church's guidance, preaching black pride, economic self-help, and civil rights. In 1927, the two men joined other black leaders to form the West Tennessee Civil and Political League—a group dedicated to black voter registration as a way of pressuring white city leaders—with Lee as president. Although the group helped elect a white candidate who promised to be more responsive to black people, the candidate turned out to be corrupt and did little for African Americans.

During the 1930s, Lee became an author. His *Beale Street: Where the Blues Began* told the story of Memphis's black history, including black entrepreneur ROBERT REED CHURCH, SR., Julia A. Hooks, who founded an integrated music school, and the many brave African Americans who helped Memphis cope with the yellow fever epidemic of 1878. He also wrote a novel, *River George*, published in 1937, and a collection of

short stories, *Beale Street Sundown*, which came out in 1942.

During the 1930s, Lee became more conservative. He stopped supporting the NAACP and focused on the Republican Party—at a time when African Americans were coming to support the Democrats, then the party of Franklin D. Roosevelt, increased social services, and a vision of national social equality.

Meanwhile, in 1946, Atlanta Life considered bringing Lee to the head office in Atlanta—but 500 Memphis citizens sent the company a letter asking that Lee remain in their city, a testament to the enormous popularity he still enjoyed. Lee also helped establish the Herndon Foundation, to

Insurance executive George Washington Lee is shown here with some of the books he wrote about the African-American community in Memphis, Tennessee. *(Library of Congress)*

ensure that Atlanta Life would remain a black-owned company. In 1948, Lee became a director of the Tri-State Bank, a black-owned bank in Memphis.

Lee eventually broke with Church, and as Memphis black leaders became more radical throughout the 1940s and 1950s, Lee became increasingly more conservative. He opposed the Civil Rights movement, and during the 1960s he traveled around the country criticizing black power. He believed that black people should appeal to white guilt rather than simply demanding their rights.

Although Lee was isolated politically by the 1970s, he was still an almost legendary figure who was easily recognized during his daily walk on Beale Street. On August 1, 1976, the 82-year-old Lee was killed in a car wreck. His legacy lives on through the books he wrote and the institutions he helped found.

Further Reading

Epsilon Phi Chapter. "Colonel George Washington Lee." Epsilon Phi Chapter of Omega Psi Phi Fraternity website. Available online. URL: http://www.epsilonphichapter.com/g_w_lee.htm. Downloaded on January 31, 2003.

Gale Group. "George W(ashington) Lee." *Contemporary Authors Online.* Farmington Hills, Mich.: Gale, 2003. Downloaded on January 31, 2003.

Tucker, David M. *Lieutenant Lee of Beale Street.* Nashville, Tenn.: Vanderbilt University Press, 1971.

Leidesdorff, William A.
(William Alexander Leidesdorff)

(1810–1848) *land speculator, merchant, financier*

William Leidesdorff was one of the founders of San Francisco and a wealthy merchant who built the city's first hotel, hosted its first public horse race, and helped establish its first public schools. He played a key role in helping to annex the Mexican territory of California to the United States. In his capacity as vice-consul to Mexico, he was probably the first African-American diplomat.

Leidesdorff was born sometime in 1810 on the island of St. Croix in the Danish West Indies, the illegitimate son of Danish sugar planter William Leidesdorff and a woman of partial African descent named Anna Maria Spark. Spark—whom some sources name as Maria Ann Sparks—had five children with the planter, who sent his son to New Orleans in 1834 to work in his cotton business. Leidesdorff became a naturalized U.S. citizen in that year, and three years later was legally acknowledged as his father's heir. As a result, he was able to inherit his father's business some two or three years later, when his father died.

Leidesdorff also worked as a ship's captain sailing between New Orleans and New York. Part of his legend includes an unsubstantiated rumor that he had an unhappy love affair with a New Orleans woman who rejected him when she realized he was of African descent. Whether or not that is true, historians are certain that he left New Orleans and went to live in New York for a while, where he became captain on a ship called the *Julia Ann.* In the days before the Panama Canal, Leidesdorff was forced to sail all the way around South America, arriving at Monterey, on the California coast, in 1841. The ship's owner then sold his vessel, and Leidesdorff became a merchant in Yerba Buena, a little village of only 30 families where he soon emerged as a leading citizen.

At the time, Yerba Buena was in Mexican territory. Five years later, it would become the U.S. city of San Francisco. In the meantime, Leidesdorff prospered as he helped the new town to develop. In 1843 he started buying property in the village, and in 1844 he established a warehouse from which he exported tallow (used in making candles) and hides (used to make clothing and shoes). Also in 1844, he became a Mexican citizen, which entitled him to land grants, including a 35,000-acre property in the Sacramento Valley, next to John Sutter's estate. He continued to buy Yerba Buena property as well, erecting the City Hotel, a large store, and his own fine home.

Historians differ about the extent to which Leidesdorff's racial heritage was public knowledge. Some of the few black citizens in Yerba Buena were certainly aware of it, and it is entirely possible that his African ancestry was widely known. This makes his rise to prominence all the more impressive, as there was a great deal of prejudice against African Americans in this era, when slavery was still legal in much of the United States.

Leidesdorff was a member of Yerba Buena's City Council, which he served as its treasurer and as a member on several committees. His education committee established the area's first public school in April 1848. He also engaged in legendary ventures, such as operating the 37-foot steamboat *Sitka*, the first such boat in San Francisco Bay. Although the *Sitka*'s first voyage on the Sacramento River took longer than it would have taken someone to walk the same distance, its notoriety increased Leisdesdorff's fame.

Leidesdorff was a Mexican citizen in 1845, but the U.S. government nevertheless appointed him vice-consul to Mexico to serve under his close friend Consul Thomas A. Larkin. At the time, there were three political factions in California: those who wanted to remain annexed to Mexico, those favoring independence, and those who wanted to become part of the United States. Leidesdorff favored the last option, and worked with others to plot the overthrow of the Mexican government, assisted by the explorer John C. Frémont. At the same time, Leidesdorff continued to accept land grants from Mexico, until President John Tyler declared war on that country in 1846. Frémont led the troops that captured Yerba Buena, while Leidesdorff headed a group of men that took the local fort and the Presidio (town headquarters). He also translated into Spanish the text of the proclamation declaring U.S. occupation of the region.

William Leidesdorff was one of the founders of San Francisco, California—and the first African-American diplomat. *(Courtesy of the California History Room, California State Library, Sacramento, California)*

After the U.S. takeover, the new city was renamed San Francisco, and Leidesdorff left his post as vice-consul to concentrate on his business activities. Then, on March 15, 1848, gold was discovered on Sutter's property as well as Leidesdorff's. In all likelihood, Leidesdorff would have established a gold mine on his estate but for the fact that he died suddenly of typhus on May 18, 1848, at the age of 38. He left no will, so there was a great deal of haggling over his estate, which became increasingly valuable as the gold rush continued. Eventually, Leidesdorff's mother established her claim to the estate, and Captain John L. Folsom bought it from her. Because the discovery of gold had raised the price of his holdings, Leidesdorff became known as America's first black millionaire, though he had certainly not possessed that much money while he was alive.

Leidesdorff's memory lives on in San Francisco through the three-block street that bears his name in today's financial district. A street and a plaza in Folsom, California, are named for him as well. He is remembered as one of the people who built a great American city and helped make California the 31st state in the Union.

Further Reading

Gale Group. "William A. Leidesdorff." *Notable Black American Men.* Farmington Hills, Mich.: Gale Research, 1998.

Haskins, Jim. *African American Entrepreneurs.* Black Stars Series. New York: John Wiley & Sons, 1998, pp. 36–40.

Lapp, Rudolph M. *Blacks in Gold Rush California.* New Haven, Conn.: Yale University Press, 1977.

Savage, William S. "The influence of William Alexander Leidesdorff on the History of California." *Journal of Negro History* 38 (July 1953): 322–332.

Thurman, Sue Bailey. *Pioneers of Negro Origin in California.* San Francisco, Calif.: Acme Press, 1952. Excerpt available online at the San Francisco Museum website. URL: http://www.sfmuseum.org/bio/leidesdorff.html. Downloaded on January 25, 2003.

"William Alexander Leidesdorff, A Rags-to-Riches Saga." *New York Amsterdam News,* February 3, 1996, p. 8.

Lewis, Byron E.
(Byron Eugene Lewis)
(1931–   ) *advertising executive*

Byron E. Lewis is the founder of UniWorld Group, Inc., one of the largest black-owned advertising agencies in the United States. He has worked with such clients as AT&T, Avon, Burger King, Coors, Eastman Kodak, Ford, Gatorade, Mars, Pillsbury, and Walt Disney. He has also handled the media relations for a number of African-American political candidates and campaigns, including Jesse Jackson's 1984 bid for the presidency. Under his leadership, UniWorld has become a diversified media company that produces television specials and engages in other media projects, as well as doing millions of dollars worth of business in advertising.

Lewis was born on December 25, 1931, in Newark, New Jersey, the son of Eugene Lewis, a house painter, and Myrtle Lewis, who cleaned homes. Byron Lewis majored in journalism at Long Island University, receiving his B.A. in 1953, but he decided not to pursue a career in the field when he realized that in those days of racial segregation (separation), he would never be hired by any major newspaper. He spent some time in the military, then in 1958 tried again to break into journalism. Unable to land a job at a mainstream newspaper, he took a job at the Harlem-based newspaper the *Citizen Call,* selling ads. The *Call's* publisher, John Patterson, became a kind of mentor to Lewis.

Unable to sell to white advertisers, the *Call* went out of business in 1960, and Lewis and other former staffers launched the *Urbanite,* a magazine intended for young, ambitious African Americans. It is extremely difficult to start a new magazine without huge reserves of cash and commitments from advertisers, and the *Urbanite* had neither. Within three months, it, too, went out of business.

Lewis took business and public relations classes at New York University during the evenings while freelancing as a sales agent during the day and selling classified ads for the *New York Times* on weekends. In the early 1960s, he was hired to sell ads for Amalgamated Publishers, an advertising broker for 153 black-owned newspapers. He went on to become vice president of advertising sales for *Tuesday,* a literary supplement geared toward African Americans that appeared in 14 urban newspapers. Once again, Lewis found that white businesses were uninterested in the black consumer market and were unwilling to direct advertising to that market.

In 1968, Lewis was one of 50 black professionals invited to a conference convened by Shearson & Hamill Investment, along with EDWARD T. LEWIS and CLARENCE O. SMITH, who founded *Essence* magazine as a result. The conference was an effort to encourage black capitalism supported by President Richard M. Nixon's Commerce Department, on the theory that black entrepreneurship would pull young black people away from the increasingly militant politics of the time. Like the founders of *Essence*, Byron Lewis, too, was inspired to start a new venture—UniWorld, an advertising agency that would target ethnic consumers.

It took Lewis a while to find investors who would back him financially, and his first clients were companies with whom he had developed relationships before founding UniWorld. His success was made possible by the emergence of black-owned or -controlled media, which also targeted ethnic markets: *Essence* and EARL G. GRAVES's *Black Enterprise;* the syndicated television show, *Soul Train;* and the black radio stations springing up around the country. A number of other black-owned ad agencies were started in the late 1960s and 1970s, but many of them went out of business in less than two years. In 1976, U.S. ad agencies did $26 billion worth of business—and less than 1 percent of that went to black-owned agencies.

Lewis was struggling to keep his business alive. In early 1974, he managed to get a loan through the U.S. Small Business Administration, but his company was still in trouble. Patterson told him to look within for more innovative ideas, and Lewis remembered listening to radio soap operas with his family as a child. He developed a radio soap opera targeted toward black-owned radio stations, *Sounds of the City*, about a southern black family that had moved to a northern city and faced the typical urban problems of unemployment, drugs, and crime. The show featured actors who would later become famous, such as Robert Guillaume, who starred on the television shows *Benson* and *Sports Night*, and Lawrence Hilton-Jacobs, who was in the film *Cooley High* and in the television show *Welcome Back, Kotter*.

Lewis convinced Quaker Oats to sponsor the show, pointing out that black families consumed many of the company's products, including oatmeal, cornmeal, pancake mix, and syrup. The company aired commercials on 27 black-owned stations for 39 weeks, providing UniWorld with much-needed funds and keeping the company afloat.

Lewis went on to develop a joint venture with National Black Network to cover the 1976 Democratic and Republican presidential conventions. At the time, AT&T was trying to reach into the affluent black consumer market, and they sponsored Lewis's coverage. In 1980, UniWorld coordinated press for the first black political convention in Gary, Indiana, which led to the company handling Jesse Jackson's presidential campaign in 1984. Just as black-owned media had made UniWorld's success possible, so did the company benefit from the increase in black political power.

Meanwhile, Lewis continued to diversify. In 1977, he formed UniWorld Entertainment to produce a number of television shows, including *This Far by Faith*, a special on the impact of the black church, at the request of Reverend Benjamin Hooks, then the head of the National Association for the Advancement of Colored People (NAACP); *Sweet Auburn*, which was done for the Martin Luther King Center; and telecasts featuring the Congressional Black Caucus. In 1984, he began producing *America's Black Forum*, an ongoing nationally syndicated news show hosted by Julian Bond.

Lewis continued to seek mainstream companies for his clients, and he occasionally benefited from firms' special needs to reach out to black consumers. In 1985, when the head of Coors Brewing Company told the NAACP that blacks "should be happy that they were brought [to America] in chains," the company responded to the criticism they received by agreeing to spend $500 million with black businesses, of which $5 million went to UniWorld. Likewise, in 1996, when Texaco was accused by company executives of making derogatory remarks to black employees, the company boosted its marketing efforts to the black community, doing $10 million worth of business with UniWorld.

In the 1980s, organizations like Jackson's Operation PUSH began pressuring white companies to work more with black-owned firms, and agencies like UniWorld benefited. But in the 1990s, two trends made things difficult for black-owned ad agencies. First, longtime attacks on affirmative action and reversals of gains made in response to the Civil Rights movement lessened the pressure on white companies to hire black firms—or black employees.

Second, UniWorld faced new types of competition—from new black-owned firms, such as RUSSELL SIMMONS's Rush Media; and from white-owned firms partnered with black celebrities, such as Spike/DDB, a partnership between black filmmaker Spike Lee and white-owned DDB Worldwide. The targeted market-share approach, in which UniWorld offered companies a chance to get their message out to various types of consumers—black, Latino, urban, young, "hip," and the like—had become commonplace in the advertising world. Ironically, people like Lewis who had pioneered this approach were now competing with others who had just begun to use it.

Lewis has continued to diversify and to focus on ever better-defined segments of the consumer market. He has created UniWorld Hispanic to reach the Latino market, and UniWorld Direct Response to target such segments as Caribbean Americans and black professionals. His company has become a sponsor of the UniverSoul Big Top Circus and has developed the annual Acapulco Black Film Festival, which is used for marketing by HBO, Eastman Kodak, and other companies.

The future of UniWorld in the changing business climate is far from clear, but the company continues to do millions of dollars worth of business in media and advertising, and to expand its diverse activities.

Further Reading

Dingle, Derek T. *Black Enterprise, Titans of the B.E. 100s.* New York: John Wiley & Sons, Inc., 1999, pp. 93–114.

Gale Group. "Byron E. Lewis." *Contemporary Black Biography,* Volume 13. Farmington Hills, Mich.: Gale Research, 1996.

"Lord Byron." *Success,* April 1999, p. 38.

Temes, Judy. "Black Ad Agencies Fail to Win Clients." *Crain's New York Business,* November 3, 1997, p. 1.

Lewis, Edward T. (1940–   ) and Clarence O. Smith (1933–   )
publishers

Edward T. Lewis and Clarence O. Smith were the founders of *Essence,* the first and most successful mass-market magazine directed to African-American women. For years, the two men published *Essence* together, and the company they founded has grown into a publishing empire that sponsors the Essence Music Festival and manufactures and markets products for black women.

Lewis was born on May 15, 1940, in the Bronx, a borough of New York City. Little is known about his parents, other than that his parents were divorced and his mother remarried. He himself attributes his entrepreneurial spirit to an uncle who had his own business and who talked to Lewis as a child about controlling his own destiny. Lewis was also affected by being a darker-skinned African American at a time when color prejudice within the black community favored lighter-skinned people.

Lewis attended the University of New Mexico on a football scholarship, which he lost when he became a controversial figure for his support of Black Power leader Malcolm X. He graduated in 1964 with a degree in political science and international relations. He then enrolled as a lecturer in the Peace Corps program at the university, worked for two years as an administrative analyst in Albuquerque's city manager's office, and received his master's degree from the University of Mexico in 1966. Lewis was devastated by flunking out of Georgetown Law School, but he went on to work at First National City Bank (now Citibank) in New York City as a financial analyst while studying in the Ph.D. program in public administration at New York University.

In 1969, Lewis was one of 50 young African Americans invited to attend a conference sponsored by the brokerage firm of Shearson-Hammill & Co., an effort to encourage black capitalism supported by the U.S. Commerce Department under the administration of President Richard M. Nixon, who thought that black entrepreneurship would pull young black people away from the increasingly militant politics of the time.

Jonathan Blount, a salesman at New Jersey Bell Telephone, suggested a magazine for black women, who at the time were virtually shut out of the publishing world. Other than JOHN H. JOHNSON's publications *Ebony* and *Jet,* black people were barely mentioned or portrayed in magazines of the era, and women's magazines featured advice, fashion, and beauty tips focusing entirely on white women. Shearson-Hammill advisers at the conference put Blount together with three other attendees: Cecil Hollingsworth, who had worked in the print industry; Clarence Smith, a sales agent for Prudential Insurance; and Edward Lewis, who brought a strong background in financial planning to the mix. The four young men worked together to raise funds, as well as putting up money of their own. Their initial investors included First National City Bank, Chase National Bank, and Morgan Guaranty Bank, and their magazine debuted in May 1970 as *Essence.* Filmmaker Gordon Parks helped provide editorial supervision.

Smith came to his participation in *Essence* by quite a different route from Lewis's. He was born on March 31, 1933, also in the Bronx, the son of Millicent Fry, a domestic, and Clarence Smith, a janitor who delivered dry cleaning. Smith's early career included a stint in the army between 1957 and 1959, and some time at New York City's

Baruch College School of Business from 1960 to 1961. Later he worked as a freight forwarder for a customs agency.

In 1963, a friend who sold him an insurance policy suggested that Smith enter sales, and Smith approached Prudential, a major insurance company that at the time had only two African-American sales agents among a sales force of 55,000—an indication of the racial segregation (separation) within the business world of that era. The company did not give Smith even a desk or a phone—yet within a year he had sold more than $1 million worth of policies.

In 1964, Smith had a fateful meeting with William Hudgins, the president of black-owned Freedom National Bank. Hudgins refused to do business with Prudential on the grounds that it and other white-owned financial institutions engaged in redlining—refusing to invest funds in black inner-city neighborhoods, even if many of their profits came from people living in those very communities. Smith was appalled at what Hudgins told him, and he began to search for other ways he might participate in the business world. He continued to work for Prudential, but he also became a registered representative with the Investor Planning Corporation, a financial services firm, so that he could help black clients put together investment packages that might eventually make them wealthy, rather than simply selling them insurance.

When Smith attended the 1968 Shearson conference, he was greatly affected by the death of Martin Luther King, Jr., earlier that year. He was deeply committed to doing something that would make life better for African Americans, particularly since by then he had married and had a one-year-old son. He was eager to work with Blount, Hollingsworth, and Lewis to found a new magazine for African-American women.

From the first, *Essence*'s focus was somewhat split. On the one hand, it was a glossy, slick fashion magazine that promoted fashion and beauty products—albeit for black women, to whom no other such magazines were marketed. On the other hand, it was a political publication that published articles like "Five Shades of Militancy." *Ebony* and *Jet* tended to present a more middle-aged and sedate view of black womanhood, but *Essence*, like such white contemporary women's magazines as *Cosmopolitan*, portrayed black women as sexy and sensual, wearing bikinis and miniskirts.

Initially, the magazine had difficulties. The first press run of 200,000 copies to be sold in 145 cities was wildly overoptimistic, as only 50,000 copies of the new magazine were sold. The first issue's editor, Ruth Ross, soon left, claiming that she was not being allowed the editorial indepen-

Clarence O. Smith helped to found *Essence*, the first major U.S. magazine for black women. *(Dwight Carter)*

dence she needed. She was later replaced by Marcia Gillespie, who was in turn replaced in 1981 by Susan L. Taylor, who as of this writing remains editorial director and is credited with much of the magazine's success.

Another major change occurred when Blount and Hollingsworth left the corporation. Lewis went on to become publisher and chair of Essence Communications, while Smith became president of the company. The two men formed a solid partnership. Lewis was the financially conservative, cost-cutting executive who kept the magazine on a sound financial footing, while Smith was the flamboyant salesman who brought in advertisers and expanded revenue. By 1975, the magazine was financially successful, thanks in part to Playboy Enterprises, which along with a number of other major corporations had made a significant contribution to the magazine's finances during its troubled early years.

Then, in 1977, Blount, Hollingsworth, and Parks sued for control of the magazine, which had just shown a second profitable year and had a projected circulation of 600,000. In 1979, Lewis ended the financial struggle by settling with the other men and taking the company private (a public company is one whose stock is sold publicly, on one of the stock exchanges; a private company is owned by investors who carefully supervise sales to specific individuals). From 1977 to 1979, *Essence* lost money, but it became profitable as soon as the lawsuit was settled.

In 1980, *Essence* started Essence Direct Mail, a direct-marketing operation. The new venture began by mailing some 20,000 *Essence* subscribers an 18-page magazine. It may then have been the only black mail-order house in existence.

Essence has always had difficulty getting its share of the advertising market, largely because black women are not a market segment respected by most mainstream advertisers. For example, even though black women buy more cosmetics than the average consumer, white cosmetics companies refused to advertise in *Essence* for many years. Smith's sales ability has been invaluable to the company, as he has managed to expand its advertising base. In 1984, Smith launched Essence by Mail, a mail-order catalog geared to appeal to an African-American audience.

In 1985, Lewis and Smith joined several other black investors to buy WKBW, the ABC affiliate in Buffalo, New York; their partners included J. BRUCE LLEWELLYN and PERCY E. SUTTON. In 1989, Essence Art Reproductions began marketing fine art by African-American artists. In 1992, Essence Communications Inc. (ECI) acquired *Income Opportunities*, a magazine geared toward people who had or were trying to start businesses, and in 1995, it started *Latina*, a widely admired magazine offering a creative blend of fashion and beauty features and political articles—all with a focus on Latinas and their heritage. ECI partners with Golden Books to publish children's books as well.

Also in 1995, Smith helped start the Essence Music Festival, a three-day event held in New Orleans. In 1996, when Louisiana was considering banning affirmative action, Smith and Lewis threatened to pull the festival—and the proposed legislation was defeated.

In 1989, Smith helped create "Essence Online," a website to reach African-American women. He has also helped create "The Essence Awards," an annual prime-time network special that honors people who contribute to the African-American community. And he was behind the creation of a weekly syndicated news magazine, also called *Essence*.

In June 2000, the Time, Inc., division of AOL Time Warner bought 49 percent of ECI. *Latina* was sold. Then, in 2002, Smith was forced out of the company by a board vote, which some observers believe was part of AOL Time Warner's takeover of the magazine. Lewis has denied that he "sold out," but he was clearly more amenable to working under the larger corporation than was Smith, who grew increasingly resistant to AOL Time Warner's control.

Essence is now owned by Essence Communications Partners and Essence Communications Holdings (ECH), new financial entities set up to preserve the 51 percent black ownership of the magazine. Susan Taylor remains editorial director, and board members include such prominent African Americans as Camille Cosby, Llewellyn, Johnson, and Frank Savage, former chair of Alliance Capital Management International. Yet since AOL Time Warner has taken over, a number of longtime staff members have been laid off, with Time, Inc., employees taking their place. Some observers have also noticed that the magazine focuses more on fashion and less on political issues of importance to black women.

The future of *Essence* remains to be seen. At the very least, the magazine's story is an example of how difficult it can be for a black-owned company to maintain a unique voice and vision in an era of ever larger corporate takeovers.

Further Reading

Block, Valerie, "Time Heads Media Majority in Targeting Minorities." *Crain's New York Business,* October 16, 2000, p. 4.

Dingle, Derek T. *Black Enterprise, Titans of the B.E. 100s.* New York: John Wiley & Sons, Inc., 1999, pp. 51–72.

Dingle, Derek T., Sonia Alleyne, Alan Hughes, Matthew A. Scott, and Sikina Spreull. "Essence of a Breakup." *Black Enterprise,* September 2002, p. 84.

Essence.com. Available online. URL: http://www.essence.com. Downloaded on January 28, 2003.

Gale Group. "Clarence O. Smith." *Contemporary Black Biography,* Volume 21. Farmington Hills, Mich.: Gale Research, 1996.

———. "Edward T. Lewis." *Contemporary Black Biography,* Volume 21. Farmington Hills, Mich.: Gale Research, 1996.

Gite, Lloyd. "Marathon Men Revisited." *Black Enterprise,* June 2002, p. 92.

Lewis, Reginald Francis
(1942–1993) *financier, business owner, entrepreneur*

Reginald Lewis was responsible for the largest off-shore leveraged buyout of its time, the $1 billion purchase of Beatrice Foods in 1987. He is known for his extraordinarily successful efforts in acquiring, managing, and selling large companies.

Lewis was born in a working-class neighborhood in Baltimore, Maryland, on December 7, 1942. His mother was a postal worker and his stepfather was a teacher. When he was 10 years old, he had his first job, delivering a local African-American newspaper. One summer, he went away to camp, leaving his mother to cover the route for him. Upon his return, he asked his mother for the money he would have earned, and she refused, saying that she had done all the work. He threatened to sue her, and she finally relented—but not before she had stressed the business lesson that she wanted her son to learn: "Set your terms up front."

Lewis was an outstanding athlete and was captain of his football, baseball, and basketball teams in high school. He dreamed of being a professional athlete, though he planned to follow a career in law or business after he turned 30. He even won a football scholarship to Virginia State College (now Virginia State University) in Petersburg, Virginia, but an injury during his freshman year led him to concentrate on his studies, which won him a place on the dean's list and a degree in economics. He then entered a Harvard Law School summer program intended to help African-American students learn more about the law.

Lewis read voraciously, learning everything he could about the law, while also identifying which faculty were involved with admissions. He so impressed them that he managed to be accepted into Harvard Law School without ever taking the entrance exam or completing an application.

Lewis graduated from Harvard in 1968 and worked for a while at the prestigious Manhattan law firm Paul, Weiss, Rifkind, Wharton & Garrison. It did not suit Lewis's personality to be a tiny part of a large operation, however, so after two years he left to set up his own practice. Based on Wall Street, Lewis's firm focused on

helping minority businesses obtain start-up capital, an activity that inspired Lewis with entrepreneurial ambitions of his own. In 1983, he set up the TLC Group (TLC stands for "The Lewis Companies"), with the goal of buying and selling companies.

In 1984, the TLC Group purchased McCall Pattern Co. in a leveraged buyout (LBO), a takeover of a company using a significant amount of borrowed money, usually 70 percent or more of the purchase price; the McCall LBO was valued at $25 million. Lewis had no experience as a chief executive and knew virtually nothing about the sewing pattern business. Nevertheless, under his leadership. McCall had the two most profitable years in its 113-year history. When Lewis sold the company in 1987 for $63 million, the personal investors who had been involved with him netted an astonishing 90-to-1 return.

Lewis was looking for even bigger quarry, however, particularly in the high-spending, speculative context of Wall Street in the 1980s. On December 1, 1987, he made financial history by purchasing Beatrice International, a food distribution and grocery products conglomerate with 64 companies in 31 countries. The corporation was being sold by Kohlberg, Kravis and Roberts through an auction conducted by Wall Street bankers Morgan Stanley and Salomon Brothers. Lewis was competing with such major corporations as Citibank, which had several dozen financial experts devoted to the project. Yet Lewis began negotiations with only four people—himself and three associates. Eventually, the deal was made, a set of transactions so complex that their completion took two days and required a team of 180 lawyers, accountants, and financial advisers. Lewis's admirer Michael Milken, the "junk bond king," put at least $400 million toward Lewis's winning $985 million bid.

Lewis set about selling the Latin American, Canadian, and Australian operations of his new company in order to bring down his debt. Beatrice—now renamed TLC Beatrice International Holdings—still operated on four continents. It was based in the United States, though, with a focus on western Europe and its headquarters in Paris.

The company was closely managed by Lewis, who might on a single day be found flying by corporate jet between Paris, Denmark, West Germany, and Ireland. He maintained expensive residences in both Paris and Manhattan, and he developed a reputation as a romantic. He once surprised his wife, Loida Nicolas Lewis, by jetting her from Paris to Vienna to hear a concert. The couple had two children.

Lewis continued to break financial records and rack up "firsts" to his credit. In 1987, TLC Beatrice reported $1.8 billion in revenue, becoming the first black-owned business to pass the billion-dollar mark. In 1992, *Forbes* magazine put Lewis on its list of the 400 richest Americans, estimating his net worth at $400 million and calling TLC Beatrice he 74th-largest privately held U.S. company. At its peak in 1996, TLC Beatrice boasted sales of $2.23 billion and 512th place on the *Fortune* 1,000 list. Lewis's company led the *Black Enterprise* roster of the top 100 black-owned businesses for several years in a row.

Lewis was also known for his philanthropy. His $3 million donation to Harvard Law School in 1992 was the largest single gift the school had ever received, leading to the creation of the Reginald F. Lewis Fund for International Study and Research. Lewis also supported Virginia State, donated $1 million to Howard University, and made contributions to several African-American politicians, including presidential candidate Jesse Jackson and L. Douglas Wilder, the first black governor of Virginia.

Lewis was looking into the possibility of acquiring Paramount Pictures and Chrysler Corporation just before his death of brain cancer on January 19, 1993, at the age of 50. Loida Lewis took over the company a year after her husband's death. Five years later, she began the process of liquidating the company.

Several years after his death, Lewis remains a legend, not only for his spectacular business successes, but also because he established a new pattern for black entrepreneurs. Traditionally, black business owners had concentrated on one or two companies, which they continued to manage for life. The strategy of buying companies, running them for a while, and then selling them became common in the 1980s, but Lewis was a pioneer of such activities in the black business community. His name lives on in the Reginald Lewis Trailblazers Award, given out each year by Jesse Jackson's Rainbow/PUSH Coalition's Wall Street Project, a prize honoring black business leaders.

Further Reading

Harper, Peter Alan. "TLC Beatrice to Liquidate." AfroCentric News.com. Available online. URL: http://www.afrocentricnews.com/html/beatrice_liquidate.html. Posted June 1, 1999.

Lewis, Reginald F., and Blair S. Walker. *Why Should White Guys Have All the Fun? How Reginald Lewis Created a Billion-Dollar Business Empire.* New York: John Wiley & Sons, 1995.

Wiley, Elliot, ed. *RFL, Reginald F. Lewis, A Tribute.* New York: Bookmark Publishing Corp., 1994.

Williams, Michael Paul. "Reginald Lewis." TimesDispatch.com. Available online. URL: http://www.timesdispatch.com/blackhistory/MGB2DVZTBIC.html. Posted February 1, 2002.

Llewellyn, J. Bruce
(James Bruce Llewellyn)

(1927–   ) *grocery store chain owner, head of Overseas Private Investment Corporation, bottling plant owner, television station owner, lawyer, entrepreneur*

J. Bruce Llewellyn is an African-American entrepreneur who came of age at a time when black businessmen faced enormous discrimination in the white corporate world and yet was a man who managed to achieve unquestionable success in a number of fields in the public and private sectors. Over the course of his career, he has owned a chain of grocery stores, a television station, and a Coca-Cola bottling plant, as well as serving as the head of a major government agency. He is credited with achieving a level of financial success that has opened doors for other black entrepreneurs, proving to white financial institutions that African-American businesspeople can indeed be good financial risks.

Llewellyn was born on July 16, 1927, in Harlem, an African-American neighborhood in New York City, the son of Charles Wesley Llewellyn and Vanessa Llewellyn, Jamaican immigrants who had come to the United States in 1921. When Llewellyn was two years old, his father left his job as printer for a daily newspaper and moved his family to White Plains, a suburb of New York, where he owned a restaurant and they lived in a segregated (divided by race) neighborhood but sent their children to integrated (multiracial) schools. Llewellyn later credited his school experience as helping him feel capable of competing with anyone, regardless of race.

The teenaged Llewellyn worked at the family restaurant and sold Fuller brushes door to door. At age 16, in the midst of World War II, he enlisted in the U.S. Army, where he served from 1943 to 1946, studying engineering at Rutgers University in New Jersey as part of his army training and becoming a second lieutenant. He used the severance bonus he received for leaving the army to buy a liquor store in Harlem, where he attended City College of New York as he worked in his store. Initially hoping to become a hospital administrator, he later studied business and law, receiving a B.S. sometime in the 1950s and going on to take classes at Columbia University's Graduate School of Business and New York University's School of Public Administration before getting his law degree in 1960 from New York Law School.

Meanwhile, Llewellyn had decided to enter the public sector, reasoning that in the 1960s,

African Americans faced too much discrimination to become successful in the corporate world. In law, on the other hand, he believed he could become a judge—and indeed, his sister later became a New York State Supreme Court justice. Llewellyn went on to hold several public sector posts, first in the New York County District Attorney's office, then at the New York City Housing and Redevelopment Board. He later became regional director of the Small Business Administration, executive director of the Upper Manhattan Small Business Development Corporation, and finally, a deputy commissioner for New York City's Housing Commission. He also formed a small law firm with a former classmate, Sam Berger, who in 1969 told him about the availability of a 10-store chain of supermarkets in the Bronx that was seeking a buyer. The Fedco chain of supermarkets was considered an undesirable property because of its location in an urban African-American neighborhood, but Llewellyn was eager to buy.

Llewellyn was willing to put up everything he owned to purchase the chain—but in addition, he needed to obtain some $2.5 million, which he sought from Prudential Insurance. Although the white-owned company was reluctant to risk so much money on a black-owned business in the inner city, Llewellyn arranged a financing scheme that was innovative for the time though it later became the norm: a leveraged buyout, in which assets in the company to be bought are offered as collateral (financial backing) for the sale. Observers consider that the deal set a precedent that helped white institutions see that they might safely engage in loans and investments with black companies.

Llewellyn's ownership of Fedco was a great success, and by 1983 it had expanded to 27 stores and $85 million in gross revenue—quite an increase over the 10 stores that Llewellyn had bought for $3 million. The chain was not without problems, however, as black consumers gave no special treatment to a black-owned business, being more concerned with obtaining the lowest prices they could and frequently struggling with economic hardship that affected their level of consumption.

Meanwhile, in 1978, Democratic president Jimmy Carter offered Llewellyn the post of secretary of the army, but Llewellyn told the president that his talents lay in business rather than the military. Accordingly, Llewellyn was made head of the Overseas Private Investment Corporation (OPIC), a government agency that helped provide insurance for companies doing business in the developing world. Under Llewellyn, the government agency made record profits, but when Republican president Ronald Reagan took office, Llewellyn had to leave, as the OPIC post was usually given to someone of the same political party as the president.

Llewellyn went on to become a partner in the Washington, D.C., law firm of Dickstein, Shapiro & Marin in 1982. In 1983 he joined former basketball star Julius Erving and television star Bill Cosby to buy a 36 percent share of the Coca-Cola Bottling Company of New York—an apparently simple transaction that actually had a complicated history. Although African Americans bought a huge quantity of soft drinks, the major soda companies had virtually no black managers or board members, and at Coca-Cola, for instance, there was only one African American among 4,000 wholesalers of Coke's fountain syrup. Thanks to political pressure from Reverend Jesse Jackson and his Operation PUSH, Coke agreed to make investment opportunities available to black people, and Llewellyn took advantage of the opening.

In 1985, Coca-Cola offered to trade shares in their Philly Bottling company for Llewellyn, Cosby, and Erving's shares in the New York company, making the 700-person Philadelphia plant one of the largest black-owned bottling plants in the country. Llewellyn's leadership of the plant was extremely successful, and in four years it went from 15th largest in the nation to number eight.

In 1984, Llewellyn sold Fedco for $20 million and moved on to a new industry: television. He bought an ABC-TV affiliate in Buffalo, New York, as he founded a new company, Queen City Broadcasting. In 1989, he bought 20 percent of one of the largest cable systems in the United States, New York Times Cable Company, which he invested in along with Camille Cosby (Bill Cosby's wife), Erving, and members of Michael Jackson's family, and of which he became chair.

When Democratic president Bill Clinton took office in 1992, new political opportunities opened to Llewellyn, who became a member of the president's Advisory Committee for Trade Policy and Negotiation, the Board of the Fund for Large Enterprises in Russia, and the U.S. Small Business Administration Advisory Council on Small Business. Llewellyn has also been an active supporter of black education, endowing a number of scholarship funds.

Further Reading

Estell, Kenneth, ed. *The African-American Almanac*, 6th edition. Farmington Hills, Mich.: Gale, 1994.

Gale Group. "J. Bruce Llewellyn." *Contemporary Black Biography*, Volume 13. Farmington Hills, Mich.: Gale Research, 1996.

———. "J. Bruce Llewellyn." Biography Resource Center. Available online. URL: http://www.africanpubs. com/Apps/bios/0275LlewellynJ.asp?pic=none. Downloaded on December 23, 2002.

M

Malone, Annie Turnbo **Malone, Annie Turnbo** See TURNBO-MALONE, ANNIE MINERVA.

McWorter, Frank
("Free Frank" McWorter)
(1777–1854) *enslaved and free entrepreneur, land speculator, town founder*

"Free Frank" McWorter was an enslaved African American who managed by his own enterprise to earn more than $15,000, money that he used to purchase his own freedom and that of 16 family members. As a free man, he became the first African-American town founder in 1836 when he established the community of New Philadelphia in Illinois.

Frank McWorter was born into slavery in 1777 in Union County, South Carolina, son of a West African–born mother, Juda, and a slave owner father, the Scotch-Irish George McWhorter. The father moved to Pulaski County, Kentucky, in 1795, taking his slaves and his family with him. In 1800, the still enslaved Frank McWorter (who had by this time changed the spelling of his last name) married Lucy, a slave on a neighboring farm. By 1810, at the age of 33, Frank McWorter was allowed to hire out his own time, and he began saving money toward the purchase of his and Lucy's liberty. (Throughout slav-

ery, enslaved people were sometimes allowed to hire out their own time or were hired out by their owners; in either case, their owners might take all or a substantial portion of their earnings.)

Eventually, George McWhorter moved to Tennessee, leaving his enslaved son in charge of the farm. During the War of 1812, Frank McWorter established a new enterprise: an extractive mining operation and manufactory for the production of saltpeter (used to help rifles fire). The enterprise proved profitable enough to enable McWorter to purchase Lucy's liberty in 1817 and his own in 1819. He became known as "Free Frank" and entered into the profitable fields of land speculation and livestock dealing.

In 1830, McWorter took his wife and four of his children to Pike County, Illinois, where he had already purchased a farm about 50 miles north of Alton. Had he not already owned land, he would not have been able to settle in Illinois without posting a $1,000 bond—legal requirement at the time for all free blacks. Since the McWorter farm stood only 15 miles from the Mississippi River, the family was in continual danger of being kidnapped and sold back into slavery.

McWorter continued to amass earnings, which he used to purchase the freedom of other relatives. In 1836 he founded the multiracial town of New Philadelphia, intended both as a haven for black citizens and as a stop on the Underground Railroad. There are at least two documented cases of McWorter's son guiding several runaways to Canada. There were other Underground Railroad towns in the antebellum era, but New Philadelphia is the only known case of a town—abolitionist or otherwise—founded by an African American before the Civil War.

McWorter went on to promote development in New Philadelphia, selling town lots, encouraging local business, and raising funds for a private school—the Free Will Baptist Seminary—that would also serve as a church. Although McWorter died in 1854, the town he founded continued to prosper, expanding rapidly in the late 1860s as newly freed slaves left their southern homes to begin a new life after emancipation.

The development of New Philadelphia slowed after the Illinois frontier closed, however, and racism led to the further curtailment of the town's fortunes. County planners rerouted a major road in another direction, while white citizens lobbied to have the railroad placed near an all-white community. The town's population declined in the 1870s and the town itself disappeared in 1885. In 1988, however, McWorter's grave was entered into the National Register of Historic Places, while in 1990, his achievements were noted in the *Congressional Record* and by the Illinois General Assembly.

Further Reading

Fraser, George C. *Success Runs in Our Race: The Complete Guide to Effective Networking in the African-American Community.* New York: William Morrow and Company, Inc., 1994.

McWhirter, Alan D. "McWh*rter Geneology." African Ancestry website. Available online. URL: http://homepages.rootsweb.com/~mcwgen/african.htm. Downloaded on February 11, 2002.

Quarles, Benjamin. *Black Abolitionists.* New York: Oxford University Press, 1969.

Walker, Juliet E. K. *Free Frank: A Black Pioneer on the Antebellum Frontier.* Lexington: University of Kentucky Press, 1983; paperback ed., 1995.

Mercado-Valdes, Frank
(1962–   ) *media entrepreneur*

Frank Mercado-Valdes is best known for being the founder and CEO of the African Heritage Network, the first minority-owned business to purchase a network series for syndication. He expanded his company from a small start-up business to a multimillion-dollar enterprise that produces original programming as well as the nationally syndicated show *It's Showtime at the Apollo.*

Mercado-Valdes was born in the South Bronx, New York. His father, a Puerto Rican, was absent during his childhood, but he was raised by his Cuban grandmother, a seamstress, and grandfather, a gas station attendant and conga player.

When Mercado-Valdes turned 11, the family moved to Miami, where the child was ostracized because of his color. The resulting fights led to his becoming a boxer who earned several Florida Golden Gloves championships while he was in high school. He graduated in 1980 with poor grades and entered the Marines. Upon his discharge in 1982, he enrolled in junior college and then went on to study political science at the University of Miami.

While still in college, Mercado-Valdes had the idea of starting the Miss Collegiate Black America Pageant ("Black America" was later changed to "African-American"). Although the pageant was originally developed by Mercado-Valdes and his fraternity brothers as a way of attracting more African-American women to their campus, Mercado-Valdes came to see the pageant as a brains-over-beauty event that would focus on black heritage and culture.

The pageant was first presented in 1985. After a number of ups and downs, including a one-week period of homelessness in New York, Mercado-Valdes managed to bring the pageant to television in 1990. Mercado-Valdes also developed "S.T.O.M.P.," a nationally televised show featuring step-dancing competitions among black fraternities and sororities.

By this time, Mercado-Valdes had established a partnership with Eugene Jackson, head of Unity Broadcasting; he was also periodically on Jackson's payroll. He became disillusioned with the partnership by 1992, however, and decided to proceed on his own with his idea for the African Heritage Network: buying up the syndication rights for old African-American movies and airing them under the banner "Movie of the Month." The program, hosted by veteran film actors Ossie Davis and Ruby Dee, started slowly, but by 1993, the series was reaching 80 markets that covered some 75 percent of the nation and 88 percent of all black households with television sets. Later, Mercado-Valdes started "AHN Prime," a series of more contemporary black movies that eventually reached 95 percent of all black television households.

In 1996, Mercado-Valdes made media history by purchasing *New York Undercover,* a police drama originally produced by Fox Network—the first time a minority-owned business bought a network show for syndication. He also bought the rights to Kensington Publishing Group's Arabesque Books, the only romance line from a major publisher to feature black characters and African-American women authors. Mercado-Valdes hoped to turn the novels into original made-for-TV movies; when the idea failed he returned the rights to Kensington (they were later purchased by ROBERT L. JOHNSON of Black Entertainment Television).

In 1998, Mercado-Valdes made an unsuccessful bid to produce *It's Showtime at the Apollo,* the rights for which were eventually obtained by Harlem media mogul PERCY E. SUTTON. In 2002, however, Mercado-Valdes was successful in his efforts to obtain rights for the show. By that year, he was also producing the syndicated program known as *The Source: All-Access,* created in conjunction with the magazine of the same name; and *Livin' Large,* with Dick Clark, a look at the lifestyles of prominent Americans of all races.

Further Reading

African Heritage Network website. Available online. URL: http://www.africanheritage.com. Downloaded on November 6, 2002.

Beech, Wendy. "Reel Soul. African Heritage Movie Network Finds Niche in Syndication of Black Films." *Black Enterprise.* August 1997. Available online. URL: http://www.blackenterprise.com/ArchiveOpen.asp?Source=ArchiveTab/1997/08/0897-08.htm.

"40 Under 40 Achievement Award Winner: Frank Mercado-Valdes." The Network Journal. Available online. URL: http://www.tnj.com/articless/tnjevent/40/mercado.html. Downloaded on November 6, 2002.

Harris, Wendy. *Against All Odds, Ten Entrepreneurs Who Followed Their Hearts and Found Success.* New York: John Wiley & Sons, 2001, pp. 113–142.

Horowitz, Craig. "How Harlem Got Its Groove Back." *New York.* July 15, 2002. Available online at New York metro. com. URL: http://www.newyormetro.com/arts/articles/02/apollo.

Simmons, Curtis. "It's Showtime for Mercado-Valdes. Heritage Networks Hopes for Long-running Show at Harlem's Legendary Theater." *Black Enterprise.* Available online. http://www.blackenterprise.com/ExclusivesOpen.asp?Source=Articles/09042002cs.html. Downloaded on November 6, 2002.

"Young Millionaires Part II. How 30 Super Achievers Grew Their Million-dollar Businesses." *Entrepreneur.* November 1997. Available online. URL: http://www.entrepreneur.com/mag/article/0,1539,267052-5-,00.html

Merrick, John

(1859–1919) *insurance company founder, bank founder, real estate investor, entrepreneur, barber*

John Merrick helped to found North Carolina Mutual Insurance Company, which was for many years the largest black-owned business in the

John Merrick helped found North Carolina Mutual Life Insurance Company—for many years the largest black-owned business in the United States. *(Courtesy of North Carolina Mutual Life Insurance Company)*

United States. He was also involved in a number of other enterprises in Durham, North Carolina, helping to develop the local African-American community in a number of ways.

Merrick was born on September 7, 1859, in Sampson County, North Carolina. Because he was born a slave, there are few records of his early life. He never knew his father, and little is known about his mother except that she was loving and supportive. Nor are there any records of the kind of education he received.

In 1871, at the age of 12, Merrick worked in a Chapel Hill, North Carolina, brickyard to support his family, and in 1877, he moved with his mother and brother to Raleigh, North Carolina, where he found work as a laborer and then as a brickmason. Although masonry was a skilled trade, Merrick wanted to become an entrepreneur, so he took a less-skilled job as a bootblack in a barber shop with the goal of becoming a barber.

Merrick's customers included the wealthy white members of the Duke family, a prominent tobacco-growing family who persuaded Merrick and his partner John Wright to start a barbershop in Durham. Although Raleigh was a more prosperous town at the time, with more black-owned businesses, Durham actually offered more opportunity in the sense of being a smaller and less-established town, with neither a black elite nor a planter aristocracy. In the absence of such social classes, new entrepreneurs actually were better poised to do things their own way and make their own rules.

In 1880, Merrick and Wright went to Durham, with Merrick working as Wright's assistant. After six months, Merrick bought a share of the shop and then, in 1892, bought Wright out completely. Meanwhile, Merrick had begun investing in real estate. He bought a lot in 1881 and built a home upon it, where he moved with his wife, Martha Hunter. Merrick continued to buy additional real estate and to expand his business, at times owning as many as nine barbershops.

In 1883, Merrick, Wright, and some other colleagues bought the fraternal order known as the Royal Knights of King David. The order was a form of black self-help to which black people paid a small sum in exchange for knowing that they would have funds for their funerals when they died. Merrick and his colleagues began to consider the possibility of providing more extensive forms of insurance, and in 1898 they formed North Carolina Mutual Insurance Company.

Merrick's decision was partly inspired by the Wilmington, North Carolina, race riots of earlier that year, in which conservative white people were angered and frightened by the thought that black people were gaining political power. The riots resulted in dozens of black people being killed, many more being wounded, and a number of black leaders being run out of town. Merrick decided that Booker T. Washington's vision was correct, that African Americans needed to avoid alienating white people by making political demands. Instead, as Washington advised, Merrick came to believe that black people should focus on their own communities and enterprises.

In response, Merrick formed a new enterprise with prominent African Americans from Durham and Raleigh, and the new company began operations in April 1899. The early years were financially difficult, but Moore hired his nephew, CHARLES CLINTON SPAULDING, to be general manager. Despite some difficult early years, Spaulding turned out to be a brilliant manager who eventually led the company to enormous prosperity.

Spaulding was the full-time manager at North Carolina Mutual, while Merrick and the others focused on businesses of their own. In the early 20th century, R. B. Fitzgerald and W. G. Pearson founded the Mechanics and Farmers Bank, each putting up $1,000 and then inviting Merrick to pledge $1,000 as well. By 1907, the organizers had raised another $7,000 and the bank opened, with Merrick serving as vice president. The founders saw their bank as a support for the black community, making funds available to local African-American homeowners and entrepreneurs. In 1920, more than 500 homes and farms in the Durham area were saved by timely loans from the bank.

Merrick went on to set up a number of other enterprises in Durham. He, Moore, and Spaulding founded the Merrick-Moore-Spaulding Land Company to own and manage the real estate he had been accumulating. In 1908, Merrick, Moore, and other black colleagues formed the Bull City Drug Company to set up drugstores in black neighborhoods. In 1914, Merrick, Moore, and Spaulding founded the Durham Textile Mill, but the enterprise had a number of difficulties: There was a shortage of skilled black labor to operate the mill, and the manager they chose to run it was

inexperienced. Merrick died, the mill in disarray, on August 6, 1919.

Merrick's legacy is complicated. On the one hand, he has been criticized for his willingness to accommodate the white power structure and to steer black people away from political activity. On the other hand, he helped found key institutions that served the African-American community. His life's work includes many of the positive and negative features of black enterprise in an era when black people faced enormous political and social restrictions in the southern United States.

Further Reading

Andrews, Robert McCants. *A Biographical Sketch of John Merrick.* Durham, N.C.: The Seeman Printery, 1920. Available online at University of North Carolina at Chapel Hill Libraries: Documenting the American South. URL: http://docsouth.unc .edu/nc/andrews/andrews.html. Downloaded on January 28, 2003.

Cline, Drew. "Business Leader Hall of Fame." *Business Leader,* November 1996. Available online at Business Leader Online. URL: http://businessleader. com/bl/nov96/cover.html.

Ingham, John N., and Lynne B. Feldman. *African-American Business Leaders: A Biographical Dictionary.* Westport, Conn.: Greenwood Press, 1994, pp. 450–457.

North Carolina Mutual Life Insurance Company. "The Company." North Carolina Mutual Life Insurance website. Available online. URL: http://www. ncmutuallife.com/company.html. Downloaded on January 28, 2003.

Metoyer, Marie-Thérèse ("Coincoin")
(1742–1816) *planter, trader, slaveholder*

Marie-Thérèse Metoyer was born into slavery but went on to become a large planter who founded a major Louisiana plantation and whose descendants were among the most prominent free people of color in Louisiana. Ironically, this former slave amassed her own fortune by becoming a slave owner, an indication of the pervasiveness of the slaveholding system before the Civil War.

Coincoin was born in Natchitoches, Louisiana, when that area was still part of a colony owned by the French. The name Coincoin was typically given to second-born daughters by the West African Ewe people, suggesting that at least one of her enslaved parents was an Ewe. Her parents, François and Françoise, were owned by Louis Juchereau de Saint-Denis, the French army officer who had founded the army post where the family resided. After his death, Coincoin—dubbed Marie-Thérèse by her owners—was left first to his widow, then to his son, and then to the son's daughter, Marie. While she was owned by the Saint-Denis family, she gave birth to five children, each of whom was sold away from her.

Coincoin was rented to the French merchant Claude-Thomas-Pierre Metoyer, who lived on Isle Brevelle in Louisiana's Red River Valley. Coincoin/Marie-Thérèse and Claude-Thomas-Pierre had four children together before her owner freed her. The law throughout slaveholding regions in North America and the Caribbean was that children followed the condition of the mother, so Marie-Thérèse's slave status meant that her children were slaves as well, even though their father was a free man. However, Claude-Thomas-Pierre freed their fourth child, then a newborn, when he freed Marie-Thérèse, and the next three children they had together were born into freedom.

When Claude-Thomas-Pierre married in 1786, he arranged for the 44-year-old Marie-Thérèse to receive a piece of land and an annual income, which she used to buy her eldest daughter, Marie-Louise. Because Marie-Louise had been crippled in a shooting accident, she cost only $300, a relatively low price for an enslaved person in those days. Marie-Thérèse could not yet afford to purchase her other children who were still enslaved, but she set to work planting tobacco and indigo and raising cattle and turkeys for mar-

ket. She also sold bear hides and grease from the bears she trapped.

In 1762, France ceded to Spain all of its lands west of the Mississippi River, including the land on which Metoyer lived. By 1794, Metoyer obtained from the Spanish a grant of 640 acres of woodland on Isle Brevelle, where she continued to raise crops and herd cattle. Eventually, she managed to purchase all but one of the enslaved children who had been sold before the time she knew Claude-Thomas-Pierre—but she was able to buy the grandchildren from the child who remained in slavery. In 1802, when Marie-Thérèse was 60 years old, she agreed to forfeit her annual income from Claude-Thomas-Pierre in exchange for the freedom of their other three enslaved children. She continued to operate her plantation until her death in 1816 at the age of 74, at which time she owned 16 slaves, a relatively modest amount for the period but enough to make her a substantial small farmer. Her descendants went on to build an agricultural empire that included nearly 20,000 acres, a dozen homes, and 500 slaves, making them one of the largest planting families in Louisiana before the Civil War. Today, Metoyer's home, Melrose Plantation, is a National Historic Landmark.

Further Reading

The Association for the Preservation of Historic Natchitoches. "Melrose Plantation." Natchitoches.net. Available online. URL: http://www.natchitoches.net/melrose/melrose.htm. Downloaded on November 3, 2002.

Hirsch, Arnold R., and Joseph Logsdon, eds. *Creole New Orleans: Race and Americanization.* Baton Rouge: Louisiana State University Press, 1992.

Jarred, Ada D. "Cane River Cachet–November 6, 2001." Cane River Heritage.org. Available online. URL: http://www.caneriverheritage.org/main_file.php/canerivercache.php/72/. Posted on November 6, 2001.

Kein, Sybil, ed. *The History and Legacy of Louisiana's Free People of Color.* Baton Rouge: Louisiana State University Press, 2000.

St. Augustine Historical Society. "M." Cane River Community of Isle Brevelle, Louisiana. Available online. URL: http://members.tripod.com/CREOLES/m.htm. Downloaded on November 3, 2002.

Micheaux, Oscar
(Oscar Devereaux Micheaux)
(1884–1951) *film producer, filmmaker, publisher, author*

Oscar Micheaux was a pioneering African-American artist, a man who created his own novels and films—and then developed his own publishing company and film company to create, promote, and distribute his work. His films appeared at a time when black people were restricted to the narrowest of stereotypes in Hollywood—buffoons and criminals—so that Micheaux was one of the few filmmakers to give African Americans a place in popular culture as heroes, cowboys, detectives, and other figures that approached the range and diversity of white film heroes.

Much of what historians know about Micheaux's life comes from his own fictionalized versions of it in his novels, which often seem like thinly disguised autobiography. It is known that Micheaux was born on January 2, 1884, the son of Calvin and Belle Micheaux, who lived on a farm near Metropolis, Illinois. The fifth of 13 children, Micheaux grew up in poverty but with huge determination to succeed. Nicknamed "Oddball" for his tendency to engage in private projects, Micheaux became an early follower of Booker T. Washington's gospel of black self-help and enterprise.

At age 17, Micheaux went to Chicago, where he worked a number of low-paying jobs, ending as a Pullman porter. Three years later, in 1904, he went to South Dakota, where the government was offering settlers land grants, or homesteads. For a while, Micheaux became an extremely prosperous farmer.

In 1909, Micheaux saw a minstrel show—a form of popular entertainment that had begun before the Civil War with white people dressing in blackface and had proceeded to putting African-American entertainers on stage—but also in blackface. Micheaux was excited, however, by seeing African Americans perform, and he decided to become a writer. In the same year, he fell in love with a white homesteader's daughter, but their racial differences eventually put an end to the affair. The theme of interracial romance would continue to fill Micheaux's novels and films. Meanwhile, Micheaux went on to marry an

Independent film producer Oscar Micheaux was a forerunner of such modern filmmakers as Spike Lee. *(AP/Wide World Photos)*

African-American woman from Chicago, but that match ended as well.

In 1913, Micheaux wrote his first novel, *The Conquest: The Story of a Negro Pioneer, by the Pioneer*, the story of "Oscar Devereaux," a South Dakota homesteader who has an unhappy relationship with a white woman. The book was published by a small midwestern press, and Micheaux sold it door to door, creating a black readership in the South and elsewhere. Later, Micheaux would use this door-to-door technique with other books as well.

Lincoln Motion Picture Company offered to make a film of *The Homesteader*, a book Micheaux wrote in 1917 and published himself. The novel is the story of a black man in love with a white neighbor while married to a black woman. Micheaux agreed on condition that he himself direct the film—a condition that Lincoln refused to meet. So Micheaux sold shares of stock for $75 each and raised the money for the film himself. This became his pattern—a grassroots fundraising effort, a film production, and then a grassroots promotion effort, in which Micheaux would personally visit owners of movie theaters that catered to black audiences, selling his current film and trying to get an advance on his next. There were other black filmmakers who attempted projects during the 1920s and 1930s, but only Micheaux managed to remain in business for any length of time.

Micheaux was frequently censored by local authorities, who objected to his frank portrayals of race. In his 1920 film, *Within Our Gates*, an African-American man is lynched by a southern white mob. The Illinois State Board of Movie Censors would not allow the film to be shown because they feared it might provoke a race riot like the 1919 riots that had just shaken the city. Eventually, the movie was shown in Chicago. In 1921, Micheaux created *The Gunsaulus Mystery*, based on the true story of Leo Frank, a Jewish man convicted of killing a young white girl and then lynched in Marietta, Georgia. The Jewish community objected to the portrayal of Frank, to

which the black press replied that many in the African-American community had objected to D. W. Griffith's *Birth of a Nation*, which portrayed black people as rapists and thieves and which showed the Ku Klux Klan as heroic defenders of white women. Yet *Birth of a Nation* had been shown, despite nationwide protests; so, argued the black press, why should Micheaux's work not be shown as well?

Some scholars believed that Micheaux made 48 full-length movies, though only about a dozen survive today. His movies were often made on a shoestring budget, with no retakes and with non-actors in a variety of parts. Micheaux did virtually everything on his films except act—he wrote, directed, edited, and marketed his work, an inspiration to later black filmmakers like Spike Lee, Robert Townsend, and Mario van Peebles. Through it all, he had an uncanny ability to find talented actors, including the great Paul Robeson, who received his screen start in Micheaux's 1925 *Body and Soul*. Robert Earl Jones, the father of James Earl Jones, also worked with Micheaux.

Micheaux has been praised for portraying black people in a variety of roles, even as he has been criticized for focusing on upwardly mobile and well-off African Americans and for his preoccupation with interracial romance. Film critic J. Hoberman has argued that Micheaux internalized U.S. racism as part of his effort to fit into American society, so that his black characters reflect racist views about black people that were current at the time.

During World War II, Micheaux had to stop making movies because many actors were going into the army and the cost of everything was rising quickly. He returned to novel writing and once again formed his own publishing company, the Book Supply Company, based in his home in New York.

In 1948, Micheaux made his last film, *The Betrayal*, one of the few to be shown in mainstream theaters rather than in the so-called ghetto theaters that catered primarily to black people. Perhaps as a result, *The Betrayal* was not particularly successful. Micheaux, meanwhile, had arthritis so severe that he was ultimately confined to a wheelchair. He continued to travel throughout the South, promoting his films and novels, and he died on tour in Charlotte, North Carolina, on Easter Monday, March 25, 1951.

Micheaux was forgotten for many years but then began to enjoy a wave of prominence, particularly as later African-American filmmakers cited him as their inspiration. The Directors Guild of America gave him the Golden Jubilee Special Directorial Award in 1986, he was given a star on Hollywood's Walk of Fame in 1987, and his grave in Great Bend, Kansas, was given a monument reading "A man ahead of his time" in 1988. The Black Filmmakers Hall of Fame calls its annual event the Oscar Micheaux Awards Ceremony.

Further Reading

Bogle, Donald. *Blacks in American Films and Television.* New York: Fireside, 1989.

———. *Toms, Coons, Mulattoes, Mammies, and Bucks.* New York: Continuum, 1994.

Dalton, Narine. "From Oscar Micheaux to Eddie Murphy: Black America's rich film history." *Ebony,* February 1988, pp. 132–138.

Duclos, Nicole. "Fade to Black." *Utne Reader,* November/December 2000, 102, p. 106.

Gehr, Richard. "One-Man Show." *American Film* 16, no. 5 (May 1991): 64.

Green, J. Ronald. *Straight Lick: The Cinema of Oscar Micheaux.* Bloomington: Indiana University Press, 2000.

Haskins, Jim. *Black Stars: African American Entrepreneurs.* New York: John Wiley & Sons, 1998, pp. 83–87.

Lowry, Mark, and Nadirah Z. Sabir. "The Making of 'Hollyhood.'" *Black Enterprise,* December 1995, p. 104.

Micheaux Society website. Duke University Program in Film and Video. Available online. URL: http://www.duke.edu/web/film/Micheaux/. Downloaded on January 28, 2003.

Sampson, Henry T. *Blacks in Black and White: A Source Book on Black Films.* Metuchen, N.J.: Scarecrow Press, 1995.

Shorock, Don. "Oscar Micheaux Home Page." Shorock.com. Available online. URL: http://shorock.com/arts/micheaux/. Downloaded on January 28, 2003.

Mitchell, John, Jr.
(1863–1929) *banker, publisher, editor, developer*

John Mitchell was a major leader of African-American society in Richmond, Virginia, during an era when the black community was under increasing attack from a white-dominated society that wanted to restrict contact between the races and limit black civil rights. Mitchell opposed this trend through his editorship of the *Richmond Planet,* even as he helped to found black enterprises that would help the African-American community sustain itself.

John Mitchell, Jr., was born on July 11, 1863, in the village of Laburnum, just outside of Richmond, Virginia, the son of slaves on the plantation of James Lyons. John and Rebecca Mitchell were house servants freed after the Civil War, when Mitchell was two years old. They left the plantation but then returned to work for Lyons, who had been a member of the Confederate Congress. Mitchell's stay on the plantation put him in contact with many prominent white families of the area, and his biographer, Ann Field Alexander, believes that he developed his own polished manners and courtly bearing from observing his parents' former owner.

Rebecca Mitchell had learned to read and write, though these activities were illegal for slaves, and when Lyons refused to let her son attend school, she taught him at home, while he worked on the Lyons plantation as a carriage boy. In 1870, a black abolitionist opened a private school for blacks, where the seven-year-old

Mitchell went to study for two years. He went on to attend the new black public schools in Richmond—in this post-slavery era, black people were allowed to educate themselves but southern schools were strictly segregated according to race. Only 20 percent of Richmond's black children were able to attend school, so Mitchell was in a distinct minority. He entered Richmond Normal and High School in 1876, which had been founded by a white northerner as part of the Freedman's Bureau, a federal agency set up after the Civil War to educate freed slaves. In 1881, Mitchell graduated from "Colored Normal," as it was called, as valedictorian (head of his class).

Mitchell tried to teach in the Richmond public schools but was unable to get a job and spent two years teaching in Fredericksburg, Virginia. When politicians more sympathetic to civil rights were elected in 1883, the Richmond school board fired 30 white teachers and hired black teachers to replace them, so that the city's teaching staff would not be white-only. Mitchell was hired to teach at Valley School, and he also began writing for the *New York Globe,* a major black newspaper.

Meanwhile, a conservative group soon regained power in Richmond and fired many black teachers, including Mitchell. In December 1884, at the age of 21, Mitchell agreed to assume the debts of the *Richmond Planet,* a local newspaper founded by politically conscious black people, many of whom had worked in the local schools—and were then fired. Mitchell's gesture led him to become the paper's editor.

At the time, the *Planet* relied on a white-owned printing company. To free it from dependence, Mitchell pushed to have the company buy its own secondhand press. He organized the Planet Publishing Company to subsidize the newspaper and eventually became publisher as well as editor.

Mitchell worked closely with WILLIAM WASHINGTON BROWNE, who was organizing a black self-help group called the Order of True Reformers. However, in 1894, Mitchell broke with Browne, and went on in 1900 to ally himself with another fraternal organization, the Knights of Pythias. Both groups subsidized the *Planet* in exchange for favorable coverage—a relationship that the paper enjoyed with many local black businesses.

Mitchell was known as a militant crusader for African-American rights, particularly through his opposition to lynching, a form of political terror that was increasing throughout the late 19th and early 20th centuries as a way of keeping African Americans from full participation in public and economic life. The *Planet's* masthead featured the drawing of a black arm with huge biceps and a clenched fist, and he once wrote that "the best remedy for a lyncher . . . is a 16-shot Winchester rifle in the hands of a Negro with enough nerve to pull the trigger." He himself was known for going armed to seek revenge for local lynchings.

Until 1902, Mitchell continued with his militant policies, urging black political participation and opposing the increasing number of "Jim Crow" laws designed to restrict black people from mainstream society. This put him at odds with Browne, who was known to be more accommodating. In 1895, for example, Mitchell had dinner at the Virginia governor's mansion, a move that white people criticized and that Browne said would make things more difficult for African Americans, by alienating whites. Mitchell defended his actions and his militancy.

In 1888, Mitchell won a two-year term on Richmond's city council, but a rigged election defeated him in 1896 and again in 1900. As black people gradually lost political power and were prevented from voting, it became virtually impossible for black politicians to be elected—and Mitchell began to take a more conservative, accommodating stance, similar to that of Browne and Booker T. Washington. Washington had advised black people to avoid direct political confrontation and instead to build up their own businesses and self-help groups.

In 1902, Mitchell followed Washington's philosophy by founding the Mechanics Savings Bank. He became the first black member of the American Bankers Association, and said at its 1904 convention, "I love the white man. There is no quarrel between me and him." His remarks seemed to symbolize the trend of black business people to accept restrictive laws and to avoid direct challenges to white society. Meanwhile, though Mitchell was also helping to organize a boycott against the segregation of Richmond's streetcars, a seven-month action that led to a short period in which Richmond was the only southern city that allowed integrated (racially mixed) seating on its public transportation.

Mitchell continued to stay active in politics as well. He was allied with the Republican Party, which in those days was seen as the party of Abraham Lincoln and civil rights. In 1921, he was nominated as a candidate for governor under the Black Independent ticket, in an effort to draw attention to black political power. By this point, some 90 percent of black voters in the region were unable to vote due to restrictive and discriminatory laws, so Mitchell won only about 5,000 votes, but his candidacy denied the Republicans a margin of victory and they lost to the Democrats. As a result, the Democratic governor promised better treatment for African Americans, though this promise was never kept.

Mitchell prospered as the bank and the newspaper he ran supported one another and provided the basis for a business empire. His many businesses included the Repton Land Corporation—formed to operate the Woodland Cemetery for blacks in an era when cemeteries were segregated by race as well; the Unique Amusement corporation, created to finance the Strand Theater, located in the white business section but intended to serve black customers; and the Pythian-Calanthe Industrial Association.

The Mechanics Bank was closed in May 1923 because of financial difficulties, and Mitchell was convicted of keeping false books. Although his jail sentence was later overturned by the Virginia Court of Appeals, the bank was doomed. The *Planet* continued to operate, however, and after

Mitchell died on December 3, 1929, it was run by his stepson, Roscoe C. Mitchell. Nearly 50 years later, Mitchell became the first black journalist chosen for the Hall of Fame of Sigma Delta Chi, a national journalist group.

Further Reading

Alexander, Ann Field. *Race Man: The Rise and Fall of the "Fighting Editor," John Mitchell, Jr.* Charlottesville: University of Virginia Press, 1993.

Ingham, John, and Lynne B. Feldman. *African American Business Leaders: A Biographical Dictionary.* Westport, Conn.: Greenwood Press, 1994, pp. 457–464.

Library of Virginia. "John Mitchell, Jr., and the *Richmond Planet.*" Library of Virginia website. Available online. URL: http://www.lva.lib.va.us/whoweare/exhibits/mitchell/ajax.htm. Downloaded on January 23, 2003.

Montgomery, Benjamin Thornton

(1819–1877) *enslaved plantation manager, inventor, cotton planter*

Benjamin Montgomery became one of the richest and most influential cotton planters in post–Civil War Mississippi and also founded and ran Montgomery and Sons, a regional market center that included a store, warehouses, and a steam-driven cotton gin and press (used for making cottonseed oil). His success is all the more remarkable because he achieved his success after a lifetime spent in slavery—though his enslavement proceeded under highly unusual circumstances.

Montgomery was born in 1819 in Loudoun County, Virginia. Because records were often not kept on enslaved people, little is known about Montgomery's parents or early life, although apparently he learned to read and write from the young son of his owner, whose companion he was.

At the age of 17, in 1836, Montgomery was sold to a trader and eventually ended up as the property of Joseph Davis, a country lawyer who had retired to his plantation, Hurricane, near Vicksburg, Mississippi. There Davis practiced his utopian ideals, based on the writings of socialist Robert Owen, who had written about the joys of cooperation. Davis tried to establish a plantation run on Owenite principles, in which enslaved African Americans were supposedly given opportunities to govern themselves. Historians have called the Davis experiment "paternalistic," meaning that Davis behaved like a father to his slaves—kindly, perhaps, but also treating them like children.

Montgomery, however, flourished under Davis's system. He was given access to the Davis library and managed to accumulate many books of his own. He became a skilled inventor, developing a type of boat propeller that enabled steamboats to better navigate in shallow water. Davis wanted to patent (license) Montgomery's invention, but the U.S. Patent Office would not recognize the right of a slave to patent an invention.

Montgomery, meanwhile operated his own retail business on the plantation, for which he eventually had his own credit line with white wholesale dealers in New Orleans. He also became the business manager for Hurricane and occasionally for Brierfield, the neighboring plantation owned by Davis's younger brother, Jefferson.

On December 24, 1840, Montgomery married the enslaved Mary Lewis. He was able to pay Davis for the cost of her labor, so that she could stay home, run their household, and raise their four children. They were concerned that their children—especially their two sons—receive a good education, and for a while, their seven-year-old boy, ISAIAH T. MONTGOMERY, was tutored by a white man who also tutored Davis's children. The integrated school was too threatening for the conservative Mississippi region, however, and was later discontinued. Isaiah went to work as Joseph's valet and private secretary, which allowed him to continue his education and gave him access to Hurricane's library.

When the Civil War broke out in 1861, Jefferson Davis was elected president of the Confederacy, and he went to live in Richmond, Virginia, the new nation's capital. Joseph Davis and his family joined them there during the summer, but life on the Davis plantation continued as before until 1862, when the Union army entered northern Mississippi. Joseph Davis left the state, with Benjamin Montgomery in charge of the plantation and Isaiah serving as his assistant. In 1863, Union admiral David D. Porter sent Benjamin Montgomery to Cincinnati, where he went to work in a boat yard.

In 1865, the Civil War ended, and Montgomery and his wife returned to Hurricane and reopened their store, now called Montgomery and Sons. They ran into opposition from Northern officials of the Freedman's Bureau, the new agency set up to help the former slaves make the transition to freedom. Again, the issue of paternalism emerged: Montgomery wished to run his enterprises, but the Freedman's official was concerned that he was exploiting his fellow black people. Montgomery turned to his former owner, Joseph Davis, for help in setting up the cotton gin he wished to establish.

Davis, meanwhile, had initially lost his land as had many supporters of the Confederacy. In 1866, however, he was pardoned by the federal government and regained ownership of his plantation, which he immediately sold to Montgomery on credit. To avoid alienating the white people in the region, Davis and Montgomery kept their arrangement secret, but in fact, Montgomery owed Davis $300,000 for the land, with interest to be paid at 5 percent in gold or 7 percent in cash.

Initially, Montgomery did well on the former plantation, hiring former slave families to work for him and producing high-quality cotton. In 1868, he was appointed a local justice of the peace, which again roused the hostility of local white people, as this was the first time an African American had held political office in Mississippi.

Isaiah had to promise local residents that his father would not rule on any cases involving white people.

By 1872, the Montgomerys were among the richest planters in the South. In 1876, they won an award at the Philadelphia Centenary Exposition for the high quality of their cotton. But falling cotton prices, floods, invasions of insects, and increasing hostility toward black people made it difficult for Benjamin Montgomery to continue running his plantation. His health began to fail and in 1877, at age 58, he died. His legacy was continued by his son, however, as well as by CHARLES BANKS, who later joined Isaiah in founding a new all-black town at Mound Bayou, Mississippi.

Further Reading

Chambers, Caneidra. "Mound Bayou: Jewel of the Delta." Department of Anthropology and Sociology, University of Southern Mississippi website. Available online. URL:http://ocean.otr.usm.edu/~aloung/mbayou.html. Downloaded on January 16, 2003.

Hamilton, Kenneth. *Black Towns and Profits*. Urbana: University of Illinois Press, 1991.

Hermann, Janet Sharp. *The Pursuit of a Dream*. Jackson: Mississippi University Press, 1981.

Sullivan, Richard Otha. *Black Stars: African American Inventors*. New York: John Wiley & Sons, Inc., 1998.

Swanson, Erik. "Benjamin Montgomery: The Slave Who Dared Invent." Inventors Online Museum. Available online. URL: http://www.inventorsmuseum.com/montgomery.htm. Downloaded on January 17, 2003.

Young, Amy L., and Milburn J. Crowe. "Descendant Community Involvement in African-American Archaeology in Mississippi: Digging for the Dream in Mound Bayou." Arkansas Archaeological Survey, University of Arkansas website. Available online. URL: http://www.uark.edu/campus-resources/archinfo/SHACyoung.pdf. Downloaded on January 16, 2003.

Montgomery, Isaiah T.
(Isaiah Thornton Montgomery)
(1847–1924) *land speculator, entrepreneur, town developer*

The legacy of Isaiah T. Montgomery is decidedly mixed. On the one hand, he achieved enormous wealth and political power, which he used to establish an idealistic all-black community in post–Civil War Mississippi. On the other hand, he helped ratify the efforts of white politicians to disenfranchise (deprive the vote and political voice of) both black and white citizens of Mississippi, in a trade-off that many black leaders at the time criticized and that he himself later regretted.

Isaiah was born at Davis Bend, Mississippi, on May 21, 1847, the son of BENJAMIN THORNTON MONTGOMERY and Mary Lewis. Although Isaiah and his parents were slaves on the Joseph Davis plantation, Davis ran the plantation according to the idealistic principle that slaves should be allowed self-government, enabling Isaiah's father to become plantation manager. Benjamin Montgomery was prosperous enough to purchase his wife's labor so that she could remain at home with her children, and Isaiah was able to receive an education at a time when most enslaved people were not allowed to read or write. For a while, Isaiah was taught alongside Davis's children, under the supervision of a white teacher. This form of integrated education was eventually discontinued when it proved too threatening for the surrounding area. The child Isaiah then had to work as Joseph's valet and private secretary—a plantation job that allowed him to continue his education and gave him access to his owner's library.

After the Union troops entered Mississippi in 1862, Joseph Davis left the plantation in Benjamin Montgomery's care. In 1863, Union admiral David D. Porter came to Davis Bend and made 15-year-old Isaiah his cabin boy and personal attendant. Later, when Isaiah became ill, Porter sent him to Cincinnati, where his parents had already gone. The family returned to Davis Bend in 1865, after the war had ended, when Benjamin Montgomery went on to become one of the most prosperous cotton planters and merchants in the state, acquiring control of several plantations in the region that had formerly belonged to the Davis family and to other rich white planters.

Starting in 1866, Isaiah Montgomery kept the family's business records, and in 1872, he managed an office staff that included a bookkeeper and a clerk. He was also running Hurricane, the largest of the family plantations, though his father was in charge of the business as a whole. In the mid-1870s, the cotton business was declining on account of falling prices, floods, and insect invasions. The Montgomery family fortunes received additional blows: Benjamin died in 1877, and in 1879, the family's retail business, Montgomery and Sons, failed, as cotton production continued to decline. Meanwhile, the family's patron, Joseph Davis, had died in 1870, and members of the Davis family tried to gain control of various plantations. By 1881, Isaiah had lost control of most of the family's lands, and by 1886, the family had left Davis Bend.

Isaiah Montgomery, meanwhile, had begun to dream of founding an all-black community, and after various false starts, he joined in 1885 with his relative Ben Green to buy 840 acres between Memphis and Vicksburg. In 1886, Montgomery and Green returned with seven other black men to start clearing the land, which was virtually a wilderness area. By 1888, the land was ready for settlement, and a number of black pioneers settled there. The new town was called Mound Bayou, after an old Indian burial mound nearby. Black people moved in from a number of areas, particularly from southern Mississippi, where political violence against African Americans was escalating.

Montgomery set up a form of government that many historians have called "paternalistic," meaning that he treated the black people who lived there as though he were their father— kindly, perhaps, but also as though they were children. In some ways, Mound Bayou was an idealistic community, founded on the principles of black self-government and self-help. But from some points of view, Montgomery was exploiting the less wealthy African Americans who lived in the community. While the profits of the community were supposed to be divided fairly, some people felt that Montgomery got more than his share. Moreover he owned either all or part of the cotton gin and warehouse, the feed and fertilizer store, the lumberyard, the burial business, and the store; he profited from lumber sales in the new community, served as town mayor, appointed the town deputy (the county had a white sheriff, however), and occasionally served as justice of the peace or postmaster.

In 1890, Montgomery made another controversial decision: He spoke at the 1890 Mississippi Constitutional Convention in favor of disenfranchising black people (depriving them of the vote). The convention had been called for the express purpose of keeping black people out of Mississippi politics, and Montgomery was the only black delegate there. He believed strongly that black people had to accommodate themselves to white political rule and withdraw from the larger society, trying to set up their own enterprises and communities. This put him at odds with many black political leaders of the time, although it led to a close alliance with Booker T. Washington, who coined the phrase "accommodationism" in 1895 to express a similar philosophy. Some historians believe that black disenfranchisement was inevitable and that Montgomery's approval of the idea made little actual difference, given the increasingly anti-black political climate. At the time, however, he was considered a traitor to his race, and he himself came to regret making the speech.

Meanwhile, Green and Montgomery disagreed over the ways the colony was being run, and in 1895 they ended their partnership. In 1896, Green was murdered by a customer in his store. Mound Bayou, however, continued to flourish. In 1900, a railroad built a depot there, and in 1904, CHARLES BANKS organized a bank there. By

1907, the town was home to 800 families who produced 3,000 bales of cotton a year, as well as corn and fodder (cattle food). The town included more than a dozen stores, a sawmill, three cotton gins, a telephone exchange, a weekly newspaper, six churches, and two private schools. (There were few public schools for black people in Mississippi at the time.)

In 1908, Banks and Montgomery worked together to sell shares in a proposed cottonseed oil mill, beginning construction of the plant in 1910. They turned to Booker T. Washington for help in raising funds, and he in turn helped them approach white philanthropists (charitable donors) in the North. Funds were raised to open the plant by 1912, but Banks and Montgomery did not have enough money to operate their business. They had to lease the mill to a local white mill owner, who may have stolen money from their enterprise; by 1915, they had to suspend operations.

Cotton prices rose during World War I, and Mound Bayou prospered. But after the war, many of the local cotton farmers were wiped out. Banks and Montgomery engaged in a divisive power struggle in which Banks's supporters won a local election and Montgomery turned to Mississippi's anti-black governor Theodore G. Bilbo to throw Banks's people out of office. The split between the two men further hurt the community, and by the time Montgomery died on March 6, 1924, Mound Bayou had fallen on hard times. The community continued to have its ups and downs throughout the decades. When the community was made an archaeological site and national historic park, there was a resurgence of interest in the town. Residents hope to restore the old Banks building downtown.

Further Reading

Chambers, Caneidra. "Mound Bayou: Jewel of the Delta." Department of Anthropology and Sociology, University of Southern Mississippi website. Available online. URL: http://ocean.otr.usm.edu/
~aloung/mbayou.html. Downloaded on January 16, 2003.

Hamilton, Kenneth. *Black Towns and Profits*. Urbana: University of Illinois Press, 1991.

———. "Founding New Towns, Creating New Opportunities." *Issues and Views*, Summer 1991. Available online. URL: http://www.issues-views.com/index.php?print=1&article=1002.

Schwartz, Don. "Biography: Isaiah Montgomery (1847–1924)." The History of Jim Crow. Available online. URL: http://www.jimcrowhistory.org/resources/biographies/Montgomery_Isaiah.htm. Downloaded on January 17, 2003.

Wormser, Richard. "Isaiah Montgomery." The Rise and Fall of Jim Crow, PBS Online. Available online. URL: http://www.pbs.org/wnet/jimcrow/stories_people_mont.html. Downloaded on January 17, 2003.

Young, Amy L., and Milburn J. Crowe. "Descendant Community Involvement in African-American Archaeology in Mississippi: Digging for the Dream in Mound Bayou." Arkansas Archaeological Survey, University of Arkansas website. Available online. URL: http://www.uark.edu/campus-resources/archinfo/SHACyoung.pdf. Downloaded on January 16, 2003.

Moore, Frederick Randolph
(1857–1943) *publisher, political and civic leader*

Frederick Randolph Moore was one of the closest associates of Booker T. Washington, and he promoted Washington's ideas of autonomous black financial institutions and black self-help throughout his long and active career in publishing and politics. For nearly 40 years he was the publisher and editor of the *New York Age,* one of the most influential black-owned newspapers.

Moore was born on June 16, 1857, in Prince William County, Virginia, the son of Evelyne or Evelina Moore, an enslaved house servant, and a white father, listed on Moore's death certificate as Eugene Moore. He was brought to the District of Columbia as a child, where he attended public schools and sold newspapers to make money.

When Moore was 18, he became a messenger in the U.S. Treasury Department, where he worked through several administrations. He served Secretary of the Treasury Daniel Manning as a confidential aide, and when Manning left government service in 1887 to become president of the Western National Bank, Moore became a clerk in that same bank. Meanwhile, in 1879, Moore married Ida Lawrence. The couple had 18 children, of whom six lived to adulthood.

Moore had grown up in the period just after slavery, when for a time it seemed as though African Americans might be able to achieve political power in the South. But later in the 19th century, a white backlash developed, taking the form of both restrictive laws and violence, particularly lynching. Two major responses to the situation developed: W. E. B. DuBois and the Niagara Movement advocated political resistance and efforts to develop full social equality for African Americans; Booker T. Washington, based at the Tuskegee Institute in Alabama, supported "accommodationism," urging African Americans to accept the political situation and focus instead on black-self help and founding independent black businesses.

Moore became a close associate of Washington's, though he took more militant stands against lynching and racism than Washington did. He helped Washington found the National Negro Business League (NNBL) in 1900 and became chair of the group's executive committee. He also worked closely with the Republican Party, which in those days was considered the party of Abraham Lincoln and Civil Rights, and for many years offered a great deal of political opportunity to African Americans. Later, however, a faction within the party called for "lily-white Republicanism," which became the dominant trend.

Nevertheless, Moore was active in the Republican Party all his life. By the beginning of the century, he had moved to New York City, where he served as a district captain in Brooklyn, a borough of New York City. In 1902 he ran unsuccessfully for a seat in the state assembly. In 1904, he had a brief political appointment as deputy collector of internal revenue (tax collector), which he left to become national organizer for the NNBL. Moore also became involved with PHILIP A. PAYTON's Afro-American Realty Company, which was instrumental in developing New York City's Harlem as a black neighborhood. Both he and Payton were believers in Washington's idea of black enterprise.

In 1905, Washington chose Moore to be editor and publisher of the Boston-based *Colored American Magazine,* which Moore relocated to New York. Washington had bought the paper in 1904 but tried to keep his involvement secret so that he would not appear to be too influential. He installed Moore, however, so that he would in fact have editorial control over the publication. The *Colored American Magazine* embodied the essence of Washington's philosophy, seeking to publish articles that showed black self-improvement, focusing on practical achievements rather than political theory.

In 1907, Moore's position as national organizer for the NNBL was abolished. In the same year, a complicated set of negotiations took place between Moore, Washington, and T. Thomas Fortune, editor and publisher of the *New York Age,* one of the nation's most important black-owned newspapers. Fortune and Moore were close friends, but Fortune was also ill, and an alcoholic. The negotiations became painful, with various charges of broken promises and misrepresentation. Eventually, Moore took control of the paper with Washington's backing, although Washington again tried to hide his involvement. Moore developed a more militant stance than Washington was comfortable with, and Washington frequently criticized him for giving too much attention to lynchings.

In 1915, Moore helped organize a protest against the D. W. Griffith movie *Birth of a Nation,* which portrayed the Ku Klux Klan as the noble defender of white people and showed African Americans as both foolish and criminal. In 1918, he opened discussions with the American Federation of Labor (AFL)—then the major organization of U.S. labor unions—on expanding wartime job opportunities for African Americans. Up to that point, the AFL's unions of skilled workers tended to exclude African Americans, and Moore's talks had little success. (A later labor organization, the Congress of Industrial Organizations [CIO], was more committed to integration.)

In 1919, Moore moved the *Age* to Harlem, further helping to establish that neighborhood as a center of black political and artistic activity. He was a huge supporter of black capitalism in Harlem, though critics question whether such policies were ultimately helpful to Harlem residents. Moore also remained active in Republican politics, attending national conventions and participating in the National Negro Republican Committee, a group designed to give black people more influence in presidential campaigns.

Despite his differences with Washington, Moore remained active with the NNBL as well as with the Colored Merchants Association (CMA), a group designed to improve the condition of black business. In 1929, the CMA of Harlem tried to develop a grocery store that would be the foundation for a nationwide cooperative association, in which black grocers join forces to purchase goods and advertise their stores. The project foundered, however, partly because of the Great Depression, which brought hard times to most businesses, and partly because white-owned businesses could offer better prices, so black customers preferred to shop there.

Moore was active with a number of other organizations that he helped found or in which he played a major role, including the National Urban League, Dunbar National Bank, and the National League for the Protection of Negro Women. In 1924, he helped nominate a black congressional candidate, and in 1927 and 1929 he served as a New York City alderman (member of the city council). In 1929, he helped elect an African American to the state assembly.

The Great Depression of the 1930s saw many more African Americans turning to the left, joining such organizations as the Communist Party and challenging the vision of black capitalism that Moore and Washington supported. By the time Moore died, on March 1, 1943, he was seen as an "Uncle Tom" who had accommodated the white power structure, while a new paper, the *Amsterdam News*, was beginning to challenge the *Age*. Yet Moore also crusaded against racism and discrimination, and his newspaper had given African Americans a powerful voice for some four decades. He lived during a difficult time for black Americans, but he was part of the process that created a new militancy in the generations that came after his death.

Further Reading

Cripps, Thomas R. "Frederick Randolph Moore." *Dictionary of American Biography, Supplement 3: 1941–1945*. American Council of Learned Societies, 1973.

Meier, August. *Negro Thought in America*. Ann Arbor: University of Michigan Press, 1963.

Thornbrough, Emma Lou. *T. Thomas Fortune: Militant Journalist*. Chicago: University of Chicago Press, 1972.

Wiseman, John B. "Frederick Randolph Moore." *Dictionary of Negro Biography*, ed. by Logan, Rayford W., and Michael R. Winston. New York: W. W. Norton & Co., Inc., 1982.

Moore, Vera
(1950–   ) *cosmetics manufacturer*

Vera Moore founded her own cosmetics company and went on to market her unique brands through Vera Moore Cosmetics, which she has built into a half-million-dollar business. In 1982, she became the first African American to rent space in the Green Acres Mall in Valley Stream on Long Island, New York; from that humble beginning she has gone to develop international partnerships in the Netherlands and elsewhere, and to be the first African American to rent space in Kings Plaza Mall, in Brooklyn, and in Queens Center Mall, in Queens (both are New York City boroughs). Her current client list includes such superstars as Lena Horne, Debbie Allen, and Phylicia Rashad.

Moore was born in Corona, Queens, a New York City neighborhood, on February 28, 1950, the daughter of Robert L. Moore, Sr., a railroad employee, and Vera Moore, a domestic worker. Neither parent ever made it past the fourth grade, and times were often hard during Moore's childhood; as a teenager, Moore slept on the couch. But the young Moore dreamed of being a singer and in the ninth grade she won a scholarship to spend her Saturdays studying opera at the Sadisburg Academy of Music in Brooklyn, New York. While attending Hunter College in New York City, she also studied at the Juilliard School of Music and sang in the All-City Chorus. When she graduated high school in 1963, she studied French and German at night in preparation for her operatic career while working as a secretary at the U.S. Customs Office in Lower Manhattan.

As Moore was promoted at the customs office, she continued to seek work as an actress while saving money to buy her mother a house. When she got a callback for a bit part in the chorus of *South Pacific* at Guy Lombardo's Jones Beach Theater, she quit her job, put a down payment on her mother's house, and landed the part, which launched her career. She performed in the summer production for two years; toured the United States with soprano Kathleen Battle; appeared in trade shows and in commercials for McDonald's, Kodak, and Pepsi-Cola; worked in a made-for-TV movie; and appeared in several soap operas. She went on to work on Broadway in various parts before returning to television in 1970 as

Former actress Vera Moore developed her own line of cosmetics for African-American women, which she sells to such clients as Lena Horne, Debbie Allen, and Phylicia Rashad. *(Courtesy of Vera Moore)*

Linda Metcalf, a nurse on *Another World*. Moore was one of the first African Americans to appear on the show and the only black person on the set at the time.

Frustrated with her makeup options, Moore created her own blend for use on the show. Moore's skin was beige, and she felt that every available shade of makeup made her look either too light or too dark. Having developed makeup for herself, in 1979, she founded Vera Moore Cosmetics, working with a chemist to design the cosmetics and drawing on the support of her husband, Barney Helms, Jr., a cosmetologist, whom she had married in 1971. In 1977, her daughter Consuella Helms was born.

In 1980, Moore brought her products to a beauty trade show in Florida, then began marketing them at her husband's hair salon in Jamaica, Queens, in New York. Moore offered free makeovers to promote her products, and the cosmetics began selling briskly. She left acting and devoted herself full-time to her makeup business, drawing on a network of friends and relatives to launch her product. Family members helped her type correspondence, answer the phones, prepare brochures, and make gift bags for the free gifts that accompany purchases. Today, Moore's niece works with her, and her daughter, Consuella, a graduate of Howard University School of Business, is planning to enter the family business as well.

In 1982, Moore moved to a location in Green Acres Mall, mortgaging her home and obtaining a $65,000 Small Business Administration–guaranteed loan to obtain the funds. Eventually, Moore moved from her 100-square-foot store to a kiosk in the mall, meanwhile expanding her makeup line, developing an online catalogue, working with a Nigerian woman in London, and developing a partnership in the Netherlands. She is the winner of the 1998 Business Award from the National Minority Business Council, and of Governor George Pataki's 1998 African American Award for Excellence. In 2002, she rented space in two New York City malls, and plans to continue expanding her business.

Further Reading

Harris, Wendy. *Against All Odds: Ten Entrepreneurs Who Followed Their Hearts and Found Success*. New York: John Wiley & Sons, 2001, pp. 163–180.

Marcazzo, Regina. "Vera Moore: Cosmetics Niche Filled with Style and Hard Work." *Networking*, May 2000. Available online. URL: http://www.networkwomen.com/archives/coverstory5_00.html.

Swirsky, Joan. "Black Women Build Businesses of Their Own." Americans for a Fair Chance. Available online. URL: http://www.fairchance.org/news/getStory.cfm?ID=97. Posted August 26, 2001.

"Vera Moore." *The Network Journal*, March 2000. Available online. URL: http://www.tnj.com/articless/March/cover/v_moore.htm.

Williams, Dr. Teresa Taylor. "Vera Moore, Vera Moore Cosmetics: Savvy Business Woman Heads for International Trade." New York Trend Online. Available online. URL: http://www.nytrend.com/movers&shakers.html. Downloaded on November 6, 2002.

Morgan, Garrett A.
(Garrett Augustus Morgan)
(1875–1963) *inventor, entrepreneur, publisher*

Garrett A. Morgan spent most of his life as a small entrepreneur, but he was also a brilliant inventor. Because of his entrepreneurial skills, he was able to form new businesses to make and sell his inventions; he also formed a business—a black newspaper—to serve his community. Morgan's inventions include the first human-hair straightener, the gas mask, and the first modern traffic light. He started businesses to make and sell the first two products and sold the rights to the third to General Electric for what was then a remarkable sum of $40,000.

Morgan was born in Paris, Kentucky, on March 4, 1877, the son of Sydney Morgan, a farm laborer, and Elizabeth (Reed) Morgan, a former slave who had been freed by the Emancipation Proclamation. He was the seventh of their 11 children and spent his childhood working on the family farm while attending school. At the age of 14, he traveled north to Ohio in search of a better education, settling first in Cincinnati and then in Cleveland, supporting himself by working as a handyman. In Cleveland, he learned how sewing machines worked, going on in 1907 to open his own sewing machine store, where he sold new machines and repaired old ones. In 1908, he married Mary Anne Hassek, with whom he eventually had three sons.

Morgan opened a tailoring shop in 1909, where he made and sold coats, suits, and dresses. He noticed that sometimes the automatic sewing machine needle moved so quickly that it scorched the thread of woolen fabrics, and he decided to develop a liquid that might polish the needle and reduce friction. Inadvertently, he invented a hair-straightener instead, and went on to market the product as the GA Morgan Hair Refining Cream, sold by his newly formed GA Morgan Refining Company.

In 1912, he set out to develop a device he called first a "safety hood," then a "breathing device," but which is known today as a gas mask—a hood that fits over the head to protect the wearer from breathing poisonous gases in the atmosphere. He formed the National Safety Device Company to make and sell the product, but sales did not really take off until after July 24, 1916, when Morgan and his brother Frank wore the devices in an effort to rescue the 32 workers trapped in a tunnel being dug under Lake Erie by the Cleveland Water Works. The tunnel was filled with smoke, dust, and poisonous gases that threatened the workers and would-be rescuers alike, but with the aid of the gas masks, the Morgans were able to save at least some of the workers. Morgan received national publicity as well as local and international awards for his invention and his rescue efforts. Initially, orders poured in for the device from fire and police departments nationwide, though when some buyers learned that Morgan was black, they cancelled their orders. Later, the U.S. Army bought gas masks to protect soldiers from poison gas used in World War I.

By this time Morgan was comfortably off, but he went on to create a third major invention, a traffic safety light designed to prevent the many accidents common in the early days of the automobile, when cars and carriages shared the roadways. Morgan's device had three settings: "Go," "Stop," and a "Stop" setting that arrested traffic in both directions, allowing pedestrians time to cross the street. Morgan sold the device to the General Electric Company, winning acclaim from many influential people, including the tycoons John D. Rockefeller and J. P.

Morgan, for whom he named one of his sons. He then turned his efforts to help the African-American community, in 1920 founding the *Cleveland Call*, the city's first black paper (it was later renamed the *Call & Post*), which he operated through 1923, and serving as the treasurer of the Cleveland Association of Colored Men, which later merged with the National Association for the Advancement of Colored People (NAACP). In 1931 he ran unsuccessfully for Cleveland City Council. In 1943, he developed glaucoma, an eye disease that eventually cost him 90 percent of his vision, and he died on July 27, 1963, in Cleveland. A Harlem public school has been named in his honor, as have numerous awards and scholarship programs.

Further Reading

Brown, Mitchell C. "Garrett Augustus Morgan." The Faces of Science: African Americans in the Sciences, Princeton University. Available online. URL: http://www.princeton.edu/~mcbrown/display/morgan.html. Downloaded on November 11, 2002.

"Garrett Morgan." The Black Inventor On-Line Museum. Available online. URL: http://www.blackinventor.com/pages/garrettmorgan.html. Downloaded on November 11, 2002.

Lemelson-MIT Awards Program's Invention Dimension, The. "Garrett A. Morgan (1875–1963). The Gas Mask." Massachusetts Institute of Technology. Available online. URL: http://web.mit.edu/invent/iow/morgan.html. Posted February 1997.

Science Museum. "The Inventions of Garrett Morgan." Science Museum website. Available online. URL: http://www.sciencemuseum.org.uk/collections/exhiblets/morgan/start.asp. Downloaded on November 11, 2002.

Morgan, Rose Meta
(Rose Morgan)
(ca. 1912–   ) *hair salon owner*

Rose Meta Morgan founded her House of Beauty salon at a time when African-American women were dominated by "white" standards of beauty, encouraging them to value silky straight hair and light skin and to be frustrated with what was popularly called "bad" hair—hair that was curly or wavy. Morgan's entrepreneurial success was founded on a philosophy that every woman is beautiful in her own way, and that every type of hair is "good" hair. Morgan's attitude helped her maintain a highly successful beauty business for more than half a century, winning her international acclaim.

Rose Morgan was born sometime around 1912 in the small rural town of Shelby, Mississippi (in those days, good records were not kept on rural African Americans, so there is no exact birthdate available). Although she always felt homely, she relied on the ongoing support of her father, Charlie Morgan, who adored her and encouraged her in all her endeavors.

Charlie Morgan had been a sharecropper in Mississippi—someone who farmed another person's land, paying for the privilege with a portion of his own crop. Most sharecroppers of the era were extremely poor, but Charlie Morgan was relatively prosperous, and when Rose was six years old, he was able to move his family of 13 to Chicago. There he continued his own successful activities as an entrepreneur, as the young Rose started her own small businesses. When she was 10, she made artificial flowers and organized neighborhood children to sell them door to door. She also worked in a laundry. At age 11, she started styling hair, and by 14, she was earning money at it. It is unclear whether Morgan ever finished high school, though she herself has said proudly that she was a dropout whose real education came at Chicago's Morris School of Beauty.

Morgan rented a station in a neighborhood salon and began dressing hair full time. In 1938, she met singer and actress Ethel Waters, who was so pleased with Morgan's work that she invited Morgan to come to New York with her. Morgan fell in love with the city but was unwilling to relocate without her family's blessing. When her

father offered his support once more, Morgan moved permanently to New York, where her hairdressing business took off almost immediately. Within six months, she had opened a beauty shop in a renovated kitchen in a friend's apartment, and soon she had hired five stylists to work under her. She and her friend Olivia Clark signed a lease on a run-down mansion that was known locally as a haunted house. Within three years, the Rose Meta House of Beauty was the world's largest African–American beauty parlor. The salon was known for its integrity, as stylists refused to give women haircuts or treatments that they thought would be unattractive, preferring to lose a customer than to send someone out into the world with an unflattering style.

Morgan's entrepreneurial gifts included a keen understanding of what black women needed in order to feel beautiful and special. At a time when there was widespread discrimination, and when U.S. magazine and movie images of glamour were exclusively white, Morgan found ways to promote opportunities for African-American women to feel beautiful, fashionable, and glamorous. In the late 1940s, she staged fashion shows at huge halls in Harlem, with her employees and customers serving as designers and models. Also in 1946, Morgan began selling Rose Meta cosmetics, geared towards African-American women.

By this time, the House of Beauty was serving some 1,000 customers a week and employing 29 people, including 20 hairstylists, three licensed masseurs, and a registered nurse. Morgan was also developing an international reputation, traveling to Paris to demonstrate her technique and promote her slogan: "To glorify the woman of color." In 1955, despite difficulties with white banks that refused to lend her money, she managed to raise funds for renovating her salon, making it more fashionable and including a dressmaking department, a diet and body department, and a charm school. A trademark was the cologne that was blown regularly through the building so that the air would smell sweet. Soon, Morgan opened a wig salon as well, including a pickup and delivery service so that women could get their wigs styled at home.

Although Morgan had been married for a year in Chicago, she remained single for most of her career. In 1955, she married heavyweight champion Joe Louis, with whom she tried to start a men's cologne business, but the venture was ahead of its time and the couple proved to be incompatible, though they parted with great affection and respect. In 1957 they separated and in 1958, the marriage was annulled. Later, Morgan married lawyer Louis Saunders, with whom she founded a New Jersey savings and loan association. She and Saunders also separated after a relatively short time, and lived apart until Saunders died.

In 1965, Morgan founded New York's only black commercial bank, the Freedom National Bank, in which she was a significant shareholder. In 1972 she opened yet another beauty-related business, a franchise operation called Trim-Away Figure Contouring. When she retired, she had been in the beauty business for some 60 years, proud of her efforts to help African-American women see themselves as beautiful.

Further Reading

Gale Group. "Rose Meta Morgan." *Contemporary Black Biography*, Vol. 11. Farmington Hills, Mich.: Gale Research, 1996.

The HistoryMakers. "Rose Morgan." StyleMakers The HistoryMakers. Available online. URL: http://www.thehistorymakers.com/biography/biography.asp?bioindex=167&category=styleMakers. Downloaded on December 22, 2002.

"House of Beauty." *Ebony*, May 1946, pp. 25–29.

Moore, Mike. "Rose Morgan: Success in Grand Style." *Essence*, June 1981, pp. 34–44.

Murray, Albert (1921–   ) and Odetta S. Murray (1921–2002)
innkeepers

Albert and Odetta S. Murray triumphed over the highly segregated atmosphere of the Poconos resort area in Pennsylvania by founding and running the Hillside Inn, the first—and today, the only—black-owned resort hotel in the region. Until Odetta's death in 2002, the two of them made their inn a symbol of black self-reliance, playing the typical role of black entrepreneurs who provided a service to the black community that the white community was unwilling to provide. Ironically, integration and the financial success of the black middle-class has meant that the black customers who once flocked to the Hillside have gradually turned to the more expensive and prestigious white-owned resorts in the area—as well as vacation spots elsewhere—but as of this writing, the Hillside continues to flourish.

Albert was born on March 15, 1921, the son of Roland Murray, a sharecropper, and Lucille Johnson, a farmer. Although he grew up in a poor family in the segregated South, his father encouraged him to dream big. After he finished the sixth grade, he went to live with an aunt in Augusta, where he attended A.R. Johnson High School and Paine College High School while working a number of difficult jobs to support himself. Albert met Odetta during his third year at Paine.

Odetta, meanwhile, had been born on May 8, 1921, in Augusta, Georgia, the daughter of Samuel Sanders, a minister, and Julia Sanders, a farmer. Her family was so well off that she rode to church in a black limousine—yet she and Albert fell in love. Albert finished high school in 1942 and enrolled at Paine College, though his studies were interrupted when he was drafted into the armed forces at age 21. Odetta graduated in 1943 and joined the army, where she became a nurse. The couple were married in 1944.

The couple later moved to New York, where Albert attended Long Island University and Brooklyn Law School in 1948 to 1952 and passed the New York State bar exam with the goal of starting Brooklyn's first black law partnership. Instead, he ended up going into business with Abraham Kaufman, a maverick investor and businessman who worked in law and real estate. The partners obtained a 109-acre lot in the Poconos as part of a foreclosure deal, complete with a small rooming house. They dreamt of turning it into a resort, but Kaufman's unexpected death ultimately resulted in the Murrays' sole ownership of the property.

Odetta had gotten a B.Ed. from Paine College, an interior design degree from the New York Institute of Design in 1948, and a master's in early childhood education from New York University in 1950. She worked as supervising nurse of the surgical unit at Bushwick Hospital in Brooklyn from 1948 to 1951, but she and Albert both dreamed of establishing a luxury resort on their Pennsylvania property. Although they had difficulty obtaining financing and were discouraged from settling by local residents who were not happy to have black landowners in the area, the Murrays went on to add such amenities as a lake, tennis court, and golf course to their property while also selling off lots around the edge of the property to black professionals who wanted to become homeowners. They opened the Hillside Inn in 1954.

Albert worked in the city during the week, advancing from lawyer to assistant U.S. district attorney to, eventually, judge, becoming the first black person appointed to the Brooklyn criminal court bench. Odetta ran the inn, which faced various difficulties, including the refusal of local mainstream newspapers to advertise black-owned businesses. The Murrays advertised in the black press and slowly built up a return clientele.

Although Hillside closed in 1982 as business was declining, the Murrays expanded and improved the property in 1988 and reopened in August 1989. Hillside has continued to operate ever since, through the efforts of their son, Sonny, an assistant U.S. attorney in Scranton, Pennsylvania. Despite Odetta's death in East Stroudsberg, Pennsylvania, on January 30, 2002, the facilities at Hillside have been renovated and expanded. In 2005, the Hillside Inn will celebrate its 50th anniversary.

Further Reading
Garrett, Kellye M. "Hillside Inn Spreads Its Wings." *Black Enterprise*. December 1998, p. 165.

Harris, Wendy. *Against All Odds, Ten Entrepreneurs Who Followed Their Hearts and Found Success.* New York: John Wiley & Sons, 2001, pp. 203–227.

"Obituaries: Mrs. Odetta Murray." *The Augusta Chronicle.* February 1, 2002. Available online. URL: http://www.augustachronicle.com/stories/020102/obi_020102-37.shtml.

Murray, Joan
(1941–   ) *founder of advertising agency, newscaster*

Joan Murray is an example of the type of African-American entrepreneur who pioneers breakthroughs in a number of different fields. She was not only the first African-American woman to be part of a major network news show, but she also founded and operated a successful advertising agency. Her entrepreneurship and her journalistic breakthroughs were part of the same pattern, both stemming from the realization that as an African-American woman coming of age in an era of racial discrimination, she would have to make her own opportunities.

Murray was born on November 6, 1941, in Ithaca, New York, the daughter of Isaiah Murray, a Fulbright scholar, and Amanda Pearl (Yates) Murray, about whom no published information is available. Murray has an identical twin sister and a younger sister with whom she grew up in Ithaca. She went on to attend Ithaca College for a year, then moved with her twin, June, to New York City, where she attended Hunter College and the New School for Social Research. Her education also included a stint at Harvard University.

When the Murray sisters moved to New York, their goal was to find work in commercial television. In the late 1950s, however, the industry was still highly segregated (separated by race), while women of any color were unusual in journalism and the other professions. Both as a black person and as a woman, Murray was taking a pioneering role—and facing discrimination of various types. Thus, she began her career not as a journalist but rather as a court reporter, someone who records the words spoken in court and prepares transcripts of the trial. She later worked as a secretary in the CBS-TV press department, where her reputation as an excellent secretary spread throughout the organization.

In 1959, Murray went on to work as secretary to Allen Funt, a prominent figure in the entertainment industry who created the show *Candid Camera,* in which ordinary citizens were surprised with various stunts recorded by a hidden camera. Murray stayed with Funt for about six months while also appearing on the camera in various television shows. Her good looks enabled her to work as a model, and she and her twin appeared in commercials together. In this era, television commercials were virtually all-white, rendering African Americans essentially invisible as both performers and consumers, but Murray and her twin appeared in the first series of black-oriented television commercials.

In 1963, Murray spent some time on the other side of the camera, writing for *Women on the Move,* an NBC daytime show hosted by popular television personality Kitty Carlisle. She continued to appear on air, however, presenting so-called "women's stories"—stories focusing on the home, family, and fashion—along with other light news.

Murray was eager to break into more serious television journalism, a resolution supported by the 1965 cancellation of Carlisle's show. It was at this point that she realized that, as she put it in a 1996 *Sepia* article, "I would have to make my own opening." Consequently, she wrote a letter to CBS-TV explaining why she was qualified to work

as a news broadcaster. The station auditioned her and hired her a week later, making her the first African-American woman to appear on a major network show. CBS was actually the last of the three major networks to use a black on-air reporter on its evening news, since both ABC and NBC had hired black reporters. All three networks were gradually beginning to respond to the Civil Rights movement's demands for increased black participation and visibility, but for many years, Murray was the only black on-air face at CBS, where she worked on both the 6 P.M. and 11 P.M. newscasts and contributed to various other news-related shows and productions.

In 1969, Murray sought a new challenge when she left CBS to found Zebra Associates, a successful advertising agency whose national clients included General Foods, Gillette, Gulf Oil, and Miller Brewing. Over the course of her career, she has won many awards, including the Mademoiselle Award for Outstanding Achievement, the Urban League's Certificate of Merit, and the Mary McLeod Bethune Achievement Award. She is also the first African-American woman to enter the Powder Puff Derby, a race for small planes flown by women.

Further Reading

Gale Group. "Joan Murray." *Notable Black American Women,* Book 1. Farmington Hills, Mich.: Gale Research, 1992.

Mapp, Edward. *Directory of Blacks in the Performing Arts,* 2nd edition. Metuchen, N.J.: Scarecrow Press, 1990.

Sepia. "Joan Murray: CBS Girl on the Go." *Sepia,* February 1966: 28–33.

N

Napier, James Carroll

(1845–1940) *lawyer, banker, politician, activist*

James C. Napier was one of the most prominent and beloved figures in the African-American community of Nashville, Tennessee. Napier was a lawyer and politician, the founder of a bank, and a fighter for African-American political and social equality.

Most historians state that James Napier was the freeborn son of parents who had recently been freed, but Herbert L. Clark, who seems the most reliable source, argues that he was born a slave and that his family was not freed until 1848, when their owner died and called for their freedom in his will. In any case, James was the son of William Carroll Napier and Jane E. Napier, who had been slaves on the plantation of Dr. Elias W. Napier. The Napiers were "privileged slaves," however, as James's grandmother, Judy, had been Dr. Napier's seamstress and mistress, bearing him five children. Dr. Napier's relationship with Judy is almost certainly the reason her family was freed on his death as well as the reason they received "a certain sum of money" on the condition that they leave the county. Accordingly, by March 1, 1849, the Napiers bought a farm near Cincinnati, Ohio. Later they purchased a farm in New Richmond, Ohio.

Then William Napier moved back to Nashville with his family, founding both a livery business and an illegal school for black children that was later closed by a group of white vigilantes. Although the school was reopened for a time under the leadership of a free black man, a race riot in 1856 forced it to close again, and it was not reopened until Union troops occupied the city in February 1862.

Accordingly, William sent his wife and two sons back to Ohio, where James and his brother attended first Wilberforce University, then Oberlin College, where James stayed until his junior year in 1867. By then, Reconstruction was in full force, and African Americans began to enter politics in large numbers, so the 22-year-old Napier went back to Nashville, where he worked as a page in the Tennessee State Senate. The following year, he was appointed to a government post by Governor William G. Brownlow.

Soon afterward, John Mercer Langston met Napier and urged him to attend Howard University, the black institution where Langston served as dean. Langston was a powerful Republican politician in his own right, a member of Congress from Ohio, and his patronage was to become very important to Napier. He helped Napier get various government jobs until he graduated from Howard in 1872 and returned to Nashville, where he found other government posts and began his entrepreneurial career. Napier bought and sold real estate, which over the course of his lifetime provided him with a steady and respectable income.

In 1878, Napier married Langston's daughter, Nettie, in a wedding considered to be the black social event of the season. The same year he was elected to the Nashville City Council, holding his seat for three terms, until 1884, when he became a kind of unofficial financial adviser to the city.

Napier used his City Council position to ensure that Nashville hired its first black schoolteachers—an important advance in a city where both black and white children attended the public schools. Education was still segregated in those days, so Napier also made sure that modern schools were built for black students. He also had the city's fire department hire its first black firefighters and made sure that the police department hired black detectives. Napier was the first African American to preside over the council.

Napier continued his influential career within the Republican Party, which in those days was considered the party of Abraham Lincoln and black political rights. In 1882, he was elected to the state party's executive committee, later advancing to the prestigious positions of secretary and chairman of the committee. He ran—unsuccessfully—for state legislature and for county circuit court clerk. In 1898, he was the Republican candidate for Congress, though he lost the general election. He was frequently a delegate to the Republican National Convention during the period 1880–1912.

Meanwhile, Reconstruction was ending, and black people's political and social rights were being rapidly curtailed. During this period, Napier became close friends with political leader Booker T. Washington, whose doctrine of self-help, black self-sufficiency, and African-American entrepreneurship was congenial to the budding entrepreneur. Both Napier and Washington were

known as "accommodationists," people who advocated trying to accommodate to, or get along with, the prevailing conditions of discrimination and inequality, working gradually to change things without alienating white people, rather than making more militant and urgent demands. In 1900, Washington founded the National Negro Business League to promote black businesses, and Napier was a delegate to the league's first convention. He organized the first Tennessee chapter of the group in 1902 and remained extremely active in its affairs, taking over as president in 1915 when Washington died.

In 1903, Napier joined with local entrepreneur RICHARD HENRY BOYD, undertaker Preston Taylor, and six other community leaders to found the One-Cent Savings Bank (later the Citizens Bank), one of the first black-owned banks in the nation. For several years, Napier served without pay as the bank's chief cashier (manager) and pledged his own money to guarantee the bank's operations during its first year. He let the bank operate temporarily in

Banker and entrepreneur James Napier helped lead a 1905 boycott of the streetcars in Nashville, Tennessee, to protest segregation. *(Fisk University Franklin Library, Special Collections)*

Napier Court, an office building he owned in downtown Nashville that he made the city center for black business activity. Because many small banks closed or encountered financial crises during that era, the One-Cent Savings Bank operated very conservatively, trying to build consumer confidence and maintain its operations, which it was successfully able to do for many years.

In 1903, Napier also took part in a controversy over segregation on the West Nashville trolley line. When the streetcar company added an extra car for black workers traveling to local fertilizer plants, it gave support to those who were demanding that all travel on the streetcar be segregated, with separate seating areas for black and white passengers. In 1905, the state legislature wrote this segregation into law, and Nashville leaders began organizing a boycott in protest. Meanwhile, Napier and his colleagues also founded the Union Transportation Company, which they hoped would provide an alternative to the segregated trolley.

The new business did not have enough funds to operate properly, especially as the city responded by levying huge taxes on the new buses. It was also difficult for the company to serve local African Americans, who were scattered widely throughout the area. Still, the company continued for approximately a year, until July 1906, by which time the boycott had also been given up. Although the effort was ultimately unsuccessful, it provided a model that would be taken up a half-century into the future, when bus boycotts became a powerful weapon against segregation in Montgomery, Alabama, and other towns.

Napier was not precisely the leader of these efforts, but he played an important role in them. While the other activists were seen as quite militant, Napier was perceived as "reasonable," and white people often wanted to negotiate with him rather than the others. His visibility in both the black and the white communities also helped bring attention to the issue.

Napier involved himself in many other community activities, including serving on the board of the Anna T. Jeanes Foundation in 1908. The foundation had a $1 million trust fund to establish black schools in the South, and Napier's fellow board members included future U.S. president William H. Taft (then secretary of war), Massachusetts financier George Peabody, and Pittsburgh steel tycoon Andrew Carnegie.

Napier got on the foundation board with the help of Booker T. Washington, who also helped him become registrar of the U.S. Treasury, the highest government position than an African American could hold in those days. The job basically consisted of being the official U.S. bookkeeper. Although the process of getting the job was long and slow, with various presidents offering less prestigious posts that Napier refused, Napier finally became registrar in 1911—appointed by Taft. As a result, he was the first African American whose signature appears on U.S. currency. Napier held the post until Woodrow Wilson took office in 1913 and began to establish a strictly segregated policy in all federal departments. When Napier received President Wilson's order that black and white bathrooms in the Treasury Building should heretofore be separate, Napier refused to comply and the president asked for his resignation.

Then 68 years old, Napier returned to Nashville. In 1913, he helped created the Tennessee Agricultural and Industrial School (later Tennessee State University). In 1914 he was elected to Nashville's Board of Trade, a self-improvement group for African Americans. He served as a trustee of the black institution Fisk University, and in 1930 he represented black people on the Nashville Housing Authority. In 1940, the city named a new housing project J.C. Napier Court in his honor. He died on April 21, 1940.

Further Reading
Clark, Herbert. "James C. Napier (1845–1940)." Available online. Tennessee State University website. URL: http://www.tnstate.edu/library/digital/napier.htm. Downloaded on November 23, 2002.

———. "James Carroll Napier: National Negro Leader." *Tennessee Historical Quarterly* 49 (winter 1990): 243–252.

Ingham, John, and Lynne B. Feldman. *African American Business Leaders: A Biographical Dictionary.* Westport, Conn.: Greenwood Press, 1994, pp. 483–491.

Norris, James Austin
(1893–1976) *founder of law firm, newspaper founder, publisher*

James Norris was the senior partner of the Philadelphia law firm of Norris, Schmidt, Green, Harris, Higginbotham, and Associates, the premier black law firm in the city and a key power base for Philadelphia's black entrepreneurial and professional class. A number of leading lawyers, judges, and public officials came out of that firm, which was known for its civil rights work, its support of black entrepreneurs, and its work on community development in Philadelphia's impoverished neighborhoods.

James Norris was born of working-class parents in the small rural community of Chambersburg, Pennsylvania. He later moved to Pittsburgh, graduated from a Methodist high school, and went on to attend Lincoln College at the University of Oxford in England, where he studied the classics and received a degree in 1912. He went on to Yale Law School, getting a degree in 1917, and came to Philadelphia in 1919. He was a major black business leader in the sense that he served corporate clients through his legal work and moved to expand the number of black people in professional and service jobs. When he joined the law practice of Schmidt, Green, Harris, and Higginbotham, he helped turn that firm into a major city institution that played a vital role in the city's economy.

In the 1920s and 1930s, Norris built up his own political base through founding an enterprise of his own, the *Philadelphia American,* which helped him accrue political influence and patronage and which led to him becoming one of the state's first deputy attorney generals. He also served as the lawyer for black nationalist Marcus Garvey and headed a campaign for President Franklin D. Roosevelt. In 1937, he was the first African American to be appointed to the Board of Revision of Taxes, a leading political post in Philadelphia, and one that Norris held for 30 years.

In the 1950s, Norris's firm helped black bar owners incorporate helped to establish the Father Divine Tracy Hotel in Philadelphia, and helped establish the principle that if a governmental unit confiscated private property, such as a restaurant and bar, it had to pay compensation.

The firm of Norris et al. also played a leading role in civil rights issues. In 1954, the Supreme Court had ruled in *Brown v. Board of Education* that black students had the right to attend white schools. Members of Norris's firm worked to integrate local schools and colleges, showing once again the relationship between the black business community and civil rights: Without a law firm of their own, black activists might have had a more difficult time pursuing civil rights issues.

The law firm also produced a number of black business leaders, including Doris Mae Harris, one of the first African-American lawyers to serve as counsel to the Small Business Administration (a federal agency that supports small and minority-owned businesses), and Mansfield Neal, who held high positions with General Electric. James Norris died in 1976.

Further Reading
Porter, Aaron C. "James Austin Norris." *Encyclopedia of African American Business History,* ed. by Juliet E. K. Walker. Westport, Conn.: Greenwood Press, 1999, pp. 432–435.

O'Neal, Stanley
(E. Stanley O'Neal)
(1951–) *corporate president*

Stanley O'Neal has risen to become the head of Merrill Lynch, the largest securities company in the world. One of the top African-American corporate leaders in the United States, he is credited with helping Merrill Lynch turn itself around during a difficult period in the company's history, winning acclaim from the business company in general and from the African-American community in particular.

O'Neal was born in Roanoke, Alabama, on October 7, 1951, the grandson of a former slave and the son of a farmer. His mother worked as a domestic, cleaning houses. He grew up in the deeply segregated rural community of Wedowee with three younger siblings and attended a one-room schoolhouse. When he was 12, his father got a job with General Motors in Doraville, Georgia, and moved his family to Atlanta, Georgia, where O'Neal became one of the first black students at West Fulton High School.

O'Neal had picked cotton and delivered newspapers to help earn money as he grew up, but when his father told him he would never be a good farmer, he went on to get a B.S. in industrial administration from Kettering Institute in 1974, alternating college semesters with a job on a General Motors assembly line in Doraville. He went on to earn an M.B.A. from Harvard in 1978 and to work in General Motors' Treasury Office.

In 1986, O'Neal became an investment banker at Merrill Lynch because he was impressed by how much money such people made. He worked in a number of positions at Merrill Lynch, for a time selling junk bonds, a high-risk bond that offers a high yield and is often issued to finance a company takeover. He also led the company's capital markets and investor services groups. In 1998, he became Merrill Lynch's chief financial officer, a position that allowed him to make many much-needed changes at the company.

For years, Merrill Lynch had relied on its reputation as the largest company of its kind. To retain that position, it often accepted less-profitable accounts simply to maintain its huge volume. Then the company's position was challenged by discount brokers like Charles Schwab Corp., which offered lower fees for the same stock trades. O'Neal started by trying to match Schwab's low prices but then switched strategies. Instead of seeking the discount market, he decided to target high-end clients, avoiding the small individual investments that Schwab was trying to attract and focusing on clients who could invest $1 million or more.

O'Neal made a number of other changes at the venerable company. In February 2000, he fired

Stanley O'Neal heads Merrill Lynch, the largest securities company in the world. *(Courtesy of Merrill Lynch & Co., Inc.)*

some 2,000 of the company's 15,000 brokers, earning himself the nickname of "axman." In December 2002, he was made chief executive officer of the company; in April 2003 he became chairman. Under his presidency, he eliminated thousands more jobs. Critics have accused him of running an elaborate campaign to eliminate his competition and take over the company—but they also acknowledge that he may be the only person who can bring about the changes necessary for the success of the company, including the shutting down of unprofitable operations in South Africa, Canada, Australia, and Japan. As one of the top African-American corporate leaders in the United States, he is being watched closely by

business analysts who consider his promotion a watershed moment in U.S. corporate history.

Further Reading

Beckett, Paul. "Merrill Lynch Executives Depart As New CEO O'Neal Takes Helm." *Wall Street Journal,* December 9, 2002, p. C9.

Cose, Ellis. "It's a Watershed Moment." *Newsweek,* December 17, 2001, p. 46.

———. "Rethinking Black Leadership." *Newsweek,* February 18, 2002, p. 40.

Daniels, Cora, and Martha Sutro. "The Most Powerful Black Executives in America." *Fortune,* July 22, 2002, p. 60.

Eisenberg, Daniel, and Eric Roston. "And Then There Were Two." *Time,* July 29, 2002, p. 32.

Gale Group. "Stanley O'Neal." *Biography Resource Center Online.* Farmington Hills, Mich.: The Gale Group, 2002. Available online. URL: http://www.galenet.com/servlet/BioRC. Downloaded on December 28, 2002.

Gasparino, Charles. "Merrill's President Making History, Will Become CEO." *Wall Street Journal,* July 23, 2002, p. C1.

Hughes, Alan. "Stepping Up." *Black Enterprise,* October 2002, p. 35.

Lucas, Peter. "Dream Job or Continuing Nightmare." *Journal of Business Strategy* 23, no. 5 (September/October 2002): 28.

"Merrill Has to Face the Music." *BusinessWeek,* August 12, 2002, p. 116.

Norment, Lynn. "3 at the Top." *Ebony,* February 2002, p. 133.

Rynecki, David, and Patricia Neering. "Can Stan O'Neal Save Merrill?" *Fortune,* September 30, 2002, p. 76.

Overton, Anthony

(1864 or 1865–1946) *cosmetics maker, insurance company owner, banker, real estate speculator, publisher*

Anthony Overton rose to business success at a time when African Americans were facing an overwhelming barrage of legal and social restrictions after the end of Reconstruction in the 1870s and before the beginning of the Civil Rights movement in the 1950s and 1960s. He was involved in a number of enterprises and, until the stock market crash of 1929, achieved enormous prosperity.

Anthony Overton was born into slavery on March 21, 1864 or 1865 (different historians cite different dates), on a plantation near the small town of Monroe, Louisiana. Although legally slavery in the Confederacy had ended on January 1, 1863, with the signing of the Emancipation Proclamation, practically speaking, slaves in Louisiana were not free until the defeat of the South in the Civil War. Thus Anthony's parents, Anthony and Martha (Deberry) Overton, were enslaved on James Masterson's plantation until the war ended, when their former owner gave them 60 acres of land.

As a free child, young Anthony studied with a black woman neighbor until he was 7, when a one-room school for African Americans was established in the region. No black high school existed anywhere within 100 miles, so in 1877, Overton's father joined the "Exodusters," an exodus (mass departure) of black people out of the South and into the state of Kansas, which had never known slavery. The Exodusters feared the erosion of black civil rights that they knew would come as soon as federal troops were pulled out of the South, ending the guarantee of black political rights that had been part of Reconstruction.

As a result of the move, Anthony was able to attend school in Topeka, Kansas, an unusually high level of education for anyone at the time, and particularly for an African American. Overton worked at a local grocery store while going to school—and his talent for business was such that the store showed a profit for the first time in its existence.

In 1881, Overton graduated from South Side High School and went into the fruit business, where once again his flair for business led him to success. For example, he often went to growers directly so he could get the best of their crop.

In 1883, Overton's mother died and his father moved back to Louisiana. Anthony remained in Kansas and sent money to his family. At age 23, he fell in love with Anna Tone, who died of tuberculosis in 1887. Overcome with despair, Overton sold his business and left Kansas for a long trip. When he finally returned to Topeka, he enrolled first in Topeka's Washburn College and then in the University of Kansas, where in 1888 he received a bachelor of law degree. That same year, he married Clara Gregg.

Overton practiced law in Topeka for a while, then became a judge of municipal court in Shawnee County, Kansas. In 1892, he was elected treasurer of Kingfisher County, Oklahoma, where he and his wife had moved. Overton preferred business to government service, however. First he bought a general store in Oklahoma City; then he started the Overton Hygienic Manufacturing Company in Kansas City, Missouri, in 1898.

Overton's business got a slow start, making and selling only a single product, but he soon went on to make cosmetics for African-American women, which for a time he himself sold door to door. His early business efforts had their ups and downs, but in 1911, Overton moved his enterprise to Chicago, where his real success began. He soon was marketing a full line of cosmetics and perfumes under the name "High Brown," as well as baking powder, shoe polish, flavoring extracts, and hair preparations. By 1915, the company had 32 full-time employees, a line of 62 products, and assets of $268,000. By 1927, the company was worth more than $1 million and was offering a vastly expanded product line. Despite competition from ANNIE MINERVA TURNBO-MALONE in St. Louis and Chicago and MADAME C. J. WALKER in Indianapolis, Overton's business flourished.

Overton invested the wealth from his enterprise into a new venture: the *Half-Century*, a magazine he founded in 1916. This monthly publication—though sometimes it came out only every other month—espoused Booker T. Washington's philosophy of black self-help, advocating a virtually separate black society and economy within the larger domain of the United States. Unlike ROBERT SENGSTACKE ABBOTT's rival paper, the *Chicago Defender*, Overton's publication opposed the current migration of African Americans from South to North, advocating accommodation with the segregated world of the South, rather than either escape from it or political efforts to change it. When Chicago's anti-black race riots erupted in 1919, leaving dozens of people dead and hundreds of people injured, the *Half-Century* began to take a more militant tone and even supported W. E. B. DuBois's civil rights group, the National Association for the Advancement of Colored People (NAACP). By 1922, however, Overton's magazine had returned to its previous stance: Protest was futile, and African Americans would do better to focus on business than on politics.

On April 18, 1925, Overton stopped publishing the *Half-Century* and started a weekly newspaper in its place, which he called the *Chicago Bee*. The *Bee* was meant to be a direct challenge to the more militant *Defender*. However, the *Bee* tended to appeal to a more middle-class audience, while the *Defender* remained the paper of poor and working people. The *Bee* was popular enough to survive the Great Depression and continue publishing into the 1940s.

Overton, meanwhile, moved into banking in 1922 with Douglass National Bank, the first black-owned bank to receive a national charter. (A charter is a contract with the federal government that sets up the terms for the bank's opera-

tion.) The bank did very well during the 1920s but was unable to weather the depression, closing for good in 1932.

In the 1920s, however, Overton was still expanding his enterprises, and in 1923 he founded Victory Life Insurance Company, which for a time was also quite successful. During the 1920s, the Chicago real estate market was booming as thousands of black families migrated North, and Overton invested the insurance company's funds in real estate, primarily in mortgages on African-American family homes. While this move was a boon to black families who needed a place to live, it proved disastrous for Overton after the stock market crash, when real estate values fell, people were unable to pay their mortgages, and the insurance company's funds disappeared virtually overnight. Overton made some other unwise moves with both bank and insurance company funds, which led to him being ousted from his insurance company and being forced to close his bank. Yet his manufacturing company and newspaper survived, and Overton managed to live a comfortable life until he died in Chicago on July 3, 1946.

Further Reading

Ingham, John N., and Lynne B. Feldman. *African-American Business Leaders: A Biographical Dictionary*. Westport, Conn.: Greenwood Press, 1994, pp. 492–500.

Obituary. *Journal of Negro History* 32, no. 3 (July 1947): 394–396.

Stoner, John C. "Anthony Overton." *Encyclopedia of African-American Culture and History*. 5 vols. New York: Macmillan, 1996.

P

Pace, Harry H.
(Harry Herbert Pace)
(1884–1943) *publisher, music executive, insurance company cofounder*

Harry H. Pace was the owner of the first black-owned and -operated recording company, Black Swan, after which he went on to organize the merger of three insurance companies, creating a newly successful business. He was considered an innovative business leader who made new inroads in every field he entered, developing new opportunities for African-American entrepreneurs.

Pace was born on January 6, 1884, in Covington, Georgia, the son of Charles Pace, a blacksmith, and Nancy Francis, about whom little is known. When Pace was an infant, his father died, but he managed to get a good education, finishing high school and college at an early age and graduating with an A.B. from Atlanta University in 1903.

At Atlanta Pace met noted black intellectual and civil rights leader W. E. B. DuBois, then a professor who dreamed of founding a national African-American journal. In 1905 DuBois talked Pace into giving up his dream of attending law school to become business manager of the *Moon Illustrated Weekly,* a Memphis-based small magazine. DuBois remained in Atlanta, and Pace threw himself into the Memphis enterprise, doing everything from editing articles to dragging bundles of magazines to the post office. After initial difficulties, DuBois withdrew his support, leaving Pace with a magazine that failed miserably. DuBois, Pace, and other staff people had put considerable sums of their own money into the magazine, so at 22, Pace was completely destitute and was actually considering suicide. He was saved by the unexpected arrival of a telegram, which arrived collect. Luckily, a local black businessman was in Pace's office at the time and offered to pay the fee. The telegram was a job offer for Pace to teach Latin and Greek at Lincoln University in Jefferson City, Missouri. He taught there in 1906 and went on in 1907 to become cashier (manager) at Solvent Savings Bank in Memphis. Although he had to take a salary cut, he felt some responsibility to help a black-owned business get on its feet, as the bank was running at a $7,000 deficit with assets of only around $50,000. Four years later, under Pace's management, the bank had $600,000 in assets and Pace's salary had doubled.

In 1912, DuBois started another publishing venture, the *Crisis,* the official journal of the civil rights group the National Association for the Advancement of Colored People (NAACP), and he again invited Pace to join him. Perhaps because of his previous experience, Pace refused DuBois's offer though he remained close to DuBois and the

NAACP. Instead, he went on to work as secretary of Standard Life Insurance Company in Atlanta.

Standard Life prospered under Pace's leadership, who profited from the opportunity to work closely with Atlanta's black leaders, many of whom served on the company's board of directors: Henry A. Boyd of the National Baptist Publishing House in Nashville, Tennessee; Morehouse College president John Hope; and Booker T. Washington's secretary, Emmett J. Scott. In 1916, Pace helped to found the Atlanta branch of the NAACP, which he served as president.

In 1917, Pace married Ethlynde Bibb, with whom he later had two children. While on their honeymoon, Pace learned of some internal political maneuvering at Standard Life that caused a rift between him and company president Heman Edward Perry. Three years later, Pace finally left the company and moved to New York, where he capitalized on his relationship with blues pioneer W. C. Handy, whom he had known since 1907 in Memphis. Handy considered Pace a "first-rate" lyricist and had heard him sing at church and community parties. In 1913, the two men published some songs together as Pace and Handy Music Publishers. In 1918, at Pace's urging, Handy brought the company to New York City, with Pace as president, his brother Charles as vice president, and himself as secretary-treasurer. They hired famed bandleader Fletcher Henderson to promote their songs and prominent composer William Grant Still to arrange their music. The first song they published was "A Good Man Is Hard to Find," which was a huge success.

Pace threw himself into the company when he came to New York, but in 1921, he and Handy dissolved their partnership and Pace went off to found Pace Phonograph Corporation, the first African-American recording company. He then formed Black Swan records to promote African-American artists. Henderson and Still left Handy's company, renamed Handy Brothers Music Company, to join Pace Phonograph, which Handy somewhat resented.

Pace's achievements at Black Swan were numerous, despite the efforts of white-owned companies to frustrate his success. At one point, for example, he tried to buy a record-pressing plant, but a white company bought it to prevent his purchase. Eventually, however, Pace's company was able to acquire a recording laboratory and pressing plant, making his the first African-American company to produce its own records.

Pace's real success with Black Swan came when he signed Ethel Waters, who eventually became a legendary singer. However, he rejected Bessie Smith, whose style he considered too "nitty-gritty." Pace was apparently trying to walk a fine line: On the one hand, he was building a black-owned company to produce African-American artists; on the other hand, he was reluctant to seem "too black."

Black Swan did very well in the early 1920s, but then the advent of radio destroyed the company's future as well as threatening many white-owned record companies with bankruptcy: Once people could hear music for free, they were less likely to buy records. Pace responded by selling Black Swan to Paramount Records, which continued to record many of his artists. However, white-owned record companies generally failed to preserve the authenticity of African-American music as they maintained virtually all-white management. Not until BERRY GORDY, JR., formed Motown Records in 1959 would another black-owned record company make a dent in the U.S. music business.

In 1925, Pace went on to found Northeastern Life Insurance Company in Newark, New Jersey, along with a number of other well-to-do African Americans. In 1929, he had the idea of merging the company with Supreme Life and Casualty of Columbus, Ohio, and Liberty Life Insurance of Chicago, combining the resources of three major northeastern black-owned life insurance companies. Pace became president and chief executive officer of the new company, known as Supreme Liberty Life.

The new company had trouble surviving the Great Depression: The resulting unemployment was even higher among black people, who had difficulty paying their insurance premiums. In addition, the company had invested in the real estate market, financing mortgages for black homeowners. But as unemployed and underemployed black people had difficulty making their mortgage payments, the company risked acquiring numerous properties that, in the depressed market, it would be unable to resell.

Pace found innovative ways of coping with these financial difficulties, as did corporate counsel EARL BURRUS DICKERSON, and the company became increasingly profitable in the late 1930s. Meanwhile, Pace fulfilled his lifelong dream of attending law school, which he did from 1930 through 1933, while running Supreme Liberty Life. He joined the firm Bibb, Tyree, and Pace, where he remained for the rest of his life. He also supported black insurance companies through his activities with the National Negro Insurance Association. Indeed, throughout the 1920s and 1930s, he was a major spokesman for the black insurance industry.

Pace also received a number of government appointments. In 1933, he was made a member of the U.S. secretary of commerce's advisory committee on black business, and in 1935, he became assistant counsel of the Illinois Commerce Commission. He was active in the NAACP, the Urban League, the Episcopal Church, and the Citizens Civic and Economic Welfare Council of Chicago. He also wrote a book of inspirational essays called *Beginning Again* and a serial novel that was published in the black newspaper *Chicago Defender*.

Pace's friend and admirer JOHN H. JOHNSON reported that in Pace's last year, he attempted to pass for white. According to Johnson, Pace had opened a law office in downtown Chicago and moved to a white suburb, angering black employees at Supreme Life. They planned a demonstration at Pace's home to embarrass him, which upset Pace enormously. Johnson wrote that Pace became "a changed man" as a result, "more cautious, more withdrawn, more secretive." Indeed, Pace's life ended in such secrecy that his actual death date is not available, though he is known to have died in 1943. No matter what happened at the end of his life, however, Pace had amassed an impressive record of achievement and had made many contributions to the black community. His designation as a "race man"—someone who proudly and publicly helped improve conditions for African Americans—is an indelible part of his biography.

Further Reading

Dixon, Robert, and John Godrich. *Recording the Blues.* New York: Stein and Day, 1970.

Gale Group. "Harry H. Pace." *Notable Black American Men.* Gale Research, 1998. Reproduced in *Biography Resource Center,* Farmington Hills, Mich.: The Gale Group, 2002. Available online. URL: http://www.galenet.com/servlet/BioRC. Downloaded on December 22, 2002.

Handy, W. C. *Father of the Blues: An Autobiography.* New York: Macmillan, 1941.

Johnson, John H. "Succeeding Against the Odds." *Ebony,* November 1992, p. 34.

Puth, Robert C. "Supreme Life: The History of a Negro Life Insurance Company." *Business History Review* 43, no. 1 (spring 1969): 1–21.

Sampson, Henry T. *Blacks in Blackface: A Sourcebook on Early Black Musical Shows.* Metuchen, N.J.: Scarecrow Press, 1980.

Parks, Henry G.

(1916–1989) *president and founder, Parks Sausage Company*

Henry G. Parks founded the first black-owned company to be publicly traded, Parks Sausage Company, whose memorable ad campaign featured a child saying, "More Parks sausage, Mom . . . pleeease?!" Parks won acclaim both for his company's success and for his innovative marketing techniques. He also served on the boards of Magnavox, First Penn Corp., Warner Lambert Co., and W. R. Grace Co., and was a trustee of Baltimore's Goucher College.

Parks was born on September 20, 1916, to poor parents working as domestics in Atlanta, Georgia. When World War I broke out, the Parks were among the many African Americans who went north looking for the newly available industrial jobs. They settled in Dayton, Ohio, where Parks attended public schools and then received a B.S. degree from Ohio State University, going on to study marketing as well.

Parks wanted to own his own business, a dream that in the 1930s was considered so unattainable for African Americans that a college counselor advised Parks to change his name and go to South America to acquire a Spanish accent. Parks refused to disguise himself, but his early years in business were marked by difficulty. He owned and operated several businesses in New York, including a theatrical booking agency, and he tried to market Joe Louis Punch through the soft drink company he formed with black boxing champion, Joe Louis. When none of his ventures caught on, Parks moved to Baltimore, where he variously ran a cement block plant, worked in real estate, and owned a drugstore. Success eluded him until 1951, when he founded Parks Sausage Company, intending to market southern-style sausage to Baltimore's black community using an old Virginia recipe. The company grew from two employees into 240, from a small venture into a multimillion-dollar operation with annual sales of more than $28 million.

Parks was known as an unusual businessman from the start, inviting federal meat inspectors into his plants before he was required to do so and coding his products to indicate when they should no longer be sold. Unlike many employers, he also welcomed labor unions into his company.

In 1969, Parks Sausage became the first publicly traded black-owned company. Parks worked with well-known African-American broadcaster Hal Jackson to develop a marketing plan that involved hiring women to stand in front of grocery stores, offering free sausage samples. Jackson would then interview satisfied consumers on live remote. The campaign was an overwhelming success, and by 1971, Parks had contracts with every major supermarket chain on the East Coast—12,000 stores, 75 percent of which were in white suburbs.

Parks sold his interest in the company for $1.58 million in 1977, though he remained on the board of directors until 1980. He died on April 14, 1989, at a time when his business was in a slump. On May 24, 1996, Baltimore's largest black-owned business filed for bankruptcy, but it was purchased for $1.7 million and the assumption of most of the company's $9 million debt by football superstars Franco Harris and Lydell Mitchell. The sports figures were unable to save the company, however, which was sold in 1999 to Pennsylvania deli meat producer Dietz & Watson. The new owners planned to outsource the manufacturing portion of the business to concentrate on sales and marketing.

Further Reading

Dominguez, Alex. "In Business World, Hall of Famer Isn't Afraid to Take Chances." *The Standard-Times.* Available online. URL: http://www.s-t.com/daily/ 12-96/12-15-96/f07bu167.htm. Posted December 15, 1996.

"Hal Jackson: Biography." TopBlacks: Positive Profiles of People of Color. Available online. URL: http://www.topblacks.com/entertainment/hal-jackson.htm. Downloaded on November 4, 2002.

Haskins, Jim. *Black Stars: African American Entrepreneurs.* New York: John Wiley & Sons, 1998, pp. 109–113.

Hocker, Cliff. "Is Less More for Parks Sausage? Sale of the Baltimore Plant Marks Last-ditch Effort to Keep Company Afloat." Blackenterprise.com. Available online. URL: http://www.blackenterprise.com/ ArchiveOpen.asp?Source=ArchiveTab/1999/05/0 599-01.htm. Posted May 1999.

"(Parks, Jr.) H. G. Parks Inc." Black Inventors: Then and Now. Available online. URL: http://members. bellatlantic.net/~vze3wm4u/page52.html. Updated on July 25, 2002.

Parsons, Richard Dean
(Richard Parsons, Richard D. Parsons)
(1948–   ) *corporate president*

Richard Parsons rose rapidly through the ranks of a number of U.S. businesses to head Time Warner, Inc. After America Online (AOL) and Time Warner merged in 1999, Parsons went on to take over the new company, winning applause for his low-key, consensus-building management style.

Parsons was born on April 4, 1948, in Brooklyn, New York, the son of Lorenzo Locklair and Isabelle Parsons. He grew up in the New York neighborhood of Queens, where he graduated from public high school at the age of 16, going on to become a student at the University of Hawaii, where he played varsity basketball and became social chairman of his fraternity. Parsons was talented but lacking in ambition until he married Laura Bush, whom he credits with giving him "focus." She convinced him to enroll in Union University of the University of Albany Law School, where he worked part-time as a janitor and an aide in the state assembly to help pay for school, going on to graduate first in a class of more than 100 students and to score highest among 3,600 lawyers when he took the state bar exam in 1971.

Parsons's first job was as an aide on the legal staff of New York governor Nelson Rockefeller, a liberal Republican whose influence led to Parsons's own association with the Republican Party. When Rockefeller became vice president under President Gerald Ford in 1974, Parsons went with him, first as general counsel, then as associate director of his Domestic Council, where he worked on drug issues. In 1977, when Deputy Attorney General Harold R. Tyler, Jr., became partner in the prestigious New York City law firm

Patterson, Belknap, Webb & Tyler, he invited Parsons to join the firm—and Parsons made partner in only two years, even though such a rise usually takes seven years.

Parsons remained with Patterson, Belknap for 11 years, winning fame as both corporate lawyer and civil litigator, and serving as counsel for a number of clients, including New York's Dime Savings Bank. In 1988, he was made chief operating officer of the bank, a position he claimed to have accepted at the urging of his wife. The first African American to manage a lending institution of such a size, Parsons came on board at a difficult time, for Dime had suffered enormous losses due to the devaluation of New York City real estate in the late 1980s. Yet Parsons reorganized the bank's labor force and lowered the bank's bad debts from $1 billion to only $335 million. Colleagues came to respect him for his low-key, respectful management style, and he went on to become the bank's chair and CEO. In 1995, he arranged a merger with Anchor Savings Bank to create Dime Bancorp., the fourth-largest thrift institution in the United States.

Parsons's Republican politics continued to draw attention, as in 1993 he supported Republican mayoral candidate Rudy Giuliani over his African-American opponent, Democrat David Dinkins. When Giuliani emerged victorious, he made Parsons head of his transition council and later offered him the post of deputy mayor of economic development. Though Parsons declined the latter job, he did serve as chair of the city's Economic Development Corporation.

Parsons became a board member for many corporations and institutions, including Philip Morris, TriStar Pictures, Howard University, the Metropolitan Museum of Art, and Time Warner. In fall 1994, he was offered the post of Time Warner president by the company chair, Gerald Levin, a controversial move that many predicted would end in disaster for Parsons when he assumed office in January 1995. Parsons had no experience in the world of media, and Time

Warner's record division was having financial problems. Moreover, the Seagram Companies, which owned 15 percent of Time Warner stock, was believed to be planning a takeover, and Time Warner carried significant debt.

Yet Parsons once again reorganized a company in trouble, overhauling the company's financial and administrative operations and winning Levin's further trust. When AOL merged with Time Warner in 1999, Parsons became the company's co-chief operating officer along with Bob Pittman. In 2001, Levin named Parsons as his successor, to assume office in May 2002. In January 2003, Parsons also became chairman of the company's board.

The Time Warner-AOL merger was extremely controversial. The new company did not do well, partly because the two companies coexisted uneasily at best, and in active competition at worst. Reportedly, top executives at AOL never accepted Parsons's leadership, predicting that he would soon be removed from office. Yet Parsons continued to be viewed with enormous respect, by the business community as a whole as well as by key people in the AOL Time Warner hierarchy. His future as a corporate leader remains to be seen, but he retains an impressive track record.

Further Reading

Burroughs, Todd Steven. "Black Man's Appointment to Run Media Giant 'Another Sign of Progress.'" *New York Amsterdam News*, December 20, 2001, p. 4.

Cohen, Adam, Michael Duffy, Frank Gibney, Dan Kadlec, and Eric Roston. "Can a Nice Guy Run This Thing?" *Time*, December 17, 2001, p. 59.

Cose, Ellis. "It's a Watershed Moment." *Newsweek*, December 17, 2001, p. 46.

———. "Rethinking Black Leadership." *Newsweek*, February 18, 2002, p. 40.

Daniels, Cora, and Martha Sutro. "The Most Powerful Black Executives in America." *Fortune*, July 22, 2002, p. 60.

Eisenberg, Daniel, and Eric Roston. "And Then There Were Two." *Time*, July 29, 2002, p. 32.

Kirkpatrick, David. "AOL's Top Job Goes to a Veteran of Time Warner." *New York Times*, January 17, 2003, p. C1.

———. "Question of New Chairman at Top of Board's Agenda." *New York Times*, January 14, 2003, p. C1.

Lowry, Tom, Catherine Yang, and Ronald Grover. "What the Shocker Means." *BusinessWeek*, December 17, 2001, p. 38.

Mermigas, Diane. "Parsons Aims to Calm Fears." *Electronic Media*, May 20, 2002, p. 34.

Roberts, Johnnie L. "AOL's Board Is Digging In." *Newsweek*, August 19, 2002, p. 40.

———. "How It All Fell Apart." *Newsweek*, December 9, 2002, p. 53.

"10 Most Powerful Blacks in TV." *Ebony*, October 2002, p. 86.

Payton, Philip A.
(Philip A. Payton, Jr.)
(1876–1917) *realtor*

Philip A. Payton was known as the "father of colored Harlem" for his efforts to open up New York City's Harlem to African-American residents in the early 20th century. His Afro-American Realty Company was for a time quite successful, and it began the process of turning Harlem into one of the most exciting African-American neighborhoods in the United States, a center for black politics and culture.

Payton was born on February 27, 1876, in Westfield, Massachusetts, the son of Philip Payton, Sr., a merchant and barber, and a mother about whom little is known. Payton attended public schools in Westfield and went on to graduate from Livingstone College in Salisbury, North Carolina, in 1899. Then, like thousands of other African Americans, Payton decided to move to New York City.

The end of the 19th century and the beginning of the 20th were difficult times for African

Americans in the South. After a brief period during Reconstruction when black people attained a measure of political power, African Americans faced a severe backlash from the white community: discriminatory laws, lynching, and a lack of economic opportunity. Many African Americans came north looking for more freedom and better jobs, and such cities as Chicago and New York experienced huge migrations from the South. In 1900, there were 60,666 African Americans in New York; by 1910, nearly half as many black people had moved to the city, for a population of 91,709. Most black residents were unskilled laborers, but there was also a small professional elite. Both types of black people faced enormous discrimination in housing, however. When Payton arrived in the city, Harlem was largely a white neighborhood and a fairly luxurious one. However, developers had overextended themselves, and when they could not get enough white tenants, they were forced to rent to black people.

Payton initially worked in a department store as an attendant at the weighing machine—customers could weigh themselves for a penny—and the "picture machine," a device that took photographs for a small fee. He lost that job and worked for a while as a barber. In 1900, he became a janitor at a real estate firm and resolved to start his own real estate company. In October 1900 he and a partner opened the Brown and Payton Realty Company. The partner left the company; Payton faced hard times and was evicted twice. With typical flair, he billed himself as a manager of colored tenements: "colored" was an acceptable term for African Americans in those days; "tenements" were a type of apartment; and Payton's designation came from the fact that housing was generally segregated.

Despite self-promotion, he did not have a colored tenement to manage until 1901, when two white landlords were in dispute over a Harlem property. One landlord took revenge by giving Payton the management of the building and the instruction to fill it with "colored tenants." This actually gave Payton his start in the real estate business. He went on to advertise his specialty of managing "colored tenements," so that in a 1917 obituary in the New York Age, a black-owned newspaper, he was called the first African-American entrepreneur to see the value of the media.

In 1904, Payton and his new partner, James C. Thomas, formed the Afro-American Realty Company. Thomas was a mortician, another example of how black funeral homes provided an early source of capital for African-American enterprise. The two men won fame when they blocked the efforts of a white company to evict black people from three homes that the company had sold them in Harlem. White people in a more luxurious part of Harlem were upset about having to live so close to African Americans—but Payton and Thomas were able to save the homes they had sold.

Payton was praised for his actions by Booker T. Washington, the black leader who preached black self-help and economic independence. However, Washington refused to invest in Payton's company, despite repeated efforts of Payton to solicit his help. Payton was able to attract other investors, including FREDERICK RANDOLPH MOORE, publisher of the New York Age and a close associate of Washington's.

Many people criticized Payton's methods. He would gain control of a property that had previously been all-white and fill it with black tenants, to whom he charged rents that were higher than the market value. Black people, desperate for somewhere to live, were willing to pay the higher prices, and Payton claimed that he had no choice: It was harder and more expensive for him to raise money than for white companies, he said, and he had to pass those costs along to his tenants. He himself, however, prospered, and his business raised questions about the pros and cons of black capitalism as a means for improving the black community. On the one hand, black people were able to live in new neighborhoods that had not been open to them before. On the other hand, they were paying high prices—and Payton was making money, at least temporarily.

Certainly, the Afro-American Realty Company continued to acquire more properties for a few years, and Payton made some headway selling investment shares to black residents of New York. However, he misrepresented the dividends that these shares would pay, and he tended to buy more property than his company could actually afford. When he was hit by the recession of 1907–08, his company foundered. Payton sought help from Washington, who refused it. He asked Washington to introduce him to Andrew Carnegie, the prominent white philanthropist, and Washington refused that as well. Payton approached Carnegie directly, but with no success. Meanwhile, a group of investors had sued Payton in 1906, and in 1907 he was arrested on charges of fraud. By 1908 his company had stopped doing business.

Payton continued operating privately, with modest success and frequent periods of struggle. His last deal was his biggest: In 1917, he bought six apartment buildings valued at $1.5 million. Payton died a month later, on September 4, 1917, and the Payton Apartments Corporation was founded in 1918 to manage the buildings. But the buildings had no heat, and the owners were unable to profit. The development of Harlem was left to two of Payton's former salesmen, John E. Nail and Henry C. Parker, who became known as the "Little Fathers" of Negro Harlem. They continued Payton's work of making that New York City neighborhood a political and cultural capital for African Americans.

Further Reading

Gale Group. "Philip A. Payton, Jr." *American Decades*, CD-ROM. Farmington Hills, Mich.: Gale Research, 1998.

Haskins, Jim. *Black Stars: African American Entrepreneurs*. New York: John Wiley & Sons, 1998, pp. 79–82.

Johnson, James Weldon. *Black Manhattan*. Cambridge, Mass.: Da Capo Press, 1991.

Osofsky, Gilbert. *Harlem: The Making of a Ghetto*. New York: Harper & Row, 1963.

"Philip Payton: Harlem Realtor." *Issues & Views*. Spring 1992. Available online. URL: http://www.issues-views.com/index.php/sect/1000/article/1011. Downloaded on February 4, 2003.

Perry, Christopher James (1854–1921) and Eugene Washington Rhodes (1895–1970)
publishers, political leaders

Christopher James Perry was the founder of the *Philadelphia Tribune*, a major black-owned newspaper in turn-of-the-century Philadelphia. When Perry died, the paper ultimately went to his son-in-law, Eugene Washington Rhodes, who ran it for many years. Although the *Tribune* has been criticized for being representative primarily of Philadelphia's African-American middle class and elite, ignoring working-class black people, the paper has survived through decades of change and is still in existence today.

Christopher James Perry was born on September 15, 1854, in Baltimore, Maryland. Although slavery was still in force, Perry's parents, Christopher and Rebecca (Bowser) Perry, were freeborn African Americans who saw that their son was educated in the city's public schools. In 1873, he went to Philadelphia, where he worked for a white family during the day while attending night school at Lombard Street Presbyterian Church. He soon began writing a column for the *Philadelphia Sunday Mercury*, known as "Flashes and Sparks." He was promoted into a number of different positions and then made editor of the paper's "Colored Department." When the paper finally went out of business in 1884, he began publishing his own journal, the *Philadelphia Tribune*. In the same year, he also married Cora Harris.

Philadelphia had a large and well-established black middle-class that could support a number of African-American-owned newspapers, but the

Tribune quickly became the city's largest black weekly. Its popularity was increased by the crusading temper of its editor, who fought for better jobs and working conditions for African Americans, more black representation in city government, and against political corruption generally. He also pushed for a "cleanup" of poor black neighborhoods, a campaign that was successful despite the fact that black political influence in Philadelphia declined seriously in the 1890s and early 20th century.

Perry himself enjoyed a certain measure of political power. An active member of the Republican Party (then seen as the party of Abraham Lincoln and civil rights), Perry had been made the first African-American clerk in the sheriff's department, a post he held for 15 years; he also served three years as inspector in the highway department. In 1895, he was elected to the common council (the city council).

Like many other northern cities, Philadelphia saw a huge influx of black immigrants fleeing the racial discrimination, violence, and lack of job opportunities in the South. Black people had trouble finding housing, in part because of their poverty and their numbers, in part because of racial discrimination. Perry and his paper supported a number of civic groups that worked to increase housing as well as economic opportunity for these black immigrants. And in 1916, the *Tribune* came out in favor of a broadly based black boycott of white-owned businesses on South Street, a major Philadelphia street, to protest the physical attacks on black people that were increasing as the city's black population rose.

Perry's paper prospered and he became a rich man. He invested in real estate and served as treasurer of the Conservative Company, a firm that bought, sold, and managed real estate.

Perry died unexpectedly in May 1921 (the exact date is unknown), leaving behind a wife, four daughters, and a son. One daughter, Beatrice Perry, became president of her father's publishing company, while his daughter Bertha became managing editor and women's editor, and his son Christopher, Jr., worked as composing room foreman. For a time, Perry's associate, Grant Williams, was the paper's editor, but when he too died a year later, Eugene Washington Rhodes took the post.

Rhodes was born on October 29, 1895, in Camden, South Carolina, the son of Charles Rhodes, a carpenter, and Laura Boykin, a committed mother who drew on the family's small savings to send Eugene to a Presbyterian private school in Camden, then to a preparatory school for black people known as Benedict College, in Columbia, South Carolina. In 1918, Rhodes went on to Lincoln University in Pennsylvania, from which he graduated with a bachelor's degree in 1922. While in school he worked at a number of odd jobs, including selling advertising space for the *Tribune* during the summer. He also wrote editorials for the paper, hoping to work there full-time when he finished school.

Thus Rhodes was relatively inexperienced when he took over the editorship in 1922, but he was about to run a paper that by this time had virtually no competition. When Rhodes married Bertha Perry in 1923, he further strengthened his position and went on to expand the paper, buying new equipment and a new building.

During the 1920s, the *Tribune* continued to do well by representing the city's black elite and black middle-class, preaching the virtues of education, thrift, hard work, self-improvement, and black capitalism. Republican politics were by now becoming increasingly conservative, and Rhodes's own politics fit in well with this trend. Meanwhile, in 1926, Rhodes received his law degree after part-time study at Temple University, and the Republican administration made him assistant U.S. attorney for the Eastern District of Pennsylvania, a job he held until the Democrats took office in 1933. He was also a law partner in the firm of Nix, Rhodes and Nix.

Rhodes's conservatism was expressed in his support for various types of segregation, which he felt would be good for black business owners; he reasoned that as long as African Americans and white people led separate lives, black entrepreneurs would be needed to serve their community. Rhodes did not support separate schools, however, because he felt that under segregation, black schools were always inferior. He pressed for black members of the board of education, and indeed, in 1932, Philadelphia saw its first African-American school board member. Rhodes also criticized the shortage of black police, whose numbers were actually declining.

At the same time, Rhodes attacked black civil rights groups for not being able to work together, and was particularly critical of the National Association for the Advancement of Colored People (NAACP). Although many black-owned newspapers tended to be somewhat more conservative than the majority of African Americans, the *Tribune* was known nationwide as being particularly conservative. Thus when the far more radical *Philadelphia Independent* was founded, the *Tribune* faced serious competition: The *Independent* went from 10,000 readers in 1931 to 30,000 in 1935. The *Independent* appealed to the majority of black people, who supported President Franklin D. Roosevelt, a Democrat, and his social service programs. Rhodes and the *Tribune* attacked Roosevelt and his programs, particularly those requiring employers to pay minimum wage; Rhodes feared that such requirements would cause bosses to fire lower-paid black workers and replace them with white workers. The president's supporters, on the other hand, believed that minimum wages meant that lower-paid black workers would now be making more money.

The *Tribune* continued to grow, however, and in 1941, it went from a weekly to a twice-weekly paper. Rhodes's own power continued to increase, and in 1958 he became the second African-American member of the Philadelphia Board of Education. By the time Rhodes died on June 24, 1970, his paper had a circulation of 50,000. Although there are criticisms of the role that he and Perry played in black politics, his newspaper continues

in existence today, a voice for at least one segment of black Philadelphia.

Further Reading
Ingham, John, and Lynne B. Feldman. *African American Business Leaders: A Biographical Dictionary.* Westport, Conn.: Greenwood Press, 1994, pp. 525–533.
The Philadelphia Tribune website. Available online. URL: http://www.phila-tribune.com/. Downloaded on February 4, 2003.

Pettiford, William Reuben
(1847–1914) *educator, pastor, banker, realtor*

William Reuben Pettiford was a talented entrepreneur who became a business leader in Birmingham, Alabama, almost by accident; although he had come to that city as a pastor, he ended up founding and running one of the largest and most successful black-owned banks of the era. Pettiford saw his involvement with the Alabama Penny Savings and Loan Company as part of a larger mission: to teach the virtues of thrift and frugality to black workers, to help black people own their own homes, and to create black-owned institutions that could help sustain the African-American community within the often hostile white world of the South.

Pettiford was born on January 20, 1847, in Granville County, North Carolina, to free black parents, the farmers William and Matilda Pettiford. In 1857, when young William was 10, his father moved the family to Person County, North Carolina, where he bought another farm. Young William, the oldest of four children, had to stay out of school to work on the farm, but he encouraged his younger siblings to teach him what they had learned and also sought lessons from a district schoolteacher who lived with the family.

Pettiford was interested in business from a very early age. When he was 17, working on his father's horse farm, he bought a pig from his brother and started raising hogs on some land that his father had given him. He also started a tanning enterprise. However, his savings from these two profitable ventures were all in Confederate money, which he lost at the end of the Civil War.

When Pettiford was 20, in 1867, he went to work on a Roxbury, North Carolina, tobacco farm, a job he found extremely boring. He continued on with a number of low-paying jobs. In the summer of 1868, he became a religious Christian and decided to pursue the life of a pastor.

It took several years of studying and working—often as a schoolteacher or principal—before Pettiford was ordained as a minister. During that time, he was married three times—to Mary Jane Farley, in 1869, until she died later that year; to Jennie Powell who died in 1874; and to Della Boyd, in September 1880. After his ordination, he worked at various churches and schools before he finally settled in Birmingham, Alabama, to preach at the Sixteenth Street Baptist Church. It was here, in Birmingham, that he found success as an entrepreneur and community leader.

Birmingham in the 1880s was a boomtown, with hundreds of uneducated and impoverished rural African Americans pouring into the town to work at the white-owned coal, iron, and steel companies. (One small black-owned coal mining company was owned by Reverend T. W. Walker.) Pettiford saw these men much as Booker T. Washington saw them—as people who did not understand how to manage their money, partly because of their own lack of training and partly because they had been so exploited by ruling-class white people that they had never had the chance to own anything. Many of these rural black people had bad experiences with white-owned banks and entrepreneurs who had cheated them in various ways. Providing these workers with a trustworthy black-owned institution that could educate them about how to deposit their money safely and perhaps even apply for a home or small-business loan seemed like a worthy goal to Pettiford—and to many other leaders of the Birmingham African-American community.

Accordingly, a group of those leaders met in 1890 to form the Alabama Penny Savings and Loan Company. Initially, the group wanted an incorporated bank—one that was recognized by the state of Alabama. The group did not properly follow the legal procedures for incorporation, however, so they decided to open as a private bank. At the time, there were only three other black-owned banks in the United States.

Pettiford served the bank as president, a post he would hold for 23 years. He soon had to resign from his pastor's job to focus on his financial duties, but he always insisted, "I'm still a preacher," and indeed, he preached the virtues of thrift and home ownership. His management skills enabled the Penny Savings and Loan to withstand the Panic of 1893 (a "panic" is a kind of financial crisis that can lead to a depression), even though 110 banks were forced to close during that period. When a bank closes, the people who have deposited their savings in it lose all their money. Sometimes a closed bank hands out certificates instead of cash, in the hope of being able to pay later. Penny Savings's ability to remain open when so many other banks were closing caused it to win the respect and trust of the black community, and the admiration of many white people as well.

In 1895, Penny Savings was finally able to incorporate, and Pettiford began investing the bank's holdings in various real estate projects. Once he had the bank buy a building for $6,500 and then sell it for $20,000 one year later; another time he had the bank buy an $18,000 house that was worth $35,000 a few years later. In 1905, the bank had 8,000 depositors, 1,000 of whom owned homes, most of whom were black.

In 1913, the bank built its own home, which Pettiford had designed by a black architect and erected by a black construction company. Both the building and the process by which it was created were a symbol of pride in Birmingham's African-American community, as well as a sign of the self-sufficiency advocated by Washington.

In 1900, Washington had founded the National Negro Business League, to promote black entrepreneurship, and Pettiford was active in support of that group. He himself helped found the National Negro Bankers' Association in 1906, and for a time served as the group's president. In 1901, he also helped establish Industrial High School (later Parker High School), the first black high school in Birmingham (in those days, schools were strictly segregated, or separated, by race). In addition, he was president of the Ministerial Association in Birmingham, and headed the Negro American Publishing Company, which published the *Negro American Journal*. At his death, on September 21, 1914, he was considered one of the richest black men in Alabama, and both black people and white people attended his funeral.

Further Reading

Feldman, Lynne. *A Sense of Place: Birmingham's Black Middle-Class Community, 1890–1930.* Tuscaloosa: University of Alabama Press, 2000.
"The Entrepreneur's Preacher." *Issues and Views.* Fall 1997. Available online. URL: http://www.issues-views.com/index.php/sect/1000/article/1010.
Simmons, William. *Men of Mark.* Cleveland, Ohio: Geo. M. Rewell & Co., 1887, pp. 460–465. Available online at University of North Carolina at Chapel Hill Libraries: Documenting the American South. URL: http://docsouth.unc.edu/neh/simmons/simmons.html#p460. Downloaded on November 24, 2002.

Pinchback, P. B. S.
(Pinckney Benton Stewart Pinchback, Pickney Benton Stewart Pinchback)
(1837–1921) *politician, entrepreneur, editor, land speculator*

P. B. S. Pinchback was one of the most interesting and controversial figures of the Reconstruction era, the period after the Civil War when African Americans had a chance to influence state and local politics in the region where they had until recently been held as slaves. As it turned out, this opportunity was short-lived—Reconstruction effectively ended in 1877, and black political power declined after that—but while political opportunities existed, P. B. S. Pinchback made the most of them. He held a variety of government posts and, for a little over a year, he served as acting governor of Louisiana—making him the first African-American governor.

Pinchback was born on May 10, 1837, near Macon, Georgia, the son of white plantation owner Major William Pinchback, and the enslaved Eliza Stewart, who was of mixed African, American Indian, and white ancestry. Pinchback and Stewart had one of the long-lasting semi-marital relationships that sometimes occurred in a system where it was illegal for African Americans and white people to marry. Pinchback did not marry, and his relationship with Stewart lasted many years and produced eight children. When he decided to relocate to a new plantation near Holmes, Mississippi, he emancipated (freed) Stewart, which meant that her subsequent children would also be free. On the way to Mississippi, P. B. S. Pinchback was born.

The young Pinchback received his early education on the plantation, but in 1846, when he was nine, he and his older brother, Napoleon, were sent to Gilmore's High School in Cincinnati, Ohio. A year and a half later, their father got sick and they returned to the plantation. The older Pinchback died soon after that, and the administrator of his estate warned Stewart that his heirs would try to enslave her and her children. Stewart fled to Cincinnati, where Napoleon was soon put in an asylum for the mentally ill and the 12-year-old Pinchback became his family's sole support.

Pinchback got work as a cabin boy on the canal boats operating on the Ohio canals around Miami, Toledo, and Fort Wayne. From 1854 to 1860, he worked on the Mississippi River steamboats, rising to become a steward—the highest position allowed to an African American at the time—and then becoming a gambler and con man under the protection of George Devol, an older white man. Pinchback also worked as a personal servant to Devol and another gambler, "Canada Bill" Jones. Rumors abounded about various women in Pinchback's life, but what is certain is that in 1860, he married the 16-year-old Nina Emily Hawthorne, with whom he had six children in a marriage that lasted the rest of his life, despite later rumors of other affairs.

By 1862, the Civil War had begun, and New Orleans, Louisiana, had fallen to Union troops. That year, Pinchback left his steamboat at Yazoo

P. B. S. Pinchback was the first African-American governor, a post he held in Louisiana during the Reconstruction years after the Civil War. *(AP/Wide World Photos)*

City, Mississippi, and made his way to New Orleans with the intention of fighting for the Union. He soon was attacked at knifepoint by his brother-in-law for mysterious reasons, fought back, and spent two months in the local workhouse. When he was released, he volunteered to serve in a white regiment, the First Louisiana Volunteer Infantry. However, the Union army was rigidly segregated (separated by race), and Pinchback was asked to recruit black volunteers for a Corps d'Afrique (French for "African unit"; French was a common language in New Orleans). Although he himself was made the captain of one of the companies, he soon discovered that all the other officers were to be white, not black as he had originally thought. Pinchback protested and eventually resigned.

In 1863, Pinchback continued his agitation for civil rights, addressing a meeting of "Free Colored Citizens" in the city, urging them to demand the vote. He did not, however, press for full social equality, reasoning that political equality would eventually make that possible. Pinchback went on to approach General Nathaniel P. Banks for permission to raise a company of black troops and spent $1,000 of his own money on recruitment after Banks approved the idea. However, Pinchback's own commission as an officer of that company was ultimately not approved, and Pinchback stopped trying to serve the Union army.

He had not given up on the cause of civil rights, however, and in 1865 went to Washington, D.C., intending to press President Abraham Lincoln on the matter. Lincoln was assassinated while Pinchback was there, so he went to Alabama, where for two years he spoke to recently freed black audiences, rallying their support for the Radical Republicans. This was a faction of the Republican Party that stood for black political rights, despite the opposition of other segments of the Republican Party and of the Democratic Party, which dominated the white citizens of the South.

Reconstruction, however, shifted the political balance of forces, depriving people high in the

Confederate hierarchy of the right to run for office and calling for new state constitutions throughout the South. When the so-called Reconstruction Acts were passed in Louisiana in 1867, opening the door to political reform, Pinchback returned to New Orleans, where a number of ambitious black politicians and entrepreneurs seemed to be doing well.

Pinchback organized a local Republican club to serve as his political base, which some historians consider the first African-American political organization in Louisiana. As this club's leader, he was elected to the state constitutional convention, where he played a leading role drafting the new constitution. It was an exciting time, as the entire political and social system of slavery and black oppression seemed on the verge of being overthrown, African Americans working side by side with white people to draft an entirely new foundation for state government based on the freedom rather than the enslavement of African Americans. The new constitution established free public schools, extended the vote regardless of race or property ownership, and granted civil rights to black people on public transportation, in public facilities, and in places of business. When the convention ended in March 1868, a new social order seemed to be in the making—and Pinchback was poised to be one of its leaders.

In November 1868, the governorship went to Henry Clay Warmoth, a white man from Illinois who had come to New Orleans in 1865. His lieutenant governor was the African-American former slave Oscar J. Dunn. Pinchback ran for state senate and was at first defeated, but when he demanded a recount, it turned out that he had won. Throughout his political career, this would be Pinchback's pattern: He would either win or lose narrowly, and the defeated candidate would demand a recount whose outcome probably had more to do with political influence than with the actual number of votes cast. Certainly, Pinchback lost more elections than he won.

Meanwhile, however, Pinchback took his seat in the state senate and soon became a target for white resentment of black political power. He was often accused of corruption, and it is difficult to distinguish charges based in fact from those that sprang from the political frustrations of people who had lost power.

Pinchback went on to engage in various entrepreneurial activities. In 1869, he and fellow state senator CESAR CARPENTIER ANTOINE opened a cotton-selling business under the name Pinchback and Antoine. At the end of that year, the two men started the *New Orleans Louisianian,* a semiweekly newspaper that Antoine left two and a half years later, leaving Pinchback to run it alone until 1881, when it closed. Although some other black journals were more militant, the *Louisianian* was the longest-lasting and therefore the most influential.

Pinchback also engaged in a number of transactions that allowed him to profit from his service in the legislature. In 1870, he helped pass an act establishing the Mississippi River Packet Company (a packet is a small boat used to transport passengers), theoretically to help black people travel up and down the Mississippi River. Pinchback was one of the founders of that company, and he was able to benefit from the $250,000 appropriation that he helped pass the following year. Antoine was another member of the company, as were other black Radical Republicans.

During this time, Pinchback and Antoine were also involved in a scheme that made use of their position as city parks commissioners. Charged with finding a site for a public park, Pinchback and Antoine made a down payment on some property, divided it in half, sold part of it to the city at a profit, and transferred their debt to the city. Antoine later accused Pinchback of somehow cheating him out of $40,000 in this transaction, and the two men broke with each other.

Politics in Louisiana continued to become more complicated, partly due to the widespread corruption, partly because of the various political factors that vied for power. In 1871, Lieutenant Governor Oscar Dunn died, and, with Governor Warmoth's backing, the state senate chose Pinchback to take his place in an extremely close election. In 1872, there was a factional fight within the Republican Party, with Antoine on one side and the governor on another. Pinchback agreed to support the white William Pitt Kellogg for governor, with Antoine as his lieutenant governor. He himself ran as a congressman at large. The election was so fraught with complications that President Ulysses S. Grant had to install Kellogg in office. Meanwhile, though, impeachment proceedings had begun against Warmoth, who fled the state to avoid them. His absence meant that Pinchback, as lieutenant governor, became acting governor, a post he held from December 9, 1872, through November 30, 1873. Even as he held the posts of congressman and acting governor, the state legislature elected him to become a U.S. senator (in those days, senators were chosen not by direct election but by state legislatures). Pinchback never went to either the U.S. House of Representatives or the U.S. Senate, since both elections were contested and charges of corruption abounded. Eventually, Pinchback received pay equal to a U.S. senator's salary, though he did not serve.

Pinchback was known for his refusal to agree to prevailing customs of segregation and discrimination. The streetcars in New Orleans had "white" and "colored" cars, but Pinchback refused to sit in the colored car. The conductor would then clear all white people from his car, and Pinchback rode alone. In 1871, he bought a ticket for his wife on the Jackson Railroad that the company would not honor, and he sued the company. The matter was settled when the railroad apologized. In 1874, he was refused service at a local saloon where he had gone for years, and he began a crusade for equal rights in the *Louisianian*. By 1875, however, Pinchback was counseling black people to be patient in their struggle for civil rights, an attitude that at least one historian believes held back the cause.

In 1879, there was another state constitutional convention, to which Pinchback was elected a delegate. There he sponsored a bill to create Southern University, a black institution, for which he received extensive criticism from the black Creole community, light-skinned African Americans with French heritage. The Creoles believed that creating a black university meant that they had accepted segregation, agreeing to be shut out of the white schools in exchange for being given an undoubtedly inferior school of their own.

Even as he accommodated himself to the changing climate, Pinchback became discouraged. Although from 1882 to 1885, he served as surveyor of customs at the Port of New Orleans—a position that involved regulating goods that came into the city—he could see that the political future for African Americans was limited, as the white power structure reestablished itself and curtailed black rights. In 1885, at age 48, Pinchback entered Straight University Law School. He graduated a year later and was admitted to the Louisiana bar, though he does not seem to have practiced.

Sometime in the early 1890s, Pinchback moved his family to New York City, serving there as a U.S. marshal, and then relocated to Washington, D.C. There he worked with the relatively conservative black leader Booker T. Washington to win some political appointments for African Americans, including fellow New Orleans entrepreneur WALTER I. COHEN. After Washington died in 1915, Pinchback's influence fell sharply, and his health declined. He and his wife were cared for by their grandson, Jean Toomer, who went on to become one of the leading authors of the Harlem Renaissance, a cultural movement in Harlem in the 1920s. Although Pinchback was relatively obscure when he died on December 21, 1921, he stands as a key figure for those who wish to understand the complicated era of Reconstruction.

Further Reading

Bontemps, Arna. *One Hundred Years of Negro Freedom.* New York: Dodd, Mead, 1961.

Devol, George H. *Forty Years a Gambler on the Mississippi.* Cincinnati, Ohio: Devol and Haines, 1887.

DuBois, W. E. B. *Black Reconstruction in America.* New York: Free Press, 1999.

Haskins, James. *The First Black Governor: Pinckney Benton Stewart Pinchback.* Lawrenceville, N.J.: Africa World Press, 1996.

Kerman, Cynthia Earl, and Richard Eldridge. *The Lives of Jean Toomer.* Baton Rouge: University of Louisiana Press, 1987.

———. *Pinckney Benton Stewart Pinchback.* New York: MacMillan, 1973.

Pleasant, Mary Ellen

(1814–1904) *real estate speculator, boardinghouse owner, entrepreneur*

Mary Ellen Pleasant's life is the subject of enormous speculation, with a number of conflicting versions based on rumor, unreliable newspaper accounts, and accusations leveled by former friends and associates. In 1993, noted historian Lerone Bennett, Jr., published an extensive two-part account of Pleasant's life in *Ebony*. During the 1990s, researcher Susheel Bibbs also looked into Pleasant's life, using the material she found to create a one-person show, write a pamphlet, give speeches, and curate exhibitions about Pleasant. At some points, Bibbs and Bennett's accounts conflict, though they largely agree. To make matters still more confusing, Pleasant herself often provided different accounts of her own life, for reasons that are unclear. The following profile is based primarily on the work of Bennett and Bibb.

Pleasant may have been born on August 19, 1814, or as late as 1817. She may have been born in Philadelphia, or near Augusta, Georgia. By some accounts, she was the daughter of a Haitian enslaved woman and the white son of a Virginia governor.

Pleasant herself said that she was sent away sometime around the age of six to Nantucket, Massachusetts, where she lived with a Quaker, Mary Hussey, who had a small shop. Although her father gave the Husseys money for her education, they kept it for themselves. The Husseys seem to have been abolitionists and they apprenticed her to a Boston tailor.

As a young woman, Pleasant may have gone to New Orleans and Cincinnati. At some point, she married a man called either James W. Smith or James Henry Smith. There are numerous disagreements over Smith's identity: Some reports have him as a carpenter and contractor with his own business; others call him a landowner and merchant, and say that he was a supporter of William Lloyd Garrison's abolitionist newspaper *The Liberator*, and an agent of the Underground Railroad, an informal network that helped enslaved people escape north to freedom.

In any case, after four or five years, Smith died, leaving his widow a substantial amount of money, which she used to further the abolitionist cause. Sometime around 1848, she seems to have married a former slave named John James Pleasant, who may also have been called Pleasants or Pleasance (people were far less careful about spelling in those days). John Pleasant may have been a cook, a seaman, or both.

Some historians believe that Mary Ellen Pleasant and her husband continued to rescue slaves until slave owners began to make life dangerous for her, so she went back to Nantucket, and then to New Orleans, where she studied voodoo with priestess Marie LeVeaux. At some point, she gave birth to her only child, Elizabeth (Lizzie) Smith.

Many abolitionists were migrating to San Francisco during this period, and eventually, the Pleasant family went with them. Pleasant arrived in San Francisco sometime between 1848 and 1852, when she worked as a housekeeper for rich merchants and saved her money to invest in the stock and money markets. By her own account, she arrived in San Francisco with $15,000 in gold coin that had been left to her by her first husband, and she rapidly amassed a fortune by speculating in silver and gold. ("Speculating" means to buy and sell an item without actually using it, intending to make money only on the trade.)

Bibbs says that Pleasant used two identities in California, so that she would not be captured under a law that allowed any black person without "free papers" to be sold into slavery. Under the name "Mrs. Ellen Smith," she worked at a boardinghouse owned by white people. As Mrs. Pleasant, she ran her own businesses, which eventually included a chain of boardinghouses, a chain of laundries, a tenant farm, a dairy farm, livery stables (where horses and carriages were rented), and a moneylending business. Bibb believed that she also ran houses of prostitution, though Bennett says there is no evidence that she did so.

What is certain is that Pleasant was an extremely talented businesswoman who was remarkably able to obtain and use information, and to turn that information into profitable deals. Some people believed that she had a network of African-American servants to spy on the wealthy, using the information she picked up as the basis for her own enterprises. Pleasant was also known as extremely generous and committed to both women and African Americans. She spent huge sums to help both free and enslaved African Americans reach San Francisco, and then she loaned them money, found them jobs, or helped set them up in small businesses. She was also extremely protective of women, who were in a very vulnerable position in the San Francisco of that time. Young unmarried or widowed women, without male protection and with few legal ways to earn a living, could easily become prostitutes or find themselves severely abused. Pleasant rescued women in dangerous situations and helped them find places for children they could not care for.

Meanwhile, Pleasant supported the Underground Railroad and fought discrimination in California. In 1858, she went east—by some

accounts, to help free a brother-in-law from slavery. Pleasant herself insisted that she had gone to meet John Brown, the white abolitionist who was trying to organize an interracial uprising that he hoped would provoke a massive revolt that would eventually end slavery. Harriet Tubman supported Brown, and so, apparently, did Pleasant. She claims to have met him in Chatham, Canada, and to have given him a significant amount of money for his cause. Although there is no evidence to support this claim, Pleasant never ceased to repeat it, and she requested that her tombstone read, "She was a friend of John Brown."

Meanwhile, in 1858, Pleasant's money and leadership were central in defeating a California law that did not allow African Americans to testify in court. In 1865, she refused to comply with racial segregation on San Francisco's streetcars, staging a sit-in that year and winning a legal case on the matter in 1868. Another historian, Sue Bailey Thurman, has called her "the Mother of Civil Rights in California."

In 1867 or 1868, Pleasant opened her first boardinghouse, which soon evolved into a chain. One facility in particular became known as the most fashionable place to stay and to eat in San Francisco. In 1871, her boarder Newton Booth was elected governor of California, and Pleasant hosted a huge gala for him at her house.

At some point Pleasant made the acquaintance of Thomas Bell, a white stockbroker with whom she joined forces. Certainly they were business partners; rumors abounded that they were also lovers. In any case, they made a fortune together, using some of Bell's money and some of Pleasant's, with Bell amassing a $30 million fortune and becoming known as the Quicksilver King of the West. ("Quicksilver" is another name for mercury.)

Eventually, Bell married a white woman named Teresa Hoey or Teresa Percy, and again, accounts vary. Bell may have discovered her in a house of prostitution and married her, or Pleasant may have taken her from such a house and tried to help her become a lady. In any case, the three went on to live together, in a huge mansion designed and furnished by Pleasant with Thomas Bell's money.

Another famous scandal is associated with Pleasant. A young woman named Sarah Althea Hill claimed that she and former U.S. senator William Sharon had signed a secret marriage contract. Sharon, for his part, claimed to have paid Hill $500 per month for sexual favors but denied having married her. Pleasant testified in the case that she had seen the contract and talked about it with Sharon. In 1884, a San Francisco judge ruled in Hill's favor, but a federal court later overturned the ruling.

In 1892, Thomas Bell died. Initially, everyone in the household agreed that while sick, he had gotten up in the night, become dazed, and fallen over the stairway railing, eventually dying of the fall. He left nothing to Pleasant in his will, though it transpired that much of his property had been in her name before his death. In 1899, Mrs. Bell ordered the 85-year-old Pleasant out of the house they still shared. Later, Bell accused Pleasant of murder, at a time when Bell was known to be actively hallucinating and, according to Bennett, was clearly mentally ill.

Meanwhile, Pleasant left the Bell house, which was actually in her own name but which was tied up in the legal entanglements that had resulted from Thomas Bell's death. She ended up living in poverty, alone, rescued at the last minute by a white friend named Olive Sherwood, who took Pleasant into her own home, where she died about two months later, on January 11, 1904.

During her life, Pleasant was sometimes referred to as "Mammy" Pleasant. She considered the nickname racist and demeaning, and always demanded to be called "Mrs. Pleasant." Another rumor—if true—testifies to Pleasant's strength, integrity, and strong sense of honor. Although she was known to be privy to many of the most scandalous secrets in San Francisco high society, she never revealed what she knew. In her days of

poverty, a man reportedly came and offered to pay for her secrets. Pleasant proudly refused, sending the man away. Today, the increased attention being paid her by historians and writers is a testament as well to her courage and independent spirit.

Further Reading

Bennett, Lerone, Jr. "The Mystery of Mary Ellen Pleasant, A Historical Detective Story, Part I." *Ebony*, June 1993, p. 56.
———. "The Mystery of Mary Ellen Pleasant, A Historical Detective Story, Part II." *Ebony*, September 1993, p. 52.
Cliff, Michelle. *Free Enterprise.* New York: Plume, 1996.
Crowe, Steve. "Mary Ellen Pleasant: Unsung Heroine." *(The New) Crisis* 106, no. 1 (January/February 1999): 35.
Katz, William Loren. "Pioneer Sisters." *Essence*, February 1994, p. 108.
Museum of the City of San Francisco. "Favorite S.F. Ghost Story About Mammy." Reprinted from *The San Francisco News*, October 14, 1935. Museum of the City of San Francisco website. Available online. URL: http://www.sfmuseum.org/hist10/mammy.html. Downloaded on November 15, 2002.
San Francisco Arts Commission. "Mary Ellen Pleasant: Mother of Civil Rights in California." San Francisco Arts Commission website. Available online. URL: http://sfac.sfsu.edu/gallery/pleasant.html. Downloaded on November 15, 2002.

Plinton, James O., Jr.
(Jim Plinton)
(1914–1996) *airline executive, aviator*

James O. Plinton was the first African-American top executive at a major airline, a pioneering figure in the corporate world. He was also the first African American to help organize and operate an airline outside the United States.

Plinton was born on July 22, 1914, in Westfield, New Jersey, the son of James O. Plinton, Sr., who had a dental laboratory, and Mary Williams Plinton, who worked at home. He graduated in 1935 with a bachelor's degree in biology from Lincoln University in Lincoln, Pennsylvania, and went on to serve in the Merchant Marine and to work at the U.S. Post Office.

Then Plinton enrolled in the University of Newark's Civil Pilot Training Program in Newark, New Jersey, the only African American in a class of 35. It was so unusual for African Americans to enter the field of aviation that the head of the school's aeronautic division spent half an hour trying to convince Plinton not to enter the program. Plinton nevertheless completed the initial course with honors and went on with the top one-fourth of his class to receive further training. After receiving his commercial pilot's license and his flight instructor's rating, he was one of six students chosen out of more than 200 to get further training in cross-country flight and flight instruction.

In February 1941, Plinton became one of the first black flight instructors at Tuskegee Institute in Alabama, where a corps of African-American fighter pilots was being trained, the 99th Pursuit Squadron, also known as the Tuskegee Airmen. By 1943, he was assistant director of Tuskegee's aeronautics division, put in charge of the War Training Service program and one of Tuskegee's airports. He also served as assistant chief pilot.

The U.S. Army Air Forces Training Command chose Plinton as the first of four black pilots to receive further training so that they could be commissioned as advanced army flight instructors and service pilots. He then became one of the first black army flight instructors at Tuskegee Advanced Army Air Base, where he taught the man who was to become America's first black four-star general, Daniel "Chappie" James, Jr.

In 1944, Plinton began working in the Caribbean, helping to organize Andesa, the national airline service of Ecuador. In 1948 he went to Haiti to establish and operate Quisqueya,

Ltd., a commercial flight service based in Kingston, Jamaica, and serving several Caribbean islands. He also had a dry cleaning and laundry chain in Haiti, which he started with only $5,000 but which grossed $250,000 each year.

After almost a dozen years in Haiti, Plinton returned to the United States to seek work in the budding field of commercial aviation. In the late 1950s, this field was segregated (separated by race), as were so many others in the United States, and black pilots, flight attendants, and airline executives were virtually unknown. Plinton, however, became the first African-American executive at a major airline when Trans World Airlines (TWA) hired him in 1957 to work in personnel and industrial relations. Plinton used his position to hire the first African-American flight attendant and the first black pilot for a major airline.

One of Plinton's achievements at TWA was to develop a targeted marketing plan that identified different consumer groups according to income, age, professional status, ethnicity, and personal interest. This type of marketing was highly unusual in the 1960s and early 1970s, and TWA did not accept it. In 1971, Plinton was passed over for a promotion that he believed he should have gotten, so he moved on to become vice president for special marketing affairs at Eastern Airlines. In 1975 Eastern promoted him to vice president for urban and international affairs, and then, in 1976, to vice president for marketing development, a position he held until his retirement in 1979.

Plinton was active in civic affairs throughout his life, serving as president, vice chair, and community chairman of the board of the YMCA between 1973 and 1981. He served on other educational and museum boards and received a number of honors and awards. He died of cancer in Lake Wales, Florida, on July 4, 1996. His *New York Times* obituary acknowledged him as a pioneer in breaking the color barrier, opening new opportunities for other African Americans.

Further Reading

Gale Group. "James O. Plinton, Jr." *Notable Black American Men.* Farmington Hills, Mich.: Gale Research, 1998.

"James Plinton Jr., Pioneer Airline Exec., Dies at Age 81." *Jet,* July 29, 1996, p. 57.

Salpukas, Agis. "James Plinton, Jr., 81; Broke Color Barriers at U.S. Airlines." *New York Times,* July 14, 1996, p. 32.

Ward, Francis. "Jim Plinton's Flight to Corporate Success." *Black Enterprise,* September 1979, pp. 59–60.

Poe, Kirsten N. (Kirsten Noelle Poe)
(1965–) and
Renee E. Warren (Renee Elaine Warren)
(1965–) *media consultants*

Kirsten Poe and Renee Warren are two best friends who are also business partners, founders, and operators of Noelle-Elaine Media Consultants. Their public relations firm, founded in 1993, has handled such prestigious clients as ROBERT L. JOHNSON's BET Holdings, Inc.; the Calvert Group; Prince; senator and 2004 presidential candidate Carol Mosely Braun; and General Colin Powell (prior to when he became secretary of state). They also handled the book tour for EARL G. GRAVES's book *How to Succeed in Business Without Being White.*

Renee Elaine Warren was born on March 11, 1965, in Chesapeake, Virginia, the daughter of Lewis McCoy Warren, Sr., who once operated a real estate company, and Viola (Faltz) Warren. Warren's father ran his own contracting firm and later created Seven Seas Investment Corp., a real estate investment firm based in Norfolk, Virginia, where he served as chief executive officer (CEO) and president. After he retired, he became an associate minister at First Baptist Church Crestwood in Chesapeake, Virginia.

Renee's mother, Viola Warren, was a nurse before having four children, whom she left nursing to raise. Later, she went back to school and earned a business management degree from Tidewater Community College in Chesapeake, Virginia, eventually becoming office manager for her husband's investment firm.

Renee received her B.S. in criminal justice and speech communications in 1987 from Old Dominion University in Norfolk, Virginia. Warren began her career as a reporter for the *Daily Press* in Norfolk, moving on after eight months to the much larger *Virginian Pilot* in the same city. In 1988, she went on to work for Dow Jones & Company's wire service, Professional Investor Reporter, in New York City. In 1990, she moved to an associate producer job at CNBC, while freelancing for *Black Enterprise* and *Essence.*

Poe was born on March 30, 1965, in the Bronx, a borough of New York City. Her mother, Dolores Poe, was an administrator at the Social Security Administration. Her father, Robert Poe, Jr., was a space analyst (currently retired) for the city of New York. In the summer of 1985, while still a college student, she interned at Manhattan Cable (now Time Warner Cable). In December of that year, she graduated from Syracuse University's Newhouse School of Public Communications with a degree in television, radio, and film management. One month later, she was working as a sales assistant at Manhattan Cable and attending graduate school part-time at New York University. In 1987, she went on to an unpaid internship producing public affairs programming at WNBC-TV in New York City, where she eventually received paying jobs first in program operations, then in sales administration. She received her M.A. in media ecology from NYU in 1988.

In October 1991, Warren and Poe met at CNBC, where Poe had just begun working as a media relations associate. They became friends immediately and in 1993 planned to travel together to Aruba. Because they could not afford the vacation they wanted, they threw an extremely successful fundraising party at a Harlem restaurant. The party drew more than 200 guests, including the vice president of CNBC, suggesting that the women had a definite flair for producing and publicizing events.

By this time, Warren was a senior producer at CNBC, producing 10 live financial shows each weekday and two shows over the weekend. Poe was media relations manager, in charge of all press-related activities for the network. When they returned from their trip, the manager of the Harlem restaurant asked them to promote an event involving Sherman Hemsley, star of the 1970s–80s television show *The Jeffersons*. Although that project never panned out, the two women decided to open their own public relations firm, setting up their office in Warren's studio apartment and continuing to work at CNBC until May 1994, when they left to operate their company full-time.

The fledgling company had hard times at first, but in 1995, they landed their first corporate client, BET Holdings, Inc., the parent company of Black Entertainment Television, which hired them to plan publicity for the BET/Michael Jackson Walk of Fame, a gala event honoring the pop singer. That year the company also produced a documentary for the U.S.-Africa Chamber of Commerce, *Africa: An Emerging Market for the 90s*, which won a Telly Award. In 1996, they organized events for the National Association of Black Owned Broadcasters, the Minority Corporate Counsel Association, and the New York Association of Black Journalists.

Although the company struggled for a while, even borrowing money from the women's parents, they achieved financial stability by 1998, when their revenues hit the $1 million mark. The company continues to receive a great deal of business from black-owned companies and African-American organizations, but they have also worked for such mainstream clients as the Disney company and *Money* magazine.

Further Reading

Capuano, Tiffany. "Friendship Is Formula for Success at New York City Media Consulting Firm." *Old Dominion Alumni News* 4, no. 1 (winter 1998). Available online. URL: http://www.odu.edu/ao/alumni_magazine/issue3/reneewa.htm. Downloaded on January 12, 2003.

Gale Group. "Renee Elaine Warren." *The Complete Marquis Who's Who*. Marquis Who's Who. 2001. Reproduced in *Biography Resource Center*, Farmington Hills, Mich.: The Gale Group, 2003. Available online. URL:http://www.galenet.com/servlet/BioRC. Downloaded on January 12, 2003.

Harris, Wendy. *Against All Odds, Ten Entrepreneurs Who Followed Their Hearts and Found Success*. New York: John Wiley & Sons, 2001, pp. 181–201.

Newsome, Melba. "PR Power." *Black Enterprise*, August 1999, p. 28.

Noelle-Elaine Media, Inc. website. Available online. URL: http://www.noelle-elaine.com/index.html. Downloaded on January 12, 2003.

Thomas, Myra A. "Dynamic Duo Hits Paydirt with Media Consulting." MBJ Online. Available online. URL: http://www.citynewsnetwork.com/mbe/genx1.htm. Posted February 1997.

Posey, Cum
(Cumberland Willis Posey, Jr.)
(1890–1946) *baseball team owner*

Cum Posey was the owner of the one of the great black baseball clubs in U.S. history, the Homestead Grays. U.S. baseball was highly segregated (divided by race) throughout its history, until white owner Branch Rickey brought black player Jackie Robinson onto the Brooklyn Dodgers in 1947. Before that time, black players had separate teams—and Posey owned one of the best.

Posey was born in Homestead (then called Harding Station), Pennsylvania, on June 20, 1890, the grandson of a slave freed after the Civil War and the son of Cumberland Willis Posey, Sr., who rose from the humble job of deck sweeper to become the first black licensed riverboat pilot and engineer, and who eventually owned a fleet of barges, the Diamond Coal and Coke Company, and part of ROBERT LEE VANN's *Pittsburgh Courier,* the major black newspaper in Pittsburgh. Posey's mother was Angelina Stevens, the first black teacher at Ohio State University and an artist whose paintings decorated Posey's home.

Although Posey grew up in an elite black family, he himself was more interested in sports than in school. He played and coached in the Homestead basketball program while attending local schools. He studied chemistry at Pennsylvania State University for a time but quit after being dropped from the basketball team for low grades.

Back in Homestead, Posey and his older brother Seward ("See") organized the Monticello-Delaney semipro basketball team at a time when the sport enjoyed little popularity. In 1911, Posey's team played the varsity champions of all-black Howard University, in the first black game played in Pittsburgh. When Posey's team won a surprise victory, he was called the best black player in the country. From 1911 to 1915, Posey starred on his team, managed its finances, and promoted and booked its games.

Meanwhile, in 1910, he had signed up to play in the outfield of the Homestead Grays, a local black baseball team whose members were mainly steel- and brickworkers at local plants who played on weekends at a local park. Posey played both baseball and basketball for a number of years. He also married Ethel Truman, with whom he eventually had five daughters.

For a time, Posey enrolled at the University of Pittsburgh. Then he transferred to Holy Ghost College (now Duquesne University) under an assumed name so he could stay eligible to play on a college team. He became his school's top scorer in basketball and the captain of its golf team.

In 1917, Posey became manager of the Grays while working full-time for the Railway Mail Service. Finally, in 1920, Posey decided to devote himself full-time to sports, attracting the best local players he could and pushing out the part-time players who had once filled the team. To compete with William "Dizzy" Dismukes, owner of the Pittsburgh Keystones, Posey needed to start paying his own players, so he approached club president Charlie Walker in 1916 and got him to come up with money for salaries.

The local all-white professional team was the Pittsburgh Pirates, who played in Forbes Field. Posey arranged to use their park for his team's games, though his team was not allowed to use the locker rooms. Still, the salaries, top players, and use of the field enabled Posey to drive the Keystones out of business.

In 1923, the Eastern Colored League was formed, operating until 1929. But for Posey, it was more profitable to have his team stay out of the league and continue to barnstorm—to travel around the United States playing games wherever they could. Touring was difficult and uncomfortable. The players rode a vehicle like a schoolbus, on which it was difficult to sleep. Yet black players of the time were usually not allowed to stay at white-owned motels or eat at white-owned restaurants.

Still, by the late 1920s, the Grays were coming into national prominence. Posey stopped playing in 1927 at the age of 37 and focused on building the team. In 1930, he brought in Josh Gibson, a catcher and one of the greatest baseball players that ever lived. The Grays were profiting, and Posey became head of the Greater Pittsburgh Colored Baseball League.

But 1930 was also the year that GUS GREEN-LEE's Pittsburgh Crawfords came onto the scene, a development that ultimately spelled disaster for Posey. Not only did Greenlee have a strong team, but also his illegal activities gave him the bankroll to keep his players going, while Posey was suffering from the Great Depression that had begun in 1929 and continued throughout the decade. In 1933, Greenlee resurrected the Negro National League (NNL), but Posey refused to join until 1935. By then, he, too, had to seek gangster money to finance his sports activities, working with Rufus "Sonnyman" Jackson, who ran the numbers racket in Homestead just as Greenlee did in parts of Pittsburgh. (The numbers racket was a kind of lottery in which three-digit numbers came up every day. Poor people could bet small amounts of money on the numbers—a highly profitable but illegal business for black organized crime.)

Posey's team was being raided by Greenlee, who offered high salaries to attract the best players. But when Jackson put his money into Posey's team as a way of hiding his illegal gains from the police, Posey managed to hold on to some of his stars. In 1937, Gibson and top hitter Buck Leonard went back to the Grays. Then 10 top Greenlee athletes went to join the Dominican League in the Dominican Republic, devastating Greenlee's team.

Also in 1937, Posey was elected secretary of the NNL. In 1940, his team began to rent Washington, D.C.'s Griffith Stadium, home of the major-league Senators. With the Greenlee team out of business since 1938, the Grays dominated black baseball, playing in both D.C. and Pittsburgh and drawing huge crowds—more than 3 million in 1942. Posey claimed that his team was the largest black-owned enterprise in the world outside of black-owned insurance companies.

World War II was hurting baseball, however—black as well as white—as players from all teams were being drafted or going to work in defense plants. Moreover, after the war, white professional baseball would gradually become integrated, spelling the death of the Negro Leagues.

Cum Posey did not live to see the end of black baseball, however, for he died on March 28, 1946, two months after Josh Gibson died tragically of a drug overdose and only three weeks before Jackie Robinson made his debut as the first black athlete to play ball with a white team, the Montreal Royals. The following year, Robinson would play with the Brooklyn Dodgers, leading See Posey to disband the team he and his brother had built. Many of Posey's players went on to enter the Baseball Hall of Fame in Cooperstown, New York, and in 1988, the Pittsburgh Pirates and the Pittsburgh city government honored Posey with a plaque commemorating his team and that of Gus Greenlee, who had "made Pittsburgh the center for Black Baseball in America during the years when the color line barred blacks from the major leagues."

Further Reading

Holway, John B. "Cum Posey and Gus Greenlee: The Long Gray Line." *Blackball Stars*. Westport, Conn.: Meckler Books, 1991, pp. 299–328.

———. *Josh and Satch: The Life and Times of Josh Gibson and Satchel Paige*. Westport, Conn.: Meckler Books, 1991.

Leonard, Buck, with James A. Riley. *Buck Leonard: The Black Lou Gehrig, the Hall of Famer's Story in His Own Words*. New York: Carroll & Graf Publishers, 1995.

Monroe, Al. "Panic Is Seen Within the Ranks of Organized Baseball." *Abbott's Monthly*, August 1932, p. 16.

Peterson, Robert. *Only the Ball Was White*. Englewood Cliffs, N.J.: Prentice-Hall, Inc., 1970.

Ribowsky, Mark. *The Power and the Darkness: The Life of Josh Gibson in the Shadows of the Game*. New York: Simon & Schuster, 1996.

Santa Maria, Michael. "King of the Hill." *American Visions*, June 1991, p. 20.

Procope, Ernesta G.
(Ernesta Bowman, Ernesta Forster)
(1929–   ) *insurance company owner*

Ernesta G. Procope is known as the "First Lady of Wall Street," in honor of the fact that she owns E.G. Bowman Co., Inc., the largest minority-owned insurance brokerage in America, which is also the largest female-owned such company and the first black-owned commercial brokerage to establish an office on Wall Street.

Ernesta Forster was born in 1929, the daughter of Elvira, from St. Lucia, in the West Indies, and Clarence, who was born in Barbados. As a child, she was a musical prodigy who played piano on the stage of Carnegie Hall at age 13 and graduated from New York City's High School of Music and Art. She went on to Brooklyn College and married Albin Bowman, a Brooklyn real estate developer who encouraged her to enter the insurance business as a way of handling his properties. Bowman enrolled in Pohs Institute of Insurance, passed the state broker's test, and went on to insure her husband's properties. The Bowmans' activities were centered in the Bedford-Stuyvesant neighborhood in Brooklyn, at the time, a largely African-American working-class area with a solid base of homeowners who may not have had much money but who were solid, reliable customers.

Bowman's husband died in 1953, but Ernesta Bowman continued to work in both insurance and real estate. She went on to marry John Procope, a former advertising executive who later became publisher of the *Amsterdam News,* New York City's major African-American paper.

Bowman prospered throughout the 1950s, insuring homes and small businesses in Bedford-Stuyvesant. Then in the mid-1960s, race riots spread through the nation—and banks and insurance companies reacted by withdrawing their financial support for black neighborhoods. Suddenly insurers were "redlining" certain areas—acting as though they had circled particular areas on a map in red and refusing to insure any home or business within that area.

As a broker, Procope's job was to obtain insurance from companies for her clients. Within two weeks, some 90 of her policies were cancelled by insurance companies who were suddenly unwilling to insure properties in a black neighborhood. Many of these policies were for fire insurance, and without them, banks had the legal right to foreclose on these black-owned homes and businesses.

Fearing for the future of both her community and her own business, Procope approached New York governor Nelson Rockefeller, whom she encountered at the swearing-in ceremony of a friend. She explained to the governor the dire situation in New York City's black neighborhoods, and Rockefeller responded by holding hearings on the issue. Procope was joined at the hearings by union members as well as representatives of New York City's police, sanitation, and fire departments. As a result, the New York State legislature passed the New York State FAIR plan in 1968, guaranteeing that homeowner insurance will be available in low-income neighborhoods. Subsequently, 26 other states passed similar legislation.

Procope, however, was shaken by the riots and the economic devastation that followed. She decided to move into a more lucrative area, becoming a commercial broker who would serve corporate clients as well as government agencies, churches, small businesses, and nonprofit groups.

Procope continued to receive acclaim for her groundbreaking entrepreneurship. In 1972 she was named "Woman of the Year" by First Lady Pat Nixon, and a few years later she was appointed Special Ambassador to Gambia, a West African nation, by President Gerald Ford.

In 1979, Procope moved her business from Brooklyn onto Wall Street, where it became the first black-owned business in the neighborhood. The change in location enabled Procope to attract more upscale clients, who would not have been comfortable visiting her in Bedford-Stuyvesant. In 1982, Procope's husband came to join her firm. He eventually served as chairman of the board, even as Procope holds the titles of president and chief executive officer (CEO).

Also in 1982, Procope faced a city scandal when her firm was accused of mishandling the insurance for the city's Human Resources Administration. Before John Procope joined the firm, he had written editorials criticizing New York City mayor Ed Koch, who was widely perceived as unsupportive of African Americans and Latinos, so the Procopes believed that the accusation was manufactured for political reasons. Procope fought the charges, and the city later admitted in a *New York Times* article that it had made a mistake.

Despite these setbacks, Procope's company has counted many corporate giants among its

Ernesta Procope founded the largest minority-owned brokerage firm in the United States and is known as the "First Lady of Wall Street." *(Courtesy of E. G. Bowman Company, Inc.)*

clients, including 80 of the "Fortune 500" companies (corporations named as the top 500 in the United States by *Fortune* magazine), including American Express, Avon Products, General Motors, IBM, Philip Morris, Pepsico Inc., and Tiffany & Co., as well as numerous small businesses, churches, colleges, and social agencies. She herself has served on the board of directors of Avon, Columbia Gas, and the Chubb Group, another insurance company, as well as on the boards of Cornell University and the Bronx Zoo.

Procope faced another scandal resulting from her role as chair of the Board of Trustees at Adel-

phi University, where she was the first woman and the first African American to hold such a position. In February 1997, she and other board members were accused of mishandling funds and committing improprieties, which in Procope's case centered on the idea that she had urged the school to buy insurance from Chubb, on whose board she served, even though that company was not the lowest bidder. Procope was one of 18 trustees ousted from the 19-member board, and many observers considered it a political move. Conservative columnist Hilton Kramer, one of the dismissed trustees, claimed that the conservatism of the trustees and the president they had chosen was the real issue, not any wrongdoing on the part of the board. In any case, Procope's stature in the financial community was so great that the scandal left her virtually untouched.

Procope's other achievements include insuring the Fulbright Scholars for the U.S. Information Agency (in the Fulbright program, U.S. scholars receive grants to teach abroad for a year) and insuring the U.S. portion of the Alaska Pipeline. She has also founded Procope Capital Management, a successful money management firm. She and John Procope have rehabilitated more than 500 brownstone buildings in low-income communities in Brooklyn, and have developed the Brinkerhoff Homes, a low-income community in Jamaica, Queens, in New York City.

Procope has received numerous honors for her achievements: She was selected in 2002 by *Crain's* as one of New York's 100 most influential women in business; received the Trumpet Award (to honor African-American achievement in medicine, education, literature, politics, sports, business, and entertainment) from the Turner Broadcasting System; and deemed one of the 100 leading women in the insurance industry in 2000 by the journal *Business Insurance*.

Despite her successes, however, Procope has expressed disappointment and frustration over how long it is taking for African Americans to become accepted into the mainstream of U.S.

society, particularly within the business world. She has said that when she first founded her company, she expected African-American progress to proceed very quickly, yet she has encountered far more barriers to full acceptance and equality than she expected. Nevertheless, she continues to be optimistic about the future of her company, which she expects to continue long after she is gone.

Further Reading

Bowers, Barbara. "First Lady of Wall Street." *Best's Review* 103, no. 3 (July 2002): 39.

Branch, Shelly. "A Premium Asset on Wall Street." *Black Enterprise,* December 1993, p. 100.

"Ernesta G. Procope." The Network Journal Online. URL: http://www/tnj.com/articless/tnjevent/25_2001/procope.htm. Downloaded November 24, 2002.

Prufer, Diana. "A Premium Life." *Savvy* 9, no. 10 (October 1988): 40.

Proctor, Barbara Gardner
(Barbara Gardner)
(1933–) *advertising entrepreneur*

Barbara Gardner Proctor literally rose from rags to riches, coming from a small, southern, rural community to head her own advertising agency. Her clients have included Jewel Food Stores; Sears, Roebuck & Company; Alberto Culver; E.J. Gallo Winery; Kraft Foods; and G. Heileman Brewing Company.

Barbara Gardner was born in Black Mountain, a rural community outside of Asheville, North Carolina, on November 30, 1933, the daughter of William Gardner and Bernice Baxter. The couple was unmarried, and Gardner was basically raised by her grandmother, Coralee Baxter, while her mother went to secretarial school. She won a scholarship to attend Talladega College in Alabama, working part-time and receiving some assistance from her mother to cover her expenses. She graduated in 1954, with a degree in English

literature and education as well as a degree in sociology and psychology.

Initially, Gardner planned to return to North Carolina to become a teacher. After a summer job at the Circle Pine Center camp in Kalamazoo, Michigan, she stopped in Chicago on her way home and spent all her transportation money on clothes. She was forced to remain in the city, where she took a job as a social worker with the Chicago Union League.

Gardner found social work depressing and went on to work as office manager for the Oscar C. Brown Real Estate Company. The six-year stint at office work gave her time to become a freelance writer, creating profiles of such jazz greats as Nancy Wilson, Cannonball Adderley, and Ray Charles, and becoming a freelancer for the prestigious *Downbeat*, a jazz magazine. She also wrote a column for a South Side newspaper (the South Side was an African-American neighborhood in Chicago), contributed to seven books on jazz, and wrote the scripts for several television specials. She went on to write blurbs on album covers for the Veejay Record Company, which eventually made her director of its International Division. Her job took her to Europe several times a year to seek new acts to sign, and she was the person responsible for bringing the Beatles to America in 1964, part of a deal that involved sending the Four Seasons to Europe.

For two years, Gardner was married to Carl Proctor, the road manager for jazz singer Sarah Vaughn. When she divorced Proctor, she also left her job at Veejay Records and went into what she described as a "battle with destiny" in which she looked for a new career. Eighteen months later, she decided to work in advertising.

Gardner, who had never stopped using her maiden name, was turned down by the Leo Burnett Agency as "overqualified" but was able to get work in 1964 at the Post-Keyes-Gardner agency, where she started at the bottom, writing labels for various household products and learning what was for her a new business. Because one of the partners in her new company shared a last name with her, she was forced to use Proctor, her married name, to distinguish herself, and from then on she was known as Barbara Gardner Proctor.

Proctor won 21 awards in three years at Post-Keyes-Gardner, enjoying a growing recognition within the industry. In 1969, she worked for a time at Gene Taylor Associates as a copy supervisor, then went on to a similar position at North (later Grey-North) Advertising. Proctor was not happy at Grey-North, however, for she felt that she was limited there to dealing with the traditional women's accounts in beauty and household products. She had a lifelong objection to being stereotyped or restricted in any way, as either an African American or a woman, and she began to think of how she could create her own type of business. Her dissatisfaction was fueled by her criticisms of the company's advertising methods, which she felt focused on pleasing the client rather than on selling a product.

In 1970, therefore, Proctor began her own agency, the first African-American woman in Chicago to do so. At the time, a number of other black-owned agencies were getting started, including the one founded by THOMAS J. BURRELL, also in Chicago. The combination of the Black Nationalist movement's focus on black pride and the Civil Rights movement's pressure for companies to feature new, positive images of black people in their ads made the time seem right for black-directed advertising campaigns. Moreover, companies were starting to become aware of the black consumer and looking for ways to reach this specific segment of the market, as they realized that "the public" was not a homogenous bunch of consumers but rather a mosaic of many different types of markets—black, women's, youth, and so on.

Proctor named her company Proctor and Gardner Advertising, Inc., hoping that the name would fool customers into believing that a man was involved as the second partner; in 1970, the idea of a woman-owned business—particularly a black-woman-owned business—still seemed

threatening to many people. As many small businesspeople do, Proctor had a hard time finding financing for her new venture, but she convinced the Small Business Administration to give her an $80,000 loan, which enabled her to open a small four-person agency above a restaurant in February 1971.

By 1972, the company had moved to a fancier location in downtown Chicago. Proctor, working seven days a week and doing almost everything herself—writing and selling all the copy and chairing all the client meetings—was determined to make her venture a success. She was mainly given accounts that required her to sell generic products to African-American customers, a difficult task, since black consumers preferred to buy brand-name products and considered generic items inferior. Proctor was successful, however, winning $4.5 million in billings for her company in 1973, a figure that had risen to $12.2 million in 1981.

In 1984, Proctor and Gardner suffered a setback when its largest client, hair-care products company Alberto-Culver, left the agency, taking 20 percent of the agency's billings as it went. Proctor responded by reorganizing her company, firing many longtime employees, and seeking new people.

Proctor is known for her strong sense of integrity, which made hers the only black-owned advertising agency not to handle cigarette ads. She has refused to promote negative images of African Americans and has asserted her wish not to be limited by her gender or her color. When President Reagan praised her in 1984 as a symbol of the U.S. "spirit of enterprise," Proctor responded by stressing that she had received government support to start her company in the form of a loan from the Small Business Administration, pointing out that the very opportunities that had made her success possible were currently at risk. Yet she has also said that many African Americans cannot run good businesses and has argued that many of the enterprises funded by the Small

Business Administration should never have been in business in the first place.

Proctor has received a number of honors and awards, including the citation by President Ronald Reagan in his 1984 State of the Union address and Reagan's inclusion of her in the 1986 special report "Risk to Riches: Women and Entrepreneurship in America." The Smithsonian Institution has featured her in its "Black Women Achievement against the Odds" Hall of Fame. She has received the 1980 Headliner Award from the Association for Women in Communications, and she is a member of the Leadership Academy of the Chicago Young Women's Christian Association (YWCA).

Proctor is also a lifelong member of the civil rights group the National Association for the Advancement of Colored People (NAACP). In 1976 she was elected the first African-American woman to head the Cosmopolitan Chamber of Commerce, the nation's largest interracial trade group. She was president of the National League of Black Women from 1978 to 1982; and in 1983–84 served as cochair of the Gannon-Proctor Commission, appointed by the governor of Illinois to study the Illinois economy. Her agency's techniques have been featured in university textbooks on advertising, and Proctor herself has received national recognition for her role as a black woman entrepreneur, including a segment on the news program 60 *Minutes.*

Further Reading

Bird, Caroline. *Enterprising Women.* New York: W. W. Norton & Co., 1976.

Birmingham, Stephen. *Certain People: America's Black Elite.* Boston: Little, Brown & Co., 1977, pp. 72–78.

CBS News. *Getting to Know Barbara.* Interview on 60 *Minutes.* Carousel Films, 1984.

Ingham, John, and Lynne B. Feldman. *African American Business Leaders: A Biographical Dictionary.* Westport, Conn.: Greenwood Press, 1994, pp. 564–571.

Rich-McCoy, Lois. *Millionairess: Self-Made Women of America.* New York: HarperCollins, 1978.

R

Rhodes, Eugene Washington See PERRY, CHRISTOPHER JAMES and EUGENE WASHINGTON RHODES.

Rhone, Sylvia M.
(1952–   ) *music industry executive*

Sylvia M. Rhone has a number of "firsts" and "onlys" to her name. Currently the chair and chief executive officer (CEO) of Elektra Entertainment Group (EEG), she is both the only African American and the first woman to rise so high in the recording industry. Her 21-year career in the music industry is full of similar landmark breakthroughs in the areas of gender and race. Among the artists Rhone has put on the Elektra label are singer Tracy Chapman; rapper Busta Rhymes; rhythm and blues singer Gerald Albright; and Natalie Merchant, the former lead singer for 10,000 Maniacs (who were also signed to Elektra).

Sylvia M. Rhone was born on March 11, 1952, in Philadelphia, Pennsylvania, the daughter of Marie Christmas Rhone, a schoolteacher, and James Rhone, a prominent attorney and political adviser to New York governor Nelson Rockefeller. The Rhones' friends included several famous musicians, so Rhone grew up surrounded by people like composer Duke Ellington, singer Nancy

Wilson, and jazz greats Cab Calloway and Lionel Hampton. Rhone attended parochial school and then chose to study at Wharton Business School at the University of Pennsylvania, where she graduated in 1974 with an undergraduate degree in economics and marketing. She started her working life in a traditional business setting—the management training program at Bankers Trust in New York—but lasted there for less than a year because of her unwillingness to accommodate herself to the prevailing corporate style. Her decision to wear pants to work, for example—a somewhat unconventional choice for a woman in the mid-1970s—alienated her employers. Rhone was so frustrated at what she considered their narrow-mindedness that she took a significant pay cut to work as a secretary with Buddha Records, an independent label.

Rhone took to the music business with enthusiasm, showing a particular talent for promotion. She became Buddha's promotion coordinator and then rose to taking charge of the label's national promotions. In 1976, she went to ABC Records, where she worked as a regional promotion manager until 1978. In 1979, she took the same job at Ariola Records. The following year, she moved to Elektra, where for three years she served as northeast regional promotion manager in change of special markets and as director of marketing until 1985.

It was in 1986 that Rhone's career really took off. Her mentor, Doug Morris, chose her to head the black music division of Atlantic Records (who hold Elektra as a separate division). Atlantic's black music division had once been a prosperous operation but had since fallen on hard times, and Rhone gratefully seized the challenge of returning the label to its former greatness. Indeed, under her leadership, Atlantic's black music department went on to hold the largest U.S. market share for a division of its kind, as well as becoming a profitable operation. Rhone's work was rewarded with her promotion to senior vice president in 1988.

Rhone started a new division, Atlantic Street, that focused on rap groups, and went on to develop a stable of rap stars, including En Vogue, MC Lyte, and D.O.C. The experience enabled her to go to Morris in 1990 and ask for her own label, preferably one that did not focus exclusively on African-American acts. Morris made her the first African-American woman to head a major record company, naming her CEO and president of Atlantic's EastWest Records America division.

In 1991, EastWest was merged with Atco Records, and Rhone became chair and CEO of first Atco/EastWest and then EastWest Records/ America. With her staff of more than 40 people, she was able to carry over the group En Vogue from Atlantic, shepherding them to their ultimate success. She created similar triumphs for Gerald Levert, Pantera, and DasEFX, as well as furthering the career of the rock band AC/DC. Four years later, Rhone's label was bringing in $90 million a year.

In August 1994, Rhone racked up another first—the first African-American woman to become head of a major record label—when she was named chair of Elektra/EastWest. In 1996, she took charge of the Elektra Entertainment Group, the result of a new merger bringing East/West, Elektra, Asylum, and Sire under the umbrella of the conglomerate Time Warner (now AOL Time Warner).

When Rhone had taken charge of Elektra in 1994, the company's sales were less than $200 million. Her goal was to raise that number to $300 million by 1997. She faced some difficulties, including the loss of singer Anita Baker to the sister label Atlantic. But she had a number of successes that seemed to result directly from the strong personal interest she took in her artists' projects, including Tracy Chapman's comeback album *New Beginnings* (1995), which went on to sell more than 3 million copies, and Natalie Merchant's solo debut, *Tigerlily* (1995), which sold equally well. Rhone was also able to hold on to Metallica, a heavy metal band responsible for approximately one-fifth of Elektra's revenues, and she helped enable the

Elektra chair and CEO Sylvia Rhone has made the careers of many recording artists, including Tracy Chapman, Busta Rhymes, Gerald Albright, and Natalie Merchant. *(Courtesy of Elektra)*

Rembrandts' success. In addition, she launched several successful new artists, including Better Than Ezra, Adina Howard, Ol' Dirty Bastard, and Kut Klose.

In 1995, Time Warner fired her mentor, Doug Morris, who went on to head MCA Records. Rhone was offered a job there but chose to stay at Elektra, reaching her $300 million target in 1996—the only head of a Time Warner label to reach her financial objective.

By the end of the 1990s, Rhone was widely recognized as a powerful figure in the music industry, cited in 1997 by *Entertainment Weekly* as the most powerful female executive in the music business. In 1998, *Essence* named Rhone one of the year's image makers, while *Entertainment Weekly* praised her for the triple platinum sales of Third Eye Blind.

In 1999, Rhone's contract with Elektra was up, and rumors flew that she might join Morris, who was now at Universal/Polygram. But Rhone has stayed at Elektra, where gospel artist Yolanda Adams is one of her latest discoveries.

In addition to her business activities, Rhone participates in community affairs. In 1996, she organized a fund-raising benefit for the Burned Churches Fund, a project sponsored by the National Council of Churches to rebuild churches destroyed in that year's flurry of church-related fires. She is a board member with a number of cultural groups that support African-American and other artists, including Jazz at Lincoln Center, the R&B Foundation, Alvin Ailey American Dance Theater, and the Studio Museum of Harlem, as well as serving on the boards of the Recording Industry Association of American (RIAA) and the Rock and Roll Hall of Fame. In 2001, *Ms.* magazine named her one of their women of the year. In 2002, *Crain's* business magazine named her one of New York's 100 most influential women in business, and the National Association of Black Female Executives in Music and Entertainment has called her a "Shero" for her achievements in music.

Further Reading

Gale Group. "Sylvia Rhone." Biography Resource Center. Available online. URL: http://www.africanpubs.com/Apps/bios/1200RhoneSylvia.asp?pic=none. Downloaded on November 23, 2002.

Robey, Don
(1903–1975) *recording industry entrepreneur, restaurant owner*

A decade before BERRY GORDY, JR., was developing Motown Records, Don Robey was marketing rhythm and blues (R&B), soul, and gospel to mainstream audiences, pioneering the crossover of what had previously been called "race music" to white listeners. The musicians whom Robey helped to reach a wider audience include Johnny Ace, Bobby "Blue" Bland, Big Mama Thornton, Clarence "Gatemouth" Brown, the Dixie Hummingbirds, O. V. Wright, Carl Carlton, the Five Blind Boys of Mississippi, Inez Andrews, Memphis Slim, Little Junior Parker, and Joe Hinton.

Robey was born on November 1, 1903, in Houston, Texas. He dropped out of high school to become a professional gambler, then married and had a son. In response to his new family, he started a taxicab business, then went on to fulfill his passion for music by promoting ballroom dances. At the end of the decade, he went to Los Angeles, where he opened the Harlem Grill night club and ran it for three years. He returned to Houston, where in 1945 he opened the Bronze Peacock Dinner Club, a venue where he chose some of the top jazz bands and orchestras of the day.

The club was a huge success, and Robey used some of the profits to open a record store. In 1947 he went on to become a talent manager. His first client was the great Clarence "Gatemouth" Brown, a 23-year-old singer and guitarist whose hard-edged sound made him popular with African-American audiences but was then considered too "rough" for white listeners used to the smoother sounds of pop singers.

Like many African-American artists, Brown was not well treated by the white-owned recording industry, and Robey was so frustrated with Brown's label that he decided to start his own company. Robey named Peacock Records after his club, choosing Brown as his first artist. In those days, single-song records were common (with one song on each side), and in late 1949, Brown had two hits on one record: "Mary Is Fine," No. 8 on the R&B charts on one side, and "My Time Is Expensive," which was No. 9, on the other. Perhaps ironically, Brown eventually left Robey's label, charging that Robey was taking advantage of him.

Robey went on to have more hits, including Marie Adams's No. 3 R&B song "I'm Gonna Play the Honky Tonks," Floyd Dixon's No. 8 R&B "Sad Journey Blues," and Willie Mae "Big Mama" Thornton's No. 1 R&B hit, "Hound Dog." Thornton's song was later recorded by Elvis Presley and helped catapult Presley into superstar status and cemented the relationship between white pop success and African-American musical roots. Robey also represented Memphis Slim, a jazz and blues player.

In 1952, David J. Mattis and Bill Fitzgerald formed Duke Records in Memphis. In August of that year, Duke and Peacock joined in a partnership under Robey's leadership, under the name Duke-Peacock. Robey took over full control of the label in 1953 in a chapter of his life that caused some to accuse him of shady dealings. Meanwhile, Robey took full advantage of Duke's roster of artists, which included legendary blues singer Johnny Ace, who had three top R&B hits: "My Song," which stayed at the top of the charts for nine weeks in the fall of 1952; "The Clock," which held the top spot for five weeks in the summer of 1953; and "Pledging My Love," which was No. 1 for 10 weeks in 1953. Ace released a number of other singles that all made the top 10 R&B list: "Never Let Me Go" (No. 9), "Anymore" (No. 7), "Please Forgive Me" (No. 6), "Cross My Heart" (No. 3),

and "Saving My Love for You" (No. 2). Ace's legend—and his record sales—grew when the singer was fatally shot during a game of Russian Roulette played backstage at Houston's City auditorium and Ace died the next day, December 25, 1954. (Russian Roulette is a game in which a single bullet is placed into one of the six chambers of a revolver; the player spins the chamber and then shoots himself, not knowing whether the shot will be fatal.)

Roscoe Gordon was another Duke-Peacock star, as was Little Junior Parker, a singer and harmonica player whose first hit with Robey was "Next Time You See Me," which was No. 7 on the R&B charts in 1957. Gordon produced several other top-10 hits, including "Driving Wheel," "In the Dark," and "Annie Get Your Yo-Yo."

The biggest star at Duke-Peacock, however, was Bobby "Blue" Bland, who had been with Duke before the merger. In 1957, Bland hit the charts with "Farther Up the Road," which was a No. 1 R&B hit that fall. Bland sang several more top 10 R&B hits for Robey, including "Little Boy Blue," "I'll Take Care of You," "Lead Me On," "Cry, Cry, Cry," and "I Pity the Fool."

Robey relied heavily on his colleagues. His partner, Evelyn Johnson, had done the original research that convinced Robey to start a record label and had helped to expand the night club into booking, management, and song publishing. Joe Scott was a producer and arranger who produced Bobby Bland's "Farther Up the Road" and many other Robey hits. Other Robey producer/arrangers included Johny Otis and Bill Harvey, while Dave Clark and Irving Marcus were his promotion and sales representatives.

Robey also began issuing gospel records on Peacock, with a roster of singers that many critics believe were the true stars of his business. His acts included the Dixie Hummingbirds, the Sensational Nightingales, the Mighty Clouds of Joy, and the Five Blind Boys of Mississippi. The Hummingbirds, whose career stretched into the 1990s, had an R&B hit with their song "Loves Me Like a Rock," later singing backup for Paul Simon's gold-record version of the same song.

In 1957, Robey started his Back Beat label, which became a soul music label in the 1960s, producing Joe Hinton, O. V. Wright, and Carl Carlton. The label also included the Texas rock-country group Roy Head and the Traits, and the Rob Roys, one of whose members was composer-producer Charles Fox, the author of "Happy Days." Carlton—who later went on to write the huge hits "She's a Bad Mama Jama" and "Everlasting Love"—got his first big break through Robey.

Robey was often criticized by artists and colleagues for ruling his company with an iron fist and for sometimes working underhandedly, accused of stealing his artists' royalty money and taking a share of publishing rights to songs he never wrote. However, his behavior was not particularly unusual for the often rough and shady music industry of the time.

Eventually, Robey sold Duke-Peacock to ABC-Dunhill Records. Although the sale took place on May 23, 1973, Robey remained as a consultant with ABC, which went on to reissue the Duke-Peacock catalogue. In the 1980s, the legacy would pass to MCA, which continues to release various Robey hits. Certainly the musical legacy that Robey made possible—both the styles that shaped a generation of music and the ability of African-American-run record companies to reach broad audiences—has continued through Gordy's work at Motown and SYLVIA RHONE's tenure at Elektra. Robey himself died on June 16, 1975, in Houston.

Further Reading

Edwards. David. "Don Robey's Labels." Both Sides Now Publications website. Available online. URL: http://www.bsnpubs.com/robey.html. Last updated September 4, 1997.

Gart, Galen, and Roy C. Ames. *Duke-Peacock Records: An Illustrated History with Discography*. Milford, N.H.: Big Nickel Publishing, 1990.

Govenar, Alan, and Benny Joseph. *Early Years of Rhythm and Blues*. Houston, Tex.: Rice University Press, 1991.

Houston Blues Society. "Don Robey." Houston Blues Society website. Available online. URL: http://www.houstonbluessociety.org/donrobey.html. Downloaded on November 24, 2002.

Morthland, John. "Record Label of the Century." *Texas Monthly* 27, no. 12, p. 182.

Rogers, John W., Jr.
(1958–) *founder, capital management company*

John W. Rogers, Jr., started investing in the stock market at age 12, and he has built his passion for investment into a multimillion-dollar investment company, Ariel Capital Management. (An investment company finds profitable places to invest an individual's or a group's money so that the funds will grow over the years.) During the recession of 2001–02, when other investment companies' stock portfolios were falling, Ariel's investments continued to earn sizable profits, winning widespread acclaim for Rogers and his company within the industry.

Rogers was born on March 31, 1958, in Chicago, Illinois, the son of John W. Rogers, Sr., a judge, and Jewel S. Lafontant, an attorney and government official whose business connections would prove extremely valuable to her son's later business ventures. John, Sr., gave his son shares of stock from the time he was 12, and John, Jr., soon became an eager investor. At the age of 16, he sold refreshments at baseball games in Comiskey Park—and then invested his earnings in stock. He graduated from the prestigious University of Chicago Laboratory School in 1976 and went on to major in economics at Princeton University, where he graduated in 1980. He spent two years as a stockbroker at William Blair & Company, a Chicago investment banking firm, and then, at the age of 24, he went out on his own, forming Ariel Capital Management.

Rogers received significant help from his mother, an early investor in the firm and a trustee of Howard University who helped him obtain his first major account, $100,000 of the school's endowment fund. (An endowment fund is the money that a nonprofit organization invests in stock, hoping that money made from the investment will support the group's work.) Within six months, Rogers and his one employee had raised another $190,000 in investment capital, however, and by 1986 the firm's assets had grown to $45 million. Clients included Revlon and Mobil, two corporations on whose board of directors his mother served. He also managed the city employees' retirement funds for Chicago, Detroit, Los Angeles, and the District of Columbia.

Known for his extremely conservative and targeted approach to investment, Rogers made a specialty of doing huge amounts of research and choosing companies carefully. When he was starting out, he tended to focus on smaller, lesser-known companies, often in unpopular industries, as well as businesses that were having temporary setbacks or had just been spun off from other companies. He avoided industries with many ups and downs, such as heavy machinery, steel, and automobiles, and also shunned commodities, such as gas, oil, and precious metals, which are also likely to rise and fall. Unlike many of his colleagues in the 1990s, he avoided start-up companies (new companies), since he could not measure their track record.

Rogers was also known for his socially conscious attitude toward investment, which led him to avoid cigarette companies, weapons makers, environmentally harmful companies, nuclear power plants, and defense companies. During the period when apartheid (racial separation) was the law in South Africa, Rogers refused to invest in any company that did business with that country.

As Rogers's company grew bigger, he had to be careful in choosing smaller companies to invest in, since buying up a significant portion of their stock would push their price up artificially high. In 1988, Rogers began working with the socially conscious Calvert Group to create two mutual funds. (A mutual fund is a group of stocks in which an individual can invest; that way, people who cannot afford to buy stocks in several different companies can still spread their smaller investments out over several companies at once.) In 1994, however, he severed his ties with Calvert, paying $4 million, or about 1 percent of the funds' assets, to break off the relationship.

Breaking with Calvert led to hard times for Ariel, as many customers pulled out of the company without the support of the larger firm. As a result, Ariel lost $100 million in assets. Around the same time, it became popular in the investment world to invest with start-up companies and high-tech stocks that promised huge, quick fortunes. Because Ariel's strategy remained more cautious and disciplined, the company lost business, going from $2.3 billion to $1.1 billion in assets over a short time.

When the recession of 2001 hit, however, Ariel's strategy paid off, and Rogers's approach to investment was praised by industry analysts. In 2002, Lipper, a mutual fund research firm, gave the Ariel Fund its highest rating, as did Morningstar, another mutual fund research firm. Rogers's company currently manages the retirement plans for the National Basketball Association (NBA) Players Association, Coca-Cola, Mitsubishi, and Johnson Publishing Co. Rogers plans to continue expanding his company's activities to become a "full-service" investment firm, handling all kinds of retirement and college-fund accounts.

Further Reading

Ebony. "Mothers and Sons." *Ebony*, May 1995, p. 42.
"John Rogers' Ariel Capital Management Recognized as Top Fund Management Firm." *Jet*, April 8, 2002: 34.
"John W. Rogers Jr. appointed to boards of First Chicago and First National Bank of Chicago." *Jet*, March 9, 1998, p. 32.

McCoy, Frank. "A $100 Million Manager for $1,000." *Black Enterprise*, November 1995, p. 64.

McCoy, Frank, and Mark Lowery. "Mature and Independent." *Black Enterprise*, October 1992, p. 22.

Scott, Matthew S. "The Fruits of Discipline." *Black Enterprise*, June 2002, p. 238.

Ruggles, David

(1810–1849) *bookstore owner, publisher, activist*

David Ruggles was the first publisher of an African-American magazine and the owner of the first black bookstore in New York. He was an active member of the abolitionist movement, which sought to end slavery in America. A public school in Brooklyn, New York, has been named in his honor.

Ruggles was born of free parents in Norwich, Connecticut, on March 15, 1810. History has recorded little about his early life, but it is known that Ruggles left home at the age of 17 to come to New York, where he started a grocery store. He became involved in the temperance movement—a movement to oppose drinking liquor—and refused to carry liquor in his store. He also became an abolitionist and was one of five African-American traveling sales agents for *The Emancipator*, the weekly newspaper published by the American Antislavery Society under the leadership of Boston abolitionist William Lloyd Garrison. Ruggles published his own abolitionist articles and pamphlets, and in 1835, he was one of 400 delegates at the convention to organize a New York branch of the society.

Meanwhile, in 1834, Ruggles had opened a bookshop and library at 67 Lispenard Street in lower Manhattan, becoming the first African-American bookseller. From 1835–39, he served as secretary and general agent for the New York Committee of Vigilance, an interracial organization founded to help runaway slaves. Ruggles helped more than 1,000 people escape, including Frederick Douglass, whom he sheltered for nearly two weeks and helped to establish himself in New Bedford, Massachusetts.

Ruggles's activism occasionally involved civil disobedience (the peaceful breaking of laws considered unjust), as in 1841, when he refused to sit in the "colored" section of a steamship headed to Nantucket. In the same year, he was dragged off the "white" car at a railway station, to which he responded by suing the company.

Although New York–born African Americans were not enslaved after 1827, the state cooperated with slave owners in a variety of ways. A slave owner might bring his or her human property into the city, for example, although state law required any slave who remained in the state for nine months to be freed. So Ruggles went door to door in rich neighborhoods, seeking those who had passed the nine-month mark. The state also jailed and tried slaves who had run away from their owners in other states, so Ruggles visited runaways in jail and attended their trials, seeking to show public support for them. Slaves were occasionally smuggled into the city, and Ruggles used to board ships to search for slaves. As a consequence of his activism, Ruggles was jailed many times before he turned 30, which undermined his health and caused him to lose most of his eyesight.

In the fall of 1835, a fire destroyed Ruggles's bookstore. Ruggles and others suspected that the fire had been set by white people who supported slavery. Two months later, a man who identified himself as "Mr. Nash" knocked on Ruggles's door early one morning. When Ruggles refused to open the door, the man returned with others, who broke down the door of Ruggles's house. By then, however, Ruggles had left. He believed that the men had intended to kidnap him and sell him into slavery, a common practice at the time, even among black people in the free states of the North.

In 1837, Ruggles founded *Mirror of Liberty*, an abolitionist newspaper. In 1838, he opened a reading room for black people at 36 Lispenard, "because Negroes were not given free privileges in the libraries of New York." From 1845 to 1847,

Ruggles edited another New York abolitionist newspaper, *Genius of Freedom.* In 1846, he opened a center where he treated people with hydropathy, a water-based treatment popular at the time. He died in Florence, Massachusetts, on December 26, 1849, at the age of 39.

Further Reading

Bennett, Lerone, Jr. *The Shaping of Black America.* New York: Penguin, 1993.

Frazier, DuEwa M. "Bed-Stuy Facts: David Ruggles." Bed-Stuy Online. Available online. URL: http://bedstuyonline.com/BedStuyFACTS/davidruggles.htm. Downloaded on November 4, 2002.

Harding, Vincent. *There Is a River: The Black Struggle for Freedom in America.* New York: Harvest Books, 1993.

Ottley, Roi, and William J. Weatherby, eds. *The Negro in New York.* New York: New York Public Library, 1967.

Stewart, James Brewer. *Holy Warriors: The Shaping of American Abolitionism.* New York: Hill & Wang, 1997.

Russell, Herman J.
(Herman Jerome Russell)

(1930–   ) *contractor, real estate and construction manager and developer, politician, philanthropist*

Herman J. Russell has built one of the largest black-owned businesses in the nation, the construction and real estate firm H. J. Russell and Company. Russell's multimillion-dollar business has also been a source of support for the Civil Rights movement and for African-American political candidates such as Maynard Jackson, Atlanta's first black mayor.

Russell was born on December 23, 1930, the son of Roger Russell, a plasterer, and Maggie (Googson) Russell, a maid. When he was eight, he earned money shining shoes and delivering papers in downtown Atlanta, contributing a portion of his earnings to the household income.

When he was 12, his father brought him into his own business, Russell Plastering Company, to teach him the plastering trade. Three years later, Russell was a skilled worker, and soon he became an entrepreneur as well. While still a junior at David T. Howard High School, he bought his first piece of land for $125 and worked with his friends to construct a duplex on it. The rent from the duplex helped finance his college education at Tuskegee Institute in Alabama, from which he graduated in 1956 with a degree in building construction. Meanwhile, he began his own plastering company, H. J. Russell Plastering Company, and then H. J. Russell Company, his own subcontracting firm (a subcontractor contracts with a larger construction company to do specialized work).

One of Russell's key experiences came early in his career, when he approached Home Federal Savings and Loan for a loan in 1955. Although it was virtually unheard-of for white-owned institutions to lend money to black businesses, president Don Hollowell decided to lend Russell money for one of his projects. Russell received the financial backing he needed—and he also learned not to make assumptions about what kinds of barriers he might face.

In 1962, Russell incorporated as a general contractor (someone who can hire subcontractors). His booming business attracted the attention of the Atlanta Chamber of Commerce, which assumed he was white and invited him to join. Russell accepted the invitation—becoming the group's first black member.

Throughout the 1960s, Russell continued to build residential housing, moving gradually from duplexes to slightly larger buildings and eventually, to complexes whose units numbered in the hundreds. He also met civil rights leader Dr. Martin Luther King, Jr., and became a strong behind-the-scenes supporter of the Civil Rights movement. Because Russell was in a vulnerable position as a black businessman in the segregated South, movement leaders agreed that he should not picket or take a public position on controversial issues. But when King and his colleagues were put in jail, Russell was always available to put up his properties as security to raise bond money for them. However, because white-dominated courts could not believe that a black person owned so much expensive property, Russell would almost always have to go to court to demonstrate his ownership.

The turning point for Russell's company came in 1968, when he was given the contract to do the fireproofing and other work on the Equitable Life Assurance Building, which was going to be the largest building in downtown Atlanta. No African-American-owned firm had ever worked on a project so big, and when Russell finished his work on time and within budget, his reputation was made.

Also in 1968, the Department of Housing and Urban Development began to sponsor the construction of low- and middle-income housing. Russell went on to construct hundreds of units of such housing, most of which he retained and managed through other companies he set up. Many construction companies simply build units, but Russell always wanted to diversify. He built housing, office projects, public buildings, and airports; managed properties; and entered other businesses as well, including airport concessions, television, beverage distribution, grocery and liquor stores, and nursing homes.

Meanwhile, Russell continued to stay active in politics. In 1974, he became the finance director for Maynard Jackson, who was elected Atlanta's first black mayor. Russell also supported Jackson's reelection in 1978. In 1980, Russell continued to break new ground by serving as the Atlanta Chamber of Commerce's first black president.

Russell went on to build or participate in the construction of a number of projects, including Hartfield International Airport, the Georgia Power Company headquarters, the Coca-Cola Company world headquarters, and the Georgia Dome Stadium, all in Atlanta. He benefited from a number of government programs, including the HUD subsidies to low- and middle-income housing and the vigorous affirmative action programs promoted by Jackson, which required white construction firms and contractors to include at least some black subcontractors or partners in their endeavors if they were to win city contracts. When Russell participated in such joint ventures, he always made sure that his company had a genuine role and was not simply a front or a token.

In 1996, at the age of 66, Russell decided to retire, which he has said means working nine hours a day instead of 16. His son, H. Jerome Russell, is president of his company, although he is still chairman of the board. His other children, Michael and Donata, are involved in various aspects of the family business as well, and Russell has said that the company will remain in the family.

Meanwhile, Russell continues to be an active philanthropist. In 1999, he donated $1 million to each of three historically black institutions—Tuskegee University, Clark Atlanta University, Morehouse College—and to Georgia State University, so that these schools could educate future black entrepreneurs. Russell has supported a number of other institutions, including the hospital where he was born in a low-income Atlanta neighborhood. Russell continues to maintain that the reason to be in business is to "give something back"—to provide jobs, services, housing, and resources for the African-American community.

Further Reading

Dingle, Derek T. *Black Enterprise, Titans of the B.E. 100s.* New York, John Wiley & Sons, Inc., 1999, pp. 155–172.

Gite, Lloyd. "Marathon Men Revisited." *Black Enterprise,* June 2002, p. 92.

H. J. Russell Company. "About Us." H. J. Russell Company website. Available online. URL: http://www.hjrussell.com/about.htm. Downloaded on February 4, 2003.

S

Scott, Cornelius Adolphus (1908–2000) and William Alexander Scott II (1902–1934)
publishers

William Alexander Scott II founded one of the most important black newspapers in the United States, the *Atlanta World,* one of the only black-owned papers to publish daily. He also founded a chain of black newspapers in several cities and developed a black newspaper syndicate with other black papers throughout the South. His brother, Cornelius Adolphus Scott, went on to run the publishing empire that his brother founded after William Scott was murdered. The *Atlanta World* is still in existence today, run by Cornelius Scott's granddaughter, Alexis Scott.

William Alexander Scott was born on September 29, 1902, in Edwards, Mississippi. His father was William A. Scott, Sr., a preacher and the owner of the Progress Printing House, a religious print company; his mother, Emeline Southall, worked as a printer in her husband's business. William Scott II worked in his father's print shop, too, doing odd jobs, until he went on to Jackson College, a junior college for black people (in those days, education in the South was rigidly segregated, or separated by race), from which he graduated in 1922. In 1923, he married Lucille McAllister, with whom he already had a son and whom he soon divorced; in his short life, he married four times.

Meanwhile, William Scott II enrolled in Morehouse College, a black institution in Atlanta, Georgia, where he was a top athlete, student, debater, and musician. He never graduated from Morehouse, however, leaving in 1925 to work as a railway clerk in Jacksonville, Florida, and then publishing the *Jacksonville Negro Business Directory* in 1927.

In 1928, William Scott II returned to Atlanta with plans of starting a newspaper of his own. Although the city already had a black-owned newspaper, the *Atlanta Independent,* he proceeded with his own enterprise. He managed to get Citizens Trust Bank to let him use some printing equipment they owned, for either a small fee or none, and started publishing on August 5, 1928.

A talented sales agent and entrepreneur, William Scott II was extremely effective at soliciting advertisements first from black-owned businesses, then from white-owned companies. He was able to gain the advertising business because he hired a number of sales agents and launched a door-to-door campaign to sell subscriptions to his paper—a tactic that black newspapers had not used before. With a guaranteed circulation for the paper, advertisements were easier to sell, and the paper began to prosper. He was able to treat his paper as a business enterprise, whereas the owner of his rival paper considered his own publication as primarily a political effort.

Scott's paper began as a weekly, but he started publishing twice a week in 1930 and three times a week in 1931, when he also began three other papers: the *Chattanooga Tribune*, the *Birmingham World*, and the *Memphis World*. Although the Memphis paper went out of business, the others survived for 40 years, thereby creating the first black newspaper chain.

In 1932, the Atlanta paper became a daily. This enabled the *World* to publish a Sunday newspaper and a rotogravure section—a popular newspaper feature of the time that included lots of photographs. Because white-owned papers tended to ignore African Americans, one of the few places where African Americans could see images of themselves was in the *World*'s rotogravure. William Scott II published comic strips as well.

He also created the Scott Newspaper Syndicate, an arrangement with small black weeklies throughout the nation who used stories from his papers and provided him with local news. His Atlanta printing plant also printed many of these newspapers.

Scott was a colorful and flamboyant figure, and he made many enemies. One January night he was shot in the back and died eight days later, on February 7, 1934. Although nothing was ever proven, a prime suspect was the brother of his fourth wife.

Although there was quite a battle over Scott's estate, he had asked his younger brother, Cornelius A. Scott, to assume ownership and editorship of the newspaper enterprise, which is eventually what happened. Cornelius Scott was born on February 8, 1908, and grew up in Jackson, Mississippi, and Johnson City, Tennessee. He attended Morris Brown College in Atlanta in 1928, and enrolled in Morehouse from 1929 to 1931. He studied journalism at the University of Kansas from 1931 to 1932, then returned to Atlanta for good to work in his brother's business, which he had been doing throughout his studies.

Cornelius Scott was a conservative, quiet family man, quite unlike his brother. He walked a fine line with the *World*, taking a firm stand on race relations—but focusing on issues outside the city so as not to offend either black or white advertisers. He gave a lot of attention to black-on-black crime, an unpopular topic with many in the black community. He also took a strong stand on the so-called Scottsboro boys, several black youths who were falsely convicted in Alabama for allegedly raping a white woman. His paper came out against poor treatment of black soldiers during World War II, as well as opposing segregated schools.

However, although most black people supported the New Deal social-service programs of President Franklin D. Roosevelt, Cornelius Scott opposed them. He thought that black people needed jobs, not government funds to help them survive times of being unemployed; and he opposed the establishment of a minimum wage, which he feared would lead to black workers being fired from low-wage jobs. Over the years, Scott and his paper became increasingly conservative, and in 1952, he began supporting Republican candidates for president. Perhaps as a result, Atlanta was for a time the only city in which black people tended to vote Republican in national elections, although eventually, Scott's conservatism led to the gradual alienation of Atlanta black readers from the paper.

A major blow to the paper was Scott's refusal to support the civil rights activists who sat in at various businesses to end segregation. Afraid to alienate advertisers, Scott criticized the activists—and lost more readers. Meanwhile, in 1960, the more radical *Atlanta Inquirer* was founded, with the support of HERBERT J. RUSSELL, a strong advocate of the Civil Rights movement.

The *World*'s circulation fell rapidly, and the paper foundered, eventually becoming a weekly. In 1997, Scott retired at the age of 89, leaving the paper in the care of his granddaughter, Alexis Scott. Cornelius Scott died on May 7, 2000, while Alexis made several changes that have begun to boost circulation: changing the paper from a pro-

Republican to a pro-Democrat institution, starting an online edition, connecting to the Internet for research services, and a number of other alterations to modernize the paper and connect it to a more militant black community. The future of the *World* remains to be seen, but the Scotts' legacy—and their family business—lives on.

Further Reading

African-American Press. "Atlanta Daily World." Father Ryan High School homepage. Available online. URL: http://www.fatherryan.org/BlackPress/html/atl.htm. Downloaded on February 4, 2003.

Gale Group. "Cornelius Adolphus Scott." *Contemporary Black Biography.* Vol. 29, edited by Ashyla Henderson. Farmington Hills, Mich.: Gale Research, 2001.

Northington, Hope. "Ten years or $10 Million." *George Trend* 17, no. 6 (February 2002), p. 65.

York, Pat. *Going Strong.* New York: Arcade, 1991.

Simmons, Jake, Jr.
(1901–1981) *oil entrepreneur*

Jake Simmons, Jr., was the founder of an oil brokerage business that drew on his knowledge of the Texas and Oklahoma region, where he grew up. Simmons was also instrumental in brokering deals between U.S. oil companies and the emerging African oil suppliers, including Nigeria and Ghana. In 1978, he was awarded Ghana's Grand Medal for his services to that nation's economy as an agent for Phillips Petroleum, the U.S. oil company.

Simmons was born on January 17, 1901, in Muskogee County, then a part of Indian Territory (later, a part of Oklahoma) under the jurisdiction of the Creek Indians. Simmons's grandfather, Cow Tom, was a slave who had been brought to the region in 1837, but the Creek treated their slaves with unusual dignity, and Tom had risen to become one of the Creek nation's black chiefs. His daughter, Rose Jefferson, married Jake Simmons, Sr., a half-Creek, half-black rancher who had been born in a Confederate refugee camp during the Civil War. Their children grew up on the family ranch in the predominantly black Muskogee region.

Jake, the ninth child, was still a boy when he—and every other member of the Creek nation—received a 160-acre freehold from the U.S. government as part of the dissolution of Indian sovereignty. Simmons was a skilled rider by age 10 and was soon put to work training his father's racehorses. In 1914, he went to Tuskegee Institute in Alabama, where he became a disciple of Booker T. Washington's self-help philosophy. He also secretly married classmate Melba Dorsey, with whom he had a child in 1915. The couple settled in Detroit, where Simmons worked as a machinist for the Packard auto factory, patenting a new type of windshield defroster he had invented. He soon realized, however, that his employers did not take seriously the idea of a black inventor.

Meanwhile, Simmons, Sr., ordered his son to either divorce Melba or be disowned. Simmons left his wife and returned home, where in 1920 he married Muskogee resident Eva Flowers and began to interest himself in the oil boom. He drilled for oil on his own land, bought oil-rich land from black neighbors, and began to broker deals between the African Americans and American Indians who owned land in the region. By ensuring that local landowners got a good price from the oil developers, Simmons also assured himself of a larger commission.

Despite Simmons's growing wealth, he was unable to win election to public office in the increasingly white and anti-black region. Simmons had a strong sense of racial pride and frequently told his children, "You are equal to anyone, but if you think you're not, you're not." He was also fond of saying, "One-tenth of the folks run the world. One-tenth watch them run it, and the other 80 percent don't know what the hell's going on."

When African nations achieved independence after World War II, Simmons expanded his brokering activities into the international arena. The Simmons Royalty Company moved into Liberia in 1952, Ghana in 1965, and Nigeria and Ivory Coast in the 1970s, negotiating multimillion-dollar oil leases for Phillips, Texaco, and other U.S. oil giants. Simmons was a multimillionaire when he died on March 25, 1981, leaving his business in the care of his son, Donald.

Further Reading

Cook, Carol L. "Use of John Johnson's Life Story in Conjunction with Other Black Entrepreneurs as Role Models for Potential Black Businessmen." Yale-New Haven Teachers Institute website. Available online. URL: http://www.yale.edu/ynhti/curriculum/units/1991/3/91.03.04.x.html. Downloaded on September 15, 2002.

Greenberg, Jonathan D. *Staking a Claim: Jake Simmons and the Making of an African-American Oil Dynasty.* New York: Atheneum, 1990.

Haskins, Jim. *Black Stars: African American Entrepreneurs.* New York: John Wiley & Sons, 1998, pp. 97–100.

Simmons, Russell
(Rush Simmons)
(1957–   ) *music and media executive*

Russell Simmons is probably the individual most responsible for the national prominence of rap and hip-hop as a mainstream phenomenon in music, video, and fashion. Through his rap label Def Jam, he has brought to national attention such groundbreaking rap acts as Run-DMC, Public Enemy, and LL Cool J, defining a sound, an attitude, a musical style, and an approach to fashion. Although he sold the DefJam label, he continues to help define rap and related styles through his position as founder, chair, president, and CEO of Rush Communications.

Russell Simmons was born on October 4, 1959, in Hollis, New York, son of Daniel Simmons, a public school attendance supervisor. Simmons and his two brothers grew up in a middle-class neighborhood in the New York City borough of Queens, where he graduated from August Martin High School in 1975.

Simmons went on to study sociology at City College of New York, where he first became aware of rap music. In the mid-1970s, rap was just getting started and was confined almost exclusively to young inner-city African Americans. Rap was a genuinely popular form of music created from the ground up, with young men—and a few women—joining in parks and on street corners to perform their own complex and rhythmic rap lyrics to spontaneously gathering crowds. The performers, known as "MCs" (after the term "master of ceremonies"), were very much involved with their audiences, telling stories about the inner-city life they all shared, criticizing the poverty and problems of the ghetto, and celebrating the almost superhuman power of the rappers to triumph over all obstacles.

Taken with this new musical form, Simmons left college to promote local rap artists. He produced recordings on minuscule budgets and organized "rap nights" at Queens and Harlem dance clubs. In 1984, he joined with Rick Rubin to form Def Jam Records, which in 1985 won a $600,000 distribution deal with CBS Records. By 1988, Def Jam had become a major force in the music world, with such influential albums as the Beastie Boys' *Licensed to Ill,* LL Cool J's *Bigger and Deffer,* and Run-DMC's *Raising Hell.* Simmons's younger brother Joseph is a member of Run-DMC.

Simmons was a hands-on music executive, managing all Def Jam acts and making sure that his artists "kept it real" and maintained their authentic connection to his urban audience. Simmons has defended rap performers as positive role models for black youth, despite the criticism that rap has occasionally received for promoting violence, glorifying gangsters, and expressing negative attitudes toward women.

In 1985, Simmons produced *Krush Groove,* his first film, a version of his own story as founder of Run-DMC. His partner, Rick Rubin, played himself, while Blair Underwood played Simmons. The movie featured a number of Def Jam acts and made $20 million despite receiving poor reviews. Later, Simmons produced several other films, including *The Addiction* (1995), *Gridlock'd* (1997), and *Def Jam's How to Be a Player* (1997).

Meanwhile, in 1993, Polygram bought 60 percent of Def Jam for $33 million. Simmons continued to supervise the company, but rap and the music world had changed since the 1980s, and Simmons reportedly felt constrained by the new financial pressures of operating in an industry that was dominated by a few big players. In 1999, Simmons sold his remaining interest to Universal Music Group for $100 million and focused on Rush Communications, as well as his Phat Farm fashion company for men and its spinoff for women, Baby Phat. Simmons's wife, the former model Kimora Lee whom he married in 1998, is creative director of Baby Phat. Simmons has also joined with Donny Deutsch of advertising agency Deutsch Inc. to form dRush, an advertising agency targeted to youth. For many years, Simmons produced *Def Comedy Jam* for HBO. Simmons later began producing *Def Poetry Jam,* an HBO television program featuring rap poets, with a theatrical version opening in New York City in 2002.

Simmons's role in the rap community has expanded in recent years to include a leadership role in convening a "Hip-Hop Summit" and lobbying for rappers' First Amendment rights to use the language and the imagery that they choose. Some politically conscious rap figures have criticized Simmons, claiming that he is taking credit for inspiring a grassroots political consciousness in hip-hop that actually already exists. But Simmons has also won admiration for his efforts to combine the power and prestige of his entrepreneurial position with a concern for education, civil rights, community safety, and peace.

Further Reading

Brown, Eryn. "From Rap to Retail: Wiring the Hip-Hop Nation." *Fortune,* April 2000, p. 530.

Chappell, Kevin. "The CEO$ of Hip-Hop and the Billion-Dollar Rap Jackpot." *Ebony,* January 2001, p. 116.

Dingle, Derek T. *Black Enterprise, Titans of the B.E. 100s.* New York: John Wiley & Sons, Inc., 1999, pp. 73–92.

Farley, Christopher John. "The Pop Life: Hip Hopping to the Church on Time." *Time,* December 12, 1998, p. 48.

Muhammed, Tariq K. "Hip-Hop Moguls: Beyond the Hype." *Black Enterprise,* December 1999, p. 78.

Ogg, Alex. *The Men Behind Def Jam: The Radical Rise of Russell Simmons and Rick Rubin.* London: Omnibus Press, 2002.

Roberts, Johnnie L. "Mr. Rap Goes to Washington." *Newsweek,* September 2000, p. 22.

Simmons, Russell, with Nelson George. *Life and Def: Sex, Drugs, Money and God.* New York: Crown, 2001.

Stark, Jeff. "Russell Simmons." Salon.Com. Available online. URL: http://www.salon.com/people/bc/1999/07/06/simmons. Posted July 6, 1999.

Sims, Naomi

(1949–) *fashion model, wig and cosmetics manufacturer*

Naomi Sims is a good example of an African-American woman who made breakthroughs in the entertainment field and then capitalized on her success with an entrepreneurial spirit. Sims was the first black fashion model to achieve mass-market success, and she used what she learned and the connections she made to become a maker of wigs and cosmetics, founding the Naomi Sims Collection and Naomi Sims Beauty Products, Ltd.

Sims was born on March 30, 1949, in Oxford, Mississippi. She later moved to Pittsburgh, where she graduated from Westinghouse High School. Other information about Sims's past has been contradictory and confusing, since Sims has given several accounts of her early life, each at odds with the other in key ways. What is certain is that after graduation, Sims went to New York to live with her sister, Betty, who worked at first as an airline stewardess and then as a model. Sims got a scholarship to study merchandising and textile design at New York City's Fashion Institute of Technology (FIT) and another small stipend to study psychology at night at New York University. When Sims needed more money, an FIT counselor suggested modeling. Without knowing how to proceed, Sims contacted Gosta Peterson, a major fashion photographer, and somehow obtained a meeting. Peterson was dazzled by the tall and beautiful Sims, and asked his wife, *New York Times Magazine* fashion editor Patricia Peterson, to help promote his new discovery. Sims had landed a high-profile spread in her first modeling session, and her subsequent fashion career followed the same breathtaking path.

For years, black women had been shut out of modeling opportunities, but in the wake of the Civil Rights movement and the Black Power movement of the 1960s, the time was suddenly right for their acceptance. Indeed, even after her *New York Times* debut, Sims got the cold shoulder from the top white agencies and chose instead to work with Wilhelmina Cooper, who was just starting her own agency. Within a week after signing with Wilhelmina, Sims was doing a national television commercial for AT&T; she went on to a six-year career in which she was featured on the cover of virtually every major fashion magazine and won numerous awards. She was also the first black person to be featured on the cover of a major woman's magazine, *Ladies' Home Journal,* and the first to be in a multicolored spread in *Vogue.*

By 1973, though, at the age of 24, Sims was tired of modeling, which she saw as a superficial and shallow industry. She left her career to pursue her longer-term goal of starting her own enterprise. In 1973, wigs available to African-American women were all made of Caucasian hair, and

Sims began experimenting with synthetic fibers that would match the various colors and textures of African-American hair. She eventually convinced Metropa Company, an import-export firm, to put up some money for the Naomi Sims Collection, which she also invested in. When she developed Kanekalon Presselle, a synthetic fiber that resembled straightened African hair, her business took off. Although white buyers refused to acknowledge the difference between "black" and "white" hair, Sims found a way to educate her clientele, and her first-year sales reached $5 million. Since 40 percent of black women wear wigs, Sims had a ready-made market. By the early 1980s, she was selling wigs in 2,000 department stores in the United States, Canada, Great Britain, the West Indies, and Africa.

Sims also published a 1976 book called *All About Health and Beauty for the Black Woman,* based on interviews with 100 black women. The book sold well and helped to promote her further. She went on to develop a black-oriented cosmetics line in 1985, which, like the wigs, proved to be a tough initial sale to white businesses but grossed $5 million by 1988. In 1989, white cosmetics firms were starting to compete for the black market, but Sims has managed to keep her company afloat.

Sims eventually married art dealer Michael Alistair Findlay, an English emigré with whom she has a son, John Philip. She has written other books for black women and remains active in black community affairs. She has had her share of criticism by those who accuse her of exploiting black women's wish to conform to white notions of beauty, as well as by feminists who are critical of what they perceive as an exaggerated focus on a woman's appearance. Sims herself stands by her work, saying that her products give women confidence and help to empower them.

Further Reading

Gale Group. "Naomi Sims." Biography Resource Center, African American Publications. Available online. URL: http://www.africanpubs.com/Apps/bios/1150Naoi.asp?pic=none. Downloaded on September 15, 2002.

Naomi Sims Online Store. Available online. URL: http://naomisims.com. Downloaded on September 15, 2002.

Sims, Naomi, with Norma Goodwin. *All About Health and Beauty for the Black Woman.* New York: Doubleday, 1986.

Smith, Ada Beatrice Queen Victoria Louise Virginia   See BRICKTOP.

Smith, Clarence O.   See LEWIS, EDWARD T. and CLARENCE O. SMITH.

Smith, Joshua I.
(Joshua I. Smith, Sr., Joshua Isaac Smith, Joshua Smith)
(1941–) *founder of computer systems and management company, computer consultant*

Joshua I. Smith was the creator of MAXIMA Corporation, which was once one of the largest minority-owned businesses in the United States. The company that Smith built eventually failed, in part because of conflicts with his son, Joshua I. Smith II. Yet Smith's reputation endures as the man who built a huge computer systems and management company—hardly a traditional field for African Americans, and one in which Smith succeeded admirably for many years.

Smith was born on April 8, 1941, in Garrard County, Kentucky. He graduated with a B.S. from Central State University in Wilberforce, Ohio, in 1963, going on to teach biology and chemistry at Ohio's University of Akron, where he also studied law for a time and where he first became interested in the growing field of computers. In 1969, he became manager of Plenum Publishing's data book division in New York, and in 1970, he went on to work at the American

Society of Information Science in Washington, D.C., where he eventually became executive director.

Smith was fascinated with the ways that computers and information science might be applied to business, so he took courses in management at the University of Delaware and at Central Michigan University. In 1977, he became vice president at Herner & Co., a consulting firm, where he began to realize that there was a growing opportunity for someone who could tailor his work to the special computer needs of government agencies.

Smith had married Jacqueline Jones, with whom he had one son, Joshua I. Smith II, and whom he later divorced. In 1978, he used the $15,000 that he received in the divorce settlement to form the MAXIMA Corporation, which was dedicated to "maximizing information for effective decision-making." Unusually for the time, MAXIMA offered all three key elements of the computerization process: hardware, software, and service.

When Smith began his company, he was the only employee and his office was one small room in Bethesda, Maryland, a Washington, D.C., suburb. He started by registering with the Small Business Administration (SBA), whose 8(a) program enabled minority-owned businesses to bypass the laborious bidding process, allowing these struggling companies to approach government officials directly in search of contracts. As soon as he won 8(a) acceptance, he began to make substantial profits, growing from $321,000 in revenue in 1979 to $28 million in 1985. MAXIMA had contracts with the U.S. Navy, Air Force, and Department of Energy.

In 1982, Smith branched out to commercial contracts, forming the Library Resources Company to help libraries computerize as well. But libraries were not interested in Smith's services and in 1983, the company folded, costing MAXIMA $300,000. In 1984, consequently, Smith sold 18 percent of his company for $1 million to defense contractor Martin Marietta.

MAXIMA was still doing well, however, and in 1985, *INC.* magazine called it one of the fastest-growing privately held companies in the nation (a privately held company does not sell stock), while the Commerce Department's Minority Business Development Agency called it federal government contractor of the year. Smith began to buy other companies, including a computer manufacturing company, a computer supplies distributor, a direct mail firm, several retail computer stores, and a science and health information company.

Then, in 1986, trouble hit, as the SBA told MAXIMA it had become too large and profitable to participate in the 8(a) program. As a result, Smith lost some $30 million worth of contracts that had been in the works, though he managed to save $70 million in contracts. For a while, sales continued to increase, but in the late 1980s, the recession caught up with MAXIMA, leading Smith to make some dramatic changes. He cut 400 people from his staff and fired the president and chief operating officer; he moved from his Bethesda offices to a smaller and less prestigious suburb; he sold 22 percent of his company to Edelson Technology Partners; and he borrowed money from National Westminster Bank. He also shifted his company's focus from the federal government to the county level.

Smith continued to enjoy the regard of the federal government, as in 1989 President George H. W. Bush appointed him to chair the U.S. Commission on Minority Business Development, a position he held until the committee released its report in 1992. Smith's company was facing hard times, however, doing more business but making less profit.

In 1993, Smith faced another blow as his own son, Joshua Smith II, along with two other employees, was accused of misappropriating some $675,000 in company funds to start their own business. Smith had to fire his son, and MAXIMA sued the three men, who in turn countersued

MAXIMA for $60 million. MAXIMA had not earned a profit since 1991, and its revenue had been falling steadily since that year as well. Smith fought to keep MAXIMA alive but finally, in June 1998, he declared bankruptcy, going on to become chairman and managing partner of the Coaching Group, a consulting firm that works with fast-growing companies, helping them to manage their growth.

Smith continues to enjoy a great deal of prestige in the business world. He is on the board of directors of three Fortune 100 companies (the United States's 100 largest companies as rated by *Fortune* magazine)—Caterpillar, Inc.; FedEx Corp.; and Allstate Insurance Corp.—and serves as director of Cardiocomm Solutions, Inc., a Canadian company. He is also a member of the Maryland Stadium Authority and on the board of directors of the National Black Chamber of Commerce. Although Smith's loss of his 20-year-old company was a bitter one, his continued success in the business world is a tribute to the respect he has won.

Further Reading

Black Data Processing Associates. "Joshua Smith." BDPA National. Available online. URL: http://www.bdpa.org/speakers2002.cfm?section=bio3. Downloaded on December 22, 2002.
"Commission Calls for Revamp of Federal Minority Business Plan." *Jet*, July 6, 1992, p. 8.
"Fed. Minority Business Programs Probed during Capitol Hill Hearing." *Jet*, August 17, 1992.
"Joshua Smith, Chairman and CEO of Maxima Corp., Fights with Son over Business' Monies." *Jet*, January 24, 1994, p. 18.
"MAXIMA Corporation's Father-Son Legal Battle Settled." *Jet*, May 19, 1997, p. 13.
NNA, Inc. "Joshua Smith." NNA website. Available online. URL: http://www.nextnetnordic.com/jsmith.html. Downloaded on December 22, 2002.
Singletary, Michelle, and Alfred Edmond, Jr. "The Big Mess at Maxima." *Black Enterprise*, May 1994, p. 15.

Smith, Stephen

(ca. 1797–1873) *lumber merchant, coal merchant, real estate speculator, banker, minister, philanthropist, abolitionist*

Stephen Smith was born a slave, yet he managed to buy his own freedom and become a respected entrepreneur in the city of Philadelphia, so much so that his contemporary, the abolitionist and researcher Martin Delany, called him "decidedly the most wealthy colored man in the United States." Smith made a fortune in lumber, coal, real estate, and the buying and selling of bank notes (loans), but he was also an avid abolitionist (opponent of slavery), political activist, and philanthropist. He is a good example of the way that black entrepreneurs provided financial support to the African-American community, creating a base from which slavery might be opposed as equal rights were pursued.

Smith was born sometime around 1797 (the poor condition of slave records makes it difficult to determine exactly when), the son of the enslaved woman, Nancy Smith, and an unknown father. On July 10, 1801—when Smith would have been around four years old—he was indentured to General Thomas Boude, a lumber merchant who had been a hero in the Revolutionary War. (To indenture someone is to hire out their labor for several years, in exchange for room, board, and perhaps some kind of fee.) As a teenager, Smith was managing Boude's lumber business in Columbia, Pennsylvania, even though he was still a slave at the time.

Somehow Smith obtained a loan of $50, which he used to buy his freedom on January 3, 1816. In November 1816 he married Harriet Lee, a free woman of color. He went on to establish his own lumber business while his wife ran an oyster and refreshment house in Columbia. The 19-year-old Smith, who clearly had a talent for business, began buying and selling real estate.

In 1834, white people rioted against black people in Columbia, and Smith's office was attacked by a mob. In 1835, white people who envied his business success tried to get him to leave the community, but the support of other white people allowed him to stay in Columbia a few years longer.

In 1842, Smith expanded his operations to Philadelphia, where he moved his family into a house that he bought from his friend, Robert Purvis, the son-in-law of sailmaker and abolitionist JAMES FORTEN, SR. Smith also opened a large coal and lumber yard, which he ran in Philadelphia with his partner, Ulysses B. Vidal, while his longtime partner and cousin WILLIAM WHIPPER kept the businesses going in Columbia.

Smith did well in Philadelphia, acquiring some 36 properties in 10 years, investing in securities, and expanding his coal and lumber business. By 1849, his and Whipper's company was the largest stockholder in the Columbia bank, a major stockholder in the Columbia Bridge Company, and the owner of 22 cars running on the rail line from Columbia to Philadelphia. Smith himself owned 52 brick houses in Philadelphia as well as real estate in Philadelphia and sizable holdings in lumber and coal.

Throughout the 1850s, Smith continued to prosper, by some accounts grossing $100,000 each year in sales. By 1864, his net worth was reportedly $50,000. Nevertheless, Smith was keenly aware of the costs of racism, and he committed himself to fighting for equal rights throughout his life. He subscribed to the *Freedman's Journal,* an antislavery paper, and he contributed articles to that paper and to the *Emancipator,* a major abolitionist journal. In 1831 he had organized a meeting among free black people in Columbia to protest against the policies of the American Colonization Society, which sought to send freed slaves to Africa. The following year he had contributed a building to the Mount Zion African Methodist Episcopal Church, one of the earliest black churches in the nation, founded in response to the discrimination that African Americans suffered in white-run religious institutions.

Smith became a member, then a minister with the African Methodist Church. He was active with the Underground Railroad in Columbia and Philadelphia, working with Whipper and with WILLIAM STILL. He was active in a number of anti-slavery groups, and on March 15, 1858, hosted a meeting at his home for white abolitionist John Brown and a group of African-American leaders to discuss Brown's plan for organizing an armed insurrection against slavery. He contributed to a number of local charities and religious groups, leaving $15,000 in his will for the Stephen Smith Home for the Aged in West Philadelphia. He died in Philadelphia on November 4, 1873.

Further Reading

Bethel Harambee Historical Services. "Historical Figures." The Underground Railroad, A Living History. Available online. URL: http://www.livingtheundergroundrailroad.com/historicalfigures.htm. Downloaded on February 4, 2003.

Ingham, John, and Lynne B. Feldman. African American Business Leaders: A Biographical Dictionary. Westport, Conn.: Greenwood Press, 1994, pp. 597–599.

Logan, Rayford W., and Michael R. Winston. Dictionary of Negro Biography. New York: W. W. Norton & Co., 1983.

Walker, Juliet E. K. "Racism, Slavery, and Free Enterprise: Black Entrepreneurship in the United States before the Civil War." Business History Review 60 (Autumn 1986): 353–354.

Worner, William Frederic. "The Columbia Race Riots." Lancaster County Historical Society Papers 26 (October 1922): 175–187.

Spaulding, Charles Clinton
(1874–1952) insurance executive

Charles Clinton Spaulding helped to found the North Carolina Mutual Insurance Company, one of the major black-owned businesses of the 19th and 20th centuries. Although his career took place during an extremely restrictive time for African Americans, Spaulding pushed the limits of what was possible for black people and black entrepreneurs.

Spaulding was born near Whiteville in Columbus County, North Carolina, in the Wilmington region. He grew up in a community of free black people who had settled there during slavery times in the early 19th century. His father was Benjamin McIver Spaulding, a farmer who was also a blacksmith and artisan. His mother was Margaret Ann Virginia (Moore) Spaulding who worked on the farm and raised the 14 children in the family. Later, the white media referred to Spaulding as the son of an ex-slave, but his father and grandfather were both born free, although the family had once been slaves on a Wilmington-area plantation.

Spaulding received very little education as a child, working on the family farm until he moved to Durham, North Carolina, at age 20 in 1894. His uncle, Dr. Aaron McDuffie Moore, helped Spaulding become literate and educated as the young man enrolled in Whitted School and worked as a dishwasher, bellhop, waiter, and eventually as the cook for a wealthy white family. In 1898 he had acquired the equivalent of a high school diploma and began working in a cooperative grocery store that had been founded by 25 local African Americans who each invested the then substantial sum of $10. When the company ran into financial difficulties, however, most investors withdrew their funds and Spaulding was responsible for $300 worth of debt.

Meanwhile, in 1898, Spaulding's uncle and JOHN MERRICK had founded the North Carolina Mutual Insurance Company, which was also on the verge of financial collapse in 1900. Moore offered Spaulding, then 26, the chance to manage the company. Spaulding remembered coming in each morning and sweeping out the office before beginning work, but he was also a remarkable salesman and he built up the company's business by going door to door selling insurance policies to black families. In those years, white-owned insurance companies, especially in the South, would often avoid black customers, so black-owned insurance companies were the only choice that many African Americans had for financial security.

Spaulding soon had brought in enough business to hire a sales force that worked on commission (a percentage of sales), recruiting respectable community leaders such as ministers and teachers in 28 North Carolina towns. Moore and Merrick had other enterprises to support them, but Spaulding was entirely dependent on the insurance company, so he suffered financially during the years that the company was struggling to find its footing. However, in 1900 he married Fannie Jones, John Merrick's half sister.

In 1901 and 1902, Merrick and Moore had to advance funds to the company on two separate occasions, but by 1903, North Carolina Mutual had become a profitable venture and Spaulding became a salaried employee rather than someone living on commissions. The company began to develop several plans for expansion. Spaulding published a company newspaper, the *North Carolina Mutual*, which came out every month and helped advertise the business. Spaulding convinced the wealthy white Duke family, local tobacco growers, to contribute a printing press. He also developed novelty items to advertise the company, including pencils, matches, fans, thermometers, blotters, and calendars with black subjects. He expanded the types of insurance that the company offered, began doing business in South Carolina, and constructed a new office building in Durham's largely white downtown. The company eventually moved into even more modern and luxurious quarters in 1921, a six-story building that became a symbol of the company's prosperity—and of the achievements of black business in general.

The insurance company supported the black community by making its funds available for various projects, including Lincoln Hospital, North

Charles Clinton Spaulding was one of the founders of North Carolina Mutual Life Insurance Company, for many years the largest black-owned firm in the United States. *(Courtesy of North Carolina Mutual Life Insurance Company)*

Carolina Central Hospital, a library, and three newspapers. It also supported local churches. Although John Merrick's death in 1920 meant a transition from the original leadership, North Carolina Mutual continued to flourish, although it did experience financial problems during the Great Depression of the 1930s. During World War II, however, Spaulding led the company to greater prosperity, and by the time he died, North Carolina Mutual was the largest black-owned business in the United States, a position it held for many years.

Spaulding was a vital force within the National Negro Business League (NNBL), which had been founded by Booker T. Washington in

1900 as part of Washington's advocacy of black self-help and black enterprise. The NNBL was failing by 1938, but Spaulding helped revive the group and served as its president for many years. He also supported the Durham community in many ways, particularly through his involvement with the Durham Committee on Negro Affairs, a civil rights group founded in 1935 that helped win rights for African Americans at a time when both laws and customs in the South sought to keep black people in an isolated, inferior position in political and economic life. Spaulding found his own ways of fighting for black equality even while he seemed to agree that white people should retain their political power.

After Spaulding died on August 1, 1952, thousands of people attended his funeral. In 1980 he was the first African American to be inducted into *Fortune* magazine's national Business Hall of Fame. The company he helped to found continues to survive, and he is still remembered as an important figure in Durham's African-American community.

Further Reading

Cline, Drew. "Business Leader Hall of Fame." *Business Leader*, November 1996, cover story. Available online. URL: http://businessleader.com/b1/nov96/cover.html.

Gale Group. "Charles C. Spaulding." *Notable Black American Men.* Farmington Hills, Mich.: Gale Research, 1998.

Haskins, Jim. *Black Stars: African American Entrepreneurs.* New York: John Wiley & Sons, 1998, pp. 74–78.

Ingham, John N., and Lynne B. Feldman. *African-American Business Leaders: A Biographical Dictionary.* Westport, Conn.: Greenwood Press, 1994, pp. 387–402.

North Carolina Mutual Life Insurance Company. "The Company." North Carolina Mutual Life Insurance website. Available online. URL: http://www.ncmutuallife.com/company.html. Downloaded on January 28, 2003.

Still, William

(1821–1902) *abolitionist, writer, businessman, banker, store owner*

William Still is best remembered for his activities as an abolitionist (opponent of slavery) and his work on the Underground Railroad, the informal but highly effective network set up by abolitionists in the 19th century to help enslaved people escape to freedom. Historians believe that Still may have helped as many as 60 runaway slaves per month, and the detailed records he kept of his activities became the basis for *The Underground Railroad,* a book he published about his activities in 1872. After the Civil War, Still also became a successful businessman who was so influential and respected in his home of Philadelphia that he was elected to the predominantly white Philadelphia Board of Trade. He also served as the first president of Philadelphia's first black-owned bank, the Berean Savings Association, which had been founded by his son-in-law, Reverend Matthew Anderson, in 1888.

William Still was born on October 7, 1821, near Medford, in Burlington County, New Jersey, the son of Levin and Charity Still. Levin, whose last name was then Steel, had been a slave in Maryland but was allowed to buy his own freedom in 1807, when he left his wife and family to move to New Jersey, where many of his relatives lived. He was able to help his wife, Sidney, escape with two of her daughters. Sidney changed her name to Charity and the family changed their name to Still in order to avoid being caught and returned to slavery.

William was the youngest of 18 children. He grew up on his father's farm, doing farm work at home and being hired out to chop wood and work in the area's cranberry bogs. He was able to get only a few hours a year of formal education, but he loved to read and spent his free time with books whenever he could. In 1841, at the age of 20, he left home to work on a nearby farm. In 1844, he went to Philadelphia, where he worked as a day laborer and started two unsuccessful businesses:

an oyster store and a secondhand clothing business. He also worked at a variety of jobs, including handyman, waiter, and brick worker. In 1847, he married Letitia George, who became the mother of his four children—and he took the job that would change his life, as clerk at the Pennsylvania Anti-slavery Society.

The society was an organization dedicated to ending slavery, and Still became an active abolitionist. He worked with fellow abolitionists Harriet Tubman and John Brown and supported Brown's efforts to start an insurrection at Harpers Ferry, West Virginia. He also helped numerous slaves move through Philadelphia to freedom, often harboring them in his own home. One of his most dramatic encounters took place in 1850, when he interviewed a tired, bedraggled man who had been a slave for more than 40 years and then had somehow managed to make his way from Alabama to Philadelphia, where he hoped to find his mother. Still discovered that this man was his long-lost brother, Peter Still.

When the Civil War began, the society temporarily closed its doors, and Still started a secondhand stove business in his old offices at the society. He expanded the business to become a coal-seller, then to make gas stoves, boilers, heaters, and other large appliances. By 1864, he was running a successful enterprise—but he left to take the prestigious position of sutler (someone who supervises the army's horses and mules) at Camp William Penn outside Philadelphia. After the war, Still expanded his coal business by buying a deserted site, building a shed, laying railroad tracks to enable the delivery of coal, and buying several wagons so that he could deliver coal all over town. He quickly achieved success, which he used to support his continuing activities for civil rights. A campaign he began in 1859 to end segregation on Philadelphia's streetcars was finally successful in 1867. He remained active in politics in other ways, and remained the president of the Pennsylvania Anti-Slavery Society until one year before he died in Philadelphia on July 14, 1902.

Today he is known as "the father of the Underground Railroad."

Further Reading

Bentley, Judith. "Dear Friend": Thomas Garrett and William Still, Collaborators on the Underground Railroad. New York: Cobblehill, 1997.

Khan, Lurey. "One Day, Levin . . . He Be Free": William Still and the Underground Railroad. New York: iUniverse, 2002.

Still, William. The Underground Rail Road: A Record of Facts, Authentic Narratives, Letters and Narrating the Hardships, edited by Susan W. Dickinson-Kaun. Chicago: Johnson Publishing Company, Inc., 1975.

The Underground Railroad: The Story of Freedom's Trail. "William Still: Father of the 'Railroad.'" The Journal News.com. Available online. URL: http://www.nynews.com/blackhistory/still.html. Downloaded on November 14, 2002.

William Still Underground Railroad Foundation Inc. Available online. URL: http://www.undergroundrr.com. Downloaded on November 14, 2002.

Sutton, Percy E.
(Percy Ellis Sutton)
(1920–) *media executive, government official, lawyer, civil rights activist, publisher*

Percy Sutton has had a long and varied career. He has served several terms as borough president of Manhattan in New York City, worked as a lawyer to defend Malcolm X and the Black Panthers, and operated as head of Inner City Broadcasting Corporation, a media company. He is part of a group that for many years was at the heart of all major political and commercial activity in Harlem, and is credited with spurring much of the revitalization of that famous African-American community.

Sutton was born on November 24, 1920, near Prairie View, a small town in eastern Texas. He was the youngest of 15 children born to S(amuel)

J. Sutton, a former slave, and Lillian Sutton, an educator. Sutton's father went on to become an entrepreneur, activist, and the principal at the San Antonio high school attended by all of his children. One of his most lucrative investments was a parcel of land near the center of a tiny cattle town—which eventually became a high-priced section of downtown San Antonio.

Percy Sutton attended public schools while continuing in his family's activist tradition. At age 12, a police officer slapped him for handing out flyers for the National Association for the Advancement of Colored People (NAACP), and Sutton responded by kicking the officer in the shins. As a result, he was beaten severely. The following year, he was arrested for sitting in the white-only section of a segregated bus.

Sutton went on to attend the all-black Prairie View College after being denied entry to a veterinary school that did not accept black students. He later studied agriculture at Hampton Institute in Virginia and at Tuskegee Institute in Alabama, both black schools. He also learned to fly and earned money doing stunts at county fairs. When World War II began, he tried to enlist in the Army Air Corps as a skilled pilot, but white southern recruiters would not accept him. He went to New York City, where he was accepted. He served with the famous Tuskegee Airmen, winning combat stars for his service as an intelligence officer. He was discharged in 1945 at the end of the war with the rank of captain.

Sutton then enrolled in Columbia University—where once again, race became a factor. Sutton staged an informal sit-in to force his acceptance, and then went on to work two eight-hour jobs while attending classes. He followed a similar schedule at Brooklyn Law School, where he earned an L.L.B. in 1950. He passed the New York bar the following year, and served as an air force intelligence officer in Washington, D.C., during the Korean War. He eventually became the air force's first black judge advocate, a position in the armed forces legal system for which special training is required.

In 1953, Sutton left the military for good and began his civilian career. He, his brother Oliver Sutton, and a colleague named George Covington set up a law partnership in Harlem that continued over the next four decades. Eventually, Sutton defended the Black Panthers and Malcolm X, and still later, he represented Malcolm's widow, Betty Shabazz, and Betty's 12-year-old grandson, Malcolm Shabazz. During the 1960s, the firm represented numerous civil rights activists who were arrested in the South, and Sutton acted as a consultant to the Student Nonviolent Coordinating Committee (SNCC). In New York, Sutton was active in the NAACP, serving as local president in 1961 and 1962.

In 1954, Sutton had begun a political career that at first seemed strikingly unsuccessful. In that year, he was defeated in a race for assemblyman, and he continued to be defeated in several other elections, for assemblyman, district leader, and state committeeman. Finally, in 1964, he was elected assemblyman. In 1966, he introduced new divorce laws and the first modern abortion reform bills.

Also in 1966, Constance Baker Motley stepped down as Manhattan Borough president to become a federal judge, and Sutton was chosen by the New York City Council to complete her term. He continued to serve as borough president until 1977, winning his subsequent elections by huge majorities. Overwhelmingly popular with African-American voters, Sutton was also popular with his mostly white constituency. It was this popularity that led him to believe he would be a logical candidate for mayor.

Although it was known as a liberal city, New York had never had a black mayor, though by 1977, a number of other cities had elected African Americans to that post. Sutton entered the race in a highly publicized bid, but he lost to Ed Koch, who served for the next three terms. Koch was not defeated until then Manhattan borough president David Dinkins ran against him in 1989, with the support of Sutton and other Harlem figures, to become New York City's first black mayor.

Meanwhile, Sutton had continued to be active in the business world. In 1971, while he was still borough president, he and some political allies had founded AM-NEWS, Inc., a group of black investors who wanted to change the portrayal of African Americans in the media. In those days, the media was almost entirely dominated by white-owned companies, and in New York, one of the few exceptions was the *Amsterdam News*, a Harlem-based, black-owned paper. The AM-NEWS group bought the paper, with a number of prominent African-American politicians taking posts in the new corporation. As the second-largest stockholder, Sutton owned 37 percent of the company. He sold his stock in 1975, however, as it was awkward for him to be in office and yet to be held accountable for the paper's editorial decisions.

Later in 1975, Sutton founded Inner City Broadcasting Corp. with many of the same colleagues with whom he had created AM-NEWS. The new company bought WLIB-AM, a radio station that had a history of supporting the Civil Rights movement. WLIB—the "lib" was short for "liberation"—was allowed to broadcast only during the day, so Inner City bought WBLS, an FM station, which proved to be an extremely profitable decision. The WBLS format was redesigned so as to appeal to white listeners—and it quickly moved into the top of the local ratings charts. WLIB, meanwhile, was converted to all news and talk, and gained a reputation of being a place where black New Yorkers could find trustworthy news and relevant opinions on issues important to the black community.

During the 1980s, Inner City bought stations in San Francisco/Berkeley, California; Detroit, Michigan; Los Angeles, California; and San Antonio, Texas. In 1988, the company sold its Detroit station to finance a new venture that had begun in 1983—a cable franchise in Queens. In that year, Inner City joined with the black-owned Unity Broadcasting Network to create Queens Inner Unity Cable Systems, with the goal of pro-viding one-third of the New York City borough of Queens with cable. The new company had great difficulty getting the financing for its venture, however, and was unable to succeed until it joined with Warner Communications (now AOL Time Warner).

Throughout his media ventures, Sutton remained politically active on both a local and a national level. In 1984 and 1988, he was legal adviser and fund raiser to Jesse Jackson's presidential campaigns, and he has continued to work with Jackson in his later endeavors.

Another area of interest to Sutton has been the Apollo Theater, long a cultural landmark where many famous African-American stars had gotten their start. The theater was bankrupt in 1980, when Sutton bought it for $220,000, a move that was widely viewed as an effort to rehabilitate the depressed area of Harlem. In 1983, the Apollo obtained federal, state, and city landmark status, and in 1985, the theater reopened. In 1987, Sutton's company began to produce *It's Showtime at the Apollo*, a syndicated variety show that aired nationwide. Although Sutton saw the Apollo as a valuable Harlem resource, he ran it at a deficit for most if not all of the time he owned it.

Meanwhile, in 1991, at the age of 71, Sutton retired, becoming chairman emeritus (retired) of Inner City Broadcasting. Even in retirement, Sutton was occupied with a number of causes, however, serving in high positions at the Greater Harlem Chamber of Commerce, working with the Harlem Business Alliance, and supporting a number of political candidates.

Also in 1991, the state of New York acquired the Apollo, ultimately creating a new controversy for Sutton. Although Inner City Broadcasting continued to produce *It's Showtime at the Apollo*, the theater now came under the auspices of a nonprofit group called the Apollo Theater Foundation, currently headed by RICHARD PARSONS, head of AOL Time Warner. In 1998, a foundation member sued Sutton for allegedly mismanaging funds. The dispute provoked a Pulitzer Prize–

winning series of editorials in the *New York Daily News*, but the paper received extensive criticism from both the journalism and the African-American communities when it transpired that the dispute was essentially over an error in contract language and Sutton was completely cleared of any wrongdoing.

Nevertheless, in 2002, Inner City Broadcasting lost the contract to produce the syndicated show at the Apollo. Instead, the contract for producing the show went to SUZANNE CELESTE DE PASSE and BERRY GORDY, JR., former colleagues at Motown, and the distribution deal went to FRANK MERCADO-VALDES's African Heritage Network.

Sutton has declared his intention of producing a rival program, *Showtime*, elsewhere in New York City. In 2003, the National Broadcasting Company (NBC) suggested that it might take over producing and distributing the program. Sutton has come out against that possibility, saying that control over what happens at the Apollo should remain within the Harlem community, of which he and Inner City Broadcasting are a part.

Meanwhile, Sutton remains an influential figure in New York City politics and media, even if two or three new generations of black media executives have superseded him. In these days when ROBERT L. JOHNSON's Black Entertainment Television is available on cable, and when New York City's major newspapers include African-American reporters and editors, it is hard to fathom the significance of Sutton's revitalization of the *Amsterdam News* and his black-oriented programming on two radio stations. Sutton's position at the forefront of the Apollo controversy shows that he is still a force to be reckoned with.

Further Reading

Arango, Tim. "Apollo Slugfest." *New York Post*, January 28, 2003, p. 27.

Boyd, Herb. "Apollo Showdown." *New York Amsterdam News*, August 22, 2002, p. 1.

———. "Percy Sutton Fights Back." *New York Amsterdam News*, August 22, 2002, p. 1.

"Charles Rangel and Percy Sutton Cleared of Wrongdoing in Apollo Theater Business Case." *Jet*, September 27, 1999, p. 25.

Dingle, Derek T. *Black Enterprise, Titans of the B.E. 100s.* New York: John Wiley & Sons, Inc., 1999, pp. 193–212.

Pristin, Terry. "Percy Sutton's Company Loses 'It's Showtime at the Apollo.'" *New York Times*, August 16, 2002, p. 83.

Pryce, Vinette K. "'Showtime at the Apollo' or 'Showtime Live.'" *New York Amsterdam News*, August 22, 2002, p. 19.

Rangel, Charles B. "A New Beginning for the Apollo Theatre." Congressman Charles B. Rangel website. Available online. URL: http://www.house.gov/apps/list/hearing/ny15_rangel/apollonewbeginning.html. Posted October 14, 1999.

Spitzer, Elliot. "What the Apollo Means for Harlem." *New York Times*, August 26, 1999, p. A16.

Tatum, Wilbert. "Rangel, Sutton, Cleared." *New York Amsterdam News*, August 26, 1999, p. 1.

T

Thomas, James
(1827–1913) *barber, real estate developer*

James Thomas was born a slave, became a prominent and wealthy business leader, and then died penniless, in a dramatic life story that exemplifies many of the challenges and achievements typical of African-American entrepreneurs in the 19th and early 20th centuries. He achieved prominence in both Nashville and St. Louis, and before he lost his fortune, became wealthy first as a barber, then as a real estate speculator.

Thomas was born sometime in 1827 (accurate records were not kept on most enslaved people) in Nashville, Tennessee, the son of Judge John Catron and his African-American slave Sally. Catron sold Sally and his son, and the two eventually lived in Virginia, the property of Albemarle County planter Charles Thomas, from whom James took his last name. When Charles Thomas died, Sally and James were sold to John Martin, who brought them back to Nashville, where he tried to sell James. Sally, the owner of a clothes-cleaning business, was able to put up $350 towards her son's $400 purchase price, and she managed to convince Tennessee planter Ephraim Foster to loan her the rest. Since Tennessee state law required freed black people to leave the state, Thomas was in danger of being returned to slavery, so he was technically considered Foster's property. Still, he continued to live as before, running errands for his mother, assisting a local doctor, and attending school during the winter.

In 1841, Thomas became an apprentice to Frank Parrish, a former slave who worked as a barber. (An apprentice signs on to work for small or no wages for several years in exchange for learning a trade.) After his five-year apprenticeship ended, he acquired his own shop, where he established a high-paying clientele of influential whites. In 1848, he attracted the attention of Andrew Jackson Polk, the cousin of President James K. Polk, who asked him to travel north as his personal servant, threatening to buy and shut down Thomas's business if Thomas did not agree.

Thomas enjoyed his travels but was shocked by what he saw as the North's hypocrisy: Despite the absence of slavery, he found that public places were segregated (separated by race), while he himself was harassed and once thrown out of a theater. A number of Nashville laws had been passed to segregate the city and restrict African-American activities, but Thomas was apparently able to evade or ignore those restrictions. Indeed, in 1851, he convinced Davidson County to allow him to become emancipated (freed) and then to let him stay in the state despite the laws against free blacks.

Thomas continued to prosper as a barber but he also hungered for new adventures. In 1856, he joined his boyhood friend William

Walker, who was invading Nicaragua in the hopes of becoming a dictator there. When Thomas realized that Walker wanted to reinstate black slavery, he left for home and began closing up his Nashville business. After traveling to Wisconsin and down the Mississippi River, he settled in St. Louis, Missouri, in 1857, where he began working as a waiter and barber on the luxury steamboat, the *William Morrison.*

In St. Louis, Thomas met Antoinette Rutgers, the 20-year-old daughter of Pelagie Rutgers, who was then the richest free black person in Missouri. James and Antoinette were married in 1868, which further increased Thomas's fortune.

For many years, Thomas ran a St. Louis barbershop with Cyprian Claymorgan, another wealthy African American. In the 1870s he opened his own shop in the luxurious downtown Lincoln Hotel. He also began buying and selling real estate, amassing a fortune of $400,000 by 1879. Eventually, he owned two mansions and became known for his luxurious lifestyle.

In the 1870s Thomas also became financial adviser to the St. Louis Freedmen's Savings and Trust Bank, until that institution failed (went out of business) in 1874. In 1879, he helped organize the Colored Immigration Association to help the African Americans flooding into the city to escape the racial discrimination and restrictive laws of the South.

Thomas retired in 1890, at the age of 63. Then, in 1893, the nationwide depression reduced the value of Thomas's holdings, a decline that worsened when the St. Louis tornado destroyed much of his property in 1896.

In 1897, Thomas's wife died and he went to live with his daughter and son-in-law in Chicago. His finances continued to worsen, and in 1898 he returned to St. Louis to live in one of his own apartment buildings. He was plagued by illness and further financial troubles, and on December 17, 1913, he died of influenza that had become pneumonia. Despite his poverty, several hundred mourners came to his funeral and the *St. Louis Globe-Democrat* ran a front-page obituary in his honor.

Further Reading

Schweninger, Loren. "The Free-Slave Phenomenon: James P. Thomas and the Black Community in Antebellum Nashville." *Civil War History* 22 (December 1976): 293–307.

———. "A Slave Family in the Antebellum South." *Journal of Negro History* 60 (January 1975): 29–44.

———. "Thriving within the Lowest Caste: The Financial Activities of James Thomas in the Nineteenth Century South." *Journal of Negro History* 63, (1978): 353–64.

Thomas, James. *From Tennessee Slave to St. Louis Entrepreneur: The Autobiography of James P. Thomas,* edited by Loren Schweninger. Columbia: University of Missouri Press, 1984.

Thomas-Graham, Pamela
(Pamela Thomas)
(1963–   ) *media executive, business consultant, writer*

Pamela Thomas-Graham is president and chief executive officer (CEO) of CNBC, the cable financial news channel affiliated with the National Broadcasting Company (NBC), making her the highest-ranking woman heading a division at that network. She is also the author of a series of mystery novels.

Pamela was born in Detroit, Michigan, in 1963, to a mother who was a social worker and a father who was an engineer. Her parents were highly influenced by the Civil Rights movement and urged their daughter to excel.

After completing her studies at Lutheran High School West, Thomas went to Radcliffe College in Cambridge, Massachusetts, where she originally intended to study pre-law. She became more interested in economics and business, however, graduating in 1985 with the Captain Jonathan Fay prize, the school's highest honor.

While an undergraduate, she did summer internships, worked in politics, assisted a professor, and interned at Chase Manhattan Bank in New York. She went on to get both a J.D. (law degree) and an M.B.A. (business degree) from Harvard University in 1989, where she was an editor on the *Harvard Law Review.*

After she graduated, Thomas started work as an associate at McKinsey and Company, a New York City management consulting company. She eventually became the first African-American woman partner in the company and one of only three black partners in a firm of some 3,000 consultants. She also rose to be head of the firm's media and entertainment practice. In that capacity, she advised the heads of various Fortune 500 companies (companies named as the country's 500 largest by *Fortune* magazine).

Thomas met Lawrence Otis Graham at Harvard, and the couple dated for six years. In 1992, they were married, and Thomas became Thomas-Graham. She has worked as a strategist for her husband's congressional campaign and continues to support his political aspirations. The couple has one son.

In 1998, Thomas-Graham also began a writing career with the publication of *A Darker Shade of Crimson*, a mystery novel featuring African-American Harvard economics professor Nikki Chase, followed by *Blue Blood* in 1999, in which Nikki investigates a death at Yale.

In 1999, Thomas-Graham wanted to move on from McKinsey, so she arranged to meet General Electric chairman Jack Welch, whose company owned NBC and CNBC. At that time, CNBC.com was primarily a promotional tool for the CNBC cable channel, and Welch wanted to make it a full-service financial site in its own right. He invited Thomas-Graham to head CNBC's online operations—a new move for Thomas-Graham, and one that drew criticism from some observers. Thomas-Graham, however, pointed out that at McKinsey she had advised a number of media companies and did indeed understand the industry.

In February 2001 she was promoted to president and chief operating officer (COO) of the cable network, managing editorial, production, marketing, communications, and technology for CNBC while still supervising the website. In July of the same year, she became president and CEO of the cable network and soon afterwards, executive vice president of NBC.

Thomas-Graham is also active in civic affairs, serving on the board of directors of the New York City Opera and the American Red Cross of Greater New York, among others. She has received numerous awards and honors and seems poised for continued corporate success.

Further Reading

Beatty, Sally. "NBC Selects Pamela Thomas-Graham to Be CEO of Business-News Network." *Wall Street Journal,* July 24, 2001, p. B4.

Bernstein, Paula. "CNBC CEO Takes Reins in Hard Times." *Variety,* September 3, 2001, p. 24.

Clarke, Robyn D. "Excellence by the Graham." *Black Enterprise,* September 2001, p. 78.

National Broadcasting Company. "Pamela Thomas-Graham." NBC.com. Available online. URL: http://www.nbc.com/nbc/header/Executive_Bios/thomas-graham_pamela.shtml. Downloaded on January 29, 2003.

"10 Most Powerful Blacks in TV." *Ebony,* October 2002, p. 86.

Thomas-Graham, Pamela. *Blue Blood.* New York: Simon and Schuster, 1999.

———. *A Darker Shade of Crimson.* New York: Simon and Schuster, 1998.

———. "Reflections on Success." The Black Collegian Online. Available online. URL: http://www.black-collegian.com/issues/30thAnn/reflectpgraham2001-30th.shtml. Downloaded on January 28, 2003.

Toney   See WESTON, ANTHONY.

Toussaint, Pierre
(ca. 1756–1853) *hairdresser*

Pierre Toussaint went from being a slave on a Haitian sugar plantation to one of the most prominent hairdressers in New York City. He helped provide funds to build orphanages, religious schools, and a religious order for women in Baltimore. He was also a major financial supporter of the construction of St. Patrick's Cathedral and St. Vincent de Paul Church. In 1992, New York City's Cardinal John J. O'Connor began the process of declaring him a saint.

Toussaint was born in the French colony then known as Saint-Domingue, where he worked as a house slave for his owners, Jean and Marie Bérard. There is controversy over his age, largely because good records were not kept for enslaved people. Unusually for the time, he learned to read and write.

In 1792, enslaved people in St-Domingue joined with free people of color to stage the first successful slave revolt in history. Eventually, they changed their country's name to Haiti and established freedom for all. In 1793, the Bérards, like many other slaveholders, left the island, bringing with them Toussaint; his younger sister, Rosalie; his aunt, Marie Bouquement; and two other house slaves, as well as two sisters of Bérard's wife.

Expecting the revolt to fail, Bérard brought with him only enough funds to support his family for a single year. After establishing himself in a rented house on Reade Street in Lower Manhattan, he apprenticed Toussaint to one of the city's leading hairdressers. Throughout Toussaint's long career, black people were never allowed to ride the city's segregated public horsecars, so Toussaint always had to walk back and forth to work.

When Bérard returned to his Haitian plantation in an effort to regain his property, he died of pleurisy. He had invested his family's money in a New York City business that later collapsed, leaving Marie Bérard penniless. According to some accounts, Toussaint refused the freedom that Marie Bérard offered, choosing instead to postpone his own marriage and to support her household through his earnings as a hairdresser. He eventually began working with such prestigious clients as the wife of leading politician Alexander Hamilton and the daughters of General Philip Schuyler, the officer who had defeated the British at Saratoga. During a time when $10,000 a year was considered a large income, Toussaint had clients who paid him as much as $1,000 per year. He supported the Bérard household even after Marie married another Haitian refugee planter, Gabriel Nicolas, who also suffered financial difficulties.

In 1807, Marie Nicolas died, freeing Toussaint on her deathbed. Toussaint went on to buy the freedom of his fiancée, Juliette Noel, and to marry her in 1811; he also bought Rosalie's freedom and raised her daughter, Euphemie, after she died. He worked 16 hours a day to buy the freedom of several other slaves, opened his home to black orphans and refugees, and risked his life to nurse those stricken with cholera and yellow fever during the city's many plagues. Toussaint was also known for his religious faith, inspiring admiring biographies by white writers before and after his death, during times when it was rare for black people to be recognized in the white world.

Toussaint's wife died in 1851, and Toussaint died two years later, on June 30, 1853, at the age of 87. He was first buried in the cemetery of St. Patrick's Old Cathedral on Mott Street, but his remains are now interred in a crypt beneath the floor of St. Patrick's Cathedral.

Further Reading

Jones, Arthur. "Pierre Toussaint, a Slave, Society Hairdresser, Philanthropist, May Become Nation's First Black Saint." *National Catholic Reporter*, August 25, 2000. Available online. URL: http://www.natcath.com/NCR_Online/archives/082500/082500a.htm.

Jones, Arthur. *Pierre Toussaint.* New York: Doubleday, 2003.

Lee, Hannah Sawyer. *Memoir of Pierre Toussaint, Born a Slave in San Domingo.* Hanover, Penn.: American

Society for the Defense of Tradition, Family, and Property, 1992.

"Pierre Toussaint." Black Saints Project website. Available online. URL: http://www.churchaction.org.uk/pierre_toussaint.html. Downloaded on November 3, 2002.

Tarry, Ellen. *Pierre Toussaint: Apostle of Old New York.* Boston, Mass.: Daughters of St. Paul, 1998.

Travis, Dempsey J.
(Dempsey Jerome Travis)

(1920–   ) *realtor, insurance executive, banker, publisher*

Dempsey J. Travis rose to become a major real estate tycoon in Chicago, though the practices he engaged in were questionable to some: He profited from the controversial urban renewal of the 1960s, helping to clear poor black neighborhoods in a program that most African Americans strongly opposed as destroying black communities. Nevertheless, Travis considered himself not a capitalist but a humanist, believing strongly that wealthy African Americans had to take responsibility for their people, and he was considered a "race leader" by many Chicagoans.

Travis was born in Chicago on February 25, 1920, the son of Louis Travis, a laborer in Chicago's stockyards, and Mittie Sims, the daughter of slaves from Birmingham, Alabama. Travis grew up in great poverty, though he later recalled that the family always had enough to eat and clean clothes. Louis's method of punishing Dempsey was to refuse to let his son work, so Dempsey grew to consider work a privilege. Louis died in 1943, but Mittie continued to offer Dempsey enormous support, living across the hall from him until she died at the age of 93.

Travis grew up on Chicago's black South Side. His father had been a pianist, and young Travis began playing at age six at a local Baptist church. As a teenager, he formed his own trio and played at clubs. He graduated from Du Sable High School in 1939 and found great difficulty getting a job, since many employers at the time refused to hire black people. He actually paid $10 to be hired as a porter and later cleaned toilets for $11.20 a week at the Apex Box Company.

In 1942, Travis joined the army and became a band conductor for the United Service Organizations (USO), until a sergeant insisted that Travis pay him a half-pint of whiskey each week, a demand that Travis refused. As a punishment, Travis was transferred to Shenango, in western Pennsylvania, a completely segregated (separated by race) facility. At one point, white troops actually fired on black solders, with Travis shot twice and the man next to him killed instantly. The incident led to several more transfers, landing him finally at Maryland's Aberdeen Proving Grounds, where he was made manager of the post exchange, won the Best Manager's Award, and became the first black man there to have white people working for him.

In 1946, Travis left the army and tried to enter college on the G.I. Bill, a program to help returning veterans go to college. To his dismay, he discovered that the education he had received at his high school was completely inferior and no college would accept him as a student. He managed to enter various two-year colleges while working at the stockyards and preparing tax returns until he was finally eligible to enter Roosevelt, from which he graduated in 1949, the same year in which he married his wife, Moselynne.

After toying with the idea of becoming a lawyer, Travis decided that black people could make more money in real estate, since most black lawyers at the time could only enter small-time criminal defense work. He became a broker, borrowing half of the $50 fee from his mother. He did not make his first sale until May 1950, but he was a superlative salesman and soon began to prosper.

African Americans faced difficulties in the real estate market of that time, however, for most banks and insurance companies would not finance their mortgages—including those insurance companies who made millions of dollars from black customers. As a result, black homeowners often had to take "land contracts," under which if a family missed even one payment, they could be evicted and lose their entire investment.

In 1953, Travis formed the Sivart (Travis spelled backward) Mortgage Company to help make mortgages available to African Americans. He sent thousands of letters to black families whose homes were being torn down in urban renewal programs, offering to find them homes in white neighborhoods, while writing to white residents offering to sell their homes to black buyers.

Real estate tycoon Dempsey Travis is also a noted author and Chicago community leader. (Courtesy of Dempsey Travis)

His actions were controversial, not only because of his involvement in urban renewal but also because many white people at the time panicked at the very thought of black people moving into their neighborhoods, quickly offering to sell their homes at bargain prices.

Nevertheless, Travis prospered with his so-called blockbusting activities, and he continued to fight to make mortgages available to African Americans. He served as president of the Dearborn Real Estate Board and of the local chapter of the National Association for the Advancement of Colored People (NAACP). He also helped organize Martin Luther King, Jr.'s first Chicago protest march in 1960. Also in the 1960s, Travis helped found Seaway National Bank.

Travis saw a kind of victory when President John F. Kennedy, elected in 1960, appointed an African-American secretary of housing and urban development (HUD), Robert C. Weaver, followed by an executive order mandating that federal housing agencies stop discriminating against black people as they offered mortgages. Since black bankers were not allowed to join the all-white Mortgage Bankers Association, Travis responded in 1961 by organizing the United Mortgage Bankers of America for black bankers to increase their influence. Not until the late 1960s did the Mortgage Bankers Association open its ranks to black members.

Travis continued to seek financing for his own mortgage business, obtaining funds in 1960 from the black-owned insurance company Chicago Metropolitan Assurance, and in 1962 from the International Ladies Garment Workers Union. He went on to get funding from the Central National Bank, Equitable Life Assurance, the New York Bank for Savings, and a number of other white-owned businesses.

In 1972, HUD's policies changed and Travis became unable to obtain their approval for some of his low-income housing projects. He accused the federal agency of favoring development in the suburbs over urban development, a policy that siphoned more federal funds to white people at black people's expense. In response, he tried to get middle-income black people to move back to the inner city, proposing a kind of black self-help that appealed to few well-off black people at the time. Some people saw his focus on black neighborhoods as a kind of segregation in reverse, while others saw it as a version of black empowerment.

Meanwhile, Travis had become enormously successful and was making some $15 million a year in real estate and insurance business. His Travis Realty Company was the city's largest black-owned real estate firm, and his influence increased with the election of Mayor Harold Washington, one of Travis's boyhood friends, who appointed him head of the mayor's real estate review committee. Seaway also received a boost from Washington's election, loaning $149,000 to the mayor's campaign in 1983 and then expanding rapidly after his victory (by the 1990s, it was the largest black-owned bank in the United States).

In 1995, Travis received Ameritech's Small Business Community Service Award and in the same year was inducted into the Junior Achievement Chicago Business Community Hall of Fame. He has been a financial editor of *Dollars and Sense* magazine and a contributing writer for *Ebony* and *Black Scholar*.

Further Reading

"Developer Dempsey Travis Starts $15 mi. Townhouse Complex in Chicago, Ill." *Jet*, December 17, 1990, p. 13.

Dwyer, Ann. "Chicago Police." *Crain's Chicago Business*, November 19, 1996, p. 50.

Travis, Dempsey J. *An Autobiography of Black Chicago*. Chicago, Ill.: Academy Chicago Publications, 1999.

———. Dempsey Travis website. Available online. URL: http://www.dempseytravis.com. Downloaded on January 11, 2003.

———. *I Refuse to Learn to Fail: The Autobiography of Dempsey J. Travis*. Chicago, Ill.: Urban Research Press, 1992.

———. *Racism: Revolves Like a Merry-Go-Round*. Chicago, Ill.: Urban Research Press, 2002.

Turnbo-Malone, Annie Minerva (Annie Turnbo Malone)

(1869–1957) *beauty products manufacturer, beauty college founder*

Annie Turnbo-Malone is the earliest recorded female self-made millionaire. She made her fortune by pioneering beauty products for African-American women. The better-known MADAME C. J. WALKER actually imitated Turnbo-Malone's products as well as her business organization, and indeed, Walker got her start as a sales agent for Turnbo-Malone's products. Turnbo-Malone was also a pioneering black philanthropist who gave huge sums to black colleges, orphanages, and other charities.

Annie Minerva Turnbo was born August 9, 1869, in Metropolis, Illinois, the daughter of Robert and Isabella (Cook) Turnbo, farmers who may have once been enslaved. The family believed that Robert Turnbo had served with the Union army, while his wife and children fled slavery in Kentucky; the family was later reunited in Metropolis, where Turnbo grew up as the second youngest of 11 children, raised by her brothers and sisters when her parents died. She attended public elementary schools in Metropolis and public high school in Peoria, Illinois, where she went to live with a married sister. During her high school years, however, she suffered from an illness that caused her to withdraw from school, which she never finished.

In 1900, while living in the all-black town of Lovejoy, Illinois (now known as Brooklyn), Turnbo began to make and sell "Wonderful Hair Grower," a product designed to help hair grow. She went on to develop hair straighteners as well, since the products available at the time were either homemade—grease, lard, and the like—or chemicals that induced burning and damaged the user's hair. Turnbo worked at home on her own to come up with a better formula, drawing on her own studies of chemistry.

In 1902, she moved to St. Louis, which included a thriving black middle-class community—a logical place for Turnbo to make and sell her beauty products, which were part of an entire vision of beauty that included "ladylike" behavior and elegance. The black business community of St. Louis was also conducive to Turnbo's business, which relied upon a network of sales agents who in effect ran their own individual enterprises selling her products.

Turnbo was enterprising in her efforts to get her business started. Because the standard retail and wholesale distribution channels of the time were closed to African Americans, Turnbo found other ways to reach potential customers. Working with three assistants, she went door to door selling her products. If a woman was interested, Turnbo offered a free hair and scalp treatment to further convince the customer to make a purchase. In 1903, Turnbo married a Mr. Pope—no information is available for his first name—but she filed for divorce soon after, citing his interference in her business as a cause.

The St. Louis World's Fair brought Turnbo a certain amount of acclaim, on which she capitalized in 1904 with a huge advertising campaign. She also toured the South, reaching out to African-American women as both customers and sales agents. So many people imitated her that she renamed her company in 1906 with the copyrighted trade name "Poro," a Mende (West African) word that refers to an organization dedicated to enhancing the body physically and spiritually.

By 1910, Turnbo's company was doing so well that she moved to larger quarters. Although she had a number of competitors, her system of franchising sales agents was the most efficient, and her company was selling better than the others.

In 1914, she married Aaron Eugene Malone, a former teacher and traveling Bible salesman.

This marriage would eventually prove her undoing, as Malone seems to have struggled with Turnbo-Malone for control of her vast enterprise. For many years before their eventual divorce, he worked to build support for his own interests within the black community.

Meanwhile, however, Turnbo-Malone's business was flourishing. In 1918, she completed the construction of Poro College, a five-story factory and beauty-training school in one of St. Louis's most prestigious black neighborhoods, which included classrooms, auditorium, cafeteria, bakeshop, dormitory, guest rooms, roof garden, and offices, as well as facilities that could be rented by various organizations. In the racially segregated climate of the early 20th century, it was difficult for African-American groups to find elegant accommodations for their conventions and events, or even to eat at many of the city's restaurants or hotels; Poro College soon became a social center for the middle- and upper-middle-class black community in St. Louis as well as an educational institution. The National Negro Business League (NNBL)—founded by Booker T. Washington to promote black enterprise—chose the college for its headquarters in 1927, in part because Turnbo was an active member of the NNBL. Poro College was eventually known as the "Showplace of St. Louis."

In 1922, Turnbo added additional beauty products to her list: soaps, cold cream, and skin bleaches. Her products were eventually sold by almost 75,000 agents in Canada, the Philippines, Africa, and South America, as well as Baltimore, Maryland; Chicago, Illinois; Cleveland, Ohio; Detroit, Michigan; and Washington, D.C. She rewarded her agents with a diamond ring after five years service, as well as with other luxurious gifts. She also supported civil rights activities, including supporting the *Crisis*, a magazine founded by African-American activist W. E. B. DuBois. Although Du Bois and Washington were at odds politically, Turnbo seems to have found something to admire in each of them.

Turnbo was also a generous philanthropist who donated huge sums to a number of charities, including the St. Louis Colored Orphans' Home, which was later renamed the Annie Malone Children's Home. She gave to African-American branches of the Young Women's Christian Association (YWCA), and to black hospitals and old-age homes—all significant forces in St. Louis's black community.

Some people have criticized the kind of beauty culture that Turnbo-Malone and her imitators represented. They claimed that the hair straighteners and skin bleaches she and others promoted undermined black pride by promoting white standards of beauty. Others, including Turnbo-Malone herself, defended her work as helping black women feel better about how they looked and giving them easier, more convenient ways of taking care of themselves.

In 1927, Turnbo-Malone divorced her husband in a legal battle that split the black community. Malone claimed that it was his own business abilities that had made his wife's success possible, and he demanded half her assets. Poro College went into receivership (a system in which an institution is operated by a government-appointed "receiver"—a person, bank, or other institution). Black leaders in the Republican Party (then considered the party of Abraham Lincoln and civil rights) supported Malone, while black church leaders, the black press, Poro employees, and other national figures supported Turnbo-Malone, including Mary McLeod Bethune, the black educator and leader of the black club women's movement (a movement of middle-class women to form clubs that became active in civic affairs).

Eventually, Turnbo-Malone settled with her ex-husband out of court for a certain amount of cash and real estate (the total was not made public). Although she was legally entitled to run her business again, Turnbo-Malone left the scene of her difficulties by relocating to Chicago in 1930. There she bought a city block known as the Poro Block and started her enterprise again. Yet she was never able to repeat her former success. The depression of the 1930s meant that black customers had less money to spend, while competitors like Walker and SARAH SPENCER WASHINGTON cut into her business. In 1937, she lost a suit filed many years before by a former employee who claimed that he had been promised a share of the company's profits—a loss that required her to sell the St. Louis property.

Turnbo-Malone had also relied upon dishonest and incompetent managers who caused her to lose much of her fortune. She was also unwilling to pay all the taxes levied against her, and between 1933 and 1951, she was frequently sued, until the government eventually took over her business. She lost her Chicago property as well, although when she died on May 10, 1957, her fortune still totaled approximately $100,000, while Poro College operated in more than 30 cities.

Turnbo-Malone is still remembered through the May Day parade hosted by the Children's Home in St. Louis that bears her name, as well as by the many charities she helped support. She created a vision of black female entrepreneurship that changed the lives of thousands of African-American women and formed a central part of St. Louis's black community.

Further Reading

Byrd, Ayana D., and Lori L. Tharps. *Hair Story: Untangling the Roots of Black Hair in America.* New York: St. Martin's Press, 2001.

Herman, Steve. "Cosmetics: The Lost Years." *Global Cosmetic Industry* 166, no. 4 (April 2000), p. 54.

Porter, Gladys L. *Three Pioneers in Beauty Culture.* New York: Vantage Press, 1966.

Wilkerson, J. L. *Annie T. Malone: Story of Pride, Power, and Uplift.* Kansas City, Mo.: Acorn Books, 2003.

V

Vann, Robert Lee
(1879–1940) *publisher*

Robert Lee Vann is best known for publishing the *Pittsburgh Courier*, which, along with ROBERT SENGSTACKE ABBOTT's *Chicago Defender*, was one of the only national voices for African Americans before JOHN H. JOHNSON began publishing *Ebony* in 1945. The *Courier* helped to encourage the huge migration of black southerners to northern industrial cities such as Pittsburgh, as African Americans sought more economic opportunity as well as freedom from the intense discrimination and the violent lynchings of the U.S. South.

Vann was born on August 27, 1879, in Ahoskie, a tiny town in Hertford County, North Carolina. Nothing is known of his father, but his mother, Lucy Peoples, was the daughter of ex-slaves who ran a small local general store. When Vann was born, Peoples was working as a cook and housekeeper for the white Albert Vann family, and, as was the custom, gave her son their last name while keeping her own.

When Robert Vann was a few years old, Peoples married Joseph Hall, a field hand working on the farm where she was a cook. Hall deserted her and Robert, however, and when Robert was six, Peoples went on to work as a cook for an affluent family.

For a few years, Vann attended Springfield Colored School, a local elementary school for African Americans. In 1892, Peoples married John Simon, a local farmer. Vann was unable to continue school because he was expected to work on his stepfather's farm.

In 1895, Vann began working as janitor and part-time clerk at a nearby post office, which enabled him to save enough money to leave home and get an education. He attended the Waters Training School in Winston, North Carolina, a Baptist institution, whose tuition he paid by working as a waiter in Boston during the summers or taking a summer off to labor in the local tobacco fields. In 1901, he graduated Waters at the head of his class and went on to Wayland Academy in Richmond, Virginia. In 1902, he enrolled in Richmond's Virginia Union University. He also met JOHN MITCHELL, JR., the *Richmond Planet*'s editor and publisher.

In 1903, Vann graduated from Virginia Union—but he felt that he still had not received an adequate education, partly because he had attended only all-black colleges, which he thought were not the equal of mainstream white schools. He won a scholarship to Western University of Pennsylvania (now the University of Pittsburgh), where he was one of the only black students. He won renown there as an orator, debator, and editor of the school newspaper.

When he graduated in 1906, he was also chosen class poet. To support himself, he worked summers at a resort in Bar Harbor, Maine.

In the 1906 election, Vann worked for the local Republican Party machine. In those days, the Republican Party was considered the party of Abraham Lincoln and civil rights. Vann's association with the Republican Party lasted until 1932, when, like many African Americans, he switched his allegiance to President Franklin Delano Roosevelt and the social programs he offered.

Meanwhile, in 1906, Vann had finally gotten his B.A. He received a law degree from the University of Pittsburgh in 1909 but found it difficult to make money as a lawyer. White people would not turn to a black lawyer, and even black clients went to white lawyers for large and serious cases.

In 1910, Vann married Jessie E. Matthews. He also got involved with the *Pittsburgh Courier* when a group of Pittsburgh African Americans asked him to draw up the incorporation papers for their new venture, which they basically intended as a vehicle to publish the poems of a local worker at the H.J. Heinz pickle factory. Later that year, Vann became the *Courier's* publisher and editor for a salary of $100 a year, to be paid in *Courier* stock.

The *Courier* was Pittsburgh's only black newspaper, despite the city's sizable black population. By 1914, Vann had gotten the paper into fairly good shape, and he hired Ira Lewis as his full-time aide. Vann provided a forum for African-American issues, especially important at a time when the white press either ignored African Americans or promoted negative images of them.

Vann took on a number of crusades, protesting segregation on public transportation, in restaurants and theaters, and in other public places. Indeed, in 1915, partly as a result of his pressure, the state legislature passed a law outlawing such discrimination, but the governor vetoed it. Vann continued to press—unsuccessfully—for such legislation until 1923.

Meanwhile, in 1917, Vann was made assistant city solicitor at a respectable salary, as a reward for the work he had done to help elect Republican candidates. Lewis received a clerkship in the sheriff's office.

Most African-American papers criticized U.S. involvement in World War I, seeing that war as a fight between two European factions who were both at fault. The *Courier* endorsed the war and suppressed the news of black soldiers rioting in Houston in 1917 over the poor treatment they had received. In 1919, when the U.S. government was investigating so-called Communist conspiracies in a number of areas, the *Courier* took a strong pro-government stance. This conservative position meant that, unlike other African-American and political groups, the *Courier* was never investigated.

Vann was doing well with the *Courier*, but he was not yet rich—and that was at least partly his goal. He tried to start a glossy, illustrated magazine for a national audience, but *The Competitor: The National Magazine* survived for only a brief time. In 1936, a white version of the magazine, *Life*, became extremely successful, and in 1945, Johnson's *Ebony* played that role in the black community, so perhaps Vann had merely been ahead of his time.

In 1925, Vann supported efforts to invest on Africa's Gold Coast, inspired by the back-to-Africa movement of Marcus Garvey. These attempts were unsuccessful, as were Vann's efforts to start a black-owned bank in Pittsburgh.

During the 1920s, Vann made several key improvements in the *Courier*, notably, hiring the white-owned Michael B. Ziff Company, an advertising broker that worked for many black-owned papers. Ziff brought in ads from nationally known white companies, which contributed both revenue and an aura of respectability to the *Courier*. Vann also engaged in a number of crusades: a protest against the popular radio show *Amos 'n' Andy*, which he accused of using black stereotypes; support for Marcus Garvey's campaign for black and African pride; and promotion of Joe Louis, the heavyweight fighter who symbolized

Publisher Robert Lee Vann's *Pittsburgh Courier* was one of the few national voices for African Americans during the years before World War II. *(Carnegie Library of Pittsburgh)*

that black people could indeed defeat white opponents, even if only in the boxing ring. He also pressed for better treatment of African Americans in the armed forces, including more black officers to command the segregated units of black soldiers.

Vann continued to support the Republican Party until 1932, when he made a famous speech at a Cleveland rally, in which he advocated that African Americans switch their allegiance from Republican to Democrat. "I see millions of Negroes turning the picture of Lincoln to the wall," he said famously, evoking the legacy of

Abraham Lincoln that most black people still associated with the Republican Party. Vann was rewarded with the position of special assistant to the U.S. attorney general in Washington, D.C., a post he held until 1935. He eventually became disillusioned with the national Democratic Party and turned to local Democrats instead.

Local white businesspeople began giving Vann a measure of respect and acclaim. In 1937, he was elected vice president of Allegheny County's Associated Weekly Publishers. In 1939, after having tried unsuccessfully to join the Pittsburgh Chamber of Commerce for many years, he was finally invited to join.

In 1940, Vann was operated on for abdominal cancer, a disease of which he died on October 24, 1940. After his death, the *Courier* had a checkered career, but it is still published, under the name *The New Pittsburgh Courier.* Meanwhile, Robert Vann is remembered as the man who helped create a national voice for African Americans.

Further Reading

Birmingham-Pittsburgh Traveler Newspapers. "The Old Pittsburgh Courier." North by South. Available online. URL: http://www.northbysouth. org/2000/Media/Old%20Courier/OPC%20Page.ht m. Downloaded on February 7, 2003.

————. "Robert L. Vann." North by South. Available online. URL: http://www.northbysouth.org/2000/ Media/Kyle's%20stuff/Robert%20Vann.htm. Downloaded on February 7, 2003.

Buni, Andrew. *Robert L. Vann of the Pittsburgh Courier.* Pittsburgh, Pa.: University of Pittsburgh Press, 1974.

The Black Press: Soldiers Without Swords "Newspapers: The Pittsburgh Courier." PBS Online. Available online. URL: http://www.pbs.org/blackpress/ news_bios/courier.html. Downloaded on February 7, 2003.

Walker, Antonio Maceo
(1909–1994) *insurance executive*

Antonio Maceo Walker's family arrived in Memphis as newcomers in the early 1920s and went on to rise to the top of the city's African-American elite, controlling the city's largest black business and one of the largest black-owned companies in the nation: Universal Life Insurance. The Walker family was in a sense the successor to the family of ROBERT REED CHURCH, SR., which had begun to dominate the Memphis black elite during Reconstruction.

Antonio Maceo Walker was the son of Joseph Edison Walker, a doctor, president of the Delta Penny Savings Bank, and the third president of the Mississippi Life Insurance Company, a position he assumed in 1917, when Antonio was eight. However, this company was based in Indianola, Mississippi, where the climate was increasingly hostile to black people. The elder Walker moved to Memphis in 1920, seeking more opportunity. He organized the Universal Life Insurance Company and opened for business on September 6, 1923.

Antonio, meanwhile, had been born on June 7, 1909, in Indianola, where he attended elementary schools, and moved with his parents to Memphis, where he attended LeMoyne Institute, now LeMoyne Owen College. He went on to get a bachelor's degree from Fisk University, in Nashville, and then to enroll as the only black graduate student at New York University, where he graduated with an M.B.A.

He also enrolled at the University of Michigan, where he studied actuarial science. Actuarial science lies at the heart of the insurance industry. When a person buys a life insurance policy, the company figures out how long that person can be expected to live and to pay premiums. The rate of the premiums is based on the length of time that the company expects to receive them. If the company imagines that a person will live to age 65 and he or she dies at age 50, the company has lost 15 years of expected income. So actuarial tables, which predict how long people are likely to live based on their age, health, and other factors, are crucial for making insurance profitable.

During his school vacations, Walker was a field auditor for his father's company, and when he finished school, he became an actuary there— the second black actuary in the nation, and the first black M.B.A. in Tennessee. One of Walker's first contributions to the company was to revise its actuarial tables. Since black people at the time had shorter lives than white people by about seven or eight years, Walker realized that using the tables developed by white companies would cost his company money: Black customers were not living long enough to pay as many premiums as they were supposed to. He recalculated the tables, and the company began doing better financially.

In 1944, Walker implemented a data-processing system for Universal Life, an innovative feature for companies at the time. In 1946, he helped found Tri-State Bank as another means by which the insurance company could invest its funds. Tri-State is still in operation today.

In 1952, Walker took over as president from his father and began to expand the company. He tried to win a larger share of the Memphis area market for Universal Life and, to that end, increased the sales force. He also invested some of the company's assets in bonds, and began offering mortgage loans for homes and churches. Again, this was part of the traditional role played by many black insurance companies, who amassed capital through selling insurance policies and then put that capital back into the black community through loans, the founding of banks, and other types of investment, enabling African Americans to own homes and businesses that white financial institutions would not have financed.

Universal Life also acquired a number of other insurance companies: Excelsior Life of Dallas in 1958; Louisiana Life of New Orleans in 1961; Richmond Beneficial Life of Richmond, Virginia, in 1963; Afro-American Texas Debits in 1975; and Union Protective of Memphis in 1980.

The Walkers had always supported civil rights and black equality. When the National Association for the Advancement of Colored People (NAACP) opened its Memphis chapter early in the century, the group got free office space at Universal Life. Throughout the 1950s and 1960s, Antonio Walker and the company he headed supported the Civil Rights movement. Walker provided bail money for political leaders, supported the 1964 integration of formerly all-white Memphis State University, and offered funds to qualified African-American students who wanted to attend the school. He also was the first African

American to sit in the "all-white" section of Memphis's Malco Theater. His company has financed three low-income housing projects, including one named for Walker's father, the J. E. Walker Housing Projects, served by the nearby J. E. Walker School.

In 1961, J. E. Walker was appointed to the all-white Transit Authority. He, Antonio Walker, and other colleagues organized the Non-Partisan Voters' Registration Club to build black voting strength. In 1973, the NAACP named Antonio Walker "Man of the Year." In 1979, Universal Life invested $200,000 in a pilot project to help six black colleges increase their endowments (the funds that colleges invest so that they can use the dividends and interest for their activities).

In 1983, Walker stepped down as president of Universal Life to be succeeded by Patricia Walker Shaw, his daughter, the first woman to head a major U.S. life insurance company. Walker remained with the company as chairman of the board. However, in 1985, Shaw died of cancer, and Walker took over as president at age 75, a position that he continued to hold until G. T. Howell took over in 1990. Walker was not idle during his last five years in the presidency, however: In 1986, he bought Security Life Insurance of Jackson, Mississippi, for $2 million.

Walker was always a strong supporter of racial integration, yet his company has only black policyholders, while 98 percent of Tri-State Bank's customers are black, as are all the employees at both companies. To some extent, this is a legacy of the South's overwhelming history of segregation (separation by race). It is also true that insurance companies who traditionally serve black customers charge higher premiums based on their customers' shorter life expectancy, and that Walker's businesses may pay lower salaries than elsewhere in Memphis.

Walker remained chairman of the board of Universal Life until his death on June 8, 1994, holding the same position at Tri-State Bank. His death merited an extensive front-page obituary in

Memphis's main paper, the *Commercial Appeal*—a tribute to his significance as a community leader.

Further Reading

Ingham, John, and Lynne B. Feldman. *African American Business Leaders: A Biographical Dictionary*. Westport, Conn.: Greenwood Press, 1994, pp. 655–670.

Robinson, Quintin, and Lela Garlington. "Civil Leader, Businessman Maceo Walker Is Dead at 85." *Commercial Appeal*, June 9, 1994, p. A1.

Walker, Madame C. J.
(C. J. Walker, Sarah Breedlove Walker, Sarah Breedlove McWilliams Walker, Sarah Walker)
(1867–1919) *hair-care products manufacturer*

Madame C. J. Walker was born into a poor family and was a washerwoman until she was 38. By the time she died at age 51, she had built one of the most successful black-owned businesses ever seen in the United States. Her company enabled thousands of African-American women to make new lives for themselves as sales agents with her company, as well as transforming how African-American women viewed themselves and their appearance.

Sarah Breedlove was born on December 23, 1867, in Delta, Louisiana, the daughter of Owen and Minerva Breedlove. The Breedloves were former slaves who had become sharecroppers—farmers who worked on other people's land in exchange for most of the crop they raised. The family was very poor, and Walker worked in the cotton fields as a child, and later as an adult.

By the time Sarah was seven, both of her parents had died, and she went to live with her older sister, Louvenia, who worked as a maid. A few years later, Louvenia's family moved to Vicksburg, Mississippi, taking Sarah with them. Sarah was given an extremely limited education, and Lou-

venia's husband was often cruel to her. At age 14, Sarah married Moses McWilliams, mainly to escape an intolerable situation. In 1885, at age 18, she gave birth to Lelia, who later called herself A'Lelia. In 1887, Moses McWilliams was killed—perhaps lynched during a race riot—and the 20-year-old Sarah was left to care for her daughter by herself.

Opportunities for African Americans in the late 19th-century South were extremely limited. The South was an impoverished region by this time, and African Americans faced an enormous number of political and social restrictions. Sarah McWilliams decided to leave Mississippi and went up the river to St. Louis, Missouri, where a network of black-owned businesses and black professionals offered new opportunities to African Americans.

St. Louis was also home to the National Association of Colored Women, which ran an orphanage and had a day-care center for working women. The day-care center helped McWilliams care for her daughter and eventually made it possible for her to send A'Lelia to Knoxville College, a black private school in Tennessee.

Sarah McWilliams had to work extremely hard in St. Louis, and she often put in 14- to 16-hour days, six or seven days a week, washing clothes in harsh chemical solutions that burned her skin and caused her to lose her hair. She began to wonder whether she might come up with a product that would help hair to grow. After her daughter left home, she developed a formula that she always kept a closely guarded secret. She herself claimed to have received it in a dream from an African man, whereas other more cynical observers suggested that she had simply stolen the formula from ANNIE MINERVA TURNBO-MALONE's Poro Company.

Sarah McWilliams herself claimed to have been more interested in helping hair to grow than in straightening hair. In any case, in 1905, she began selling her formula door to door in St. Louis. A few months later, she moved to Denver,

Colorado, where her recently widowed sister-in-law was living. She began working in a laundry once more, selling her products house-to-house in her spare time. She also met Charles J. Walker, a reporter and publicist, whom she married and who helped her with what was to become an extensive advertising campaign. Charles Walker suggested that she call herself Madame C. J. Walker, to give the products a respectable air and to keep from being referred to as "Aunt Sarah." In those days, it was often difficult for African Americans to assure themselves of being called "Mr.," "Mrs.," or "Miss," as opposed to being referred to by their first names or as "Aunt" or "Uncle." "Madame C. J. Walker" was assured of being treated with more respect.

The Walkers were successful in Denver, with Charles handling the advertising and promotion as Sarah sold door to door. She also trained agents—whom she called "hair culturists" or "scalp culturists"—who taught customers her methods and sold them her products. Through this system of agents—also initially developed by Turnbo-Malone—Walker expanded her business rapidly while giving the agents a chance to earn income for themselves at a new kind of work for black women.

As Turnbo-Malone had done before her, Walker toured the South and the East, reaching out to black women at churches, homes, and schools. In 1906, she put her daughter in charge of mail-order operations in Pittsburgh, where she herself moved in 1908. Madame Walker and A'Lelia founded the Lelia College, where for $25 women could receive lessons in the Walker method through the mail.

In 1910, Walker relocated her company to Indianapolis, where she built a large manufacturing plant, and eventually, a laboratory and a beauty school. Separated from her husband, in 1912 she divorced him, claiming that he had too limited a vision of what her company might become. She, had big plans, and she worked long hours every day to fulfill them, developing a full line of hair products and educating her agents and customers about personal hygiene (cleanliness) and care for their appearance.

When Walker met Freeman B. Ransom, a Columbia law student who was working as a train porter, she hired him to run the manufacturing plant and supervise the administrative side of the business in Indianapolis. A'Lelia then moved to New York City, opening another Lelia College and expanding business on the East Coast.

Walker started to organize her agents into clubs that did charitable work, known as Walker Clubs, with prizes to the clubs that accomplished the most. She brought her sales agents together at national conventions that served as motivational sessions as well as a chance for women to meet other professional black women and to travel a bit. Although her company was run as a business, Walker thought of it as a family, with herself as the mother. She also saw herself and her company as having a duty to the African-American community. Thus she took stands against lynching, while supporting black women's right to become educated and involved in the business world. She moved her sales agents to take political stands as well: In 1917, they sent a telegram to President Woodrow Wilson, asking him to make lynching a federal crime.

The Walker company offered various types of protection to its agents. For example, women paid 25 cents per month membership dues, and then when they died, they received $50 towards funeral expenses. Women were also encouraged to see their appearance as a source of pride—though this was a controversial point, then and later. Both contemporaries and those who came afterwards have criticized Walker for promoting white standards of beauty, encouraging African-American women to straighten their hair so that they would look more like white women. Walker herself saw her work as uplifting African-American women and instilling a sense of race pride.

Walker worked occasionally with Booker T. Washington and the National Negro Business

League (NNBL), which Washington had founded to promote black enterprise. Although Walker was a successful businesswoman by the time she first attended an annual NNBL convention, she was treated with a marked lack of respect, largely because she was a woman who ran a women's business. Eventually, however, the convention acknowledged her, and she won Washington's endorsement, as she had hoped.

Walker also worked with the National Association of Colored Women, the organization led by Mary McLeod Bethune. Walker and Bethune became close friends, and Walker made substantial donations to Bethune's Cookman College for women in Florida.

Walker took a wide variety of political stands. She and MAGGIE LENA WALKER were both part of a delegation to Washington, D.C., to protest President Wilson's efforts to segregate employees within the federal government. She protested segregation on the local, national, and international levels, and she supported the National Association for the Advancement of Colored People (NAACP). She also donated large sums of money to many charities, with particular interest in setting up a school for girls in West Africa.

As her wealth increased, Walker bought more property, including building a luxurious mansion for herself in Irvington, New Jersey, then a country town near New York City. Meanwhile, though, she suffered from health problems, including hypertension, kidney failure, and exhaustion from the long hours she worked. In 1919, while visiting St. Louis, she became very sick and died on May 25, 1919.

Further Reading

Bundles, A'Lelia. *On Her Own Ground: The Life and Times of Madam C. J. Walker.* New York: Scribner, 2001.

Byrd, Ayana D., and Lori L. Tharps. *Hair Story: Untangling the Roots of Black Hair in America.* New York: St. Martin's Press, 2001.

Haskins, Jim. *Black Stars: African American Entrepreneurs.* New York: John Wiley & Sons, 1998, pp. 63–66.

Herman, Steve. "Cosmetics: The Lost Years." *Global Cosmetic Industry* 166, no. 4 (April 2000): 54.

Lommel, Cookie. *Madame C. J. Walker.* Los Angeles: Holloway House Publishers, 1999.

Peiss, Kathy. *Hope in a Jar: The Making of America's Beauty Culture.* New York: Henry Holt, 1998.

Porter, Gladys L. *Three Pioneers in Beauty Culture.* New York: Vantage Press, 1966.

Walker, Maggie Lena
(Maggie Draper, Maggie Mitchell)
(1867–1934) *banker, philanthropist, civic leader*

Maggie Lena Walker was the founder of one of the most successful black banks in the United States, as well as the leader of a religious order that helped to support the political, social, and economic needs of African-American women for many years. The first woman bank president in the United States of any race, Walker achieved renown as a leader in racial affairs, civic matters, and local business.

Maggie was born on July 16, 1867, in Richmond, Virginia, the daughter of Elizabeth Draper, a former house slave and at that time a cook in the home of Elizabeth Van Lew, one of the few white Southern abolitionists (opponents of slavery) and reportedly a conductor on the Underground Railroad, the informal network of people dedicated to helping enslaved people escape to freedom. Family legend had it that Maggie's father was Eccles Cuthbert, a Northern abolitionist and writer, though little is known for sure. Van Lew, meanwhile, was the local postmistress. Draper married William Mitchell, a butler who worked for Van Lew.

When Mitchell became a headwaiter at the St. Charles Hotel, he moved his family from the Van Lew household to a small cottage on a street that was later named Maggie Mitchell Alley in

Walker's honor. There, Maggie's mother gave birth to a son, John. A few years later, Mitchell disappeared. His body was found a few days later, floating in the James River, the apparent victim of a robbery and murder.

Maggie's mother had to work full-time as a laundress to support her family, with Maggie caring for her brother. She was able to attend Lancaster School, however, a local elementary school for African-American children across the street from the jail. Reportedly, the southern white women who taught there were remarkably free of the prejudice that characterized other parts of the community, and Maggie received a reasonably good education.

At age 11, Maggie became a Baptist. She went on to teach Sunday School. At age 14, she joined the Independent Order of St. Luke, a women's organization with which she would be active for the rest of her life, engaging in numerous civic and entrepreneurial activities for the benefit of her community.

Meanwhile, she went to Armstrong Normal School, a black high school whose graduation ceremonies were held at a local black church, while the white school's ceremony was held in the city theater. Maggie led a protest against the segregation, which eventually resulted in the black school's graduation ceremony being held in the school's auditorium.

Maggie then taught at Lancaster School for three years while studying accounting and working part-time for the Women's Union, an insurance company. In 1886, she married Armstead Walker, a man involved in his father's construction business, with whom she eventually had two surviving sons, Russell and Melvin. The custom of the time expected Maggie Mitchell to stay home and raise her family—but Mitchell had too much energy and ambition to be satisfied with such a private life. She turned to the Order of St. Luke as an acceptable outlet for her energies.

The Order had been founded in 1867 as a women's group, though eventually men were admitted, too. Walker later became a national deputy to the group, and in 1889, three years after her marriage, was made executive secretary. In 1895, she organized a juvenile branch to focus on the problems of youth.

In 1901, Walker called for the group to sell burial insurance, collecting small amounts from members in exchange for a guarantee that their funeral expenses would be paid. Walker was inspired by the work of WILLIAM WASHINGTON BROWNE and his Order of True Reformers. She also helped found the *St. Luke Herald*, which became an influential local paper.

While still a high school student, Maggie Lena Walker protested segregation in her hometown, before going on to become a teacher. *(Courtesy of National Park Service, Maggie L. Walker National Historic Site)*

In 1903, Walker helped organize the St. Luke Penny Savings Bank, intended to help poor black women save their small wages and, eventually, to use both their savings and the bank's mortgage funds to acquire homes of their own. Depositors in the bank were encouraged not only to start savings accounts but also to buy a share of the bank themselves, at $10, so they could be part-owners of the institution that held their money. Walker said that the bank would "take nickels and turn them into dollars."

In 1904, the *Herald* joined JOHN MITCHELL, JR.'s, *Richmond Planet* in fighting the segregation (separation by race) of passengers on the local streetcar system. Segregation and discriminatory legislation against African Americans was common during this period throughout the South, as part of the backlash against the improved political and economic status that black people had achieved during Reconstruction. Black people fought the trend to restrict them to separate accommodations in public places, but they were often unsuccessful. Walker, Mitchell, and their followers resisted the white community's effort to insist on separate seating on local streetcars, but they ultimately lost that fight. Undaunted, the *Herald* continued to come out against lynching, restricted educational opportunities for black people, and many other forms of discrimination.

In 1905, the Order of St. Luke established the St. Luke Emporium, a department store intended to provide affordable products to black women, employ black women as clerks, and educate black women about business. The store eventually closed, a failure that some blamed on managerial incompetence. Others, however, pointed to the efforts of local white businesses to crush the store, as part of white opposition to all black-owned businesses.

In 1906, Walker fell and broke her kneecap, which eventually meant she had to resort to a wheelchair. Nevertheless, she remained extremely active. Her *St. Luke's Herald* often worked with Mitchell's *Planet* on various political crusades, but

Maggie Lena Walker was the first woman bank president in the United States. *(Courtesy of National Park Service, Maggie L. Walker National Historic Site)*

sometimes the two publications were at odds, particularly after 1910, when Mitchell's True Reformers Bank failed, even as Walker's Penny Savings Bank succeeded.

Like the Emporium, the bank employed many black women, as did the St. Luke's office and a local shop set up to make uniforms and insignia for St. Luke's. Walker and other St. Luke's women also joined with the National Association of Wage Earners, a group intended to unite housewives and women who worked outside the home in a common effort to improve the economic status of black women. And in 1912, Walker founded and headed the Richmond Council of Colored Women, a fund-raising group for such institutions as the Girl's Industrial School in Peaks, Virginia, and the Community House in Richmond, with the motto "Lifting as we climb."

In 1915, Walker dealt with a personal tragedy—her son, Russell, mistook his father for a burglar, and accidentally shot and killed him. After two exhausting trials, Russell was cleared, but he died the following year. Meanwhile, the rival *Planet* published allegations of foul play, which made trouble for Walker within the Order of St. Luke.

Nevertheless, throughout the 1920s, Walker worked to promote black and women's suffrage (voting). The local voter registration drive that she helped organize was so successful that in 1920, the first election in which women were allowed to vote, some 80 percent of local black voters were women. Walker was also president of the Virginia chapter of the National Association for the Advancement of Colored People (NAACP) and a board member of the National Association of Colored Women's Clubs. In addition, she helped found the Negro Organization Society, a group focused on the black community's health needs.

During the Great Depression of the 1930s, Walker engineered the merger of her bank with the Second Street Savings Bank and the Commercial Bank and Trust Company, under the name of the Consolidated Bank and Trust Company. Walker served as chair of this bank's board until her death of diabetic gangrene on December 15, 1934.

Walker was mourned at one of the largest funerals in Richmond's history, and she continues to be honored by the African-American community. In 1979, her home was made a national historic site and museum, and in the 1980s and 1990s, she received increasing attention as an historical figure who had been a pioneer of the "womanism" that Alice Walker and other black feminists would promote several decades after her death.

Further Reading

Branch, Muriel Miller, and Dorothy Marie Rice. *Pennies to Dollars: The Story of Maggie Lena Walker.* North Haven, Conn.: Linnet Books, 1997.

Haskins, Jim. *Black Stars: African American Entrepreneurs.* New York: John Wiley & Sons, 1998, pp. 69–73.

National Park Service and Susie Sernaker. "Maggie L. Walker." National Park Service: Park Net. Available online. URL: http://www.nps.gov/malw/home.htm. Last updated July 12, 2000.

Scott, Robert C. "Bobby." "Women's History Month Remarks by Congressman Robert C. Scott, March 27, 2001: Maggie Lena Walker." U.S. House of Representatives website. Available online. URL: http://www.house.gov/scott/remarks_maggie_walker.htm. Posted March 27, 2001.

Virginia Historical Society. "Education: Learn About Virginia: Maggie Lena Walker." Virginia Historical Society website. Available online. URL: http://www.vahistorical.org/education/maggiewalker.htm. Downloaded on February 7, 2003.

Walker, Sarah Breedlove McWilliams   See WALKER, MADAME C. J.

Warren, Renee E.   See POE, KIRSTEN N. and RENEE E. WARREN.

Washington, Alonzo
(1967–   ) *comic book company owner*

Alonzo Washington has combined social activism with entrepreneurship through the comic books he produces, which he creates in order to provide positive role models for black youth. In 2002 his firm Omega7, Inc., became the first black-owned comic company to reach its 10-year anniversary.

Alonzo Washington was born on June 1, 1967, in Kansas City, Kansas, the son of Grover Washington, a retailer, and Millie Washington, a teacher. He loved comic books and began collecting them by age 10. By age 12, he realized that the black characters that appeared in the comics he read were all either stupid or criminal, whereas the positive characters were uniformly white. He responded by creating his own comic characters, many of which became the basis for the characters he writes about today. He would also buy action figures and press homemade clay Afros onto their heads, paint their faces, and then sell them to local children, to whom he also sold his homemade comics.

Washington attended Catholic elementary school and public high school, from which he graduated in 1985. At the age of 16, he formed the Black National Congress, a group intended to keep young African-American men out of gangs. He also took part in a two-year course called the KC Media Project, which helped him realize that he could affect society by making his voice heard through the media. He went on to Kansas City Community College and then to Pioneer Community College in Penn Valley, Missouri, where he majored in liberal arts.

After his graduation in 1989, Washington began producing a community affairs show on a local cable station, in response to a chapter of the Ku Klux Klan that had recently begun producing a show of its own. He funded his show himself, with some help from local black businesses. He also began holding rallies among area youth and giving speeches to a number of local groups.

In 1992, Washington sold advance orders to finance the printing of his first comic book, "Original Man," a story about a black superhero and scientist who travels back from the future to fight criminals from another planet. Somehow he managed to scrape together the funds to print the first 3,000 copies, which he brought to a bookstore event in Kansas City, Missouri. He sold 1,000 comics in one afternoon, taking in $2,000; perhaps more importantly, he was featured in a *Newsweek* article that brought in orders from all over the country. His first issue ultimately garnered $30,000 in sales and he set up a permanent operation in his den.

Washington has gone on to create five more series, as well as a line of related products. Eventually, the Minneapolis-based Diamond Comic Distributors, Inc., began selling Washington's products,

as did United Brothers and Sisters Communications Systems. Although some retailers were reluctant to carry the politically minded comics, such mainstream groups as the Kansas City (Missouri) Police Department have used Washington's trading cards as part of their war on crime.

In 1997, Washington became the first black-owned comic entrepreneur to create an action figure, Omega Man. He went on to add related products such as T-shirts, cups, watches, clocks, and candy, as well as to create several other positive black characters, male and female. He continued to receive widespread media coverage, which helped him place his action figures into such major retailers as Toys 'R' Us, Kaybee, and Wal-Mart.

Comic-book author and publisher Alonzo Washington is the creator of such African-American superheroes as Original Man, Original Woman, and Omega Man. *(Dana D. Washington)*

In 2002 Washington made two additions to his product line: the Omega Man bobble-head doll and the Original Woman action figure. He has received extensive media coverage, both for his comics and for his social activism, which in 2002 included efforts to bring national attention to the plight of missing black children. He is married to Dana Washington, a consultant and health coordinator for the Red Cross who also works for Omega. The couple has six children.

Further Reading

Harris, Wendy. *Against All Odds, Ten Entrepreneurs Who Followed Their Hearts and Found Success.* New York: John Wiley & Sons, 2001, pp. 93–112.

Robinson, Bryan. "Coming to a 'Forgotten' Child's Rescue." ABCNews.com. Available online. URL: http://abcnews.go.com/sections/us/DailyNews/comics_missingkids020930.html. Posted September 30, 2002.

Shaffler, Rhonda. "Super Entrepreneur." CNN.com. Available online. URL: http://www.cnn.com/2000/books/news/08/17/omega.man. Posted August 17, 2000.

Walker, Jerry. "Local Entrepreneur/Community Activist Gains National Attention." The Call: Internet Edition. Available online. URL: http://www.kccall.com/news/2002/0927/KCK_Community/012.html. Posted September 27, 2002.

Washington, Alonzo. "Press Release—September 1, 2000: Black on Black Comic Book Violence." Omega 7 Inc. website. Available online. URL: http://www.omega7.com/html/PressRelease_09_01_00.html. Posted September 1, 2000.

Washington, Sarah Spencer
(Sara Spencer Washington)
(1889–1953) *hair-care entrepreneur*

Sarah Spencer Washington set up a hair-care system and related industries in Atlantic City, New Jersey, and around the world, following in the footsteps of beauty entrepreneurs MADAME C. J. WALKER and ANNIE MINERVA TURNBO-MALONE. One of the few black women millionaires of her time—or any time—she stood as a symbol of black achievement to African-American women across America.

Washington was born on June 6, 1889, in Berkley, Virginia, the daughter of Joshua and Ellen Douglass Phillips. She attended public schools in Berkley, going on to the Lincoln Preparatory School in Philadelphia, Pennsylvania, and Norfolk Mission College in Norfolk, Virginia. She also took classes in beauty culture in York, Pennsylvania, and later studied advanced chemistry at Columbia University in New York City.

Washington's career began in 1905, when she went to work as a dressmaker, an enterprise she maintained until 1913. Although her family wanted her to become a schoolteacher, she insisted upon entering the then-new field of beauty culture, opening a small hairdressing shop in Atlantic City in 1913. She worked as an operator in her own shop during the days while going door-to-door in the evenings, selling the beauty products that she herself had developed. She also developed her own beauty system, which she taught to other beauty operators.

In 1919 or 1920, Washington founded her own Apex News and Hair Company in Atlantic City, a beauty school that went on to establish branches across the country: in Manhattan and Brooklyn in New York City; Philadelphia; Chicago; Washington, D.C.; Atlanta, Georgia; Richmond, Virginia; Baltimore, Maryland; and Newark, New Jersey. She also founded international branches of her school, including an office in the Bantu World Bank in Johannesburg, South Africa. Each year, more than 25,000 students graduated from these schools.

From 1937 to 1939, Washington constructed her own laboratory in Atlantic City, where she made some 75 different products. Thus Washington had founded a kind of empire, in which beauty operators across the country learned to administer her system, using her products, while sales agents went door to door, also selling her products. Washington saw her system of agents as a public service, providing black women with a job that allowed them to become small entrepreneurs of a sort, selling her products on commission (for a percentage of the price).

Concerned about unemployment and seeking to provide as many jobs to the black community as possible, Washington opened a number of other ventures, including Apex Community Drug Store and Apex Rest and Tourist Home. Although the stock market crash of 1929 was hard on Washington, as on so many others, she was able to rebuild her company and thrive for the rest of her life. In 1939, she was awarded a medallion at the New York World's Fair for her achievements in international business.

Washington was a committed philanthropist (charitable giver), and she is credited with supporting a number of charities, including the Ellen P. Hunter home for Girls in Atlantic City, named for Washington's mother, and the Betty Bacharach Home for Children in Longport, New Jersey, an institution that helped children from many races. She donated 20 acres of her own farm in Egg Harbor, New Jersey, as a campsite for black youth under the auspices of the National Youth Administration (NYA), one of the New Deal programs established by President Franklin D. Roosevelt. She even reportedly gave coal to poor families when the winter weather was particularly cold.

By the time of her death in April 1953, Washington's enterprise was worth more than a million dollars and employed some 500 people, in addition to the 45,000 people who she claimed worked as Apex agents, selling her products door to door. She herself exemplified her company's slogan: "Now is the time to plan your future by learning a depression-proof business."

Further Reading

Davis, Marianna E. *Contributions of Black Women to America*, vol. 1. Columbia, S.C.: Kenday Press, 1982.

Dawson, Nancy J. "Sarah [Sara] Spencer Washington." *Encyclopedia of African American Business History*, edited by Juliet E. K. Walker. Westport, Conn.: Greenwood Press, 1999, pp. 593–595.

Gale Group. "Sarah Spencer Washington." *Notable Black American Women*, vol. 1. Farmington Hills, Mich.: Gale Research, 1992.

Porter, Gladys L. *Three Pioneers in Beauty Culture*. New York: Vantage Press, 1966.

Wasow, Omar

(1970–   ) *Internet analyst*

Omar Wasow is one of the new generation of Internet pioneers who is bringing an African-American perspective to cyberspace. He is currently executive director of BlackPlanet.com, an online community for African Americans that debuted in 1999 and that now calls itself "the largest black site on the Web," with almost 7 million members. Wasow is also an Internet analyst for New York's local NBC-TV station and for National Public Radio.

Wasow was born on December 22, 1970, in Nairobi, Kenya, the son of Bernard Wasow, a white Jew, and Eileen Wasow, an African American. Both parents were teachers, and as a child, Wasow lived in Bangladesh, Australia, and Puerto Rico, among other international locations. Wasow credits his mixed-race family background and his multicultural childhood with giving him a broad perspective on cultures and ethnicities.

Wasow began computer programming at age 11 and was online from age 12. He spent his high school years at Stuyvesant High School in Manhattan, the top-rated public high school in New York City, accessible only through a special entrance exam. He recalls that a party he attended in New York City's Greenwich Village, at which computer users shared stories and software, gave him his first inkling that computers could create community.

Wasow designed his own major at Stanford University, in race and ethnic relations. He grad-

Internet pioneer Omar Wasow has created multiracial online communities while exploring the new possibilities for African Americans in cyberspace. *(Courtesy of Omar Wasow)*

uated in 1992 and went on to work with Freedom Summer '92, a 22-city voter registration drive. After traveling to various countries, he returned to New York City in 1993 and cofounded New York Online with former Stanford classmate Peta Hoyes, a Jamaican who lived in the New York City borough of Queens. Through the corporation Diaspora Inc. ("diaspora" means dispersal and can refer to the scattering of people of African heritage throughout the world), Wasow and Hayes were able to set up their Internet service, which they saw as a haven for people of color and women, in contrast to the usual white-male domination of the cyberspace. Wasow financed the service himself for $50,000, which he raised from his savings, credit cards, and loans.

New York Online soon attracted a number of prestigious clients as well as a diverse customer base. Some 50 percent of its subscribers were people of color, while 40 percent were women. His first corporate client was *Vibe* magazine, which had been cofounded by QUINCY DELIGHT JONES, JR. Diaspora eventually divided into a consumer online service, a web development division, and a new media consultant division. In 1996, while he was still in his mid-20s, Wasow was touted as an expert in online ventures and a major influence in cyberspace. He built websites for such prestigious clients as *Consumer Reports*, the *New Yorker* magazine, Martinique Promotion Bureau, *Latina* magazine, Pfizer, Samsung, and the College Board. The venture won Wasow acclaim from the *New York Times*, which called him a "pioneer in Silicon Alley," and from *Newsweek*, which dubbed him one of the "fifty most influential people to watch in cyberspace."

In 1997, Wasow began working as a commentator for MSNBC, the television network cofounded by Microsoft and NBC. In 1999, the staff of New York Online merged into a new company, Community Connect, Inc., to launch Black-Planet.com, where he works as executive director.

Wasow also has a strong interest in charter schools (publicly funded schools developed by private citizens) and is the co-chair of the Coalition for Independent Public Charter Schools. In fall 2003, a school he helped found opened in Wasow's hometown of Brooklyn, New York.

Further Reading

Gale Group. "Omar Wasow." African American Publications, Biography Resource Center. Available online. URL: http://www.africanpubs.com/Apps/biosd/0435WasowOmar.asp?pic=none. Downloaded on November 4, 2002.

Green, Noah. "The Sixth Borough: A Bulletin Board Grows in Brooklyn." *The Village Voice*, July 12, 1994, p. 1.

Haskins, Jim. *Black Stars: African American Entrepreneurs.* New York: John Wiley & Sons, 1998, pp. 160–163.

Imperato, Gina. "Old Media, New Star." *Fast Company.* December 1997. Issue 12, p. 270. Available online. URL: http://www.fastcompany.com/online/12/newstar.html. Downloaded on November 4, 2002.

Marketing Opportunities in Business & Entertainment. "Profile: OmarWasow, Executive Director, BlackPlanet.com." MOBE.com. Available online. URL: http://www.mobe.com/next/bio/omarw.html. Downloaded on November 4, 2002.

Richardson, Lynda. "Entrepreneur Takes Black-Oriented Site Out of Red." *New York Times,* November 27, 2002, p. B2.

Sicko, Dan. "The Mix Is the Message." *Wired.* Issue 3.04, April 1995. Available online. URL: http://www.wired.com/wired/archive/3.04/streetcred.html?pg=12.

WNBC. "Omar Wasow: Internet Analyst." wnbc.com. Available online. URL: http://www.wnbc.com/wnbc/1169229/detail.html. Downloaded on November 4, 2002.

Waterford, Janet   See BRAGG, JANET HARMON.

Weston, Anthony
(Toney)
(ca. 1800–1876) *millwright, slave owner*

Anthony Weston's story reveals some of the contradictions in the slaveholding system. He was a former slave who not only became a slave owner but also joined with 22 other prominent African Americans in the Charleston, South Carolina, elite to sign a document on the eve of the Civil War swearing their allegiance to the "white race" and to the state of South Carolina—the state that would soon secede from the Union and become the leader of the Confederacy in an effort to protect the slave system.

Originally known as Toney, Weston was born sometime around 1800 (because records of slaves' lives were so badly kept, exact dates are not available). Little is known about his background, but he was recorded as a "mulatto"—someone of mixed race—so it is likely that he was the son of an enslaved mother and a white father, perhaps his owner, Charleston planter Plowden Weston. Indeed, Plowden Weston acted as many fathers of enslaved children did, giving his offspring more leeway than other slaves and making arrangements for his eventual emancipation (becoming free): When Plowden died in 1820, his will asserted that Toney had been allowed to hire out his own labor as a millwright (skilled repairperson and engineer) between May and November of each year, and that this arrangement should continue for six years, when Toney would then either be freed or allowed to leave the state. However, an 1820 state law required that the South Carolina state legislature approve any manumission (setting a slave free), so Toney's legal status was never entirely certain. The 1840 and 1860 censuses listed the man—now called Anthony Weston—as a free colored person, but there are no documents to prove that he ever legally received his freedom.

Nevertheless, he was allowed to live as a free person after 1826, and he went on to amass a small fortune, first by working for himself as a millwright, then by expanding his business through the purchase of slaves. At some point he married a house servant, Maria, who was also a slave of Plowden's. Maria's freedom was recognized, so she was actually the one who held title to all of the couple's possessions. Weston also bought the freedom of his brothers, Samuel and Jacob.

In 1831, Weston was working as a mechanic and millwright for a local planter, Benjamin Franklin Hunt, for whom he not only rebuilt a threshing machine but also rendered the device twice as efficient. From that point on, Weston's reputation grew, and he made a good living building and repairing rice mills. Rice was an enormously profitable crop in the Charleston area, and one that had enabled many large slaveholders to make huge fortunes. Weston followed their example in his own business, having Maria spend $8,950 between 1834 and 1845 on the purchase of some 20 slaves, including artisans who worked for him.

Unlike such black slaveholders as ANDREW DURNFORD and WILLIAM ELLISON, Weston seems to have shown some compassion towards his slaves. He seems to have avoided selling them, for example, suggesting that he respected their right to establish themselves in families and communities with some security. He also seems to have known several of the slaves his wife bought, and he may have given them the kind of license that Plowden gave him, even permitting them to live apart from him. Even as Weston profited from his slaves' labor, he may have tried to ease the difficulties of slavery.

Yet certainly, Weston profited from the slave system, and, on the eve of the Civil War, publicly supported it. Historians cannot determine whether Weston and his colleagues signed their pro-Confederacy document out of fear at a time when it was quite dangerous to be a free person of color in South Carolina, or whether he and the other free African Americans genuinely identified with the goals and values of the slaveholding South.

In any case, by 1860, the federal census had recorded that Weston's estate was worth more than $48,000, including the value of 14 slaves. And even five years after slavery had ended, in 1870, his property was worth more than $30,000, still a considerable sum. He still owned several houses in Charleston, which he rented out to maintain the income that sustained him until he died in 1876.

Further Reading

Johnson, Michael P., and James L. Roark. *Black Masters: A Free Family of Color in the Old South.* New York: W. W. Norton & Co., 1986.

Koger, Larry. *Black Slaveowners: Free Black Masters in South Carolina 1790–1860.* Columbia: University of South Carolina Press, 1995.

Powers, Bernard E., Jr. *Black Charlestonians: A Social History, 1822–1885.* Fayetteville: University of Arkansas Press, 1994.

Schweninger, Loren. *Black Property Owners in the South, 1790–1915.* Urbana: University of Illinois Press, 1990.

Whipper, William

(ca. 1804–1876) *lumber merchant, real estate speculator, coal merchant, philanthropist, abolitionist*

William Whipper and his cousin, STEPHEN SMITH, were two of the wealthiest African Americans in pre–Civil War America, prosperous businesspeople in Philadelphia and Lancaster County, Pennsylvania, who used the resources amassed in their successful enterprises to support the abolitionist cause. After the Civil War, Whipper was involved in a number of businesses that likewise provided support for African Americans in the new postwar era.

William Whipper was born on February 2, 1804, in Drumore Township, Pennsylvania (some sources say Little Britain Township), the son of "Nance," a female enslaved house servant, and her owner, a white lumber merchant of Columbia, Pennsylvania. Little is known about Whipper's early life, but by 1828, he had moved to Philadelphia, where he worked cleaning clothes in an early form of dry cleaning. In 1834, he opened a grocery store dedicated to "temperance," the movement to abolish alcoholic beverages. Many people at the time believed that drinking was the root of many of society's problems and that making liquor illegal would abolish poverty and other social ills.

In Philadelphia, Whipper became involved in literary and political circles, and in 1833, he was one of the founders of the Philadelphia Library for Colored Persons, an important institution at a time when society's institutions were highly segregated (separated by race) and when enslaved

African Americans were not permitted to read or write. Making books available to African Americans—free or enslaved—was a powerful statement, part of Whipper's overall commitment to "uplifting the race," improving society, and winning civil rights for African Americans.

In 1830, Whipper began attending the National Negro Convention, an annual national meeting of African Americans dedicated to ending slavery and achieving equal rights, whose constitution he wrote. In 1835, he tried to start a new group, the American Moral Reform Society, dedicated to the notion that improving the morals of society would lead to the end of slavery and to more ethical—that is, equal—treatment of black Americans. He wrote the Reform Society's constitution, too, and went on to edit their journal, *National Reformer,* becoming the first African American to edit a magazine. The Reform Society lasted only until 1841, but Whipper continued to be active in the National Negro Convention, which he attended in 1848, 1853, and 1855.

Meanwhile, in 1836, Whipper moved to Columbia, Pennsylvania, where he went into business with his close friend and cousin, Stephen Smith, in a business known as "Smith and Whipper, Lumber Merchants." By 1849, their company was the largest stockholder in the Columbia Bank, a major stockholder in the Columbia Bridge Company, and the owner of 22 cars running on the rail line from Columbia to Philadelphia. Whipper also bought a home in Columbia in 1847 and began to accumulate other properties.

Whipper and Smith were abolitionists, dedicated to ending slavery. Each of them was a major supporter of the Underground Railroad, the network of antislavery individuals who helped escaped slaves find safety and freedom. Whipper and Smith assisted escaped slaves, helping them go west to Pittsburgh, Pennsylvania, or north to Canada; or they would use their own railroad cars to help African Americans reach Philadelphia.

In 1853, Whipper bought property in Dresden, Ontario, where he helped several relatives settle. Having property there also enabled him to settle escaped slaves in a welcoming community. Indeed, Whipper himself was planning to immigrate to Canada when the Civil War broke out.

Committed to ending slavery, Whipper helped support the Union cause. When the Civil War ended in 1865, he terminated his relationship with Smith to go into business with James Whipper Purnell, his nephew. In 1868, he moved to New Brunswick, New Jersey, where he also bought property, and where the 1870 census recorded that he had a fortune of $108,000.

In 1873, Whipper returned to Philadelphia, where he had been serving as the cashier of the Philadelphia branch of the Freedman's Savings Bank from 1870, a position he held until the bank closed in 1874. The Freedman's Savings Bank was a black-owned institution set up after the Civil War to provide investment capital for the African-American community and the newly freed slaves. Although it was unable to stay afloat for very long, it served as a model and inspiration for other black-owned banks.

Whipper died on March 9, 1876, leaving his estate to Purnell's son with the express hope that the son would change his own name to "William Whipper" to keep Whipper's memory alive. Several descendants of the Whippers and Purnells continue to live in Dresden and in Lancaster County. Whipper's memory continues to be honored as that of a man whose business interests gave him the wherewithal to help the black community fight against slavery and for equal rights.

Further Reading

Bethel Harambee Historical Services. "Historical Figures." The Underground Railroad, A Living History. Available online. URL: http://www.livingtheundergroundrailroad.com/historical figures.htm. Downloaded on February 4, 2003.

Ingham, John N., and Lynne B. Feldman. *African-American Business Leaders: A Biographical Dictionary.* Westport, Conn.: Greenwood Press, 1994, p. 599.

Zimmerman, David. "William Whipper in the Black Abolitionist Tradition." Underground Railroad in Lancaster County, NMC Regional Center at Millersville University. Available online. URL: http://muweb.millersville.edu/~ugrr/resources/columbia/whipper.html. Downloaded on February 4, 2003.

Willis, Gertrude
(Gertrude Pocte Geddes-Willis)
(1878–1970) funeral home director, life insurance executive

Gertrude Willis was one of the first African-American female funeral directors in New Orleans. When she married Clem Geddes, she became part of the huge network of businesses owned by the DeJoie, Geddes, and Misshore families, who formed a kind of Creole business dynasty in 20th-century New Orleans.

Willis was born on March 9, 1878, in Louisiana's St. Bernard Parish, near the small fishing community of Happy Jack. She was one of three daughters of Oscar and Louise Pocte. While Gertrude was still a child, the family moved to New Orleans, where she attended elementary school.

Gertrude's first husband was Clem J. Geddes, who had inherited a mortuary from his father. In 1909 he went into partnership with a local barber, Arnold Moss, to establish a burial association. This business was a kind of insurance agency: Customers paid a regular fee in exchange for knowing that their funeral expenses would be covered when they died. Gertrude was active in both enterprises.

Black-owned funeral homes and burial associations were indispensable for African Americans during the 19th and much of the 20th centuries. White businesses, especially in the South, would often refuse to serve black customers, or would offer them second-class treatment. In the climate of racial hostility and disrespect that character- ized the pre–civil rights era, especially in the South, black people were often made to feel unwelcome at white businesses and particularly in their time of grief needed a funeral business that would make them feel comfortable and be responsive to their needs. Moreover, many black families did not have the resources to pay for funeral expenses when a loved one died. A burial society allowed them to put away a small amount of money at a time so that eventually, their families could be buried in a religious ceremony in a marked grave.

Clem died on August 22, 1913, and Gertrude went on to run their business by herself. Then, in 1919, she married dentist and entrepreneur Dr. William A. Willis, who joined her in the enterprises she had run with Clem. In 1940, they reorganized the Gertrude Geddes Willis Burial Association, with William Willis serving as the head of that association, as well as vice president of the funeral home. In 1969, they opened the Gertrude Geddes Willis Funeral Home in New Orleans. Ironically, the Civil Rights movement meant that many white businesses began serving African Americans on an equal basis, undermining the need for black-owned businesses. Yet the enterprises that Gertrude Willis helped to run are still active in New Orleans and the surrounding region, claiming over a century of continuous service.

Gertrude Willis was a devout Catholic who was active in her local church and in the Ladies Auxiliary Council of the Knights of Peter Claver, the black Catholic organization founded by GILBERT FAUSTINA. She and her husbands were social and political leaders in the New Orleans black community, and were active with the local National Association for the Advancement of Colored People (NAACP), a major civil rights group. Willis was affectionately known as "Miss Gert" by many who knew her, a testament to her position as beloved leader and role model among African Americans in New Orleans. She died in New Orleans on February 20, 1970, and was buried in St. Louis Cemetery No. 3, alongside both of her husbands.

Further Reading

Borders, Florence. "Gertrude Willis." *Black Women in America: Business and Professions*, edited by Darlene Clark Hine. New York: Facts On File, 1997, pp. 164–165.

Ingham, John N., and Lynne B. Feldman. *African-American Business Leaders: A Biographical Dictionary*. Westport, Conn.: Greenwood Press, 1994, pp. 174, 178–180.

Winfrey, Oprah
(Oprah Gail Winfrey)

(1954–   ) *television talk show host, actress, television and film producer, publisher*

Oprah Winfrey is one of the most powerful African-American women in media. Capitalizing on the enormous popularity of her daytime talk show, she has gone on to win control of the show, found her own production company, start her own magazine, and engage in a number of other media-related projects. She has used her fame and financial position to promote literature, particularly by African-American authors; to make sure that worthy projects reach film and television audiences; and to take a stand on political issues that matter to her, such as child abuse.

Winfrey was born on January 29, 1954, on a farm in Kosciusko, Mississippi, the child of 20-year-old Vernon Winfrey, a soldier, and 18-year-old Vernita Lee. The two were barely acquainted, and supposedly, Vernon learned of Oprah's birth when he received a birth announcement in the mail along with a scrawled note, "Send clothes!" Oprah was named for Orpah, the sister of Ruth in the Old Testament, but the name apparently was entered incorrectly on the birth certificate.

Oprah's mother left Mississippi soon after her daughter was born, leaving Oprah with her grandparents, who raised her in a stern but loving environment. When Oprah was six, she was sent to Milwaukee, Wisconsin, to live with her mother, who was working as a housecleaner. Oprah's mother was frequently at work, and Oprah resorted to imaginative and outlandish stories to get her mother's attention, even staging a fake burglary.

When Oprah was nine, she was sexually abused by a teenage cousin. The abuse continued for several more years, and her abusers later included other male relatives and friends—an experience she shared in 1991 on her talk show and later wrote about in an article for *Essence* magazine. The abuse ended when Oprah, at age 14, was sent to live with her father and his new wife, Zelma, in Nashville, Tennessee, an experience she credits with "saving" her. In Milwaukee, she felt, she had been heading for trouble, wearing provocative clothes, breaking curfews, and taking the road to becoming a criminal. In Nashville, Vernon Winfrey was now a barber, a city councillor, a grocery store owner, and a church deacon. He and his wife supervised Oprah closely and expected her to do well in school.

Oprah blossomed under the attention. She joined the drama club and won a $1,000 scholarship for a speech on "The Negro, the Constitution, and the United States." She became Nashville's Miss Fire Prevention—the first African American to do so—and Miss Black Tennessee. In 1971, she was a part-time radio newscaster on Nashville's WVOL.

Winfrey went on to enroll in the University of Tennessee, where in 1973, as a 19-year-old student she was recruited to work as a reporter and anchor at WTVF-TV, the CBS affiliate in Nashville. In 1976, she went on to work as a news anchor at Baltimore's ABC affiliate, WJZ-TV, but she was soon fired. By her own account, she was not ready to take such a job in a major market— but she soon found her niche as cohost of *People Are Talking*, a morning talk show. She held that job for several years, loving the work but experiencing a number of personal problems that resulted in a dramatic weight gain. Part of her difficulties stemmed from the ways that the producers of her show tried to convince her to change her look as well as her name. When Oprah finally left Baltimore in 1983, she vowed that she would never again let anyone have that kind of influence over her.

In January 1984, Winfrey became the cohost of *AM Chicago,* a morning talk show that was doing very poorly against the rival *Phil Donahue Show.* Within a year, Donahue moved his show to New York City and to an afternoon time slot, leaving room for Winfrey to become a successful local personality. Meanwhile, in 1985, film and music producer QUINCY DELIGHT JONES, JR., happened to be in Chicago to testify in a lawsuit and saw Winfrey's show. He was producing the movie *The Color Purple* at the time, which was adapted from the Alice Walker novel, and he immediately arranged for Winfrey to audition for Sophia, a part that later won her Golden Globe and Academy Award nominations for Best Supporting Actress.

In 1986, the *Oprah Winfrey Show* went national, and within five months, it was the third-highest rated syndicated show in the nation, outstripped only by *Jeopardy!* and *Wheel of Fortune.* Since its debut, Winfrey's show has won several Daytime Emmys.

Meanwhile, Oprah had formed Harpo Productions—the name comes from "Oprah" spelled backwards—through which she produced a number of television specials based on black-authored stories and novels. In 1988, Harpo took over the ownership and control of Winfrey's show, which also enabled her to promote projects that would not necessarily be profitable, but that she felt needed to reach an audience. Thus, in 1989, she coproduced and starred in *The Women of Brewster Place,* a television miniseries based on the Gloria Naylor novel about the African-American women in a poor urban neighborhood. She tried to turn the series into a weekly program the following year, but it went off the air in the first season. Winfrey later admitted that she had overextended

herself, hoping to succeed "on the strength of her own will" rather than being more realistic about what she might accomplish.

By 1991, Winfrey was earning $80 million, putting her on *Forbes* magazine's list of the richest U.S. entertainers. She also saw her work as a public service, making an effort to hire as many minority technicians and artists as possible, calling her work a "minority training program" in an interview with *Ms.* magazine.

Meanwhile, she was continuing to gain and lose weight in a very public arena, an issue that became part of her public persona as well. As part of sharing her personal life with the public, Winfrey made a public disclosure of the abuse she had undergone as a child, hoping that her acknowledgment would help other people come to terms with their own painful experiences.

In 1998, Winfrey helped produce and starred in the film version of *Beloved,* Toni Morrison's Pulitzer Prize–winning novel. Although the film was a commercial and critical failure, Winfrey plans to continue bringing stories that she considers important to film and television. Also in 1998, Winfrey became involved with Oxygen Media, whose women-oriented cable television station went on the air in 2000. She and Gayle King, her best friend, created a series called *Oprah Goes Online,* with computer adviser OMAR WASOW, explaining how to use the Internet. From 1999 to 2001, Winfrey also taught a course called "Dynamics of Leadership" in conjunction with her partner, Stedman Graham, and has been developing the course curriculum for Internet publication.

Winfrey has also become a serious force in the publishing world. In 1996, she started Oprah's Book Club, a segment of her television show that became so popular, it turned the books she recommended into instant best-sellers. Winfrey was known for focusing on serious literary works, such as books by Nobel Prize–winner Toni Morrison, as well as more commercial products. In 2001, she ended the book club, claiming that she no longer had time to do so much reading—a huge blow to the publishing industry, which had begun to rely on both her specific suggestions and on the general interest in reading created by her club. In 2003 she began talking about restarting her club in a more limited way.

Meanwhile, in 2000, Winfrey began publishing O, a women's magazine, while staying involved in a number of other enterprises. She is part owner of various network-affiliated television stations, and of the Eccentric, a Chicago restaurant. She has also started or participated in a number of charities, and made donations to black colleges and other institutions.

Talk-show host, producer, and actress Oprah Winfrey arrives at the 2002 *Vanity Fair* Oscar party in Hollywood, California. *(AP/Wide World Photos)*

In 2001, Winfrey was named one of the Forbes 400—one of the 400 richest people in the United States according to *Forbes* magazine. In 2002, she became the first recipient of the Bob Hope Humanitarian Award, a special Emmy (award for television excellence) that acknowledged her work for humanitarian causes.

One of Winfrey's trademarks has been her willingness to grow, change, and take new risks. She continues to find new projects and new areas of expansion, and she maintains that her money and influence are important not in themselves but for the opportunities they provide to make positive changes in the world.

Further Reading

Bayles, Martha. "Bookends: Imus, Oprah, and the Literary Elite." *New York Times Book Review,* August 29, 1999, page 35.

Berthed, Joan. "Here Comes Oprah! From *The Color Purple* to TV Talk Queen." *Ms.,* August 1986.

Dedman, Bill. "Personal Business: Professor Oprah, Preaching What She Practices." *New York Times,* October 10, 1999, Section 3, page 9.

"Dumbing Up: How Oprah Has Influenced People to Read More Through Her Television Show." *The Economist,* October 17, 1998.

Farley, Christopher John. "Queen of All Media." *Time,* October 5, 1998.

Glimpse, Marcia Ann. "Winfrey Takes All." *Ms.,* November 1988.

Haskins, Jim. *Black Stars: African American Entrepreneurs.* New York: John Wiley & Sons, 1998, pp. 147–150.

Kindles, Bridgett. "The Oprah Effect." *Publishers Weekly,* January 20, 1997.

"Oprah on Oprah." *Newsweek,* January 8, 2001.

Oprah.com. Available online. URL: http://www.oprah.com. Downloaded on February 6, 2003.

"10 Most Powerful Blacks in TV." *Ebony,* October 2002, p. 86.

White, Mimi. *Tele-Advising: Therapeutic Discourse in American Television.* Chapel Hill: University of North Carolina Press, 1992.

Woods, Granville T.

(1856–1910) *inventor, manufacturer*

Although Granville T. Woods had to leave school at the age of 10, he is the creator of more than 60 inventions, primarily in the field of electricity and communications. Woods was unable to get work as an electrician, however, so he developed his inventions, first in his own electrical shop and then in the Woods Electrical Company, which he co-owned with his brother, Lyates.

Woods was born free on April 23, 1856, in the city of Columbus, Ohio. Although slavery had always been illegal in the Northwest Territory, Ohio became the first non-slave state to enact "black laws," which set up many legal barriers to African-American participation in society. For example, Woods had to have white friends check out books from the library for him.

Woods attended school in Columbus until the age of 10, then served as apprentice (trainee) in a machine shop, becoming a skilled machinist and blacksmith. In 1872 he became a fireman on the Danville and Southern Railroad in Missouri, where he later was made an engineer. In 1874, he moved to Springfield, Illinois, to work in a rolling mill. In 1876, he moved east, where he worked part-time as a machinist, studying mechanical and electrical engineering at night. Because of his color, however, no one would hire him in those fields, so in 1880, he took a job as engineer aboard the British steamer *Ironsides*, where he was promoted to chief engineer two years later.

Continually held back by racial prejudice, Woods founded his own shop in Cincinnati, where in June 1884 he obtained his first patent, for an improved steam boiler furnace. In December 1884, he obtained his second patent, for a telephone transmitter. Because he lacked the capital to make and market these inventions, the patents were assigned to someone else. If Woods was to become a recognized inventor in his own right, he needed money.

Woods then developed a new apparatus that combined features of the telephone and telegraph and could transmit messages in either Morse code or voice, via electricity. He sold this device to Bell Telephone Company in Boston, which seemed to have provided the funds he needed to found Woods' Railway Telegraph Company in Cincinnati. Through this company, he patented his Synchronous Multiplex Railway Telegraphy, which was designed to prevent accidents by keeping trains informed of each others' whereabouts by enabling telegraph communication to and from moving trains.

The famous inventor Thomas A. Edison had cofounded the Edison and Phelps Company, which was also working on a railway telegraph, and the larger company sued Woods, claiming credit for the invention. Woods won the court case, however. Woods and Edison met in court on another dispute, and when Edison lost that case, he offered Woods a job. Instead, Woods formed his own manufacturing company with his brother, Lyates, the Woods Electrical Company. He continued to invent communications systems, which he sold to Bell and other large companies.

In 1890, Woods moved to New York City, where he patented many improvements to the city's electric-powered streetcar system. He invented a grooved wheel that allowed the car to receive electrical current while reducing friction. The wheel was called a troller, and from its name, the word *trolley* evolved. In 1902, Woods invented an automatic air brake, whose patent was eventually purchased by the Westinghouse Air Brake Company. Woods was also responsible for the third rail system in subways that is still in use today, an overhead conducting system for electric railways, an automatic safety cutout for electric circuits, an electric-powered incubator, a new type of battery, a steam boiler furnace, and many other electrical inventions. He was known by some as the "black Edison." He died on January 30, 1910, in New York City.

Further Reading

Aaseng, Nathan. *Black Inventors.* New York: Facts On
File, 1997.

Brown, Mitchell. "Granville T. Woods: Inventor."
The Faces of Science: African Americans in the
Sciences. Available online. URL: http://www.
princeton.edu/~mcbrown/display/woods.html.
Last updated on February 6, 2003.

Cefrey, Holly. *The Inventions of Granville Woods: The
Railroad Telegraph System and the Third Rail* (19th
Century American Inventors). New York: Pow-
erkids Press, 2003.

James, Portia P. *The Real McCoy: African-American
Invention and Innovation, 1619–1930.* Washington,
D.C.: Smithsonian Institution Press, 1989.

Sullivan, Otha Richard, and James Haskins. *African
American Inventors* (Black Stars Series). New York:
John Wiley & Sons, 1998.

Swanson, Erik C. "Granville T. Woods: Genius Inventor." Inventors Online Museum. Available online.
URL: http://www.inventorsmuseum.com/woods.
htm. Downloaded on November 4, 2002.

Wallace, Sidney. *Black Inventors.* Bloomington, Ind.: 1st
Books Library, 2001.

Woods, Sylvia
(Sylvia Pressley)
(1926–) *restaurant owner, food and beauty products entrepreneur*

Dubbed "the queen of soul food" by the *New York Times,* Sylvia Woods has won international acclaim with Sylvia's, her Harlem restaurant, which she expanded from a tiny luncheonette in 1962 to its current size of almost an entire city block. Since 1992, Sylvia's has expanded to include additional restaurants, a line of canned foods, a line of hair and skin products, and a proposed entertainment division to produce music and documentaries.

Sylvia Pressley was born on February 2, 1926, in Hemingway, South Carolina, the only child of Julia Pressley, a midwife, and Van Pressley, who died three days before she was born. Her grandfather had been lynched two decades earlier, so her grandmother, also a midwife, and her mother ran the family farm, bartering the "woman's work" of washing, mending, and cooking for their male neighbors' help with plowing and other heavy chores. When Pressley was three, her mother went to New York to work as a laundress so that she could save money to build a house of her own. In 1933, she returned to Hemingway, bought the property next to her mother's house, and within two years, built her own four-room house. Meanwhile, the young Pressley picked cotton, tobacco, and string beans.

At age 11, Sylvia met Herbert Woods, a boy of 12. As the couple tells the story, they fell instantly in love, though Herbert was not allowed to begin courting until Sylvia was 14. Meanwhile, in 1941, Pressley's mother interrupted her daughter's 10th-grade education to send her to New York to study cosmetology. In 1943, Pressley returned to Hemingway, pregnant with her first child. She built and ran a beauty parlor on her mother's farm. In 1944, she and Herbert married. Sylvia continued to work as a beautician, washing and curling hair for $1.50 per customer, while Herbert served as a cook in the U.S. Navy.

In 1945, Herbert was discharged from the navy and the couple moved to Harlem, where they worked at a number of jobs and tried their luck in a number of different cities. In 1950, they had settled permanently in New York, where Herbert drove a cab and Sylvia eventually got work as a waitress at Johnson's Luncheonette, a tiny establishment with six stools and four booths. When the owner relocated, she ran the restaurant herself. In 1962, she took her own savings and the money that her mother had raised from mortgaging the family farm and bought the little restaurant. Six months later, she renamed it Sylvia's. In addition to the standard hamburgers and french fries, Sylvia's also offered such soul food specialties as neckbones, pig's tails, fried chicken, collard greens, and black-eyed peas.

Restaurant owner Sylvia Woods is known as "the queen of soul food." *(Compliments of the Woods Family)*

In 1968, riots over the assassination of Martin Luther King, Jr., shook the Harlem community where Sylvia's was located—but the restaurant itself, beloved by the community, was untouched. Ironically, the devastation caused by the riots enabled Herbert and Sylvia to purchase a larger site at 126th Street and Lenox Avenue, where their restaurant remains today. Over the years, the establishment expanded, greatly helped by a rave review published by premier restaurant critic Gael Greene in *New York* magazine in 1979. The review led to vastly increased customer business, arrangements with national and international tour groups to visit the restaurant, and eventually, expansion to a total of three dining rooms.

In the early 1990s, Sylvia's expanded further, as the Woods formed Sylvia Woods Enterprises LLC to sell a food line that eventually included some 40 soul-food items. In 1992, the foods were marketed to gourmet stores, but Van DeWard, the Woods' oldest child and head of the new company, soon placed the products in supermarkets: BI-LO in 1993, Pathmark in 1994, and eventually, A&P/Food Emporium, Stop & Shop, Shop & Save, and other major East Coast chains.

Woods also published two cookbooks, opened new operations in Atlanta and at New York City's Kennedy Airport, founded Sylvia's Catering, and started a beauty products line. Although such outside investors as J. P. Morgan have contributed financing and the company has made use of outside consultants, Sylvia's and its many spin-offs remain very much a family business, with the Woods children and many of the grandchildren holding key positions in the enterprise.

Further Reading

Harris, Wendy. *Against All Odds, Ten Entrepreneurs Who Followed Their Hearts and Found Success.* New York: John Wiley & Sons, 2001, pp. 1–19.

Mantas, Marylena. "Sylvia Woods: The Queen of Soul Food." *Education Update*, February 2002. Available online at Education Update Online. URL: http://www.educationupdate.com/archives/2002/feb02/htmls/cover_sylvia.html.

Payne, Helena. "Landmark Harlem Eatery Turns 40, Celebrates Community Revitalization." *Naples Daily News*, August 16, 2002. Available online on naplesnews.com. URL: http://www.naplesnews.com/02/08/business/d804346a.htm.

Sisterfriends. "Sylvia Woods: Queen of Soul Food." Sisterfriends.com. Available online. URL: http://www.sisterfriends.com/swoods.htm Downloaded on November 5, 2002.

Sylvia's: Queen of Soul Food. Available online. URL: http://www.sylviassoulfood.com. Downloaded on November 5, 2002.

"Sylvia Woods—Entrepreneur." South Carolina African American History Online. Available online. URL: http://www.scafam-hist.org/calendar.asp?Month=8&Year=1998. Posted in August 1998.

Woods, Sylvia, and Melissa Clark. *Sylvia's Family Soul Food Cookbook: From Hemingway, South Carolina, to Harlem.* New York: William Morrow, 1999.

Woods, Sylvia, and Christopher Styler. *Sylvia Woods' Soul Food: Recipes from the World-Famous Harlem Restaurant.* New York: Hearst, 1992.

Wormley, James
(1819–1884) *hotelkeeper*

James Wormley established Wormley's Hotel, one of the most fashionable hotels in Washington, D.C., during the later part of the 19th century. Besides making a fortune at a time when it was very unusual for African Americans to be entrepreneurs at all, Wormley is memorable for the universal respect he seems to have commanded in Washington society and for the dignity and racial pride that he projected.

James born on January 16, 1819, in Washington, D.C., the son of Peter Leigh Wormley and Mary Wormley, African Americans who had lived as free people on a Virginia plantation before coming to Washington in 1814. Peter had been a coachman on the plantation, and by the time James was a child, he had established a livery business (a place that rented horses and carriages). He was moderately prosperous and raised a family of five children.

Historians know little about James Wormley's childhood, but he began working as a driver for his father at an early age, then bought his own carriage and started his own business. He went on to become a steward, first on a U.S. oceangoing ship, then on various Mississippi steamships. In 1849 he went for a while to try his luck in the California gold rush, but returned to Washington, where he took a job as steward at the Metropolitan Club, a prominent city establishment.

Just before the Civil War began in 1861, Wormley began his own catering business, located next door to the candy store run by Ana Thompson, whom he had married in 1841. Catering was

a business in which many black entrepreneurs had established themselves, as it had the reputation of being a "servile" enterprise: Rich families would contract a catering company to provide all or most of their daily meals. Wormley, however, was known for the sense of pride he brought to his business, and for the respect he won among both whites and blacks. He was so successful that he was able to expand his establishment in the mid-1860s and to include a restaurant there that quickly became the favorite spot of the city's Radical Republicans, a group of white politicians who believed in abolishing slavery and establishing the political rights of African Americans. One of the leading Radical Republicans was Senator Charles Sumner, who became such a close associate of Wormley's that Wormley named a son for him. Wormley was also close to Vice President Henry Wilson, who ran on the ticket with President Ulysses S. Grant.

For a while, Wormley went to England in the service of Reverdy Johnson, ambassador to the Court of St. James (that is, to England). There, Wormley won acclaim for his American gourmet food, especially a dish of diamondback terrapin (an animal like a turtle), which was native to the D.C. area's Chesapeake Bay and Potomac River. Wormley spent some time in Paris studying cooking before returning to Washington, where his new international reputation further increased his popularity. He expanded his property to include what became known as Wormley's Hotel, turning to Massachusetts congressman Samuel Hooper for help with the financial arrangements.

Wormley's Hotel and the associated restaurant became a favorite of the Washington elite, and a number of prominent politicians stayed there, including both U.S. and foreign officials. The hotel was known for having an elevator and one of the capital's first telephones. It was also the location chosen for a famous political meeting that produced an arrangement known as the "Wormley Agreement," though history books today refer to it as the Compromise of 1877. The presidential election of 1876 had been extremely close. The Democratic candidate, Samuel Tilden, had more votes in the electoral college than the Republican candidate, Rutherford B. Hayes, but Tilden did not have the majority he needed to claim the presidency. At that time, federal troops were stationed in many southern states in order to keep the leaders of the former Confederacy from rising again, and to guarantee African-American political rights. In the Wormley hotel, politicians brokered an agreement whereby federal troops would be withdrawn in exchange for some electoral votes going to Hayes. Hayes became president, troops were withdrawn—and African-American political rights in the South quickly disappeared under an avalanche of racially specific laws that established segregation. Wormley, of course, had no part in the arrangement and probably had never heard of it, but, ironically, the agreement was named for his hotel.

Wormley continued to expand his properties, secured a patent (license) on a device that made boats safer, and fought to improve educational opportunities for black children. On October 18, 1884, he died in Boston after an operation for kidney stones. One year later, a public school was named in his honor.

Further Reading

"Everywhere You Look: German-American Sites in Washington, D.C." Goethe Institut. Available online. URL: http://www.goethe.de/uk/was/vtour/dc1/A2/26/en_tmb_1.htm. Downloaded on November 12, 2002.
"The Exhibit Hall: African-American Family Photograph Collection." Cleveland Public Library. Available online. URL: http://www.cpl.org/ExhibitHall.asp?FormMode=ExhibitGraves. Last updated January 29, 2001.
Hollis, Nicholas E. "A Hotel for the History Books." *Washington Post*, March 18, 2001. Available online. URL: http://www.innercity.org/columbiaheights/newspaper/03_18_01_wormely.html.
James Wormley Recognition Project. The Agribusiness Council. Available online. URL: http://www.agribusinesscouncil.org/jameswormley.htm. Downloaded on November 12, 2002.
Logan, Rayford. *Dictionary of American Negro Biography*. New York: W. W. Norton, 1983.
Wynes, Charles E. "James Wormley of the Wormley Hotel Agreement." *Centennial Review*, Winter 1975, pp. 397–401.

Wright, Richard Robert, Sr. (1853–1947) and Richard Robert Wright, Jr. (1878–1967) bankers

The Wrights were an extraordinary father-and-son team who founded a major financial institution when the elder Wright was 68 years old and while the younger Wright was deeply involved as an official of the African Methodist Episcopal (AME) Church. Although banking was not the major activity of either of their lives, their establishment of the Citizens and Southern Bank and Trust Company represented their greatest business success and an impressive achievement.

Richard Wright, Sr., was born on May 16, 1853, a slave on a plantation near Dalton, Georgia. His father was Robert Waddell, the family coachman, and his mother, Harriet (who had no last name, as was the custom with many enslaved people), was a house servant. In 1855, Wright's father ran away to freedom, and he and his mother were sent to Cuthbert, Georgia. There Harriet married Alexander Wright, who also ran away during the Civil War to join the Union army. When the war was over, Harriet moved to Atlanta where she opened a boardinghouse, while Richard entered the Storrs School of the American Missionary Association.

Wright went on to attend the preparatory school set up by Atlanta University, a recently established school intended to educate the many freed African Americans after the Civil War. He taught during the summers to support himself while studying and became valedictorian (first in his class) of Atlanta University's first graduating class in 1876, despite threats from the Ku Klux Klan, who saw Wright as a civil rights leader. Also in 1876 Wright married Lydia E. Howard.

The couple moved to Cuthbert, Georgia, where Wright became principal of an elementary school, organized local farmers' cooperatives, established the state's first county fair for black people, and, in 1878, organized the Georgia State Teachers Association, serving as its first president. He also founded the *Weekly Journal of Progress,* later the *Weekly Sentinel.* In 1879, he founded Ware High School in Augusta, Georgia, the first public high school in the state that African Americans could attend.

Wright became active in Republican politics (the Republican Party was then considered the party of Abraham Lincoln and black civil rights), and in 1891 his political activity led to his appointment as president of the Georgia State Industrial College, an institution recently set up to offer vocational education to black people. Many white people at the time felt that black people should be taught only "practical" subjects rather than getting the traditional classical education, and many industrial and vocational schools were founded toward that end. For the same reason, the Georgia state legislature cut off funds to Atlanta University in 1887, supporting the vocational school instead. White citizens protested the proposed location of Athens, so the school was moved to Savannah.

Wright formed the National Association of Teachers in Colored Schools to try to improve conditions in black education. Nevertheless, his school received poor ratings, perhaps because of lack of support from the white board of trustees. Meanwhile, Wright became involved in real estate and gradually prospered. He first had the idea of founding a bank when his daughter, Julia, was treated rudely at Savannah's Citizens and Southern Bank, where a teller insisted on calling her by her first name and said he would never call an African American "Miss." Wright contacted his son, Richard, then living in Philadelphia, and proposed founding a bank there.

Richard Wright, Jr., had been born on April 16, 1878, in Cuthbert, Georgia, attended the Haines Institute in Augusta, and became the first graduate of his father's school in 1898. He attended the University of Chicago, earning a bachelor of divinity degree in 1901 and an A.M. in 1904, going on to get his Ph.D. from the University of Pennsylvania in 1911, as well as studying at the universities of Berlin and Leipzig in 1903 and 1904. In 1909 he married Charlotte Crogman.

Wright taught Hebrew and New Testament Greek, served as a pastor, edited church publications, and became manager of AME Book Concern, a church publishing company, which gave him his first real experience in business and where he worked until 1912. He also served as secretary of the black-owned People's Savings Bank in Philadelphia, which was organized in 1907 and survived until 1917. Later he became involved in the real estate business in Philadelphia, eventually owning some 50 houses in the city.

In 1920, the Wrights started a private bank (a bank without a state charter), with Richard, Sr., as president, Richard, Jr., as secretary-treasurer, and Richard, Sr.'s daughter, Lillian, as teller. Richard, Sr., then returned to Savannah, but he soon resigned his college presidency and in 1921 settled in Philadelphia at the age of 68 to become a banker.

By 1924, the Wrights had raised enough money to incorporate as a joint stock venture (a bank financed by investors). Several local ministers were put on the bank's board in order to give it legitimacy with Philadelphia's black community. However, few native Philadelphia black people trusted the small bank, having more faith in Brown and Stevens, the city's other black bank, a much larger and more commercial institution.

Wright, Sr., saw his bank as another vehicle for education, with the goal of teaching working-class black people how to save their money and budget their low incomes. In those days, many white institutions either would not accept black customers, or, as Julia Wright found, treated them rudely. Wright, Sr., was committed to making things different for the black community of Philadelphia, and his institution eventually offered insurance and mortgages so that black customers could receive a full range of services.

Wright, Sr., joined the Pennsylvania Bankers Association in 1922 and the American Bankers Association in 1923. He went on to found the National Association of Negro Bankers (later the National Bankers Association) in 1926, and served as the group's first president. His conservative policies enabled the bank to purchase Keystone Bank in 1927, renaming his own institution the Greater Citizens and Southern Bank and Trust Company. Remarkably, he was able to survive the Great Depression of 1929, despite the many failures of other larger banks.

Wright, Sr., also organized the Haitian Coffee and Product Trading Company in 1935. In 1940, he was central in getting the U.S. Post Office to issue the first stamp honoring a black person—educator and activist Booker T. Washington. When he died on July 2, 1947, the bank he had founded had more than $3 million worth of deposits.

Wright, Jr., meanwhile, had become president of Wilberforce University in 1932, a post he held until he became a bishop in the AME church in 1936. He served as bishop in South Africa, then in Kentucky and Tennessee, until 1956, when he became AME church historian. As a religious leader, he built some 50 churches and schools, and founded the R. R. Wright, Jr., School of Religion and the Crogman Community Clinic in South Africa.

In the 1950s, the bank he and his father had founded became first an integrated institution, and then, in the 1960s, a white-owned bank. Although the Wrights had founded a successful, long-lived institution, it is unclear what effect it had on Philadelphia's black community as a whole. On the one hand, it treated black customers with dignity and enabled many people to obtain mortgages and buy their own homes. On the other hand, most of the city's black population continued to be poor, and to live in poor housing, despite the success of its business leaders.

Further Reading

Davis, Maryellen. "Richard R. Wright (Richard Robert), b. 1878." University of North Carolina at Chapel Hill Libraries: Documenting the American South. Available online. URL: http://docsouth.unc.edu/church/wright/bio.html. Downloaded on December 27, 2002.

Patton, June O. "'And the Truth Shall Make You Free . . .': Richard Robert Wright, Sr., Black Intellectual and Iconoclast." *Journal of Negro History* 81, no. 1–4 (1996): 17.

"Richard Robert Wright, Jr." *Religious Leaders of America*, 2nd ed. Farmington Hills, Mich.: Gale Group, 1999.

BIBLIOGRAPHY AND RECOMMENDED SOURCES

Bell, Gregory S. *In the Black. A History of African Americans on Wall Street.* New York: John Wiley & Sons, 2002.

Bennett, Lerone, Jr. *The Shaping of Black America.* New York: Penguin, 1993.

Birmingham, Stephen. *Certain People: America's Black Elite.* Boston, Mass.: Little, Brown, & Co., 1977.

Blassingame, John. *Black New Orleans 1860–1880.* Chicago: University of Chicago Press, 1973.

Byrd, Ayana D., and Lori L. Tharps. *Hair Story: Untangling the Roots of Black Hair in America.* New York: St. Martin's Press, 2001.

Clarke, Marilyn. *Take a Lesson: Today's Top Black Achievers Talk About How They Made It and What They Learned Along the Way.* New York: John Wiley & Sons, 2001.

Coppock, Paul R. *Memphis Memoirs.* Memphis, Tenn.: Memphis State University Press, 1980.

Davis, Marianna W., ed. *Contributions of Black Women to America.* Columbia, S.C.: Kenday Press, 1982.

Dingle, Derek T. *Black Enterprise, Titans of the B.E. 100s.* New York: John Wiley & Sons, Inc., 1999.

Drake, St. Clair, and Horace Cayton. *Black Metropolis: A Study of Negro Life in a Northern City.* New York: Harcourt, Brace and World, 1970.

DuBois, W. E. B. *Black Reconstruction in America.* New York: Free Press, 1999.

Estell, Kenneth, ed. *The African-American Almanac,* 6th ed. Farmington Hills, Mich.: Gale, 1994.

Feldman, Lynne. *A Sense of Place: Birmingham's Black Middle-Class Community, 1890–1930.* Tuscaloosa: University of Alabama Press, 2000.

Franklin, John Hope, and Albert Moss. *From Slavery to Freedom, A History of African Americans,* 8th ed. New York: Knopf, 2000.

Gale Group. *Contemporary Black Biography.* Farmington Hills, Mich.: Gale Research, 1992.

———. *Notable Black American Men.* Farmington Hills, Mich.: Gale Research, 1998.

———. *Notable Black American Women.* Farmington Hills, Mich.: Gale Research, 1992.

———. *Who's Who Among African Americans,* 14th ed. Farmington Hills, Mich.: Gale Research, 1992.

Gardner, Robert. *Forgotten Players: The Story of Black Baseball in America.* New York: Walker & Co., 1993.

Garraty, John A., and Edward T. James, eds. *Dictionary of American Biography.* New York: Scribner's, 1974.

Gates, Henry Louis. *African-American Voices of Triumph: Perseverance.* Alexandria, Va.: Time-Life Books, 1993.

Gatewood, Willard. *Aristocrats of Color: The Black Elite, 1880–1920.* Bloomington: Indiana University Press, 1990.

Green, Richard L., ed. *A Gift of Heritage: Historic Black Pioneers.* Vol. 3. Chicago, Ill.: Empak Enterprises, 1990.

Greenwood, Janette. *Bittersweet Legacy: The Black and White "Better Classes" in Charlotte, 1850–1910.* Chapel Hill: University of North Carolina Press, 1994.

Hamilton, Kenneth. *Black Towns and Profits.* Champaign: University of Illinois Press, 1991.

Hammond, Theresa A. *A White Collar Profession: African American Certified Public Accountants since 1921.* Chapel Hill: University of North Carolina Press, 2002.

Harding, Vincent. *There Is a River: The Black Struggle for Freedom in America.* New York: Harvest Books, 1993.

Harris, Wendy. *Against All Odds, Ten Entrepreneurs Who Followed Their Hearts and Found Success.* New York: John Wiley & Sons, 2001.

Haskins, Jim. *Black Stars: African American Entrepreneurs.* New York: John Wiley & Sons, 1998.

Ingham, John N., and Lynne B. Feldman. *African-American Business Leaders: A Biographical Dictionary.* Westport, Conn.: Greenwood Press, 1994.

Johnson, James Weldon. *Black Manhattan.* Cambridge, Mass.: Da Capo Press, 1991.

Kaplan, Sidney. *The Black Presence in the Era of the American Revolution.* 1973. Reprint, Amherst: University of Massachusetts Press, 1989.

Katz, William Loren. *Black People Who Made the Old West.* Trenton, N.J.: Africa World Press, 1992.

Kein, Sybil, ed. *The History and Legacy of Louisiana's Free People of Color.* Baton Rouge: Louisiana State University Press, 2000.

Kern-Foxworth, Marilyn. *Aunt Jemima, Uncle Ben, and Rastus: Blacks in Advertising, Yesterday, Today, and Tomorrow.* Westport, Conn.: Greenwood Press, 1994.

Koger, Larry. *Black Slaveowners: Free Black Masters in South Carolina 1790–1860.* Columbia: University of South Carolina Press, 1995.

Kranz, Rachel, and Philip J. Koslow. *Biographical Dictionary of African Americans,* rev. ed. New York: Facts On File, 1992.

Logan, Rayford W., and Michael R. Winston, eds. *Dictionary of American Negro Biography.* New York: Norton, 1982.

Meier, August. *Negro Thought in America.* Ann Arbor: University of Michigan Press, 1963.

Ottley, Roi, and William J. Weatherby, eds. *The Negro in New York.* New York: New York Public Library, 1967.

Peiss, Kathy. *Hope in a Jar: The Making of America's Beauty Culture.* New York: Henry Holt, 1998.

Powers, Bernard E., Jr. *Black Charlestonians: A Social History, 1822–1885.* Fayetteville: University of Arkansas Press, 1994.

Quarles, Benjamin. *Black Abolitionists.* Cambridge, Mass.: Da Capo Press, 1991.

Savage, William S. *Blacks in the West.* Westport, Conn.: Greenwood Press, 1976.

Schweninger, Loren. *Black Property Owners in the South, 1790–1915.* Urbana: University of Illinois Press, 1990.

Simmons, William J. *Men of Mark, Eminent, Progressive, and Rising.* 1887. Reprint, New York: Arno Press, 1968.

Stewart, James Brewer. *Holy Warriors: The Shaping of American Abolitionism.* New York: Hill & Wang, 1997.

Taub, Richard. *Community Capitalism.* Cambridge, Mass.: Harvard Business School Press, 1994.

Walker, Juliet E. K., ed. *Encyclopedia of African American Business History.* Westport, Conn.: Greenwood Press, 1999.

Woodard, Michael D., Ph.D. *Black Entrepreneurs in America. Stories of Struggle and Success.* New Brunswick, N.J.: Rutgers University Press, 1998.

ENTRIES BY TYPE OF BUSINESS

ACTING/ENTERTAINING/ MODELING
Bricktop
Sims, Naomi
Winfrey, Oprah

ADVERTISING
Burrell, Thomas J.
Lewis, Byron E.
Murray, Joan
Proctor, Barbara Gardner

AERONAUTICS
Bragg, Janet Harmon
Brown, Willa Beatrice
Felton, William McDonald
Plinton, James O., Jr.

AUTOMOTIVE
Barden, Don
Farr, Mel
Felton, William McDonald
Gidron, Dick
Johnson, Albert W.

BANKING
Banks, Charles
Binga, Jesse
Blayton, Jesse
Boutte, Alvin Joseph
Boyd, Richard Henry

Browne, William Washington
Chappell, Emma
Church, Robert Reed, Sr.
Coleman, Warren Clay
Gaston, Arthur G.
Gates, Clifton W.
Hurt, James, Jr.
Merrick, John
Mitchell, John, Jr.
Napier, James Carroll
Overton, Anthony
Pettiford, William Reuben
Smith, Stephen
Still, William
Travis, Dempsey J.
Walker, Maggie Lena
Wright, Richard Robert, Jr.
Wright, Richard Robert, Sr.

BARBERING/BEAUTY SALONS/ HAIRDRESSING
Johnson, William Tiler
Merrick, John
Morgan, Rose Meta
Thomas, James
Toussaint, Pierre
Washington, Sarah Spencer

BASEBALL
Greenlee, Gus
Posey, Cum

BEAUTY PRODUCTS
Dudley, Joe L., Sr.
Fuller, S. B.
Gardner, Edward G.
Johnson, John H.
Joshua, Ernest P.
Joyner, Marjorie Stewart
Moore, Vera
Overton, Anthony
Sims, Naomi
Turnbo-Malone, Annie Minerva
Walker, Madame C. J.

BOOKSTORE
Ruggles, David

BOTTLING/BEVERAGE DISTRIBUTORS
Blayton, Jesse
Davis, Willie D.
Llewellyn, J. Bruce

BOXING
Greenlee, Gus
King, Don

CARPENTRY
Day, Thomas
Fortune, Amos

CIGARS
Faustina, Gilbert

CONSULTING
Brimmer, Andrew F.
Smith, Joshua I.
Thomas-Graham, Pamela

CORPORATE MANAGEMENT
Chenault, Kenneth Irvine
Fudge, Ann
O'Neal, Stanley
Parsons, Richard Dean

DEVELOPMENT
Faustina, Gilbert
Hurt, James, Jr.
Mitchell, John, Jr.

DRY CLEANING
Eldridge, Elleanor
Jennings, Thomas L.

ENGINEERING/CONTRACTING/ CONSTRUCTION
Alexander, Archie Alphonso
Bartholomew, Joseph Manuel
King, Horace
Russell, Herman J.

ENSLAVED ENTREPRENEUR OR MANAGER
Gray, Simon
Henson, Josiah
McWorter, Frank
Montgomery, Benjamin
        Thornton

FARMING/PLANTING
Durnford, Andrew
Ellison, William
Henson, Josiah
Metoyer, Marie-Thérèse
Montgomery, Benjamin
        Thornton

FILM
De Passe, Suzanne Celeste
Jones, Quincy Delight, Jr.
Micheaux, Oscar
Simmons, Russell
Winfrey, Oprah

FINANCE
Brimmer, Andrew F.
Chappell, Emma
Chenault, Kenneth Irvine
Fletcher, Alphonse, Jr.
Gates, Clifton W.
Holland, Jerome Heartwell
Johnson, William Tiler
Leidesdorff, William A.
Lewis, Reginald Francis
Rogers, John W., Jr.

FOOD PRODUCTS
Amos, Wally
Fudge, Ann
Gibson, Vivian
James, Charles Howell
James, Charles H., III
Parks, Henry G.
Russell, Herman J.
Woods, Sylvia

FOOD SERVICE/RESTAURANTS/ CATERING/SALOONS
DeBaptiste, George
Downing, George Thomas
Dutrieuille, Albert E.
Dutrieuille, Peter Albert
Fraunces, Samuel
Greenlee, Gus
Robey, Don
Woods, Sylvia

FUNERAL HOMES
Jefferson, Lucy C.
Willis, Gertrude

GAMBLING/RACETRACKS
Barden, Don
Greenlee, Gus
Jones, Wiley

HEALTH CARE
Bragg, Janet Harmon

HOTELS/BOARDINGHOUSES
Downing, George Thomas
Gaston, Arthur G.
Murray, Albert
Murray, Odetta S.
Pleasant, Mary Ellen
Wormley, James

INSURANCE
Antoine, Cesar Carpentier
Bartholomew, Joseph Manuel
Beavers, George Allen, Jr.
Cohen, Walter I.
Coleman, Warren Clay
Dickerson, Earl Burrus
Gaston, Arthur G.
Johnson, John H.
Kennedy, William Jesse, Jr.
Kennedy, William J., III
Lee, George Washington
Merrick, John
Overton, Anthony
Pace, Harry H.
Procope, Ernesta G.
Spaulding, Charles Clinton
Travis, Dempsey J.
Walker, Antonio Maceo
Willis, Gertrude

INTERNET ANALYSIS
Wasow, Omar

LAND SPECULATION
Durnford, Andrew
Johnson, William Tiler
Leidesdorff, William A.

McWorter, Frank
Montgomery, Isaiah T.
Overton, Anthony
Pinchback, P. B. S.
Pleasant, Mary Ellen

LUMBER
Gray, Simon
Smith, Stephen
Whipper, William

MANUFACTURING
Boyd, Richard Henry
Coleman, Warren Clay
Day, Thomas
Ellison, William
Henderson, Henry F., Jr.
Julian, Percy Lavon
Woods, Granville T.

MARITIME INDUSTRY
Cuffe, Paul
Forten, James, Sr.
Gray, Simon

MILL EQUIPMENT
Weston, Anthony

MUSIC
De Passe, Suzanne Celeste
Gordy, Berry, Jr.
Griffey, Dick
Jones, Quincy Delight, Jr.
King, Don
Pace, Harry H.
Rhone, Sylvia M.
Robey, Don
Simmons, Russell

NIGHT CLUBS/THEATERS
Bricktop
Felton, William McDonald
Greenlee, Gus

OIL
Simmons, Jake, Jr.

PUBLIC RELATIONS
Poe, Kirsten N.
Warren, Renee E.

PUBLISHING
Abbot, Robert Sengstacke
Antoine, Cesar Carpentier
Boyd, Richard Henry
Chase, Calvin
Fuller, S. B.
Graves, Earl G.
Hurt, James, Jr.
Johnson, John H.
Lewis, Edward T.
Micheaux, Oscar
Mitchell, John, Jr.
Moore, Frederick Randolph
Morgan, Garrett A.
Norris, James Austin
Overton, Anthony
Pace, Harry H.
Perry, Christopher James
Pinchback, P. B. S.
Rhodes, Eugene Washington
Ruggles, David
Scott, Cornelius Adolphus
Scott, William Alexander, II
Smith, Clarence O.
Sutton, Percy E.
Travis, Dempsey J.
Vann, Robert Lee
Washington, Alonzo
Winfrey, Oprah

RADIO
Blayton, Jesse
Brunson, Dorothy
Davis, Willie D.
Hughes, Cathy
Sutton, Percy E.

REAL ESTATE
Barden, Don
Bartholomew, Joseph Manuel
Binga, Jesse
Bush, John Edward
Church, Robert Reed, Sr.
De Priest, Oscar Stanton
Faustina, Gilbert
Gaston, Arthur G.
Gates, Clifton W.
Jones, Wiley
Lafon, Thomy
Merrick, John
Overton, Anthony
Payton, Philip A.
Pettiford, William Reuben
Pleasant, Mary Ellen
Russell, Herman J.
Smith, Stephen
Thomas, James
Travis, Dempsey J.
Whipper, William

RETAIL
Cohen, Walter I.
Eldridge, Elleanor
Fuller, S. B.
Hurt, James, Jr.
Lafon, Thomy
Llewellyn, J. Bruce
Still, William

SLAVEHOLDING
Durnford, Andrew
Ellison, William
Johnson, William Tiler
Metoyer, Marie-Thérèse
Weston, Anthony

TAILORING/DRESSMAKING
Jennings, Thomas L.
Jones, John
Keckley, Elizabeth

TANNING
Fortune, Amos

TELEVISION
Barden, Don
Bowser, Yvette Lee
De Passe, Suzanne Celeste
Gordy, Berry, Jr.
Johnson, Albert W.
Johnson, Robert L.
Jones, Quincy Delight, Jr.
Llewellyn, J. Bruce

Mercado-Valdes, Frank
Simmons, Russell
Sutton, Percy E.
Thomas-Graham, Pamela
Winfrey, Oprah

TOWN DEVELOPMENT
Allensworth, Allen
Banks, Charles
Du Sable, Jean Baptiste Pointe
McWorter, Frank
Montgomery, Isaiah T.

TRADING
Cuffe, Paul
Du Sable, Jean Baptiste Pointe
Flora, William
Metoyer, Marie-Thérèse

TRANSPORTATION
DeBaptiste, George
Jones, Wiley

ENTRIES BY YEAR OF BIRTH

1700–1749
Du Sable, Jean-Baptiste Pointe
Ellison, William
Fortune, Amos
Fraunces, Samuel
Jennings, Thomas L.
Metoyer, Marie-Thérèse

1750–1799
Cuffe, Paul
Eldridge, Elleanor
Flora, William
Forten, James, Sr.
Henson, Josiah
McWorter, Frank
Smith, Stephen
Toussaint, Pierre

1800–1809
Day, Thomas
Durnford, Andrew
Gray, Simon
Johnson, William Tiler
King, Horace
Weston, Anthony
Whipper, William

1810–1819
DeBaptiste, George
Downing, George Thomas

Jones, John
Keckley, Elizabeth
Lafon, Thomy
Leidesdorff, William A.
Montgomery, Benjamin
    Thornton
Pleasant, Mary Ellen
Ruggles, David
Wormley, James

1820–1829
Still, William
Thomas, James

1830–1839
Antoine, Cesar Carpentier
Church, Robert Reed, Sr.
Dutrieuille, Peter Albert
Pinchback, P. B. S.

1840–1849
Allensworth, Allen
Boyd, Richard Henry
Browne, William Washington
Coleman, Warren Clay
Jones, Wiley
Montgomery, Isaiah T.
Napier, James Carroll
Pettiford, William Reuben

1850–1859
Binga, Jesse
Bush, John Edward
Chase, Calvin
Merrick, John
Moore, Frederick Randolph
Perry, Christopher James
Woods, Granville T.
Wright, Richard Robert, Sr.

1860–1869
Abbot, Robert Sengstacke
Cohen, Walter I.
James, Charles Howell
Jefferson, Lucy C.
Mitchell, John, Jr.
Overton, Anthony
Turnbo-Malone, Annie
    Minerva
Walker, Madame C. J.
Walker, Maggie Lena

1870–1879
Banks, Charles
De Priest, Oscar Stanton
Dutrieuille, Albert E.
Faustina, Gilbert
Felton, William McDonald
Morgan, Garrett A.
Payton, Philip A.
Spaulding, Charles Clinton

Vann, Robert Lee
Willis, Gertrude
Wright, Richard Robert, Jr.

1880–1889
Alexander, Archie Alphonso
Kennedy, William Jesse, Jr.
Micheaux, Oscar
Pace, Harry H.
Washington, Sarah Spencer

1890–1899
Bartholomew, Joseph Manuel
Beavers, George Allen, Jr.
Blayton, Jesse
Bricktop
Dickerson, Earl Burrus
Gaston, Arthur G.
Greenlee, Gus
Joyner, Marjorie Stewart
Julian, Percy Lavon
Lee, George Washington
Norris, James Austin
Posey, Cum
Rhodes, Eugene Washington

1900–1909
Bragg, Janet Harmon
Brown, Willa Beatrice
Fuller, S. B.
Robey, Don
Scott, Cornelius Adolphus
Scott, William Alexander, II
Simmons, Jake, Jr.
Walker, Antonio Maceo

1910–1919
Holland, Jerome Heartwell
Johnson, John H.

Morgan, Rose Meta
Parks, Henry G.
Plinton, James O., Jr.

1920–1929
Boutte, Alvin Joseph
Brimmer, Andrew F.
Gardner, Edward G.
Gates, Clifton W.
Gordy, Berry, Jr.
Henderson, Henry F., Jr.
Hurt, James, Jr.
Johnson, Albert W.
Joshua, Ernest P.
Kennedy, William J., III
Llewellyn, J. Bruce
Murray, Albert
Murray, Odetta S.
Procope, Ernesta G.
Sutton, Percy E.
Travis, Dempsey J.
Woods, Sylvia

1930–1939
Amos, Wally
Brunson, Dorothy
Burrell, Thomas J.
Davis, Willie D.
Dudley, Joe L., Sr.
Gidron, Dick
Graves, Earl G.
Griffey, Dick
Jones, Quincy Delight, Jr.
King, Don
Lewis, Byron E.
Proctor, Barbara Gardner
Russell, Herman J.
Smith, Clarence O.

1940–1949
Barden, Don
Chappell, Emma
De Passe, Suzanne Celeste
Farr, Mel
Gibson, Vivian
Hughes, Cathy
Johnson, Robert L.
Lewis, Edward T.
Lewis, Reginald Francis
Murray, Joan
Parsons, Richard Dean
Sims, Naomi
Smith, Joshua I.

1950–1959
Chenault, Kenneth Irvine
Fudge, Ann
James, Charles H., III
Moore, Vera
O'Neal, Stanley
Rhone, Sylvia M.
Rogers, John W., Jr.
Simmons, Russell
Winfrey, Oprah

1960–1969
Bowser, Yvette Lee
Fletcher, Alphonse, Jr.
Mercado-Valdes, Frank
Poe, Kirsten N.
Thomas-Graham, Pamela
Warren, Renee E.
Washington, Alonzo

1970–1979
Wasow, Omar

INDEX

Boldface locators indicate main entries. *Italic* locators indicate photographs.